UNFINISHED BUSINESS

Memoirs: 1902-1988

John Houseman

APPLAUSE
THEATRE ❤ BOOKS

UNFINISHED BUSINESS

Copyright © 1972, 1979, 1983, 1989 by John Houseman

Library of Congress Cataloging-in-Publication Data

Houseman, John.
  Unfinished business : a memoir / John Houseman.
    p. cm.
  Includes index.
  ISBN 1-557-83024-X : $14.95
  1. Houseman, John. 2. Theatrical producers and di-
rectors—United States—Biography. 3. Motion picture
actors and actresses—United States—Biography. I.
Title.
PN2287.H7A3 1989
792.023'0924—dc19
[B]   88-31171
                                                              CIP

APPLAUSE THEATRE BOOK PUBLISHERS
211 West 71st Street
New York, New York 10023
212-595-4735

Again — for Joan

To say that our life is entirely what we make of it
or entirely the data we are given is to say the same thing...
As far as freedom is concerned, two things are certain:
we are never predetermined and we never change;
we can always find in our past the presage of
what we have become.

MAURICE MERLEAU-PONTY

ACKNOWLEDGEMENTS

My thanks to Diana Fleishman
and Ingrid von Essen
for making this book possible.

Contents

CONTENTS

OVERTURE
The Education of a Chameleon
1902-30

I was conceived in the second year of this century and legitimized five years after that. By then I was speaking English with my mother, French with my father and his friends, Rumanian with the household and German with a visiting governess. Two of my first four birthdays were celebrated on board the Orient Express between Paris and Bucharest, the city where I was born on September 22, 1902, of a Jewish-Alsatian father and a British mother of Welsh-Irish descent.

He first saw her in the Bois de Boulogne riding a bicycle and wearing a bright red blouse with black polka dots. A month later they were living together at Maisons-Laffitte near the race track. Six months after that, when he was sent off to manage his family's grain and shipping interests in the Balkans, she accompanied him to the shores of the Black Sea, where they occupied a large brick house on a hill overlooking the Danube.

Till I was four and a half my hair fell in long golden curls over my shoulders: the day it was cut off I was photographed twice—before and after. That same year my father's family business collapsed as the result of a great-uncle's disastrous investment in the Marseilles streetcar system. As a result he was able to marry my gentile mother and I was registered at the French consulate under the name of Jacques Haussmann. Returning to Paris, he set up in business for himself as a broker and operator in commodities. He was a gambler; for the remaining ten years of his life he rode a series of speeding roller coasters (wheat, cotton, sugar, cocoa, coffee and various sorts of vegetable oils) up and down the "futures" markets of the world. They carried him from month to month, and sometimes from week to week, from riches to ruin and back again.

Our lives followed his fortunes in sudden moves from palatial suites to furnished rooms, from the favored corners of the Café de Paris to the dented aluminum tabletops of the Bouillons Duval. Lacking security, we lived in a whirling state of conspicuous extravagance. Chinchillas and pearls, a townhouse half-decorated but never occupied, two specially designed, custom-built automobiles (a Charron and a Delauney-Belleville, both bottle green with basket-weave cabins) were ceremoniously presented to my mother, then quickly resold to meet some critical margin call or to finance some new bonanza. My memory of my father—a composite of childish impressions and fading photographs—is of a short, pink-cheeked, bald, bearded, potbellied, elegant, smiling man with beautiful white hands and a striking resemblance to Edward VII of England.

When I was a child, before passports and police regulations and total wars, Europe was a garden through which the moneyed middle class journeyed incessantly in search of health and amusement. A few reckless eccentrics raced through clouds of dust along tree-lined highways, but the rest of them did their traveling in the swaying mahogany security of the Grands Expresses Européens. Beneath racks that strained under loads of label-covered cowhide luggage, leaning back on lace doilies pinned to seats of varicolored, dusty plush which, at night, were miraculously converted into beds by men in brown uniforms, they moved in well-ordered comfort between the capitals and resorts of continental Europe: Biarritz, Deauville, Ostend, Baden-Baden. Aix-les-Bains, Nice, La Bourboule, Chamonix, St. Moritz and the Swiss and Italian lakes—these were their favorite playgrounds and, at one time or another, we visited them all. On various holidays, over the years, I was shown King Alfonso of Spain thundering by at dusk in his white Mercedes; the *Graf Zeppelin* rising from a bright green German meadow dotted with tiny running figures; Max Decugis, the French lawn-tennis champion, demonstrating Diabolo on a hotel terrace to two Scandinavian princesses. But my most persistent memories are those of Lake Lucerne, where my mother and I spent seven consecutive summers until the First World War put an end to our travels. Here at the water's edge, with the snow-capped mountains all around us, we lived in an atmosphere of continuous and extravagant celebration: tennis tournaments, regattas and races succeeded each other in scheduled profusion, culminating in gala weekends that were filled with banquets, cotillions and fireworks. In these activities I participated only remotely. Coming out of our early table-d'hôte dinner while it was still light, Fräulein and I would pause to admire the translucent meringue castles topped with Swiss flags and the fabulous ice sculptures that rose glistening from long, crowded buffets at either end of the deserted ballroom. I was half asleep when my mother came very quietly into my room at twilight, perfumed and rustling, to kiss me good-night on her way down to her mysterious excitements. When I awoke with the sun in my eyes and Mount Pilatus rising steeply across the lake, there would be wrinkled balloons and tinsel favors and, usually, a scrawled note with crosses for kisses from her at the foot of my bed.

Summer was not the only time we travelled; I have memories of extended voyages undertaken for unknown reasons—to Vienna and Budapest, Berlin, Barcelona and Rome. It was the arrivals and departures that moved me—stations and hotels rather than landmarks and monuments. By the age of seven I had been in half the celebrated cities of Europe. Of this precocious Grand Tour no clear recollections remain. I came away from Venice with a confused memory of dungeons and stagnant water and the walls of our rooms at the Danieli Palace red with blood from the crushed corpses of giant mosquitoes. In Rome the Sistine Chapel and the lobby of the Excelsior Hotel left me with identical impressions of grandeur.

My early education was erratic. At the age of six I made a brief appearance at the day school that my French cousins attended. The third time I vomited in class I was removed and resumed private instruction under a gentle, sallow, Catholic mademoiselle with whom I made the rounds of the Paris museums and a sharp-eyed Fräulein from whom I learned to recite some of the shorter works of the German romantic poets and the words and music of "Deutschland über Alles."

Six months later (while my parents were in Istanbul) I made my second institutional experiment, this time as a guest in a celebrated Parisian girls' finishing school for the daughters of the English and American rich. Within that budding grove I spent eight amazing weeks in the company of two dozen nubile, spoiled and exuberant young women. I shared their meals, their entertainments, their French and German classes, and, occasionally, their beds. To this brief, delicious sojourn and those unconsummated delights I attribute many of my emotional problems in years to come, including the deep shame of my superannuated virginity.

My third experience was less agreeable but more lasting. Soon after my seventh birthday I was sent to Bristol in the west of England to be brought up in the house of a schoolmaster, Head of the Modern Language Department at Clifton College. He was of German origin, married to a Scot, and they had six children, the youngest of whom was exactly my age. After more than half a century Eric Siepmann, the youngest of them, recalled the appearance in his home of "a French boy known as Fat Jack who arrived from Paris with a beautiful Mama in a beautiful hat that actually had three storeys. As soon as she had gone he told us that he knew everything—for example that Eskimos live at the North Pole on a diet of candles. He was a spoiled only child and it never occurred to us, because he was plump and foreign and used to riches, that he could be anything but a vulgarian. We set about him and I am surprised he ever recovered."

I was fortunate, in my first confrontation with an alien society, to encounter so intelligent and humane a family as the Siepmanns. Their persecutions were spontaneous, brief and almost entirely free of the calculated cruelties of the world's pecking orders as I came to know them later. During the four years I lived among then in their grey Bathstone house on College Road, the struggle to be accepted by them remained the principal preoccupation of my life. Some of its most savage battles were waged in the bare room with striped walls which Eric and I shared and which was known from earlier times as the Nursery. It was here, after we had said our prayers and the lights were out, that I came to know loneliness in all its icy, corrosive horror and wept in panic as the doors of my lost happy childhood slammed shut behind me. And it was here that my first male relationship was formed—an intimacy rooted in inequality and fear: inequality since this was *his* house in which I was a stranger, *his* room in which I was an intruder; fear because it was through *him* that the hope of acceptance and the menace of rejection were kept in constant suspense. This created a pattern of insecurity that has persisted through most of my life and has permanently affected my relations with other men. It left me incapable of parity—a prey to competitiveness in its most virulent form.

My mother believed that by combining the healthy austerity of my life in England with the glamour of her own cosmopolitan world, she was giving me the best of all possible lives. It didn't work out that way. Three times a year—for a month at Christmas and Easter and for seven weeks each summer—I was shuttled across the restless waters of the English Channel, from the cold reality of my days and nights at Clifton into the holiday sunshine of my childhood, back to the secret universe of fantasies and desires where my mother was queen and I was her only child. After these euphoric excursions, no gradual decompression was possible; each holiday was followed by agonizing emotional bends and each return to school became a bereavement and a violation that left me frightened and sore for weeks to come. Divided between my two worlds, I belonged to neither.

At the age of nine, wearing a grey flannel suit with short trousers, a stiff Eton collar and a cap with blue concentric circles, I became a day boy at the Clifton Preparatory School and went on from there, after two years, in yellow radial stripes, long trousers and a top hat on Sundays, to become a junior. Since four of my eleven years at Clifton College were war years, mine was not a typical experience. The rituals and routines remained unchanged but much of the adolescent violence that normally fermented under the surface of British public school life was drained off and sublimated in the more immediate anxieties of the Great War. Yet this same war presented me with another, more grievous, problem.

Regularly, three times a year, as each holiday came around, I continued to make the long and sometimes dangerous voyage from Clifton to Paris and back again. Even for so skilled and experienced a chameleon as I had become, this constant alternation grew increasingly difficult as I found myself becoming a whipping boy for the rising resentments that divided the Entente Cordiale in those first years of the war. Arriving in France for the holidays, I was challenged by members of my own family as an emissary of *"perfide Albion."* A third of France was still occupied by the enemy; 2 million Frenchmen had been killed, wounded or captured. What were the dirty English waiting for to come over and share the burden of the war?

When I returned to England (where I was an alien with a German name and had to register with the Bristol police under the Defence of the Realm Act) I faced the charge that Frogs were braggarts and cowards who expected the British to pull their chestnuts out of the fire. Also, more specifically, while Britons were tightening their belts and living on ever more stringent rations as their ships were sunk and their seamen drowned in their efforts to bring in essential foodstuffs and ammunition, the French—including me and my family—were gorging themselves on rich foods and wines. Year after year this whipsawing continued. Such was my capacity for rapid assimilation that, with each holiday and term, I was able to make a new and drastic adjustment to the prevailing mood—just in time to ensure my full distress at my next transplantation, when I again crossed the Channel and reappeared, full of the wrong loyalties, in a strange and hostile world. As a result, in self-protection, I lost all sense of patriotism in my early teens and have not regained it since.

Except for the agitations of the war, my years in the Junior School were uneventful and undistinguished. I made the rugby fifteen, partly on account of my weight, but was poor at cricket, which I played without style or pleasure. Our academic life was conducted in an atmosphere that was predominantly Philistine, following a schedule that seemed to leave time for everything except reading. It was not until my last year in the Junior School that I encountered my first good teacher—a harsh, ascetic man with a beaked nose under whom I began the study of Greek. When I came to him my brain was clogged with a thick sludge of inertia and self-love; he scared, chivvied and finally helped me to achieve my first breakthrough into sustained and organized study. Later, at different times in my life, I sought refuge in a variety of lethargies. But I never quite forgot the satisfactions of the discipline he forced upon me and only once again reverted to the depths of torpor from which his rigor has saved me.

That summer, a few months after the sinking of the *Lusitania* by a German submarine, my parents decided to vary the routine of my cross-Channel holidays with a voyage to the United States, where my father had gone as head of a French government purchasing commission. I arrived during a heat wave, ate my first grapefruit on the roof of the Biltmore Hotel, learned to foxtrot under the personal supervision of the celebrated Mrs. Vernon Castle, visited the Hippodrome, where I watched an entire regiment of chorus girls and a small herd of elephants disappear into a tank of water, and went riding in Central Park with a red-haired lady to whom my father sent roses. For added excitement, there was the Black Tom explosion in New York Harbor, a shark scare and a polio epidemic. We moved up to the Grand Union in Saratoga for the racing season, fished for black bass in Lake George, visited the dwarf genius of General Electric, Dr. Steinmetz, in his laboratory at Schenectady, where he and my father spoke in German of an electric car for the postwar European market, then continued north to Niagara Falls in our huge, double-clutching Packard Twin-Six, driven by a scowling Italo-American who had been chief racing mechanic to Ralphe de Palma and whom I worshipped. On our way back through the White Mountains we stopped at a great cream-colored caravanserai where, after my father had written his name in the register, we were politely but firmly refused admission. The next day as we drove back to New York along the Post Road, the Twin-Six was suddenly and hideously transformed from a magic coach into a speeding hearse that was carrying me back to the grim realities of school and the war—out of the holiday brightness of the New World into a region of darkness and desolation and death.

Number 30 College Road, known in my day as "Mayor's House," was one of half a dozen buildings (each housing from fifty to sixty boys) set in an irregular cluster around the main body of Clifton College. Here we lived in a state of divided allegiance. We had our school patriotism, as prescribed by our own poet laureate, Sir Henry Newbolt, whose "Clifton Chapel" and "Vitae Lampeda" we were expected to memorize and admire. But the basic unit and emotional center of our lives was the House. Here I spent four years, following the normal curve of the

British public schools' "queuing up" system—from humiliation to power—under the watchful eye of our housemaster, Henry Bickersteth Mayor. He was a shy man of great vitality and good will with a large crimson nose and a walrus moustache overhanging a sensitive mouth. My relations with him were satisfactory but precarious. Throughout my first year, since I had recently returned from the United States, he held me directly responsible for America's shameful treatment of the Red Indian. Later I committed the unpardonable faux pas of switching from classics to modern languages as my principal study.

This was the last year of my father's life. He and my mother had returned from America during the darkest days of the war, confident that with America's entry a quick Allied victory was certain. Soon after his arrival, he rented a large office on the Champs-Elysées, where he had visions of himself and his son, one day, conducting vast and brilliant international affairs. In the meantime, he staffed it with a second cousin who had been invalided out of the army and an old friend who had fallen on evil days. Here, one morning, he suddenly felt weak and sent a boy out for a cup of chocolate and a brioche. Before they arrived he fainted, then quickly recovered. But, by the time I left school after the Easter holidays, my mother had been told by two specialists that her husband was suffering from Addison's disease and had only a short time to live.

Within three months this plump man whose face had been rosy and round under his beard was reduced to a sagging, copper-colored sack of bones and skin. He was dying and he knew it, but he tried to hold death off with a final spasm of financial activity—a last, frantic gamble in which he staked his whole new-won American fortune on a desperate chance that death would not call his bluff. He began by buying $50,000 worth of Russian Imperial War Bonds (with which I was lighting fires in Rockland County forty years later), then invested hurriedly in a number of enterprises, including the controlling interest in an aircraft factory (which collapsed with the end of the war) and a trading corporation for supplying France's North African territories with American agricultural equipment (a large consignment of which was found rusting in warehouses in Algiers and Casablanca ten years after his death). But his main investment and highest hopes lay in a perfume factory, Les Parfums Sidlay de Paris. Considering the world-wide cosmetics boom of the twenties and thirties, this should have made my mother a millionairess. It never did. For the day came when my father had to give up. He lay in bed in his hotel off the Place Vendôme for a few weeks, then decided to move south. One July night, at Salies-de-Béarn, in the Basque country, my mother heard a dog howling mournfully in the street below. She went out onto the balcony for a moment. When she turned back into their room, she found my father stiff from a stroke. He died before morning at the age of forty-two.

When I reached Paris my mother was already there but the coffin, caught in a French wartime railways snarl, was still on its way. While we waited for it to arrive, the sitting room and bathroom at the hotel were filled with weeping members of my French-Jewish family spelling each other in a ceremonial sequence of mounting lamentations. The persistent moaning, nose blowing and gnashing of teeth, the hands that reached out and clutched me with possessive pity to heaving bosoms and groaning chests, the incessantly repeated commiserations and reminiscences—these all shocked and embarrassed me as I moved between the wailing figures and the bedroom in which my mother had taken refuge.

She did not attend the funeral, at which I wore black gloves and a bowler hat as I blindly shovelled the first spadeful of earth over my father's coffin in the Jewish section of the Montparnasse cemetery, under instructions from my uncle Robert (in uniform) and a black-clad rabbi whose beard glistened in the sun. Afterwards relatives and friends drove back to the hotel, where they continued their wailing far into the night. Among the noisiest of the mourners was the second cousin, my father's associate in the perfume factory. Six months later, still weeping, he confessed to having embezzled the entire capital of Les Parfums Sidlay de Paris in a disastrous speculation in alcohol futures for which my father, over my mother's protest, had given him a temporary proxy shortly before his death.

The scenes at my father's grave (so different from the restrained ceremonial of Clifton Chapel) had disturbed and shaken me but they had not cracked the insulation which, for so many years, had enabled me to "pass," whenever it suited me, among Jews and gentiles alike, without the faintest feeling of betrayal or guilt. From the repeated chameleon's maneuvers which I found myself forced to perform throughout my childhood, I had developed a mechanism of adjustment so automatic and so complete that I was honestly unaware of the denials and deceptions that these transformations required of me. On a simple semantic level, phrases like "to jew down," "don't be a Jew!," "a fat Jew," even "dirty Jew" formed part of the standard vocabulary of my schoolmates to whose customs I was so scrupulously trying to adhere. Yet I would have been horrified and hurt if I had ever heard them applied to my father while he lived, or to those cousins, uncles and aunts whose elegant Parisian apartments I visited during the holidays. Unable or unwilling to make the distasteful connection, I remained blithely unaware of the problem. (Years later, on a belated pilgrimage to the family vault in the Cimetière Montparnasse, I noticed three plaques next to my father's grave. They were those of two aunts and one cousin—MORT 1944 A AUSCHWITZ, ASSASSINÉS PAR LES ALLEMANDS.)

Some of this duplicity accompanied my reception into the Church of England. Some months earlier a letter had arrived in Paris during the Christmas holidays "reminding" my mother that I was approaching the age of confirmation and "assuming" that she would want me prepared for that event with others of my group. We discussed the matter. "You never know," said my mother, "it might come in useful one day." Some weeks later there was a second letter—from the Bishop of Bristol—asking for a copy of my baptismal certificate. Since I had never been baptized—in Rumania or anywhere else—this was an awkward request. The war saved me. It was impossible to obtain papers from a country that was under the iron heel of the Imperial German Army. I explained this to the ecclesiastical authorities and gave them a fictitious date which they accepted.

I recall my preparation for confirmation with the deepest distaste. It was conducted in hollow, sanctimonious tones by our house tutor, a muscular Christian with high-church leanings and completed, when he left to take a commission as chaplain in the RAF, by Henry Bickersteth Mayor in person. Both devoted more time and thought to convincing us of the evils of masturbation and sodomy (neither of which I practiced) than to salvation of my eternal soul. (Intercourse with the other sex was an evil so heinous and unthinkable that it was never even mentioned.)

During the confirmation service in Clifton Chapel I was oppressed by such a weight of fear and gloom that I hardly noticed the strange sensation—something between a tickling and an ache in my side—of which I first became aware just after I had sunk to my knees before the Bishop of Bristol. While I crouched there, open-mouthed, waiting to receive my little strip of bread and the metallic sip of wine from the hard edge of the silver chalice, I was pierced by a shaft of pain so intense that it was all I could do to prevent myself from rolling over at the Bishop's feet. And it came to me with terrible clarity that this was God's punishment for my baptismal fraud and that I was going to die. At two the next morning a gray-faced army surgeon, hastily summoned to the school sanatorium, removed my distended, pus-laden appendix and left me with three red rubber tubes dangling from what remains one of the most gruesome incisions in the history of appendectomy. It took me less than a month to recover from the surgery, more than nine years to get over the emasculating effects of the obscene and gloomy ritual that preceded it.

I recall my last year at Clifton as one of intense and continuous scholastic pressure; also as a time of fulfillment and satisfaction. As a prefect and a member of the school rugby fifteen, I was more secure, mentally and physically, than I had been since childhood. I founded the Clifton College Dramatic Society of which I was president and I became one of the editors of the *Cliftonian*, normally a bland, formal, pale-pink-covered quarterly, of which we devoted one whole devastating issue to reducing the Officers' Training Corps to what we considered its proper peacetime place in the life of the school. It was my first taste of the power of propaganda and I have never forgotten it. It was also my first act of subversion.

For my final vacation, in the summer of 1919, for the first time since the war, my mother and I visited Switzerland and went on from there, over the St. Gotthard Pass, to the Villa d'Este on the Lake of Como. On the way home we stopped in Milan and saw trucks in the streets filled with men in work clothes and tattered uniforms with red flags flapping in the wind. The next morning when we came out from seeing Leonardo's "Last Supper," there were more trucks, battered grayish wartime Fiats, lined up in the square outside, guarded by men in black shirts.

At Cova's, where we lunched on veal and white truffles, a middle-aged man came over to our table, kissed my mother's hand and asked if he might join us. He had been with my father in the grain business and spoke with feeling of the old days in Rumania. Over coffee he asked me about myself. I told him I was at school in England but that if I was successful in my examination for the university, I might leave at the end of the Christmas term and go travelling—possibly to Spain. Over cognac he suggested that I come instead to Argentina, where I could learn Spanish and the grain business at the same time. He gave me his card from which I noted that his name was Señor Katz and that he was a member of the Jockey Club of Buenos Aires.

In the agitations of my final term this chance meeting was quite forgotten. Early in December I travelled with the rest of Clifton's rugby team for our annual game against Wellington. I scored the winning try, spent the weekend in London and arrived in Cambridge the day before the scholarship examinations began. That night I was invited to a dinner party given by a famous university hostess, at which I sat silent, gauche and unnoticed among a dozen suave and mannered young men whose informed, sophisticated talk seemed to float, without strain or effort, far above my head. The effect of this exclusion, real or imagined, was to send me into the examination room the next morning in a state of furious determination. This may or may not have had something to do with my placement on the Cambridge scholarship list as it appeared in *The Times* of London the following week.

I had won one of the highest academic prizes of the year—the first major scholarship awarded for modern languages at Trinity College. For Otto Siepmann, as my director of education, it was a glorious victory; even Henry Bickersteth was impressed. So was everyone except, possibly, my mother, who was delighted but entirely taken up with her preparations for my South American voyage, which seemed to have materialized without my knowledge during the autumn. On my last Sunday in Clifton, divided between pride in my success and suspicion of my incomprehensible voyage, Otto Siepmann, as my director of education, outlined the bright future that lay before me: four years of advanced studies under ideal cultural conditions with some of the world's greatest scholars; a few years of travel to the leading universities of France and Germany; then, a fellowship—and he said it with bated breath—at Trinity College, Cambridge: a life of dignity and honor, of ease and universal respect. At parting he gave me a long list of carefully selected reading for the months to come. I listened to him with attention, put the list in my pocket and never looked at it again.

Two nights later, in my blue velvet School Fifteen cap with its golden tassel jiggling about my ears, I sat with fourteen other heroes high on the narrow ledge of the "big school" gallery from which we looked down, like gods, at the dark crowd in the floor below and led the singing of "The Best School of All" and "Auld Lang Syne" with our hands tightly clasped and our crossed arms pumping up and down, over and over, faster and faster, setting the rhythm for those other hundreds of rocking figures below, till the whole building shuddered and heaved and swayed on its foundations.

* * *

I sailed for South America two days later in the RMS *Almanzora*. My mother cried at saying goodbye and she was still crying and waving as the darkness swallowed up the swaying tender which was carrying her back to shore and the lights of the French coast, which I was not to see again for thirty-five years.

I imagine that, in the long, lonely hours of her train trip back to Paris, my mother must have found comfort in the thought that against bitter opposition, through peace and war, riches and poverty, separation and death, she had achieved her goal: her son was tall, blue-eyed and multilingual, with a pleasant manner and a British public-school education. From here on, with such advantages, it was up to him to make his way in the world and she never had the slightest doubt that I would.

For my part, while the *Almanzora* moved out of the Channel into the full fury of the Atlantic, I might have reflected—if a sudden, violent wave of nausea had not banished all other thoughts from my mind—that at eighteen and a half I still had not the faintest notion of what I wanted to do with my life, that I had a little less than 500 francs in my pocket, a modest but elegant wardrobe and no return ticket.

The Argentine Republic, when I arrived there, was still a colony—no longer of Spain, but of half a dozen of the great industrial powers of the Western world. Its army and police were trained by Germans; its culture was imported from France; its films and automobiles came mostly from the United States; its latest immigrants were Italians and Spaniards, while all its railroads and a great part of its industry and banking were run by Europeans—principally British. Agricultural production was native but its export was in foreign hands: the packing plants were American and grain shipments were controlled by international firms of which Señor Katz's was one.

My first home in Argentina was his *hôtel particulier* on the Avenida Alvear. He was a pleasant, shrewd, extravagant, domineering and moody man with whom, since we had nothing in common except his former association with my father, I found if difficult to communicate. My host was under the impression that he was helping his friend's son on the first step of a career in the international grain business, which he assumed I was impatient to embark on. For me the trip was nothing more than a pleasant and instructive interlude between Clifton and Cambridge. This delusion was encouraged by the dream life which I led as his guest that first month, in a lotus land whose temptations I was not disposed to resist. While my former companions at 30 College Road were being awakened by the clanging of bells, washing in ice water, answering roll calls and undergoing the horrors of cross-country "runs" and open-order drills, I was lying in bed until noon every day, breakfasting from a tray on which, once a week, I would find an envelope thick with spending money, which I had no compunction in accepting. Around noon I would rise, bathe and dress in time to be driven downtown in a long, open maroon Minerva, either to Señor Katz's office or directly to the echoing marble Exchange, where I was introduced to a number of middle-aged men who claimed to have known me as a baby on the shores of the Danube. After lunch I would accompany Señor Katz to the races at the Palermo track, where flamingos flew in orange clouds over the jockeys' heads. Later in the afternoon, while Señor Katz returned to his business, I attended chaperoned tea parties on the top floor of Harrods department store, where society debutantes, accompanied by their mothers or older sisters, sat with their brothers, cousins and fiancés in shrill, trivial, interminable chatter. Later, I accompanied those same brothers, cousins and fiancés on their regular evening rounds of the bars and brothels of the Calle Florida, where I would exhaust myself in endless tangos with the native call girls (*pour apprendre l'espagnol*) to the pumping rhythms of long, flexible concertinas, while my friends went upstairs with the newly arrived French and German girls who had been reserved for their sampling.

Know as the *niños bien* (the sons of good families), these young men were the accepted leaders of the city's night life, from which they seldom absented themselves, except when they were off doing the same thing in Paris or exiled to a distant family *estancia* following some especially unsavory scandal or racing up and down the Avenida del Cinco de Mayo in their Hispanos and Bugattis, charging into processions of protesting workers or marching strikers. Spoiled, ignorant and dangerous, they were consistently pleasant to me—so pleasant that I thought it wise to conceal three vital and shameful facts from then: a) that I was penniless (which was not apparent, with my O'Rossen suits and my Sulka haberdashery); b) that I was the houseguest of a Rumanian-Jewish grain merchant; and c) that I was a virgin.

This dream life ended suddenly one February night when I left with Señor Katz for the larger of his two *estancias*—in the north-west of the province of Buenos Aires. In an airless compartment of the Central Argentine Railways (he in the lower berth, I in the upper), just as I was falling asleep, Señor Katz began to talk to me out of the darkness. He spoke of my father: what a great gentleman he was and what a wonderful couple he and my mother had made in those happy, far-off days in Braïla. This led him, after a while, to talk of my mother's present financial situation. It was common knowledge among my father's friends, he told me, that she could not last much longer on what my father had left her—not living the way she did. When that was gone, what would she do? Had she ever discussed her situation with me? Had she talked of remarrying, ever? Soon after that he fell asleep and I could hear his peaceful breathing through the racket of the train wheels and the moaning of the racing locomotive. There was nothing surprising in what he had told me—nothing I had not been aware of for years. But now it had been said—and nothing would ever be the same again. I lay in the dark, frozen with fear, clutching at the sides of the narrow berth and hanging on for dear life while great waves of guilt and panic came sweeping over me in such a flood of anguish as I had not known since my first nights in the Nursery at

Percival House. Once again a door had swung shut behind me; I had heard the click of a trap from which I knew there was no escape.

The train made a special stop for us at Arribenos around four in the morning. There was no one at the station to meet us, and a small, bitter wind swept the empty tracks and tore at the kerosene lamp in the stationmaster's deserted office. Ten minutes later two dust-caked Model T Fords came roaring over the level crossing and stopped at the loading platform. A harried-looking man with a broad face and glasses and leather leggings jumped out and started shouting in broken Spanish at the driver of the second car to take charge of our luggage, while Señor Katz yelled at him in a shrill combination of Rumanian and German. The man answered in Yiddish that one of the Fords had blown a tire.

After we had cleared the village, the night closed in on us, except where the flickering yellow stripes from the headlights of our swaying cars lit the road ahead—the wide corridor of rutted earth between wire fences that ran in endless parallel lines before us into the darkness. Twice we had to stop with screaming brakes to avoid running into herds of sleeping horses that rose suddenly out of the ground as our lights hit them and went galloping off heavily into the night, past the wagon trains to which they belonged—towering, six- and eight-horse carts with iron-rimmed wheels 12 feet high, their long, narrow bodies loaded with grain sacks and their drivers asleep around their dying fires.

It was hard to tell, at first, when the late-summer dawn began to come up behind the wire. There was nothing to catch the light—only the slowly hardening line between the long, flat stretch of the earth and the cloudless, slowly brightening sky. Then, gradually, as color was added to the light, the varying textures of the pampa became visible—gray stubble and standing grain, sunburnt pastures and the green of young maize and, sometimes in the distance, a small island of young, straggly trees or the thin outline of a steel windmill whirring above the mud shack and the accumulation of refuse that marked a sharecropper's place.

After a while, through the roaring of our Model Ts, we began to hear the lowing of cattle and then, suddenly, rising out of the earth ahead of us, shimmering in the sun, we saw trees, taller and fuller grown than any we had seen till then, and the outlines of the buildings and windmills and water tanks of the Estancia Santa Maria. As we turned into the driveway, we could see a herd of cattle being moved slowly through a lake of green clover by four dark-skinned men sitting hunched on small horses, with what looked like bowler hats on their heads. These, said Señor Katz, were his "gauchos," and when we came

through the outer yard with its sheds and mud shacks, dogs began to
bark and children with Indian faces stared at us from open doorways
as we came to a stop before a long, dirty-white building in which two
naked light bulbs were still burning.

The Estancia Santa Maria, where Señor Katz never stayed for more
than two days at a time, was a large commercial ranch he had acquired
out of his wartime profits. Its main structures, besides the native shacks
that seemed to grow out of the earth of which they were made,
included the gray-white, brick administration building and a pink
stucco bungalow with modern plumbing set in a struggling eucalyptus
grove. Here I lived with my benefactor's half-brother, a recent arrival
from Rumania, whose resentment of me was exceeded only by his
raging envy of his more successful brother. Though he was titular
administrator in his brother's name, the Estancia Santa Maria was, in
fact, managed by his bitter enemy—an ambitious, khaki-clad
Palestinian agricultural expert named Edelstein. Working in the office
were two clerks in their twenties: one local—a Galician with a
moustache and bad teeth (an animal torturer); the other a quick,
intelligent city Jew sent out from Señor Katz's office in Buenos Aires to
recuperate, in the country air, from threatened tuberculosis. They sat
all day and half the night working over piles of tallies and bills of
lading wearing eyeshades under the naked bulbs.

These four were my trapmates. They detested each other and were
in turn resented and mocked, behind their backs, by the natives—the
Indians and Mestizos, cowhands and peons, who did the physical
work of the *estancias*. Chief of these, captain of the gauchos and father
of seven sons, was Don Bernardo—a dark, massive, bow-legged man
in a stiff black felt hat and stained leather apron, silent, slow and
awkward on the ground but agile, eloquent and formidable in the wide
sheepskin saddle on which he bestrode his string of horses—six shaggy
work ponies, one for each day of the week, and a gaited Arab stallion
which he rode with a silver-studded bridle on Sundays. In his charge
were several thousand head of cattle—Durham and Hereford—
serviced by two huge, ill-tempered and dangerous bulls, whose stalls
occupied the other half of the windowless, smoke-filled shed in which
Don Bernardo slept on the earth floor with his sons, his two wives and
half a dozen black-haired girl-children.

Running through the estate, a few hundred yards behind the
building, was a wide, shallow creek into which great flocks of
flamingos descended at dusk and stood, all night, balancing
themselves on one leg in the shallow water. Beyond it were fields of
alfalfa, alive with thousands of squirming, grunting, screeching,
cannibalistic black pigs, which were bred according to the latest

American methods in individually movable pigpens. One of the first of the bucolic duties to which I was assigned was the castration of 487 young porkers—emasculated between lunch and dinner, then dropped squealing into a strong solution of creosote. But it was in the grain operations of the *estancia* that I was expected to serve my apprenticeship, for which I received a salary of 20 pesos a week.

All through the late summer and fall, as the threshing crews moved in clouds of dust from farm to farm and the straw rose in gray-gold mounds above the stubble, we drove out in our earth-caked Model Ts to acquire what was left of the sharecroppers' grain. Unskilled, ignorant and recently arrived from the poorest farmlands of Europe, they regarded us with mute, resentful suspicion. Finally, rather than let their grain rot in the late-autumn rains, they were forced to sell us their wheat, barley and oats well below market price. This meant more paperwork and, night after night, I found myself sitting with the two clerks at their cluttered table checking contracts and bills of lading against the scrawled piles of wagon receipts.

Some nights, after we were done, the clerks would invite me to accompany them on their excursions to the neighboring villages—sad, hideous places, with streets ankle-deep in dust and mud and, invariably, off to one side (with its red light, dirt floor and scratchy gramophone), the local brothel with its changing personnel of dark, unwashed country girls and an occasional European derelict, shipped here from the Buenos Aires waterfront to die or recover in the country air. It was late when we got back from these forays, on which I was never more than an embarrassed and frightened spectator. Approaching Santa Maria, we could hear the dogs barking a long way off; they were still barking as we roared in between the silent buildings, all dark except for the red glow of Don Bernardo's eternal corncob fire and the light in the window where Señor Katz's brother sat playing solitaire on the bare dining-room table. He was devoured by loneliness, as by a cancer, and as soon as his brother had left for Europe, we were joined in the bungalow by a middle-aged German blonde whose amorous moanings were clearly audible through the beaverboard that separated our rooms. She stayed a little less than two months—exactly the time it took Edelstein to report her presence by letter to Señor Katz in the South of France and for Señor Katz, by cable, to order his brother to get rid of her or leave Santa Maria immediately. After that, since he and Edelstein were not speaking and the clerks were not allowed in the bungalow, we returned to two-handed card games and the reading of last month's papers from Europe.

I lived on the Estancia Santa Maria for eight and a half months in a state of deep mental torpor. Within a few weeks any excitement or curiosity I may have felt at the novelty of my situation had worn off. What was left was boredom, fear and a slowly accumulating desperation. The disciplines I had formed at Clifton proved entirely useless outside the limited frame for which they were intended. And, as the cold wind began to blow across the bare, treeless plains, I looked on with idle indifference while the frail structure of self-confidence I had so painfully acquired during my last year in England was frayed, torn apart and scattered over the dark, rain-soaked earth.

I do not recall a single book that I read during those months and since I was neither willing nor able to give a true description of the abominable wilderness in which I found myself, I soon stopped writing any but the most perfunctory letters. In the limbo in which I was living, news from Europe reached me as a faint, meaningless echo from a world to which I had ceased to belong. For if I was unmoved by the latest gossip from my companions at the Best School of All, how could they, on their part, be expected to thrill to reports of how two weeks of steady rain had benefited the winter wheat but damaged the pastures; that Verdun, our Negro cowhand from Paraguay, had run amok after drinking a bottle of wood alcohol and knifed two of the foreman's sons before being shot in the left thigh by Edelstein's .38; that a bright-green venomous toad the size of a soup plate with teeth like fishhooks had appeared in the bottom of our well; and, finally, that on the night of the first heavy frost 37 calves had been trampled or crushed to death around the water tank in pasture number three?

Some time in June a letter with an English stamp was delivered to me in the office of the Estancia Santa Maria, where Edelstein and Señor Katz's brother were going over the monthly inventory—each hoping to catch the other in some error or, better still, in some petty theft. The letter, which had been forwarded by my mother from Paris, bore the crest of Trinity College, Cambridge. It was from the man who was to be my tutor and contained a number of practical and academic questions and suggestions relating to my arrival at the university in October.

I put the letter in my pocket, where it stayed for several days, then laid it away in a drawer among my carefully folded Sulka shirts. Some weeks later a second letter arrived, in which my tutor expressed surprise at my failure to answer his first. Also a letter from Otto Siepmann, which I never opened.

Sometimes, looking back, I am inclined to think that I never really had a free choice: that my decision not to go to Cambridge was the logical, necessary and mathematical consequence of my birth and upbringing—an instinctive and hereditary imperative, which it was impossible for me to deny. At other times I tend to believe that if I had

had a return ticket to Europe in my pocket I would probably have used it and presented myself at Trinity for the start of the academic year.

I remained four months longer on the Argentine pampa—paralyzed, self-pitying and desperately waiting for someone to tell me what to do. No one did. Then, late in November, just as the new wheat was beginning to show green in the fields, I woke up one morning, got my bags out of the storeroom and packed my things. I arranged for one of the clerks to drive me over to Arribenos, said goodbye to everyone in fluent Argentine Spanish and caught the noon train to Buenos Aires.

Señor Katz was still in Europe. His manager, a gentle Hungarian with velvet-brown eyes, found me a job as a junior clerk in the foreign exchange department of a bank. Here, for the next five months, I pursued my education behind a calculating machine at a high desk in the international arbitrage department of the Banco Hollandes de la America del Sud. I was sitting there when a letter arrived from England which informed me that, on the recommendation of M. Katz and other former associates and friends of the late Georges Haussmann, I had been accepted as an apprentice to the firm of Wm. H. Pim, Jr., & Co., Ltd., of Bury Street, St. Mary Axe, London EC3, and that a reservation had been made for me aboard the RMS *Avon*, sailing in mid-August from the River Plate to Southampton.

* * *

My mother, whom I found waiting for me at the Savoy Hotel in a room overlooking the Thames, had two gifts for me. The first was a visit to Savile Row, where she ordered two business suits, a dinner jacket, a set of tails and a silk hat the total cost of which, added to my scholarship, would have gone a long way toward the expenses of a year at Cambridge. The second was less welcome: it was a mobilization order inviting me to report within the month to the military authorities at Besançon in the department of Doub for induction into the French Army. This summons, which I had not the slightest intention of obeying, meant that I would now be listed as a deserter and exiled from the territory of the French Republic for the rest of my natural days; it also meant that for the next eighteen months, until I could become a British citizen by naturalization at the age of twenty-one, I would be living in a state of perilous vagrancy without nationality or papers of any kind.

Two days later, at a starting salary of four guineas a week, I went to work in a shabby second-floor office overlooking the Baltic Exchange for the firm of Wm. H. Pim, Jr. & Co. Ltd. By operating as a confidential agent between the exporters of North and South America,

India, Australia and the main importing centers of continental Europe and the United Kingdom, Pim's had become the most successful grain-brokerage house in the world. Through its crusted telephones and battered ledgers passed orders and shipping papers for millions of bushels of grain, stowed in the holds of dozens of ships bound on never-ending voyages along the trade routes of the globe. Yet its employees numbered less than two dozen—including partners, traders, freight experts, clerks, secretaries, office boys, a sultry, multilingual switchboard operator and a one-armed veteran porter-commissionaire.

Pim and his heirs had long since vanished. The firm was now controlled by a florid vulgarian of enormous energy, charm and guile named George Howe. He and my father had known each other in London as apprentices and, later in Paris, as bons vivants. He combined shrewd judgement with an almost limitless capacity for drink and a persuasiveness that led clients of sharply contrasting interests to believe that he was sincerely and wholeheartedly on their side. When he died suddenly of uremia on the Riviera near the end of my first year with the firm, a Japanese client for whom he had made a fortune through a long-term purchase of Canadian wheat refused to realize his profits until he had journeyed to the edge of the new-turned earth and received George Howe's permission from beyond the grave.

My first year was spent acquiring the vocabulary and syntax of the mysterious language in which the international grain trade was conducted. This instruction took place in an airless inner room filled with high, old-fashioned wooden desks and bursting cardboard files. Here, like a gray spider at the center of his web, sat the office manager, 'Mister' Newsom, in his faded alpaca jacket. He was a celebrated figure in the trade, and Pim's paid him handsomely. Bald, pale and stooped, full of shrewd saws and shady precedents, with a cockney-drawling slit of a mouth from which four-letter words flowed incessantly past a false, vacuous smile, he chose to maintain a perverse humility that never for a moment concealed his profound contempt for the world of amateurs by whom he was surrounded.

Mister Newsom and his four clerks were my constant, intimate companions during my first year at Pim's. They treated me with indulgent and amazing patience under a system that required them to share their specialized, painfully accumulated professional knowledge with a privileged amateur soon to be elevated, through no merit of his own, to a world of wealth and power that they themselves could never hope to achieve. When, after nine months, I followed my predestined promotion to the Wheat Room, they accepted the move without surprise or resentment—but our intimacy was ended.

With my return to England I had reverted to the emotional habits of my childhood and adolescence: once again I found myself seesawing between the realities of "work" and the fantasies of my secret "holiday" world. The circumstances were changed but not the mechanism: my pattern of escape remained the same. Once again my life was sharply divided into two parts. Every morning a red bus carried me westward to my servitude, past the Inns of Court, St. Paul's and the Royal Exchange deep into the City. And every evening amid grinding gears and the stench of petrol the same red bus carried me back through the magic looking-glass that separated my two roles—from the fetid penumbra of Mister Newsom's domain into the shining region of my fantasies and desires.

In reality, few private lives could have been less glamorous or adventurous than the one I led, after office hours, during my first year in London. For a few weeks following my return from exile, I had made determined attempts to resume the relationships of my eleven years at Clifton. Of my companions from Mayor's House two were in the army, others at Oxford or Cambridge; still others (so drastically had British life changed since the war) were working for industrial and commercial concerns in the provinces and overseas. When we finally met in carefully arranged reunions we found, after our first sentimental effusions, that we had absolutely nothing to say to each other.

In my loneliness and from a desire to salvage some residue of human value from my wasted, detestable months in the Argentine, I began to record my impressions of that dark, brutal world in which I had lived for close to a year on the Estancia Santa Maria. I wrote compulsively, in response to an urgent emotional need, without any of the literary inhibitions that plagued me later, slowly and painfully at the rate of 50 or 100 words a night, deriving a sharp, pure pleasure from this secret and hopeless labor. As the months went by and the tide of loneliness receded, the necessity to write became less pressing. I still wrote one or two nights each week but without my former urgency, almost as though I were fulfilling a commitment on which I was reluctant to default. And as the pages accumulated in my drawer they changed gradually from a consolation and an escape into that concrete and alarming object—a book to be completed and shown, one day, to others.

In modest rooms, first in St. James's Place and then in Ebury Street (with George Moore on one side of me and Noël Coward on the other), I was beginning to make a life for myself. In the company of Alan Napier (who had fled his family's hardware business in Birmingham to try his fortune as an actor) I began my education in the theater, which we both attended undiscriminatingly as often as two or three times a week at prices ranging from one shilling to half a crown

My own social associations were forming gradually among the less extravagant elements of what the newspapers of the day insisted on calling "the Bright Young People." I met a pair of sisters about whom I made the astounding discovery that they were alumnae of that same finishing school for young ladies in which I had spent the most blissful weeks of my life. (I was of the class of 1907, while they belonged to a much later era during the war, when the establishment was moved from Paris to the south of England.) Eileen, the elder, with the high color and wide-set green eyes, was the Bohemian of the family—a painter of talent who left her parents' home in Mayfair to live in sin, first in Pimlico and then in Paris, where she became one of the earliest and best of the British surrealists. Winifred, the younger, with the red hair, was the "literary" one. She lent me books by authors of whom I had never heard—D.H. Lawrence, Llewelyn Powys, E.M. Forster and Katherine Mansfield; she gave me *Crome Yellow, Howard's End, South Wind, The Purple Land*, the *Criterion* and the *Adelphi* to read, presented me with *Lady into Fox* for Christmas and a thin orange book—*Jacob's Room* by Virginia Woolf—for my birthday. It was through her and her friend Bea Howe, whose family lived in a flat above Harrods and with whom I thought I was in love for some months, that I entered the magic region that was coming to be known as Bloomsbury, from which I returned to my bed-sitting room on Ebury Street—having laid eyes on Keynes and Lopokova, Roger Fry, Clive Bell, Lytton Strachey, Elsa Lanchester, Aldous Huxley and the mythical sisters, Virginia and Vanessa—with the pleasantly dizzy feeling of having been on the heights among the gods.

(One evening remains in my memory on which I attended a big party given in a house off the Fulham Road by two American girls whose beauty, energy and wealth were causing something of a stir in London that winter. David Garnett was in love with them and had just dedicated his latest book, *A Man in the Zoo*, to them both. Later, in different ways, both came to play vital parts in my life, but of that night I remember only that Mina Kirstein, the elder and more serious one, urged me to read *The Education of Henry Adams* while the other, Henrietta Bingham, known in Bloomsbury as "the Kentucky Heiress," sat on top of a piano in a purple velvet dress and played the saxophone.)

The day following my twenty-first birthday, armed with a note from Harry Siepmann on Bank of England stationery to a Home Office official, I filed my naturalization papers. I hoped for prompt action. I was disappointed. Four months were to pass before I was summoned for formal questioning and seven more before I was finally accepted as a citizen of the country in which I had spent more than twelve of the twenty-one years of my life. This was maddening for several reasons. After ten months in the Wheat Room at Pim's I was nearing the end of my apprenticeship. The next step was for me to become an assistant trader on the Baltic Exchange, which admitted only British citizens to its floor. Until my papers went through I could not even apply for membership.

I was stuck in other ways too. For more than two years now I had been a man without a country, incapable of movement in a world that lived by passports and visas. When my annual holiday fell due it was my mother who, reversing the rhythm of so many years, crossed the Channel to visit me. We spent a quiet, pleasant fortnight at Clovelly in Devonshire, where I finished the last and longest of the nine stories that were to make up my book. I had written around 40,000 words by now and I could not force myself to write another line. I made nervous, meaningless last-minute revisions and tried out several title pages, of which my final choice was:

THE PLAINS
by
John Houseman

Then I wrapped the manuscript with great care and sent it off by registered mail (receipt requested) to a typist in Bristol.

When I got back to Ebury Street, the receipt was waiting for me together with a summons from the Home Office to appear for my final naturalization proceedings. Within a month I was able to present the partners of Wm. H. Pim, Jr. & Co. Ltd. with a certificate of British nationality to go with my application for membership in the Baltic Exchange. While I anxiously awaited their verdict two things happened that made it irrelevant.

In the three years since I had started work on the book, less than half a dozen people had known of my nocturnal writing habits and only one had read more than a few pages of what I had done. This was Flora Mayor, the sister of my Clifton housemaster, Henry Bickersteth, one of the very few to whom I had kept writing during my South American exile. Plain, delicate and pathologically timid, she had poured much of her life into a novel that had been published while I was away and had been favorably received with reviews in which she was frequently compared to Trollope. It was to her, rather than to my Mayfair friends, that I brought the manuscript of *The Plains* and, on the following Sunday, under the trees of Richmond Park, received her approval. She added (and she hoped I would not mind) that she had sent it on to her own publishers, Leonard and Virginia Woolf at the Hogarth Press. I was appalled.

In the successive emotional stages I had gone through with the book I had only remotely considered the possibility of publication. This sudden, irrevocable exposure of my work to the publishers of Katherine Mansfield, T.S. Eliot, E.M. Forster, Sigmund Freud and Virginia Woolf herself shocked and terrified me. Within ten days a note arrived from Leonard Woolf saying that he and his wife had both read my book and would like to talk to me about it. He understood I worked in the City: how would Saturday tea suit me? I replied that Saturday tea would suit me very well, gave my blue suit to be pressed and carefully combed my hair for my visit to Tavistock Square.

I was received by a dark, slender, soft-spoken man who led me upstairs to a front room, where a lady whom I recognized as Virginia Woolf was seated at the tea table with a schoolboy of twelve or thirteen—a nephew, I gathered. During tea, I became aware of the incessant trembling of Leonard Woolf's hands and of the faint rattle of his cup and saucer, but it was on Mrs. Woolf that my attention was fixed. I had read *Jacob's Room*, *Kew Gardens* and *The Voyage Out* and I had seen her from afar, at night, tall, rustling and brilliant, at Bloomsbury soirées. I had heard of her wit and malice, of her shyness and melancholy. Here at home, behind her teapot, in the afternoon light, she was less formidable, with her hooded eyes and noble features, beautiful in a prematurely faded way, talkative, humorous and domestic.

Like film fogged by the brightness of the sun, my memory of that enchanted tea party is blurred and incomplete. I recall the nephew asking some question about H.G. Wells, which Virginia Woolf, smiling, passed on to me and to which I replied, flustered and unprepared, that in my opinion, Mr. Wells would be remembered for his prophetic and pseudo-scientific works. Mrs. Woolf disagreed. She maintained that Wells's early novels such as *Mr. Polly*, *Kipps* and *Tono Bungay* were works of originality and merit and the rest journalism of no interest whatsoever. Mr. Woolf shared her opinion, though less emphatically. After that the conversation became personal: I was asked questions about myself to which, in my desire to shed a more interesting light upon my writing, I gave answers that were only partially true. It was not until tea was over and the nephew had gone back to his homework that my book was mentioned. After nearly fifty years I can still feel myself in that small book-lined room, sitting breathless with delight, hardly hearing the quiet words of praise, spoken first by Mrs. Woolf and then by her consort—conscious only of the incredible and overwhelming fact that they liked my book and actually wanted to publish it!

Like most ecstasies it was short-lived. At my second meeting with the Woolfs, Leonard did most of the talking. He confirmed their liking for the work and repeated that he and Virginia would like to publish it at the Hogarth Press. However, as a small house of very limited resources, they were in no position to assume the financial risk that a commercial publisher would normally take with the first work of an author of promise. The Woolfs offered to assume one third of the cost of publication if I could supply the rest.

It must have been my sudden look of dismay that caused Mrs. Woolf to break in and explain that all her own books had been published in this way, including *Mrs. Dalloway*, which was about to appear. On the other hand, she could understand my reluctance at having to raise money for the publication of my first work; they offered to pass the manuscript on, with their recommendation, to Heinemann's, of which their close friend Desmond MacCarthy was chief editor. The weeks during which I waited for his reply were also those in which I continued to await the verdict of the directors of the Baltic Exchange. His came first—in longhand under the Heinemann letterhead: "I have just finished your manuscript. It is a pleasure to read what is so well written."

I lunched with Desmond MacCarthy at Boulestin's and found him charming and kind. He told me over brandy that he shared the Woolfs' good opinion of my book and was reporting favorably on it to Heinemann, but added that there were others to be consulted and that this would take time. As we were walking back to his office at the *New Statesman*, of which he was literary editor, I asked him on a sudden impulse if, in his opinion, I should adopt writing as a career. It was a foolish question, to which he gave me a sincere, sympathetic and realistic answer based on the experience of his own creative failure. One wrote out of necessity, he told me, not by choice. Then, as I was leaving, he suggested that I take one of the dozens of new books that were piled high on his table and chairs and review it for the *New Statesman*. I chose *A Story Teller's Story*, the autobiography of Sherwood Anderson, whose *Winesburg, Ohio* I had read and loved the year before. Utterly inexperienced in critical writing, I took more than three weeks to do the piece, working three or four nights a week. When it was finished it was more than double the length Mr. MacCarthy had requested and included most of what I knew and felt about contemporary American writing. He never acknowledged receipt of it, but when I received proof sheets some days later I found it uncut and almost unedited.

Four pieces of mine were published in the *New Statesman* that autumn, including a rather morbid short story over which the name John Houseman appeared in print for the first time. (O'Brien's *Best Short Stories of 1926* lists *The Ghoul* by John Houseman among the hundred best published British and Irish stories of the year.) As a result, during those last few months of my time in London, the rift which had been widening under the surface once again broke open and I found myself torn apart by the two warring and irreconcilable fantasies that continued to wage their dubious battle inside me for the next ten years.

As Jacques Haussmann, I continued to live my mother's image of me—a blend of English gentleman and continental merchant prince, a member of the world's international élite. So vague and grandiose were my expectations in this role that they made it almost impossible for me to face reality in any form. Hence the alternating waves of aimless megalomania and passive despair which formed the continuing pattern of my years in the international grain business.

As John Houseman my dreams were no less wild but at least they were my own. From the day of my arrival at Clifton among the Siepmanns, throughout the eleven years of my middle-class, Anglican, public-school education, I had developed vague cultural yearnings to which were added a deep, unreasoning distaste for the activities of the mercantile world into which I had been born. Repressed or dormant during my Argentine exile, this fantasy had gained strength during my years in London till, in the months following my first small literary successes, it had become the dominant influence in my life. Like my Trinity scholarship, with its vision of a distinguished academic career, this proved to be an illusion. At the first real test of strength, it was, once again, the inherited image of the merchant prince that prevailed. While the directors of the Baltic Exchange were still arguing over my application, I received an invitation one morning to come to the Ritz Hotel to the apartment of Monsieur Fribourg of Paris. I knew precisely what he was going to say to me and what my reply would be.

René Fribourg, a dapper man with a fuzzy moustache, received me cordially, inquired after my mother and then asked me how I would like to go to the United States where his company needed executive personnel for its rapidly expanding operations. I said yes before he had finished speaking and, in that instant, slammed the door shut on everything I had most desired during the past year.

My roots in London lay loosely in shallow soil and my farewells were sentimental but painless. Among my colleagues at Pim's, Jim Mitchell (a thin-lipped, ambitious Scot with a fleshy nose and a bulbous forehead), whose assistant I had been in the Wheat Room, expressed the hope that we would work together again some day. Desmond MacCarthy, when I called upon him to thank him for all he had done for me, admitted what I had long suspected—that he had lost the script of my book before showing it to anyone at Heinemann's. He asked if I had another copy and I said yes and he urged me to send it to him. I never did, for I had other things on my mind.

* * *

I sailed on the *Mauretania* with my new British passport and a special commercial visa issued to Jacques Haussmann under the Anglo-American treaty of Commerce and Navigation. I arrived in New York dreaming of adventures and triumphs that had not the faintest relation to the realities of my situation. I spent the weekend with one of my mother's friends in his Park Avenue apartment, was driven through the flaming Indian summer of the Hudson Valley, lunched at Voisin's under the hanging canary cages and dined with my aunt, looking out over the East River and Brooklyn Bridge, in the apartment she occupied on the top floor of the Beekman-Downtown Hospital, of which she had just been made superintendent. Then, on Monday morning, in pouring rain, I set out for the offices of the Continental Grain Corporation in the Produce Exchange at 1 Broadway. In the next five years that vast, low, red-brick building became hatefully familiar to me: I can see it still (through the towering structure of glass, steel and tile that has long since taken its place) as I first looked upon it in fear on that gray November morning on which my dream of America ended and reality began.

The Continental Grain Company's office was on the second floor and it was there, in the sweet-stale stench of rotting grain samples, wooden partitions, dried ink, glue and rubber stamps together with various kinds of paper (ledgers, carbons, ships' manifests, bills of lading, insurance certificates and warehouse receipts) and the tired bodies and sour breath of sedentary clerks, that I was interviewed by my new employers, who sat at a double desk in a small glass-enclosed room under a rain-streaked window overlooking the river. The senior director, Joseph Feuer, who said he had known me as a child in Rumania, was short, bald and potbellied with red-rimmed eyes and a duck-bill nose overhanging thick, dry lips, through which issued a strong Eastern European accent that remained constant in all of his many languages. He was also—as I discovered later when I was less completely blinded by disappointment and loathing—a man of great charm and culture, a strategist with a fertile imagination, which had enabled him, in less than five years, to build the Continental into one of the most active and progressive grain-handling firms on the North American continent. I listened to him, nodding and smiling, staring past him at the dirty, wrinkled water of New York Harbor and the Statue of Liberty beyond, while he outlined a future that in no way resembled the glamorous fantasies that I had come trailing across the Atlantic. Beginning the next day, I was to go to work in the office at a starting wage of $50 a week, learning the business once again "from

the ground up." In the spring, if he felt I was ready, I would be sent to
Chicago and from there to Kansas City, Winnipeg and the Pacific
Coast. What I was being offered, I knew, was the opportunity to
advance rapidly, along the accepted nepotistic route, to the top of the
fastest-growing company in the international grain trade. But all I
could hear, as I sat sunk in self-pity in the stale air of that cramped and
squalid office, was the snap of the trap which I had myself baited with
false dreams and megalomaniac fancies.

On the advice of an English actor friend, I had moved into a
monolith known as the Shelton Tower. With its thirty-two floors of
identical cells, this was a new kind of hotel—antiseptic, impersonal
and functional. At seven each morning the phone rang with my
wake-up call. Through the single window of my overheated cubicle I
could see the astonishing variations of New York's winter sky; leaden
clouds full of rain and snow alternating with pure, icy blue such as I
had never seen anywhere before. At 7:15 a.m. a soughing elevator
plunged me down to the Olympic pool in the basement where I swam
in chlorinated water before returning to my cell to dress. Then I was
whirled up to the cafeteria on the roof, where I joined the jostling herd
of men and women who stood tensely in line with their aluminum
trays before gleaming counters, from which young men in the
uniforms of hospital orderlies dispensed rustling cereals, canned fruit
juice, stewed prunes and pale-yellow mounds of dry scrambled eggs.
Then down again and along the freezing corridor of Lexington Avenue
into the stale warm mouth of Grand Central Station and the
exhilarating rush-hour frenzy of the IRT's South Ferry downtown
express.

My cell at the Shelton was on the twenty-third floor and here, in
the evenings, I made a few vain attempts to resume my writing. Soon
after my arrival I had sent a short story, hurriedly transplanted to U.S.
Soil, to the *Dial*, which returned it with a note from the poet Marianne
Moore in which she regretted that it was "not that of which we are in
search." I switched envelopes and sent it off to the *New Masses*, which
printed it opposite a cartoon by William Gropper but did not pay me.

It soon became apparent that the Tower was unsuited to creative
work—especially after dark. For, with the coming of night, those same
men and women with whom I had stood in line on the roof at dawn,
constipated and separate, sullen from forced awakenings and rigid
with apprehension of the day ahead, seemed to become liberated and
transformed. Filled, now, with a feverish awareness of each other's
presence and a collective lust that spread like wildfire through the thin
walls, across air wells and corridors, from cell to cell and from floor to
floor, they began to communicate with each other by phone or—if they

faced the inner court of the building as I did—by signs, grimaces and
gestures, through the brightly lit windows, from one face of the tower
to the other. These salutations went through various stages, from
preliminary approaches and rejections to smiles and assignations. And,
as the evening wore on, the corridors and safety stairs of the Shelton
Tower became alive with furtive migrants, each making his cautious
but determined way, in defiance of floor supervisors and house
detectives, to or from the cell of a fellow resident. I observed this
mating dance with fascination, but since there was only one logical end
to these maneuvers (one that I was still incapable of consummating)
my participation remained that of an enervated voyeur.

In England, where sexual backwardness such as mine was not
exceptional, I had succeeded, without too much embarrassment or
difficulty, in finding intellectual and sentimental palliatives for my
chastity. In America, where sex seemed to play a more direct and
aggressive part in the national life, my nagging concern with my
condition was harder to bear. Aggravated by boredom and loneliness,
it became my main preoccupation and involved me in romantic
sublimations and sentimental obsessions which have no place in a
factual narrative such as this. At their center stood the figure of a tall
girl with blue eyes—or, rather, the image of her I had formed to suit
my own urgent emotional needs. For the next two years, during most
of which we were thousands of mile apart, there was hardly an hour of
my days and nights that was not permeated by dreams of her. Looking
back through the mists of hope, ambition and frustrated yearning with
which I surrounded her, I find it impossible to separate the memory of
the real Henrietta Bingham—with whom I fell in love my first
Christmas in New York and with whom I finally lost my virginity in an
English seaside hotel with a crystal chandelier and red damask walls
sixteen months later—from the fantasy of her that I created in the
loneliness of my first wander-years in America.

I left New York in mid-March of 1926 on the Twentieth Century
Limited. As a travelling representative of the Continental Grain
Corporation and one of its future directors, I was supposed to
familiarize myself with the workings of the two great wheat
markets—Chicago and Winnipeg—and their relation to the flow of
grain from the Western prairies through the elevators of the interior to
the main coastal shipping points. I was no longer an apprentice: my
salary was doubled and I was given a generous living allowance.

Yet, so deep was the division inside me that, as the train carried me
through the night, it was still unclear to me whether it was the exciting
prospect of a brilliant career in the grain-export business that kept me

awake in my lurching lower berth or the exhilaration of entering that vast, enchanted land—the America of Whitman and Sandburg, Dreiser, Sinclair Lewis, Frank Norris and Sherwood Anderson—of which I had already formed such a vivid literary image and which I was now impatient to discover for myself.

At dawn, through the dining-car window, I watched the gray, sprawling steel mills of Gary, Indiana, and, soon after, as we clanged slowly through the yards, the littered desolation of the Chicago slums. I first saw the Loop, deserted on that Sunday morning—the air tainted with a faint, sickening smell of putrefaction from the stockyards. There was a motion-picture convention at the Drake Hotel when I arrived and the lobby was jammed with men with Western hats and cigars and women who looked like Clara Bow, with pillboxes on their shingled heads. When I got to my room I could see the vast expanse of Lake Michigan through my window, its shimmering, wind-swept water stretching out beyond the breakwater for what seemed like an infinite distance into the sky.

The Continental Grain Corporation's Chicago office occupied two small, crowded rooms in an annex of the Chicago Board of Trade. It was run by a slender, serious, opinionated man with dark, sharp eyes and prematurely white hair named Simon Mayer. It was he who gave me my first vision of the Chicago Wheat Pit.

I had been aware of the Pit's existence and felt its remote power in the Wheat Room at Pim's; I had read Frank Norris's account of it. Looking down on it for the first time from the visitors' gallery, confused by the reverberating howl that filled the building, I was aware only of a dark, circular motion below me—as of a huge pot boiling. Then, as I grew accustomed to the movement and the continuous roar, I came to realize that this seething mass was the sum of the movements of hundreds of human beings—of waving arms, struggling bodies and, occasionally, an upturned face distorted in a grotesque expression of passion. For five hours, each day, in this bowl of heaving flesh, furious battles were fought by men in business suits, alpaca jackets and shirtsleeves—deadly single combats in which opponents sought each other out, slashing their way through the struggling mass as they approached each other with threatening gestures, moving closer and closer till finally they stood face to face, straining for each other's throats, grappling, grabbing, tearing at each other's clothes, their mouths twisted, screaming inaudible words which they punctuated with wild, spastic gestures that indicated to those who were familiar with the Pit's mysterious sign language the price and delivery date of imaginary masses of wheat.

Multiply this action by hundreds and you had a normal morning's activity in the Chicago Wheat Pit. And over it hung that cloud of sound—the roar of hundreds of human voices which, combined, expressed the collective emotion of the moment: the sharply rising modulation that goes with a bull market and the barking, descending tone which indicates that the bears are in command—so that even an outsider like myself could soon tell by ear, from the sound that rose out of the Pit, whether the wheat market was, at that moment, rising or falling.

Long after the first physical thrill had worn off and I had begun to understand the inner workings of the international wheat-futures markets, I continued to derive excitement and pleasure from the action of the Pit itself and from the realization that its fluctuations occurred in response to influences that went beyond immediate considerations of supply and demand and included the meteorology of four continents, national and international politics, greed, fear, money, power and, sometimes, nothing more than collective hysteria.

New York had overwhelmed me with its violence; in Chicago it was the extremity of the contrasts that fascinated me. These began with the weather and included every aspect of the city: the old and new side by side, the beautiful and the indescribably hideous, the sickening poverty and the exaggerated, flaunted wealth—all in a state of rapid and continuous flux. Close by my hotel, along the luxurious Lake Shore Drive, stood the great houses of the very rich. And here, each Sunday, in the first exploding heat of the Midwestern spring, I watched the proletariat take over. They came in the thousands—Italians, Jews, Czechs and Poles, gray from their long hibernation in their dark crowded tenements—an untidy flood darkening the sidewalks, flowing past the locked doors and shuttered windows of the millionaires' mansions, irresistibly drawn to the waters of the lake, where they lay all day on the narrow public beaches, devouring huge Old World meals and washing their pale, hairy bodies in the dark-green, restless waters.

My memory of Kansas City, where I arrived in early June, in time for the start of the wheat harvest in western Kansas, Oklahoma and the panhandle of Texas, is colored by two dominant impressions—loneliness and heat. Nowhere else had I experienced such unbearable heat—harsh and dry like the blast from an open furnace, the air radiated from the brick and concrete walls of buildings, rose trembling from the pavements and melting asphalt of the streets and lay over the mouth like a blanket, drying the saliva and forcing the breath back into the throat. Much of the city's life during July and August seemed devoted to finding ways of defeating or evading the heat. The surest refuge was to be found in the newly constructed movie palaces: vast, freezing, red-carpeted caverns of marble and gold which, in addition to the icy escstasy of excessive refrigeration, offered three hours of variegated entertainment. These were the last great years of silent films supplemented by swooping and thrilling performances on the Wurlitzer and, in the larger theaters, by ineffably tedious "stage shows." Other places of refuge were the several "roofs" atop Kansas City's newer hotels where couples left their thin, tepid jellied consommé, limp lettuce smeared with creamy dressings, and melting ice cream to shuffle around in dank, joyless circles in the mistaken belief that they would feel the heat less if they moved. The same craving for motion motivated the hundreds of thousands of miles of driving that took place in and around Kansas City throughout the summer nights. For some it was a prelude to lovemaking; with others it led to roadhouse crap games and the spiked-beer joints on the Kansas side of the river. But, for most of them, it was a hopeless attempt to postpone the insomnia that played such an essential part in Kansas City's summer life. I, whom war, bankruptcy, and the preoccupation of sex have seldom prevented from falling asleep within thirty seconds of my head's hitting the pillow, would lie trapped hour after hour in my creaking, rumpled, sweat-dampened Murphy bed on the seventh floor of the Ambassador Hotel, caught between the lights of the streaming traffic in the street below and the muted, persistent pounding of the dance bands on the roof above. And when the bands were finally still and most of the cars were off the streets, a new sound would take over—the dry crackling and rolling thunder of the endlessly circling electric storms that nightly shook the overheated Missouri River bottoms and, far from relieving the heat, seemed to aggravate and intensify it.

Loneliness was nothing new. I had known it for much of my life—in its most painful form in my early years at Clifton, in its most dismal and damaging shape on the Estancia Santa Maria. In Kansas City, from the time I left the office in midafternoon till the next morning when I took a green Broadway bus to work, I was almost always alone; over the weekends I would go for sixty hours without speaking a word to anyone except a waitress or a bus driver. Even during the week my work with the Continental, which I continued to do conscientiously but with ambivalent feelings, occupied only part of my time and none of my emotional energy. To fill the void of my days and nights, besides writing endless, yearning, tear-drenched letters to Henrietta wherever she happened to be, I engaged in curious activities of my own: I found myself singing "Brighten the Corner Where You Are" with 10,000 of Billy Sunday's adherents in one of his monster revival meetings; I attended the dog races, walked for hours in the railroad yards, paid weekly visits to the Columbia Burlesque Wheel and to the Wednesday evening testimonies at the Christian Science churches that abounded in Kansas City. When these palled I found myself resuming my interrupted education: I began to read compulsively in English, French and occasionally in German with an appetite that grew with the months, following no organized plan or order but letting one book lead to another, one writer suggest another, one area of interest bleed into another and create the desire and the necessity for further reading.

Chicago and Kansas City were the first stops in the chain of travel which, for the next two and a half years, carried me back and forth across the North American continent to such places as Kansas City (three times), Winnipeg, Duluth, Calgary, Vancouver (three times), Seattle, Portland, Minneapolis, Wichita, Fort Worth, Galveston (four times), New Orleans and St. Louis (twice).

I made few friends on my travels: a fifty-year-old Mormon in Vancouver, BC; an anarchist hobo from New York, who had known Emma Goldman and who followed me from Kansas City to the Coast and taught me IWW songs; a nigger-hating shipowner's son in Galveston, Texas—these were the temporary associates with whom I ate and talked and went for walks. They remain vague figures on the edges of my memory but my true companions of that time—besides my own dream figures and fantasies—were the ideas and the characters I discovered in the pages of the books I was reading.

My memories of the places that I passed through are still related to what I was reading while I was there and form a strange emotional geography of their own. I discovered the wonders of *The Golden Bough* on a hill of tall grass and yellow daisies in a public park overlooking the Missouri River; *The Brothers Karamazov* on a peeling, green bench in a Kansas courthouse square on which I sat waiting all afternoon for a bus. I read the first two volumes of Proust in a maroon Pullman car of the Canadian Pacific Railroad crossing the snow-white prairie from east to west; the first hundred pages of *Das Kapital* in a sand- and soot-filled lower berth close behind a wood-burning Southern Pacific locomotive speeding at night along the Gulf Coast; Rilke and *Bateau Ivre* in the cabin of a camp in the Ozarks, which I shared with an insurance salesman from St. Joseph, Missouri; Michelet's *Histoire de la Révolution Française*, *Tom Jones*, *The Possessed* and the *Revelations of St. John the Divine* under the rain-laden winter skies of the Pacific Northwest; *The Conquest of Mexico* in a hotel room on the main street of Joplin, Missouri, where I found myself spending the night of the Fourth of July, 1926, amid the patriotic explosions of torpedoes and crackerballs.

***

My twenty-fifth year saw the consummation and the final agony of my love affair with Henrietta Bingham. This coincided and probably triggered the sudden, violent reassertion of some long-buried Alsatian trader's instinct. Leaving John Houseman to his mooning, I became, almost overnight, one of the most successful young traders in the North American grain-export business. It began with the effective campaign I conducted for the Continental Grain Corporation in the Pacific Northwest. This first success filled me with exultation: the merchant prince was taking over. The following summer, on my second visit to Kansas City, I showed great energy and skill in anticipating and exploiting an unusually early movement of American winter wheat to the Gulf of Mexico. Once again I overwhelmed the competition and made a killing for the Continental Grain Company, which, surprised and delighted, doubled then trebled my salary and sent me personal congratulations from the main office in Paris.

This was not enough for me. During my years of frustration I had built up a head of steam that was now driving me forward at a speed I could no longer control. For years I had felt not the slightest material ambition; I made up for it now with a ravenous appetite for money that I made no attempt to control. From an insecure, reluctant apprentice I had been transformed in twelve months into a confident, arrogant young proconsul moving from one provincial victory to another. Now I was becoming impatient for my triumphal entry into the capital.

I spent the last part of that summer in St. Louis, supervising our shipments of wheat down the Mississippi to New Orleans; having an affair, on the rebound, with an Olympic swimming champion whose lust and energy almost equalled my own; and preparing for my next move. Then, one evening, while I was listening to Al Smith on the radio, I received a long-distance call from Winnipeg. It was from Jim Mitchell, the shrewd, thin-lipped Scot with whom I had worked in the Wheat Room at Pim's. He said he needed to talk to me on a most urgent matter before returning to London.

We met secretly in his suite at the Plaza Hotel in New York. He had just concluded a deal with one of the leading grain-elevator chains in Western Canada; now he was looking for someone to set up a New York office and to run the North American branch of his firm. Two weeks later I was president and managing director of the Oceanic Grain Corporation at a guaranteed salary of $20,000 a year plus 5 percent of the profits.

My parting from the Continental was traumatic. When I first handed in my resignation the directors figured it was a maneuver to get more money out of them and offered to match whatever I was offered elsewhere. When they realized that I really intended to leave, they were hurt and furious: in their eyes my desertion was more than a commercial infamy; it was a personal and racial betrayal. I listened politely, unable to explain to them that the more reckless and insane my action appeared, the more irresistible and exhilarating I found it.

The Oceanic Grain Company was incorporated in the state of Delaware with a paid-up capital of $250,000, most of which was also being used in London to finance Mitchell's European operations. Our opening offensive would be launched during the winter from the Canadian Pacific coast, where I had already demonstrated my skill. The Vancouver season did not start till December, when the Eastern waterways froze over; this gave me time to start setting up an organization and to make my personal adjustment to life in New York.

I had been surprised, on my return, to find my foster sibling, Eric Siepmann, living on 12th Street, three blocks form the Brevoort, where I was staying. He had come to the United States as a correspondent for the London *Times*, thrown up that job on an alcoholic caprice but remained in New York as an editorial writer for the New York *Post*. He was living with a woman named Magda—a painter who made her living doing drawings of children's clothes and whom Eric had described to me as "a catlike beauty with a small round head, huge black eyes, little hands like claws and thin legs of the American kind though she was brought here form Hungary at the age of six."

They led an uneasy but fascinating life on the margin of Greenwich Village; most of my evenings—after so many months of provincial solitude—were spent in the company of their friends, who included e. e. cummings, Heywood Broun, Jimmy Light from the Provincetown Theater, Edmund Wilson and Magda's sister, Zita, who was seldom around because she was rehearsing a play.

It was to see her that we went one night, all dressed up, to the Plymouth Theater to my first Broadway opening. *Machinal*, by Sophie Treadwell, was a sentimentalized, epressionistic version of the highly publicized Snyder-Gray murder case. But the evening really belonged to a dark, slender, totally unknown girl by the name of Zita Johann, who illuminated the play's feminine clichés with a deep, tragic tenderness of her own. (It also belonged, in a lesser degree, to a tall, dark, relaxed, sexy young man with big ears who was making his Broadway debut that night under his stage name of Clark Gable.) We went backstage after the show and took Zita out to supper while we waited for the reviews. I found her beautiful and exciting and vulnerable, with flowing dark eyes and a smile which, on that first evening, when she was flushed and bewildered by her sudden success, was irresistibly moving.

Five days after the opening of *Machinal*, Zita and I became lovers. She was living on West End Avenue in a room with a studio couch. It was the first time in my life I had lived with a woman, spent each night with her—our bodies restless and intertwined in that narrow bed—made love half-asleep in the dark and awakened beside her at dawn. We were apart during the day and met again at dusk. Since she had to be in the theater by seven, we ate at strange hours in curious places. After the performance she was completely wrung out and wanted only to be taken home. But several times, after her Saturday night show, we took a late train to Long Beach and spent the night and the next day in a curious and awful hotel (under the name of Mr. and Mrs. John Wolf) overlooking the deserted boardwalk and the beach and the gray, rolling Atlantic breakers.

In mid-November, while *Machinal* was still running, I left for Vancouver. I was to be gone for three months and, when her play closed, Zita was to join me on the coast. It did close early in January but she went off, instead, to California—to the MGM studio in Culver City where Irving Thalberg, then at the height of his inflated fame, was courting her with golden promises of stardom. In February, on my way east, I visited her in Santa Monica, where she was enjoying the sun and the beach and living in reasonable luxury for the first time in her life. When I got back to New York, I began to search for an apartment. In a bare penthouse on the roof of 66 Fifth Avenue, where an old man lay dying, I found what I was looking for. I signed a two-year lease and asked a French lady of my acquaintance to decorate it. She assumed I wanted it *"moderne"* and I made no objection.

My first season with the Oceanic had gone well. With the Western Canadian wheat available to us through our grain-elevator association, I had succeeded, once again, in dominating the field. And, by supplying Mitchell in London with a continuous flow of saleable cargoes, we had helped him to build up his sales organization into one of the finest in Europe. As a result, when the Oceanic opened its New York office in March in a half-furnished, newly painted office on the third floor of the Produce Exchange and we started cabling our first offers of open-water Canadian wheat from the Eastern seaboard, we found ourselves almost immediately doing a huge business in that, too. I had designed the Oceanic as a flexible, streamlined organization capable of operating with a lower overhead and at a smaller profit margin than our competitors. This worked even better than I had expected and our business took a further jump in June when the American winter-wheat crop began to move to market and we once again outpaced the field. However, by the end of July, I was becoming seriously concerned over the extent of our success.

There was nothing speculative about our operation. Each of our trades was made at a profit and each purchase and sale was instantly and automatically covered in the futures markets of Chicago and Winnipeg. It was the sheer mass of our business that worried me. This was the mad summer of 1929—the last feverish spasm of the great boom of the twenties. Inevitably, spiralling stock prices had affected commodities. Speculators were pouring their easy money into anything they could find—including grain, which had become part of the international crap game.

One morning in mid-August, Mr. Weaver, our office manager—his jowls gray and flaccid from sitting all night over his calculating machine—walked into my office, closed the door and pushed a slip of paper across my desk. It indicated that our loans had reached the astounding total of over $8 million—more than thirty times our declared capital.

Late in August Zita returned from California. In her six months with MGM she had made money but no pictures. She arrived, with a Russian wolfhound and a Croatian cook, just in time to move into the penthouse, which, though far from finished, was becoming habitable. We never succeeded in recapturing the wonder of those first weeks on West End Avenue, but we were pleased to be together again and fascinated by the strange environment that was forming around us—the sheer white walls, the gray-and-black built-in cabinetwork, the black-glass and chromium tables, the tubular metal chairs and the vast shiny cork surface of our outer terrace.

Living in sin among all these gleaming and costly belongings required more nerve than either of us possessed; in mid-September, a few days before my twenty-seventh birthday, we went down to City Hall one morning and got married, with my aunt and one of her ambulance drivers as our witnesses. Early in October we gave our first party. A few weeks later, on the morning of what came to be known as Black Thursday, I stood on the floor of the Produce Exchange and watched the market collapse—saw it first, with fascinated, incredulous horror, on the overhead blackboards where the Chicago and Winnipeg wheat-futures quotations were falling so fast that, within an hour, trades were no longer being recorded. After that we huddled around the grinding ticker tape, and, when that too fell hopelessly behind, stood leaning across the telegraph counter listening to the dry clacking of the keys and the flat voices of the operators reporting orders executed at prices that could not be believed. The panic could be seen most clearly on the faces of the men who rushed to answer the constantly ringing bells in the private phone booths and who came out, seconds later, blind and shaking and looking suddenly as though they wanted to die.

Nothing like it had ever been seen or imagined. Infected by the stock-market panic, wheat futures lost more than a tenth of their value in two hours and double that in the days to come. Holding no speculative position on the market, Oceanic was not directly affected by the Crash—or so I thought.

Our huge wheat sales had been made at pre-Crash prices to various parts of Europe with delivery dates that extended over a period of several months. This meant that until we got paid, we had to carry several million bushels of wheat, financed at prices so far above their present value that we were being pressed on all sides to make up the difference. In normal times, with fractional fluctuations, this would have presented no particular problem. For the Oceanic—overextended, undercapitalized, precariously balanced on its frail pyramid of shrinking credit—it became a catastrophe.

All through November and early December, still only partially aware of our situation, I continued to navigate a vessel whose decks were already awash. Every day I sat at my desk signing checks which I hoped were good and listening to bad news that grew steadily worse. Our accountant, gray and glassy-eyed, was fighting desperately to keep us afloat—juggling collateral, postdating checks, ignoring calls, acting dumb, using every technicality to put off the inevitable moment when a note would be presented or a loan called and we would have to admit our inability to meet it.

Just before Christmas the last of the imported furniture—a gray, fur-lined armchair—was delivered to the penthouse at 66 Fifth Avenue. That same day our accountant had a nervous breakdown and spent the next two days visiting the nation's leading manufacturers of office equipment and ordering $500,000 worth of calculating machines in my name. He died of a brain tumor three weeks later.

And, some weeks after that—wearing an appropriately sober suit and a black knitted tie—I appeared in the Arbitration Room of the New York Produce Exchange before the assembled creditors of the Oceanic Grain Corporation. To the questions that were put to me as president of the stricken corporation I gave sincere and straightforward answers in a voice that was muted with remorse. Since blood cannot be squeezed out of a stone, the creditors were reproachful but lenient. It had already been determined that there was no ground for criminal action and no material advantage to anyone in a forced bankruptcy. So they lectured me on my folly, then excused me while they made the final tally of our losses (which amounted to between $200,000 and $300,000, mostly to banks) and settled the details of the liquidation. I thanked them with hatred in my heart and left the room—a picture of modesty and repentance.

I walked down the long corridor with the faint, familiar rumor of the Exchange floor on my left and went on down the steps that wound around the antique iron elevator shaft to the street level, past the newsstand, the telegraph office, the spittoons and the shoeshine stands, on through the swinging doors into the cold air of Battery Place, past the customs House, through the early afternoon traffic into Battery Park with its bare winter trees, across the burnt grass, among the fluttering pigeons, sandwich wrappings and paper cups—the lunch-hour leavings of secretaries and office boys.

Seated on a bench, looking past the Aquarium across the river to the Jersey shore, as the exhilaration of disaster slowly ebbed away, I held a small, private liquidation meeting of my own over the affairs of Jacques Haussmann and concluded that there, too, the liabilities greatly exceeded the assets. He had had his big chance and muffed it; at twenty-seven he was thoroughly discredited in the only activity in which he had any training or experience or connections. His cash position was deplorable; against the few thousand dollars he had managed to salvage, he had personal debts of over $20,000 including the money he had borrowed to acquire his now worthless stock in the Oceanic. His emotional situation was little better: involved in a marriage that he had never really desired, he found himself committed to a way of life that he could no longer afford but from which he saw no way of disengaging himself. Other liabilities included his mother in Paris, to whose support he had been contributing for the past two years and who, by her own account, was once again down to her last few thousand francs. Last, and by no means least, was the disturbing realization that with the dissolution of the Oceanic Grain Corporation and the consequent loss of his commercial visa, Jacques Haussmann was, as of this moment, an illegal resident of the United States of America, subject to arrest and expulsion, and with little likelihood (as a native of Rumania whose immigration quota was filled for years to come) of ever achieving legal entry to the only country in the world to which he had any sense of belonging.

It was a dismal catalog of defeats—one that filled him with a sudden sense of overwhelming despair. In spite of the cold, he remained seated on his bench for more than an hour, while the red mass of the Produce Exchange darkened behind him. Finally, after the street lights had been turned on, he got up and moved slowly through the small, deserted park, between the bare trees and the pigeons, back toward Battery Place and the Bowling Green subway station of the Broadway IRT. It was late afternoon and the rush hour was just beginning. At the head of the stairs he hesitated for a moment and turned to look for a cab. Seeing none, he went on down the steps and, once and for all, out of the pages of this history.

I
Four Saints in Three Acts
1934

From Jacques Haussmann, the merchant prince, I inherited five business suits, a black Auburn convertible, a penthouse with sixteen months of its two-year lease still to run, four languages, perfect health, a beautiful and talented wife, and an extensive collection of fantasies, the most persistent and dangerous of which was the notion that I was a long-repressed creative artist who would now, at last, have a chance to follow his true vocation as a writer. The three years I spent trying to reconcile this yearning with the realities of the world were among the worst of my life.

Seated on my imported tubular metal chair at my black-glass and chromium table, I soon made the horrifying discovery that I had absolutely nothing to write about. I sat there day after day and then week after week, through the spring and early summer of 1930, with a pile of crumpled paper at my feet, darkening sheet after sheet with words that only vaguely reflected my own confused private fantasies and could be of no conceivable interest to anyone else.

All this time my money was running out and my personal situation was getting worse by the hour. My relations with my wife—even in the days and nights of our first romantic and physical ardor—had been based on the mutual assumption that we were a unique and glamorous couple, wonderfully and peculiarly suited to each other. Lovely, sensitive, much admired and publicly acclaimed, Zita Johann was the perfect mistress for a successful, sensitive young executive at the height of his powers; she also supplied a vicarious outlet for my frustrated artistic aspirations. I offered equivalent attractions: a young man of a kind she had never known, handsome, self-confident, cultivated and rich, performing mysterious miracles in the international markets of the world; I also represented security—her permanent protection from the hazards of a notoriously precarious profession.

Now suddenly I had broken my part of the contract and she woke up to find herself in bed with a frightened, ruined man in his early thirties who seemed intent upon groping his aimless and anxious way into a new life for which he had no apparent qualifications. What was worse—he seemed quite content, after his savings were gone, to live indefinitely on her earnings.

Yet it was Zita who broke up the inertia into which I was sinking and who first brought up a possibility that I had never even considered: that my future might lie in the theater. She suggested one night that we try writing a play together.

It happened quickly and it came out surprisingly well, flowing easily out of our combined subjective experience. It was a story of unrealized love between two insecure, ill-suited young people—a lonely girl and a boy with a frightened, possessive mother—and it took place in a small hotel by a lake that blended some of the nostalgic elements of my own Swiss holidays with Zita's memories of the times when she had waited on the tables of summer resorts in her teens. It was derivative, low in energy and quite European (somewhere between *Grand Hotel* and *The Seagull*), but it had a depth of personal feeling that makes it unlike anything I ever wrote before or since. We finished it in six weeks and Zita typed it and gave it to Alexander Kirkland, who ran the Berkshire Playhouse at Stockbridge, Massachusetts. He agreed, if Zita would appear in it, to present *The Lake* during their summer season, between *Romeo and Juliet* and *The Admirable Crichton*. After the first dress rehearsal, Aline MacMahon told me that the play made her feel as though she had grown hair on her teeth during the evening. But, once again, Zita was much admired, and we got sympathetic reviews from one New York critic who was vacationing in the neighborhood.

While we were in Stockbridge a call came from Jed Harris, the producer, then at the height of his sulphurous fame. He wanted Zita for the part of Sonya in his production of *Uncle Vanya*, which he was sending on tour. After weeks of negotiating—Jed wooing, Zita fleeing; Zita relenting, Jed cooling, then pursuing again—she signed her contract and departed. During her absence I started looking around for a congenial collaborator to work with while she was away.

I found him in the person of Lewis Galantière, a multilingual Franco-American, a few years older than myself, who worked for the Federal Reserve Bank and had acquired some reputation for his translations and critical writings. Erudite, myopic and gregarious, he saw himself following the great European literary tradition of the bureaucrat-intellectual and man about town. We decided to write a play together: something between a Restoration comedy and Parisian boulevard farce. We both knew and admired Sacha Guitry's *L'Illusioniste*, from which we purloined the basic idea: that of a man so charming and persuasive that he can talk any woman he desires into loving him and, when he is tired of her, talk her painlessly out of love. It was all very Gallic and we took our title *Lovers, Happy Lovers* from the last stanza of La Fontaine's fable *Les Deux Pigeons*. The structure—the least interesting part of the work—was mine: the dialogue and the style were mostly Lewis's. We worked during weekends and at hours when he was free from the bank, either at my glass-and-chromium table or in Robert Benchley's apartment, where Lewis was living. Lewis protested periodically that such foolery was not for him, but he was having a good time; as a small fastidious man with thick glasses, he found vicarious satisfaction in the gambits of our philandering hero.

We progressed slowly and we were barely halfway through the second act when Zita returned from her *Vanya* tour, brooding over her personal and professional situation. Since her sudden triumph in *Machinal* nothing had been offered her in the theater that she considered worthy of her; her experience in Hollywood had been profitable but disturbing. Convinced, like all theater people, that each engagement was the last, she was filled with growing resentment over my fecklessness—especially when I admitted that, during her absence, I had been unfaithful to her and had been offered a job on the Produce Exchange which I had turned down. We had scenes that alarmed even our savage Croatian cook. Then suddenly, out of the blue, she was offered the starring role in Philip Barry's new play, *Tomorrow and Tomorrow*, opening on Broadway early in the new year.

Rehearsals began almost immediately and Zita was able to transfer some of her rage from me to Gilbert Miller, her producer-director, who never for one moment concealed the fact that he had cast her at the author's insistence and that he himself felt she was all wrong for the part. Spoiled by the loving permissiveness of Arthur Hopkins's direction in *Machinal*, she reacted to Miller's bellowing coarseness with sullen Hungarian fury.

Tomorrow and Tomorrow was not one of Barry's brightest successes. Zita was commended for giving it "distinction with the fragility and radiance of her personality," and it was still running when Lewis Galantière and I finally finished our comedy. Within a week, to our stupefaction, three major Broadway producers had offered to buy it and it had been sold to Gilbert Miller as a vehicle for New York's leading romantic star and matinée idol, Leslie Howard. Under the Dramatists' Guild contract the standard price for a six-month option was $500, of which I received one half. With what I had made on *The*

Lake and after deducting the agent's commission, my total earnings for the year amounted to $275.

My situation was desperate, but I was not dissatisfied. In twelve months I had worked on three plays and now I was starting on a fourth—another collaboration. I had made the acquaintance, soon after my arrival in New York, of a former newspaperman, A.E. Thomas, the author of several successful Broadway comedies. He was no longer young and, shaken by the convulsions that were changing his world, he was looking for a partner with an idea for a contemporary play. He found it in a notion I suggested to him after borrowing it from Jules Romains, who had used it in two of his plays: that, with the multiplying means of publicity in our modern world, almost any idea or personality can be sold to a sufficient number of people to make it seem real. My plot—by no means a brilliant or original one—showed an aging, indigent and alcoholic street musician being elevated through human credulity and corruption and the machinations of a high-powered publicity agent to the status of an international celebrity.

I remember our collaboration with embarrassment. With incredible arrogance I set about correcting this veteran playwright's work. When he questioned some of my amendments, I snatched the script from him and proceeded, without consultation or permission, to rewrite whole sections of it before sending it off to my agent, who immediately sold it for production at the Cleveland Play House during the following season.

With the sale of *A Very Great Man* my earnings had risen to $410 in fifteen months—hardly enough to justify renewing the lease on the penthouse, which, besides, had been the scene of too many miseries and disasters. Still, it was saddening to watch all that costly, built-in cabinetwork ripped out and carted off, together with the glass-and-chromium table and the fur-lined armchair, to a warehouse, where they remained until they were sold at auction for non-payment of storage years later.

Zita and I moved for the summer to a small house in New City in Rockland County on the west shore of the Hudson River, from which she was driven at dawn each day to the studio where she was working on her first film—for D.W. Griffith. The great man had sent for her during the run of *Tomorrow and Tomorrow*, interviewed her in his New York hotel room (in a fine, old-fashioned way, with the lights so arranged that she sat in brightness while he remained concealed in the shadows) and announced to the world that he had chosen her above all other young actresses in America to star in his latest picture—*The Struggle*.

His fortunes were at the lowest possible ebb. From somewhere he had raised not quite enough money to make this, his last film, in a small, ill-equipped studio in the Bronx. It was an unhappy engagement, during which Zita found herself working in outrageous conditions with none of the charismatic inspiration that Lillian Gish and so many others had found in earlier films with the Old Master. She would return late at night, green with exhaustion from chasing her alcoholic husband in the film from saloon to saloon in pouring rain—drenched, shivering, wind-whipped and deafened by the old-fashioned wind machines—and sit hunched before our midsummer fire, drying out and mumbling bitterly through her tears as she chewed her cold supper that she should never have done the lousy picture and that she was ruining her career and her health to hold our marriage together. She was still trying to hold it together in the fall when she insisted that I accompany her on the tour of *Tomorrow and Tomorrow*, which was being sent out to the principal cities of the East and Midwest. I resisted. I wanted to stay quietly in the country where it cost me almost nothing to live and work. By the time she got back we would both have had a chance to test our crumbling relationship and, possibly, with one or more of my plays in production, to redress my ignominious financial situation. Zita refused: she would not go on the tour unless I went with her. After days of argument I gave in.

I have always found travel exciting. For all my loneliness and frustration, my three years of wandering for the Continental had been rich in personal discoveries. But this tour was a nightmare: seven Middle Western cities in the dead of winter. For Zita there was the stimulation of facing new audiences eight times a week. For me there was nothing but the tedium of sitting in identical, overheated hotel suites, pretending to work but, in fact, reading the papers and sleeping and, when I could stand it no longer, walking the frozen streets.

My gloom was not entirely personal. On my earlier visits to many of these same cities in the twenties I had breathed an air that was vigorous and lively and rich with hope. Now all that was changed. The Great Depression had the country by the throat. Everywhere in the streets, in that winter of 1931, there was the bitter, pervasive smell of fear and despair.

Then one morning we woke up in our drawing room aboard the Santa Fe Superchief and saw the orange groves and palm trees of the San Bernardino Valley racing by. An hour later, with flashbulbs popping, we were basking in the bright sunshine of Hollywood. Zita had signed a new contract, this time with Howard Hawks for a picture called *Tiger Shark*, in which she was to appear, as a tuna fisherman's wife, with Edward G. Robinson. We lived for two weeks in Los Angeles, then moved to San Diego for location work with the tuna fleet. The day we arrived, the corpses of the two 18-foot tiger sharks that had been caught off the coast of Baja California were hauled out of the deep freeze and wired for action. The company moved across to Catalina Island, where we lived in bungalows at the water's edge. I spent my days on the set, learning what I could about the making of motion pictures until one day, in the Catalina Channel, while Robinson was playing his final sequence on the deck of the tuna boat (after the tiger shark had chewed off his leg), he refused to continue his death scene with Zita until I had been removed and rowed to shore.

When we returned to the mainland we moved into a small beach house we had rented in Malibu. It was elegantly decorated in blue and white with nautical motifs and had been used by Joan Crawford for her honeymoon with Franchot Tone. From here Zita was driven to work each morning, across the mountains to Burbank, in her secondhand, sixteen-cylinder Cadillac, while I chugged along the coast to Culver City in the Chevrolet roadster I had bought for $200—with my first week's earnings at the MGM Studio, where, through the efforts of Zita's agent, I had been engaged to work on a film about the Kansas wheat fields, on which he had assured them I was an expert. I sat in my cell in the Writers' Building in Culver City and no one came near me or told me what the movie was about. After three weeks the producer summoned and fired me.

I sat on the sand at Malibu making revisions on one of my plays, watching the gulls and the pelicans make their regular flights up an down the coast and waiting for Zita to come home. On weekends or when she did not have to work the next day, we dressed up and went to openings and to parties which I attended as the Star's husband. She was having her usual fights with the Studio: unable to find a film that was mutually acceptable, they had loaned her out again—this time to Universal for *The Mummy*, in which she appeared as a reincarnated Egyptian princess pursued by Boris Karloff.

Our last months in Hollywood were spent at the Garden of Allah, where we occupied the suite with a black marble bathroom that had been designed by Nazimova when this was her home. Neighbors complained that we kept them awake with our nocturnal quarrels. Twice I started to leave and twice Zita begged me to stay with her until she had finished her film. Finally, in late October, we set out for New York in the Cadillac with a White Russian couple whom Zita had found at the studio and engaged as her maid and chauffeur. It took us eight days to cross the continent, including the detour we made in Ohio, from Columbus to Cleveland, to catch a performance of my play—*A Very Great Man*—at the Play House. Al Thomas had sent me

the reviews, which were better than I expected, together with the news
that the play was about to be optioned for Broadway. The next day we
crossed the Appalachians in driving rain with two of our sixteen
cylinders out of commission and the transmission barely holding
together as we crawled through the Holland Tunnel into New York.
Three weeks later when RKO summoned Zita back to the Coast, I did
not go with her.

I spoke to her twice in the next ten months. The first time was
when I saw her photograph one night on the front page of the bulldog
edition of the *Daily News* under the headline BEAUTY MARRED and
read that she had been injured by flying glass in an auto crash with
John Huston in the Hollywood hills. I called the hospital and she said it
was nothing and thanked me for calling.

* * *

New City, where I spent five months of that winter and spring, is the
first place in the world I ever thought of as a home. At that time,
before the Geroge Washington Bridge was built, it was a remote
village with a courthouse, an inn, half a dozen stores, two churches
and one garage. Three miles north, running along the foot of a low
mountain that ended at the edge of the Hudson River was the South
Mountain Road, where, among the farms and broken-down houses of
the original settlers, a so-called artists' colony had sprung up after the
war.

I had fallen in love with the Road during the difficult summer I
had spent there with Zita. Now I returned to it in the dead of winter in
search of peace. The house I lived in was a former farmhouse with
huge trees all around it, which I had persuaded my aunt to rent (for a
few hundred dollars a year) as a refuge from the pressure of the great
hospital of which she was superintendent. That winter, except for an
occasional weekend visit when she arrived, loaded with huge steaks
and bottles of Canadian rye, I had it all to myself.

I had never lived in the country or in a house alone. In New City,
surrounded by snow, the silence of the day and the deeper silence of
the night, I found some of the peace I was looking for. It began with
simple, immediate things. For years, ever since my nights in the
Nursery at Clifton, I had been afraid of the dark. In the freezing
darkness of that isolated house, with my nearest neighbor a quarter of
a mile away, these night fears grew to such an unbearable pitch of
violence that I knew I had to break through them or go mad. When
they finally scattered and dissolved, they drained away some of those
other deeper terrors—of rejection, poverty, death and annihilation—
that had haunted me for so many years of my life.

No miracle took place during those lonely months; no sudden vision came to me of what I was going to do with my life. But with the ebbing of my fear it became easier, as the months went by, to adapt my fantasies (in which I continued to indulge) to the realities of the world around me. I was aided in this adjustment by the friends I made that winter on the South Mountain Road. The house I was living in was owned by Bessie Breuer, who had left it when she married Henry Varnum Poor and moved to the stone house he had built with his own hands two miles up the road. Henry was a strong, gentle man, an athlete who retained his physical grace and power in his work and in his life. Born in Kansas, educated in California and in Paris, he began as a painter; then, discovering that he could make a more secure living as a potter, he became one of the great American ceramists of his time. He continued to paint, wrote books and designed and built several beautiful and original homes (including the one he later built for me) along the South Mountain Road. With his soft-spoken, blond craftsman's serenity, he was the exact opposite of Bessie, who was dark, garrulous, loving, impulsive and acutely sensitive to the vibrations of those around her. She had been a successful journalist and feature writer; after her marriage she became a short-story writer and a novelist. With her daughter Anne and their son Peter, the Poors became, after the Siepmanns, the nearest thing to a family I had known. Every day, in good weather and bad, I walked the two miles that separated our two houses, sometimes for a brief greeting if Henry and Bessie were both at work, sometimes for a meal or a drink by Henry's big fireplace before staring back on my long walk home.

With the last of the snow, from what was left of my option money, I bought a battered Model A Ford which I used to get in and out of New York. On the nights when I stayed in town, there was a small circle of friends (the Mielziners, the Malkiels, the Lights) on whose hospitality I could count and in whose apartments I billeted myself in rotation as I began to pick up the threads I had left dangling during my absence. One of these was a German theater piece called *Gallery Gods*, owned by a friend who asked me to work on it with her. We were delighted when Harold Clurman, one of the directors of the Group Theatre, saw in it an opportunity for ensemble acting and took and option on it for the coming season. The other was a French farce, *Trois et une*, a Boulevard success of which William Harris, Jr., needed a quick adaptation. He was one of Broadway's leading commercial producers, specializing in sex comedies; he was also notoriously parsimonious. For $250 each, against 1 percent of the gross, Lewis and I did a hurried job for him, without pride or pleasure, in the hope that, with seven characters and one set, it might achieve some sort of a Broadway run.

In July Harold Clurman called from the Adirondacks, where the Group Theatre was spending the summer in an adult camp known as Green Mansions. In exchange for entertaining the guests four nights a week and on weekends, members of the Group, including dependants, designer, choreographer, voice teacher and other associates to the number of fifty, received free board and lodging during the months of July and August. Harold said there were still a few places open and suggested that we come up, watch preliminary rehearsals of *Gallery Gods* and make whatever textual changes seemed desirable. I leaped at this chance to extend my theatrical education and spent two enthralling weeks in a world that was unlike anything I had ever known. I was familiar with the Group's artistic and social attitudes and beliefs; it was another thing to see them at work and in their collective life.

It was a summer (the third since their formation) which, according to Clurman, was more full than usual of personal upsets and dissensions. I followed their rehearsals, sat with them at meals and attended their meetings, which were all highly emotional. I listened while members of the Group had their regular outbursts against the tyranny of the directors and were answered by Lee Strasberg, who habitually spoke for two hours at the top of his voice. And I was present at the first, half-hearted reading of a new play, *I've Got the Blues*, by one of the Group's younger members—Clifford Odets—which, later, under the name of *Awake and Sing*, ensured their place in theatrical history.

From the Adirondacks I moved to Provincetown on Cape Cod, where *A Very Great Man* was being tried out for the alcoholic young millionaire who had it under option. No two worlds could have been more widely separated than that of the Group, with its contentious, obsessive dedication, and this cheerful band of summer actors, who laughed and made love and smelled of salt from continually diving off the pier for a swim between scenes. Richard Whorf, who was directing, had cast himself in the part of the publicist; his wisecracking secretary was played by a vivacious beauty of Armenian descent who called herself Arlene Francis. Together they gave the play the kind of energetic, slapdash treatment it deserved and it turned out to be one of the summer's most popular shows. On the day of the opening, I received a registered letter from Zita, forwarded from New City. It contained some enclosures in Spanish—applications for a Chihuahua divorce—which she asked me to sign right away because she was anxious to get married again.

Soon after Labor Day, at Lewis Galantière's suggestion, I moved into the building in which he was living at 125 East 57th Street. With its grand staircase, scarlet carpet, mahogany panelling and brass elevator cage, it had once been one of Manhattan's most elegant apartment houses. In what had been the servants' quarters, on the top floor, I occupied a cell with a washstand, a table and chair and a bed just wide enough to make love in. Down the hall Lewis had a larger room with an alcove, a bath, a telephone and some Schnabel recordings which he allowed me to use by day while I waited for my theatrical ships to come in.

Whorf confidently predicted a pre-Christmas Broadway opening for *A Very Great Man*. I doubted that and I did not really desire it. I had no great hopes for *Gallery Gods*. *Three and One* was already in rehearsal. I went to the theater and watched William Harris at work and was filled with irritation and gloom. My only stimulation came from a pale-faced, garrulous, exhaustingly eager and ambitious young lighting expert just out of Carnegie Tech. His name was Abe Feder—professionally abbreviated to Feder. *Three and One* opened in mid-October, got mediocre reviews and ran to modest business for 120 performances. Lewis and I made less than $400 apiece from it.

So now my hopes were fixed on *Lovers, Happy Lovers*, which was touring the British provinces before coming into the West End of London. I rose before dawn after a sleepless night, went down with my coat over my pajamas to the newsstand on the corner, then burst triumphantly into the darkness of Galantière's room and read him the brief cabled report of our play's successful London opening. Lewis took the news more calmly than I did and was less disappointed when it closed after five weeks. In a note that accompanied their final statement, its managers assured us that they were in no way disheartened and intended to bring the play to New York soon after the turn of the year.

In a letter to my mother in Paris I wrote hopefully of their coming as the possible solution to all my problems. I doubt if I really believed that. Through luck, shrewd associations and my knowledge of languages I had managed to gain a slippery toehold in the theater and to earn the few hundred dollars of option money and advances on which I was managing to subsist. But it was not a way of life and I knew it. Quite soon now I must find regular work in a profession in which I had no training, no craft, no special skill or experience of any sort. In normal times there would have been little reason for anyone to employ me; in mid-Depression, with so many thousands of theater people out of work, it was unthinkable—all the more since I myself seemed to have no clear notion of the capacity in which I was offering myself for hire.

Yet, for all my anxiety, I was leading a fairly agreeable and gregarious life in New York that fall. To eke out the last of my option money I had rationed myself to $25 a week, on which I managed to subsist without humiliation or hunger. Most of my social activity seemed to be theatrical: intimate and intellectual in Rosamond Gilder's apartment on Gramercy Park; turbulent and alcoholic around the Neighborhood and Provincetown playhouses in the Village; soul-searching, very personal and argumentative with members of the Group Theatre in Stewart's Cafeteria after the show. There were weekends at Sneden's Landing, in the house of my friend Pare Lorentz, where I listened to writers and journalists arguing over the New Deal and the State of the Union; all-night poker games for negligible stakes in Lee Miller's photographic studio to which I was drawn less by passion for gambling than by an unrequited lust for my beautiful hostess.

My breakthrough came quite soon, accidentally and from an unexpected quarter. One day in mid-November Lewis asked me to go with him to someone's house for a drink the following Sunday afternoon, to meet his friend Virgil Thomson, who had recently arrived from Paris with an opera he had done with Gertrude Stein, on which he needed theatrical advice. I almost didn't get there. I had arranged with my aunt to drive to New City for the weekend. At the last moment some crisis at the hospital changed her plans and I accepted Galantière's invitation—nervous, as always, at the prospect of entering a world I did not know.

I had read Gertrude Stein's *Three Lives*, some of *Tender Buttons* and more recently *The Autobiography of Alice B. Toklas*; I knew nothing about Virgil Thomson except what Lewis told me as we walked the four blocks to 61st and Third Avenue. Born in Kansas City, he had been to Harvard, then to Paris during the twenties, where Galantière had known him as an associate of the poets, painters and musicians of the neoromantic movement. And I had never heard of the Askews, at whose brownstone house we arrived shortly before six. From the small, cork-lined library in which we were invited to shed our coats I could hear, through the half-open door of the next room, the modulated hum of three or four dozen cultivated voices.

The Askews' Sunday "at homes" were not parties: they were a continuing, well-organized operation with a clear and consistent objective. This weekly gathering, known to its habitués as "the Askew Salon," conformed to the dictionary's definition of that word as "a reunion of notabilities in the house of a lady of fashion." The lady, Constance Askew, was a New England woman of means, of broad cultural experience and striking beauty. With her generous, unfashionable bosom and coils of light hair that were just beginning to turn gray, she gave a spendid, Junoesque solidity to a world that might easily have seemed effete. Her consort, Kirk Askew, small, bright-eyed, with carved ivory features, was one of a band of young men—art dealers, historians, curators, musicians and painters for whose artistic and professional benefit the Salon existed and functioned. This group, which came to exert such a dominant modernistic influence in the art fashions of its day, included at one time or another almost every famous figure in the art world of its time.

These "reunions" were held each Sunday afternoon (during the R months, like oysters) from five o'clock on in a large drawing room overlooking a garden. Leading off this and serving as a cloakroom and a place for serious artistic or personal dialogue was the small library which the hostess used as her study on weekdays. Its cork walls, where they were not covered with books, were hung with original drawings, paintings and historic photographs. Through these two rooms circulated the "notabilities," some four or five dozen each Sunday, evenly divided, as a rule, between the sexes. They flowed in revolving eddies over the brown-purple carpet, between the massive Victorian furniture. From time to time this human stream seemed to get caught against some physical object—the tail of the piano or the curve of a love seat—or it would become congested around some particularly eloquent or glamorous guest. Then Kirk Askew would appear, smiling and efficient, and start the traffic back into its normal flow. Tea was served, also cocktails and whisky, though never in quantities that would interfere with the serious business of the gathering. Shop talk was permitted up to a point; so were politics, if discussed in a lively and knowledgeable way. Flirtation (homo- and heterosexual) was tolerated but not encouraged.

Such was the new world I entered that Sunday in November, nervously, as I had entered Bloomsbury ten years before. I met my host and hostess and received a drink. There were a few familiar figures in the room but, before I could join them, I was led toward a small, vivacious man several years older than myself, with a pale face, a piercing voice, precise articulation and a willpower that became evident within thirty seconds of meeting him, who immediately propelled me through the crowd toward a free spot in the curve of the piano, from which we moved after a moment to a sofa in the library under a photograph of Sarah Bernhardt in the role of Phèdre. Here we talked or, rather, he talked for close to an hour about the opera he had written with Gertrude Stein which was to be performed in Hartford in ten weeks' time.

Virgil Thomson in his autobiography has described the various stages which *Four Saints in Three Acts* went through between its composition in Paris in 1927 and its première in Connecticut on February 7, 1934. Miss Stein has given her own account of its conception:

Virgil Thomson had asked Gertrude Stein to write an opera for him. Among the saints there were two saints whom she had always like better than any others—St. Teresa of Avila and Ignatius Loyola and she said she would write him an opera about these two saints. She began this and worked very hard at it that spring and finally finished *Four Saints* and gave it to Virgil Thomson to put to music. He did. And it is a completely interesting opera both as to words and music.

For the next five years Thomson performed it, singing all the parts himself, first in Paris and then in a succesion of New York drawing rooms including that of Carl Van Vechten, who found it "as original in its conception as *Pelléas et Mélisande.'*" But it was not until 1933 that the leaders of the rising group that frequented the Askew Salon finally rallied behind the opera and decided to ensure its production. A.E. (Chick) Austin, curator of the Hartford Athenaeum, undertook to present it in the small theater he was building into the wing he had just added to house his considerable acquisitions of baroque and modern art. The opera would be the museum's inaugural presentation to coincide with the opening show—the first retrospective Picasso exhibition ever to be held in the United States. With a budget of $10,000 guaranteed by a Hartford organization known as the Friends and Enemies of Modern Music, it was, for the composer, "the ultimate in dream fulfillment—a production backed by enlightened amateurs and executed by whatever professional standards I chose to follow."

By the time I arrived at the Askew Salon, Thomson had already set most of the elements of his production, but he still lacked a director. A number of professionals had shown little interest or faith in the work since it resembled nothing they knew. Besides, the composer had very clear and positive theatrical ideas of his own, which he outlined to me as we sat on Mrs. Askew's couch. He was pleased to discover that I was "a European, a product of French lycées and an English public school." He asked me what I had done in the theater and I told him the truth, which did not seem to disturb him. He invited me to come and hear the opera the next morning at the Hotel Leonori, where someone had lent him a room with a piano.

> To know to know to love her so.
>
> Four Saints prepare for Saints
>
> It makes it well fish
>
> Four Saints it makes it well fish.

So sang Virgil Thomson, banging away at the piano and filling the small room with his thin, piercing tenor voice. He sang for close to two hours—arias, recitatives, choruses, stage directions and all. And I sat there trying to look intelligent and appreciative and hoping with all my soul that he would invite me to work with him. He did so and I accepted. He explained there was no money in it and asked me when I could start. I said immediately and so began the busiest and most decisive weeks of my life.

I soon discovered that what Virgil needed was not just someone to stage his opera but some sort of director-producer-impresario who would combine, coordinate and regulate the various artistic elements he had already selected. I accepted the assignment without diffidence and without question. We had $10,000 and nine and a half weeks in which to find a cast, coach and rehearse them in two hours of unfamiliar music and complicated stage action, to execute scenery and costumes, to rehearse a new score, and to move to Hartford into an unfinished theater with an orchestra of twenty and a cast of forty-three and there to set up, light, dress-rehearse and open cold before one of the world's most sophisticated audiences. With the slightest theatrical experience I would have realized the impossibility of our task. In my total ignorance I assumed the job in a mood of irresistible euphoria.

Virgil had given me an outline of a scenario that had been jointly developed by his friend Maurice Grosser and himself and accepted by Gertrude Stein: the next step was to find out what the opera was going to look like.

Florine Stettheimer, a member of the Askew Salon, whom Virgil had chosen to design it, was one of three daughters of a distinguished and wealthy New York family. She had been painting for years, mostly family portraits of her sisters, her mother, herself and her friends—in colors of a clean and extraordinary brilliance. She also painted pictures of New York City—including a photographic likeness of Mayor Walker—in which she anticipated many of the elements of Pop Art. She had heard Virgil sing the opera and admired it. When he invited her to design it she asked for time to consider the idea. Some months later she began her research. One of the elements that struck her was the portal of the cathedral at Avila with stone lions chained to a stone cathedral. The following year she painted a portrait of Virgil Thomson which has, in the background, an arch and a lion chained to a rainbow sitting on a cushion like a poodle dog. Also in the picture is a toy theater floating in the air, a bird bringing a bouquet, a big black flower in an upper corner, the Holy Ghost in various forms and a shaft of light pouring down on St. Virgil. Much of this imagery found its way into her designs for the opera, of which I got my first glimpse when Virgil conducted me one afternoon to her studio. Its windows were hung with cellophane curtains and chairs and tables were all white and gold. The tables were glass and gold and there were lamps streaming with white beads and gilt flowers in vases. The windows of the little balcony that looked down on the studio were hung with Nottingham lace.

Florine herself, frail and elegant amid all this elaboration of gold, crystal and lace, proved formidable but enchanting. From a closet she brought out three boxes swathed in shawls and gauze and, when she had removed these, I saw that they were cellophane-lined models of the three acts of the opera and that they were inhabited by tiny dolls draped in cardinals' and other religious costumes—all in primary and secondary colors; red, purple and green for the first act; white for the second; yellow and Spanish black-and-white for the third. With slender fingers she set in place an arch of crystal beads, a golden lion with a cellophane chain around its neck, an emerald grass mat and palm trees of white and pink tarlatan.

All this seemed a far cry from Virgil's next artistic choice, which was to have his Spanish saints played by black singers. His reasons were simple and basic: quality of voice, clarity of speech and an ability to move with dignity and grace. Remembering his own happy experience with Negro church choirs, Virgil decided that they were the right persons to sing in his opera. When Miss Stein was informed of his decision she was shocked, "assuming there would be some sexuality inherent in the opera's being done by Negroes." Miss Stettheimer was pained on the simpler ground that brown faces and hands would interfere with her color scheme; she suggested they be painted white.

Thomson had already selected for his musical director Alexander Smallens, assistant to Leopold Stokowski. Now he came up with one final artistic suggestion which he had been reluctant to express until he had a director. In our first interview he had told me, "I don't really want them to act. I want them to be moved about." Since I had never staged a play, let alone an opera or a musical, he suggested that I might welcome the aid of a choreographer, to which I agreed. He had first considered Agnes De Mille, who was not available, then switched to a young English dancer-choreographer with whose work at Sadler's Wells he was familiar. His name was Frederick Ashton; he knew the opera and was eager to work on it. A cable was sent to London inviting him to come over immediately. He arrived within ten days and moved into the Askews' guest bedroom that had just been vacated by the Irish novelist Elizabeth Bowen. That and the $10-a-week pocket money he received during rehearsal were his only remuneration. He was a delight to work with: except for occasional brief spasms of homesickness, he was gay, free, self-confident, infinitely resourceful and imaginative and dearly beloved by everyone with whom he worked.

Our next urgent task was to assemble singers and chorus. To advise us in this we engaged an elegant, soft-spoken, very thin young

Negro named Edward Perry. It was Perry who pointed out that the
famed Hall Johnson singers, whom Virgil so admired in *Run Little
Chillun!*, rehearsed and sang mostly by rote. He then suggested a lady
named Eva Jessye, whose singing group was small but of high musical
standards. Virgil met her, interrogated her, heard her singers and
approved. From then on, daily auditions were held—for the chorus
uptown by Miss Jessye, for the principals by Virgil himself in the
Askews' living room.

Our first and easiest casting was for the part of St. Ignatius.
Edward Matthews was a short, light-skinned baritone, a concert singer
of some reputation whom Virgil engaged immediately. Most difficult
to find was the soprano—St. Teresa I. We interviewed a celebrated diva
named Caterina Jarboro: she received us in her apartment with her
agent, voice coach and accompanist in attendance and, after much
conversation, sang for Virgil, who thought she had a fine voice. But,
about that time, someone discovered in a church in Brooklyn a high
soprano named Beatrice Robinson-Wayne. She was a plain,
middle-aged lady, pug-nosed and pigeon-toed; but her voice was
sensational and she had all the things Virgil was looking for—the clear
speech and the rapt, simple, dedicated quality of a saint.

We engaged her and never regretted it. And we teamed her with a
contralto St. Teresa II, a voluptuous, lethargic girl whose lover, a
liveried chauffeur, used to collect her at rehearsals and beat her from
time to time. The Commère and Compère, being constantly on stage,
required presence, variety and charm, which we found in the persons
of Abner Dorsey, a former small-time vaudeville performer, and
Altonnell Hines, a lovely, slender, honey-colored young woman—very
dignified and very chic in the red paillette evening dress which Florine
designed for her in the first act, white tulle ruffles in the second and
black paillettes for the third. The Compère wore a stiff black Spanish
hat and tails.

Rehearsals started in mid-December in an atmosphere of love in
the basement of St. Philip's Episcopal Church on 137th Street. It was
the first time I had worked in Harlem—almost the first time I had seen
it by day. Every morning I rode north on the Lexington Avenue
express; twice each day I made the underground transition from white
to black in the morning and back to white in the evening. North of
125th Street I found another world, a world of poverty and desolation
and fear where the winter winds seemed to blow twenty degrees
colder than downtown and one could smell decay and despair in the
uncollected garbage in the streets. But in our clean, stuffy church
basement, all through Christmas and into the new year, we were
crowded and warm and secluded and busy. Visitors came up from

time to time: Alexander Smallens appeared periodically, listened, consulted his score and departed. Feder, the passionate lighting expert from Carnegie Tech, showed up with an assistant and pads on which they scrawled page after page of notes and diagrams. Lee Miller came with flashbulbs and took our pictures.

One of the main problems of rehearsing in Harlem, I had been warned, was keeping the company together amid the intolerable poverty and harassment in which most of them were living. We arrived at a figure of $15 a week to be paid from the first day of rehearsal. We had a few inevitable dropouts, but we succeeded in holding together, for seven weeks, a company of eighteen principals, a chorus of twenty and six dancers. This was attributable partly to our unusual rehearsal pay but, even more, I believe, to the excitement they were beginning to feel in their work. Here was a chance to get away from the usual musical-comedy, vaudeville and nightclub routines, the standard spirituals and church music they were accustomed to singing. And the people they worked with were different; for Virgil, with his clipped, meticulous severity, they developed a growing musical and personal respect; they found me formal but sympathetic and fair; Freddy was funny, adorable and quite unlike anyone they had ever known. As rehearsals progressed, they seemed to get the feeling that they were involved in something unique and memorable.

This sense of excitement grew steadily throughout the final weeks of rehearsal. Soon after the New Year we started run-throughs of the first and second acts with Virgil conducting and a very small black girl with thick glasses thumping away on the piano. Meanwhile, the other elements of the production were gradually coming together. My working arrangment with Virgil Thomson was unspoken and simple: in all musical matters and in those areas where his artistic choices had already been made, I deferred to his judgments and did my best to understand and execute them. For the rest he showed complete faith in me and supported without question the countless decisions I was forced to make day by day and sometimes hour by hour.

I spent half my day supervising rehearsals, the other half dealing with problems that were technical, economic and personal. Florine Stettheimer, for one, could never quite accept the limitations of the theater and of our budget. She was disappointed that the tiny glass beads she had strung on a wire loop to represent the cathedral portals on her model could not be translated into huge cut-crystal balls on the stage. She worried about the expression on the face of the lion. She wanted an antique lace frame around the proscenium arch and spurned the machine-made stuff that Kate Lawson, our technical director, managed to supply at a reasonable price. Finally, there was the sky—the dazzling cellophane cyclorama, which measured one foot square on her model and 1500 square feet on the stage. Cellophane was a comparatively new substance that had never been used in the theater. It took Kate two weeks to find a manufacturer who was willing to mount it on a cotton mesh strong enough to sustain, without tearing, the huge weight of those thousands of square feet of tufted and festooned cyclorama. It would take another three weeks to make and deliver it. This brought us dangerously close to our dress-rehearsal date of February 3, but we had no choice.

Early in January I made one final addition to the participants in our project. Our original sponsors—the Friends and Enemies of Modern Music—were having trouble raising their promised $10,000. Any further financing would have to come from New York and I knew enough of the theater to realize that no regular Broadway producer or angel would touch us. Harry Moses was no regular producer. Having made his pile in ladies' hosiery in Chicago, he had arrived in New York with his wife (an eager, talkative lady with artistic aspirations) and, before long, had become the principal backer and co-producer with Herman Shumlin of Vicki Baum's enormously successful *Grand Hotel*, followed by a production of *The Warrior's Husband* that had made a star of Katharine Hepburn. Since then he had been waiting for something prestigious to strike his fancy. I called on him and invited him and his wife to St. Philip's Church to one of our advanced rehearsals. They were impressed by what they saw and heard and by the artistic and social tone of the enterprise. And they were agreeably surprised to discover that I was not asking them for money but only for their interest in bringing the opera to New York if it proved successful in Hartford.

By mid-January we were deep into the third act. Freddy caught the flu and was away for two days; I took over and staged the vision of the Holy Ghost to Virgil's satisfaction. Then it was my turn to be absent for a day on personal business—theater business.

The comedy I had written with Lewis Galantière (its name changed to *And Be My Love*) had reached Canada soon after the New Year and was announced to open in New York in the last week in January. Three months earlier it had carried all my theatrical hopes: now I awaited its coming without excitement or pleasure. I attended its one and only dress rehearsal and it depressed me. I went to the first night by myself, watched it as though it were someone else's work, hated almost every moment of it, thanked the cast and walked home alone in the rain.

Next morning's notices were less lethal than I had feared. Brooks Atkinson of the *New York Times* found it "a flawless comedy, though dull." It ran for a few weeks to small business before it closed. But, by then, I was beyond hurt in Connecticut, wholly absorbed in the final rehearsals of *Four Saints in Three Acts.*

* * *

The temperature in Hartford was near zero when we arrived and it grew colder from day to day. Each evening thousands of starlings, chirping piteously, sought refuge under the eaves of the Wadsworth Athenaeum. But, inside, all was light and beauty and warmth. Unlike most new buildings the Avery Memorial Wing was complete and ready for its inauguration. It was all magically illuminated as we arrived; so were the upper galleries in which the Picasso retrospective (with pictures ranging from before the pink and blue periods to the newest, classic giantesses and two small rape scenes hardly larger than postage stamps) was already hung—violent and startling in its brilliant variety against the white walls.

Austin was there to welcome us and proudly took us on a tour of the museum, ending with his new theater in the basement. Then he drove us to his house for dinner, the last serious meal I was to have in a week. Over brandy, under the seventeenth-century Venetian panels which were his latest acquisition, he informed us with a boyish smile that the Friends and Enemies were in trouble. The ticket sale was going swimmingly; we were already sold out for three of our five performances. Unfortunately most of the tickets had been ordered by out-of-towners and would not be paid for until the people arrived. I pointed out that the cast and technicians expected to be paid before the weekend. Chick said he would try to think of something. Then he drove me back to the theater where Feder and his men were at work spotting lines and hanging equipment on the empty stage. They were a curious crew: his close friend and counsellor, Teddy Thomas (born Tomashevsky of the illustrious Yiddish theater dynasty), and a silent apprentice whose name I never knew—not even when he sliced off the tip of his finger while cutting gelatins at five in the morning and we had to drive him to the hospital to have it sewn back on while Feder kept abusing him for getting blood on the equipment. Chief of the local helpers was a gargoyle of a man, bald as an egg, with a huge beak of a nose, a former acrobat and escape artist, whom Chick used as an assistant and victim in his magic shows. He never complained but, during one of our interminable night shifts, we were startled by a loud, continuous, hollow banging overhead. It was the escape artist, high up on a 20-foot ladder, bashing his head against the back wall of the theater to keep himself awake.

Since the theater lacked rigging, ropes, pipe, cable and many of the necessities of a professional stage, several cars and a truck were in constant motion between New York and Hartford, bringing urgently needed equipment, over 200 costumes, our fragile props and the huge mass of our cellophane firmament, which arrived with Kate Lawson on Thursday morning and took all of that day and most of the following night to install.

The company arrived by bus at noon on Friday. They were greeted by the Negro Chamber of Commerce and billeted in black households all over town. That afternoon we began transferring our rehearsal movements to the stage. We worked until midnight, then sent the company home. As the singers left, the technicians moved in and began their nightly task of lighting the show.

Abe Feder was the first of the prima donnas in the American lighting field. *Four Saints* was his big chance, and he was determined to make the most of it at no matter what human cost. Florine Stettheimer's décor with its dazzling, diamond-bright background was, in Feder's words, "a creeping bitch" to light—especially the first act, which she wanted inundated with pure white light. In vain Feder attempted to explain (to Florine, to Virgil, to me, to anyone who would listen) that there was no such thing as white light in the spectrum—that it was obtained by the expert mixing of primary colors projected through various shades of red, blue and yellow gelatin in the 200 or more projectors with which he had covered the ceiling and sides of Chick's theater. Florine repeated that she wanted clear white light—as in her model. For three successive nights he had the escape artist and his crew clambering up and down ladders, changing gelatins, which he then blended with infinite care and skill at diverse intensities. And each morning, when he proudly exhibited his night's work to Florine, she would say quietly that what she wanted was clear white light. Reluctant and unconvinced, he finally gave it to her at dress rehearsal and she was grateful.

On Sunday afternoon we held a dress parade—act by act. (Florine was pleased on the whole but horrified to discover that the Saints' hands were bare—and dark! White gloves were rushed from New York for the opening.) This was followed by a run-through in costume with props. When it was over, I invited the company to meet me in the main court in front of the baroque marble nude. Against this impressive background, at 1:30 in the morning, I told them of the Friends and Enemies' financial straits. They looked at me and said nothing. I said we would be most grateful if they could wait until opening night for their money. Though most of them must have been penniless, not one of them demanded payment.

The next morning Alex Smallens and his orchestra of twenty arrived from New York and held their first musical reading in the pit, which could barely hold them. The next day we held full dress rehearsal with orchestra. It ran far into the night with only one major blow-up—the classic conflict of conductor and director over performers so placed on the stage that they had difficulty in following the beat. Smallens was a bully and a shouter. His yelling drove Freddy Ashton up the aisle in tears, stopping long enough to shout "I have worked with Sir Thomas Beecham! A genius! And he never spoke to me as you have!" before leaving the theater. Since it was -15 degrees outside, he returned almost immediately and the rehearsal continued.

On February 7 and 8 the New Haven Railroad added extra parlor cars to its afternoon train for the New York fashionables, the press and members of the international art world coming to Hartford to honor the new wing's opening and to see the Picasso show and the opera. I remember that evening vaguely as through a bright, heavy haze: the terrible cold outside as the cars began to arrive and the starlings screaming their heads off and the galleries overhead filled with people in evening dress with champagne glasses in their hands moving among the strong colors of the Picasso canvases.

Backstage everyone except me seemed surprisingly confident and relaxed. Fifteen minutes before curtain time I went out to get a breath of air. The birds were still screeching, and as I stood in the street for a moment, pierced by the icy wind, I became aware of an astonishing thing: silently, as in some German film of the early twenties, there appeared out of the darkness a huge smooth object unlike anything I had ever seen. Black and shiny and shaped like a gigantic raindrop, it came to a stop before the museum; and from a sliding panel in its side stepped two beautiful ladies, one blonde and one dark, in shimmering evening dresses, accompanied by a small, wiry, balding man in a dinner jacket who, I discovered later, was Buckminster Fuller, creator of the Dymaxion car (of which this was the first specimen), escorting Dorothy Hale and Clare Boothe. Leaving their vehicle at the curb they entered the building and disappeared into the crowd that was beginning to flow down from the galleries into the theater.

Downstairs the Saints were assembling on the stage, ascending their pyramids and checking their costumes and props. At 8:47 Chick Austin appeared to tell us that everyone was seated and we could begin. We embraced each other. Then the Saints took their opening positions and waited for the sharp drum roll that announced the start of the opera.

Since I spent the entire time of the performance rushing around backstage, checking entrances, light cues, props and effects, I do not have the faintest recollection of how the opera looked or sounded that night. Virgil was pleased and so, apparently, were our distinguished audience and critics.

A music critic, in a review headed ECCLESIASTICAL RAG, found the opera replete with "hints of blues songs, Negro spirituals, folk carols and recitatives with an ecclesiastical flavor." The dance critic of the *New York Times* found it "the most interesting experiment that has been made here in many seasons and the most enlightening." An excited gentleman in tails was heard to declare, "It's like Grand Opera only it's got more sense!" The United Press informed its millions of readers that the show might anger and annoy them, but like a war or a flood, they would regret having missed it. Stark Young pronounced it "the most important event of the season—important because it is theater and flies off the ground, most important because it is delightful and joyous and delight is the fundamental of all art, great and small."

But it was Lucius Beebe, columnist for the *Herald Tribune*, who gave the premier its most vivid sociological coverage:

The curtain was conveniently late and everyone had a chance to make at least two grand entrées and some of the more enterprising got around as many as five times. But the real show was at the intermissions. For the first five minutes conversation was as guarded as that in a Pullman smoker in wartime. But, as soon as Messrs. Kirk Askew and Julien Levy burst into unabashed tears because they "didn't know anything so beautiful could be done in America," the hysteria was on and a blizzard of superlatives was in progress, with little groups letting down their back hair and crying quietly in corners for beauty...There were curtain calls by the score. Professor Hitchcock smashed his opera hat with gay abandon and called for Mr. Thomson. Mr. Thomson made a bow. Professor Hitchcock tore open his collar and shouted for Mr. Austin. Mr. Austin made a bow to a bedlam and a sea of fluttering handkerchiefs. After that everyone went on to an enormous party at Mr. Austin's—not forgetting to take their programs which contained a portrait of Mr. Thomson by Miss Stein beginning "Yes ally yes as ally"—and called it a night.

The party, unlike the performance, is quite clear in my memory, with Salvador Dali, seated in a love seat beside the wife of one of Hartford's most enlightened young art lovers, gazing intently at the mother-of-pearl buttons on the bosom of her dress and inquiring courteously, as I happened to pass by, if they were edible. ('*Madame, ces boutons, sont-ils comestibles?*') In the next room Nicolas Nabokov, the composer, exasperated by the triumph of the international epicenes, sat at a piano thumping out Russian folk songs, in which he was joined by a male chorus that included the poet Archibald MacLeish and other red-blooded Americans. The next night we danced till dawn at a ball given by the Negro Chamber of Commerce and on Saturday we gave our two final performances to sold-out, cheering houses.

By then two things had happened: the cast had been paid in full and Harry Moses, throwing caution to the winds, had announced our

New York opening for Tuesday, February 20 at the enormous 44th Street Theater, half a block from Times Square.

With that, our struggle against seemingly impossible odds began afresh. We had exactly one week to transfer a production that had been conceived and designed for a miniature theater to one of the largest musical-comedy houses on Broadway. To reduce the immense stage opening we rented a black velour portal and hung a new red-velvet inner curtain, brighter and twice the size of the first. We doubled the size of our cellophane sunburst and the number of our tarlatan trees. Our greatest difficulty was with the sky, which now reached barely halfway up the back wall of the 44th Street Theater. A squadron of seamstresses added several hundred square feet of cellophane and redraped the entire firmament in huge festoons that rose 50 feet into the air. To illuminate this enormouse surface Feder emptied New York's electrical supply houses of projectors and cable, which he added to already lavish equipment.

We opened in a blizzard. Snow had begun to fall in the night and became thicker and heavier through the day. By midafternoon there was more than a foot of it in the streets and traffic came to a stop all over the city. But the press and the 1400 "members of the Social Register and Intelligentsia" who formed our opening-night audience were made of sterner stuff.

Our curtain went up almost half an hour late. Once again I stood breathless, backstage, waiting for the sharp opening drum roll and for the crimson curtain to rise on the lone purple figure kneeling at the edge of the stage. When it did, it was immediately apparent from the difference in the sounds out front how dissimilar the mood of these Broadway first-nighters was from the knowledgeable intimacy of our audiences at the Athenaeum. They applauded the opening tableau, but the early scenes of the two Teresas in Avila, "half in and half out of doors," were received, as they had not been in Hartford, with ripples of self-conscious and slightly embarrassed laughter. It was only gradually, as the two ladies in their red cardinal's robes went about their saintly business "seated and not standing half and half of it and not half and half of it seated," while the chorus explained that

Saint Teresa could be photographed having been dressed like a lady and then they taking out her head and changed it to a nun and a nun a saint and a saint so

that the magic of the opera really began to work. With the entrance of St. Ignatius in green moiré silk, the issue was no longer in doubt. As the curtain fell on the first act, I ran out the stage door through the snow and arrived in the lobby just in time to meet the first wave of emerging fashionables. Five minutes later I raced back to give the cast the news that all was well.

I went out front once again near the end of the last act. Anxious to see the effect of our funeral procession on a large stage before a full house, I joined the crowd of standees that had accumulated in the rear of the theater. From there I watched the front of the double line appear far downstage left, chanting as they advanced slowly—all forty-four of them, moving from left to right across the stage, their black-and-white cloaks and hoods and banners silhouetted against the livid sky, till they filled the entire proscenium and stood there swaying gently in their solemn, syncopated, baroque funeral march:

> With wed led said with led dead said
> with dead led said with said dead led
> wed said dead let dead led said wed

they sang fervently, their eyes raised to heaven then, almost imperceptibly, their swaying became once more a slow forward motion till they were lost to sight and their voices died away in the darkness of the wings.

The closing scene of the opera was short and bright and melodious. And as the crimson curtain fell quickly on the Chorus's final, abrupt exclamation—"Which is a fact!"—I heard for the first time in my life that most wonderful of all backstage sounds—the brief, terrifying silence followed by the sudden crash of applause from a huge, invisible audience, breaking in great waves against the velvet wall behind which it could be heard beating like an angry, insistent flood. When the curtain finally rose again it was as though a dam had burst. With a triumphant roar, through which I could vaguely distinguish the sharper tones of cheers and bravos, it came rushing at us out of the darkness, sweeping over the brightly lit stage, overwhelming the small, solemnly bowing figures of our astounded Saints.

I have no idea how many curtain calls we took that night. Flowers were handed up in the best operatic tradition as bow followed bow. Still, the audience refused to budge and we went on bowing and smiling as wave after wave of sound swept over us, and the sweating stagehands, like demented bell ringers, hauled away at their ropes, sending the huge curtain up and down, up and down till, finally, in sheer exhaustion, they stopped and the audience slowly evacuated the theater. And when it was all over and the Saints had gone off to their dressing rooms and the crew had cleared the deck on which a single, bare worklight remained burning, I found myself alone in the sudden stillness, lying front and center of that vast, dark, empty stage, with my face against the splintered wooden floor, sobbing like a child.

***

Four Saints in Three Acts ran for four weeks in the vastness of the 44th Street Theater in what was at the time (before *Porgy and Bess*) the longest continuous run ever enjoyed by an American opera.

In our fourth week, we had what *Variety* described as "a hearty jump considering weather" and Harry Moses became so encouraged that he decided to extend our run. Since the 44th Street was already booked for an incoming musical, we moved to the Empire Theater three blocks away, for an additional two weeks.

The Empire was everyone's favorite New York theater and I was proud and excited at the idea of occupying it, even for a short time. In that glamorous and perfectly proportioned house, with Virgil Thomson conducting his own work, the Saints looked and sounded better than they ever had before. We played to fair houses the first ten days, then to standing room only for the rest of the run when it became known that this was the public's final chance to see this astonishing work. Our last night was wildly emotional, with much embracing and shedding of tears.

Lying in my narrow bed on 57th Street the morning after our closing I felt like a man reluctantly awakening out of a delightful dream. For fifteen enchanted weeks I had been wholly absorbed in the opera and its production, committed without reservation to a creative project in which I was playing an indispensable part with people whom I loved and admired.

Now suddenly it was over. The small world to which I had belonged for four months was breaking up: Freddy Ashton had returned to England; Kate Lawson was back with the Theatre Guild; Feder was ranging Broadway in search of new electrical miracles. Only Virgil remained through our run at the Empire: then he too sailed away to make his report to Miss Stein in Paris.

After the final curtain I watched the Saints clear the dressing rooms of their scant personal belongings before vanishing into the night. With their going I suffered a sentimental and physical loss; I had become accustomed to their warm, rich world of color and scent and resonance; its sudden withdrawal made the all-white world to which I was returning seem pale and arid and cold. And when it was all over and the trucks had driven off with the last of the scenery, a deep gloom descended upon me. In four months I had become used to friendship, responsibility and power. Now these were being taken from me. Once again I was alone and, though my tide of fear never again reached its earlier high-water mark, I was aware of its constant, hateful murmur as I found myself beginning to worry, once again, about my future.

II
Panic
1935

Nathan Zatkin, who had done such a brilliant job publicizing *Four Saints*, was a short, forbidding-looking man with curly blue-black hair, a beard that needed shaving three times a day and a small bulbous nose that was perpetually wreathed in smoke from the evil-smelling cigars he held clamped between his nutcracker jaws.

With the success of *Four Saints* Nathan Zatkin had tasted theatrical blood. Publicity was no longer enough for him. He was seized with a raging desire to become a producer. Almost immediately, from a surprising quarter, the opportunity presented itself. He had an acquaintance, the granddaughter of one of New York City's most illustrious mayors; she had been considered for a time one of the more promising ingénues in the American theater (she had come close to creating the part of Saint Joan for the Theatre Guild), but, at twenty-six, she found herself—beautiful, intelligent, well-bred, talented and unemployed. It was at this point that a friend of the family, a platonic admirer and a man of means, offered to finance her to the tune of $15,000 to be used entirely at her discretion, for her appearance on Broadway in any part her heart desired. She turned for advice to Nathan Zatkin who set about helping her to plan her production, which very soon became *his* production. One of the first things he did was to persuade her that, no matter what play she wanted to do, there was only one man worthy of directing her: his friend, the hero of *Four Saints in Three Acts*—John Houseman.

The trouble was—*she* knew exactly what play she wanted to do. Diffident in most respects, she revealed a will of iron in her choice of the piece on which she was about to spend her benefactor's money. Following in the steps of Eleanora Duse, she decided to attempt Ibsen's *The Lady from the Sea*. For a young woman of limited experience to undertake such a part in the New York commercial theater was an act of madness. We let her do it; we encouraged her and abetted her in her preparations. I am not too proud of my part in this conspiracy; I have always felt that in agreeing to direct *The Lady from the Sea* I participated in a con game in which Mary Hone was the willing dupe.

Zatkin had no such qualms. To be known as the producer of a serious play on Broadway he would, without hesitation, have assassinated his nearest and dearest. Besides, as a press agent by training and inclination, he had the capacity to persuade himself of whatever it was necessary for him to feel for the efficient execution of his job. Having once accepted the notion of presenting Mary Hone in *The Lady from the Sea*, he was no more capable of giving it up than a hungry dog is of dropping a half-eaten bone. In the end, he proved the less dishonorable of the two. As publicist for the production he fulfilled his function beyond reproach. As its director, I did not.

Amateur though I was, I had intelligence, taste, a sense of style and a certain superficial competence, which I exercised in the selection of designer and cast. My failure lay not so much in the production, which had a certain fluidity and style, as in my inability to bring any clear or unified concept of Ibsen's play onto the stage. Here, for the first time in my life—alone, incompetent and unprepared—I faced the challenge of translating a script of notorious difficulty into some sort of viable theatrical performance. In my own opinion, as in that of most of the critics, I failed to meet it.

It took more than a dozen years of humiliation and suffering for me to assemble enough technical and psychological knowledge to walk into a rehearsal with a real, rather than a simulated confidence in my ability to control all the elements of a production. In *The Lady from the Sea* my shame and fear were almost unbearable, my ineptitude so glaring that I could conceal it from nobody—least of all myself. The chief victim of this insecurity was Mary Hone. I had no experience in shaping a role of such magnitide and no technical or personal resources on which I could draw to sustain this sensitive but emotionally and professionally immature young woman in her time of need. We opened to reviews that were generally poor with most critics divided between their distaste for the play and for my production. Most severe was Brooks Atkinson of the *New York Times*, who was exasperated by the pallid performance of "folk who frankly seem to be lacking in thyroid." Stark Young, the critic whose opinion I most valued, was a bit kinder to my direction, which he found "easy, graceful and right." But by the time his review appeared in the *New Republic*, our raked platforms and stormy backdrops had already been reduced to ashes and I was moving towards the next painful stage of my theatrical education.

* * *

New City was hot and agreeable that summer with several swimming holes within walking distance of my aunt's house. One was Wally Fleischer's, peopled by his wife, Millia Davenport (who later designed two shows for us at the Mercury), and a dark, slender beauty, his daughter, married at the time to Donald Friede, the publisher, for whom I had a burning desire but could never find a convenient time or place in which to satisfy it. Another was Maxwell Anderson's on the South Mountain Road. Fed by springs that became the headwaters of the Hackensack River, it was filled with children of various ages, to whom Mab, Max's new wife, was trying to be an acceptable stepmother while fulfilling her other, multiple and delicate duties as mate, mistress, secretary and inspiration to that large, vain, industrious man, her husband. Up the road lived my friends the Poors. Their stone house in the woods was, once again, a place of release and refuge—my emotional home, that summer, as it had been two years before. Only, this time, Bessie went beyond sympathy and encouragement: she became my champion, secret agent and broker. Through her intervention and due entirely to her machinations, before the summer was over, I had achieved the impossible: I had signed a contract to direct a major production for America's leading producer—the Theatre Guild.

The Guild, in 1934, stood high in prestige and power. It was the country's most active and distinguished theatrical organization—the accredited producer of O'Neill, Shaw, and Lunts and, more recently, Robert Sherwood and Maxwell Anderson. Its reputation was high with the public, less good with theater people for whom it occupied an equivocal position between an art theater and a commercial management. What I encountered when I went in to sign my contract as co-director of *Valley Forge* was a strained situation of which I only gradually became aware.

Maxwell Anderson was a soft, kind, possessive, competitive man with a gigantic ego. He had written his first play after attending a reading by one of his neighbors on the South Mountain Road and deciding that if John Howard Lawson could write a play—so could he. He had had several successes with the Theatre Guild but now he was beginning to have the same feeling about production and direction as he had had about writing—that he could do it better himself.

When he offered the Guild his new play *Valley Forge* in the summer of 1934, he insisted on a degree of artistic control they had never given before. This led to recriminations and long negotiations at the end of which (since they badly needed the play for their subscription series) they capitulated to what they sincerely regarded as his ungrateful and imprudent demands. And here again Max's ego came into play. Now, reluctant to submit his work to a strong, opinionated director, he was looking for someone through whom he could exercise total control of his play.

The South Mountain Road, in those days, was one big family. It did not take Bessie long to convince her neighbor Max that I was heaven-sent to fill his present need. I was given a script of *Valley Forge* to take home and read. I read it in bed that night at the other end of South Mountain Road and, although I disapproved of what I felt to be Max's derivative abuse of the Elizabethan iambic pentameter, I felt that *Valley Forge* contained some of his most eloquent writing about the dream and the reality of America's vision of freedom. I detested all the episodes involving Washington's supposed first love, Mary Philipse, and did my diplomatic best, before and during rehearsals, to get her thrown out of the play. I failed but I got the job.

The Theatre Guild, when Max presented my name, yelled bloody murder. They investigated my brief career in the theater and received reports that were generally, though not unanimously, unfavorable. However, they had no choice. Some time in August I signed my contract as director and received, for my first payment, a sum greater than any I had yet earned in the theater. But my position in this production was, from the first, an untenable one: to the Guild I was a nuisance, something that had been shoved down their throats by an egomaniacal playwright. To Anderson I was, mainly, a buffer between himself and the Guild's opinionated and domineering executives—particularly Lawrence Langner. To the cast I was a mystery; and if there is one thing that upsets actors, it is a mystery—particularly if he is inexperienced, pretentious and ingratiating, with a strong smell of fear about him.

It was during rehearsals of *Valley Forge* that I received my most painful lessons in the human relations of the theater—that strange process of meeting and parting, wooing and testing, trusting and knifing that forms part of the business of getting a play onto the stage. In *The Lady from the Sea* I had gone into production unprepared. I arrived at rehearsals of *Valley Forge* with every move, tempo and reading of the first act worked out—on paper. This preparation gave me self-confidence, though it was not to the taste of the hardened Broadway professionals who formed our company. Where I failed most miserably was in the scenes involving our star, Philip Merivale, who was in no mood to accept detailed and specific direction from an amateur of my kidney. He was suffering, throughout rehearsals, from a severe attack of hives, which I felt he attributed somehow to my presence. It was not until later that I discovered that much of what I took to be personal hostility was, in fact, the normal professional behavior of this moody, sentimental and frustrated man. My patent inability to deal with him confirmed the Guild in its misgivings about me and helped to undermine what authority I might have had with the rest of the company.

It was unfortunate, too, that halfway through rehearsals, I had to leave for four days to supervise the production of *Four Saints in Three Acts* in Chicago. When I got back to New York I found *Valley Forge* falling apart. Max Anderson had been conducting rehearsals in my absence and the Guild had deliberately chosen the eve of my return for a run-through which, from what I was told the next day, could not have gone worse—particularly the romantic scenes. The Guild's automatic reaction was to replace the actress who was playing them. Since she and our star were, by this time, amorously involved, her tears improved neither his hives nor his temper. We continued to rehearse in an atmosphere of animosity and defeat.

Our première in Pittsburgh ten days later had a raw, unfinished look—partly the result of my total inexperience with out-of-town openings. The military scenes, which Max had continued to improve and develop, had a certain energy and eloquence; the sentimental interludes and, more particularly, the Philadelphia society scenes seemed shoddily written and ineptly directed—as indeed they were.

That night, immediately after the show, over whisky and sandwiches in a suite of the hotel where Duse had suffered her final illness, Lawrence Langner fired me from *Valley Forge*. The meeting was brief and deadly, though I had known before the curtain went up that my replacement was sitting in the theater, watching the performance. Langner spoke for the Guild. Ignoring me completely, he addressed himself to Max who, shocked and defeated by the first public reaction to his play, was in no state to withstand his calculated attack. Things were bad, he said, but not hopeless. The situation could still be saved—on certain conditions. Till now, against their better judgment, the Guild had given Max everything he asked for. Now they insisted that they be allowed to take back the production into their own experienced hands. It was at this point that I asked for the floor. Soberly, in a style not unlike that in which I had addressed the creditors of the Oceanic Grain Corporation, I pointed out to Max what he and everyone else in the room already knew—that he had no choice in the matter. With becoming modesty, after thanking him for the chance he had given me and regretting my failure to give him a successful opening performance of his play, I resigned as director of *Valley Forge*. Max protested vaguely while my successor, Herbert Biberman, who had been waiting in his room on the floor below, was called and asked to join the meeting. Soon after his entrance and after chivalrously wishing him the best of luck, I withdrew. But, for me, the evening was not yet quite over. I was walking away, blasted and brokenhearted, down the long hotel corridor, when I heard footsteps padding behind me. As I stook waiting for the elevator, half-blinded with tears, I did not immediately recognize the dark-clad figure that silently entered the cage and rode down with me towards the lobby. When he spoke I realized it was Lawrence Langner. He said I must be a bit upset but things like this happened all the time in the theater and I mustn't take it too hard because, on the whole, I'd done a good job on a weak play under difficult conditions and he hoped I would remain with the production. He then added, while I stared at him open-mouthed, that, while he admired Biberman's vitality, he was not at all sure of his taste. For that reason he urged me, during the critical days to come, to continue to observe rehearsals and, if I saw anything of which I disapproved, to report to him personally. Then, without waiting for a reply, Lawrence Langner cheerfully wished me good night, re-entered the elevator and went back up to the conference with his new director.

This was my first exposure—but by no means my last—to a duplicity so constant and innate that it could not, in fairness, be described as treachery since it left its owner unaware of the ghastly things he was doing to others. With this went a certain sensitivity and kindness, a tireless and eager brain, a curiosity, a tenacity and a lack of moral principles that made Lawrence Langner one of the leading patent lawyers of the world and placed him, for forty years, at the heart of almost every new and significant movement in the American theater. He is one of the very few men in my life whom, in spite of a grudging admiration, I have devoutly and consistently detested.

Some weeks later I attended the New York opening of *Valley Forge*, which still had my name on it as co-director and which did rather better, critically, than expected. The *New York Times* found it "a grandly motivated drama" and commended Maxwell Anderson for having "mind enough to perceive honest heroism in a great character." This was not sufficient to overcome the allergy that afflicts the American public each time the Father of his Country appears on stage or screen. *Valley Forge* closed after less than five weeks—by which time Max was well into his next play and I was, once again, in search of work.

*　*　*

The year 1934 was not ending as well as it had begun. The previous Christmas I had been completely absorbed in a collective enterprise, which, for all its apparent recklessness, had been carefully planned and efficiently executed in an atmosphere of confidence and love. Since then I had suffered two serious personal defeats, from which I emerged with an almost total loss of faith in my own creative ability. I also became aware that, besides the usual hazards of inexperience, I was facing the dangerous consequences of my own opportunism, through which I had worked myself into theatrical jobs that I was incapable of executing. By moving too fast beyond my capabilities I had done myself what seemed like irreparable harm.

Yet, in the circumstances, what choice did I have? Having entered the theater from the top after the age of thirty in the confusion of the Great Depression, I had no alternative but to try to maintain myself at the top, learning my trade as I went along and hoping I would not break my neck in my repeated and inevitable falls. Even if I had been willing to take a stage manager's or assistant's job, where I might have learned the technical rudiments of my profession, no such job was available to a man who had already directed a play for the Theatre Guild. (Besides, I was even less capable of stage-managing a professional production than I was of directing it.)

If my prospects of making a living on Broadway seemed bleak, they were no less discouraging in the other places where theater was practiced at the time. I had learned, during my brief stay at Green Mansions, that I did not belong in the collective but exclusive world of the Group Theatre; I was even more remote and alien from the other left-wing organizations that had sprung up with the Depression. The Theater Union had been in existence for almost a year and had produced three plays, of which the last, *Stevedore*, was a solid success. It already had more liberal-intellectual amateurs on its staff than it needed. Alfred Saxe's Workers' Lab (renamed the Theater of Action) was a youthful proletarian group in which I had friends (Nicholas Ray and Elia Kazan among them) but to which I was quite obviously unsuited.

I waited and hoped. Against all reason I continued to cherish the conviction that once again, any day now, some golden opportunity would present itself and that I must be alert and resourceful enough to grasp it when it appeared. When it did, it came, once again, from an unpredictable quarter and by a circuitous route. On the night of December 21, 1934, Jo and Annie Mielziner invited me to the opening night of Katharine Cornell's *Romeo and Juliet*, for which Jo had designed the sets and costumes.

That glossy and successful evening was marked for me by one astonishing vision: not Miss Cornell's fervent Juliet, nor Edith Evans's admirable Nurse, nor Basil Rathbone's polite, middle-aged Romeo, nor Brian Aherne's Mercutio exuberantly slapping his yellow thighs as he strutted through Jo's bright Italianate scenery—those were all blotted out by the excitement of the two brief moments when the furious Tybalt appeared suddenly in that sunlit Verona square: death, in scarlet and black, in the form of a monstrous boy—flat-footed and graceless, yet swift and agile; soft as jelly one moment and uncoiled the next, in a spring of such furious energy that, once released, it could be stopped by no human intervention. What made this figure so obscene and terrible was the pale, shiny child's face under the unnatural growth of dark beard, from which there issued a voice of such clarity and power that it tore like a high wind through the genteel, modulated voices of the well-trained professionals around him. "Peace! I hate the word as I hate Hell!" cried the sick boy, as he shuffled along, driven by some irresistible interior violence to kill and soon himself, inevitably, to die.

Orson Welles's initial impact—if one was sensitive or allergic to it—was overwhelming and unforgettable. Michael MacLiammoir, the Irish actor, in his memoir *All for Hecuba,* has described the impression received when he and his partner, Hilton Edwards, were first confronted on the stage of the Gate Theatre in Dublin by a young man looking "larger, taller, softer and broader" than anyone they had ever seen, who bounded on stage with glaring, Chinese eyes and, in a tearing rage, began to enact for them the part of the Duke in *Jew Suss:*

It was an astonishing performance, wrong from beginning to end, but with all the qualities of fine acting tearing their way through a chaos of inexperience. His diction was practically perfect; his personality, in spite of his fantastic antics, was real and varied; his sense of passion, of evil, of drunkenness, of tyranny, of a sort of demoniac authority was arresting; a preposterous energy pulsating through everything he did.

Such extreme reactions were personal; in the professional evaluations of a fashionable opening night, Welles's appearance created no special stir. His reviews the next day were not outstanding and, when I went backstage with the Mielziners and stood politely in the background while the proper amenities were exchanged with Miss Cornell, I looked around vainly for a glimpse of the red and black costume.

I left without seeing him; yet, in the days that followed, he was seldom out of my mind. My agitation grew and I did nothing about it—in much the same way as a man nurtures his sense of excited anticipation over a woman the sight of whom has deeply disturbed him and of whom he feels quite certain that there will one day be something between them. In the meantime, I found myself eagerly absorbing that considerable body of personal legend—partly apocryphal but largely authentic—which already formed about Orson Welles before the age of twenty.

The prodigious son of a Chicago beauty and a society playboy, who made his first acting appearance as the baby in *Madama Butterfly*

and a rabbit in a Marshall Field's Christmas show; who at the age of
five had confounded theatrical scholars ten times his age; who, at
twelve, played Marc Antony, the Soothsayer *and* Cassius in a
prize-winning school production of *Julius Caesar*, which he also
directed and of which, a few years later, he edited, illustrated, printed,
and published his own acting version; of his voyage, as a painter,
through Ireland in a donkey cart, from which he descended, at the age
of sixteen (claiming to be a well-known star of the New York theater)
to play leading parts in Dublin's Gate Theatre; of his departure, when
they would not let him play Othello; of the total neglect which awaited
him on his return to his native land till the afternoon, at a cocktail party
in Chicago, when he met Thornton Wilder, who sent him to New York
via Alexander Woollcott to Katharine Cornell, by whom, after one
reading, he was engaged to play opposite her on her national repertory
tour. His conduct, on that tour, was a legend in itself—a sequence of
brawls, debauches, missed trains and breaches of discipline which
were without precedent in a company known for its outward propriety
and decorum. When the company returned to New York, he was
considered too immature at nineteen to play a metropolitan Mercutio.
His fury at being recast as Tybalt was not entirely histrionic.

The period of waiting, during which the conditions of my meeting
with Orson Welles were ineluctably shaping themselves, was about
three weeks. But the event which finally brought us together had been
germinating for months. The previous summer among the guests at
Mina Curtiss's Sunday lunch party at Chapelbrook had been Archibald
MacLeish, who spoke of the new directions to be taken by American
poetry, including his own, and mentioned that he was in his final
weeks of work on a play with a contemporary American theme.

I may have reported this to Nathan Zatkin one day as we were
raking over the coals of past and future projects. Knowing Nathan, I
should not have been surprised, a week later, when I discovered an
item, prominently featured in that greenhouse of theatrical fantasies,
the Sunday drama section of the *New York Times*, reporting that
Archibald MacLeish, the eminent poet, Pulitzer Prize winner and editor
of *Fortune* magazine, had completed a play in verse on a contemporary
theme and had entrusted its production to Nathan Zatkin and John
Houseman as the first presentation of their newly formed Phoenix
Theater. I called Zatkin, who professed utter, unconvincing
amazement. Two days later I received a sharp note from the poet, to
which I replied with an abject apology and the hope that his legitimate
indignation would not prevent him from letting me read the play when
it was ready.

In the months that followed, I learned that he had submitted it to the Theatre Guild, to Jed Harris and, finally, to the Theater Union—without results. Then one morning, soon after the New Year, came a letter from the poet asking if I still wished to read his play. Two Sundays later it was once again announced in the drama section of the *New York Times* that *Panic*, a play in verse on a contemporary subject by that eminent poet Archibald MacLeish, would be presented by John Houseman and Nathan Zatkin as the opening production of their newly formed Phoenix Theater. This time, the announcement was authorized by the poet.

I had nothing to lose and, by my own mysterious calculations, a lot to gain by rushing in where every other New York management, Right and Left, feared to tread. The fact that MacLeish's play was so patently uncommercial and presented such obvious and apparently insurmountable production problems gave me a kind of perverse protection and made it essential that I produce it immediately. Unable to function within the patterns of the existent commercial, social or art-theater setups, I had found it necessary to create the image of a man who would undertake what no one else would venture. *Panic* was the perfect vehicle for such a demonstration.

Besides, I had found in *Panic* a personal empathy that excited me. Without identifying myself with the doomed tycoon McGafferty I, too, had felt the thrill of the "creeping ruin." Re-evaluating the play today, fifty years later, with a full awareness of its historical and social fallacies and of its prosodic and dramatic limitations, I still see merit in *Panic*. For all its tricks and poses and its literary attempt to impose upon the economic incident of the Crash the fatality of a Greek tragedy, it carries the unmistakable mark of deep personal shock—the despairing fear a man feels at the sudden, inexplicable collapse of a world of which he himself has been a secure and confident part.

Taking off with the speed of desperation, Zatkin and I managed to raise $500, half of which we presented to the poet as an advance payment, incorporate ourselves as the Phoenix Theater and have a telephone installed in the squalid one-room office that we rented by the month on the second floor of a burlesque house on 42nd Street. This became the headquarters of the Phoenix and it was from there that an eager, harassed and unpaid secretary began to mail out the innumerable and astonishing releases that poured from Zatkin's fertile brain till, within a fortnight of our first announcement, *Panic* seemed well on its way to becoming one of the main theatrical events of that spring.

After that we came to a sudden stop—for two good reasons. We had no money and we had no leading man. The latter was the more serious. To announce *Panic* without a McGafferty was like preparing to put on *Lear* without the king. And like Lear, McGafferty was an almost impossible role to cast in the American theater—a formidable J.P. Morganesque figure "in his late fifties, the leading industrialist and financier of his time," who was expected to convey an almost legendary greatness through speech after speech of rhetorical and frequently repetitive verse.

It was at this point that I paid a visit one evening backstage at the Martin Beck Theater, where *Romeo and Juliet* was playing. I appeared around ten o'clock—by which time I knew that Tybalt was dead and Orson Welles off the stage, waiting for his curtain call. While the doorman, with my 50 cents clutched in his hand, slowly climbed the stairs to announce me, I could hear the voices from the stage; they continued to rise faintly from below as I entered the cramped and cluttered cubicle where he sat, naked to the waist, before his mirror under the glaring bulbs, waiting for his long-delayed curtain call. His black-and-scarlet Tybalt costume, stiff and heavy with sweat, lay over the back of a chair. The beard was off and, under the viscous, mottled slime of greasepaint and the multiple lines and shadings round the eyes and the false nose, it was still impossible to distinguish the real face from that of the "King of the Cats." But the hands were extraordinary; in life as on the stage, they were pale, huge and beautifully formed, with enormous white palms and incredibly long, tapering fingers that seemed to have a life of their own. There were sheets of paper scattered among the greasepaint, the bottles and the beard, all covered with large, well-formed writing, doodled figures and gruesome faces—vague caricatures of himself. (A play he was writing about the Devil, he explained, smiling.) I left to wait for him in a bar across the street.

It was always a shock to see Welles without the make-up and the false noses behind which he chose to mask himself. When he walked in, with his hair combed, in a sober, dark suit, I did not know him for a moment; then, as he moved towards me, I recognized his shuffling, flat-footed gait, which I had found so frightening in Tybalt and which was really his own. I could see his features now, finally; the pale pudding face with the violent black eyes, the button nose with the wen to one side of it and the deep runnel meeting the well-shaped mouth over the astonishingly small teeth. Against the darkness of the wooden table I was conscious once more of the remarkable hands and the voice that made people turn at the neighboring tables—startled not so much by its loudness as by its surprising vibration.

We had one old-fashioned and then another while I told him of our project and gave him a copy of the play and my telephone number.

Afterwards I walked across town with him towards Grand Central Station, then watched him vanish, with astonishing speed, into the tunnel leading to the Westchester commuter trains. After he had gone, I was left not so much with the impression of his force and brilliance as with a sense of extreme youth and charm and of a courtesy that came very close to tenderness.

Orson called at twelve the next day to say he wanted to play McGafferty. When did rehearsals begin?

Twenty-four hours later I saw MacLeish's eyes narrow in exasperation as a tall nineteen-year-old boy in gray pants and a loose tweed jacket entered our bare, one-room office over the burlesque house to read for the role of the aging tycoon. I gave him the hardest part first: the last despairing phase when McGafferty, harried and weakened with fear, becomes convinced, through the suicide of his last trusted associate, that his own end is near.

Sitting stiffly in that small grimy office (with only two wooden chairs, so that Zatkin and I sat on the floor with our backs against the wall), hearing that voice for the first time in its full and astonishing range, MacLeish stared incredulously. And, an hour and a half later, the poet had heard his play, including the choruses, read as he would never hear it again. After Orson had left (there was a matinée of *Romeo*), while the walls were still echoing with the sweet thunder of that fabulous recital, Zatkin asked the glowing poet if he had any idea where we could borrow $2000. The next morning a bank draft was delivered, by hand, from the office of Robert Lovett, of Brown Bros., Harriman & Co., for $2500. This, with another $1000 that we borrowed later from MacLeish himself, constituted our entire financing for a production that had nothing modest or experimental about it.

The script ot *Panic* called for twenty-five speaking parts, to which we added a chorus of twenty-three. These fifty-odd persons were to appear on a stage which, according to the author, showed "a bank president's office, raised by several steps and enclosed, on the sides, by open square columns, at the back by a double door" and "a street before an electric news bulletin of the Times Square type"—the whole to be "impersonal, bare, huge, on a scale to dwarf the shapes of men and women." To achieve this titanic effect, we managed to rent, for ten days, the most desirable musical-comedy stage in New York—that of the Imperial Theater. To create our décor I conned one of Broadway's leading designers, Jo Mielziner, into working for nothing. The set was plain but enormous and called for a raised, sharply raked platform separated from the forestage by a trench or pit, 40 feet long and two feet wide, which we hacked out of the expensive linoleum-covered stage flooring and filled with electric projectors whose beams, shooting straight into the air and blending with another bank of lights pouring down from behind the proscenium arch, formed an opaque wall or curtain of light between the upper and lower parts of the stage. (Later, in the Mercury *Julius Caesar*, we came to refer to them as "Nuremberg lights" after Hitler's use of similar lighting tricks in some of his Nazi night ceremonies.)

To regulate traffic on the forestage I persuaded Martha Graham to join us. (I had known her since 1929 when we both lived at 66 Fifth Avenue.) Virgil Thomson agreed to supply music for the sum of $100—later reduced to $50 when he decided that the only sounds needed were a real telegraph key tapping out real Morse code and a metronome. With a special dispensation from Actors' Equity that allowed us three weeks' rehearsal in exchange for a guarantee of one week's salary at Equity minimum ($40 in those days) and including the cost of a whirl-wind promotion and subscription campaign and $100 apiece for Zatkin and myself, the total estimated cost of *Panic* came to around $4500.

In three performances before diversified audiences in a large theater, we hoped to draw whatever spectators we could reasonably expect to attract to a play as special as *Panic*. By restricting our run we were able to cut our production cost virtually in half; also, by limiting our call on the actors' time, we were able, in the words of one reviewer, "to beguile a large company of excellent and willing actors into donating their services to an unusual artistic cause."

For our first reading on the bare stage of the Imperial Theater we had, in fact, assembled a huge and quite surprising cast. Besides Welles as McGafferty, Richard Whorf as his principal henchman and my ex-wife Zita Johann (back from Hollywood for a while) as his loyal mistress, our cast and chorus featured a number of distinguished American actors, including several visitors from the Group Theatre and the celebrated black actress Rose McLendon—attracted by this rare opportunity to speak contemporary verse on the stage.

After our first general reading, until the final run-throughs began, we rehearsed at different times and places: the street scenes under Martha Graham, the personal scenes under the direction of James Light. I had intended to stage the play myself but, overcome by the responsibilities of producing and promoting this monster-on-a-shoestring (and having, besides, lost what little self-confidence I had in the fjords of Norway and the snows of Valley Forge), I had withdrawn, before the start of rehearsals, in favor of James Light, whose talent I had admired since the days of the Old Provincetown. Except on the days when they were sawing up the floor or moving in scenery and lighting equipment, the stage of the Imperial was occupied mostly by Miss Graham, her chorus, her metronome and her incredible energy.

Actors who worked with her during those exhausting three weeks talked with awe of the disciplined fervor and the rigid perfectionism with which she drove them—with charley horses and screaming tendons—through the slow, angular ballet that grew before our eyes out of the moods and rhythms of MacLeish's unrelenting three-beat lines.

This use of the chorus, "the attempt to use the crowd as an actor which results in a chorus speaking, not with the single voice of a Greek chorus, but with the many voices of the American street," constituted the most challenging element of the production. Stark Young wrote that the best thing in *Panic* was Martha Graham's arrangements of the crowd groups and that "a considerable amount of firmness appeared in the pattern that these people in the street sought to establish for their numerous and gradually less exhilarating scenes." A critic of the Left, on the other hand, accustomed to the more realistic motions of "agitprop," felt that "in the mass-scenes, Martha Graham...slows down the figures and masses of the chorus into a Grecian frieze."

The office scenes, which revolved around the doomed figure of McGafferty, were rehearsed mostly underground in the lounge of the Imperial and on the stage after the battered chorus had been sent home. I had heard hair-raising stories of Welles's behavior in rehearsal. With us, from first to last, his conduct was perfect. Towards James Light, who regarded him with continually growing amazement and admiration, he was respectful and courteous; he remained understanding and gentle when Jimmy started to crack up in the final, harrowing days of rehearsal. With his fellow actors he was considerate and, perhaps for the only time in his life, punctual. With Zita, who was nervous and disturbed over her difficulties with the rigid, unfamiliar verse in a role that she found affected and unmotivated, he was helpful and patient. And, to his own part of the sexagenarian McGafferty, he brought us, as a free gift, the strength, the keen intelligence, the arrogance and the prodigious energy of his nineteen and a half years.

It was a gift for which I was truly grateful, for, almost from the first day of rehearsal, it had become evident where the principal dangers of *Panic* lay: McGafferty, as MacLeish had written him, was not so much a man as the symbol of a condemned class—a stiff, inflexible figure with little emotional growth, whom neither his enemies nor his entourage of partners, lieutenants, lawyer and mistress could ever quite warm into theatrical life. Add to this my gradual realization that, by the spring of 1935, *Panic* was already out of tune with its time. The climate had changed since the bank closings. The days of window jumpers, apple vendors and bonus marchers were over; blind fear and passive acceptance were things of the past. By 1935 the rage to live was returning to the American people; as they started to thrash their angry and untidy way back to plenty, there was one thing they were united in abhorring: the contemplation of their own immediate and shameful past.

For our three performances of *Panic* we had tried to mobilize three quite distinct kinds of audiences. Our third and last night was already disposed of—sold for $1000 to *New Theater*, a left-wing magazine intended to aid in "the mass development of the American theater to its highest artistic and social level—a theater dedicated to the struggle against war, fascism and censorship" which, in general, closely followed the cultural line of the American Communist Party. *New Theater* and *New Masses* firmly and deliberately supported *Panic*, pressed the sale of tickets and, as an added attraction, offered a symposium on the stage after the show, featuring Archibald MacLeish in debate with three leading intellectuals of the American Left.

Our first performance was a "subscribers' preview," open to members of the nonexistent Phoenix, friends of the cast and of MacLeish. They were respectful, impressed by the magnitude of our effort, mildly admiring but, also, worn and confused. No such generous feelings animated the audience that attended our second performance—the official first night of *Panic* on March 15, 1935. At the then astronomical price of $5.50 a seat, we had succeeded in half-filling the theater with a grimly elegant and forbidding opening-night audience. They applauded Jo's set when the curtain rose. After that, for any number of reasons (including the lack of an intermission and their bitterness at being reminded, by one of their own, of things they were trying so hard to forget), they generally detested what they saw and heard.

Some of this atmosphere of resentful gloom was reflected in the press the following morning. Brooks Atkinson of the *New York Times* gave the poet and his producers a good mark for effort; he congratulated the youthful Phoenix for reviving "an impulse that our middle-aged theater has long been lacking'" and praised the poet for "the terse beauty of his bare, lean verse, which is modern in choice of words and vigor of sound." He had kind words for Orson Welles's "excellent performance," and for the "crisp and forceful thrust" of James Light's direction. After which, Mr. Atkinson confessed his perplexity at Mr. MacLeish's basic theme "that the collapse of industry is no rational disaster but a visitation of fate, the furies and the Gods." He also expressed reservations as to the theatrical quality of Mr. MacLeish's verse. *Variety*, the organ of show business, described *Panic* as "ultra-contemporaneous—a highly effective and forceful dramatic interpretation of the big-banking, busto-crusto days of March 1933."

The following night, *Panic*, for the first and only time, played to a packed house before an audience swept by one of those ground swells of excitement that were characteristic of the period and that had found its most recent expression in the first public performance of Odets's *Waiting for Lefty*. It was a Depression phenomenon through which, for a short time and for large numbers of predominantly young people, the theater became far more than entertainment or even artistic release. It seemed to offer them an escape from the anxiety and squalor of their own lives and a direct participation in that "joyous fervor" that accompanies the creation of a brave new world.

Panic was no *Waiting for Lefty*; in style, emotional content and dramatic tone no two works could have been further apart. Yet, some echoes of that same excitement (if not of the warmth and the joy) filled the Imperial Theater on that Saturday night, for what was by far the best of our three performances. Not all that excitement was theatrical; some of it was frankly political and much of it had been quite deliberately induced and encouraged by the operators of the Communist Party's cultural apparatus.

Their plan was clear, if a trifle ingenuous: to capture alive America's most fashionable poet and put him to work, eager and eloquent, on the side of the Revolution. To accomplish this, the intellectuals of the Party assembled their strongest and subtlest forces on the stage of the Imperial Theater for a ceremony which seemed to fall somewhere between an exorcism and a conversion, a kidnapping and an auto-da-fé.

The playwright John Howard Lawson led off the debate; Burnshaw, the pedant of the Party, followed with a tedious academic paper. But the main attraction, who finally rose at last and moved slowly down to the footlights, was the head of cultural activities for the American Communist Party—V.J. Jerome. His face was pale, his eyes sorrowful, his voice gentle and cultivated with a faint trace of Whitechapel cockney accent. He began quietly enough: "Last night, in this theater, I saw *Panic* at its première performance. As I sat in the audience I heard hissing from the front rows, where tickets were priced at $5.50. That will help you to appreciate who the majority of those first-nighters were." There was some laughter at that, but he quickly continued, "I am not here to discuss the ethics of the hiss, though its aesthetics cannot altogether be separated from its politics. One thing I did feel, however—that the hiss of the bourgeoisie is the applause of the proletariat!"

When the clapping and the laughter had subsided and after an unflattering reference to "that court singer of British imperialism, Rudyard Kipling," the speaker got down to the serious business of the evening: "MacLeish has taken for his subject matter a certain moment in the

economic crisis of American capitalism and has dealt with it in a
manner that is new to him and something of a shock to those who have
hitherto been his followers." He glanced back at the poet before continuing, "MacLeish's play has as its theme the doom of capitalism, a doom
that proceeds out of the very being of capitalism, organically, by an inex-
orable dictate. In this sense *Panic* is an anticapitalist play and represents a
significant transition in the career of Archibald MacLeish as a writer."

There was loud applause at that. The speaker waited, raised his
hand for silence, then continued more quietly, a thin smile playing
about his lips as he drew attention to the "significant" fact that in
MacLeish's play "the bankers are endowed with lines of *five* accents,
while the proletariat received only minced, *three*-accented lines!" He
smiled knowingly at Archie, as one cultivated man at another. "I
should say in justice to MacLeish that this differentiation was probably
not intended as a belittlement of the workers; it is due, as he himself
tells us, to the fact that the unemployed constitute the element of
chorus and, as such, traditionally, I dare say, do not need full extension
of speech." The smile lingered for a moment, then vanished. The tone
rose. "But his error lies precisely in this conception of the unemployed
as *chorus*—not as *Dramatis Personae*! Hence the fatalism that pervades
the play; hence the pallor and the showiness of the workers. When the
playwright fuses into his blood the red corpuscles of faith in the
revolutionary power of the proletariat—then and not till then will his
unemployed workers be given flesh and blood and muscle; will his
chorus emerge from the background and assume the position of the
protagonist!" There was some applause but he did not stop for it.

"Archibald MacLeish has given evidence, I believe, of his sincere
desire to proceed along that road. I think the play we have seen this
evening justifies us in expecting to see him advance from his present
point of splendid, lonely poet to sing the epic of the proletariat
advancing through day-to-day struggle to power, to be one of the poets
that the American working class has drawn into its ranks—to work as
poet, singing the epic of the New Conquistador!"

With that, V.J. Jerome sat down amid loud and prolonged
applause, which faded down, then broke out again, swollen by
cheering, as the poet rose to his feet and moved slowly to the front of
the stage—a slim, lithe elegant figure, seriously and modestly
acknowledging their bravos. This was the high point of the evening,
the climax to which everything else had been prelude. So they
continued clapping and cheering for a time, while MacLeish stood
there, facing them and waiting. Then, gradually, the sounds died away
and the house was silent—waiting for the poet to make his statement.

What did they expect? Did they seriously believe they had him trapped? Backed into a corner from which the only exit lay in a public conversion to Marxism? Did they really expect to see him hit the sawdust trail? Or did they hope that in the agitation of the moment, out of embarrassment or vanity, he would let slip an irretrievable condemnation of his capitalist associates or some rash, irrevocable hope for the triumph of the Proletariat? If so, they did not know their man.

The poet's voice, as he began to speak, was soft but clear, full of sincerity and charm. He opened with expressions of gratitude; he thanked his collaborators—his actors, his director, his choreographer, his producers and, last but not least (with a slow, emotional look around the jammed and silent theater), his audience. Contrasting the arid, jaded gang of the previous night with the eager, intelligent and vital crowd he saw before him, he let them share his dream of a new theater in America.

"The American theater is dead! And the American theater is now alive!" he announced dramatically. "For the first time since I knew anything about such matters, there exists in this country a theater in which dishonesty is not demanded, in which hokum and sex are not compulsory ingredients. There is offered, in other words, a theater for art—a theater for people!"

There was solid applause after that. When it had subsided the poet turned to his fellow panelists in the stage and thanked them for their constructive consideration of his work. After that, he repeated his thanks to all those who had helped make the occasion possible, including the editors and subscribers of New Theater. It was during this final expression of gratitude that he uttered what turned out to be his most radical sentiments of the evening.

"Social injustice is no novelty in the world. What is new is the recognition of social injustice; the recognition, specifically, that it *is* injustice and that it *is* hateful!"

He sat down amid scattered applause. It was after midnight and everybody was tired and the theater emptied quickly as people went for their subways and taxis.

Two days later, by appointment, Zatkin and I visited the poet in the offices of Fortune magazine high up in the Chrysler Building, showed him our figures and explained that we saw no possible way of repaying the money we had borrowed from him and from Mr. Lovett. He behaved admirably and undertook to explain the situation to his friend. On my way uptown I bought an evening paper. It was full of stories of real panic in the streets—the Harlem riots. Though the outbreak was over, with one dead and many injured, tension remained high and Governor Lehman had been asked to send military assistance. The

Mayor had opened an investigation during which the District Attorney blamed it all on the Reds: "Let the Communists know they cannot come into this country and upset our laws!" Meantime more than 500 police, in cars and on foot, continued to patrol the Harlem area in which we had rehearsed *Four Saints* the year before and the streets through which the massed bands of the Monarch Elks were to march one year later to celebrate our grand opening of the Negro *Macbeth*.

My immediate preoccupation, now that the excitement of *Panic* was past, was once again with the constant and pressing problem of what I should do next with my life. At long last, after so many false starts and frustrations, I was beginning to find in the theater a possible realization of those hopes and ambitions that had previously existed only in my most fantastic dreams. The passage from fantasy to reality remained a slow and precarious one: it was made easier for me that winter and in the months to come by the presence of Mina Curtiss and by the certainty that her intelligence, her instinctive understanding and her warmth were available to me without embarrassment or reservation whenever I urgently needed them.

I collaborated that summer with Nathanael West (who had already written *Miss Lonelyhearts*) on a revue based on traditional American musical and dramatic material of the kind that was so successfully exploited in the decades that followed. No manager showed the slightest interest and West departed for Hollywood, where he wrote *The Day of the Locust* before he was killed with his wife in a motor accident.

But my best times, that spring and early summer, were those I spent with Orson Welles. In the frenzy of rehearsing and opening *Panic* we had had little chance to talk. It was not until after he had come out from behind his sexagenarian's wig and putty nose that we began to meet and to make plans for the future. He and Virginia, the beautiful young wife he had found in Chicago the previous year, had moved into a curious one-room residence on Riverside Drive. I went there one day to collect Orson for lunch. He said he had been working all night and when I arrived he was still in his bath—a monstrous, medieval iron cistern which, when it was covered at night with a board and mattress, served them as a marriage bed. Orson was lying there, inert and covered with water, through which his huge, dead-white body appeared swollen to gigantic proportions. When he got up, full of apologies, with a great splashing and cascading of waters, I discovered that his bulk owed nothing to refraction—that he was, in reality, just as enormous outside as inside the tub which, after he had risen from it and had started to dry himself, was seen to hold no more than a few inches of liquid lapping about his huge, pale feet.

Since neither of us had a residence suited to serious conversation, we spent hours drinking coffee in odd places until Nathan Zatkin one day presented us with the key to a large suite in the Sardi Building on 44th Street, the abandoned headquarters of the Mendelssohn Society of America. A bronze bust of the composer, an enormous oak table and four straight chairs were the only furnishings of what became the temporary headquarters of the moribund Phoenix Theater. Here Orson and I spent hours, talking, dreaming, laughing and vaguely developing schemes for making bricks without straw. "Planning" is the wrong word for what we did together—then or later. Of the manifold projects we cooked up in the five and a half years of our association—the ones that succeeded and the ones that failed, the ones that were begun and abandoned and the ones that never got started at all—each was an improvisation, an inspiration or an escape: our response to an emotional impulse rather than the considered execution of a plan.

Now, towards the end of April 1935, sitting in our bare office in West 44th Street, we were seized with a sudden, compulsive urge to produce a play together. It did not matter too much what it was nor that it was too late in the season nor that we had no way of financing it. Orson's dominant drive, at the moment, was a desire to expose the anemic elegance of Guthrie McClintic's *Romeo and Juliet* through an Elizabethan production of such energy and violence as New York had never seen. For this demonstration, we hesitated between Marlow's *Tragical History of Doctor Faustus* and John Ford's *'Tis Pity She's a Whore*, which we finally selected.

Welles spent a weekend in and on his bathtub devising a handsome and extremely complex Italian street scene (complete with balconies and interiors) in which the stage became a theatrical crossroads where the physical and emotional crises of the tragedy converged. After that he began to produce costume sketches in great number. The rest of our time was taken up with the sociable business of casting. During the weeks of our occupancy, the premises of the Mendelssohn Society of America had become a sort of lighting place and refuge for young actors of our acquaintance on their weary and discouraging rounds of Broadway's theatrical offices. Now, in addition to serving them tea or coffee (brought in at their own expense from the drugstores on Times Square), we set them to reading Elizabethan verse, for their own benefit and ours. These exercises—readings, dialogues and staged scenes—went on for several weeks, long after it had become painfully clear that no production would result. One day we reluctantly announced that we were closing the office and Orson and Virginia went off to Wisconsin to see a man about a summer theater.

We parted friends—without promises or commitments and with no particular reason to believe we would ever be associated again. Yet our time together had not been wasted.

To me, those weeks were a revelation. I was almost thirty-three years old. Welles was twenty. But, in my working relationship with this astonishing boy whose theatrical experience was so much greater and richer than mine, it was I who was the pupil, he the teacher. In certain fields I was his senior, possessed of painfully acquired knowledge that was wider and more comprehensive than his; but what amazed and awed me in Orson was his astounding and, apparently, innate dramatic instinct. Listening to him, day after day, with rising fascination, I had the sense of hearing a man initiated, at birth, into the most secret rites of a mystery—the theater—of which he felt himself, at all times, the rightful and undisputed master. I watched him, with growing wonder, take John Ford's mannered and decadent work, bend it to his will and recreate it, on the stage of his imagination, in the vivid, dramatic light of his own theatrical emotion. *'Tis Pity She's a Whore* served its function—that of a dry run for productions that followed. Through it we learned each other's language and laid the foundation and set the form and tone of our future collaboration.

I missed Orson when he left. Then, as the spell lifted, I resumed my life of plots and maneuvers, of watching and waiting for my next chance. In this, my last fallow summer before the raging activity of the years ahead, I divided my time between my attic room on 57th Street and the little house on the South Mountain Road. Halfway between New York and New City, and a frequent resting place for my throbbing Model A, was Sneden's Landing, where Pare Lorentz had just moved into a house high up the hill. Pare, besides being America's liveliest movie critic, was becoming increasingly concerned with the changing state of the nation under the New Deal. After a series of magazine articles, he had turned to documentary films to tell his story: he was working on the first of his films, *The Plough that Broke the Plains*, in which he dealt dramatically and poetically with the calamity of soil erosion in Texas and Oklahoma—on those same burning plains over which I had travelled during my first Southwestern summer. Pare was a man of exasperating eloquence who was outraged if you broke off a conversation before four in the morning; in the years during which we were friends and occasionally worked together, he taught me a lot about America and the painful but exciting realities of its growth.

So passed another anxious, idle summer in the green, steaming heat of the Hudson Valley. Twice I drove with Lincoln Kirstein into the

Berkshires and once Mina came down and spent three days with me in
New City. Defying the copperheads with which the South Mountain
Road abounded that summer, other ladies paid platonic visits. Lewis
Galantière came once but found the atmosphere too rustic for his taste.
Walking down the center of the South Mountain Road at hours set
aside "pour la promenade," in his light flannel trousers, straw hat and
jacket, he surprisingly resembled photographs of Marcel Proust.

By the middle of August the last of my savings were gone and I
was nervous and anxious to get back to town to work I did not have.
The little house in New City, which had been my refuge, two years
before, against the devastating winds of national and personal
catastrophe, no longer served my needs. The time for a storm cellar
was over. Things were on the move all around me and, outsider
though I was, I must move with them or perish. When my opportunity
came it was, once again, from an entirely unexpected quarter—from
the government of a country in which I had been, for more than five
years, an illegal resident.

III

Voodoo Macbeth
1935-36

By 1935, halfway through the energetic confusions of Roosevelt's first term, the outline of the New Deal had begun to appear. One significant symptom was the changeover from relief—from a national acceptance of "defeated, discouraged, hopeless men and women, cringing and fawning as they came to ask for public aid"—to the revolutionary and humane idea of work-relief. To 20 million Americans dependent on public charity (amid cries of socialism, communism and worse), work was to be supplied by the federal government within their own skills and trades. This mutation took place during the dog days, with only moderate attention on my part; it was not till September that the Works Progress Administration, newly formed under Harry Hopkins, received its allocation of $5000 million of federal funds. Of this a small fraction (less than 1 percent) was to be devoted to the arts—including the theater.

The Federal Theater of the Works Progress Administration, which came to play such a vital part in so many of our lives, was not primarily a cultural activity. It was a relief measure conceived in a time of national misery and despair. The only artistic policy it ever had was the assumption that thousands of indigent theater people were eager to work and that millions of Americans would enjoy the results of this work if it could be offered at a price they could afford to pay. Within a year of its formation the Federal Theater had more than 15,000 men and women on its payroll at an average wage of less than $20 a week. During the four years of its existence its productions played to more than 30 million people in more than 200 theaters as well as portable stages, school auditoriums and public parks the country over.

To guide and administer this, the most controversial of all his work projects, Harry Hopkins had chosen a national director who was not drawn from the commercial hierarchy of Broadway but from among the dreamers and experimenters—the eggheads of the American theater. Hallie Flanagan, like Hopkins a graduate of Iowa's Grinnell College and head, since 1925, of Vassar's famed Experimental Theater, was a wild little woman who believed and publicly stated her conviction that "the theater is more than a private enterprise; it is also a public interest which, properly fostered, might come to be a social and an educative force"; a fanatic, armed with millions of taxpayers' dollars who, on assuming office, had heretically announced that "while our immediate aim is to put to work thousands of theater people, our more far-reaching purpose is to organize and support theatrical enterprises so excellent in quality and low in cost and so vital to the communities involved that they will be able to continue after federal support is withdrawn." To those who were fortunate enough to be a part of the Federal Theater from the beginning, it was a unique and thrilling experience. Added to the satisfaction of accomplishing an urgent and essential social task in a time of national crisis, we enjoyed the excitement that is generated on those rare and blessed occasions when the theater is suddenly swept into the historical mainstream of its time.

My own connection with the project began quite suddenly one evening in Rosamond Gilder's apartment on Gramercy Park. As associate editor of the *Theater Arts Monthly*, she had come to form part of the inner circle of Hallie Flanagan's aides and advisers. She said my name had come up in discussions over the formation of the New York WPA Negro Theater. She asked if I would be interested; I told her I would. Two weeks later my friend Rose McLendon, the great Negro actress, called and asked me to meet her in Hallie Flanagan's office. She was late as usual and I spent half an hour alone with Mrs. Flanagan—a small, forthright, enthusiastic lady with strong teeth, whose matted reddish hair lay like a wig on her skull and who seemed to take her vast responsibilities with amazing self-confidence and sang-froid. When Rose arrived there was a meeting at which I was offered and accepted the post of joint head—with her—of the Negro Theater Project in Harlem.

In the confusion of transferring 3.5 million men and women to the federal payroll before Christmas, it was not noticed that I was not only an alien but also illegally residing in the United States under a false name. Or maybe nobody cared. My application went through as urgent, non-relief, executive personnel at a salary of $50 a week. It was not until many months later that I understood the true circumstances of my nomination to a job which I took on with only a confused awareness of its hazards and implications.

I had known Harlem in the mid-twenties as a late-night playground; I had found it again, eight years later, as the scene of my first and happiest theater experience, *Four Saints*. Both times, in different ways, I had been made sharply aware of the corrosive misery that filled its streets and houses. Harlem had a church on every other corner; it also had the highest crime rate in the city. Gambling in its various forms was a Tammany political preserve of long standing; rents were double or more what they were in any equivalent white area of the city, with no leases given, no control or inspections enforced and an organized landlords' blacklist against protesting or "troublesome" tenants. Local businesses and stores (many of them survivals from the days when Harlem was a white, bourgeois suburb) refused, almost without exception, to employ Negro help. Unemployment had long been endemic in Harlem; with the Depression, it became critical. Under the spur of despair, passive resignation turned into active resentment—stirrings of revolt in which the Left found fruitful ground for its expanding activity. The first Negro unemployed demonstrations had been met with police brutality; soon after that, the Harlem edition of the *Daily Worker* began to call itself the *Liberator* and the Communist Party's vice-presidential candidate in the two next national elections was a Negro. Yet the Party's influence remained limited, for Harlem followed the typical minority pattern: united in misery, it remained fragmented in every other respect. Father Divine was in his heyday. The churches, with their multiple denominations, continued to perform an important and soothing function in the life of the community, though many of their preachers were considered old-fashioned, in some cases mercenary, and generally suspected of "Uncle Tom" attitudes. "Segregation" and "integration" were still academic words, in use among the intelligentsia. (The word "black" was generally taboo. "Negro" was in official and general use.) Economic discrimination, on the other hand, was general and acutely felt; it was the main and immediate cause of the rage and fear that filled Harlem's littered and neglected streets during the worst of the Depression. "Don't buy where you can't work!" had become a battle cry long before the riots which were inevitable—a spontaneous explosion of despair rather than part of any organized campaign of protest. Now, six months later, the New Deal's continuing increase in federal relief and the promise of local works projects on a large scale had taken some of the fever out of the Harlem crisis without curing its underlying causes. Discrimination and rent-gouging continued; so did the bitterness and the disunity.

The Negro Theater Project of the Works Progress Administration was announced in mid-September and immediately became Harlem's leading topic of agitated dispute. It was known that between seven and eight hundred actors, technicians, service personnel and theater staff were about to be hired: this would make the project the city's largest employer of Negro workers in one unit, with activities that promised to be far more attractive than leaf-raking, street-cleaning, construction or office work. For years show business had occupied a special place in Negro city life as one of the few open roads to self-expression and fame: here was a chance to enter it—at government expense. No wonder that from the first day and, increasingly, as rumors began to fly, the question was asked in curiosity, suspicion and anger: now that Harlem was finally to have its own WPA project—who was going to run it?

There were three theatrical factions in Harlem at this time. The first centered around the former Lafayette stock company, which had enjoyed a long and successful career (before talking pictures) in that same theater building in which the WPA was now about to house its project. Ex-members of the Lafayette Players and their friends felt that the government's effort to revive Harlem theatrical life should be entrusted to veterans who had run their own show once before without a white man—and who needed one now?

They were opposed by a second, larger and more influential group. Among the intelligentsia—the teachers, social workers and race-relations experts—there was a general feeling of condescension towards Negroes in show business, who were felt to be lacking in the experience, the education and the vision required to administer a major Negro project in a white man's world. This group recommended the appointment of a white man "of stature," flanked by Negro advisers, whom they were eager to supply. Between these two stood a third, small but powerful group of successful Negro performers, respected union members whose talent had won them full acceptance in the white world. Many of these were now torn between a desire to lead their people into the theatrical promised land and a reluctance to be sucked back into the Harlem broil from which they had only recently emancipated themselves. They, too, for all their strong racial feeling, were generally of the opinion that without a white man at its head—with connections in government circles and some reputation on Broadway—the Negro unit would receive scant recognition or respect in Washington or New York.

There was one other element which, finally, came to exert a considerable influence in the choice of a project head for the Negro Theater. This was the Communist Party, which, having few acceptable candidates of its own, threw its support behind those Negro "names" who had shown a willingness to collaborate with United Front organizations. One such name was that of my friend Rose McLendon. Rose was not well—ravaged already by the cancer that carried her off some months later. When the job of heading the Negro Theater Project was offered her, she demurred, then finally accepted on one condition: that a suitable white associate be found who would work with her, on a basis of complete equality, as her artistic and executive partner. Asked if she had any suggestions to make, she gave my name as that of someone she knew and trusted.

Our collaboration was never put to the test. In the early days of the project she made one or two formal appearances before she fell finally and hopelessly ill. My visits to her bedside after we got under way gave her a feeling of participation, but soon she was too ill even for that. By then the project was so far advanced that no one was willing to risk the delays and confusions that would have resulted from a change of leadership.

Our first month had been devoted to one single activity—getting people off relief and onto the project. This transfer took place in a temporary building on lower Madison Avenue, where, day after day, the hallways, elevators, stairways and improvised waiting rooms were jammed with hundreds of men and women, many with children, who arrived and stood around in herds, sent by their local relief agencies to be interviewed, processed and transferred to WPA jobs for which they were more or less qualified.

Besides the established relief cases, hundreds of new applicants suddenly appeared, excited by rumors of jobs and opportunities in a work area where skills and credentials were almost impossible to verify. Anyone with an authentic relief status was hired, sight unseen; as the days passed and the rolls began to fill up, our task was to make sure that men and women with legitimate theatrical backgrounds got on the project even if their relief status (through pride or bureaucratic confusion) was not entirely satisfactory.

In making these vital and sometimes distressing decisions about people with whose background and circumstances I was totally unfamiliar, I had to rely on the advice of two Negro aides. One was Edward Perry, my stage manager from *Four Saints*; the other, who became my counsellor, protector, instructor, deputy and intimate friend, was Carlton Moss. One of the Negro "new generation," a graduate of Morgan College in Baltimore, he had directed a community project for the New York Public Library and written for radio. When he came to work for the WPA at the age of twenty-five, he was already a bitter and skeptical man. But behind his smiling pose of self-protective sarcasm lay a deep and sympathetic understanding of the inner workings of the Negro world. He was my Machiavelli— briefing me before every meeting, sitting by my side and whispering to me or slipping me scribbled notes along the table each time he saw me getting ready to make a fool of myself or to surrender some essential point of which I had failed to grasp the importance.

These meetings were held in various places—in vestries, board rooms and the back rooms of shady bars. And each was entirely different. Around the polished table of the Urban League, sober, conservative, well-spoken men and women were interested mostly in employment, culture and decorum and were worried lest the Negro unit's behavior be considered radical or immoral. On the other side was the more progressive National Association for the Advancement of Colored People which had long ago rejected the policy of "gradualism" and demanded immediate racial equality. Finally, there was the Communist Party, which wanted no "handkerchief-heading" on the project, demanded plays of social protest in our program and a voice in the assignment of executive jobs.

Sometimes this variegated patronage led to curious situations—especially in the deals we found ourselves making with the Party which, of them all, was the most insistent and capricious in its demands.

(Two minor executives, both white and both appointed at the insistence of the Communist Party, lasted less than three months in their jobs. Following some mysterious internecine dispute which not even Carlton Moss could clarify, the Party suddenly demanded their instant dismissal on charges of "white chauvinism." Since they had worked hard on the project and had done nothing wrong, I refused to fire them and this led to bad feeling and threats of reprisal until finally both men, under intolerable pressure, requested and obtained transfers to other projects.)

Hallie Flanagan believed that she would "find on the relief rolls people with the energy, ability and talent to achieve any program we set up." But, to ensure the artistic and professional standards of the Arts Projects, a special dispensation was granted which permitted each unit to hire up to 10 percent of its creative and executive personnel from outside the relief lists, though still at relief wages. In our case, that meant actors, directors, technicians from the professional theater and, in a few cases, experienced administrators. But most of our non-relief appointments—black and white—were on the creative side. These included a number of the country's best Negro actors, whom pride and an obstinate sense of status had kept off the relief rolls. Their names appear with honor on the cast lists of that year's Lafayette productions.

A few of our artistic staff came from among my own associates (including Virgil Thomson and Abe Feder) who joined, certainly not for $30 a week, not primarily out of friendship for me, but because they saw in the project a wide-open field for those creative activities which they were denied within the narrow limits of the commercial theater; also, perhaps, out of a vague, undefined feeling that, as cooperating members of the Negro Theater Unit, they were helping to start something new and significant in the cultural life of their country.

Late in October 1935, about the time Mussolini was invading Ethiopia, the Negro Theater Project, with its more than 750 men and women and its battered desks, chairs and filing cabinets, began its move from lower Madison Avenue to Harlem. Soon after that, while the Japanese were invading the Chinese mainland, we started to take down the rotting boards which had long covered the doors and windows of the old Lafayette Theater on Seventh Avenue between 132nd and 133rd Streets. Built around the turn of the century when Harlem was a theatrical tributary of Broadway, the Lafayette was a sordid, icy cavern—with peeling plaster, a thick accumulation of grime, burst bulbs, rotting carpets and broken seats in the hairy recesses of which lurked rats, lice and other horrors. Within a month the auditorium had been restored to some semblance of respectability and warmth. On stage, behind the lowered, flaking asbestos safety curtain, equally miraculous changes were being wrought by a stage crew that was the equal in zeal and skill to the best of Broadway. Consistently refused admission to the Stagehands' Union on the ground of color, these carpenters and electricians had been forced to make their living for years outside the theater. Now they were back in their chosen profession: the miles of new rope and cable that Feder had requisitioned, the scores of up-to-date electrical units hanging overhead and the six portable dimmer boards with their dozens of multicolored switches and levers were a source of excitement and pride that made theirs the most consistently enthusiastic department of the project.

Of our 750 workers, almost half were officially classified as actors, singers or dancers. Of these approximately one third had never acted, danced or been on a stage or a concert platform in their lives. This left us with around 200 professional performers, including African drummers, veteran stock actors, Broadway stars and locally celebrated elocutionists like Venezuela Jones. To devise productions in which we could properly employ even a fraction of such variegated talent became my main challenge as the project got under way.

None of the tired and obvious ways would work. In the current temper of the Harlem community, the old "stock" pattern of performing Broadway hits with Negro casts was undesirable, if not downright offensive. Equally unsuitable, for different reasons, was the revival of such celebrated Negro successes as *The Emperor Jones, In Abraham's Bosom, All God's Chillun* or even *Porgy,* which Harlem audiences had applauded downtown but would resent on the stage of their own community theater. This same inhibition semed to apply to the revues and musicals that had long been the Negro performers' main source of theatrical fame and employment; they were regarded as "handkerchief- head" and so, for our purposes, anathema.

In the solution of this problem, Virgil Thomson, with whom I was sharing the first of the five Manhattan apartments we inhabited together over the next two and a half years, was of inestimable aid to me. He reminded me that our casting of *Four Saints* had been done on purely artistic and theatrical grounds. Our black singers had justified our choice and this encouraged me in the position I now took—that our only hope of functioning in a vital and constructive way lay in dividing the performing personnel of the Negro Theater into two separate, though still interrelated, halves. One would be devoted to the performance of plays written, directed and performed by and for Negroes, in Negro locales and, preferably, on contemporary Negro subjects. The other would devote itself to the performance of classical works of which our actors would be the interpreters, without concession or reference to color. The choice of which group they joined was to be made by the project members themselves, with the clear understanding that they could, if they chose, shift their allegiance from production to production. This would give diversity to our shows, increase our use of manpower and stimulate public interest in our activities. It would also arouse a feeling of emulation that would, I hoped, act as a sharp and constant spur to our morale.

For this fine scheme to work, there was one essential condition—that the quality of these "classical" productions be unquestionably high. It would be fatal to undertake the risky and difficult business of producing Shakespeare in Harlem until I had found a director of whose creative imagination and power I was completely confident. Unfortunately no black director had been given the opportunity to direct classics in recent years—if ever. This is why I found myself one evening visiting the basement apartment on West 14th Street into which Orson and Virginia Welles had just moved. Orson had spent a feckless summer in Wisconsin—his impresario having gone broke even before he opened. On his return to New York, in order to keep himself and Virginia alive, he had been forced into what soon became a meteoric career in radio, where his magnificent voice was put to such base uses as *The Shadow*, the *voice of chocolate pudding* and *The Great McCoy*, besides his weekly impersonations on the March of Time of such diverse characters as Haile Selassie, Hindenburg, Sir Basil Zaharoff and the Emperor Hirohito.

I told him of my plans for the Negro Theater and formally invited him to join us. I suggested that our dream of staging a whirling Elizabethan drama might now be realized under unusual but attractive conditions—with Uncle Sam as our angel. Orson called me at two in the morning to announce that Virginia had just had an inspiration: our first production would be *Macbeth*, laid in the island of Haiti in the early nineteenth century, with the witches as voodoo priestesses! Within a week he had constructed out of Plasticine, on a sheet of laundry board, a scale model of what later appeared on the stage of the Lafayette as the basic unit of *Macbeth*. At the same time he and Nat Karson, the designer, with Virginia as their legman, began to amass research on Directoire modes, Napoleonic uniforms and tropical vegetation.

As soon as it was known that we were considering doing *Macbeth*, it became a matter of general controversy in Harlem. The community was fascinated but wary: some thought this Shakespearean venture a white man's scheme deliberately hatched to degrade the Negro and bring the Theater Project into disrepute. Our first auditions tended to confirm these misgivings. I had announced that we would hear anyone who wished to try out for the classical wing of the project. For the best part of a week, they followed each other onto the platform of a large recreation hall belonging to the Ancient Order of Monarch Elks: old and young, male and female, singers, dancers, semiliterates and intellectuals—some in deadly earnest, some giggling in self-conscious embarrassment; still others came suspiciously, regarding the whole thing as an elaborate hoax. By the end of the week more than 300 had been auditioned and classified under mysterious symbols that signified rejects, dancers, soldiers, witches, walk-ons and principals. Within another week *Macbeth* was in rehearsal.

For obvious reasons it was desirable to open the Lafayette with an "indigenous" and, preferably, a realistic contemporary Negro work. And here, immediately, I had encountered our first predictable hazard—the absence of performable Negro scripts. Of the many scripts submitted to us, two were possible, though far from good: *Turpentine* was a stereotyped play of protest laid in a turpentine-workers' camp in South Carolina; Frank Wilson's *Walk Together Chillun!*, which he was eager to direct himself, was a hodgepodge of theatrical clichés, complete with church scene, dance-hall sequence, comedy routines and a preachment that could offend absolutely no one. Wilson was one of America's best-known black actors, the creator of Porgy, a church member and a man whose confused and voluble sincerity had won him the patronizing approval of most organized sections of the community. I chose his play for tactical reasons, fully aware of its weaknesses but equally aware of its advantages for our opening show. My assignment, as head of the project, was not, primarily, the production of masterpieces. I had been instructed to find suitable theatrical activity for the hundreds of needy men and women on our payroll and to find it quickly. *Walk Together Chillun!* seemed to meet this requirement.

For all their many divisions, every member of the project seemed to agree on one thing: that the Negro Theater must be the first New York unit to open its doors to the public. With this objective very much in mind, we put *Walk Together Chillun!* into rehearsal early in December, first in a church, then on the reconditioned stage of the Lafayette. And, in spite of our difficulties with the play and the problems normally attendant upon the opening of a dark theater, it soon became evident that we would, in fact, be the first major project to present a WPA Federal Theater production in New York City.

Walk Together Chillun! opened with a suitable official flurry on the night of February 5, 1936. Its reception was cordial but not enthusiastic. Harlem was relieved that the Project's opening show was neither a disaster nor an "Uncle Tom" piece and proud that the first Federal Theater play in New York should be a Negro production. People who remembered the old Lafayette were impressed by the condition of the house, the size of the pit band led by Joe Jordan and the lavishness of the new technical setup—the lighting particularly. Downtown was generally uninterested.

This, our opening production, ran for less than a month to moderate attendance. Our second—also from the "contemporary" wing of the project—was *Conjur Man Dies* by Rudolph Fisher, a well-known Harlem physician and novelist. It was less earnest than its predecessor and a lot more fun—a comic murder mystery whose theme song was "I'll Be Glad When You're Dead, You Rascal You!" It opened on March 11 and it was a smash. Unlike Wilson's ingenuous preachment, this was big-city entertainment—fast-moving, topical, crammed with inside allusions and bitter minority jokes.

From every practical point of view, even from that of those who disapproved of it, *Conjur Man Dies* was good programming, an asset to the project and a welcome escape from the many stresses and anxieties that continued to harass us. Its success allowed me to turn all my attention to our next opening—the first production of our classical wing, which was generally referred to, by this time, as the *Voodoo Macbeth.*

My functions on the Negro Project, so far, had been essentially administrative and diplomatic. Though I had personally supervised both our contemporary shows, I had not identified myself creatively with either of them. The gauge of my success, so far, had been the efficacy and harmony with which the project was conducted, rather than the theatrical or artistic quality of its productions. Now, suddenly, with *Macbeth*, all this was changed. For, besides its potential value to the project in opening up new fields for black performers, I could not help regarding this production as a direct, personal challenge and the first serious test of my theatrical collaboration with Orson Welles, on which I was setting such high hopes and on which I was preparing to risk not only my own future but that of the Negro Project as well.

Whenever I visited the Elks' Hall where Welles was rehearsing, what I heard and saw delighted but in no way astonished me. I had never seriously doubted the company's ability to speak Elizabethan blank verse when they encountered it under the right conditions and, though he had never professionally staged a play, I had complete faith in Welles's ability to direct them. We had chosen the cast together: Jack Carter, the creator of Crown in the original *Porgy*, was the Thane, with Edna Thomas as his murderous lady. For the Macduffs we had Maurice Ellis and Marie Young; J. Louis Johnson was the Porter, Canada Lee was Banquo and Eric Burroughs (a graduate of London's RADA) played Hecate, a composite figure of evil which Welles had assembled out of fragments of witches' lines and to whose sinister equipment he presently added a 12-foot bullwhip. Our supernatural department was very strong. In addition to the witches and sundry apparitions called for by the bard we had a troupe of African drummers commanded by Asadata Dafora Horton (later Minister of Culture of the Republic of Sierra Leone). Except for their leader, who had a flawless Oxford accent, they spoke almost no English: the star of the troupe, Abdul, an authentic witch doctor, seemed to know no language at all except magic. Their first act, after they had been cast in *Macbeth*, was to file a formal requisition for five live black goats. These were brought into the theater by night and sacrificed, huggermugger, according to approved tribal ritual, before being stretched into resonant drum skins.

This supernatural atmosphere added to the excitement that was beginning to form around our production of *Macbeth*. By the end of February it had become the most debated subject in Harlem—one on which the entire future of the Negro Theater Project was felt to depend. Partly, this had to do with the nature of the show—probably the first full-scale, all-professional Negro Shakespearean production in American theatrical history. Partly it was the effect of sheer mass. Our *Macbeth* had grown steadily with the months until it had become an undertaking of such magnitude that the whole project was beginning to sag under its weight. Backstage at the Lafayette, to make room for the huge slabs of scenery and acres of painted backdrops that continued to arrive from the shops, *Conjur Man Dies* was gradually being edged down towards the footlights, to the fury of Joe Losey, its director. And, in the basement, the glow of hundreds of Karson's gorgeous uniforms, stiff with gold braid, the sheen of satin ball gowns and the gnarled and hairy horror of the witches' hides could not fail to arouse the envious resentment of members of the project's contemporary wing, who were confined to the realistic drabness of street clothes and denim. Soon ugly rumors began to fly: someone had been told downtown by an authoritative source that *Macbeth* would never open; so much of the project's money had been spent on Orson's "folly" that all future productions of the Negro unit had been cancelled. And a stale but dangerous whispering campaign was revived: that what was being so secretly prepared was, in reality, a vast burlesque intended to ridicule the Negro in the eyes of the white world. As a result, Orson was attacked one night, as he was leaving rehearsal, by four alcoholic zealots determined to prevent this insult to their race.

Including his regular midtown radio jobs, to which he commuted by taxi (sometimes two or three times a day), Orson was now working about twenty hours out of the twenty-four. When he was not drilling the company in mass scenes of battle, revelry or witchcraft, or rehearsing individually with Macbeths and Macduffs, he was working with Virgil on music, Karson on costumes, Feder on lights or Asadata on voodoo.

It was during the preparation of *Macbeth* that Orson revealed his surprising capacity for direction. For all the mass of his own ego, he was able to apprehend other people's weakness and strength and to make creative use of them: he had a shrewd instinctive sense of when to bully or charm, when to be kind or savage—and he was seldom mistaken. With Feder, who was a garrulous masochist, Orson was abusive, sarcastic and loud. At light rehearsals he would set him impossible tasks, then howl at him, shamefully and continuously, before the exhausted company, who were so delighted to hear someone else (a white man, especially) catching hell that they persevered with their own stage maneuvers long after their normal span of patience had run out. With Virgil Thomson it was less easy. For here Orson was dealing with an intelligence and an attitude of a kind he had never encountered. Virgil was wary of the boy genius:

You brought Orson to the flat where we were living on 59th Street. We argued late one night and as an older man I tried to beat him down because I felt he was full of bluff and because his verbalization of what he wanted to do in the theater was not entirely convincing. I argued hard and not always fairly against Orson and you told me later to stop it because he was a very, very good man in the theater. You were the one that believed in him...

Then, as they began to work together, things got easier.

Orson was nearly always likeable. He was never hateful or brutal with me, though I was terrified of his firmness. He was extremely professional and he knew what he wanted. He knew it so well and so thoroughly that I, as an older musician with a certain amount of pride, would not write him original music. I would not humiliate myself to write so precisely on his demand. On the other hand, I respected his demands dramatically. So, as your employee, I gave him sound effects and ready-made music—trumpet call, battle scenes and percussive scores where he wanted them—and, of course, the waltzes for the party scene.

Orson and I never quarreled—as you and he did; but we never really agreed. We used to take each other out to elaborate dinners; and it was I who taught him to drink white wine and not whisky at rehearsals...

Another quite different set of problems arose during our collaboration with Asadata Dafora Horton and his troupe of African drummers. With the exception of Abdul, the witch doctor, who several times during rehearsals fell into deep and agitated trances from which not even his fellow witches could rouse him, our voodoo contingent was thoroughly professional, adaptable and eager to please—except in the matter of spells. One day after Orson, Virgil and I had been auditioning their voodoo numbers, we complained to Asadata that his chants did not sound evil enough. Virgil, as usual, got right down to the point.

"Are those really voodoo?"

"Oh yes. Yes, indeed, sirs. That is absolutely real, authentic voodoo."

"They don't sound wicked enough."

"Sirs, I..."

"Sometimes for the theater you have to exaggerate."

"I am sorry, sirs. You can't be any more wicked than that!"

I stayed behind with Virgil and the drummers. As fellow musicians they argued for most of the afternoon. Finally Asadata admitted what those chants of his really were: they were strong spells intended to *ward off* the beriberi—not to induce it. He dared not give us the real thing, he explained. It might work.

The *Macbeth* troupe, including cripples, children and dependents, finally numbered 137. Orson led them with an authority that was extraordinary in a boy just out of his teens. He had the strength; but had also had the infinite and loving patience which, in my experience, distinguishes the great from the competent director. And he displayed a capacity for total concentration without which our whole perilous venture could never have been brought off. For this *Macbeth* troupe of ours was an amazing mishmash of amateurs and professionals, church members and radicals, sophisticates and wild ones, adherents of Father Divine and bushmen from darkest Africa. It was one thing to handle them administratively and paternalistically as I did (firm but understanding, not always truthful but generally fair) and quite another to lead them creatively through unknown country during months of rehearsal in an atmosphere of gathering enervation and doubt. Orson kept them going by the sheer force of his personality. His energy was at all times greater than theirs; he was even more mercurial and less predictable than they were—driving and indolent, glum and gay, tender and violent, inflexibly severe and hopelessly indulgent. I once estimated that half of his growing radio earnings, during *Macbeth*, went in loans and handouts to the company; and to the purchase of props and other necessities (including a severed head) held up by bureaucratic red tape; a quarter went for meals and cabs; the rest was spent on the entertainment of Jack Carter.

Jack Carter was the most furious man I have ever known. Six foot four, elegant and malevolent in his bespoke shoes and his custom-made English suit, he had bright blue eyes and a skin so light that he could pass as white anywhere in the world, if he'd wanted to. He didn't. The son of one of the famed beauties from the original Floradora Sextet, born in a French chateau, unaware of his own Negro blood and brought up in the lap of European luxury, he had never heard of a race problem until he returned to America in his teens. What he then discovered made an outlaw of him; he became a pimp, a killer and finally an actor. As Crown in *Porgy* he scored a big personal success, which was soon threatened by bouts of misbehavior. (His favorite diversion on tour was to register, as a white man, in a town's leading hotel, then invite his black friends, male and female, up to his room and fight till the blood flowed when they were denied admission.) He had not worked much in recent years but made a living somehow through his underworld connections in Harlem. His life was a nagging torment, not knowing whom he despised and hated most—his mother's people for submitting to humiliation or his father's for inflicting it.

When it became known that Jack had been cast for the part of Macbeth, in which he would be directed by a twenty-year-old white man, eyebrows were raised all over Harlem and people waited with mixed emotions for the outcome of their first encounter. From the moment, after the first reading, when Orson threw his arms around Jack, his eyes brimming with tears of gratitude and admiration, a close and passionate friendship had sprung up between these two giants who, together, measured close to 13 feet. For four months they were seldom apart. Jack appeared at every *Macbeth* rehearsal, whether he had been called or not and, when work was over, at four or five in the morning, they went roaring together through the late-night spots and brothels of Harlem till it was time to rehearse again. (I used to wonder, sometimes, seeing Orson returning from these nocturnal forays, if they did not perhaps evoke some echo of those other long, wild nights which he had spent as a boy, with his father, in the red-light districts of the Mediterranean, Hong Kong and Singapore.) This curious intimacy proved of inestimable value to the project. In the state of anxiety and exhaustion which the company had reached by the beginning of April, Jack Carter's loyalty was a major factor in sustaining morale. Not only was he above reproach in his own behavior, but he constituted himself Orson's champion with the company—scornful of its fatigue, quick to detect signs of revolt and to crush movements of disaffection.

This zeal sometimes got us into trouble. One night, not long before opening, around four in the morning, a minor mutiny broke out on stage. In sheer exhaustion, weighed down by the heavy uniforms in which they had been working for almost ten hours, the company exploded suddenly into open anger and refused to go on. First their stage manager, then I, then Orson—sweating and gray with fatigue—pleaded with them, explaining that, for technical reasons, certain stage movements must be fixed that night or not at all. They shook their heads and started to scatter. At that moment a tall figure, superb in full Napoleonic regalia, vaulted onto the parapet of Glamis Castle and began to harangue the rebellious troops. Jack was in a towering rage; he looked and sounded magnificent, full of the unrestrained fury which Orson had been trying to infuse into the last act of *Macbeth*. He told them he was tired too for he had a bigger part than they did; they might have worked for nine hours but he had been rehearsing for thirteen—and, anyway, what was a little fatigue when the whole future of the Negro Theater was at stake? Here was the chance they had never been given before; the opportunity for which they had never even dared to hope. If these men (Orson and I, Harry Hopkins and the President of the United States) were willing to risk their reputations on such a project—to work on it as Welles had done, night and day, month after month, on their behalf, when he could easily have been earning a fortune in radio, as they goddamn well knew—there was only one thing that they, as self-respecting Negro actors and human beings could do: follow him, unquestioningly, to the ends of the earth and stop screwing up his wonderful production with their fucking stupid complaints. If they were tired, let them rest after opening! Because, if the opening was a bust and the production failed through their fault—they'd have the rest of their goddamn lives to rest in!

The company listened in silence. When he finished they began to pick up their props and to drift back into their positions; the mutiny was over; they were ready to rehearse till dawn or longer. It was then that the demon that drove Jack Carter made him add one more sentence to his oration.

"So, get back to work!" he yelled. "You no-acting sons of bitches!"

In the brawl that followed, some scenery was smashed and a court lady was slightly injured when she was thrown off the stage. And no more work was done that night.

Finally, not an hour too soon, the end of rehearsals drew near for Orson Welles and his *Macbeth* company. April 14 was announced as our opening date: it promised the Harlem community an emotional release such as they had not known since the riots of 1935. Little else was talked about. The news that Haile Selassie's troops were in headlong flight before Mussolini's mechanized army and air force made no stir at all in a week that was entirely monopolized by the activities of the Lafayette Theater.

Some of this excitement was spontaneous; some of it was induced and stimulated. Three days before opening, Harlem woke up to find MACBETH stenciled in luminous paint on every street corner from 125th to 140th—from Lexington to Broadway. The Tree of Hope, a gnarled relic that survived with difficulty on Seventh Avenue in front of the Lafayette Theater and which was credited with magic properties, was festooned with garlands and bright-colored ribbons for luck. By April 10 every seat in the theater (except those reserved for U.S. Government officials and the press) had been sold, sometimes twice over, as ticket scalpers became active in Harlem's fancier bars. From the WPA press department came word that every first-string critic in town would attend. (One of them, tactfully, requested that he and his wife should be seated, if possible, "not next to Negroes.")

On opening night, just before dusk, the massed bands of the Monarch Lodge of the Benevolent and Protective Order of Elks, in uniforms of light blue, scarlet and gold, began to march in two detachments through the streets of Harlem behind two huge, crimson banners that read:

McBETH
by
William Shakespeare

By 6:30 they had converged before the theater where they continued to play around the Tree of Hope, while 10,000 people milled around them and dozens of police, including some on horses, tried in vain to keep a way clear into the Lafayette. As reported in the *New York Times*: "All northbound automobile traffic was stopped for more than an hour, while, from trucks in the street, floodlights flared a circle of light into the lobby and cameramen took photographs of the arrival of celebrities."

When the curtain finally rose it was on a jungle "luxuriant, savage and ominous with shadows," where the trees met "in a great overhead arch of twisted trunks that suggested a gigantic, living skeleton." Within five minutes, amid the thunder of drums and the orgiastic howls and squeals of our voodoo celebrants, we knew that victory was ours.

The Witches' scenes from *Macbeth* have always worried the life out of the polite, tragic stage; the grimaces of the hags and the garish make-believe of the flaming cauldron have bred more disenchantment than anything else that Shakespeare wrote. But ship the witches into the rank and fever-stricken jungle echoes, stuff a gleaming naked witch doctor into the cauldron, hold up Negro masks in the baleful light—and there you have a witches' scene that is logical and stunning and a triumph of the theater art.

The next scene to stop the show was that of the Macbeths' royal reception immediately following the murder of Banquo: dozens of shimmering couples in their court finery swirling with wild abandon to the crashing rhythms of our Thomson-orchestrated nineteenth-century waltzes—then, suddenly, a wild, high, inhuman sound that froze them all in their tracks, followed by Macbeth's terrible cry as the spirit of Banquo, in the shape of a huge luminous death mask, suddenly appeared on the battlements to taunt him in the hour of his triumph.

For Birnam Wood, Central Park and half of Rockland Country had been stripped of their burgeoning boughs, till the floor of the stage became a moving forest above which Macbeth, cornered at last on the highest platform of his castle, first shot down the "cream-faced loon" who brought him the news of Macduff's approach, then kicked him, for an 18-foot drop, into the courtyard below. It was here that the defiant hero vainly emptied his pistol into the body of the tall, dark, bearded man whose wife and children he had murdered and of whom he discovered, too late, as they closed for their final duel, that he had been "from the womb untimely ripped." A moment later, as Macbeth's head came sailing down from the battlements, a double cry rose from the stage—of jubilation from Macduff's army over the tyrant's death and of triumph from the assembled members of the Negro Theater Project over the successful outcome of their long and agonizing ordeal.

The notices the next morning were a joy to read: they spoke of "an Emperor Jones gone beautifully mad," of "the dark sensual rhythms, the giant tropic fronds" and of "a tragedy of black ambition in a green jungle shot with such lights from heaven and hell as no other stage has seen," of the "childlike austerity" of the performance: "With all their gusto they play Shakespeare as though they were apt children who have just discovered and adore the old man."

Roi Otley, a militant Negro journalist, was less concerned with these picturesque aspects than with the racial significance of the production:

The Negro has become weary of carrying the White Man's blackface burden in the theater. In *Macbeth* he has been given the opportunity to discard the bandana and burnt-cork casting to play a universal character...

From the point of view of the community, Harlem witnessed a production in which the Negro was not lampooned or made the brunt of laughter. We attended the *Macbeth* showing, happy in the thought we wouldn't again be reminded, with all its vicious implications, that we were niggers.

Like all WPA productions, *Macbeth* was judged by standards that were not purely theatrical. Percy Hammond, dean of New York drama critics, representing the city's leading Republican journal, the *Herald Tribune*, wrote what was not so much of a review as an attack on the New Deal:

The Negro Theater, an offshoot of the Federal Government and one of Uncle Sam's experimental philanthropies, gave us, last night an exhibition of deluxe boondoggling.

He went on to ridicule the whole idea of a popular theater supported by government funds, citing the size of our cast, the brightness of our costumes and the loudness of our music as evidence of criminal extravagance and presumptuous folly. As an example of political polemic it was savage but eloquent; as a theatrical notice it was irrelevant and malignant. It did not surprise us nor were we unduly disturbed. But there were some that were.

The next day I was formally visited in my office by Asadata Dafora Horton and his corps of African drummers, including Abdul, the witch doctor. They were perplexed, he said, and desired guidance. He then produced a sheaf of clippings from which he detached the *Herald Tribune* review. He had read it to his men, he declared, and it was their opinion, and his, that the piece was an evil one. I agreed that it was.

"The work of an enemy?"

"The work of an enemy."

"He is a bad man?"

"A bad man."

Asadata nodded. His face was grim as he turned to his troupe, to Abdul in particular, and repeated what I had said. The men nodded, then silently withdrew. Excited by waves of praise and a line a block long at the box office, Orson and I attended that night's performance, which was better played and no less enthusiastically received than the first. We thanked the company, had one of our usual brief, violent personal rows on the sidewalk, then went home to get some sleep.

When we arrived at the theater around noon of the next day it was reported to us by our disturbed house manager that the basement had been filled, during the night, with unusual drumming and with chants more weird and horrible than anything that had been heard upon the stage. Orson and I looked at each other for an instant, then quickly away again, for in the afternoon paper which we had picked up on our way uptown was a brief item announcing the sudden illness of the well-known critic Percy Hammond. He died some days later—of pneumonia, it was said.

Macbeth played for ten weeks at the Lafayette with never an empty seat, then moved downtown to Broadway where it remained through the long, hot New York summer before being sent on a triumphal national tour. In Indianapolis Macbeth fell ill. Orson flew out and played the role in blackface for the rest of the week.

* * *

In the months since we had started work on *Macbeth*, I had come to think of my association with Welles as a continuing and possibly a permanent one. Already I was totally committed to that unreasoning faith in his theatrical genius that was an essential condition of our partnership. Then and later, friends and intimates used to reproach me for what they considered my subordination to Orson and for devoting so much of my time and energy to promoting his achievements rather than my own. It was difficult to explain to them (since I was not entirely clear about it myself) that if I did subordinate myself, consciously and willingly, to a man twelve years younger than myself, this was the price I was willing to pay for my participation in acts of theatrical creation that were far more stimulating and satisfying than any I felt capable of conceiving or creating myself.

Macbeth had been such a creation. I knew there were others to come. I also knew that Orson was already dreaming of new worlds to conquer and that he had no intention of undertaking another long grind in Harlem that, at best, could only bring him a repetition of his first triumph.

This forced me to choose between two alternatives. One was to let Orson go on his dazzling way while I stayed on as the successful head of Harlem's Negro Theater unit, fostering and encouraging the "indigenous" projects as best I could while I tried to follow up our first classical achievement with what must inevitably be diminishing returns. My second course was to leave on a note of triumph, to abandon my position of power with the Negro Theater (turning it over to those to whom it rightly belonged) and risk my future on a partnership with a twenty-year-old boy, in whose talent I had unquestioning faith but with whom I must increasingly play the combined and tricky roles of producer, censor, adviser, impresario, father, older brother and bosom friend.

If I chose the latter (and it was inevitable that I should) I had not a moment to lose. I must immediately supply those new theatrical opportunities of which he dreamed and find fresh scope for Orson's terrible energy and boundless ambition before someone else did or before he became wholly absorbed in the commercial success-mill which was beginning to grind for him.

I called Hallie Flanagan and requested a meeting with her. I told her of my feeling about the Negro unit: that it was now viable and ready to be placed entirely in Negro hands. I also told her that Orson Welles and I wished to devote ourselves to forming and running a new federal unit, to be known as the Classical Theater. Her answer came within a few days. If I could set up my succession in Harlem, I was authorized to start organizing a classical theater immediately. I was offered Maxine Elliott's Theater at 39th and Broadway which the WPA had just rented. (And privately I was told to waste no time, for the freewheeling days of the Arts Projects were nearing their end and drastic reductions seemed certain in the months to come.) To take my place I left a triumvirate with Carlton Moss in the center of it. It worked well for what remained of the life of the Negro Project. For my own part, at the last moment, I was filled with that sense of loss and sorrow and guilt that I have felt with each of the many departures and desertions of which my life is the sum.

Our final farewells were long and emotional, full of protestations of love. Orson's parting scenes were particularly passionate. He and his company had been through hell together and come out victorious: he had given them a vision of theatrical magic which none of them would forget and few of them would ever glimpse again.

Viewed in the perspective of time the accomplishments of the Negro Theater appeared to be far from impressive. Theatrically its final effects were almost nil; Negro playwriting was not appreciably encouraged by our efforts and Negro actors (with a few notable exceptions) were held, for another twenty years, within the galling bounds of stereotyped roles. The theater technicians whom Feder had trained remained excluded from every professional theatrical union in America except as cleaners or janitors and went back into other trades. No Negro company came into existence for thirty years after the dissolution of the Federal Theater and no Negro audience clamored for a continuation of the entertainment they had apparently enjoyed under the auspices of the WPA.

Now, years later, I have changed my opinion. I now believe that many of the welcome changes that took place in the late fifties and early sixties had their deep invisible roots in the achievements, on so many levels, of the WPA federal projects of the thirties.

For me personally it had been a wonderful time. My two years on the project had been among the busiest, happiest and proudest of my life; they also represented the period during which I had come nearest to being God. I had enjoyed my power and out of chaos I had created a comparatively well-ordered and smooth-running universe. Through the rear window of the cab that was carrying me to my new domain in the basement of Maxine Elliott's Theater, I looked back at the worn and dirty face of the Lafayette and saw what I had wrought. And it was good.

IV
Project #891
1936-37

Maxine Elliott's Theater had been built at the turn of the century by J.P. Morgan for his favorite actress and many famous productions had been presented there. After years of abuse and neglect, with its yellowing marble and discolored brocades, it retained traces of its former splendor and seemed particularly glamorous after the moldering squalor of the Lafayette.

Leading to the ladies' toilet in the basement was a large powder room with a worn Aubusson carpet and walls of faded rose-pink velvet. Here, amid remnants of the original furnishings (an ormolu bureau, a cerise tailor's dummy and two tall mirrors) I had set up my office. Feder and his aides did their paperwork at the foot of the opposite staircase, in the white-tiled area surrounding the men's room. Backstage, between rehearsals and radio shows, Orson occupied the star dressing room, which had a bath and a small sitting room with a bed.

My first activity, after moving in, was to assemble a staff and a company of actors to the full limits of our appropriation. Hundreds came to be interviewed, most of them rejects or fugitives from older and lesser WPA theater projects—vaudeville and circus, tent shows and units in dissolution. It was a bizarre collection of aging character actors, comics and eccentrics that delighted Orson's heart. We also took on a number of middle-aged, garrulous ladies with bright-colored hair whom no one else wanted and several young females, among them a strangely beautiful waif from Brooklyn with olive skin and a Cretan profile named Paula Lawrence.

The special character and the obvious limitations of this hastily collected troupe may have helped to influence us in the choice of our first play, but mainly, I believe, it came from a refusal to do what was expected of us. Soon after our arrival downtown Orson and I sat in the powder room one afternoon lamenting our inhibiting title of "classical theater." We tried various alternatives: "repertory" was inaccurate, "people's theater" pretentious. While we were talking, a requisition was put on my desk which I signed as managing producer of WPA Project #891. Orson was looking over my shoulder and, in that instant, we had our name. Soon after that, Project #891 announced its first two productions: *The Italian Straw Hat* by Eugene Labiche, with Marlowe's *Tragical History of Doctor Faustus* to follow. Among the ideas we filed for future use were a modern-dress *Julius Caesar*, Ben Jonson's *The Silent Woman*, Dekker's domestic comedy *The Shoemaker's Holiday* and *The Duchess of Malfi*.

To justify our first choice we explained that nineteenth-century situation farce ("*le vaudeville*") was a classical theatrical form "taught in schools" and that Labiche was its recognized master. Having made our point, we changed the name of the piece to *Horse Eats Hat* and began to plan its production. At Virgil Thomson's suggestion I entrusted the adaptation to Edwin Denby, a poet-critic and dancer recently returned from Europe, where he had made a name for himself in advanced theatrical circles. Aided, driven and abetted by Welles, he inflated and expanded Labiche's text to astonishing proportions; he also devised a prologue, known as the "horse ballet," in which he himself appeared as the rear half of the offending hack.

The plot is that of a horse that eats a hat and the owner of the horse, a bridegroom on the way to his wedding, must find the hat's owner a similar hat immediately because she, the hat's owner, cannot go home to her husband without it...

This is the only cold-blooded attempt anyone seems to have made to tell the plot of *Horse Eats Hat*. It was written by a man who never saw it.

Scenery and costumes, like those for *Macbeth*, were flamboyantly designed by Nat Karson. The score was by Paul Bowles, aided in his orchestrations by Virgil Thomson. An enormous amount of music was needed and we ended up using thirty-three men in the pit and a grand piano in each of the lower boxes, plus pianola, lady trumpeter and gypsy orchestra. For the rest—the dances, the marches, the chamber music, the piano solos and some added songs—we used existent compositions by Bowles or popular pieces from public domain.

Our cast of dozens was drawn from among our recent recruits, to whom we added as many non-relief actors as we could get into the project under the 10 percent special talent ruling. Orson Welles played the bride's ferocious father, Virginia the shy bride, Hiram Sherman her libidinous cousin and Joseph Cotten the harried bridegroom. Paula Lawrence was the unfaithful wife whose Leghorn straw hat the horse chewed up while she lay behind a bush in the Bois de Boulogne with a dashing hussar. Arlene Francis played Tillie, the glamorous modiste, in whose seven-doored shop the hat had been bought. Other characters included the world's grandest countess, its most corrupt valet and an aging cuckold with the gout. There were also wedding guests, party guests, a bevy of Tillie's girls and two regiments of Zouaves.

Sitting in my pink underground lair, deluged with paperwork for the new project, negotiating with WPA administrators and representatives of the Workers' Alliance and City Projects Council, I listened enviously to the wild and wonderful sounds of rehearsal on the stage above. For, besides the hazards of starting and running another government project with more than 200 employees, I had problems of my own to occupy me that summer.

During the fall of 1935—about the time I was setting up the Negro Theater—I was introduced to Leslie Howard, who was passing through New York on his way from England to Hollywood. He was preparing to produce and perform *Hamlet* on Broadway and when I met him he had already gone quite far in the planning of his production: he had chosen Stewart Chaney to design the sets and costumes and Schuyler Watts, a glib and passionate young man fresh out of Yale, to arrange and edit the text. Now he was looking for someone to help him on the production and direction of the play.

My conferences with Leslie Howard were agreeable if only moderately productive. I had long admired the skill and delicacy that had made him one of the most successful drawing-room actors of his time. His voice was thin but under perfect control, his stage presence remarkably organized and effective. I saw no reason, if he remained true to his own personal qualities, why he should not be a fascinating and moving Hamlet. Before he left for California to appear in the film of *The Petrified Forest* (which he had created on Broadway), I had, without telling Orson, signed a contract to co-direct his *Hamlet* the following spring. Then, within a month of his arrival in Hollywood, Howard accepted an offer to co-star in a film of *Romeo and Juliet* with Norma Shearer, and our *Hamlet* date had to be moved forward to another season. By that time I was full of my own excitements with the Negro Theater Project and welcomed the postponement. But I was delighted, with *Macbeth* already in rehearsal, when Howard invited me to fly out and visit him in California to discuss plans for a late summer tryout and a late fall opening of *Hamlet* in New York. Since the mention of any theatrical activity except his own provoked in Orson an automatic reaction of ridicule or rage, I did not tell him where I was going. I stayed with the Howards in Beverly Hills and spent my days at MGM on the set of *Romeo and Juliet* talking to Leslie between set-ups. I remember seeing Norma Shearer on a large stone balcony and Howard moving towards her through acres of artificial orchard across the false grass, while a carefully measured rain of apple blossoms fell on him from the branches as he passed.

I flew back to New York the following day, convinced that there would be no *Hamlet* production till fall. Two months later, after the opening of our *Macbeth*, Leslie and Ruth Howard passed through New York on their way to England, where he was to spend the summer on his estate, "preparing" himself for *Hamlet*. We discussed casting and I came up with a list of actors who seemed to complement his own virtues and limitations. Leslie listened attentively, then boarded his ship for England, inviting me to join him there at some time during the summer. I accepted, knowing I would not go.

(My commercial visa, issued to me in the name of Jacques Haussmann as a naturalized British citizen under the Anglo-American Treaty of Commerce and Navigation, had become invalid with the dissolution of the Oceanic Grain Corporation. Having been born in Rumania, I was, according to U.S. Immigration rules, a Rumanian; and, since the Rumanian quota was minimal and perpetually filled, there seemed to be no way in which I could ever inhabit the United States as a legal and working resident. As an indigent playwright and freelance director this had not bothered me. But now, for over a year, I had been conducting a large, official and partly political operation for the U.S. Government in direct violation of the country's laws and in an exposed position from which it would have taken no more than one single anonymous postcard addressed to the Department of Justice to have me summarily deported, without hope of return.)

Project #891 had been formed and *Horse Eats Hat* was already in rehearsal when I learned, through cautious inquiries, that now, finally, after four years of international depression, the Rumanian quota was open. Canada was the nearest foreign territory and a series of urgent letters from the heads of the WPA to the U.S. Department of Labor and the consulate in Toronto had won me the firm assurance, by late July, that I was qualified for readmittance to the U.S. as a permanent resident.

I drove to Toronto in my Model A on the first Sunday of August, 1936, telling everyone I would be back the following Wednesday at the latest. I drove all night and, after the sun came up, I had to slap my face every few minutes to keep awake in the rising heat. At 9:30 I crossed into Canada over the International Bridge at Buffalo. Behind me through the rear-view mirror, I saw the gate close between me and country in which I had lived for eleven years—in which I had been successful and bankrupt, married and divorced and in which everything I possessed and held precious was waiting, in a state of suspended animation, for my return.

The U.S. consulate in Toronto was closed for lunch when I arrived. I took a room at the Royal York, bathed and shaved and returned to the consulate at two o'clock. By three my papers had been examined and pronounced in order. I was just beginning to regret having taken a room and planning to be halfway back to New York by nightfall, when the blow fell. I could have my visa, the vice-consul assured me, just as soon as I obtained a quota number. This, he explained, was not in his province, but in that of the U.S. consulate in Bucharest, Rumania. How long would that take? He was vague. I showed him my contract with Leslie Howard and Hallie Flanagan's urgent letter addressed to the Department of Labor in Washington, D.C.

The vice-consul was not moved. He said that if I was willing to pay the cost, a cable could be sent to Bucharest in which case we might receive an answer within two days. But he warned me not to expect too much. With the utmost luck, he said, I might obtain a quota number by September 1; on the other hand, there might be a delay of several months. I paid the money and the cable was sent.

The next forty-eight hours were among the worst of my life. Sleep was out of the question. I lay fully dressed on my bed in the Royal York Hotel, listenting to the trains below, too frightened to move, while the whole carefully planned and precariously balanced structure of my life shivered and swayed around me. I was filled with self-pity; I had been right to be afraid all my life. Just when it seemed that I had finally achieved acceptance I was, once again, being harshly and coldly rejected. I went downstairs and collected newspapers and magazines from the hotel lobby. Back on my bed I learned that the Eleventh Olympiad had opened in Berlin, with Hitler as host to a worldwide gathering. Hope for peace had been voiced during the opening ceremonies and Jesse Owens had won the 100-meter dash in record time.

Early in the morning I went out, found two continuously grinding movie houses and spent the rest of the day there. Between programs I ate and paid a visit to the vice-consul, who rather curtly told me not to come back till the afternoon of the following day because the cable, assuming it came, would not be decoded till then. I saw three more films before midnight, then returned to my hotel room with a pile of detective stories. Around noon of the next day I bathed, shaved and combed my hair with propitiatory care. There was a decoded cable waiting for me at the consulate with a Rumanian quota number, good on September 1—more than three weeks away. As I made an appointment for 9:30 of that distant morning, the vice-consul wished me a happy holiday. He suggested the Laurentian Mountains as a region of great natural beauty and bracing air.

Back at the Royal York, I wrote to Hallie Flanagan to explain my absence and, later that evening, called Welles at home. He was out but Virginia said not to worry; the way Orson was directing *Horse Eats Hat* they'd all be in jail anyway. That night I slept like a baby and early next morning, having conceived a lasting horror for the city of Toronto, I started east, driving at water level beside the St. Lawrence, roughly along the route I had once taken, with my father and mother, twenty years before. In Montreal there was a money order waiting for me at the desk of the Ritz-Carlton Hotel with a letter reporting that all was well on the project. That afternoon I drove east again to Trois Rivières, then north by slow stages into the Laurentians, where I spent four days in a family hotel by a lake. On the fifth day I grew restless and turned south and east again. On the river road, I passed a speeding black Bentley convertible which seemed curiously familiar. At the Ritz-Carlton mail desk in Montreal there was a cable from Leslie Howard that confirmed his arrival in New York on September 14, ready to begin rehearsals. There was also an unstamped note, left that morning, in a small, crabbed writing I had almost forgotten. That evening I drove back to Trois Rivières, where Henrietta Bingham was waiting to drive me to her family's fishing camp in the mountains where she was spending the rest of the summer.

So this voyage which had begun as a nightmare ended in a dreamlike holiday reunion beside a dark mountain lake high in the Laurentian hills. It was more than nine years since we had lost our virginity together; we talked of the curious turns our lives had taken since then: of mine in the theater and hers as an ambassador's daughter in London. Certain things had not changed at all: the color of her eyes and skin, the warmth of her voice, the way she wore a tailored suit and her hands held the wheel of her car. But there was one major difference—I was no longer in love with her.

Early on the morning of September 2, 1936, I was back in New York (still an alien but now legally resident) in my rose-colored powder room at Maxine Elliott's Theater. A letter from Leslie Howard awaited me in which he listed the all-English company he was bringing over with him. The only name I knew was that of Lady Forbes-Robertson, the former Gertrude Elliott, sister of the lady for whom the theater we were occupying had been built. She was to play the Queen.

My reaction to this communication and to the selection of a cast in complete disregard of my opinions and advice took much of the pleasure and excitement out of my work on Howard's *Hamlet*. Other displeasures were to follow during production, but this, my first gloom, soon melted in my joy at being back among friends and by the gleeful, frenetic tempo of the proceedings on stage where *Horse Eats Hat* was entering its final weeks of rehearsal. To the endlessly repeated refrain of Myrtle's wedding song sung to the tune of "Les fraises et les framboises" were added women's screams, cries of jealous rage and outraged virtue, the thump of falling scenery, Orson's bellowing, Feder's answering howls and the oom-pah-pah of the pit band rehearsing under Virgil's baton. All these were reassuring and homelike sounds.

One week later we held our first preview. As madness followed madness through two crowded acts—with actors by the score hurtling across the stage in endless, circular pursuit, in carriages and cars, cycles, tricycles and roller skates, walking, trotting and galloping, leaving ruin in their wake, scattering the rubber plants in Myrtle Mugglethorpe's suburban home, dispersing the gorgeous, squealing models in Tillie's modish millinery establishment, terrorizing the Countess's elegant guests as they turkey-trotted to the strains of a red-coated gypsy ensemble—our left-wing audience laughed but it was not altogether at ease. Its uneasiness grew as the wildest scene of the evening got under way. This had for its finale one of the most extravagant accumulations of farcical horror ever assembled behind the proscenium arch of a respectable American theater. I can still see Joe Cotten, wearing his bright yellow leather gloves, with the coveted straw hat grasped firmly between his teeth, caught between the Countess's indignant guests and the vengeful pursuit of the wedding party, leaping from sofa to table to piano top to chandelier which, at that instant, started to rise like a great golden bird, carrying him upward in a wild, 40-foot flight till he vanished into the fly-loft, while a three-tiered fountain flung a giant jet upward at the seat of his pants and Cotten himself, clinging to the rising chandelier with one hand and grasping a siphon in the other, squirted streams of soda water over the madly whirling crowd below.

Horse Eats Hat opened officially on September 26, 1936, to "mixed" notices. Some reviewers were shocked (like our left-wing audiences) and, in some cases, offended by the extravagant frivolity of the production. The Hearst press used it as a stick with which to beat the New Deal: "Does the U.S. Sanction Vulgar Play?" asked a front-page headline in the *New York American*. And the answer was emphatically yes. Senator Dirksen (Republican, Illinois) described it officially, in the *Congressional Record*, as "salacious tripe." On the other hand, there were groups of sophisticated New Yorkers who found in *Horse Eats Hat* a source of unending, zany delight and who came to see it (at a 55-cent top) as often as ten, fifteen and, in one case, twenty-one times in a row.

After the launching of *Horse Eats Hat* there was a lull in the operation of

Project #891. Orson had signed a Broadway contract to play the juvenile lead in Sidney Kingsley's ill-fated antiwar play, *Ten Million Ghosts*, and Leslie Howard was finally ready to begin rehearsals.

Here another surprise awaited me when it became evident, at the first reading, that our star's vaunted summer preparations for *Hamlet* had not included a serious study of the name part. This, I discovered, was consistent with his nature and with the phenomenon of his stardom. Leslie Howard impressed me, during the months that I worked with him, as the most fatalistic man I had ever met. He was secretly and sincerely convinced, I believe, that his sudden, miraculous success was due to some mysterious accident—some error in the celestial filing system—to which his own efforts had contributed little and which would one day be discovered and corrected. This seemed to explain the curious combination of humility and egotism, indolence and obstinacy that marked his personal and professional behavior. In the role of Hamlet these inconsistencies were not without their dramatic value. In the presence of his father's ghost, the conflict between suspicion and devotion was fascinating to watch; the Ophelia scenes were, at once, kind and cruel; the baiting of Polonius had a careless, chilling venom and the calm after the grave scene, before the final duel, was ominously equivocal.

It had been agreed that Howard and I would share the work and the credit of direction; he was so busy learning his lines that the staging—within the limits of Chaney's handsome unit set—became almost entirely mine. Rehearsals were courteously but firmly conducted under the devoted eye of Eddie McHugh, stage manager to the Barrymores for two decades. As one of his assistants, in charge of light cues, I engaged a small, smiling child with a boyish haircut named Jean Rosenthal, recently out of Yale, whom I had discovered working under Feder in the basement of the Maxine Elliott. A few of the company (including eight of the most gorgeous court ladies in history), had been cast by me in New York; the principal parts, with the exception of Horatio and Osric, were held by English actors whom I had not met and whose work I had never seen. Some of them gave me agreeable surprises. Pamela Stanley was a joy to work with—one of the best Ophelias I have ever seen. She would have been even better if Howard, in his scenes with her, had managed to conceal the fact that he did not find her physically desirable. But it was with the royal couple that I had my real problems. Our Claudius was a massive stock leading man with a large voice who presented no emotional threat to his stepson. As for the Queen, it was evident from the first day of rehearsal that her casting was a catastrophe.

Gertrude Elliott was in her middle sixties when Howard invited her to appear with him in *Hamlet*, in which she had first played Ophelia with her illustrious husband, Sir Johnston Forbes-Robertson, thirty-seven years before. Not only was she of an age to be Leslie Howard's grandmother, she had a theatrical tone (full of echoes of Sir Johnston's golden voice as I had heard it at Clifton in my teens) which bore not the slightest relation to the subtle and intimate style of Leslie's playing. The closet scene, in which Hamlet pursued this frail sexagenarian with accusations of criminal lust, was such an embarrassment that, after we had staged it, Leslie refused to rehearse it again for days. At the end of each day I would ask him what he was going to do about it and Leslie would sigh and shake his head and smile, as though to say that it was not for him, a former Hungarian bank clerk, to fire Lady Forbes Robertson from a Shakespearean production.

She was still with us when we arrived in Boston. At our first dress rehearsal she and Leslie played the closet scene amid appalled silence. At two in the morning I took Leslie aside: the most I could achieve was permission to go to New York and retain somebody who was familiar with the part as a possible replacement. I found Mary Servoss, who had played the Queen with Raymond Massey six years before, and asked her to get up on her lines. Back in Boston the next afternoon I called a rehearsal of the closet scene; Leslie did not appear and Lady Forbes-Robertson and I walked stiffly and politely through the business. We were due to open on Tuesday. Then, suddenly, a little before noon on Sunday, I was told to summon Mary Servoss immediately. Miss Elliott had vanished. Mary went on that night after one walk-through with the company; the next day Leslie rehearsed with her for two hours and again, briefly, the day after that. Then we opened and he never rehearsed with her again.

(It was not until days later that I discovered what had happened to poor Lady Forbes-Robertson. Among Leslie's many romantic involvements with his leading ladies, there had been a particularly tender one, during the London production of *Berkeley Square*, with Jean Forbes-Robertson, considered the most brilliant young actress on the British stage. Now, learning that she was on her way to America, he had appealed to her by radiophone, in mid-Atlantic, in the name of their former affection, to help him and her mother out of their hideous impasse. The day she landed she had come up to Boston, witnessed one rehearsal and, on grounds of health, taken her mother back to New York with her.)

The dress rehearsals and the out-of-town opening of *Hamlet* took place in the immensity of the old Boston Opera House. As Stewart Chaney's massive eleventh-century sets began to go up and his rich costumes to be loudly admired at dress parade, it became clear that here, too, we were in trouble. The show would be impressive and beautiful and we would all receive bouquets for a notable production—which we did. But these qualities of grandeur made it the worst possible background against which to present Leslie Howard's delicate and tender prince. In the end, to counteract the archaic splendor of the setting, we were forced to play most of the personal scenes far downstage, on steps or narrow platforms. The evening's most memorable moment, visually, was that of Hamlet standing far upstage in the prow of the ship that was to carry him to England. It was a lovely sight, but the soliloquy which he delivered on high was barely audible.

For our music I had turned, as usual, to Virgil Thomson, who had just finished recording *The Plough that Broke the Plains* with Pare Lorentz. The score he now composed for us—for kettledrums, open trumpets and bagpipes—was a model of theater music, which I used again in Stratford twenty years later. But it was this *Hamlet* collaboration that almost put an end to our friendship and threatened to break up an artistic association that has, finally, endured for more than forty years.

The play scene in *Hamlet* is a notorious trap; few theatrical areas are so cluttered with the bones of bright and pretentious ideas. Agnes De Mille (engaged by Howard in Hollywood where she had choreographed the dances for *Romeo and Juliet*) was determined to make a "mime" of it, while Virgil insisted that it must be performed as *"mélodrame"* with the speeches chanted to a formal musical accompaniment. While Leslie was off in his hotel room trying to learn his lines I, like Solomon, was trying to arbitrate the insoluble conflict between composer and choreographer which ended when both Virgil and Agnes resigned and left, in separate rages, for London and Paris.

Our Boston reviews were satisfactory and our business was terrific. But two things disturbed me. One was the realization that, in that large auditorium, Leslie had begun to lose those qualities which alone made his Hamlet worth doing. Egged on by his entourage he began to "broaden" and "enlarge," to project and posture. And, gradually, what might have been a subtle, sinuous and intelligent performance began to look like ineptitude and bombast. My other, more immediate, concern was that John Gielgud had just opened triumphantly in New York with a performance of Hamlet that had taken ten years to mature. For Leslie to appear against him would inevitably give the impression of a contest—a contest in which Howard, who barely knew his lines, could only be the loser.

I urged Leslie to switch, before it was too late, from a New York opening to a national tour. The huge business he was doing in Boston indicated how profitable this would be. Late in the spring, with his investment recouped, fortified by the prestige of a triumphal national tour and Gielgud forgotten, he could enter New York with a virtual assurance of success. This was one of the times when I saw Leslie's fatalism most clearly at work. He listened attentively (as he always did where money was concerned), agreed with every point I made, thanked me for my frankness—and opened three weeks later in New York.

"*Hamlet* with the Hamlet left out"; "Comparisons are not inevitable, they are impossible"; "It is quite unnecessary to discuss the performance with any idea this is an interpretation of Hamlet"—these were among the savage wisecracks that appeared in the press the next morning. The most temperate review was Brooks Atkinson's in the *New York Times* where he commended Howard for his courage and described the production as "thoughtful and beautiful."

Leslie was resigned, by now, to an unfavorable press, but the lack of business stirred him into drastic action. He packed up his huge, handsome *Hamlet*, opened it in Chicago on Christmas Eve and toured it for four months, with cut-down scenery and a shrunken harem of court ladies, from one end of the continent to the other. By the end of the tour he had recouped every cent of his $90,000 loss and salvaged his national reputation. And, as his anxiety diminished, his performance improved: by the time he reached the West Coast he was once again playing Hamlet as we had rehearsed it in the beginning—in the only way in which he was capable of playing it.

Orson had chosen to regard my *Hamlet* activity as I had regarded his appearance as the juvenile lead of *Ten Million Ghosts*—as a sort of absurd and shameful betrayal of which the least said the better. It was more than two years before I undertook any new theatrical work of my own. For, by now, I was completely committed to my partnership with Welles and happier within the creative excitement of that collaboration than I could be, by myself, on the outside. I returned to Project #891 in time for the closing performance of *Horse Eats Hat* and rehearsals of *Doctor Faustus*. It was pleasant, after the big-time frustrations of *Hamlet*, to find myself back in my faded-rose basement, with the normal bureaucratic agitations of the WPA enveloping me once again in their reassuring confusion.

The holidays, both Christmas and New Year's, were spent in the darkness of Maxine Elliott's in an atmosphere that was sulphurous and grim with the presence of demons. Struck, carted off and demolished were our bright Parisian sets. Their places were taken by acres of funereal velour, dun and drear in the hard glare of the worklights which illuminated rehearsals by night and the labors of the construction crews and electricians by day. Downstage, spanning the orchestra pit, a tapering apron was built to Orson's specifications. Into its surface and into that of the entire stage, traps were cut—with a deafening hacking of axes, screeching of saws and banging of hammers—holes of all shapes and sizes, some too small for midgets, others vast, yawning pits, mouths to the nether regions, capable of holding whole regiments of fiends and lakes of flame. Since Orson insisted on rehearsing in the theater, he and his actors could be seen, nightly, threading their way between deadly chasms and mountains of lumber as they moved from one stage position to another. Surprisingly, except for one sprained ankle (Welles's) and one exhausted electrician who fell off a 30-foot ladder at four in the morning, no one was injured.

Faustus was the third of eight shows Orson and I produced together in a partnership in which our mutual functions were only vaguely defined and of which it is difficult, after so many years and so much recrimination, to describe the creative workings with any degree of honesty or accuracy. Looking back, it seems that my two main functions (beginning on the WPA projects, uptown and downtown and, later, through the first triumphal year of the Mercury Theater) were, first, to supply Orson, beyond the limits of prudence and reason, with the human and material elements he required for his creative work; second, to shield him not only from outside interference but, even more, from the intense pressures of his own complicated and destructive nature.

What direct creative aid I was able to give him on our productions was exerted mainly during the early stages of conception and preparation and, then again, during the final crises of dress rehearsals and previews. Throughout Orson's main periods of rehearsal, during which he jealously guarded his intimacies with his actors, I did not appear unless he specifically invited me. I had my own secret and intuitive ways of following his progress but run-throughs were unheard of. Welles, like most imaginative directors, had a pathological reluctance to submit work in progress to the cruel test of another man's viewing—especially mine, whose taste he trusted and whose premature judgments he therefore doubly feared. Our relationship became particularly strained on productions, like *Faustus*, in which Orson himself was playing a leading role. At such times I became not merely the hated figure of authority, to be defied and outwitted as I refused further delays and escapes, but the first hostile witness to the ghastly struggle between narcissism and self-loathing that characterized Orson's approach to a part.

Once this barrier had been cleared, I was welcome again. Indeed, during the latter stages of production, there were times when Orson refused to rehearse unless I was in the theater. As the nights dragged on and our long agony was stretched to the breaking point, it became my main responsibility to preserve him from exhaustion and confusion, to disentangle the essentials of the production as he had originally conceived it from that obsessive preoccupation with insignificant detail in which he was inclined to seek refuge when fatigue or self-doubt had begun to wear him down.

Of all the shows we did together, *Faustus* looked the simplest and was the most complicated; it was also the most brilliantly executed. In its acting style, its sound patterns, its scenic conception, its costumes (which Orson designed), its props and its magic tricks, it gave unified and vivid expression to Welles's very special theatrical talent.

In all his theatrical work (from his schoolboy *Julius Caesar* to the nights, during the Second World War, when he sawed Marlene Dietrich in half at the Hollywood Stage Door Canteen) Orson was always, at heart, a magician. His production of Marlowe's tragedy was designed and executed as a magic show, employing as its basic technique one of the oldest and most effective of stage magicians' deceptions—the trick professionally known as "black magic." Used for vanishing acts and miraculous appearances, it exploits the absorbent properties of black velvet so that, under certain lighting conditions, not only do black surfaces became totally invisible against each other, but all normal sense of space, depth and perspective becomes lost and confused in the eye of the spectator. Orson, with Feder's assistance, extended and elaborated this device. By using almost no front light and crisscrossing the stage with parallel light curtains and clusters of units carefully focused from the sides and from overhead, he was able to achieve mystifications that would have impressed the great Thurston.

Far away, from depths of darkness, Faustus is disclosed, surrounded by his diabolical books, while Mephistopheles is first seen as two gigantic horrible eyes which Faustus conjures into a human head,

wrote one perplexed reviewer.

There were other equally magical effects, culminating in Faustus's reception by the Pope in Rome. Here a procession of scarlet and purple princes of the Church and their servants, carrying golden platters piled with roasts and sweetmeats, paraded across the stage to ceremonial music on their way to the banquet hall. Suddenly, under the Pope's nose, a suckling pig was seen to rise from its golden dish, fly straight up to a height of 12 feet, execute a few steps of an obscene dance, then melt into thin air. A haunch of beef followed, then two fat chickens and a gaudy pudding. In consternation, the procession faltered. At that moment, to the accompaniment of subterranean thunder, three cardinals' hats flew off like giant saucers. When the Pope's own mitre rose from his head and a flash box exploded under his skirt amid cries of terror and fiendish laughter, the procession broke up, leaving Faustus alone on a stage that was suddenly and completely bare.

This mystification was accomplished with the aid of eight dancers, dressed from head to foot in black velvet, moving alongside the procession, just far enough upstage to be out of the blaze of the light curtain and thus completely invisible to the audience against the darkness of black velvet. In their black-gloved hands, they held, like fishing poles, thin, black, flexible steel rods whose ends were affixed to the meats, the pudding and the episcopal headgear that were marked for flight. On cue the boys in black swung those loaded rods up over their heads and brought them down behind them, where their own black costumes formed a screen for them till they were able to leave the stage unobserved in the confusion of the dissolving parade.

Still another form of magic was achieved through trap doors which permitted characters to enter and exit as though they were rising or sinking through the solid black floor of the stage. Among their users was that sinister puppet troupe, the Seven Deadly Sins, who appeared, one by one, through holes in the apron—obscene, diminutive specimens of evil that flapped and wriggled and squeaked their lewd temptations at the doomed doctor's feet. These, together with the explosions, subterranean rumblings and jagged sheets of lycopodium flame that swept the stage with bursts of hellish brightness, were the gaudy theatrical devices with which Welles adorned his revival. But underneath, at the center of the production, there was deep personal identification which, across a gulf of three and a half centuries, led him to the heart of the work and to its vivid recreation on a contemporary American stage.

The truth is that the legend of the man who sells his soul to the devil in exchange for knowledge and power and who must finally pay for his brief triumph with the agonies of eternal damnation was uncomfortably close to the shape of Welles's own personal myth. Orson really believed in the Devil. This was not a whimsy but a very real obsession. At twenty-one Orson was sure he was doomed. In his most creative, manic moments, in his wildest transports of love or on the topmost peak of his precocious victories, he was rarely free from a sense of sin and a fear of retribution so intense and immediate that it drove him through long nights of panic to seek refuge in debauchery or work. Quite literally, Orson dared not sleep. No sooner were his eyes closed than, out of the darkness, troupes of demons—the symbols of his sins—surrounded and claimed him, body and soul, in retribution for crimes of which he could not remember the nature, but of which he never for a moment doubted that he was guilty. Neither running nor hiding could save him from their clutches. And, when they had seized him with their bleeding claws, they would drag him off into some infernal darkness, there to inflict upon him, through all eternity, those unspeakable torments which he felt he so richly deserved.

Some of this anguish found its way nightly onto the stage of Maxine Elliott's Theater. Amid the rank fumes and darting flames, there were moments when Faustus seemed to be expressing, through Marlowe's words, some of Orson's personal agony and private terror. This sense of conviction was heightened by Welles's inspired casting of the fiend Mephistopheles, played by the Negro actor Jack Carter, who had been our Macbeth. Years later, Carter's appearance with Welles was cited as an early and successful example of integrated casting. It was that and far more. Their presence on the stage together was unforgettable: both were around six foot four, both men of abnormal strength capable of sudden, furious violence. Yet their scenes together were played with restraint, verging on tenderness, in which temptation and damnation were treated as acts of love. Welles was brightly garbed, bearded, medieval, ravenous, sweating and human; Carter was in black—a cold, ascetic monk, his face and gleaming bald head moon-white and ageless against the surrounding night. As Orson directed him, he had the beauty, the pride and the sadness of a fallen angel. He watched Faustus sign his deed in blood and, later, officiated at his destruction and listened to his last gasping pleas for respite:

Ah, Faustus,

Now has thou but one bare hour to live

And then thou must be damned perpetually!

with the contemptuous and elegant calm of a Lucifer who is, himself, more deeply and irrevocably damned than his cringing human victim.

There is only one woman's part in *Doctor Faustus*. Paula Lawrence was transformed from the Parisian adulteress of *Horse Eats Hat* into a silent Helen of Troy which she played, far upstage, in a gray mask and pale gray velvet gown, "looking like Diane de Poitier on a tapestry in a silver moonlight."

Faustus was due to open early in January. New Year's Eve and the first nights of 1937 were spent in technical rehearsals. Despite their satanic complication, I remember those unending electrical sessions with pleasure as a time when we were all very close together—in our work and in our lives. Around two in the morning the stage crew went home and Orson, his face still swollen with make-up, was ready to start lighting. The company had been dismissed by then, except for our stage managers, a few insanely devoted volunteers and a handful of girlfriends and wives (led by Virginia Welles) who remained to the end, taking turns dozing and "standing in" for actors—moving back and forth, up and down on the bare, perforated stage while Orson, Feder and I yelled at them and at each other, and electricians on tall, shaky ladders focused lamps overhead and the men on the switchboard tried to get the feel of those sequences of delicately overlapping light cues upon which the movement of the show was so wholly dependent. Around four in the morning hamburgers, milkshakes and brandy were brought in from Times Square. Between seven and eight we quit, partly because we couldn't see any more but also because Welles usually had a radio call at nine.

That was my winter with a Viennese girl with gray eyes who was born in the same hour of the same day of the same year as Orson and whom it seemed to me, for a time, that I loved. Since she insisted on spending every night at the theater, we had taken a room in a small hotel on 39th Street to which we returned in the late winter dawn, made love, had breakfast and slept together for an hour or two before I reappeared in the powder room of the Maxine Elliott, ready to deal with the list of the day's emergencies.

Item: It has been reported to Mrs. Flanagan that the baggy-pants routine in the second clown scene is in bad taste, if not actually indecent. Please investigate and, if necessary, speak to Welles.

Item: The Workers' Alliance has complained to Actors' Equity about the excessive rehearsal hours on Project #891. Equity, in turn, has called Mrs. Flanagan.

Item: Mr. Murphy at the bank says several checks of yours are going to bounce for lack of funds.

Item: The Fire Department is disturbed over the open flames in the final scene. They are threatening to cancel the lease of the theater. Please deal with this.

On the evening of our first dress rehearsal Hallie Flanagan noted in her journal that the Maxine Elliott had become "a pit of hell...total darkness punctuated by stabs of light, trap doors opening and closing to reveal bewildered stagehands and actors going up, down and around in circles; explosions; properties disappearing in a clap of thunder and, on stage, Orson muttering the mighty lines and interspersing them wth fierce adjurations to the invisible but omnipresent Feder."

Welles's dress rehearsals and previews were nearly always catastrophic—especially if he was performing. I think he enjoyed these near disasters: they gave him a pleasing sense, later, of having brought order out of chaos and of having, single-handedly, plucked victory from defeat. It is also true that, suffering more than the usual actor's fears, Orson welcomed and exploited these technical hazards as a means of delaying the hideous moment when he must finally come out on the stage and deliver a performance.

By the third preview the show had begun to work, though Welles's own performance did not finally emerge until opening night. Though the *Daily News* and the Hearst press continued to involve us in their dispute with the New Deal, a majority of the daily press approved of us—especially the *New York Times*.

Everyone interested in the imaginative power of the theater will want to see how ably Orson Welles and John Houseman have cleared away all the imposing impedimenta that makes most classics forbidding and how skillfully they have left *Doctor Faustus,* grim and terrible, on the stage...They have gone a long way toward revolutionizing the staging of Elizabethan plays and a good many people will now pay their taxes in a more charitable frame of mind.

Stark Young was astonished to find Marlowe's tragedy, "with all the radiance of its ambition and the spell of its audacity," coming "straight over the footlights to an audience whose attention is such as I have not seen elsewhere in the theater this year."

The Tragical History of Doctor Faustus ran from January 8 to May 9 to a total of 80,000 paying customers not including standees. One night, about halfway through the run, Harry Hopkins appeared unannounced and bought a seat far in the rear of the theater before he was recognized by the agitated and obsequious house staff. At the close of the performance, after Faustus had sunk howling into a lake of flame, I led the head of the New Deal's Works Progress Administration between gaping stage traps, through sulphurous fumes, backstage, to where Welles lay—huge and half-conscious on a broken sofa—gasping and sweating from his descent into Hell. After the usual backstage amenities, Hopkins asked us one official question. Were we having a good time on the Federal Theater? We told him we were.

V

The Cradle Will Rock
1937

It was customary, after each of our successful openings, for Orson and me to drift apart for a time, relieved at being suddenly free of one another after so many days and nights of shared and enforced intimacy. With the triumph of *Doctor Faustus* our estrangement lasted longer than usual. This gave me a chance to catch up on my sleep and to try to pick up the pieces that remained of my personal life after almost two years of Federal Theater.

Of my world of the early thirties little was left. The couples were separated, the women married. Lee Miller was an Egyptian princess residing in Cairo; Anna Friede was the wife of a labor leader in Detroit; Henrietta Bingham back in Kentucky breeding race horses; Mina Curtiss at Smith College, teaching. Virgil Thomson, with whom I was once again sharing an apartment, was working day and night on the music for Pare Lorentz's second film, *The River*. The Viennese lady was gone: she had left suddenly for Paris to model a collection, then moved on to Rome, from where she sent me gay, tender letters and a snapshot of herself in the seat of an Alfa-Romeo roadster whose owner she presently married. No one replaced her. The physical and sentimental adventures with which I continued to fill my nights and weekends provided only mild satisfactions compared to the sustained excitements and violent consummations of my life in the theater.

Now there was a lull. My days were still spent in the powder room dealing with the increasingly difficult administrative problems of Project #891. And several times a week, for all or part of the evening, I was drawn back to *Faustus* and its dangerous beauty. (During the four months of its run I never heard the clanging of fire engines in the streets at night without feeling sure that our lakes of lycopodium flame had finally set the Maxine Elliott alight.) Sometimes I would go backstage to Orson's dressing room and we would talk vaguely about our next production.

In part, this inertia reflected the deep collective unease with which the Federal Theater was becoming infected. Flushed with our early successes, hailed by the critics as "the chief producers of works of art in the American theater," we had lived and worked, for eighteen months, under the growing illusion that we formed part of a permanent theatrical organization—pioneers in the development of a nationally supported popular Art Theatre. Now we were harshly reminded, from outside and inside the Project, that the institution to which we belonged was, in fact, nothing but a temporary relief agency, born of poverty and fear in a time of national calamity. The irony of our situation lay in this—that as the economic panic receded and the misery and the human need began to diminish, so did the social need for our work. By the end of 1936, it was becoming clear that the national economy was finally turning that long-awaited corner. This was bad news for the Project: with each new sign of recovery, the government came under increasing pressure to cut back on the vast, costly machinery of work relief and, in any such reduction, it was evident that the Arts Projects would be the first to suffer.

Ever since its belated formation as a "classical theater," Project #891 had been the most purely theatrical, the least social-minded or politically involved of the New York Federal Theater's major theatrical units. Now, in the high wind that was beginning to blow all around us, this isolation was swept away. Caught between demoralizing rumors of reduction and liquidation and the rising tide of desperate, organized resistance among project workers who felt their very lives threatened by the impending cuts, we found it daily more difficult, in spite of our past successes, to preserve the morale and muster the energy for creative work on a project in whose future we ourselves were ceasing to have faith.

Our torpor lasted for almost two months. Then, overnight, in one of those sudden, total reversals that formed one of the few consistent patterns of our erratic collaboration, Orson and I launched Project #891 on a huge new production that bore absolutely no relation to anything either of us had done before and which was guaranteed, in the circumstances, to land us both in the most serious possible trouble.

The Cradle Will Rock, which its author, Marc Blitzstein, described as "a play with music" (while others, at various times, called it a labor opera, a social cartoon, a marching song and a propagandistic tour de force), had been written at white heat one year earlier—in the spring of 1936. (I had known Marc slightly in the late twenties, soon after his return from Europe, where he had gone from a substantial, middle-class Philadelphia home and the Curtis Institute of Music to study

composition, first with Schoenberg and then, in Paris, with Nadia
Boulanger. A musical sketch of his—"Triple Sec"—had been admired
in the *Garrick Gaieties* but, generally, he was considered a sophisticated
composer of "serious," "modern" music.)

Marc's political conversion and its creative expression came late,
after the advent of the New Deal. In the summer of 1934 he was
swimming in the Mediterranean with his wife; one afternoon, as they
lay drying in the sun on a beach at Majorca, he said to her, "I don't
think I want to stay here any more. I want to be working in my own
country. There are things going on there I want to be part of." "I've
already packed," Eva said.

The next year, at Provincetown, Marc wrote a dramatic sketch,
"The Nickel Under the Foot," which, later, formed the basis of the
streetwalker's scene in *The Cradle Will Rock*. He showed it to Bertolt
Brecht, who was in New York and who approved but said it was not
enough. "To literal prostitution you must add figurative prostitu-
tion—the sell-out of one's talent and dignity to the powers that be."
Nine months later, soon after Eva's death, Blitzstein wrote *The Cradle
Will Rock* in five weeks—partly in a friend's house in Connecticut,
partly in his sister's home at Ventnor, New Jersey—and dedicated it to
Brecht.

The Cradle Will Rock was originally announced for production by
the Actors' Repertory Company, a left-wing group which had
successfully produced Irwin Shaw's *Bury the Dead* the previous spring. I
was not present when Welles and Blitzstein met backstage during the
run of *Horse Eats Hat*, to discuss the possibility of Orson's directing
Marc's play. Apparently, it was love at first sight. Marc was entranced
by Orson's brilliance and power; Orson was excited by the challenge of
this, his first contact with musical theater. I remember listening
jealously, with an ill-concealed sense of rejection, to Orson's enthusiastic comments about the piece (which I had not heard) and to his ideas
for casting and staging it, which he elaborated for my annoyance.
Hamlet had opened and closed and *Faustus* was deep in rehearsal when
the Actors' Repertory Company abandoned *The Cradle* for lack of funds.

So things stood early in 1937 when, as part of the complicated game
of one-upmanship that Orson and I were constantly playing together, I
suggested one night in his dressing room that if I were ever invited to
hear Marc's work, I might conceivably recommend it for production by
Project #891. I did. And, soon after that, with Hallie Flanagan's
approval, *The Cradle Will Rock* was officially announced as the next
production of Project #891. There was some feeling, later, in New York
and Washington, that Hallie had been irresponsible in allowing so
controversial a piece to be produced. She had no way of guessing (none

of us had) that a double accident of timing would project us all onto the front pages of the nation's press; but she did sense which way the political winds were blowing and realized, better than her more timid colleagues, that in the storm into which the Arts Projects were headed, there was no safety in prudence and no virtue in caution.

Work on *The Cradle* started calmly enough. We had singers and dancers on the project, but Will Geer was brought in from the outside to play Mr. Mister, the lord of Steeltown, and Howard da Silva to be the proletarian hero—Larry Foreman. To make up our chorus of thirty-two, we borrowed or traded singers from other units. Lehman Engel, our conductor, came over daily from the Music Unit, where he was working, to sit in on rehearsals. Orson, between radio shows, spent hours learning the music and working with his designer on an extravagant scenic scheme that called for a triple row of three-dimensional velour portals between which narrow, glass-bottomed, fluorescent platforms, loaded with scenery and props, slid smoothly past each other as the scene shifted back and forth from the night court to a street corner, a church, a drugstore, a hotel lobby, a faculty room, a doctor's office and the front lawn of the finest home in Steeltown, U.S.A.

Marc had created *The Cradle Will Rock* in haste, out of a burning conviction which he never quite recaptured in his subsequent work. Its prime inspiration, admittedly, was *The Threepenny Opera* by Brecht and Weill, to which Marc added "whatever was indicated and at hand. There were recitatives, arias, revue patters, tap dances, suites, chorales, silly symphony, continuous incidental commentary music, lullaby music—all pitchforked into it without a great deal of initiative from me." There were also patches of Gilbert and Sullivan and echoes of the Agitprop experiments of the early thirties.

The style of the piece as it began to take form at rehearsals fell somewhere between realism, vaudeville and oratory: the singing ranged from *Sprechstimme* to arias, patter and blues. A few of our more established performers were vaguely uneasy in their satirical roles but, for most of them, the piece had the fascination that goes with the creation of something new and unusual in the theater. And almost from the first day there were strange, prophetic stirrings in the air—a turbulence that grew with the weeks as the harsh realities of the national crisis met the rising theatrical excitement that was being generated on our bare, worklit stage. As opening night approached, those winds reached tornado force. How they finally blew *The Cradle* right out of our theater onto another stage twenty blocks uptown has become part of American theatrical history.

Now, after a world war, Korea, Vietnam and thirty years of cold war and inflation, it is not easy to recreate the world we lived in during the midthirties. 1937 was, in some ways, the most confused and disturbed of those difficult years—a time of transition between the end of the great Depression and the beginning of the slowly gathering industrial boom that accompanied our preparations for World War II. It was also the year in which labor violence vied for space with international news on the front pages of the nation's press.

The week we opened *Doctor Faustus*, sit-down strikes closed seven major automobile plants in the Middle West and the auto union voted a general strike against all plants of General Motors, whose president, Alfred Sloan, Jr., had just announced his refusal to deal with "labor dictators" or to consider their "demands for union recognition." The day *The Cradle Will Rock* went into rehearsal there were riots in Akron and Pontiac and strikes halted work in the Chrysler and Hudson auto plants.

By May the main battleground had shifted from autos to steel; five mills of Republic Steel were struck and picketed. At Canton and Massillon, strikers prevented night-shift workers from reaching plants. On May 29 in south Chicago, 1000 steel workers marching on a mill of the Republic Steel Corporation were beaten back by police after a sharp fight. Two days later ten were killed and eighty-four hurt as strikers again battled police in Chicago. The crowd used guns and rocks; the police employed clubs, tear gas and bullets.

During the first week of June, as we were starting our technical rehearsals, 5000 CIO sympathizers invaded the business section of Lansing, Michigan, forced the closing of factories and stores and blocked all traffic in protest against the arrest of pickets. Later that same week Johnstown, Ohio, was placed under martial law.

These national disturbances were echoed in the small, special world of the Arts Projects of the WPA. Rumors of cuts and pink slips filled the air. These were resisted by administrators who, like Hallie, sincerely believed that the Federal Theater, through its good work, had earned the right to live on as a form of national theater. Fanning the fear and the anger were the extremists on both sides. On the one hand, there were those, in and out of Congress, who had never ceased to feel that relief workers were parasites, encouraged by a "socialist" administration to believe that the world owed them a living and who regarded the Arts Projects as a particularly dangerous form of Trojan horse, loaded with screwballs and Reds. On the other, there were those for whom the projects and their human problems had, from the first, formed useful beachheads for political action—those who now saw in the relief reductions a weapon of agitation and propaganda of which they were determined to make the widest possible use.

It was in this tense but appropriate atmosphere that we conducted our final rehearsals of *The Cradle Will Rock*. On May 27 many members of the project had taken a day off when a one-day, citywide strike of all WPA work had been called in protest against threatened cuts. Seven thousand joined the stoppage. Asked to comment, the following day, Hallie Flanagan replied that the Federal Theater workers had struck "for what was once described as life, liberty and the pursuit of happiness...If we object to that method, I feel that some word should come from this gathering as to a better one."

Then came the announcement everyone had been dreading: a cut of 30 percent in the New York Theater Project, involving the immediate dismissal of 1700 workers. In protest, a number of sit-downs were called: in Harlem hundreds of members of the Negro unit sat with members of the audience through the night while other sympathizers formed a picket line outside.

Such action was not for us. Project #891 had a challenge of its own which we were determined to meet—to get Marc Blitzstein's play with music onto the stage of the Maxine Elliott Theater against a variety of odds. These included all the hazards that normally went with the opening of Orson's productions. By the end of May our three great portals were in place and our illuminated glass-bottomed floats were cruising across the stage, pursued by panting players, trailing yards of black, writhing cable in their wake. Actors accustomed to an open stage and four months of piano accompaniment were startled to find themselves confronted by gliding platforms and a 28-piece orchestra between themselves and the auditorium. There were the customary scenes of recrimination and reconciliation. But our real perils were not theatrical. Already, some weeks earlier, following reports in Washington that the opera was "dangerous," a special envoy had arrived in New York, watched a run-through with Mrs. Flanagan and pronounced it "magnificent." Now, ten days before our opening, with more than 18,000 tickets sold, a new set of rumors began to fly. We ignored them and continued rehearsing and selling tickets. Our first public preview was scheduled for June 16. On June 12, the blow fell—in the form of a routine memorandum received by all national directors prohibiting "because of impending cuts and reorganization, any new play, musical performance or art gallery to open before July 1."

As producers, Orson and I were not noted for our punctuality. Our *Macbeth* opening had been postponed five times, *Horse Eats Hat* twice, *Doctor Faustus* three times. Normally, we would almost certainly have postponed the opening of *The Cradle*. But now, suddenly, we became demons of dependability. Hallie called Washington and tried to get an exception to the ruling. When she failed, Orson and Archibald MacLeish, to whom we had turned for help, flew to Washington and visited the WPA administrators just as they were preparing to meet a Congressional committee to obtain funds for the coming year. Hopkins was not available. In a sharp scene with his assistant Orson informed him that if *The Cradle* failed to open as advertised under government auspices, he and I would launch it privately. The interview was brief and Orson was back in time for that night's dress rehearsal—the one before the last.

Early next morning we started telephoning; we called everyone we could think of—Right and Left, professionals and outsiders—and invited them to that night's run-through which, we intimated, might be their last chance to see *The Cradle Will Rock*. I remember little of the evening except that I felt it was not going too well. The glass wagons slid in and out—not too precisely; the actors, concerned with finding their places and lights, still lacked the fervor and energy of our earlier run-throughs; Lehman Engel, our conductor, was still struggling to establish a balance between their untrained voices and the twenty-eight not so subtly orchestrated instruments in our shallow pit. Near the end of the evening, the piece came suddenly alive: I can still see Howard da Silva as Larry Foreman, with his dirty-blond toupee, his fist clenched and his jaw jutting out around his flashing teeth as he sang, with the chorus behind him, right over the blaring band into the faces of the cheering audience:

> That's thunder, that's lightning,
> And it's going to surround you!
> No wonder those stormbirds
> Seem to circle around you...
> Well, you can't climb down, and you can't sit still;
> That's a storm that's going to last until
> The final wind blows...and when the wind blows...
> The Cradle will Rock!

The audience which left the Maxine Elliott that night, filing out past the guards in the doorways and the Workers' Alliance handbill distributors on the sidewalk, was the only one that ever saw and heard Marc's work performed in its entirety. After they had left, the lights were turned out and the doors of the theater were locked. For us, they were never reopened.

The next day, June 15, a dozen uniformed WPA guards took over the building in force. Project members arriving to sign in found their theater sealed and dark. The Cossacks, as they came to be known, guarded the front of the house and the box office; they hovered in the alley outside the dressing rooms with orders to see that no government property was used or removed. This included scenery, equipment, props and costumes: Howard da Silva, who attempted to retrieve his toupee (purchased with federal funds) had it snatched from his head at the stage door and confiscated. But there was one place in the building from which the Cossacks were excluded—the pink powder room in the basement, which now became headquarters in the fight to save *The Cradle*. Here we lived for the next thirty-six hours, sustained by food and drink brought in by well-wishers from the outside, for we were afraid to leave the theater lest the Cossacks prevent us from returning. Our telephones had not been cut off and we made the most of them.

The authorities had notified the organizations which had bought our previews that these were cancelled. We called them back and urged them to show up in full force. They needed no urging, for most of our advance sales were to organized theater parties of the Left—young and generous and eager to participate in the excitement which the stage alone seemed to offer them in those uncertain times. We were determined to keep faith with them and the authorities were determined that we should not.

In fact, Orson and I had been so busy asserting our integrity that we hadn't given much thought to the problems of performance. Members of our orchestra had already been notified by their union that, if they wished to perform under the management of Houseman and Welles, they must sign new contracts at full union scale for rehearsal with a two-week guarantee of performance. Since neither Welles nor I had five cents to our names, this was out of the question. The next morning Actors' Equity, in a special meeting of its board, reached a similar decision. Our actors were forbidden to appear for us on stage unless they too were paid in full for three weeks of rehearsal.

We felt betrayed and defeated. We could give a show without scenery and costumes and, if need be, without an orchestra—but not without actors. Marc's despair at this point was ghastly to behold. He who had come within a day of seeing his work presented by the director, the conductor and performers of his choice, amid elegant setting, in a Broadway theater, with a cast of sixty and an orchestra of twenty-eight, had seen these gifts snatched from him one by one, until, now, he was back where he had started a year ago. And the unkindest cut of all came with the realization that the final, fatal blows had been dealt him by those very unions in whose defense the piece had been written.

On June 6 the temperature in New York was in the upper 80s. Midday found us in the powder room, still blithely announcing the opening of *The Cradle*. We summoned an agent—a small, seedy man in a black felt hat who specialized in distressed theaters. He had a long list of available houses. Five hours later, their number had shrunk to zero. It was mid-summer and not one was available. Every half-hour or so he would look up from the phone we had put at his disposal at our secretary's desk under the lavender mannequin and announce that we had a theater. And each time, a few minutes later, it would turn out not to be so. Once, early in the afternoon, we closed a deal for a house only to discover, as we were about to take possession, that its management was deep in a dispute with the Stagehands' Union and that we would have to cross a picket line to get in. After that the man in the black hat was ordered from the powder room in disgrace. He stayed on, unnoticed, making futile calls and, occasionally, trying to attract our attention.

By midafternoon the press had begun to collect in our powder room. They were invited to wait while we held an emergency meeting in the ladies' toilet next door. Jean Rosenthal (back on the Project after her tour with Leslie Howard) had been sent out with a $10 bill and instructions to acquire a piano. She called to say that she had got one (a battered upright) and what should she do with it? We told her to hire a truck, load the piano onto it, then call for further instructions. After that we turned to face the press—Orson radiating confidence, I looking worried and Marc, recovered from his state of shock, looking pale but determined and eager for martyrdom. We told them that *The Cradle Will Rock* would be presented that night, as announced, even if Marc had to perform it alone on a piano and sing all the parts. When they inquired where this tour de force would take place we suggested they stay around and find out. Then we went up to talk to the actors who were still waiting, sitting and lying around in the darkened auditorium under the disapproving glare of the Cossacks. I told them of our decision and explained the fine legal point we had evolved in the ladies' toilet: that while they were forbidden by their union to appear *on* stage, there seemed to be no interdiction against their playing their parts from any other position in the theater. "There is nothing to prevent you from entering whatever theater we find, then getting up from your seats, as U.S. citizens, and speaking your piece when your cue comes," we told them.

Their reaction was mixed. The stalwarts, Will Geer, Howard da Silva and the rest of the non-relief 10-percenters, were enthusiastic. Others—especially our older members and the predominantly Negro chorus—were understandably reluctant to risk the loss of the small weekly income that alone kept them and their dependents from total indigence through a quixotic gesture for a cause which they did not really understand or altogether approve. On these (on the chorus especially) we were careful to exert no pressure or moral suasion. Each had his own personal problems and each must do what seemed sensible or right, regardless of collective or personal loyalty. Amid applause and tears we returned to the powder room, where Archibald MacLeish in a white linen suit had now appeared. The man in the black hat was still in his corner, looking glum and intimidated, and Jean Rosenthal was on the phone again. She reported success: after standing on the corner of Broadway and 37th Street, in the heart of the garment district, for forty minutes, propositioning New Jersey trucks headed home across the river, she had found one, hired it by the hour with its driver and loader and hoisted the piano aboard. Now, what should she do? "Keep riding around," I said, "and call in every fifteen minutes for orders."

Around seven Orson and I came out through the stage door and gave our personal assurance that the show would go on—"Somewhere! Somehow!" By now, sensing excitement, a considerable crowd had assembled on 39th Street; they formed little indignant knots, between which members of the City Projects Council circulated, distributing handbills:

YOUR FRIENDS HAVE BEEN DISMISSED!
YOU MAY BE NEXT!

At 7:20, as the swelling crowd began to get restless, several of our actors appeared on the sidewalk and offered a brief preview of the show to come. With their shadows lengthening in the early summer twilight, Hiram Sherman sang "I Wanna Go ter Honolulu" and Will Geer (veteran of many a union picnic and hootenanny) enacted one of Mr. Mister's more repulsive scenes.

Meanwhile, inside the theater, the gloom deepened. In the pink powder room a hopeless silence had fallen, broken only by the uneven whir of a single fan that barely stirred the stale air of the overcrowded basement. It was 7:30—a half-hour from curtain time; our piano, with Jean Rosenthal on top of it, had been circling the block for almost two hours and the driver was threatening to quit. Clearly, this was the end. After all our big talk, for lack of a theater, The Cradle would not be performed—on this or any other night.

It was then that the miracle occurred. The man in the black felt hat, the down-at-heel theatrical real-estate agent, rose from his corner and moved towards the stair. In the doorway he paused, turned and spoke. It was an exit speech, uttered in a weak, despondent tone. No one, later, could remember exactly what he said, but the gist of it seemed to be that since there was nothing more he could do, he might as well go home. Only he still couldn't understand what was wrong with the Venice Theater. With a sigh he turned and started up the stairs. He was already halfway up when he was seized, turned, dragged down, shaken and howled at. What was he talking about? What Venice Theater? He then explained in a flat, aggrieved voice that for three hours he had been offering us a theater that was open, empty, available, reasonable, unpicketed and in every way suitable to our requirements—but that none had listened to him. He held a rusty key in his hand which, he assured us, would admit us to the Venice Theater on Seventh Avenue at 58th Street at the cost of $100 for the night. The key was snatched from him and he was paid with money borrowed from members of the press.

Within seconds, Abe Feder, our lighting director, was in a cab, headed uptown. Jean Rosenthal, reporting for orders for the fourth time, was told to route her truck at full speed up Seventh Avenue. She got there first and four firemen from the hook-and-ladder station next door helped her to break into the abandoned theater and hoist the piano up onto its deserted stage. Meantime Orson and I went upstairs where our cast was patiently sitting in the auditorium under the disapproving glare of the Cossacks. We told them we had found a theater and invited them to accompany us uptown.

We went out into 39th Street, informed the audience of our move and, since our adopted theater was three times larger than our own, suggested they each invite one or more friends. On the way uptown—a distance of twenty-one city blocks—our audience trebled. They arrived by cab, by bus, by subway and on foot—2500 of them, including Mrs. Flanagan. A few of our own people stayed behind in the theater, signed out and went quietly to their homes. Others who remained in doubt were willing to risk the voyage; they entered the Venice Theater and took their seats, not knowing whether they would take part in the performance as spectators or performers. Howard da Silva made a final attempt to recapture his government toupee, failed, rushed home to get his own, could not find it, and still managed to be one of the first to arrive on 58th Street. Lehman Engel, our conductor, was among the last to evacuate the Maxine Elliott. Two of the Cossacks, sweating gently in the early summer heat, must have been surprised to see him leaving the building in a large overcoat, but failed to search him. If they had, they would have found, clasped against his stomach, the piano and vocal score of *The Cradle Will Rock*.

By 7:50 the Maxine Elliott was dark. Only a few guards and workmen remained to patrol its emptiness. Orson and I left with Archie MacLeish in someone's white Nash roadster with never a look back at the building in which we had prepared three shows together and opened two. Driving up Broadway through the light summer traffic, MacLeish seemed troubled; he was afraid we were going too far in our insubordination, yet he was reluctant to abandon us. Besides, there was a strong smell of history in the air which he was unwilling to miss.

There were no ticket-takers that night, no ushers and no program. We had changed our curtain-time to 9 p.m. but by 8:50 there was not an empty seat in the house; in defiance of the Fire Department, standees were beginning to clog the back of the theater and the side aisles.

At 9:01, like partners in a vaudeville act, Orson and I made our entrance "in one" in front of a shabby curtain that depicted Mount Vesuvius smoking above the Bay of Naples. We thanked our audience for making the long voyage uptown and related the full history of *The Cradle Will Rock*. We were not subversives, we insisted, but artists fulfilling a commitment. We told them how the show would have looked and sounded and described the characters they would *not* be seeing. In conclusion, "We now have the honor to present—with the composer at the piano—*The Cradle Will Rock*." As we left the stage, the curtain rose on Marc Blitzstein sitting pale, tense but calm at our eviscerated piano.

The Cradle starts cold, without an overture. Behind us, as we dashed into the house, we could hear Marc's voice, setting the scene:

A Street Corner, Steeltown, U.S.A

followed by a short vamp that sounded harsh and tinny on our untuned upright.

Then an amazing thing happened. Within a few seconds Marc became aware that he was not singing alone. To his strained tenor another voice, a faint, wavering soprano, had been added. It took Feder's hand-held spotlight a few seconds to locate the source of that second voice: it came to rest on the lower stage-right box in which a frail girl in a green dress with red-dyed hair was standing glassy-eyed, stiff with fear, only half-audible at first in that huge theater but gathering strength with every note. It is almost impossible, at this distance in time, to convey the throat-catching, sickeningly exciting quality of that moment or to describe the emotions of gratitude and love with which we saw and heard that slim green figure. Her name was Olive Stanton; she had been cast as "the Moll" almost by default and I knew that she was entirely dependent on the weekly check she was receiving from the WPA.

Years later Hiram Sherman wrote to me: "If Olive had not risen on cue in that box I doubt if the rest of us would have had the nerve to stand up and carry on." But she did—and *they* did.

The next character to appear was a bit-actor known as "the Gent."

Once again Marc was preparing to speak his lines and once again they were taken out of his mouth by a young man with a long nose who rose from his seat somewhere in the front section of the orchestra and addressed the girl in the stage box.

GENT

Hello, baby!

MOLL

Hello, big boy.

GENT

Busy, baby?

So a scene which, three nights before, had been played in atmospheric blue light, under a prop lamppost, downstage right, was now played in the middle of a half-lit auditorium, by two frightened relief workers standing 30 feet apart. From then on it was a breeze.

Nothing surprised the audience or Marc or any of us after that, as scenes and numbers followed each other in fantastic sequence from one part of the house to another. Blitzstein played half a dozen roles that night, to cover for those who "had not wished to take their lives or, rather, their living wage, into their hands." Other replacements were made spontaneously, on the spot: Hiram Sherman, word-perfect, took over for the Reverend Salvation, whose unctuous part he had never rehearsed, and later repeated this achievement, from an upper box, in the role of Professor Scoot, "an academic prostitute." Scenes were played, at first, wherever the actors happened to be sitting so that the audience found itself turning, as at a tennis match, from one character to another and from one part of the house to the other. Then, as the act progressed and their confidence grew, the actors began to move around, selecting their own locations, improvising their actions, while instinctively communicating with each other from a distance. No one later remembered all that happened. But I do recall that Mr. Mister, Editor Daily and the Mister children sang and danced "I Wanna Go ter Honolulu" in the same center aisle in which Mr. Mister and his stooges later played their big bribery scene. Mrs. Mister did her big scene upstairs in a balcony loge from which she wafted down imaginary "donations" to the Reverend Salvation, who stood in the orchestra floor at the head of the aisle with his back to the stage facing the audience, as did Ella Hammer later for her "Joe Worker" number. Our black chorus—all twenty-eight of them—sat clustered in the third and fourth rows, surrounding Lehman Engel, where they presently provided another of that evening's memorable moments.

Just before leaving 39th Street I had made a last round of the theater, thanked the members of the chorus for their loyalty and urged them not to take any unnecessary chances. It was all the more startling, therefore, in Scene Three, to hear the Reverend Salvation's booming pieties:

> Righteousness conquers! Iniquity perishes!
>
> Peace is a wonderful thing!

answered by an "Amen" reverently intoned by two dozen rich Negro voices. Without rising, taking their beat from Lehman Engel, they sang like angels. Melting into the half-darkness of the crowd, they were not individually distinguishable, and this gave their responses a particularly moving quality.

Another surprise came when Marc suddenly became aware that, instrumentally, he was no longer performing alone. Of the twenty-eight members of Musicians' Local 802, not one was to be seen that night at the Venice—but one was clearly heard. Somewhere, high up in the balcony, Rudy, the accordionist, sat hidden among the audience with his instrument open on his knees, playing along with his composer in passages where he felt it would help.

During the intermission the crowd milling around the jammed lobby and spilling out onto Seventh Avenue was agitated and happy but not overexcited. They kept meeting friends and inquiring how they got there and telling each other how splendid it all was. It took a long time to get them back inside—which was just as well, for Marc was limp with exhaustion.

The second act went like a house afire. The "inflammatory" scenes of *The Cradle Will Rock* occur cumulatively, towards the end. And then, finally, the showdown: Larry Foreman confronting Mr. Mister and his Liberty Committee in the crowded night court. Only this night they were all on their feet, singing and shouting from all over the theater as they built to the final, triumphal release:

> When you can't climb down, and you can't sit still;
> That's a storm that's going to last until
> The final wind blows...and when the wind blows...
> *The Cradle Will Rock!*

There were no "bugles, drums and fifes" that night—only Marc's pounding of an untuned piano before a wrinkled backdrop of the Bay of Naples. As the curtain fell and the actors started to go back to their seats, there was a second's silence—then all hell broke loose.

It was a glamorous evening and the cheering and applause lasted so long that the stagehands demanded an hour's overtime—which we gladly paid. We made the front page of every newspaper in the city and ran for eleven performances at the Venice Theater to packed houses. Then the entire cast returned to the Maxine Elliott where, under WPA regulations that limited absences to twelve days, the Federal Theater had to take them back.

* * *

The weeks that followed found Project #891 in a state of disgrace and uncertainty. The Cossacks had departed but we had nothing in rehearsal and no plans for the future. Our 238 workers continued to report daily, signed their time sheets and went home while they waited to be fired or transferred to other units. (Orson had already resigned and I was about to be dismissed for being an alien.) Personally Welles and I had little to say to each other. Our immediate response to the success of *The Cradle Will Rock* was the usual need, on both our parts, to prove that each of us could exist without the other. We both got our chance—quite soon. Needless to say, it was Orson who got the first and more sensational offer.

It came from Arthur Hopkins, still the most highly esteemed producer on Broadway. It had been Hopkins's dream, early in the twenties, to found a great American classical acting company with the Barrymores at its center. *Macbeth* and *Richard III*, followed by John Barrymore's celebrated *Hamlet*, had encouraged him in this hope, which had foundered finally on the rocks of the Barrymore temperament. Now, fifteen years later, Hopkins saw a chance to revive his dream around the figure of the fabulous 21-year-old Orson Welles. He proposed *King Lear* as a starter and Orson, flattered and excited, accepted. They had several meetings at which visions were exchanged, after which Orson went to work with Pavel Tchelitchev on a production scheme which he assumed Hopkins would approve. By the first week of August announcements of the Welles-Hopkins *Lear* had begun to appear in the theatrical columns, where I read them with a distaste that was all the more acute since my own future was far from brilliant.

For twenty months, first in Harlem and then on 39th Street, I had been so wholly absorbed in collaboration—not only with Welles but with all the human elements that went to form the organism of the Federal Theater—that the thought of working alone again was repulsive and terrifying to me. For three years the Federal Theater had been my life. Within its peculiar structure I had found myself wielding authority and power such as I was unlikely to find again elsewhere; as its leading producer I had been responsible for a series of creative achievements which had been remarkable for their variety and success. Now all this had been taken from me.

This was my state of mind when I got a call from Hallie Flanagan, asking me to come over and see her. It was the first time we had spoken since the night of *The Cradle* opening and I assumed that the purpose of her summons was to explain my dismissal from the Project. I was right. Hallie thanked me for my contribution and expressed the hope that Orson and I would continue our fine work elsewhere. For her own part she must stay on and fight what she knew to be a losing battle to retain some of the gains achieved by the Federal Theater under her direction. Meantime, she explained, she was still head of Vassar's Experimental Theater Production Department which she had founded and left to join the WPA. She asked me if I would consider taking the job for a year. I thanked her and agreed to drive up to Vassar College and speak to the president.

Driving back down the Hudson Valley one August evening, I stopped off at Sneden's Landing, where Orson and Virginia were spending the summer in a small house in the woods. When I told Virginia, who was two months pregnant, that I was about to become an associate professor of English at Vassar College for girls she laughed so hard that she had to be sent off to bed. Orson was too preoccupied with his sketches and models for *King Lear* to hear what I was saying. But, later that week, after I had accepted Hallie's offer, I found him sitting glumly in his bed, glaring at a letter that had just been delivered by hand. In it Arthur Hopkins released him from his commitment and reluctantly abandoned all plans for *King Lear*. His main reason was a newspaper interview in which the Wonder Boy, without referring to Mr. Hopkins, had informed the world of his plans for the production of *King Lear*. "It's like prematurely uncorking a vintage wine," Hopkins wrote. "It is no longer worth drinking." Was this the whole or the true reason for his change of heart? Or did he run into difficulties finding backing in mid-Depression for an expensive production of a difficult classic with an unknown star? Orson never found out. But, three days later, when I passed Sneden's Landing on my way to New City for the weekend, all his models and sketches for *Lear* had disappeared. And after supper, as he was walking me out to my car between the trees, Orson said suddenly, "Why the hell don't we start a theater of our own?" I said, "Why don't we?" and I did not go home that night or the next day or the day after that.

VI
Mercury
1937

To start a repertory theater in New York City today would take $1 million, months of high-minded discussion, a major real-estate operation, city, state and federal involvement and the benevolent participation of two or more gigantic foundations. The Mercury Theater was conceived one summer evening after supper; its birth was formally announced ten days later and it opened on Broadway within ten weeks in a playhouse bearing its own name with a program of four productions, a company of thirty-four and a budget of $10,500.

We had no difficulty formulating a program: we had already announced our favorite plays the previous winter on the Federal Theater and our tastes had not changed. We found our name on the cover of a two-year-old magazine in the corner of an empty fireplace at Sneden's Landing; we were registered and incorporated four days later in Albany as the Mercury Theater, Inc., with a paid-up capital of $100. It was mid-August and if we wanted our theater for the 1937-38 season we had not a moment to lose.

Our first step, once we had a name, was to find a theater. Our search led us downtown to Second Avenue, where we looked at huge, desolate playhouses left over from the boom days of the Yiddish theater. We got excited for a few days over an abandoned medical amphitheater in the East Forties. Then one morning someone called and suggested we visit the Comedy Theater on 41st Street and Broadway. One look—and we knew we had found our home.

The Comedy, an intimate, rococo, two-balcony theater with 687 seats and a fair-sized stage, was for many years one of Manhattan's most elegant and intimate playhouses; it had been used mainly for small musicals, which accounted for the narrow orchestra pit and a booth for follow spots high up in the rear of the second balcony.

Jean Rosenthal was hastily summoned. While we made our way by flashlight through cobwebs and scuttling rats, exploring the twilit, long-abandoned desolation of our new home, our business manager hurried off to make inquiries about its availability. He returned in half an hour with a confused report that the house was currently controlled by an Italian known as the "Commendatore" who ran a bar on Eighth Avenue and fronted for a gangster in Chicago. More important—it was available at the reasonable rental of $187.50 a week, on a three-year lease, so long as it was clearly understood that the owner would not spend one cent to restore or maintain it. Furthermore he didn't care what we did with it so long as the Fire Department stayed off his back. There was only one thing wrong with the deal: the first three months' rent had to be paid in advance.

So now we were incorporated; we had a theater available and a program to announce. But we had not one cent of backing and not the faintest notion of where to look for it. Clearly the time had come for a manifesto.

I made an appointment with Brooks Atkinson, drama critic of the *New York Times,* whose Olympian benediction was desirable, if not essential, for such a project. We met in the *Times* commissary, where I outlined our plans for an independent, low-priced repertory season on Broadway; he approved and offered to publish our "declaration of principles" in the Sunday drama section, where it appeared on the front page on August 29, 1937.

At the height of our success, *Time,* describing our origin, wrote that "the Mercury was at first just an idea bounded north and south by hope, east and west by nerve." Actually our venture was less rash than it seemed. We founded the Mercury with the sublime confidence of our youth and our reckless temperaments—and with a substantial accumulation of theatrical knowledge and skill. This was reflected in our "manifesto" in which I tried to avoid the tone of vague, verbose grandeur generally associated with the announcements of embryo, indigent artistic groups. In my third and final draft, completed an hour before deadline, I tried to convey an impression of self-confidence and continuity based on our successful operations of the past two years.

When its doors open early in November, the Mercury Theater will expect to play to the same audience that during the last two seasons stood to see *Doctor Faustus, Murder in the Cathedral* and the Negro *Macbeth.*

To anyone who saw it night after night, as we did, it was apparent that this was not the regular Broadway crowd taking in the "hits" of the moment. Even less was it the special audience one has learned to associate with "classical revivals." (A million people do not make a special audience.) One had the feeling, every night, that here were people on a voyage of discovery in the theater—people who either had never been to the theater at all or who, for one reason or another, had ignored it for many seasons.

By filling out the questionnaires we placed in their programs during the run of *Doctor Faustus* some forty thousand of them made their theatrical confessions to us. A large number professed themselves disappointed in the regular run of Broadway plays but stated that the theater had once again assumed importance for them with the productions of the Federal Theater. We asked for specific suggestions: the overwhelming majority of their requests was for "more classical plays," "classical plays excitingly produced," and "great plays of the past produced in a modern way."

This is the audience the Mercury Theater will try to satisfy.

With no money, no theater, no company and no organization of any sort, it was essential that our initial release be specific and credible.

We shall produce four or five plays each season. Most of these will be plays of the past—preferably those which seem to have emotional or factual bearing on contemporary life. While a socially unconscious theater would be intolerable, there will be no substitution of social consciousness for drama...We prefer not to fix our program rigidly too far ahead. New plays and new ideas may turn up any day. But we do know that our first production will be Shakespeare's *Julius Caesar*. As in *Faustus*, by the use of apron, light, sound devices, music, etc., we hope to give this production much of the speed and violence it must have had on the Elizabethan stage.

Next we hope, with George Bernard Shaw's consent, to produce what we consider his most important play, *Heartbreak House*. Also William Gillette's *Too Much Johnson*, Webster's *Duchess of Malfi*—one of the great horror plays of all time—and Ben Jonson's *The Silent Woman*. We expect to run our first play between four and six weeks. After that, without clinging to the rigid European system of revolving repertory the Mercury Theater expects to maintain a repertory of its current season's productions. However, at no time will more than two different plays be seen in one week.

We expect to occupy a theater of medium size on the edge of the Broadway district. With a top price of $2 there will be several hundred good seats available at $1 or less for every performance.

Within a few hours of our manifesto's appearance the phone had begun to ring in the hole in the wall I had rented on the mezzanine of the Empire Theater building. There were congratulations, expressions of hope and requests for employment—from members of our Projects up and downtown; from friends on Broadway and in radio; from actors and technicians we had never met but who were excited by the repertory idea; from audience groups inquiring about theater parties for November, December and January.

Seated in the airless cubbyhole which a sheet of yellow foolscap paper, glued to the outside of the door, identified as the office of the MERCURY THEATER, INC., I received visits, answered phone calls and worried about money. Accustomed to the regular payrolls of the U.S. Government, I had never learned the essential theatrical skill of money raising. I called several well-known Broadway angels and one rich acquaintance on the Produce Exchange and was politely refused. Meantime, not knowing how I was going to pay the phone bill, I continued to make plans for our future. Paralyzed with embarrassment and fear, I sat day after day radiating confidence and waiting, as I had so often done before, for a miracle to happen.

One afternoon during my second week of waiting the phone rang and a cultivated voice introduced itself as that of a man whom I remembered vaguely from the Federal Theater, where he had held a supervisory position in the fiscal department. He said he had long admired our work and was delighted to hear of our new program. If we were not fully financed would we consider him as one of our investors? As calmly as I could I asked him what kind of sum he had in mind. "Around $5000," he replied. I set a meeting in our lawyer's office for the next morning, at which he turned up, to my amazement, with a certified check for $4500. Ten minutes later, having converted the Mercury from a dream into a reality, George Hexter vanished as silently as he had appeard and I did not see him again until the opening of *Julius Caesar*.

Within a week I had landed our second angel—William Rapp, editor of *True Story* magazine, a man of great warmth and enthusiasm who brought in a retired builder by the name of Myron Falk, who put in $3500 in the name of his daughter. He was a gentle, shrewd, sincere, white-haired gentleman who plagued us with sound advice and did his best to help us, later, when we were in trouble. Another modest investor was the heir to a New England carpet-manufacturing fortune, followed by a radio director and a law student at Harvard with a passion for the theater. And that was it. Our total capitalization for the Mercury Theater amounted to less than $9000.

Treasury regulations were less stringent in those days. Legally there was nothing to prevent us from using our investors' money as it came in. And we did. Most of our first checks were spent on the day we received them. They went for advance rent on the theater, legal fees, stationery, second-hand furniture and additional telephones for our rapidly multiplying staff. We had got into the habit on the WPA of having a lot of people around; we started the Mercury with more personnel than most established, big-scale Broadway producers. From the first day, we regarded ourselves as an institution: as such it was necessary to have publicity and promotion departments long before we had a production.

(One person who worried about his premature expansion was our secretary, Augusta Weissberger, who had followed us from Harlem to the Maxine Elliott and who alone knew the real state of our finances.

This occasionally put her in an awkward situation. Soon after our move to the Empire she protested the pitiful WPA wages we were continuing to pay her for fourteen-hour-a-day work. We ignored her demands and, when she insisted, we accused her of presumption, treachery and blackmail. Pale as a sheet, she stuck to her guns. Finally we agreed to her request. Instead of gloating, she burst into tears. "But you can't afford it!" she sobbed.)

Our publicity was handled by a quiet, devoted, pleasant and competent young man named Hank Senber. Promotion was handled by Sylvia Regan, an expert in left-wing audience development and theater-party sales, who had followed us over from the Federal Theater. She brought in a myopic assistant and then an office girl to answer the telephone. (The office girl became a theater and movie star later under the name of Judy Holliday; she was fifteen at the time, received $5 a week and wept each time I used a four-letter word.)

The Comedy Theater, when we moved into it, was in even worse shape than we had supposed. The stage house, particularly, was a dilapidated, sordid and dangerous shell, caked with rust and corrosive grime. Jeannie spent a week crawling around its dangerous darkness. Then she presented me with a formidable list of absolute and immediate necessities, which included major repairs to the grid, new rigging and power lines and a new stage floor to replace the rotting planks through which huge, fearless rats could be seen emerging on their hunting excursions. I told her to go ahead and to hire whatever help she felt she needed to make the theater usable within a month.

Meanwhile, between desks in our cramped cubbyhole in the Empire, Orson and I were interviewing dozens of actors each day. They came, attracted by the chance of good classical roles, by the excitement of belonging to a theatrical organization of the sort serious actors had long dreamed of and by the reputation we had acquired over the past two years. As we auditioned and talked with them, we were thinking primarily of *Julius Caesar*, but also of an acting company and a repertory season.

It was the first time we were entirely free to select our cast; we sat with our lists in front of us, weighing each name and arguing over each choice: Orson took in Martin Gabel, with whom he had worked in radio, John Hoysradt, who had been his companion on the Cornell tour, Hiram Sherman and Joseph Cotten, who had been with us on Project #891. My candidates were Joseph Holland, who had played Horatio in Leslie Howard's *Hamlet*, George Coulouris, Grover Burgess, a fugitive from the Group Theatre, and Norman Lloyd, whom I had admired when he was playing leading roles in the Federal Theater's innovative

Living Newspaper (which dramatized current events in popular "revue" style).

To each of them we offered contracts at the Equity minimum ($40 a week for senior members and $25 for juniors) plus a dubious sliding scale based on an improbable weekly gross. No one turned us down. We exacted no monastic vows or long-term commitments; we signed no run-of-the-play contracts. They were free to quit at any time on two weeks' notice. During our first Mercury season not one of them left us or talked of leaving.

In mid-September Orson announced that he needed to go into a retreat before the start of the season. I drove him north, through woods that were turning red and gold, into the White Mountains. We arrived late in the afternoon at a huge, half-empty New Hampshire resort hotel that looked suspiciously like the one from which my father, my mother and I had been turned away twenty years before. Here I left him to his meditations. On my way back I stopped off at Chapelbrook for a weekend with Mina Curtiss, then drove to Poughkeepsie for my first formal appearance as head of the Drama Production Department of Vassar College.

When I got back to 41st Street, I was told that a quarter of a million handbills announcing:

JULIUS CAESAR
!!DEATH OF A DICTATOR!!

with an opening date of November 11 had been scattered all over town by volunteers who were bound by oath not to throw them in trash cans or empty lots, but to distribute them conscientiously in schools, colleges, cafeterias, drugstores and bookshops all over the five boroughs. Sales of theater parties were reported well into the new year. With all this activity our cubbyhole at the Empire had become so intolerably crowded and noisy that I moved over to the theater into the only space available—the former projection booth at the rear of the upper balcony. From there, squeezed between a day bed, a table, two chairs and three telephones, I conducted the affairs of the Mercury and, through the gaping hole that had once held a follow spot, followed the frantic activity below.

From the day she joined us Jean Rosenthal was not so much our technical director and lighting expert as our partner. We demanded daily miracles and she gave them to us. She also gave us love. Throughout her long and brilliant career as America's leading lighting designer one of her invaluable assets was her ability to enlist the loyalty and enthusiastic cooperation of the technicians with whom she worked. Through personal suasion, a sense of theatrical excitement and the prospect of continuous employment, she managed to sign up,

as our department heads, three of the best stagehands in New York
City. Under their direction walls were pierced and stage boxes
breached to accommodate our light towers and augmented power
lines. Amid the blue flames of blowtorches and the screeching of
power drills, a large iron platform was hung high overhead, stage
right, strong enough to hold the eight dimmer boards needed for the
elaborate light effects we were in the habit of using. Under Harry Rose,
our head carpenter, the rotting stage floor and grid were checked and
repaired, decaying hemp removed from the fly floor and replaced by
twelve sets of new, beautiful, pale-yellow lines. Over what had been
the orchestra pit a wooden apron was constructed, similar to the one
we had built for *Faustus* but wider and shallower because of the sharp
angle of the double balcony.

Bootleg painters and plasterers were brought in at night to patch
up our crumbling walls and proscenium; by day, looking down
through my peephole, I could see the shapes of women writhing in
the aisles as they stitched away at the torn red carpeting and the
frayed seats we could not afford to replace. In the basement plumbers
tinkered sceptically with our clogged, disgraceful toilets and banged
away at a furnace that was crusted with thick, dark-brown rust but
seemed to function. Remembering our landlord's warning, there was
nothing we could do but pray that it would continue to work through
the worst of the winter. The few dollars we had for decoration were
spent on the small outer lobby and box office, for which we chose
pearl-gray walls with a second-hand crystal chandelier and all the
gold leaf we could afford. One day, while the painters were at work, a
truck drove up carrying a large electric sign. For two hours all other
activities stopped while the entire organization helped to unload it
and hoist it into place. We cheered when the current was turned on
and the letters

M

E

R

C

U

R

Y

flashed pale in the sunlight. That night they could be seen shining
encouragingly all the way from Sixth Avenue to Broadway.

When Orson returned from his ten-day retreat, he brought with him a
completely re-edited text of *Julius Caesar*, including music and light

cues, and a suitcase full of notes, sketches and a Plasticine model of his production. We had four weeks in which to adapt them to the Mercury stage. At Jean Rosenthal's suggestion we engaged a young scenic designer named Samuel Leve, a fellow graduate from Yale. He was a dynamic polliwog of a man with a crew cut and a strong accent, known as "the Rabbi" because he taught shul each Sabbath at a Talmud Torah uptown. He absorbed Orson's ideas and sketches, spent a day marching around the stage with him while Jean and I watched sight lines from the balcony; then, under her technical direction, set about converting them into working drawings and blueprints.

Later, when they saw *Julius Caesar*, many people were under the impression that they were watching a play performed upon a bare stage and praised the Mercury for its return to theatrical simplicity. I have described the complications of Orson's "simplicity" in *Faustus*. In *Caesar* he called for a series of huge, subtly graded platforms that covered the entire stage floor. First came the main downstage playing area—14 feet deep including the apron—which rose in a gentle rake to meet a set of shallow steps running the full width of the stage. These led to an eight-foot plateau, the midstage playing area, then rose again through another set of steps to a final narrow crest, six and a half feet above stage level, before falling back down in a steep, fanning ramp that ended close to the rear wall of the theater. This gave the stage an appearance of enormous depth and a great variety of playing areas.

Steps and platforms were honeycombed with traps out of which powerful projectors were angled upward and forward to form a double light curtain (the "Nuremberg lights") through whose beams all actors making upstage entrances had to pass and were suddenly and dramatically illuminated before descending to the playing areas below. It was a brilliant concept but, when the first estimates for lumber, construction and additional lighting equipment were added up, they came to far more than we had budgeted or could afford. Moved by my distress, Orson agreed to do without padding on his platforms. As a result they made a hollow, drumming sound which disturbed us during rehearsal until we discovered that they added an ominous and highly dramatic element to our mob scenes.

There was also the small matter of paint. What could be simpler and more economical than a few platforms and bare brick walls daubed with the standard barn-red that Orson was demanding? Precisely because they *were* bare, it meant that hundreds of gallons of paint must be sloshed and sprayed from ladders and scaffolds over an acreage of more than 5000 square feet, including dressing-room stairs, stage door, steam pipes and fire extinguishers. The first 1500 feet were done at night by bootleg house painters. Then the union stepped in and ruled that the walls, having become scenery, must be painted by ruinous, accredited scene painters.

For our enormous platforms Jean unearthed a builder who was willing to construct them outside the New York metropolitan area in an abandoned movie studio at Fort Lee, New Jersey, where our *Julius Caesar* platforms were put together from salvaged lumber and fragments of old sets. They were solid enough but, as a result, no two sets of steps were exactly the same height or depth. When Leve pointed this out to Orson, he replied that he preferred steps to be uneven. When Leve objected that one of these steps might be as high as 20 inches, Orson said, "That's fine! We can use it to sit on!"

Costumes, fortunately, presented no problem. Our production came to be known, later, as the "modern-dress *Caesar*"' and we were commended for our shrewdness in avoiding the expense of period costumes and armor. The decision to use modern dress was not an economic one and it was not conceived as a stunt. It was an essential element in Orson's conception of *Julius Caesar* as a political melodrama with clear contemporary parallels. All over the Western world sophisticated democratic structures were breaking down; the issues of political violence and the moral duty of the individual in the face of tyranny had become urgent and inescapable. To emphasize the similarity between the last days of the Roman republic and the political climate of Europe in the midthirties, our Roman aristocrats wore military uniforms with black belts that suggested but did not exactly reproduce the current fashion of the fascist ruling class; our crowd wore the dark, nondescript street clothes of the big-city proletariat.

Uniforms were easily procured on a rental-purchase basis from the Brooks Costume Company. They were old army tunics and overcoats, dyed a uniform dark green. For the rest, the actors wore their own street clothes, supplemented by dark coats and hats picked up in second-hand clothing stores—all except Orson, who, as the aristocratic Brutus, wore a double-breasted, custom-made black pinstripe suit with a dark tie.

Rehearsals began in the first week of October with a company of twenty-one, to which were presently added twelve, then finally sixteen, extras for the mob scenes. The first reading, which was held on our still unfinished stage in the presence of the entire Mercury staff, ran for less than an hour and a half and was electrifying in its clarity and power. Our emotional casting seemed to work: Joe Holland, with his marble brow and big voice, was a pale, truculent dictator—"a mortal confusing himself with divinity and heading toward a fall." Martin Gabel, who looked neither lean nor hungry, was a violent,

angry and, finally, heartbreaking Cassius; Coulouris, no longer in his
first youth, was a political, persuasive Antony opposed to Orson's
high-minded, aristocratic liberal-intellectual Brutus. Chubby Sherman
was a smiling, cynical wardheeler of a Casca; Norman Lloyd a pitiful
astonished rabbit as Cinna the Poet. The ladies—Portia and
Calpurnia—as so often happened in Welles's classical productions,
were decorative, adequate and hardly memorable.

Our stage management at the Mercury was effective but
unorthodox: no professional could have functioned for more than a
day in the capricious, overheated atmosphere that Orson created
backstage. All technical matters, including sound and light, were
handled by Jean Rosenthal and her flock of female assistants; the rest
was in the hands of a sensitive, overstrung young man with red hair
who presently suffered a nervous breakdown. His aides, that first
season, were Richard Wilson (Welles's patient and devoted assistant
for the next eleven years) and a chinless boy with a big voice who
called himself Vakhtangov or William Alland, neither of which was his
real name. He eventually played the reporter in *Citizen Kane*. Both of
them, besides their stage managers' duties, doubled and trebled as
dressers, waiters, male nurses, messenger boys and actors.

(The manner of Alland's joining the Mercury was typical of the
climate in which we lived. The previous spring, while he was directing
Aaron Copland's *Second Hurricane* for the children of the Henry Street
Settlement, Orson had told me of a boy who called himself
Vakhtangov, who hung around day and night, working lights, holding
book, sweeping, prompting, moving pianos, talking too much and
making himself generally indispensable. In exchange for these services,
at some time in the middle of the night, he had extracted a promise of
employment in the theater. Orson was not one to remember such a
commitment. He had quite forgotten Vakhtangov's existence when a
frail, ragged figure rose out of the sidewalk one evening after dinner as
we were hurrying back to the theater, discussing our latest crisis.
Running backward ahead of us, this apparition began to harangue
Orson in an agitated and almost incomprehensible voice. Once he
tripped and fell. I told him to call me the next morning. But he picked
himself up and continued to scuffle backwards all the way to the
theater, alternately pleading and threatening, urging Orson to
remember his oath, offering to act, light, valet, pimp, clean the toilets,
steal—anything at all, so long as he was allowed to fulfill his destiny,
which his dead mother's ghost had told him lay with the Mercury
Theater. Amused, then finally exasperated, Orson brushed past him
through the stage door and hurried across the unfinished stage into the
dressing room which he used as his office. We were about to start work

when the door flew open and Vakhtangov stood before us, wild-eyed and deathly pale, slammed the door shut behind him, locked it, slipped the key into his bosom and announced that he would never surrender it until he had been heard. Then at the top of his voice he launched into a word-perfect recitation of the entire funeral oration, which so surprised us that we hired him on the spot.)

In the second week of rehearsal Orson began blocking his crowd scenes. Two days later he demanded the stage—platforms and all. Jeannie said that even if they were ready it would cost a fortune in crew bills to bring them into the theater. Orson didn't care. I did. We were virtually bankrupt already. "Where are those platforms?" Orson asked. "Across the river," Jeannie replied. So, for the next ten days, the entire company (forty strong by this time) made its way each morning by West Side subway to 125th Street, crossed the Hudson on the Dyckman Street ferry, then took a Palisades Park bus to where our platforms stood in a vast shed among mounds of moldering lumber in Fort Lee, New Jersey. Here, without a trace of heat, the mob scenes of *Julius Caesar* were rehearsed day after day amid the whir of saws, the banging of hammers and the perils of an unfinished set. To his mildly protesting troupe Orson explained that all this was for their own protection: by the time the platforms reached the theater they would be so familiar with the steps, ramps, risers and sudden drops that they would feel totally secure.

They needed every bit of this security, as it turned out. For, when they finally arrived at the theater for the first of their all-night sessions, our actors discovered that the platforms had been pierced by four large traps—gaping holes located in strategic positions, each wide enough for the passage of a human body and each supplied with a narrow, almost perpendicular set of wooden steps leading down to the basement below. These open traps provoked some grumbling among the actors, who regarded them as unnecessary physical risks— especially when they were expected to negotiate them in pitch-blackness. When they spoke to Orson about them, he was amazed and indignant. Were they not actors? And were not traps among the oldest and most consecrated devices of the stage? They must stop being amateurish and craven; they must get used to the presence of these traps and learn to use them like professionals!

At the next rehearsal, when the lights dimmed up on the assassination scene, all the conspirators were present except the honorable Brutus, who was nowhere to be found. A hurried search of a neighboring saloon (to which he sometimes retired for a quick nip) and of our mezzanine (to which he sometimes climbed to survey his staging) failed to locate him. Rehearsal stopped and the perplexed company waited for his return.

He was found five minutes later, still unconscious, in the dark, after falling through an open trap and dropping 15 feet before striking the basement floor with his chin. He was shaken but uninjured except for a slight sprain of his ankle, which got twisted as he was being helped to his feet. The next morning two of our manholes were plugged up. The others remained open and the company gradually got used to them, as Welles had predicted they would.

Throughout the run of *Julius Caesar* the problem of entrances and exits remained a tricky one on that completely open stage. All the dressing rooms except Orson's were located in a three-story cell block served by a narrow cement staircase set in the wall, from which stage left entrances could be made. All other entrances required going down into the darkened basement and coming up on the other side or through one of the traps. After some initial confusion the company became quite expert at getting into position and timing their entrances while keeping out of sight of the audience. Unfortunately they were not the only ones to use the stage. Since our stage door opened directly onto the street and we had a permissive doorman, it was not unusual for people to wander in off the street during performances. On the second night of *Julius Caesar* one critic noted the presence of a New York City fireman in uniform in the background of the assassination scene. And one Wednesday afternoon, a conscientious delivery boy, carrying a pressed suit on a hanger, made his way across the crowded stage to Orson's dressing room, where he delivered one garment, collected another and departed the way he had come without disturbing the matinee audience or the funeral oration. Other regular visitors were rats—the size of small dogs—with whom we still shared the theater and who found in Orson's Elizabethan stage traps a quick and convenient route from the basement to the street. Undeterred by the presence of forty actors, the glare of 200 projectors and the thunder of Marc Blitzstein's martial music, they trotted about the stage—singly, in troupes or pursued by impotent cats.

By November 1, I had spent all our investors' money and we were deep in debt. After two months of euphoric activity, the realities of Broadway were beginning to reassert themselves. Our advance business was encouraging: student and theater-party sales were substantial and more than half our cheap seats were already sold for the first seven weeks of our season. But this was not nearly enough. For the major part of our receipts, we would have to rely on the sale of our orchestra seats. I urged our box-office staff to try to wring some sort of an advance buy from the ticket agencies which controlled the carriage trade. They got nowhere. Some agents were benevolent but cautious;

others refused to let us put our posters in their windows on the grounds that we were "amateur stuff" and not a Broadway show.

I was sitting alone in the projection booth the evening before the first dress rehearsal, considering our situation and listening to Brutus's page singing Marc's lovely setting of "Orpheus with His Lute" on the stage below, when Jean Rosenthal and George Zorn (our company manager since the troubled days of *The Cradle Will Rock*) appeared with sober faces and presented me with the estimated cost of our dress rehearsals and previews. These were not expenses that could be swept under the rug; the unions required payment at week's end in cash—which we did not have. What about the money from our advance sales? "Spent!" said Georgie. Our deposits from the theater parties? "Gone!"

After they left I lay on my day bed for a while; then I called Mina Curtiss in the Berkshires. I asked her to lend us $1000. She said she would drive into Northampton in the morning and mail the check. After that, in desperation, I called Archie MacLeish. I told him of our crisis. Would any of his rich friends care to help us? He was at dinner and said he'd think about it. He called back at noon the next day to say that he had talked to Clare Luce; I should go to the Waldorf Towers between five and six and talk to her myself.

I had met her twice before—once at some summer theater up the Hudson on the opening night of her disastrous first play and again on the night when she had appeared at the Hartford première of *Four Saints*. Like any beautiful and successful woman, she presented two quite different images to the world: in the one she appeared as a ruthless climber who had exploited her sex and her wits to claw her way to her present position of wealth and power. Others, especially my friend Pare Lorentz, had given me a picture of a warm, generous and loyal friend. In the hour I spent with her—a mendicant in desperate need of a few dollars talking to the wife of the nation's most successful publisher, herself the author of one of the biggest hits on Broadway—I was overcome by her charm but, even more, by her instinctive, feminine capacity to bring out, even in those circumstances, a sense of my own male attraction, intelligence and power. She encouraged me to talk, listening to every word I said with an eager and fascinated absorption. She had seen our shows; she knew of our hopes for the Mercury. Just before I left, after my second Scotch-and-soda, Henry Luce, her husband, came in and she mentioned the object of my visit. Late that night, halfway through dress rehearsal, the phone rang in the box office and George Zorn came down the aisle, found me in the darkness and whispered that a "Mrs. Clare" was asking for me. She apologized for calling at such an hour, but she knew we were worried about money and thought I'd be able to watch the rehearsal more objectively knowing that she and her husband were coming in for $2500 and that the check would be sent over in the morning.

I had not discussed the details of our situation with Orson. I did not need to. We were both fully aware of the danger we were in. On the broad wings of the federal eagle, we had risen to success and fame beyond our wildest dreams; we had become dazzled with the vision of ourselves as America's youngest, cleverest, most creative and audacious producers to whom none of the ordinary rules of the theater applied. Now, suddenly, we were facing reality. With the imminent opening of *Julius Caesar*, our moment of truth had arrived. Had we soared too near the sun and were we about to get our comeuppance? Or were we about to realize our shining vision of founding a great new theater of our own, comparable to the fabled theaters of the past? Were we about to show a sceptical world that we could achieve the impossible—run a classical repertory company on Broadway? Or were we about to break our necks?

Orson Welles was a prodigious, if somewhat erratic, worker. This time he was fanatical in his preparation. Between the personal scenes, which he continued to rehearse long after they seemed to be ready, the crowd scenes which he drilled and repeated endlessly, the setting of lights and the balancing of Blitzstein's musical background, he was spending between sixteen and twenty hours a day in the theater and making scenes if I wasn't by his side for most of that time. I also had to administer the Mercury and discharge my duties as associate professor of English at Vassar College. By getting up at five in the morning two days a week, fast driving and a lot of telephoning, I was just able to fulfill my contractual obligations which, in addition to eight hours of teaching each week, called for three productions a year. (I conducted my classes informally, with limited preparation, counting on my energy, my limited theatrical experience and the glamour of our recent successes to hold the attention of some twenty young women of whom less than a third were interested in theater as a career. If I brought them anything, it was the exciting sense of big-time professional theater which I carried with me from New York as I came roaring onto the campus twice a week and slid to a screeching stop before the Experimental Theater building.)

Technical rehearsals of *Julius Caesar* were going smoothly—Jeannie's quiet, deliberate politeness, which she seemed to maintain no matter what strain was put upon her, made our lighting sessions an almost agreeable experience. The light plot was complicated and grew daily more elaborate as secondary cues and transitions were added. But the basic electrical setup, carefully conceived and imaginatively installed, was superior to anything we had known in our previous theaters and Jean's communication with Welles was more direct. Having watched rehearsals for weeks, she was familiar with the action on the stage and had carefully prepared herself for whatever effects might be required of her. (There is always an element of improvisation in theatrical lighting: one of the loveliest effects in *Julius Caesar*—known as the "orchard lights" because they were used to illuminate the moonlit scene in which Brutus is visited by the conspirators in his orchard at night—was achieved by pure accident when it was found that a worklight, left burning in the flies, threw strange, broken shadows through the grid and hanging ropes onto the blood-red floor of the stage below.)

Marc's music gave us no trouble. His flexible score for trumpet, horn, percussion and Hammond organ was strong, effective and easily cued. With this limited combination (the Musicians' Union's minimum requirement) he managed to achieve amazingly varied effects—from the distant bugles of a sleeping camp to the blaring brass and deep, massive, rhythmic beat which instantly evoked the pounding march of Hitler's storm-troopers that we were hearing with increasing frequency over the radio in the newsreels. Added to this was the ominous rumble of the electric organ on certain bass stops which set the whole theater trembling and the deep booming of a huge, old-fashioned thunder drum.

These technical elements of the production took up hours of our time, but it was on the human performances that Welles concentrated his main effort during that last week, dividing his time between the crowd scenes and the personal confrontations—particularly the relationship of Brutus and Cassius which, in his version, formed the emotional spine of the tragedy.

It would have been hard to find a man less suited, physically, to the role of Cassius, as Shakespeare describes him, than Martin Gabel: squat, broad, thick-necked with a furrowed brow and massive jaw. His gravid voice had made him, in his early twenties, one of the country's most successful and sexy radio actors. A man of deep sensitivity distorted by insatiable ambition and a furious energy, he was a reckless gambler and a compulsive operator in many fields. All of this, fermenting under the outward arrogance of a Jewish boy from New Jersey on his first dangerous venture into the classical theater, made him the perfect antagonist for Orson's high-minded and meditative Brutus. In their first moment together, waiting for Caesar to return from the Games, there was something recognizable and terrifying in the way he intruded upon Brutus, violating his privacy with his corrosive, vengeful discontent, tearing his way through that serene self-righteousness to plant the seed of murder in his ear. And, in their last scene together, in the tent before Philippi, when the final, inevitable conflict between these two irreconcilable men breaks through the frail structure of their enforced association, it was surprising to find that one's sympathy was evenly divided—between the bitter, humiliated partner caught with his hand in the till but still craving respect and affection and the self-defeating but still noble, sincere and righteous Brutus.

In his fascination with the Brutus—Cassius relationship, Welles had cut out not only the battle scenes (which no one missed) but also much of the Antony and Octavius material from the second half of the play. As a result, George Coulouris was a highly effective but one-dimensional Marc Antony. In his big scene in the Forum, following a stricken but restrained and dignified brutus, Antony's oration, as Coulouris delivered it, was a cynical political harangue, a skillfully organized and brilliantly delivered demagogic tour de force, a catalyst whose emotional effect on the Roman mob was deliberate and premeditated.

To achieve such mass reactions of pity, indignation and unbridled fury with a crowd of two dozen boys in second-hand overcoats and dark felt hats, Orson spent days and nights of detailed and patient work. One of them recalls how Welles spent hour after hour with them, orchestrating their individual and collective reactions:

He recorded the speeches of Antony and Brutus on discs and had us speak back specific lines in reaction to the main speeches. It wasn't just a matter of walking on and off the stage and making noises. We had definite lines to say and definite moments at which to speak.

Later these ad libs were replaced by appropriate exclamations collected from other Elizabethan plays, notably *Coriolanus*.

There was no realistic scenery in the production and therefore no "pulpit"—just a 10-foot rostrum covered with black velour that was wheeled up the ramp in the dark (under cover of the electric organ and the thunder drum) on which first Brutus, then Antony, seemed to float in space above the crowd gathered around Caesar's open coffin between the speakers and the audience. Their reactions during their climactic scenes were not merely verbal: Orson kept them in continuous, fluid movement which, on our hollow, unpadded platforms, gave out a constantly changing and highly dramatic sound which he exploited to the full. Yet it was one of those mob scenes that gave us so much trouble that, for a time, it seemed about to wreck the entire show.

All directors—especially the creative ones—get stuck sooner or later. There are always certain scenes which, for one reason or another, do not move forward with the rest of the work. This was particularly true of Welles. In every production we did together there were one or more scenes which came to embarrass or bore him—either because he had become disillusioned with the performers or because he realized that his own original conception of the scene had failed and he was uncertain which way to turn. In *Julius Caesar* the lynching of Cinna the Poet had become such a block.

Orson, in his editing of the play, had given the scene a special significance: he saw in it the dramatic consummation of the passions aroused by Antony's inflammatory oration. At the first reading it had seemed to do just that. Then, after a few days, it ceased to progress. Perhaps he was asking too much of the moment and got disappointed and angry when it didn't happen immediately; perhaps he was reacting unfavorably to the challenge presented by the personality of Norman Lloyd, whom I had brought into the company over some resistance by Orson. Whatever the reason—after several false starts, he simply stopped rehearsing the scene.

This was not the first time such a block had occurred. In such cases it was my function, as his partner and producer, to cajole, harass or shame Orson into going back into the scene and reworking it, sometimes even reconceiving it entirely, until it satisfied us both or I conceded that it was hopeless. With the Cinna scene I got nowhere. When I insisted that it be worked on, he turned it over to Marc Blitzstein, who rehearsed it for several days with a metronome: the rising menace was to be achieved through a crescendo in volume and an accelerating tempo with each move and speech related to a percussive beat. That didn't work either. Lloyd as the dreamy, oblivious victim was unable or unwilling to adjust his highly personal style of playing to these arbitrarily imposed, external rhythms. By this time the scene looked like a parody of Martha Graham's street movements in *Panic* and, for the first time since the start of the production, the company was beginning to get restless and querulous. So, once again, the scene was abandoned. For our first three dress rehearsals it was missing from the show.

By that time another crisis had hit us. From the start of rehearsals Orson had been telling me of an astounding soundtrack that was being prepared for him by his radio friends over at the Columbia Broadcasting System, where sound men and engineers were assembling a sequence of big-city sound effects the like of which had never been heard inside a theater. As usual where electronics are concerned, this all took longer than expected. On the Friday before opening— in time for our second dress rehearsal, the disc was finally ready. We went over to the CBS building on Madison Avenue and heard it in Studio One on the finest high-fidelity equipment in the business. It sounded terrific. But when we tried to play it back in the theater, we discovered that our rented equipment was quite incapable of reproducing it. Over the weekend Jeannie managed to find, rent and install a new turntable and six expensive speakers which we hung above and under the stage and on the sides and rear of the house. They were in place when we opened our doors for the first preview.

It was a disaster. Some of the personal scenes worked, but enough music and light cues went wrong to throw the entire cast into a turmoil. Infected by the general insecurity, the crowd scenes fell apart and the absence of the Cinna scene left a gaping hole in the structure of the play. But all these were negligible flaws compared to the catastrophe of our sound. Over our still inadequate system the fabulous big-city montage sounded like a subway train in travail. At first the audience was puzzled and irritated as the moaning and crackling of the loud-speakers interfered with their hearing of the actors' words. Then they began to giggle and, finally, to laugh out loud. Some walked out. At the end there was perfunctory applause and we took no curtain calls.

All through the following day a flock of CBS engineers was tinkering and testing. That night we tried again, with results that were only slightly less grim. Halfway through the show Orson ordered all electric equipment cut off. From then on we relied for our sound on Marc's music supplemented by our thunder drum and the pounding feet of the forty members of our cast.

Otherwise, our second preview (still without Cinna) had gone rather better than the first. The company, having recovered from its initial panic, recaptured some of the magic it had shown in rehearsal. The end of the play, as it focused on Brutus and Cassius, and, finally, on Brutus alone, had a tragic and heartbreaking quality which, following the violence and turmoil of the earlier scenes, left our audience exhausted—but still not fully involved. We had two more previews before our opening—a matinée and an evening performance.

Orson gave the company forty-five minutes for supper. Then he called them back and rehearsed the crowd scenes until morning, repeating the mob's violently changing reactions to Brutus and Antony and going on from there, time after time, into the deceptively quiet opening of the Cinna scene: the slender, red-haired figure in the dark suit, starched collar and neutral tie, emerging from the basement into a ring of light, whistling a little carefree air on his wistful way to death—

> I have no will to wander out of doors
> Yet something leads me on.

Then, suddenly, the crowd was upon him—singly at first, then in twos and threes, scuffling out of the surrounding darkness till they formed a ring around the bemused poet, moving in on him, pressing him with questions, not listening to his answers—"I am Cinna...Cinna the poet"—till, with a savage cry of "Tear him!" they swallowed him up in their idiotic, murderous frenzy.

They did it a dozen times till Lloyd and the exhausted mob were on the edge of madness. Orson used some of Blitzstein's rhythmic patterns, some of his own original staging and some of the things Norman Lloyd had patiently and obstinately worked out for himself. Forty-two hours before opening he and Orson suddenly stopped fighting each other: at four in the morning, on their seventh try, the scene began to work, getting tauter and more dangerous as the night wore on. At 5:30 we stopped and it was announced that the Cinna the Poet scene would be in the show for the matinée.

I slept in the theater that night on my day bed in the projection room. At 8 a.m. Jeannie and her crew were back, dismantling the speakers and hanging additional projectors high up on the downstage towers. The office switchboard opened at ten. Half an hour later I heard Judy Holliday's small voice announcing that a Mr. Brown was on the wire and that it seemed to be important.

John Mason Brown, to whom I had hardly spoken since the time we were both wooing Henrietta Bingham on lower Fifth Avenue twelve years before, had become drama critic of the *New York Post*, where he had established a reputation as one of the liveliest and best-informed of the men on the aisle. He was on the phone, now, with a troublesome request. Would I mind if he came to the matinée preview of *Julius Caesar*? Called out of town on an emergency, this would be his only chance to see the show and to review it himself rather than turn it over to his second-stringer. Torn between my fear of having the show judged prematurely and my reluctance to refuse an important and friendly critic, I had only one choice—to say yes. I told him we were still working on the show. He wished us luck. After some hesitation I told Orson; we decided not to tell anyone else.

The audience was already in its seats and the cast assembled in the darkened basement, in position for its first appearance on the streets of Rome, when George Coulouris announced in a voice loud enough to be heard by the entire front half of the orchestra that while he hated to be a Cassandra, it was his considered opinion that the show was a bust and would be closing on Saturday night. Since he was voicing an apprehension shared by a number of our cast, it may have been this sudden stab of fear that made such a difference to that afternoon's performance. Or, more likely, the show was primed and ready and in the presence of the right audience it burst into flame. Suddenly everything was right: individual performances, transitions, silences, progressions and climaxes—they all seemed to come together in a devastating whole.

At the end of the performance, John Mason Brown came down the aisle to where I was standing, listening to the audience as it filed out into the fading daylight. He took my hand and held it and made an unusual and unethical request. He asked to be taken backstage. Orson, sitting before his make-up table in his green military greatcoat, looked up in consternation as one of the country's leading drama critics burst into the dressing room and started to tell us such things about the production as we had not hoped to hear even in our wildest dreams. They appeared in print two days later: *Julius Caesar* was described "by all odds the most exciting, the most imaginative, the most topical, the most awesome and the most absorbing of the season's new productions. The touch of genius is upon it."

Of all the critics who later came to enthuse over *Julius Caesar*, Brown, in the first rush of his excitement, seemed to convey most vividly the look and sound of the production.

It is placed upon a bare stage, the brick walls of which are crimson and naked. That is all. And that is all that is needed. In its streamlined simplicity this set achieves the glorious, unimpeded freedom of an Elizabethan stage. It is a setting spacious enough for both the winds and victims of demagoguery to sweep across it like a hurricane...

In groupings that are of that fluid, stressful, virtuoso sort one usually has to journey to Russia to see, Mr. Welles proves himself a brilliant innovator in his deployment of his principals and the movement of his crowds...he keeps drumming the meaning of his play into our minds by the scuffling of his mobs when they prowl in the shadows, or by the herd-like thunder of their feet when they run as one threatening body. It is a memorable device. Like the setting in which it is used, it is pure theater; vibrant, unashamed and enormously effective.

We opened the next night and the following morning when I got to the theater there was a line in front of the single window of our small box office. That night we sold out and there were standees at the Saturday matinée and evening performances.

On the Monday following our opening George Zorn appeared in my office. He wished to speak to me alone: Welles was a lunatic but I was a reasonable fellow and I must listen to him. His tone was avuncular. Was I aware that *Julius Caesar* was the hottest ticket in town? With most of our cheap seats gone until January 1 and an orchestra floor of under 300 seats priced at the absurd figure of $2 (plus tax) we were in a situation that was calculated to drive any professional box-office man out of his mind with frustration and rage. To see half the tickets for the biggest hit of the season sold at an average price of a little over a dollar, while having to turn down dozens of sales of orchestra seats each day to brokers clamoring to pay five times that much under the table—this was idiotic to the point of criminality.

I asked what he would suggest. He told me: run *Julius Caesar* and cancel all other productions; burn all tickets already printed and not sold; between now and the end of December sell only to brokers; after that eliminate all cheap seats and sell the entire house for the standard Broadway price of $3 plus tax. As he spoke I could see his eyes gleaming with the vision of fawning brokers, their pockets stuffed with the green stuff and "ice" on the side for us all. What about our theater parties and student sales? To hell with them! Repertory? Screw repertory!

He supported his plea with figures. To recondition the theater and open *Julius Caesar* we had spent almost three times our entire capital. On the present basis, with every seat sold, our profit would amount to a bare $1500 a week. Thus it would take us three months to get back to solvency, without counting the expense of the second show. By following Zorn's suggestion, we could treble that weekly figure: by June 1 we would have $100,000 or more in the bank with which to present repertory and make art to our heart's content in the future.

Every word he said was true. It was also true that by going into a straight run of our current hit we would be breaking every promise made to our public and to the press. "Oh yeah?" said George. "And where would your 'public' be if you'd got lousy reviews?"

I talked to Welles and did some research of my own. From the press, personally and through Senber, I got the impression that they would be chagrined but not infuriated if we exploited a situation to which they themselves had contributed. As to the company—they had been assembled with a promise of repertory and, though a number of them might have been happy to do less work and enjoy their success, there was a strong feeling that by denying the promises made in our manifesto we would be betraying both them and the future of the Mercury. Our stockholders were divided: theatrically, they hated to see us abandon the repertory idea which had originally attracted them; practically, they would have been delighted to see us end the season with a substantial operating fund.

Neither Welles nor I was primarily interested in principles or in money. We thought of the Mercury as an instrument of artistic expression and a ladder to fame and power. To Orson, the prospect of coming to the theater nightly for seven months to play the part of Brutus was absolutely abhorrent, just as it was impossible for me to think of myself sitting in my projection booth day after day with no other activity than to administer the stable and lucrative routine of a successful Broadway run.

So we had supper at "21" and, over our second bottle of champagne, we prepared an announcement which was given to the press the next morning: the Mercury Theater was about to go into rehearsal not with one production but with two: *Shoemaker's Holiday* and a revival of *The Cradle Will Rock*.

* * *

So began the halcyon days of the Mercury: rehearsing by day, playing nightly to packed and enthusiastic houses, with enough cash coming in from the lines that wound daily around our small pearl-gray lobby under the crystal chandelier to take care of our current payrolls and accumulated bills and debts. From the stage to the boiler room, a general euphoria pervaded the Mercury during those first few months of our operation.

Our actors had everything to make them happy: they had received great collective and individual reviews: their future was assured for months to come; they were at work on two new shows. Zorn, in his box office, was happy: while personal profits were not all that could be expected from a Broadway smash hit, it was a continuing delight to be dealing all day with a line of humble customers and eager brokers.

This high state of morale extended to the meanest members of the Mercury personnel. Our house staff was touching in its devotion. Joe, the engineer, could barely speak English but he kept our furnace going and our toilets flowing throughout the winter. (He went so far as to steal hot air for us through a subterranean pipe which he somehow connected to the heating system of the bank across the street.) And, for what may have been the first time in Broadway theatrical history, the cop on our beat refused the weekly tribute normally exacted for keeping the street clear of traffic at theater time.

This same dedication was evident among the flock of volunteers (mostly young women) who descended upon us. Some were from progressive schools like Bennington which encouraged professional apprenticeship among their advanced students; others were graduates or fugitives from the drama departments of major universities. We exploited them without scruple. They did everything from bringing in coffee, running errands, distributing leaflets, pressing and repairing costumes, to holding book, cueing actors and, in some cases, performing essential technical services under Jean Rosenthal. They also had one special, rather curious but absolutely essential duty to perform.

The Mercury Theater did not have the underground splendors we had known at the Maxine Elliott. Our gents' and ladies' toilets, both located in the basement, were not fully insulated from the auditorium. Several times, at previews, a loud flushing was heard during our most tense and pregnant silences. The staff was rigorously forbidden to use the johns during performances but, since *Julius Caesar* ran for an hour and 49 minutes without intermission, there was a small, constant stream of anguished customers tiptoeing down to the basement. We tried locking the toilets, but this provoked such protests that we quickly opened them up again as the law required. We finally solved the problem by having a well-spoken girl posted at the foot of each staircase who would explain the situation as charmingly as she could, then admit the customers to the johns only during scenes so noisy that their flushing was lost in the roar of human voices or the deep vibrating chords of the Hammond organ and thunder drum.

This state of euphoria did not extend to the "extras" who constituted our crowd in *Julius Caesar*. They were a tough, energetic, quick-witted gang—a cantankerous and independent but passionately dedicated group. Their working conditions were appalling. They shared the black hole below the stage with the rats; during rehearsals they were on call for as many as sixteen hours at a stretch and, except after midnight or when Orson felt it necessary to buy their cooperation with a treat of ice cream or sandwiches, no food was provided for them. For all this they received the munificent sum of $1 per performance.

Three weeks after the opening of *Julius Caesar* the extras requested a conference. Through their spokesman, Jack Berry, they reaffirmed their devotion to the Mercury but they wanted me to know that they could not keep alive on what we paid them. I asked them to wait a few weeks. They repeated that they were hungry. I said I would think it over. When they left I felt I had the situation well in hand. Then, a moment later, Zorn came running upstairs and told me they had left the theater in a body and were on their way over to complain to their union, Actors' Equity.

The intervention of Equity was the last thing I wanted in our unorthodox affairs. I dispatched one messenger, then another, to intercept them and coax them back to the theater. Finally I pursued them into Times Square. I reproached them for their treachery and lack of faith. That made them laugh, for in that moment they knew that they had won. I asked them what they considered a living wage. They said $15 a week. I said OK—even if it broke us. That made them laugh again and the mutiny was over.

In our manifesto we had made much of our intention to present new plays on the Mercury stage on Sunday nights. By announcing *The*

Cradle Will Rock as the first offering of this so-called Worklight Theater we hoped to kill two birds with one stone—to get our experimental series started and to reaffirm our rights to Blitzstein's work, for which Marc was receiving other offers. It was not a difficult piece to put on; many of our Venice stalwarts were available and enthusiastic. Marc Blitzstein conducted rehearsals; he also continued to thomp his eviscerated piano, narrate and play a number of lesser parts.

We opened *The Cradle* in our own Mercury Theater on a Sunday night for a *New Theatre* audience and the press. We had made front-page news during the summer but we had not been covered by the drama critics of the New York press. This was now remedied:

The best thing militant labor has put into the theater yet...An exciting and savagely humorous social cartoon with music that hits hard and sardonically...It must be put down as one of the most interesting dramatic events of the season.

Following the reviews, both Blitzstein and the Mercury received offers—from labor organizations anxious to have the show run all over the country and from commercial producers eager to present it on Broadway. Marc himself was of two minds. He wanted to be a labor hero but, after so many years of hardship, he was not averse to the benefits of a Broadway run. Nor were we.

We made a deal with a dubious producer who, out of his huge profits on *Tobacco Road*, had acquired the old 48th Street Theater which he had rechristened the Windsor. We opened there in the first week of January but *The Cradle* never seemed as satisfying and dynamic at the Windsor as it had in the shabby vastness of the Venice or in the intimacy of the Mercury. It ran for fourteen weeks, but we made very little out of it and I always felt that there was something incongruous about its simplistic staging and radical sentiments in the garish luxury of a renovated Broadway playhouse.

* * *

We were deep by now into preparations for the Mercury's second production. On his return from his retreat in New Hampshire, Orson had brought back with him, besides the final text and designs for *Julius Caesar*, an edited version of Dekker's *Shoemaker's Holiday* with which we had all fallen in love. Dekker's Elizabethan domestic comedy was the perfect companion to the political melodrama of *Julius Caesar*: gay, colorful and democratic, it had a charming, nonsensical musical-comedy plot, some unusual social comment and more bawdry than Broadway was accustomed to seeing outside of burlesque houses.

We had known we would have to add to the company as the

repertory increased but *Shoemaker* called for more than we anticipated. We ended with seven additions to our weekly payroll. Among them, playing Simon Eyre, the merry shoemaker, later Lord Mayor of London, was Whitford Kane, formerly of the Abbey Theatre in Dublin; to play the philandering Master Hammond, we invited Vincent Price, who had just finished playing Prince Albert opposite Helen Hayes in *Victoria Regina*; Sybil, the busy maid, was Edith Barrett, of the great acting family of that name. (She and Vincent Price met at rehearsal and had their wedding party on our stage.)

Once again the set design was Orson's, executed by Samuel Leve under Jean's supervision. Thanks to their joint ingenuity it was possible, by rotating the whole central section of the *Caesar* platform, to give the stage an entirely new shape with a minimum of movement and expense. The set itself suggested the stylized configuration of a sixteenth-century city: from materials that were intentionally plain and rough—natural wood, burlap and unpainted strips from used orange crates—they managed to create a stage picture that struck one observer as "one third Elizabethan, one third Italian deep perspective and one third workable nonsense."

A high burlap cyclorama encircled the three framed inner stages, side by side, each shut off by burlap curtains. The central one, when its curtain was open, represented London street about ten feet wide running uphill and upstage between tall wooden houses in false perspective. The side stages were smaller; one was the interior of the Guildhall, the other Simon Eyre's shop where he and his journeymen plied their trade and exchanged their earthy jokes. The whole thing had a feeling of lightness, simplicity, gaiety and style, "very much in the tradition of Palladio's theater at Vicenza."

Our costumes, designed by Millia Davenport (my neighbor in New City) were in solid, bright colors and plain materials—wool, jersey and felt rather than silk and brocade. More interested in men's than in women's costumes, she was assiduous in her measuring of male crotches, and her codpieces (carefully tailored and personally adjusted) were among the more striking items of this generally lusty production. Music was by another member of the family—Lehman Engel, who had conducted the orchestra and chorus for *The Cradle*.

By mid-December these various elements had been brought together without too much difficulty or pain and we were ready for technical rehearsals. This was one production in which there was to be no dramatic lighting—just general illumination with minor variations as the action moved from day to night and from one part of the stage to another. Without the agony of all-night lighting sessions, there was a relaxed air of confidence and affection about the whole production that was unlike anything I had experienced with my protean partner.

On Christmas Day we gave our usual sold-out evening performance of *Julius Caesar*. After the bravos that greeted the final call, Orson stepped forward and, dropping his solemn Brutus manner, announced that, in honor of the festive season, the Mercury was offering a small Christmas gift to its customers: at midnight we would give the first preview of our next production—*The Shoemaker's Holiday* (applause and cheers) which they were all invited to attend (more applause, whistles and cheers). Since it would take about an hour and a half to make the scenic changeover, members of the audience were given the choice of going out and refreshing themselves and returning, with friends if they wished, on a first-come, first-served basis; or, if they preferred, since we used no house curtain, they could remain in their seats and watch the crew changing sets. About half the audience remained in the house and watched the city of London take form while the actors and extras, in their dressing rooms, between hot dogs and hamburgers, were changing from the drab greens and faded black of contemporary Rome into the bright, padded costumes of Elizabethan England. At 11:45, with the new set in place and Jean calling for her opening light cue, it was discovered that our two electricians, who had gone out for a quick yuletide celebration, had not returned. They were found, after a frantic search of the neighboring bars, walking up Sixth Avenue in the wrong direction. Hustled back to the theater, hoisted onto their platform and plied with cartons of black coffee, they applied themselves to their switchboards under Jeannie's watchful eye.

At midnight exactly, with a fanfare by Lehman Engel, while George Zorn tried to cope with the two or three hundred extra persons who had poured in at the last moment from Times Square, we began our first public performance of *The Shoemaker's Holiday*. Thrilled but rattled, at first, by unexpected waves of laughter and applause, the company soon settled down and went on to surpass itself. By 1:16 a.m. it was over and, as the theater slowly emptied into 41st Street for the second time that night, we knew we had another hit.

Jacques Haussmann. (Braïla, Rumania, 1906)

May Davies Haussmann— 'a beautiful Mama in a beautiful hat that actually had three storeys.' (Paris, 1909)

Georges Haussmann and family on a wartime mission to the United States for the French Government. (Niagara Falls, 1916)

J. H. (London, 1922)

Zita Johann and Clark Gable in
their joint Broadway debut.
(September, 1928)

J. H. and Zita Johann before
their marriage. (Hollywood,
1929)

'St. Virgil,' painted by Florine Stettheimer during her conception of *Four Saints in Three Acts*.

Macbeth's Castle: the Court Ball following the murder of Banquo.

Opening night at the Lafayette.
(April 14, 1937)

Hamlet (Act I, Scene 3)—Leslie
Howard on the battlements,
with Joseph Holland (Horatio)
and Edward Ballantyne, who
also played Marcellus with
John Barrymore.

Orson Welles as Doctor
Faustus.

Horse Eats Hat—Sidney Smith
as the Hussar, Paula Lawrence
as the Wife, Edwin Denby
inside the Horse and Joseph
Cotten as the desperate
Bridegroom. (1937, WPA
Project #891)

J. H., Pavel Tchelitchev, Aline McMahon and Orson Welles before the first reading of *The Duchess of Malfi*.

Mina Curtiss and her brother Lincoln Kirstein.

John Houseman and Marc
Blitzstein in conference.

The Cradle Will Rock ('oratorio'
version)—Peggy Coudray
(Mrs. Mister) and John
Hoyradt (Daubwer) with Marc
Blitzstein at the eviscerated
piano.

Julius Caesar—Norman Lloyd (right) as Cinna the Poet, with Joseph Cotten, Ross Elliot and the Mercury's three stage managers: Richard Wilson, Walter Ash and William Alland (alias Vakhtangov). (1937)

Heartbreak House, The Mercury. Left to right, Brenda Forbes, Eustace Wyatt, Orson Welles, Mady Christians, John Hoyradt, Phyllis Joyce, Vincent Price, Geraldine Fitzgerald, Erskine Sanford and George Coulouris.

Danton's Death, The Mercury.
Saint-Just and Fouquier (Orson
Welles and Eustace Wyatt.)

Five Kings—The revolving
stage in its first position:
London Street with Palace
Exterior (left) and Boar's Head
Tavern (right).

Falstaff and Prince Hal (Orson
Welles and Burgess Meredith).

J. H. and Jean Rosenthal in
their habitual position.

CBS Studio One with sound
equipment in the foreground.
Orson Welles, age 19, second
from right.

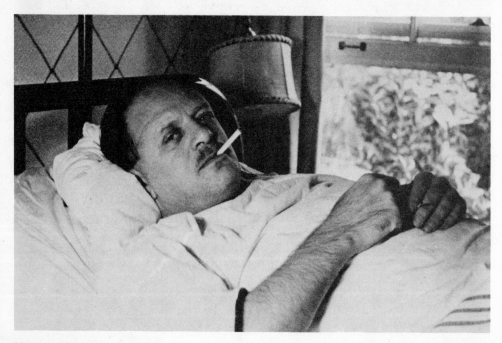

Herman Mankiewicz during
the writing of *Citizen Kane*.
(Victorville, April 1940)

VII
Mercury
1938

The Mercury came into being in mid-Depression at a time when "subsidy" and "deficit" were obscure and dirty words in the theater. Too late for individual millionaires' capricious benefactions (like those of the late Otto Kahn), too early for the calculated munificence of the foundations, we had to rely on our wits to survive. Having wrung a few thousand dollars from our friends to get us floated and having reaffirmed our determination to remain a repertory theater, we were left to sink or swim in the rough seas of the profit system.

Within a few weeks of our *Julius Caesar* opening we had been approached by a number of Broadway managements, all excited by the idea of a smash hit with no scenery and all eager to help us milk our surprise success in a large Broadway house at advanced prices. I refused all such temptations. At the same time I could not ignore the fact, of which Zorn frequently reminded me, that under the glitter of our new fame, we were headed for bankruptcy. Our advance sales continued heavy and, by supplying us with a continuous flow of ready cash, obscured the real danger of our situation. The cost of the *Shoemaker* production, though modest by Broadway standards, had absorbed the few thousand dollars of income we had made since the opening of *Julius Caesar*. Our weekly gross was limited by the size of our theater; our expenses were not. Our maximum intake at the Mercury, with every seat sold, was just under $6000 a week. Our weekly cost including rentals, promotion, house staff, stage crew and acting company (which, with *Shoemaker* in the repertory, numbered over fifty) came close to $7000. With two smash hits in our theater, the Mercury was going deeper into debt with each passing week.

To correct this absurd situation I came up with what seemed like a brilliant idea: to move the entire Mercury repertory two blocks west for a couple of months into the much larger National Theater. Since its orchestra floor was more than twice as big as the Mercury's we would finally be able to satisfy the carriage trade's clamor for our higher-priced seats; and it would permit us to sell theater parties and students' group tickets to our hearts' content. At a conservative estimate we could not fail to come out several thousand dollars a week ahead; in ten weeks we could accumulate enough to pay for our new productions and carry us through to the end of the theatrical year.

As soon as this idea became known, it was violently opposed by a minority of the company headed by Hiram Sherman. They felt we were making a fatal mistake in abandoning our home so soon after occupying it and that, in attempting to increase our audience, we were, in fact, dissipating it. We were a repertory theatre, they argued. The more people we turned away the longer we would be able to keep *Caesar* and *Shoemaker* running. And if it meant carrying them over into our second year, so much the better: it would be a protection for a season that might not be as lucky or successful as the first.

These were sound arguments and I had already made them all to myself. In the circumstances I had no choice but to override them. However, since I was well aware of the dangers of the move and anxious to avoid the charge that we were getting too big for our boots, I insisted that we retain our Mercury price scale, including our much advertised 50-cent seats. Against all Broadway precedent I made them "split" their orchestra floor: the 300 best seats in the house would sell at the regular Broadway price of $3.30 while the rest of the orchestra and the mezzanine would still be available at our original Mercury price.

On January 24, 1938 we moved our repertory to the National. After rehearsing all weekend to adapt our productions to its larger stage and auditorium, we opened with *Julius Caesar*, followed two nights later by *The Shoemaker's Holiday*.

Gypsies that we were, we soon adjusted to our new home. We may have missed the shabby familiarity of our Mercury surroundings but, in most ways, life was easier at the National. Orson occupied the star dressing room, which he also used as his office. After their sheer three-story cell block, the company's new dressing rooms seemed accessible and comfortable. The extras still dressed in the basement, which was warm, well-lit and ratless. For myself an agreeable room was found at the rear of the orchestra floor with a French window opening onto the long, curving alley that led from the stage door to 41st Street. The mounted policeman on the beat had a horse which regarded this area as its own private domain and spent hours at the glass door spying on my activities.

Business was excellent from the start. So, after their initial doubts, was the company's morale. Little by little, as the weeks went by, the specter of bankruptcy began to recede. And, in my relationship with Orson, this was a period of relative peace and affection. We had been far too busy, since the opening of *Julius Caesar*, to indulge in those spasms of hostility which so often followed the success of our projects. Tension continued (our relationship would have been unthinkable without it), but during that winter there were few of those ugly, neurotic scenes that had marked the period of our anxious beginnings and were to become increasingly frequent in the years ahead.

Though life was peaceful at the National, it was by no means uneventful. There was, for instance, the incident of the flood. We had in the company a boy of thirteen, gangling, with a long neck and prominent Adam's apple, curly hair and a nice smile. As a successful child actor on radio, he had long contributed to the support of his widowed mother. He played a Cheapside urchin in *Shoemaker*, but his main contribution was in *Julius Caesar*, in which he played the role of Brutus's page, Lucius, first in the orchard scene, then, later, in the tent before Philippi where he sang his troubled master to sleep. It was a lovely lyric interlude—a last moment of peace before the final catastrophe.

On matinée days, between his two appearances in *Caesar*, he had a long, tedious wait and it was here that he and the Mercury ran into trouble. Our first intimation that all was not well came when a chronic shortage of light bulbs was reported in the third-floor dressing rooms. The reason was soon discovered. Our boy, having played his orchard scene and finished his homework, had been conducting experiments to discover the shock-resistant powers of electric light bulbs: he had been hurling them out of his dressing-room window against the bricks of the opposite wall and comparing the different kinds of pops they made. He was ordered to desist and, being an obedient boy, he did. Instead, he started a series of new experiments: standing on his dressing-room chair one Wednesday afternoon with a box of matches in his hand, he began testing the melting point of the little copper tongues located beneath each sprinkler valve.

Two floors below, on stage, Brutus had just ascended the pulpit above the body of Caesar and was urging the crowd below to "be patient to the last." At that moment, unperceived by the audience, a few drops of rain began to fall. Intent upon the action of the play, assuming it was some kind of leak in the roof above the grid, Orson continued to address the crowd in a measured, reasonable tone:

If there be in this assembly any dear friend of Caesar, to him I say that Brutus' love to Caesar was no less than his. If then that friend demand why Brutus rose against Caesar, this is my answer...

His answer was never heard, for at that moment, what had been an accelerating drizzle turned to a heavy shower and then, within a few seconds, into a deluge of tropical rain. Brutus paused, looked up into the fly floor, glared questioningly into the wings, then turned back, as clouds of water began to envelop him and, in the sincere tones of the noble Brutus, urged the audience to remain in their seats and not to be alarmed. As the asbestos curtain began to fall and half the stage lights went out, he was seen running for shelter with the rest of the Roman citizenry through a solid sheet of falling water, while blasts of blue fire and showers of sparks flashed around them from the short-circuiting dimmer boards.

Alerted by the ringing of the fire bell, I rushed through the door that led backstage just in time to see our crew struggling with the handle that shut off the sprinkler system. Assured that there was no fire, I ran back (while others calmed the audience) to cancel the automatic call to the fire department. While I was dialing, I looked up and saw the mounted policeman galloping along the alley towards the stage door.

One minute later a pale, very frightened youth was brought into my office under guard. Appalled at the enormity of what he had done, his first instinct, when the water began to spout, had been to escape. Halfway down the alley he thought of his mother, stopped, trotted back to the stage door, slipped a coin into the pay phone and was whispering, "Hey, Mom, I'll be home early," when he was seized.

As soon as he realized he was not going to jail, he became quite calm. He was sorry for what he had done. He had $184.82 in his personal savings account which he was placing at our disposal to pay for any damage he might have caused. I ordered him back to his dressing room, still under guard, to await his cue for the last scene. He asked if he might call his mother again and I said yes.

Meantime, on stage, the crew had replaced the fuses and mopped the stage floor and platforms. Ten minutes later I stepped out from under the rising asbestos and assured the audience that the show would resume where it had left off. There was a moment of darkness and a roar from the Hammond organ. Then, as the lights dimmed up, Brutus, his hair slicked down as after a bath, his dark suit clinging damply to his body, was seen climbing slowly back into the pulpit above the drenched Roman mob. "Be patient to the last," he began—to loud applause.

On that same stage, some weeks later, a less comic incident occurred. The conspirators, when they attacked Caesar in the Senate, did so with heavy rubber daggers with aluminum-painted blades which they jabbed savagely from various angles into the dictator's dark-green coat. All except Brutus. Feeling that his final confrontation with the tyrant needed the reality of a gleaming blade, Orson used a bright steel hunting knife to deliver the decisive blow. For more than fifty performances he had held its sharp point against the cloth that covered Joseph Holland's chest; then, as Caesar clung to him in his death agony, he masked the final thrust with a turn of his body.

One spring night, without either of them being aware of it, the blade went through the cloth and slipped quite painlessly into Joe Holland's chest and through an artery in the region of his heart. As Caesar fell at Brutus's feet the conspirators surrounded him. When they scattered again after the oath one of them was seen to slip, recover himself and glance down, with a sudden look of apprehension, at the inert body of the dead dictator. This curious behavior was repeated during the scene with Marc Antony, which seemed to play faster and more nervously that night than usual. In the blackout that followed, amid the thunderous organ roar that followed Antony's "Cry havoc and let slip the dogs of war!," members of the cast carried Joe Holland's inert body directly out of the stage door and to the nearest hospital. He left behind him on the platform several pints of blood which, being roughly the same color as the stage floor, was not clearly visible from the front, but caused considerable inconvenience and dismay among the mob as it milled around the base of the pulpit. By the time the Cinna scene was over it had been pretty well spread around and was beginning to dry.

Joseph Holland was in a state of shock when he arrived at the hospital; he received transfusions and remained in bed for several days. He was admired and blamed for lying quite still for almost fifteen minutes while bleeding to death: but, in evaluating his heroism, it must be remembered that the incision was quite painless and that neither he nor Welles nor anyone else was aware of what had happened. Orson had a short, violent spasm of guilt. Then, when he learned that his victim was not in danger, he developed an angry conviction that the blame was Joe's for making a wrong move and impaling himself on Brutus's stationary blade. We paid Joe's hospital bills and he never sued us.

Our sojourn at the National was nearing its end when I received a surprise visit, one afternoon, from an unbelievably lovely young woman with dark-red Irish hair, who arrived unannounced and claimed she had been sent by Orson's former associates at the Gate Theater. Her name was Geraldine Fitzgerald. Stunned by her beauty, I asked her questions about her experience in the theater, to which she gave lying answers. Then, still bemused, I led her to Orson's dressing room and left them together to talk about Dublin. An hour later he confirmed what I already knew—that we had found the ingénue for George Bernard Shaw's *Heartbreak House*.

(Mr. Shaw's royalty terms, which were stiff, reached us in mid-April. With them came a typed note, signed GBS in ink: "You would do well to have New York City printed under your street address. My eye was caught by the word Pennsylvania and I sent the envelope to that address. Needless to say it was returned here marked 'Unknown.'" By that time we were in rehearsal, Orson's daughter Christopher had been born and we had moved back into our own theater.)

It had been decided, after much debate, that, before *Heartbreak House* opened, *Shoemaker's Holiday* would be temporarily dropped from the repertory and saved for the following season. *Caesar* was still selling out and could be counted on to carry the repertory until the hot weather forced us to close.

We were in love with *Heartbreak House* but we knew the risks it entailed. Determined to avoid the stigma of "stock" casting, we found ourselves seeking actors, once again, from the outside. Of the ten characters in the play only five, including Orson, were from our own company. The rest, four of them ladies, formed an exotic group—a far cry from the austerity of our *Julius Caesar* casting six months before. Orson, with pounds of putty and clouds of white hair all over his face, played the octogenarian Captain Shotover. And it was in this make-up, with a huge beak of a nose against a pale blue sky, that he appeared on the cover of *Time* over the caption *"From Shadow to Shakespeare, Shoemaker to Shaw,"* accompanied by a five-page story headed MARVELOUS BOY.

It was a long, flashy piece, full of *Time*'s stylistic tricks and special angles—"troubled by his asthma, not troubled by his flat feet"; "with a voice that booms like Big Ben but a laugh like a youngster's giggle"—and it was the first to give national circulation to the legends of Welles's gargantuan childhood and puberty. For the Mercury it marked the peak of the year's publicity and, if there was a note of warning in its concluding phrase—

The brightest moon that has risen over Broadway in years, Welles should feel at home in the sky, for the sky is the only limit to his ambition—

I was too exhilarated to heed it.

The *Time* cover story was timed to coincide with the opening of *Heartbreak House* which made me nervous for two reasons: first, the probability of a critical backlash after so much extravagant praise and excessive publicity; second, the nature of the production. With the performance of a very talky and quite realistic piece by a contemporary author we could not expect the explosions of enthusiasm that had greeted *Caesar* and *Shoemaker*. The best we could hope for were respectful reviews for a controversial play. And that is precisely what we got.

Heartbreak House played in repertory with *Julius Caesar* to satisfactory business. Still, summer was upon us: the Mercury was not air-conditioned and everyone was getting tired. We announced June 11 as a closing date for our first Mercury season.

We parted with all the customary sentimentalities, wishing each other a happy summer and looking forward to a reunion within a few weeks. Our closing was marked by renewed encomiums in the press:

The biggest Broadway news for 1937-38 was the Mercury Theater...To one new and adventurous group, the Mercury Theater, has gone the lion's share of the year's success...The liveliness that has marked the Mercury's race through the year may well be taken as the chief characteristic of New York's 1937-38 season.

* * *

Our books were atrociously kept, but certain facts were quite evident. With our fantastic record of four hits out of four, we had managed, with our taxes and bills still to be paid, to end the year with rather less than half of what we started with. With those few thousand dollars and a modest line of credit, I had to try and keep our organization alive through the fallow months of summer, pay our rents and finance the production of our second season—at which time the rat race would begin again, with much expected of us and the odds heavy against our repeating our recent ratio of success.

Having accepted the situation as an inevitable fact of theatrical life, I tried to plan our 1938-39 season in what seemed a practical and economical way. To keep our theater alight and maintain our identity as a repertory company, we had devised an elegant but economical production of *The Importance of Being Earnest*. It was a perfect vehicle for our small theater and for Chubby Sherman, Vincent Price and Brenda Forbes to follow up their success of the previous season. In repertory with *Shoemaker* this would keep the Mercury in profits and public favor while we concentrated on the serious work of the season—the monster know as *Five Kings*. This was a stupendous

conception of Orson's—a compressed and edited verson of all but two
of Shakespeare's historical plays to be performed on two successive
evenings. Orson predicted—when he first announced it on the 374th
anniversary of Shakespeare's birth—that it would be an unforgettable
theatrical experience.

The performance of Shakespeare's historical plays in series has
become a commonplace of theatrical showmanship. In 1938 it was a
bold and original notion. It germinated in Orson's mind as a
hybrid—by *Caesar* out of *Shoemaker*—but secretly, I always believed, as
a means of dealing a crushing blow to that English upstart Maurice
Evans, Welles's only serious local competitor in the classical field, who
had had the effrontery to follow his much acclaimed *Richard II* with a
successful Falstaff—a part which Orson regarded (as he did every great
classical role) as exclusively his own. *Five Kings*, by its sheer
magnitude, would reduce Mr. Evans once and for all to his true pygmy
stature.

For the creation of this colossus I had made what I felt to be a
valuable alliance with the Theater Guild, which would alleviate our
financial burden and give Orson the time he needed to prepare such a
massive and complicated work.

Satisfied with my arrangements, I drove into the Berkshires for a
few days of peace. The water in the Baptist's Hole was dark brown and
cool and there were wild strawberries in the woods. On the third
morning, quite early, the phone rang: it was Augusta, our secretary,
who asked me in a rather shaky voice if I had seen the *New York Times*.
She then read me the lead item in the theater column in which it was
announced that Hiram Sherman had signed to star in a new revue due
to open in September at the Music Box Theater under the direction of
George Kaufman.

I accepted this grim news as true the moment I heard it and I did
not, then or later, call Sherman to verify it or to try and persuade him
to change his mind. As I drove with a sinking heart between the
turning tobacco fields and then down through Danbury and across the
Bear Mountain Bridge towards Sneden's Landing, where Orson and
Virginia were spending the summer, I found myself weighing the
implications of his defection and trying to find an explanation for it.

Chubby Sherman had come to occupy a very special place with the
Mercury. Outside of Welles himself, his had been the outstanding
personal success of the season. From our triumphal confusion he had
emerged not only as our most versatile and valuable actor but also as
the conscience of the company and the mainstay of its morale. Most
important of all, he was Orson's oldest and closest friend.

He was fully aware of our plans: he knew what his sudden leaving would do to the Mercury. Yet he must have been negotiating for days, even weeks, without saying a word to either of us. I began to question my judgment of our entire situation. In my anxiety to keep the Mercury afloat, had I misjudged the state of the company? It had seemed to me that morale was high. There was some resentment, I knew, at Welles's increasingly overbearing ways and some irritation over my arbitrary manipulation of the repertory, of which the premature closing of *Shoemaker* was one example. Had I underestimated these murmurings? Was Sherman's departure a manifestation of this discontent? In his passionate devotion to the idea of a collective repertory company, had he, like Cassius, begun to wonder upon what meat his former friend was feeding that he was grown so great?

Later, another much simpler explanation suggested itself: for Sherman, as for so many of those who, at one time or another, worked with Orson and left him, the pace had become so wild, the mood so intense and violent as to be physically and mentally unendurable. Was Chubby, with his low threshold of fatigue and pain, merely the first of those who could not bear to stay around?

When I got to Sneden's Landing I found Orson lying limp and huge in a darkened room with his face to the wall. To him, Sherman's action was quite simply one of personal, malignant treachery: he was a Judas who could not forgive his master for having chosen him, an Iago jealous of his general's nobility. All that Orson could see in Chubby's desertion was yet another proof that, in the circle of his collaborators and intimates, there was not one who loved him, none he could trust, no one who was not waiting to stab him the moment his back was turned.

Some of this despair was histrionic, but coming, as it did, at a turning point in Welles's personal life, Sherman's perfidy hit him with exaggerated force. For the Mercury it marked the great divide between our halcyon days and the hurricane weather that followed. With Sherman gone, all plans for *The Importance of Being Earnest* had to be abandoned. Locked in his room, Orson refused to discuss the future. I spent two days in the theater cancelling our commitments before I started back to Sneden's.

I did not reach Rockland County. I was over the bridge, driving along 9W, coming down the long hill that leads down into the village of Palisades, when I saw an oversized black limousine coming up the hill at high speed. As it approached, it began to sound its horn and I became aware of Orson's huge face sticking out of the window with its mouth wide open and of his gigantic voice echoing through the surrounding woods. I parked my Ford by the roadside and got into the limousine, which rushed on towards New York. Sherman was forgotten. Crossing the Washington Bridge and driving down Riverside Drive, Orson explained that we were on our way to the Columbia Broadcasting System on Madison Avenue, where he was about to receive a phenomenal offer—an hour's dramatic radio show once a week for ten weeks on which he could do anything he pleased.

I knew almost nothing about radio and did not listen regularly except to news. But I had listened the previous summer when Orson had done a four-part dramatization of Victor Hugo's *Les Miserables*, which he wrote and directed besides playing the part of the unfortunate Jean Valjean.

I now sat in, as his partner, on his conferences at CBS, trying to look knowledgeable but understanding little of what was said. This much I gathered: the show was to be an hour long and broadcast nationally on Monday evenings; Orson was to have a free hand in the choice of material but would favor adventure—preferably familiar material in the public domain. It was intended as a prestige show of general appeal. The network's formula (all continuing radio shows had a formula) was that each of these stories would be introduced and narrated by Orson in the first person, while he also played the leading character. Under the title *First Person Singular* it was to be his show in every sense of the word: "Written, directed, produced and performed by Orson Welles."

The show was to go on the air on July 11, in less than two weeks' time. Since this didn't seem to bother Orson, I kept my mouth shut until we were sitting in "21" two hours later celebrating the deal. Orson said it would be a tight squeeze but we could make it; he seemed to assume that I would be working with him. I reminded him that I knew less than nothing about radio. He said I'd better start learning.

Our first move, naturally, after the show had been announced, was to issue a manifesto in the *New York Times*:

The Mercury has no intention of reproducing its stage repertoire in these broadcasts. Instead, we plan to bring to radio the experimental techniques that have proven so successful in another medium and to treat radio itself with the intelligence and respect such a beautiful and powerful medium deserves.

After that, I set to work to master the rudiments of a new art.

* * *

I came to radio during its short golden age, after it had been fully developed technically and before the advertisers and their agencies finally took it over and corrupted it. It was a brief period—three or four years in all—during which American radio drama created its own original forms and styles. Working in the single dimension of sound, it became a highly effective narrative medium which allowed full scope to the listener's imagination. In its time, it produced a number of valuable shows and a handful of creative directors of whom Orson was one. All these men worked at high intensity and breakneck speed—as though eager to get the most out of their new medium before it was snatched out of their hands.

Next in importance after the director (and the engineer) was the radio actor. Here the medium called for a special kind of proficiency— a capacity for sight reading and instantaneous interpretation that brought to those who possessed it an income surpassed only by that of the highest-paid movie stars. Much of the successful radio actor's time was spent "bicycling" from one studio to another. On routine shows and serials this led to curious abuses: if the actor was wanted badly enough, he was permitted to arrive just in time for a single reading before going on the air. For *The Shadow*, in which Welles played the name part for a couple of years, he would be delivered in a taxi by one of his slaves barely in time for the dress rehearsal. Having no idea what the episode was about he would sometimes, in the middle of a show, have to change his whole attitude to meet some basic situation of which he had been unaware when he started.

Welles was a high-ranking member of this elite band. With a vocal instrument of abnormal resonance and flexibility, uninhibited by that neurotic preoccupation with his own physical appearance that affected his stage performances, he was capable of expressing an almost unlimited range of moods and emotions. According to a colleague who had no reason to love him, "Welles raised the whole standard of radio acting. He carried the rest of the cast along with him and forced them through emulation to come up to his own level of intensity and color."

By agreement with the network, the first show of our series was to be *Treasure Island*, in which Orson, as narrator, would impersonate the boy-hero grown up and, of course, the villainous Long John Silver. I spent several days holed up in my one-room apartment on 61st Street going through the book, marking it up, trying to reduce it—with scissors, paste pot and pencil—to a reasonable length. It was still nothing like a radio show. Orson would drop in, between visits to the internationally famous ballerina with whom he was falling in love that summer, to see what I was doing and make rearrangements and changes. Then, less than a week before air time, he came in one afternoon to announce that our plans were all changed. Instead of *Treasure Island* we were going to open with *Dracula*, to which we had just obtained the rights—not the corrupt movie version but the original Bram Stoker novel in its full Gothic horror.

While I sent out for six copies of the book, Orson stayed long enough to describe his favorite scenes and departed. The next afternoon, two days before the start of rehearsal, he returned and we started to go over what I had done. Around eight, taking two copies of the book, several pads of lined paper, a pair of scissors, a handful of pencils and a paste pot, we moved over to Reuben's Restaurant two blocks away on 59th Street. While we worked we dined and then remained working after the table had been cleared—except for constantly renewed cups of coffee and cognac. By 10:30 we had got through the first section: the Count had just been observed crawling, batlike, down the sheer walls of his ancestral castle. Occasionally, an acquaintance passed by, paused for conversation and, receiving no encouragement, moved on.

As the after-theater crowd began to arrive, we left the Carpathian Mountains, with Count Dracula in a catatonic condition, safely nailed in his coffin of polluted earth and on his way, in a drifting abandoned coal scow, to England. By this time there was a pile of paste-stiffened paper on the edge of the table. Augusta was summoned from her bed to bring money. After she had left, with orders to start typing in the morning, we resumed work. I do not know if it was the sight and smell of food being devoured all around us or whether we were affected by the Count's desperate thirst for blood, but some time after midnight we ordered a whole new meal of our own—large steaks, very rare, followed by cheesecake and more coffee and brandy.

By 3 a.m. the place was empty again, but we did not notice it. We were now with the fly-eating lunatic in his Broadmoor cell, following his rising agitation during the great storm which drove the scow and its mysterious cargo of East European earth ashore on a deserted corner of the Cornish coast, where the Count, in the guise of a large gray wolf, leaped ashore and vanished into the woods.

It was Reuben's long-standing boast that it never closed. That night we were able to verify that claim. We saw the midsummer dawn come up over 49th Street and continued our work, turning out gluey pages by the dozen and covering them with pencilled zigzags, arrows and balloons as we moved relentlessly towards our climax. By now the last of the late revellers and scrambled-egg eaters had departed. Between 6 and 7 a.m. a team of cleaning women appeared with pails, mops and brooms. They worked around us, swabbing and scouring the floor under our feet. When they had gone we consumed eggs, bacon and a double order of kippered herring with coffee and orange juice. Then, just before eight, as a few early birds appeared for breakfast and the streets outside came to life, we nailed down the Count, with a burnt stake through his heart, and rose from our table. Three days later Dracula went on the air as the opener of what was to become a legendary radio series.

It was a pleasant surprise to find that, for our musical accompaniment, we were to have the CBS Symphony Orchestra, under Bernard Herrmann. Benny was the golden boy of music around CBS; egotistical, contentious, devoted and enormously well read, he managed, then and later, to combine a serious musical career with work for the mass media.

He and Orson had a long, tempestuous but productive relationship that culminated two and a half years later, in the score of *Citizen Kane*. Amid screaming rows, snapping of batons, accusations of sabotage and hurling of scripts and scores into the air and at each other, they understood each other perfectly. More music was used by the Mercury show than by any other dramatic show on the air: out of 57 minutes of playing time it was not unusual to have 30 to 40 minutes of music.

According to Herrmann, Orson was not a man for whom you could write an original score because of his tendency to change the show around up to the last moment. Since he never conformed to a preconceived outline, it was better to improvise with him:

Welles's radio quality, like Sir Thomas Beecham's in music, was essentially one of spontaneity. At the start of every broadcast Orson was an unknown quantity. As he went along his mood would assert itself and the temperature would start to increase till the point of incandescence...Even when his shows weren't good they were better than other people's successes. He inspired us all—the musicians, the actors, the sound-effects men and the engineers. They'd all tell you they never worked on shows like Welles's. Horses' hooves are horses' hooves—yet they felt different with Orson—why? I think it had to do with the element of the unknown, the surprises and the uncomfortable excitement of improvisation.

Some of Orson's improvisation was extremely elaborate. Among the technical and electronic devices that were being perfected in those days, sound effects, which had started out as simple indications (footsteps, windows and doors opening and closing, cars starting, etc.), were taking on increasing complexity. Orson, determined to push this further than his competitors, spent hours experimenting with new devices and combinations. Long John Silver's wooden leg was easy, but for *The Count of Monte Cristo* the two actors who played the dungeon scenes were required to lie on the stone floor of the men's room and to speak into a special dynamic microphone set at the base of the toilet seat to achieve the right subterranean reverberation, while a second microphone, placed inside a toilet

bowl at the other end of the building and constantly flushed, gave a
faithful rendering of the waves breaking against the walls of the
Château d'If.

In *A Tale of Two Cities* several hours of precious studio time were
spent on the decapitation of Sydney Carton and the fall of his head
into the basket. Various solid objects were tried under a cleaver
wielded by one of the best sound men in the business: a melon, a
pillow, a coconut and a leg of lamb. Finally it was discovered that a
cabbage gave just the right kind of scrunching resistance. In *Beau
Geste*, for the climactic Bedouin attack on the fort, Orson sent two
engineers with microphones and hundreds of feet of cable onto the
roof of the building together with four extras and a stage manager
armed with guns and with orders to fire six rounds apiece every time
he flashed a cue light from the studio. Now it sounded real—so real
that within five minutes the building was invaded by uniformed
police who burst into the studio and threatened to arrest us all for
illegal possession of firearms.

Such episodes are comic in the telling: they formed part of the
hysterical intensity amid which the show was produced each week
with an obsessive perfectionism that gradually, over the summer,
earned us a reputation for quality and imagination such as no dramatic
radio series had quite achieved before. We adhered to the formula of
first-person-singular narration but, within it, we invented all sorts of
ingenious and dramatic devices: diaries, letters, streams of
consciousness, confessions and playbacks of recorded conversations.
And, gradually, though adventure continued to be the backbone of the
show, we ventured into more varied and sophisticated material.
Dracula and *Treasure Island* were followed by *A Tale of Two Cities* and *The
Thirty-Nine Steps;* then came a show made up of three short stories
followed by John Drinkwater's *Abraham Lincoln*, Schnitzler's *Affairs of
Anatol*, *The Count of Monte Cristo* and G.K. Chesterton's *The Man Who
Was Thursday.*

We had no hired reader; the material was chosen by Welles and
myself on the basis of contrast and personal preference with occasional
suggestions from the outside. In each case we would discuss the tone
and mood of the production and then I would go off and write it. Once
again, as in the beginning of our partnership in the theater, it was
Orson who was the teacher, I the apprentice. But I learned quickly and
once I had mastered the basic techniques and tricks, I wrote all our
scripts—usually in bed, over a period of three to four days. Orson
usually accepted them with minor corrections but, once in a while, out
of caprice or ego, or because he really felt he had a superior idea, he
would make radical changes, for better or for worse, before or during

rehearsal.

Seated in the control room next to the engineer while he directed and performed in the studio, I was expected to monitor the show and pass on my impressions to Welles, who stood on a raised podium where all could see him with earphones clamped to his head through which he could hear everything, including himself. He also counted on me for the drastic, last-minute editing which took place every week just before air time, with the clock ticking over our heads, in an atmosphere of panic pressure.

It was a loose but viable collaboration and it worked with surprising efficiency. Within a few weeks ours had become the summer's leading dramatic program on the air—another bright feather in the cap of the Mercury. In my exhilaration over this new achievment I chose to ignore the change it was causing in our relationship.

Throughout my theatrical association with Orson over the past three and a half years, much of the initiative had been mine. While I never hesitated to acknowledge Orson's creative leadership, I had managed, consciously and not without effort, to maintain the balance of power in a partnership which, for all our frequent and violent personal conflicts, had remained emotionally and professionally stable. With the coming of the radio show this delicate balance was disturbed and, finally, destroyed. The formula *"produced, written, directed and performed by Orson Welles"* was one that I approved and encouraged. In the first place it was true: Mercury of the Air *was* Orson's show. In the second, it was good showmanship and sound business to publicize and exploit one dominant, magnetic personality. But its effect on our association and on the future course of the Mercury was deep and irreversible. From being Orson's partner I was becoming a senior member of his staff.

In the beginning, because it was all so spontaneous and exciting and successful and because of our deep personal affection and continued professional need of each other, the change was barely perceptible. In the tensions of the following months, under the alternating extremities of great success and dismal failure, this growing imbalance in our partnership became the main cause of its final and inevitable dissolution.

That was still more than a year away. Meantime CBS had offered to continue the show for another twenty-six weeks if the problem of suitable air time could be solved. With the reopening of the theater season our Monday evening hour had become impossible. So had every night of the week except Sunday, when the Mercury Theater was dark. But Sunday night was dominated by the rival network's long-time popular favorite—the comedian Edgar Bergen with his puppet, Charlie McCarthy. For a while this looked like an insuperable obstacle. Finally, out of necessity and perhaps as an experiment in programming, CBS decided to run us against the puppet on the off chance that we might attract a small part of his mass public in addition to our own limited but growing audience.

Such was our self-confidence and our blind faith in our own unlimited energy that, as we signed our new contract, we neither of us, for one instant, questioned the wisdom of trying to combine a weekly national radio show with the running of a full-scale repertory theater in New York City.

VIII
Men from Mars
1938

Neither Welles nor I felt really alive unless we were doing a number of things at one time. Immediately after the broadcast of *Dracula*, the Mercury Theater, which had been paralyzed since Sherman's desertion, sprang back into furious life. Our first task was to reconstruct our wrecked program for the coming season: *The Importance of Being Earnest* was out; so was *The Shoemaker's Holiday*, in which the defecting Sherman had played an irreplaceable part. We found two substitutes: the first was *Too Much Johnson*, an early twentieth-century farce by William Gillette, which had been on our list for some time. It was not my favorite piece but Orson assured me that, with a new production idea he had in mind, it would be funnier than *Horse Eats Hat*. The other was *Danton's Death*, on which we decided quite precipitately one afternoon during a radio rehearsal.

Orson's production idea for *Too Much Johnson* included two filmed interludes—both chases: the first, a prologue in which the leading characters and the basic situation (mistaken identity and a suspicion of cuckoldry) were introduced in a wild chase through the streets, parks and waterfront of New York City; the second, a comic manhunt through a Cuban jungle to be created in Palisades Park.

Shooting began in mid-July. Dressed in rented Edwardian garments and accompanied by three horse-drawn cabs, we set out for our opening day's work in Central Park. Just before the first shot it started to pour. Orson felt this would add to the excitement of the chase. The horses and their drivers felt otherwise. Frightened by the rain, a rising wind and falling branches, they refused to budge. Scowling in the shelter of a large tree, Orson, with his actors, awaited the passing of what, he assured them, was nothing but a summer shower. It turned out to be the beginning of the East Coast's worst hurricane in years and it lasted for two days. Three days later we resumed shooting.

While Orson was acquiring his first experience as a film director, I was trying to finance our new Mercury season, besides writing and producing our radio show each week. With incorrigible optimism I had hoped to eke out the summer and produce our fall season with what little was left of our original capital and then use the profits of the repertory to pay for the rest of the season. With our enforced change of plans this neat scheme fell apart. I could not go back to our original backers. After a triumphal season in which they had seen themselves described in the press as "beaming sponsors" and "Maecenases with a flair," I was embarrassed to tell them that their money was all but gone and that more was needed. Using every source I could think of and exploiting every bit of the prestige we had acquired during the previous year, I finally managed to raise enough from sundry well-wishers to carry us over into the next season.

The filming of *Too Much Johnson*, hilarious though it was, finally had to be stopped for lack of funds. Orson was determined to do his own editing; instead of renting a professional cutting room he had the film delivered to the St. Regis Hotel on Fifth Avenue where he occupied an air-conditioned apartment for his hay fever and for the amours that were beginning to play an important part in his life. He ordered a Moviola together with some film-cutting and splicing equipment and gave the floor maid a large bribe never to enter his room. As each day's new batch of developed film was brought in, it went to swell the rising pile of celluloid that lay coiled loosely all over the floor. To reach the bed, when the slaves came to rouse him for a rehearsal or for one of his radio shows, they had to wade knee-deep through a crackling sea of inflammable film.

On the nights when he was not on the air or with his paramour, Orson would sit for hours laughing at his own footage while the slaves hunted vainly for the bits of film he needed to put his chases together into some kind of intelligible sequence. He also conducted desultory rehearsals of Gillette's play which, by this time, amused him far less than the variations he had shot and which we had already announced as opening in New York in mid-September after a week's tryout in Connecticut.

On the small stage of the Stony Creek Summer Theater I found *Too Much Johnson* trivial, tedious and underrehearsed and set myself firmly against bringing it in as the opening production of the Mercury Theater's critical second season. This led to several ugly confrontations with Orson, who secretly agreed with me but who needed to play out a "sabotage" scene to salve his pride.

So, once again, we were forced to change our program, which now read *Danton's Death* followed by *Five Kings*. With this change our economic situation grew infinitely worse. *Danton*, a big and difficult show, could not possibly open till early October; this meant carrying a dark theater and the entire Mercury organization, now back on full pay, for an additional, unproductive month. Despite the prestige of our successful radio show I had made no real progress with my financing. For all our triumphs we remained an "art theater"—poison to the smart money and to regular Broadway angels.

Too Much Johnson was Orson Welles's first reversal but its effects were catastrophic. The night it opened at Stony Creek he retired into his air-conditioned lair at the St. Regis, where he lay in darkness for a week like a sick child, convinced that he was going to die, racked by asthma and fear and despair. Years later one of the slaves still spoke with pity and horror of the spiritual flagellations he had witnessed in that twilit room, of "the self-vilifications and the remorse for what he had done to those around him...for the cruelty and moral corruption with which he reproached himself."

On the seventh day he rose from his bed and returned to the world, but his troubled emotional state continued to be reflected in his creative activity: it helped to explain the indecision and doubt that were beginning to infect his work in the theater and it added to the difficulty we experienced as we tried to recapture our working rhythm at the Mercury and to restore the sense of continuity that had been snapped by our double change of plans.

Danton's Death had been written, just over a century before, by a boy who died at the age of twenty-four, leaving behind him this and two other more or less finished plays (*Leonce und Lena* and *Wozzeck*). Scribbled in a student's notebook in the attic of his father's house, where Georg Büchner was hiding it from the police repression that swept Europe after the Congress of Vienna, it is a play of keen political and human insights—one that seemed to offer us scope for creative and experimental production and, at the same time, reflected significant aspects of the modern scene. Laid in that violent period of the French Revolution when it was making the transition from new-won liberty to dictatorship, it is a very young man's play with a fragmentary and defective structure. It had been seen in New York in 1927 when Max Reinhardt presented it (in an augmented version with vast crowd effects) as one of the great successes of his American season. This success, far from helping us, made our undertaking more hazardous: it conditioned Orson's approach to the play and influenced the nature of his production. Since Reinhardt had made a mass spectacle of it and Orson himself had already demonstrated his ability to handle crowd scenes, *Danton's Death* would be performed as a "drama of lonely souls and the mob," with the mob ever present but rarely visible.

Except for such general notions, Welles came to the play unprepared and uncertain. He was a great improviser but he needed a strong structure (as in *Caesar*) or a brilliant texture (as in *Faustus*) around which to develop his inventions and variations. Both were missing in *Danton*. He brought to it, as he could not fail to do, intermittnent genius, spasmodic energy and an occasional flash of vision but none of that impregnable personal conviction that had carried him irresistibly through our earlier productions.

Danton's Death was created in an anxious mood that fluctuated between uneasy inertia and almost unbearable tension. It was rehearsed in a set of which the dominant element was a huge, curved wall formed entirely of human faces that filled the rear of the stage from the basement to the grid. Called on to execute this in a hurry and at reasonable cost, Jean Rosenthal went out and bought 5000 unpainted Halloween masks, each of which was colored by hand and glued onto a curved, stiffened canvas cyclorama by rotating crews of assistants, volunteers, slaves, wardrobe women, secretaries, visitors— anyone who could be persuaded or pressured into joining in the loathsome task. When finished and lit, it was an effective and active device that suggested different things to different people: in one light it was "the hydra-headed mob, impersonal but real, omnipresent as a reality"; in another, "it looked like a huge canopy of staring faces which gave the strange ominous effect of a rigid dance of death." At the climax of Danton's self-destruction, blood-red lights were thrown upon it; during Robespierre's midnight meditation it turned to vicious, steely gray, which made it seem, for a moment, "as though the whole pile of skulls was about to fall upon him and stone him to death." In the last scene, as Danton and his followers went to their execution, this whole rear wall opened up and revealed a narrow slit against a bright blue sky topped by glittering steel. At the final curtain drums rolled and the blade of the guillotine flashed down through the slit as the lights blacked out.

In front of this wall, starting immediately behind the forestage, was a yawning pit 30 feet long and 20 wide, hacked out of the center of the stage floor we had so lovingly and proudly rebuilt the year before. Out of this hole, rising in steep steps from the basement, like a miniature Aztec pyramid, was a four-sided structure the center of which was occupied by an elevator shaft through which a small platform travelled up and down, descending to the basement to unload and rising to a maximum height of 12 feet above the stage. This was successively used, at various levels, as a rostrum, a garret, an elegantly furnished salon, a prison cell and a tumbrel until, in the final scene, it rose slowly to its full height to become the raised platform of the guillotine.

It was a brilliant conception but mechanically it was a horror. The only kind of elevator we could afford was a swaying, rickety, man-driven contraption. When I complained to Jean of its instability, she explained that it was precisely this flexibility that made it safe. We spent days trying to make it stop at the right floors, dozens of hours lighting it at its various levels. When it was all set and lit, it looked wonderful; it was also constricting and exceedingly dangerous.

Our mood, throughout *Danton's Death*, was matched by that of the world around us. Throughout that summer and fall, if anyone in a moment of restlessness turned on the small radio that was left in the rear of the box office, it was to listen to consistently alarming news: Hitler's armies poised for invasion; Prague vowing resistance; France mobilizing; the British fleet massing. In September, while Chamberlain was flying between London and Munich to secure "peace in our time," a cloud of tragi-comic madness seemed to hang over the Mercury and its inmates. Night after night and sometimes all night, Welles would go through the motions of rehearsal—endlessly shifting the order of scenes and the sequence of speeches. Each time such a change was made, it called for a complete rerouting and relighting of that entire section of the play. The wall of faces, effective as it was, was horribly difficult to light; each of its 5000 masks seemed determined to get itself into the light. If one single lamp was moved, even slightly, to accommodate an actor's changed position on the stage, it was likely, a moment later, to illuminate a hundred masks behind him.

Days and nights went by and nobody left the theater. Mattresses were dragged into the aisles to take care of our 24-hour shifts. Jeannie grew smaller and grayer. Still Orson would not stop. He drove himself and the company with no sense of time, to no apparent purpose and with no perceptible feeling. It was as though he expected, by continuously increasing the pressure, to strike some new well of inspiration that would save us all from disaster.

It was during our third dress rehearsal that we had our first catastrophe. The night had started badly. The Longchamps restaurant next door, to which we owed several hundred dollars, had refused to release Orson's double steak and triple pistachio ice cream (which he was in the habit of eating, seated in the aisle, while conducting rehearsal) unless they were paid for in cash, and no one in the theater was able to advance the necessary sum. By 10 p.m. there was a crowd of citizens on the forestage—assorted couples, spies, drunks, market women, hawkers, agitators and lynchers—all calling for "death for those with no holes in their coats." Off stage, in the basement, they were singing "La Carmagnole." Then as the street scene faded, behind it, slowly rising out of darkness into light, the elevator came into view, revealing a delicate, civilized, eighteenth-century drawing-room scene, all silk and elegance and laughter—three men and two women drinking tea to the soft playing of a harpsichord. It had just cleared the level of the stage, swaying gently as was its wont, when it was shaken by a slight tremor, barely perceptible from the front but enough to make the actors glance at each other. For a few seconds it continued to rise—a charming sight. It had almost reached its mark when it stopped, shuddered (so that a tea cup fell off the table and smashed) and began to sink—slowly at first, but gathering speed as it vanished from sight.

There was a silence that seemed eternal, then a woman's scream, followed by a crash that shook the theater. More screams and a man's groan. It came from an elderly actor whose leg was broken; the rest were shaken but unhurt.

Jean Rosenthal, after examining the debris and determining the cause of the crash, which she said would never occur again, asked for three days to repair and reconstruct the elevator. So, once again, I called the *New York Times*, cancelled three more previews and postponed our opening for the third time—"due to technical problems."

Unfortunately, "technical problems" were not our only ones. What we now encountered came as a complete surprise in an area where we felt comparatively secure. The Mercury Theater had been created on the foundation of the Federal Theater: our public was the same as that which had attended our shows in Harlem and at the Maxine Elliott and had then followed us into the Mercury. It was a left-wing audience of whom we knew that a substantial number were Party members or sympathizers: in fact, our last-minute choice of *Danton's Death* had been motivated, in part, by our feeling that this was a political play that would appeal to intelligent left-wing theatergoers. This added to the shock we felt at what now happened to us.

Ever since *The Cradle Will Rock* Marc Blitzstein had been our close and constant collaborator. He had given us highly dramatic music for *Julius Caesar* and he was now hard at work on a score for *Danton's Death* that included Mozartian chamber music, two love songs and several choral versions of the bloodthirsty, revolutionary "Carmagnole."

Besides being our accredited composer, Marc had appointed himself our political counsellor and our cultural contact with the Communist Party. It was in this capacity that he came to me after one of our previews in a state of great agitation. Full of anguished self-reproach, he confessed that he had failed us! He should have kept in closer touch with the Party; he should have warned us before it was too late! When I urged him to be more specific he assured me that in producing *Danton's Death* at this moment in history we were guilty of a grievous and inexcusable error—one so serious that our best course would be to cancel the show immediately. Exasperated, I pressed him for a clarification, which Marc now gave me, very white about the gills, straight from the Cultural Bureau of the Party.

With the Moscow trials and purges fresh in people's minds and the Trotskyite schism growing ever wider among American Communists, how could we have failed to notice the inescapable and dangerous parallel of *Danton's Death*? Could we not see that, to the politically immature, and particularly to the younger, emotional members of the Party, Danton, the hero of the Revolution, who had raised and commanded the armies of the young republic, must inevitably suggest the renegade Trotsky, while his antagonist, the rigid, incorruptible but utterly ruthless Robespierre must, equally inevitably and unfavorably, be equated with Stalin. To the Party any such comparison was odious.

When I tried to discount Marc's fears, he assured me that, unless we did something drastic to bring our show into line and to obtain the approval of the Party, we would certainly be picketed and every one of our left-wing theater parties (which, at this time, constituted by far the greater part of our advance sales) would certainly be cancelled. He offered to set up a meeting, at the earliest possible moment, with the head of the Party's Cultural Bureau—V.J. Jerome.

I remembered Jerome as a dominant participant in the symposium that had followed the performance of MacLeish's *Panic* three years earlier. I became better acquainted with him during the numerous meetings we held in the days that followed—some of them late at night, after rehearsals, in Stewart's Cafeteria on Union Square. (I also visited him, at his invitation, in his modest apartment, just off Union Square, where tea was served in formal, middle-class English fashion by what appeared to be a spinster sister.) He was a highly cultivated man, a former rabbinical student, with dark, hollow eyes, a sallow complexion, a gentle manner and traces of a cockney accent. He knew *Danton's Death* and shared our admiration for it. But, as head of the Cultural Bureau, he was adamant in his opposition to its performance.

I told him it was too late for us to cancel and appealed to him on the basis of our past good relations with left-wing audiences and with the Party. We argued for several nights (once with Welles present) and finally reached a series of compromises—cuts, transpositions and changes of emphasis—some of which we reluctantly inserted into the production during previews where they further confused an already obscure play. In exchange, we obtained an assurance that the Party would not picket us or attack us in the *Daily Worker* before our opening.

As we limped on through our frequently postponed or cancelled previews, we continued to make theatrical and political changes in our production. We need not have bothered. Poor word-of-mouth soon achieved the damage we had feared from the Party's censors; our advance sale faltered, then collapsed, as one left-wing theater party after another was cancelled.

Our formal press opening was now set for Wednesday, November 3. It could not take place earlier because, over the weekend, we were committed to rehearse and broadcast our weekly show for Mercury of the Air. On this particular Sunday it was *The War of the Worlds*, better known as *The Men from Mars*.

We had been on the air for four months and this was our seventeenth broadcast. With the start of the theater season, since Welles and I could no longer handle the show by ourselves, we had increased our personnel by two. Our first addition was Paul Stewart, a Broadway and radio actor with ambitions to be a director, who now became our associate producer. The other was an extremely tall, spindly, hollow-eyed, earnest young man by the name of Howard Koch, who, after having had a play performed by the Federal Theater in Chicago, had abandoned his law practice and arrived in New York with his wife and two children to earn his living as a writer. He was helpless, literate and in desperate need. I put him to work immediately on a trial basis at $50 a week, which I raised to $60 after he had proved himself. As an aide and liaison I loaned him my secretary Ann Froelisch—an emphatic, pretty girl from Smith College with fine, ash-blonde hair, a rasping voice and a delicious smell of fading spring flowers.

Even with our augmented staff everyone was perpetually overworked. Shows were created week after week under conditions of soul- and health-destroying pressure. But, between us, we had gradually worked out a system—a sort of chaotic routine which was supposed to survive the eccentricities of our leader. As general editor of the series I chose the material with Welles and, when possible, discussed with him the tone and general form of the show and its casting possibilities. I then laid it out roughly and turned it over to Koch who would have a first draft ready by Wednesday night, when Orson was supposed to read it but seldom did. On Thursday Paul Stewart would put the show through its first paces, rehearsing it all day with a skeleton cast while Koch and I made whatever adjustments and changes seemed needed in the script after we had heard it spoken. Late in the afternoon, without music and with rudimentary sound, we would make an acetate recording of the show. From this record, played back later—sometimes much later—that night, Orson would give us his reactions and revisions, which we would accept or dispute. In the next thirty-six hours the script would be reshaped and rewritten, sometimes drastically. Saturday afternoon there was another rehearsal, with sound—with or without Welles. It was not until the last day that Orson really took over.

Sundays, at eight, we went on the air. Beginning in the early afternoon, when Bernard Herrmann arrived with his symphony orchestra, two simultaneous dramas were unfolded each week in the stale, tense air of CBS Studio: the minor drama of the current show and the major drama of Orson's titanic struggle to get it on. Sweating, howling, dishevelled and single-handed he wrestled with chaos and time—always conveying an effect of being alone, traduced by his collaborators, surrounded by treachery, ignorance, sloth, indifference, incompetence and—more often than not—downright sabotage. Every Sunday it was touch and go. As the hands of the clock moved relentlessly towards air time the crisis grew more extreme, the peril more desperate. Often violence broke out; scripts and scores flew through the air, doors were slammed, batons smashed. Scheduled for six—but usually nearer seven—there was a dress rehearsal, a thing of wild improvisation and irrevocable catastrophes.

After that, with only a few minutes to go, there was a final frenzy of correction and reparation, of utter confusion and absolute horror, aggravated by the gobbling of sandwiches and the bolting of oversized milkshakes. By now it was less than a minute to air time.

At that instant, quite regularly week after week, with not one second to spare, the buffoonery stopped. Suddenly, out of chaos, the show emerged—delicately poised, meticulously executed, precise as clockwork, smooth as satin. And above us all, like a rainbow over storm clouds, stood Orson on his podium, sonorous and heroic, a leader of men surrounded by his band of loyal followers; a giant in action, serene and radiant with the joy of a hard battle bravely fought, a great victory snatched from the jaws of disaster—which, in a sense, it was. For, what Orson accomplished each week in those eight terrible hours was extraordinary.

The War of the Worlds formed part of our general scheme of contrasting shows. No one, as I recall, was particularly enthusiastic about it. But it seemed good programming—following Julius Caesar (with the original Mercury cast and commentary out of Plutarch), Oliver Twist (in which Orson played both the boy Oliver and the villainous Fagin), Around the World in Eighty Days, The Heart of Darkness and Jane Eyre, and before *Life with Father,* which was to be our next show—to throw in something of a scientific nature. We thought of Conan Doyle's *Lost World* and several other well-known works of science fiction before settling on H.G. Wells's twenty-year-old novel, which neither Orson nor I remembered at all clearly. It is just possible that neither of us had ever read it.

Actually it was a narrow squeak. The Men from Mars barely escaped being stillborn. Late Tuesday night—thirty-six hours before the first rehearsal—Howard Koch called me at the theater. He was in deep distress. After three days of slaving on H.G. Wells's scientific fantasy he was ready to give up. Under no circumstances, he declared, could it be made interesting or in any way credible to modern American ears. Koch was not given to alarmism. To confirm his fears, Annie came to the phone. "You can't do it, Houseman!" she whined. "Those old Martians are just a lot of nonsense! It's all too silly! We're going to make fools of ourselves! Absolute idiots!"

We were not averse to changing a show at the last moment. But the only other script available was an extremely dreary version of *Lorna Doone* which I had started during the summer and abandoned. I reasoned with Koch. I taxed him and Annie with defeatism. I gave them false comfort by promising to come up and help. When I finally got there—around two in the morning—things were better. They were beginning to have fun laying waste to the state of New Jersey. Annie had stopped grinding her teeth. I worked with them for the rest of the night and they went on through the next day. Wednesday at sunset the script was finished.

Thursday, as usual, Paul Stewart rehearsed the show, then cut a record. We listened to it, rather gloomily, between *Danton* rehearsals, in Orson's room at the St. Regis, sitting on the floor because all the chairs were still covered with coils of unrolled and unedited film. He was dead tired and thought it was a dull show. We all agreed that its only chance of coming off lay in emphasizing its newscast style—its simultaneous, eyewitness quality.

All night we sat up—Howard, Paul, Annie and I—spicing the script with circumstantial allusions and authentic detail. Friday afternoon it was sent over to CBS to be passed by the network censor. Certain name alterations were requested and made under protest. Then the script went over to mimeograph and I went back to the theater. We had done our best and, after all, it was just another radio show.

Saturday, Paul Stewart rehearsed with sound effects and without Welles. He worked for a long time on the crowd scenes, the roar of cannon echoing in the Watchung Hills and the sound of New York

Harbor as the ships with the last remaining survivors put out to sea.

Around six we left the studio. Orson, phoning from the theater a few minutes later to find out how things were going, was told by one of the CBS sound men, who had stayed behind to pack up his equipment, that it was not one of our better shows. Confidentially, the man opined, it just didn't come off. Twenty-seven hours later, quite a few of his employers would have found themselves a good deal happier if he had turned out to be right.

On Sunday, October 30, 1938, at 8:00 p.m. EST, in a studio littered with coffee cartons and sandwich paper, Orson swallowed a second container of pineapple juice, put on his earphones, raised his long white fingers and threw the cue for the Mercury theme—the Tchaikovsky Piano Concerto No. 1 in B Flat Minor. After the music dipped, there were routine introductions—then the announcement that a dramatization of H.G. Wells's famous novel, *The War of the Worlds*, was about to be performed. Around 8:01, Orson began to speak, as follows:

WELLES

We know now that in the early years of the twentieth century this world was being watched closely by intelligences greater than man's and yet as mortal as his own. We know now that as human beings busied themselves about their various concerns they were scrutinized and studied, perhaps almost as narrowly as a man with a microscope might scrutinize the transient creatures that swarm and multiply in a drop of water. With infinite complacence people went to and fro over the earth about their little affairs, serene in the assurance of their dominion over this small spinning fragment of solar driftwood which by chance or design man has inherited out of the dark mystery of Time and Space. Yet, across an immense ethereal gulf, minds that are to our minds as ours are to the beasts of the jungle, intellects vast, cool, and unsympathetic, regarded this earth with envious eyes and slowly and surely drew their plans against us. In the thirty-ninth year of the twentieth century came the great disillusionment.

It was near the end of October. Business was better. The war scare was over. More men were back at work. Sales were picking up. On this particular evening, October 30th, the Crossley service estimated that 32 million people were listening in on their radios...

Neatly, without perceptible transition, he was followed on the air by an anonymous announcer caught in a routine bulletin:

ANNOUNCER

...for the next twenty-four hours not much change in temperature. A slight atmospheric disturbance of undetermined origin is reported over Nova Scotia, causing a low pressure area to move down rather rapidly over the northeastern states, bringing a forecast of rain, accompanied by winds of light gale force. Maximum temperature 66; minimum 48. This weather report comes to you from the Government Weather Bureau...We now take you to the Meridian Room in the Hotel Park Plaza in downtown New York, where you will be entertained by the music of Ramon Raquello and his orchestra.

On cue, Bernard Herrmann led the massed men of the CBS orchestra in a thunderous symphonic rendition of "La Cumparsita." The entire hoax might have been exposed there and then—but for the fact that hardly anyone was listening. The nation was being entertained by Charlie McCarthy.

The Crossley rating, taken about a week before the broadcast, had given us 3.6 percent of the listening audience compared with Edgar Bergen's 34.7 percent. What the Crossley Institute ignored was the healthy American habit of dial-twisting. On that particular evening Edgar Bergen, in the person of Charlie McCarthy, temporarily left the air about 8:12 EST, yielding place to a new and unknown singer. At that point, and during the following minutes, a large number of listeners started twisting their dials in search of other entertainment. Many of them turned to us—and when they did, they stayed put! For, by this time, the mysterious meteorite had fallen at Grovers Mill in New Jersey, the Martians had begun to show their foul leathery heads above the ground, and the New Jersey State Police were racing to the spot. Within a few minutes people all over the United States were praying, crying, fleeing frantically to escape death from the Martians. Some remembered to rescue loved ones, others telephoned farewells or warnings, hurried to inform neighbors, sought information from newspapers or radio stations, summoned ambulances and police cars.

The reaction was strongest at points nearest the tragedy—in Newark, New Jersey, in a single block, more than twenty families rushed out of their houses with wet handkerchiefs and towels over their faces. Some began moving household furniture. Police switchboards were flooded with calls inquiring, "Shall I close my windows?"; "Have the police any extra gas masks?" Police found one family waiting in the yard "with wet cloths on faces contorted with hysteria." One woman reported later:

I was terribly frightened. I wanted to pack and take my child in my arms, gather up my friends and get in the car and just go north as far as we could. But what I did was just sit by one window, praying, listening and scared stiff and my husband by the other sniffing and looking out to see if people were running...

In New York hundreds of people on Riverside Drive left their homes ready for flight. Bus terminals were crowded. A woman calling up the Dixie Bus Terminal for information said impatiently, "Hurry please, the world is coming to an end and I have a lot to do."

In the parlor churches of Harlem, evening services became "end of the world" prayer meetings. Many turned to God in that moment:

I held a crucifix in my hand and prayed while looking out of my open window for falling meteors...When the monsters were wading across the Hudson River and coming into New York, I wanted to run put on my roof to see what they looked like, but I couldn't leave my radio while it was telling me of their whereabouts.

Aunt Grace began to pray with Uncle Henry. Lily got sick to her stomach. I don't know what I did exactly but I know I prayed harder and more earnestly than ever before. How petty all things on this earth seemed; how soon we put our trust in God!

The panic moved upstate. One man called up the Mount Vernon police headquarters to find out "where the forty policemen were killed." Another took time out to philosophize:

I thought the whole human race was going to be wiped out—that seemed more important than the fact that we were going to die. It seemed awful that everything that had been worked on for years was going to be lost forever.

In Rhode Island officials of the electric light company received a score of calls urging them to turn off all lights so that the city would be safe from the enemy. The *Boston Globe* received a call from one woman who "could see the fire." A man in Pittsburgh hurried home in the midst of the broadcast and found his wife in the bathroom, a bottle of poison in her hand, screaming, "I'd rather die this way than that." In Minneapolis a woman ran into church screaming, "New York destroyed, this is the end of the world. You might as well go home to die. I just heard it on the radio."

The Kansas City bureau of the AP received inquiries about the "invaders" from Los Angeles, Salt Lake City, Beaumont, Texas and St. Joseph, Missouri. In San Francisco the general impression of listeners seemed to be that an overwhelming force had invaded the United States from the air, was in process of destroying New York and threatening to move westward. "My God," roared an inquirer into a telephone, "where can I volunteer my services? We've got to stop this awful thing!"

As far south as Birmingham, Alabama, people gathered in churches and prayed. On the campus of a southeastern college the girls in the sorority houses and dormitories huddled around their radios trembling and weeping in each other's arms. There are hundreds of such items, gathered from coast to coast. Several books and quite a pile of sociological literature have appeared on the subject of "the invasion from Mars." Many theories have been put forward to explain the "tidal wave" of panic that swept the nation. Two factors, in my opinion, contributed to the broadcast's extraordinarily violent effect. First, its historical timing. It came within thirty-five days of the Munich crisis. For weeks, the American people had been hanging on their radios, getting most of their news over the air. A new technique of "on-the-spot" reporting had been developed and eagerly accepted by an anxious and news-hungry world. The Mercury Theater of the Air, by faithfully copying every detail of the new technique, including its imperfections found an already enervated audience ready to accept its wildest fantasies. The second factor was the show's sheer technical brilliance. To this day it is impossible to sit in a room and hear the scratched, worn, off-the-air recording of the broadcast without feeling in the back of your neck some slight draught left over from that great wind of terror that swept the nation. Even with the element of credibility totally removed it remains a surprisingly effective broadcast.

Beginning some time around two, when the show started to take shape under Orson's hands, a strange fever seemed to invade the studio—part childish mischief, part professional zeal. First to feel it were the actors. I remember the actor who played the part of Carl Phillips, the network's special reporter, going down to the record library and digging up the recording of the explosion of the *Hindenburg* at Lakehurst. This is a classic reportage—one of those wonderful, unpredictable accidents of eyewitness description. The broadcaster is casually describing the routine landing of the giant dirigible. Suddenly he sees something. A flash of flame! An instant later the whole thing explodes. It takes him time—a full second—to react at all. Then seconds more of sputtering ejaculations before he can make the adjustment between brain and tongue. He starts to describe the terrible things he sees—the writhing human figures twisting and squirming as they fall from the white burning wreckage. He stops, fumbles, vomits, then quickly continues. Readick played the record to himself, over and over. Then, recreating the emotion in his own terms, he described the Martian meteorite as he saw it lying inert and harmless in a field at Grovers Mill, lit up by the headlights of a hundred cars, the coppery cylinder suddenly opening, revealing the leathery tentacles and the terrible pale-eyed faces of the Martians within. As they began to emerge he froze, unable to translate his vision into words; he fumbled, retched and then, after a second, continued.

A few moments later Carl Phillips lay dead, tumbling over the microphone in his fall—one of the first victims of the Martian ray. There followed a moment of absolute silence—an eternity of waiting. Then, without warning, the network's emergency fill-in was heard—somewhere in a quiet studio, a piano, close on mike, playing "Clair de Lune," soft and sweet as honey, for many seconds, while the fate of the universe hung in the balance. Finally it was interrupted by the manly reassuring voice of Brigadier General Montgomery Smith, Commander of the New Jersey State Militia, speaking from Trenton and placing "the counties of Mercer and Middlesex as far west as Princeton and east to Jamesburg" under martial law. Tension—release—then renewed tension. Soon after that came an eyewitness account of the fatal battle of the Watchung Hills; then, once again, that lone piano was heard—now a symbol of terror, shattering the dead air with its ominous tinkle. As it played on and on, its effect became increasingly sinister—a thin band of suspense stretched almost beyond endurance.

That piano was the neatest trick of the show—a fine specimen of the theatrical "retard," boldly conceived and exploited to the full. It was one of the many devices with which Welles succeeded in compelling not merely the attention but also the belief of his invisible audience. *The War of the Worlds* was a magic act, one of the world's greatest, and Orson was the man to bring it off.

For Welles, as I have said, was first and foremost, a magician whose particular talent lay in his ability to stretch the familiar elements of theatrical effect far beyond their normal point of tension. For this reason his productions required more careful preparation and more perfect execution than most; like all complicated magic tricks, they remained, till the last moment, in a state of precarious balance. When they came off, by virtue of their unusually high intensity, they gave an impression of the greatest brilliance and power; when they failed—when something in their balance went wrong or the original structure proved to have been unsound—they provoked a particularly violent reaction of unease and revulsion. The Mars broadcast was one of his unqualified successes and it could have been carried off in no other medium than radio. If, that night, the American public proved "gullible," it was because enormous pains and a great deal of thought had been spent to make it so.

In the script, *The War of the Worlds* started extremely slowly—dull meteorological and astronomical bulletins alternating with musical interludes. These were followed by a colorless scientific interview and still another stretch of dance music. These first few minutes of routine broadcasting "within the existing standards of judgment of the listener" were intended to lull (or maybe bore) the audience into a false security and to furnish a solid base of realistic time from which to accelerate later. Orson, in directing the show, extended these slow movements far beyond our original conception. The interview in the

Princeton Observatory—the clockwork ticking monotonously overhead, the woolly-minded professor mumbling vague replies to the reporters' uninformed questions—this, too, was dragged out to the point of tedium. Over my protests, lines were restored that had been cut at earlier rehearsals. I cried there would not be a listener left. Welles stretched them out even longer.

He was right. His sense of tempo, that night, was infallible. When the flashed news of the cylinder's landing finally came—almost fifteen minutes after the beginning of a fairly dull show—he was able suddenly to spiral his action to a speed as wild and reckless as its base was solid. The appearance of the Martians; their first treacherous act; the death of Carl Phillips; the arrival of the militia; the battle of the Watchung Hills; the destruction of New Jersey—all these were telescoped into a space of twelve minutes without overstretching the listeners' emotional credulity. The broadcast, by then, had its own reality, the reality of emotionally felt time and space.

At the height of the crisis, around 8:31 EST, the Secretary of the Interior came on the air, in a voice just faintly reminiscent of Franklin Delano Roosevelt's, with an exhortation to the American people.

THE SECRETARY

Citizens of the nation: I shall not try to conceal the gravity of the situation that confronts the country, nor the concern of your Government in protecting the lives and property of its people. Fortunately, this formidable enemy is still confined to a comparatively small area, and we may place our faith in the military forces to keep them there. In the meantime, placing our trust in God, we must continue the performance of our duties, each and every one of us, so that we may confront this destructive adversary with a nation united, courageous and consecrated to the preservation of human supremacy on this earth. I thank you.

Towards the end of this speech (circa 8:32) Davidson Taylor, supervisor of the broadcast for the Columbia Broadcasting System, received a phone call in the control room, creased his lips and hurriedly left the studio. By the time he returned, a few minutes later, pale as death, clouds of heavy smoke were rising from Newark, New Jersey, and the Martians, tall as skyscrapers, were astride the Pulaski highway preparatory to wading the Hudson River. To us in the studio the show seemed to be progressing splendidly—how splendidly Davidson Taylor had just learned outside. For several minutes now, a kind of madness had been sweeping the continent that was somehow connected with our show. The CBS switchboards had been swamped into uselessness but from outside sources vague rumors were coming in of deaths and suicides and panic injuries by the thousands.

Taylor had orders to interrupt the show immediately with an

explanatory station announcement. By now the Martians were across the Hudson and gas was blanketing the city. The end was near. We were less than a minute from the station break. The "last announcer" was choking heroically to death on the roof of Broadcasting Building. The boats were all whistling for a while as the last of the refugees perished in New York Harbor. Finally, as they died away, an amateur shortwave operator was heard, from heaven knows where, weakly reaching out for human companionship across the empty world:

> 2X2L Calling CQ
>
> 2X2L Calling CQ
>
> 2X2L Calling CQ
>
> Isn't there anyone on the air?
>
> Isn't there anyone?

Five seconds of absolute silence. Then, shattering the reality of world's end—the announcer's voice was heard, suave and bright:

ANNOUNCER

You are listening to the CBS presentation of Orson Welles and the Mercury Theater of the Air in an original dramatization of The War of the Worlds by H.G. Wells. The performance will continue after a brief intermission.

The second part of the show was well written and sensitively played but nobody heard it. It recounted the adventures of a lone survivor, with interesting observations on the nature of human society; it described the eventual death of the Martian invaders, slain—"after all man's defenses had failed by the humblest thing that God in his wisdom had put upon this earth"—by bacteriological action; it told of the rebuilding of a brave new world. After a stirring musical finale, Welles, in his own person, delivered a charming little speech about Halloween and goblins.

The following hours were a nightmare. The building was full of people and dark-blue uniforms. Hustled out of the studio, Orson and I were locked into a small back office on another floor. Here we sat incommunicado while network employees were busily collecting, destroying or locking up all scripts and records of the broadcast. Finally the press was let loose upon us, ravening for horror. How many deaths had we heard of? (Implying they knew of thousands.) What did we know of the fatal stampede in a Jersey hall? (Implying it was one of many.) What traffic deaths? (The ditches must be choked with corpses.) The suicides? (Haven't you heard about the one on Riverside Drive?) It is all quite vague in my memory and quite terrible.

Hours later, instead of arresting us, they let us out a back way and we scurried down to our theater like hunted animals to their hole. It was surprising to see life going on as usual in the midnight streets, cars stopping for traffic, people walking. At the Mercury the company was still rehearsing *Danton's Death*—falling up and down stairs and singing the "Carmagnole." Welles went up on stage, where photographers, lying in wait, caught him with his eyes raised to heaven, his arms outstretched in an attitude of crucifixion. Thus he appeared in a tabloid the next morning over the caption, "I Didn't Know What I Was Doing!" The *New York Times* quoted him as saying, "I don't think we will choose anything like this again."

We were on the front page for two days. Having bowed to radio as a news source during the Munich crisis, the press was now only too eager to expose the irresponsibilities of the new medium. Orson was their whipping boy. They quizzed and badgered him. Condemnatory editorials were delivered by our press-clipping bureau in bushel baskets. There was talk, for a while, of criminal action.

Then gradually, after about two weeks, the excitement subsided. By then it had been discovered that the casualties were not as numerous or as serious as had at first been supposed. One young woman had fallen and broken her arm running downstairs. Later the Federal Communications Commission held some hearings and passed some regulations. The Columbia Broadcasting System made a public apology. With that the official aspects of the incident were closed.

Of the suits that were brought against the network—amounting to over $750,000 for damages, injuries, miscarriages and distresses of various kinds—not one was substantiated. We did settle one claim, however. It was the particularly affecting case of a man in Massachusetts, who wrote:

I thought the best thing to do was to go away. So I took $3.75 out of my savings and bought a ticket. After I had gone 60 miles I knew it was a play. Now I don't have money left for the shoes I was saving up for. Will you please have someone send me a pair of black shoes size 9B!

We did. And the lawyers were very angry with us.

IX
Mercury
1938-39

So obsessive had our rehearsal pattern become on *Danton's Death* that on the night following the Mars broadcast we were back in the Mercury Theater checking light cues with Jean Rosenthal at three in the morning. We had spent half the day closeted with CBS network executives, the other half being cornered by the press in unlikely places. That evening there had been a preview of *Danton* which had not gone badly. Orson still had a few changes he wanted to make; he rehearsed the cast for two hours after the show; then we got down to light changes. At 3:20 our chief electrician fainted. He was revived and placed in a taxi. But that was the end of that night's rehearsal.

At our opening-night performance of *Danton's Death*, mingling with the press, the fashionables and intelligentsia, Marc Blitzstein identified Earl Browder, secretary of the American Communist Party; Joe Freeman, leader of the Trotskyites; and Jay Lovestone, head of still another dissident Marxist sect, all seated within a few yards of each other. The performance was the best we had given so far—the audience was restless.

Our notices were not disgraceful but there was little in the papers the next day to encourage anyone to visit *Danton's Death*. "For the Mercury the honeymoon is over" was the general tone of the reviews. Our friends on the weeklies were particularly severe: *Variety* warned that "if the Mercury's Wonder Boy hopes to retain his legit prestige, he will have to give his best to the theater, not his second best."

By the end of our first week it had become apparent that nothing could save us—not even the men from Mars. The ticket agencies ignored us; more than half of our theater parties had been cancelled; our faithful, "lower-middle-class, semi-intellectual, left-wing" audience was conspicuous by its absence. After twenty-one performances we threw in the sponge—not just for *Danton's Death* but for the Mercury Theater.

It all happened so quickly and quietly that we never knew what hit us. Even now it is difficult to explain how one single setback (which by the law of theatrical averages was long overdue) could have annihilated an organization with such a fantastic record of success and acclaim. We had planned, operated and sacrificed to form a repertory theater capable of withstanding just such hazards; at the first intimation of failure, without the slightest gesture of resistance, we lay down and died.

We were broke. With the ruinous cost of all those incessant, all-night rehearsals and the endless postponements, we had spent every cent of the money I had raised with such difficulty—and more. (For several weeks now we had been regularly issuing checks on the theory that it was all right for them to bounce once, or even twice, but that they should be made good the third time.) But it was not money, or the lack of it, that destroyed us. It is always possible to find money—somewhere, somehow. And I have always believed that if we had really wanted to save the Mercury Theater that winter, we could have done so. If we had dropped everything else (including the monstrous *Five Kings*) and used our radio money to restore to health the repertory theater to which our life had been dedicated the year before, there is no doubt in my mind that we could have done it. The truth is—we were no longer interested. In the grandiose and reckless scheme of our lives, the Mercury had fulfilled its purpose. It had brought us success and fame; it had put Welles on the cover of *Time* and our radio show on the front page of every newspaper in the country. Inevitably, any day now, the offers from Hollywood would start arriving. It was too late to turn back and we did not really want to.

In mid-December, a few days before Christmas, we abandoned the theater, for which I found a subtenant (a left-wing Yiddish workers' theater group known as ARTEF), and moved back into our cubbyhole in the Empire Theater building.

So now (although the electric sign over the door remained untouched until the building was pulled down to make room for a parking lot after the war) the Mercury Theater was no more. Like the Oceanic it had lasted a little over a year; like the Oceanic it had flown too near the sun and, when the wax melted, no one was surprised.

* * *

For two weeks after the Martian broadcast the fate of the Mercury Theater of the Air hung in the balance while executives of the Columbia Broadcasting System tried to make up their minds whether they were proud or ashamed of us. Then, just before Thanksgiving, the

Campbell Soup Company came through with an offer of commercial sponsorship at prime time and at such a figure that the network was suddenly very proud of us indeed.

Orson and I, in our most conservative suits and stiff collars, journeyed to Camden, New Jersey, and spent several hours with the president of Campbell Soups and his leading executives. Dutifully we made our tour of the plant, saw hecatombs of dead chickens and huge, bubbling vats of tomato and pea. At noon, in the executive dining room, we smacked our lips over the thin, briny liquid of which we were about to become the champions. After lunch there was a formal meeting around a long, gleaming table with pads and pencils that so awed us that Orson and I—all 400 pounds of us—sat down with perfect solemnity in the same chair. A few days later the deal was consummated and announced: the Mercury Theater of the Air had become the Campbell Playhouse.

This time we really were in the big money. Orson himself, depending on the size of the cast and the cost of royalties, stood to make between $1000 and $1500 a week. But there were disadvantages. It soon became apparent that, in some respects, life with Campbell's Soups was going to be less agreeable than when we were our own masters. Previously our only worries had been over the quality of the broadcast and the problems of getting it on the air: now we were concerned with "format" and with adjusting the commercials that riddled the broadcast. Welles, in addition to being "producer, writer, director, star and narrator" of the Campbell Playhouse, now became its leading salesman: he assumed a role of a sophisticated world traveler who, having savored all the greatest broths and potages of the civilized world, still returned with joy and appreciation to Campbell's delicious chicken-and-rice, tomato and pea. Also, since the agency felt we should enliven our own classic tastes with more popular fiction, negotiations now had to be conducted for the radio rights to current best sellers. This was also true of our casting. Gone were the happy days of our tight little stock company: each week, after endless bickering with agents and studios, one or more greater or lesser movie stars were brought in to brighten the show. While Orson was struggling with *Five Kings*, most of this added work devolved upon Paul Stewart and myself aided by Howard Koch and a flock of slaves and pieceworkers, including, on one occasion, the poet W.H. Auden, who received $100—for an "extraction" of *Pride and Prejudice*.

Our opening show for the Campbell Playhouse was Daphne du Maurier's *Rebecca*, with Margaret Sullavan as the unnamed heroine, Welles as the romantic hero with a secret tragedy in his past (later played in the movie by Laurence Olivier) and Agnes Moorehead as the

dreadful Mrs. Danvers. It was a resounding success and it was soon
followed by the inevitable *Christmas Carol*, in which Orson played both
Scrooge and Tiny Tim.

* * *

To tell the story of *Five Kings* is like trying to record the terminal
stages of a complicated and fatal disease. The name of our disease was
success—accumulating success that had little to do with the quality of
our work but seemed to proliferate around the person of Orson Welles
with a wild, monstrous growth of its own.

Published around this time and almost lost in publicity that
swirled around Orson's name, a *New Yorker* "profile" had come out. It
was better researched than the *Time* cover story, with a fuller
background and a more perceptive view of the 23-year-old Wonder
Boy. Among the elements the writer had diagnosed as decisive in.
Welles's life was the divorce of his parents: the beautiful, passionate
mother who died young and the Chicago society playboy after whom,
in his heyday, "a restaurant, a race horse and a cigar had been named."
He was a *bon vivant* who, before killing himself in a Chicago hotel
room, had cut a wide swath on three continents. Through him,
vicariously, while still in his early teens, Orson had "sampled the wine,
women and song of London, Paris, the Riviera, Singapore, Tokyo and
the island of Jamaica."

Those of us who were close to Orson had long been aware of the
obsessive part his father continued to play in his life. Much of what he
had accomplished so precociously had been done out of a furious need
to prove himself in the eyes of a man who was not longer there to see
it. Now that success had come, in quantities and of a kind that his
father had never dreamed of, this conflict, far from being assuaged,
seemed to grow more intense and consuming. Having demonstrated
his superiority as an artist and a public figure, he must now defeat his
rival on his own ground—that of Champagne Charley, the man about
town.

This helped to explain the growing wildness and the conspicuous
extravagance of Orson's behavior that winter. It was as though he was
determined to bury the ghost of Richard Welles, once and for all, under
the mass of his own excesses. Each meal was a feast; his consumption
of alcohol was between one and two bottles of whisky or brandy a
night; for his new apartment, which had a living room the size of a
skating rink, he acquired furniture so huge that it had to be hoisted by
a crane through the double windows; his sexual prowess, which he
was inclined to report in full statistical detail, was also, apparently,
immense. This dissipation reached its climax during *Five Kings* and

contributed to that calamity. It conditioned the atmosphere in which the production was prepared and helped to give the entire venture the tone of grotesque horror with which it is associated in my memory.

From the day Orson first suggested *Five Kings* as a Mercury production, it had been apparent that it was far beyond our means. I knew that the Theatre Guild was having a difficult time finding new productions for its subscribers. In the spring of 1938, in the pride of our four successive triumphs, I had offered to help them out. I explained that since our own theater was too small to hold this colossus of ours, we would consider an association with the Theatre Guild for its production and presentation during the following winter. In a meeting with my old enemy, Lawrence Langner, a deal was made for the Mercury Theater to produce the first half of *Five Kings* (which included a fragment of *Richard II*, the two parts of *Henry IV* and *Henry V*) as part of the Guild's subscription series. If successful, it was to be followed by a second evening—all three parts of *Henry VI* and *Richard III*—to be rehearsed during the run of the first. The two things he kept asking me were how long the performance would run—to which I had no answer—and how we expected to produce a $100,000 show for $40,000. Since my estimate was based on the wildest of guesses, I could only reply that the Mercury had its own way of doing things which I was not prepared to reveal.

Orson began to grow a beard for the part of Falstaff and, around Christmas, we started to rehearse on the various empty stages that the Guild was able to procure for us around town. I have always believed that if Welles had put on *Five Kings* under the same circumstances and with the same dedicated preparation as he devoted to *Julius Caesar*, it could have been one of the memorable events of the modern theater. With Jean Rosenthal as his technical director, his production scheme was brilliant—a viable theatrical solution to the problem of moving a historical play with multiple locations through an infinitely varied and mobile pattern of continuous, progressive action.

As in *Shoemaker*, the basic materials of the production were burlap and wood—but far more massive and grand. For diversity—so that the scenery could be used at all possible angles—it was double-faced with thin veneer cut into narrow slats and stained a light blue-gray without shadowing or paint of any sort. With changes of light these wooden surfaces took on an appearance of lightness and gaiety or somber mass, depending on the intensity and color of the illumination.

At the center of the production was a large revolving platform, 30 feet in diameter, which kept circling like a lazy Susan, without blackouts or visible scene-shifts, in a great variety of forms throughout the play's thirty-two scenes. The scenery was divided into two main elements: London and the countryside. A basic castle setting with huge rounded walls towered over one third of the revolving stage. The tavern set occupied the rest. Running between them was a ramped street with an open court at one end and a narrow alley at the other. Within these three revolving structures the actors would move from one scene to another in full view of the audience. A characteristic transition was that in which Prince Hal is summoned from the Boar's Head to appear before his father in the palace. By revolving slowly, with accompanying light-changes, it would be possible to keep him continuously in the movement and in view as he left the tavern, walked up the crowded alley into the castle and through the anteroom into the ailing King's presence in the council chamber. For the battle scenes the whole stage would turn around as the actors marched or fought over a series of ramps and platforms which, in different arrangements and speeds, became the Field of Shrewsbury for the English wars and Harfleur and Agincourt for the wars of France.

Costumes—codpieces and all—were once again designed by Millia Davenport. The music was Aaron Copland's, who did a professional job but suffered from a lack of communication with his director. *Five Kings* was not one of his happiest theatrical experiences.

The company was the largest we had assembled since Federal Theater days—forty-two with seven doubles and four stage managers. Among the newcomers was Robert Speaight (fresh from his London success as Becket in *Murder in the Cathedral*), whom we used as narrator of the connective material—the Chorus and the Holingshed Chronicles. John Emery was Hotspur and Burgess Meredith (who had scrawled his name on a contract at 1 a.m. on the *Ile de France* just before sailing with Franchot Tone and two women to spend Christmas in Paris) as Prince Hal, to which he brought a warmth and an energy that I have never seen equalled in the part—even by Laurence Olivier.

Rehearsals were undisciplined and desultory from the start. It was *Danton* all over again—without the tension and with a lot more alcohol. Welles had known the Histories from childhood and played in them at Todd School; now he seemed unable to organize either his material or himself. Like a magician who is unsure of his act, he masked his insecurity with procrastinations and diversions. And this time I was of little help to him. Wholly involved in the Campbell Playhouse and the financial logistics of *Five Kings*, I attended few of his early rehearsals and at those I was made to feel uneasy and unwelcome. The reports I received were increasingly disturbing. Some came from the directors of the Theatre Guild. Orson had announced that he did not want them at rehearsal: when they defied this interdiction, a bottle of Scotch, especially kept for that purpose, was produced and Orson would call a break and entertain the cast with jokes and anecdotes until they had withdrawn.

Welles had always been a prolific raconteur. Now, as one of his devices for evading rehearsal, he gave his fancy free rein. There were the set pieces—an amorous encounter with Isadora Duncan in Paris, fighting bulls in Spain, visits to the Glaoui's fortress palace in the mountains of Morocco. And there were the fantasies, invented on the spot out of sheer exuberance or to cover up some particularly outrageous piece of behavior. One night Welles burst into rehearsal, more than two hours late, in a new, extravagantly tailored dinner jacket, and announced that the Mob was after him: a gorgeous creature, the wife of a celebrated gangster, had been seized with lust for him; he had possessed her in Harlem, then fled, with the husband and his torpedoes in hot pursuit. Two stage managers were sent to mount guard before the building while rehearsal got under way.

Another time he was not two but four and a half hours late. Everyone knew where he had been—to Chicago to spend the night with the ballerina. With all regular flights grounded for the journey back, he had secured a place in a small private plane, where he found himself sitting beside the pilot. The flight was a nightmare: visibility nil, lightning bolts, downdrafts and swirling rain. The passengers, in panic, begged the pilot to turn back, but the wretched man admitted he was lost— somewhere over the northwest part of New York State. They cruised about for two hours, the passengers moaning and praying. And then it happened. A huge downdraft sent them plunging earthward and, as the clouds parted, the pilot screamed and his hands froze on the controls. Orson looked and gasped, for rising high *above* them were the waters of Niagara Falls. How Orson swung into action and swept the worthless pilot from the controls; how he seized the stick, gunned the motor and slowly, slowly lifted the brave little plane above the roaring waters of the Falls—all this was described in vivid and fascinating detail. The cast listened in silence. "Believe me, I was scared," Orson added.

Halfway through rehearsals, in addition to my deteriorating relations with Welles and with the directors of the Guild, I found myself facing new money troubles—the worst so far. We had gone into *Five Kings* without a cent in the bank and still owing money on *Danton*. When the Guild demanded that we put up our small part of the costs, I did not have it. The big money from the radio show was only just beginning to come in and Orson himself was deep in debt. In desperation I turned to two of our original backers—the sorrowful contractor and his daughter. Out of the goodness of his heart he lent us several thousand dollars and the heat was off till we got to Boston in the middle of February.

There the real horror began.

Our rehearsals were held in the Colonial Theater. By day an enormous crew occupied the stage, assembling and installing the great mass of our scenery. Orson rehearsed in lobbies and underground. At night, after the construction gang had quit, he and his troupe, half-costumed and armored, swarmed all over the unfinished set, while the prop department made experimental firings of our two huge mortars (seven feet long and 15 inches in circumference), loaded with real gunpowder and showers of flaming arrows. After midnight, light rehearsals began and continued till dawn.

Over the weekend we had our first run-through. The first few hours were encouraging; the scenes between Prince Hal, Falstaff and the hangers-on had that exciting quality of closeness that Orson sometimes achieved with his male actors. The set was impressive and the transitions looked as though they might work. But, since by 3 a.m. we had got through less than a quarter of the play, it was still too early to tell. We advanced no further the next night and only slightly further, under pressure, the night after that.

By now two things had become evident: first—that, once again, we were about to pay for our poverty. To drive our huge turntable we had an electric motor that was smaller and worked less well than it should have. It had two speeds, but even in high it did not turn fast enough to let the actors move through the scenery at their normal pace. When we tried to accelerate it, it had an alarming way of jumping into reverse at twice its forward speed and hurling masses of scenery into the orchestra pit. Second—that the second half of *Five Kings* had, literally, never been staged.

On our third day in Boston Orson came to me and announced that we would have to postpone our opening. There was nothing unusual in this request: we had postponed *Macbeth* three times, *Horse Eats Hat* twice, *Faustus* four times and *Danton's Death* seven times. Unfortunately, those days were over. I explained to Orson, as I had frequently over the past month, that we were now in the commercial big time with the Theatre Guild subscription involving tens of thousands of people and specific theater bookings. I pointed out that plenty of big shows were not ready when they opened out of town and that, if worst came to worst, I could probably persuade the Guild to give us another out-of-town engagement. By this time Orson was in a panic. He had assumed he would get his postponement as he always had before. Thwarted and betrayed, his face streaming with tears and sweat, he turned his full rage against me. In that moment I was his father and every other enemy he had ever known. I was a yellow son of a bitch—a whore, a crooked bastard who had sold him out to the Guild, milked and exploited him and then left him holding the bag! As I turned to go, he tore a telephone from the wall and threw it at me.

Such scenes took place almost daily during the final agony of *Five Kings*. Not all were ugly; some were extremely funny—like the night I tried to murder him. During the scenes in the Boar's Head Tavern, Orson, inside his hundred pounds of soaking padding, drank large quantities of steaming mulled wine. This, as he carefully explained to our property man, could be achieved only by inserting the tip of a red-hot poker into the tankard. The prop man pointed out that a brazier on stage was against the rules of the Fire Department. He suggested that the steam could be created by slipping a small lump of dry ice into the wine. Orson categorically forbade its use. The man explained that the lumps were harmless and the smoke dangerous only in large quantities. Welles ordered him to heat the poker.

At 11:30 on the night of one of our final run-throughs the prop man came to me in fear and asked what he should do about Falstaff's steaming tankard. I had just arrived from New York and knew none of the background.

"Dry ice," I said.

"But, Mr. Houseman..."

I had other cares at the moment. An hour later I was sitting in the orchestra, begging Jeannie to make the turntable move faster and thinking how wonderfully good Orson was as the Fat Knight. Suddenly he stopped in the middle of a line as the realization came to him that the steaming tankard from which he was noisily gulping was ice cold. With a fierce yell he summoned the prop man onto the stage. "Front and center!" he yelled. Then, indicating the thin wisp of smoke, Orson demanded to know what caused it. "Dry ice," whispered the prop man and, as Orson moved upon him (all 340 pounds of him, including padding) he added quickly, "Mr. Houseman said..."

That was all Orson needed. He flung the tankard from him. He clutched at his belly and groaned. Then, staggering down to the edge of the stage, he singled me out in the darkness and pointed a long, pale finger at me.

"You've done it! You've killed me! For months you've wanted to destroy me—and now you've done it! You've poisoned me!"

Shaken by terrible spasms, he started back upstage, turned to shout "Killer! Poisoner!" then reeled and fell groveling to the floor, muttering "Poisoned! Poisoned!" Someone arrived with a bottle of milk and held it to his mouth. Orson gulped it down like a man dying of thirst, then spewed it up till the stage around him was white with it. After that, still groaning piteously, he was helped off the stage and driven back to the Ritz-Carlton, having achieved his real objective which was, once again, to avoid rehearsing the second half of the play.

On Monday, February 27, without ever having had a complete run-through, *Five Kings* opened to a theater filled with Theatre Guild subscribers and the Boston intelligentsia. It ran, with two intermissions, past two in the morning. One third of the audience vanished at the first intermission; another third left during the next two and a half hours. Some had suburban trains to catch, others were exhausted; others, especially those down front, fled in terror of the explosions, flaming arrows and chunks of solid wooden scenery which Orson delivered from the stage at the final curtain. Among them were the directors of the Theatre Guild, who had watched the show in gloom and terror. The local press did little to cheer them up. The one thing they all agreed on was that the show was not ready for Broadway.

Even more painful than the reviews were the crew bills that were now presented to the directors of the Guild. With overtime and all-night rehearsals on golden hours, they carried us more than $20,000 over our original budget. Langner held me personally responsible for the disaster. He began by demanding that we pay our share of the overage; I assured him with profound sincerity that we did not have a nickel. All-night rehearsals must cease, he insisted. I told him that Welles was incapable of working by day and that his only chance of getting the show he hoped for was to let Orson function in his own way as he had in *Julius Caesar*. I explained how fine was the line between success and failure in Orson's shows. He was not appeased and, in his mouth that morning, "genius" became a dirty word. Finally, under protest, it was agreed to carry *Five Kings* as far as Philadelphia. But, from now on, if Welles wanted all-night rehearsals he must pay for them himself, in cash—which he did, during the next ten days, to the tune of several thousand dollars, borrowed against future radio earnings.

Five Kings was shortened by forty minutes during its Boston run. Slowly the show was finding itself; scenes were now staged that had been ad-libbed on opening night, and a dramatic form began to appear. Technically, too, it was smoothing out, though the accursed lazy Susan, for all Jean's tinkering, still held up transitions and slowed down the battle scenes.

We moved to Philadelphia. The Chestnut Street Theater, into which the Guild had booked us, was a large, old-fashioned theater with a sharply raked stage. Another problem we discovered was that Philadelphia's electric current was not as other currents were. For technical reasons which I never even tried to understand it was found to be incompatible with the wretched little motor that drove our turntable. Back and forth rushed Jeannie's friends, the electrical experts, from New York, New Haven, and Camden. By Tuesday afternoon no suitable mode of conversion had been discovered. If we opened that night it would be with a revolving stage that was turned by hand. I called the Guild and pleaded with them. They were adamant. We must open that night or not at all.

Once again our curtain fell long after midnight with only a small remnant of the audience present. Our Boston reviews were paeans of praise compared to what we received in the City of Brotherly Love. By Wednesday noon a new converter had been found, adapted and installed—too late. For, at eleven that morning, Lawrence Langner had officially informed me that the Guild was withdrawing its sponsorship of *Five Kings*.

Variety had been keeping the profession supplied with bulletins of our disaster. On March 22 it reported:

KINGS BENT IN PHILLY

Five Kings will fold at the end of the week and is in doubt thereafter. There is talk of opening on Broadway without Guild participation. But that is viewed as an outside possibility. From Mercury sources it was indicated that Houseman favors keeping the show off Broadway at this time but Welles wants to rehearse it this week and bring it in the week after that.

Variety was right, as usual. Now, suddenly, much too late, a frenzy had seized the Wonder Boy. Determined that his show must not die, he was up at dawn, rehearsing all day and far into the night, pouring in his radio money, trimming and vitalizing *Five Kings* for its New York opening in the same way as he was accustomed to pull his radio show together each week in its final hours. Between rehearsals he was busy on the phone, making personal appeals in all directions (including a flight to Illinois to anticipate a $20,000 trust fund he was to receive at the age of twenty-five) begging the world not to let a masterpiece perish for lack of a few thousand dollars and a few more days of work.

In his desperate attempt to salvage *Five Kings* he received little help from me. I watched its final agony with indifference, almost with relief, at the thought that it would soon be dead and buried and out of the way. I saw no hope for the show in its present form: its flaws were too deep, its wounds beyond any possibility of cure. One day, perhaps, at another time, in some other place, *Five Kings* might rise from its ashes, but I would not be there to see it.

If *Danton* marked the demise of the Mercury Theater, it was during *Five Kings* that my association with Welles moved irrevocably towards its end. Fatigue, humiliation, mutual reproaches and, through it all, our growing inability to communicate except in anger—all these were having their corrosive effect on a partnership from which all affection seemed to have been drained.

I derived personal satisfaction from a meeting I had with Robert Edmond Jones, the great designer, who invited me to direct a new American opera he was producing and for which he was designing the sets. I accepted gratefully and the three weeks I spent staging *The Devil and Daniel Webster* in New York that spring were a welcome relief from the accumulated horrors of the winter.

I continued to do my job on the radio show and I was in the theater in Philadelphia on the closing night of *Five Kings*. Still Welles would not accept defeat. The scenery—all 17 tons of it—was shipped to New York, where it was held in demurrage for several days at great expense while Orson made his last desperate bids for renewed backing. Finally he was forced to have it unloaded in a theatrical warehouse where it lay, piling up storage charges, for the next twenty years. As a final token of defiance, Orson announced that he was retaining his Falstaff beard and vowed not to shave it off until he had played the role on a New York stage.

Momentum plays a significant part in show business. The Mercury's initial triumphs had been so great and so widely publicized that our recent theatrical failures had not seriously tarnished our national reputation or Welles' luster. Our radio show continued to be a success—critically and in soup sales—and there was every indication that it would be renewed after the summer layoff. It was, by now, an almost automatic operation that made few emotional demands upon any of us. With the passage of weeks the fever of my relations with Welles had abated; we found ourselves living in a sort of Indian summer from which the threat of disaster had temporarily lifted.

In mid-May, negotiations for a film contract began with RKO in Hollywood. By early June Orson had received and accepted one of the most sensational offers ever made to an individual by a major studio. He was to receive $100,000 for one film a year—to be produced, written, directed and performed by himself, on a subject of his own choosing, with no artistic interference by the studio and the right to refuse to show the film to anyone until it was finished. Such authority was unheard of, even among veteran directors, and no other studio would have given it. But RKO was a maverick operation, the victim of a long series of financial manipulations and changing managements. Its present interim and insecure boss—a former sales manager named George Schaeffer—had little to lose and a lot to gain by putting most of his eggs into the hands of the Wonder Boy of Broadway and radio, who just might come through with a winner for him.

In the excitement of the new contract and the exhilarating prospect of fresh worlds to conquer, the rancors and miseries of recent months were hastily buried in a shallow grave. A year, almost to the day, after he had invited me to work with him on the radio show, Orson asked me to go with him to California to help with the film. I said yes. A week later, immediately after the year's last Campbell show, he left, still wearing his beard and stopping over in Chicago for what was possibly the most ludicrous venture of that whole phantasmagoric year. For a large sum of money he had agreed to make a four-day personal appearance for one week at the largest vaudeville house in the Middle West. Following in the footsteps of Sarah Bernhardt, Ethel Barrymore and other stage luminaries who had performed capsulated drama on vaudeville stages, he had decided on an abbreviated version of *The Green Goddess*, an absurd melodrama we had done on the Campbell Playhouse.

Since I disapproved of the whole project and had things to take care of in New York, I saw only the last performance, in which Orson, in a rented Hindu garment with a bejeweled turban, a mud pack for make-up and an incredible accent, was supported by a troupe in pith helmets and turbans and a blonde I had never seen before, in white riding breeches. The audience was puzzled and apathetic. On the way back to our hotel, Orson stopped the cab for a moment and pointed to an alley leading to the rear entrance of a hotel in the Loop. "That's where they brought my father out—feet first," he said.

We were met by photographers at the Los Angeles airport and lived for some weeks at the Chateau Marmont on Sunset Boulevard, then moved into a mansion in West Los Angeles, complete with swimming pool, a huge luminous jukebox, palm trees and a distant view of the Pacific Ocean. Here Orson resided for some months, tended by Alfalfa the midget chauffeur and Charles the butler (the original of Raymond in *Citizen Kane*), a sinister and idle figure, whose only accomplishment wsa making soggy crêpes Suzette. Soon, by plane, train, car and hitchhiking, the entire entourage arrived: together with a full contingent of slaves, from whose presence Orson seemed to derive security and comfort in a strange and hostile town. They descended like locusts, occupying every room in the house and, when those were all filled, camping in the cabanas that surrounded the pool. Here at night, under the bright reflectors, we would listen to the latest news of the Danzig crisis and feel the war coming closer from 7000 miles away.

Orson's position in the film colony was a peculiar one. Hollywood was still a closed society whose social, financial and professional structure, though subject to constant shifts, remained basically solid and unchanged. By the members of this established order Welles's coming was awaited with suspicion, envy and a perplexity which Orson did nothing to allay. Virginia was off in Nevada getting a divorce and soon after our arrival rumors began to circulate about the strange all-male population of the house in Brentwood. These spread following our first public appearance at a Hollywood "gala première" at Grauman's Chinese Theater. In the line of purring limousines, each with its cargo of celebrated and carefully selected couples, was an aging open Lincoln with Alfalfa at the wheel and Orson and me, with Arnold Weissberger, our attorney, sandwiched in between us, in the back. The news of Welles's well-publicized heterosexual prowess seemed not to have reached the Pacific Coast: it was as a "queer" that he was taunted one night in the Brown Derby by Big Boy Williams, a bully-boy polo player, who tried to provoke Orson to one of those trials-by-combat-in-the-parking-lot that were still a regular part of Hollywood night life and ended up by cutting off his tie with a steak knife.

But most of our time was spent at the studio, where we sat hour after hour in battered leather armchairs running one film after another. It was from John Ford, like many young directors of that era, that Orson seemed to learn the most. Between films we wandered around the sound stages and talked about *Heart of Darkness*, which Orson had just announced—with considerable fanfare and without consulting me—as his first picture.

We had done this Conrad story with only moderate success on the Mercury Theater of the Air and, while it was a wonderful title, I never quite understood why Orson had chosen such a difficult subject for his first film. I think, in part, he was attracted by the sense of corroding evil, the slow, pervasive deterioration through which the dark continent destroys its conqueror and exploiter, Western Man, in the person of Kurtz. But, mainly, as we discussed it, I found that he was excited by the device—not an entirely original one—of the camera eye. Like many of Orson's creative notions, it revolved around himself in the double role of director and actor. As Marlow, Conrad's narrator and moral representative, invisible but ever present, Orson would have a chance to convey the mysterious currents that run under the surface of the narrative; as Kurtz, he would be playing the character about whom, as narrator, he was weaving this web of conjecture and mystery.

The attractions were obvious; so were the difficulties. In this double quest—for the body of Kurtz rotting in the Congolese jungle and for the soul of Kurtz as he moved towards his final moral destruction at the heart of darkness—Joseph Conrad had used all sorts of subtle literary devices; the evil that destroyed him was suggested and implied but never shown. In the concrete medium of film no such evasion was possible. Kurtz's life and the actions that led to his downfall must be dramatized and shown on the screen.

Orson was aware of this but he had not given it much thought. He had ideas about Kurtz as a young man rather like himself, with a fiancée who was rather like Virginia. And Dick Baer was sent down to the Los Angeles County Museum to make a survey of all the primitive races of the world—their customs, peculiarities and habits, with the idea of creating a "composite native." Beyond that, it was left to me to develop Welles's ideas into some kind of first-draft motion-picture script.

I was an editor and an adapter rather than a writer. On our radio show, over the past year, I had taken finished texts of varying qualities, condensed and translated them successfully into another medium; it had been one of my virtues as an adapter that I managed to retain much of the quality and texture of the original works—including *Heart of Darkness*. But, in this new venture, I was a failure. Frightened by the demands of an unfamiliar medium, worried by the ambivalence of my own feelings for Orson and in my anxiety to give him what he wanted, I found myself unable to give him anything at all. And Orson, who was beginning to have his own doubts about the project, had the satisfaction of feeling that his partner, once again, had betrayed him.

I was spared further embarrassment by the owners of Campbell Soup who, when they renewed their option, insisted that the Playhouse continue to be produced under their direct supervision in New York City. This complicated Orson's life, but it suited me admirably. Feeling that I had no real place in Welles's movie career and that our association was drawing to a close, I proposed that I should stay in New York and work with Paul on the radio show—arguing with agency men, getting the scripts written and supervising preliminary rehearsals. Once a week Orson would fly in for the broadcast. He agreed and I returned to New York where, with the war now seemingly inevitable, my mother had arrived from Paris and moved into the back room of my Ninth Street apartment.

With the new DC-3s, commutation to California had become painful but possible. Orson would come in on the Thursday overnight flight and drive straight to the studio, where he would listen to a recording of the previous day's rehearsal while eating a second breakfast. We rehearsed all day, went on the air at 8:00 p.m. and then again at 10:00 p.m. for the Pacific Coast. Between broadcasts we ate large dinners during which we talked about the next week's show. If our talk was not ended, I would drive to Newark with him; twice I flew to California and returned the following night, by which time every member of the organization had taken me aside to tell me that there was still no sign of a script for *Heart of Darkness*. This did not seem to bother Orson: he was busy making tests of his camera-eye technique— his first experience of shooting film under studio conditions.

By mid-November, when Campbell relented and I moved back to California, the vultures were beginning to hover. With the war and the uncertainties of European business, the Studio was losing its nerve. They asked Orson to postpone *Heart of Darkness* and start with a less ambitious film. Orson, who had already spent a large part of his first $100,000, switched without protest but without enthusiasm to *The Smiler with a Knife*, an English potboiler in the Hitchcock style, written by the poet Cecil Day Lewis under the pen name of Nicholas Blake. Orson gave me the book to read and asked me to work on it. Against my better judgment I tried for two weeks, between radio shows, then gave up.

By now another crisis was forming. When the Campbell Playhouse moved to Hollywood, Orson had decided that he wanted his regular New York actors with him. Most of them were earning so much in radio that they could not afford to move to the Coast for one show a week. This was no problem, said Welles, and he instructed the Studio to put them all under contract on a film salary in addition to what they would be earning on the radio show. A number of them arrived and were welcomed with a party. Their faith in their leader was slightly shaken when they learned that *Heart of Darkness* had been cancelled. Not cancelled, Orson assured them, only postponed. Besides, there were parts for all in *The Smiler with a Knife*.

A week before Christmas, with no progress evident on *The Smiler*, a staff meeting was held in an upper room of Chasen's Restaurant in Beverly Hills. My position at such meetings was equivocal: I had little to say about Welles's film activities, yet I remained president of the Mercury and Orson's partner. As usual, when there was something unpleasant to discuss, small talk, jokes and the inevitable anecdotes occupied the first part of the meal. It was not until after the steaks that we got down to the real subject of the meeting—a notification received that morning from RKO that, after December 31, the Studio would pay no further salaries until a final script had been OKed and a firm shooting date set for Orson's film. This raised the urgent problem of what to do with our New York actors.

Orson would not admit it was a problem. If RKO didn't pay them, he would.

"But, Orson—"

"Pay them!"

"We can't, Orson. We don't have the money."

This from Schneider, formerly our agent and now our business manager. Orson stared at him. In preparation for this distasteful conversation he had absorbed more than his normal quantity of alcohol. His eyes were bloodshot, his face damp and white.

"What the hell have you done with it?"

"Orson—"

"You're supposed to be my manager. What have you done with it? Answer me! Where's it all gone?"

Schneider, an emotional man, bowed his head and stared, with tears in his eyes, at what was left of his steak. Orson turned to the rest of us.

"I work myself to the bone to earn this money and you sons of bitches piss it away! And you don't tell me! Not one of you has the decency..."

At this moment two of Chasen's waiters entered to remove what was left of the steaks. They retired quickly; but, in the fifteen seconds they were in the room, I had made up my mind. At other times, in such a crisis, I would have used the waiters' incursion to halt the debate. Then, the next day, I would have taken each of our actors aside, explained the situation to them and given them a week's notice. They would have gone home quietly, disappointed but somewhat richer through their visit, and waited to be called back when the film was ready—if something else had not come up for them in the meantime. One day, probably on the next radio show, Orson would have noted their absence. But his pride would have been spared. Not this time. I wanted a showdown. As soon as the waiters had left I asked him what he intended to do about his actors. Orson looked at me sharply.

"What would *you* do?"

"Tell them the truth for once. Stop lying to them."

"I don't lie to actors! I've never lied to an actor in my life! You're the one who lies! That's why they hate you! You're a crook and they know it! Everyone knows it! Everybody..."

I had wanted my *Götterdämmerung* and now I had it. As I rose from the table, collecting my papers and laying my napkin down carefully beside my plate, Orson picked up one of the flaming dish heaters that had been left on the table and threw it at me. It missed me by a yard and landed at the foot of a drawn window curtain behind me. Another flaming object flew by me as I moved towards the door, which had opened and in which I could see Dave Chasen, the owner of the restaurant, frozen with horror, staring at the flames that were beginning to lick at his curtains. Two more blazing dish-warmers followed me across the room. The last one crashed against the side of the door as I went through it and began to descend the stairs. Behind me I could hear Orson on the landing yelling, "Crook!" and "Thief!"

after me, his voice becoming fainter as I walked through the half-empty restaurant and out into the street.

I went back to my apartment, took the phone off the hook and went to bed. The doorbell rang during the night but I did not answer it. At dawn a four-page telegram from Orson was delivered. I did not read it. That morning I started to drive east. Crossing the Arizona desert by night, I listened on my car radio to Orson in the last Campbell Playhouse I had written. I drove fast, without stopping for sleep, filled with the initial exhilaration that I have always felt following the destruction of something that has once been supremely important in my life. At dusk I arrived, somewhat sobered, in La Luz, New Mexico, where Mina was spending the winter. And the next day I wrote two letters. The first, carefully worded, was to Orson; it was my resignation.

...Nothing that has happened recently affects the very deep affection I have for you and the delight I have found in my association with such a talent as yours. Every word I wrote to you in New Hampshire more than two years ago continues to be true for me. And it is this feeling, mainly, that prompts me to do what I am now doing. We have been through too much together and have had too much excitement and too much joy for me to let our partnership follow the descending curve of misunderstandings and mutual dissatisfactions along which I see it moving. What happened the other night merely brought to a head a situation I have seen growing worse for some time—the situation of my position with the Mercury. For the manner in which this happened I accept, personally, a good deal of the responsibility. The truth is that in the past year my position with you and with the Mercury has become something between that of a hired, not very effective manager, a writer under contract and an aging, not so benevolent uncle. Besides, there has been something between us, lately, which instead of being intense and fruitful merely succeeds in embarrassing and paralyzing us both.

So I am going back to New York. Nothing would make me happier than, one day, again to produce plays together. I have no illusions—the theater will never be as wonderful for me again as it was during those four years with you and I need not tell you that the Mercury continues to be my first love. It is simply that the present situation is hopeless and must be changed at once for both our sakes.

Love—

The second, dashed off in a hurry, was to Virgil Thomson in Paris. Like a man sucking at a sore tooth, I described our theatrical reverses of the past year:

...Failures that were sometimes honorable, sometimes idiotic and ignominious—but constant and uninterrupted! Looking back, I can see now how dearly we paid for our first success, our entry into the big time, our fame—Orson's and the theater's. We paid for it in many ways: in our personal relations and loyalties; in our changing public image, with audience-friendliness replaced by audience-challenge; in our own creative work where feelings of grandeur and what-is-expected-of-the-Mercury completely supplanted the simple desire to put on a good show. The fault is mine as much as his, since by failing to control and influence him and by letting him use the Mercury as an instrument of personal aggrandizement, I was betraying my most useful function in the partnership. *Five Kings* fell on its face (though it contained notable things and was often wonderful to look at and gave Orson a chance to be a magnificent Falstaff) not just through lack of time and technical inadequacies, as Orson likes to tell it himself, but because it was a half-baked project in which size and competitive "notions" took the place of love and thought.

We started the year fertile, successful, happy, foolish perhaps, but in love with ourselves and each other and the theater and the public. We ended it, tired to the point of sickness, full of hatred and distrust of each other, of our audience, of our theater—weary and full of fear and loathing for the whole business of producing plays together in the theater. And it left me, personally, without the fervor and, worst of all, without the love and faith which, during its brief, brilliant career, was the essential quality of the Mercury and before that of Project #891 and before that of the Negro Theater and before that of our *Four Saints*...

In its place we have had publicity in unbelievable quantities, snowballing to the point where Orson has become a public figure only less frequently and massively projected into the news and the national consciousness than Franklin D. Roosevelt, N. Chamberlain and A. Hitler. This new fame has grown in inverse proportion to the success of our recent artistic endeavors. It is unrelated to our work. In fact, it is just about fatal to our work. That is the main reason why, for seven months now, a picture (under one of the most magnificent contracts ever granted an artist in Hollywood) has been "about to be made," talked of, wondered about, defended, attacked, announced, postponed and reannounced in hundreds of publications with hundreds of thousands of words—without the picture itself (either on paper or even in Orson's own mind) having got beyond the most vaguely conceived first draft.

If and when it does get made, I shall not be there to see it. Because—not suddenly but after much painful communion with myself—I have decided to end our association.

If yours is the first letter I have written since the break, it is because you are one of the few—perhaps the only one since you were there from before its beginning—capable of understanding just how much of an uprooting the dissolution of this artistic marriage means to me. It was you who gave me my first taste of work-in-the-theater-by-those-who-have-faith-in-and-love-for-each-other; I know that you have regarded the direction I have taken with the Mercury and with Orson—if not with disapproval, then certainly with doubts. You have always disliked the notion of work produced on schedule and under compulsion—compulsion of any kind, whether of ambition or desperation or greed or the pressure of publicity or anything else. And you were right when you warned me that neither creative work nor human values could stand up under the kind of pressure to which Orson and I were subjecting them...

It is my great virtue that I can impart terrific initial acceleration to any project to which I am a part; it is my great weakness that I am unable (or unwilling) to control its speed once it is under way. Instead, there comes a day when I suddenly find myself disliking the direction in which it is moving and sick from the speed which I have helped to impose upon it. At that instant, having made quite sure right along that there is a safety-hatch open and working, I am likely suddenly to abandon ship. That is what I am now doing. For I am fond of Orson still and I retain much of my admiration for his talent: but our partnership is over for good and with it an exciting chapter of my life. It has been very wonderful and very painful and I am very glad that it is ended...

Reviens, donc! What are you doing in Europe, with a war on, that is half as important as returning home to influence the cultural life of your time? L'Amerique a besoin de toi. Moi surtout...

Je t'embrasse,

John

Virgil did not return until six months later, when he left Paris a week ahead of the Germans with fourteen pieces of luggage containing his scores, his collection of paintings and his new Lanvin suits. But I felt better, having written to him, and drove on after two days, through a snow-white desert, which I recognized in the newsreels five years later when it became the scene of the world's first atomic explosion. Four days after that I was in New York.

Back in my apartment on Ninth Street, with my mother as my house guest, divided between relief at my liberation and an almost unbearable sense of loneliness, I set about trying to fill the sudden vacuum in my life. I did not get very far. At five one morning I got a call from Chicago. It was from Orson. Would I meet him for lunch at "21"?

It was the first time we had seen each other since the night of the flaming sternos. After three dozen oysters, some jokes, sentimental amenities and an overwhelming display of charm, Orson came to the point. Things were getting grim at RKO; with *Heart of Darkness* still on the shelf and *The Smiler with the Knife* stalled, the miraculous contract had three and a half months to run and there was no film in sight. There was one faint glimmer of hope: Herman Mankiewicz had come up with a project—little more than a notion, but an exciting one. If it could be developed into some sort of screenplay in the next ten weeks, the situation might still be saved. Mankiewicz was notoriously unreliable: I asked Orson why he didn't take over the idea and write himself. He said he didn't want to do that. In the name of our former association he pleaded with me to fly back with him to California, talk to Mankiewicz and, if I shared his enthusiasm, stay and work with him as his collaborator and editor till the script was done. It was an absurd venture and that night Orson and I flew back to California together.

X
Citizen Kane
1940

Herman Mankiewicz was a legendary figure in Hollywood. The son of a respected New Jersey schoolteacher, one of a brilliant class at Columbia, he had fought in the war as a Marine, worked for the *World* and the *New York Times*, collaborated on two unsuccessful plays with two otherwise infallible playwrights, George Kaufman and Marc Connelly, came to California for six weeks to work on a silent film for Lon Chaney and stayed for sixteen years as one of the highest paid and most troublesome men in the business. His behavior, public and private, was a scandal. A neurotic drinker and a compulsive gambler, he was also one of the most intelligent, informed, witty, humane and charming men I have ever known.

His career would have been inconceivable anywhere but in the motion-picture business. At $2000 to $3000 a week, he had served B.P. Schulberg at Paramount, Louis B. Mayer at MGM and Harry Cohn at Columbia. But, since to employ him was to incur his contempt and deadly hate, he had goaded them, one by one, into barring him from their lots until, finally, there was nowhere left for him to go. Of the millions he had earned, nothing was left except debts. Of his numerous credits as writer and producer there were not more than half a dozen he was prepared to acknowledge; these included the early Marx Brothers pictures and *Million Dollar Legs*, with which he had bamboozled the entire industry (and delighted the intelligentsia of the Western world) by producing the first American surrealist film with W.C. Fields, Ben Turpin and Jack Oakie. Reduced to utter penury, with the bailiffs camped on the lawn, he had demeaned himself to the extent of writing a couple of our radio scripts, which I had edited rather harshly. Then, in his midforties, in twelve and a half weeks, for a few thousand dollars, he wrote *Citizen Kane*.

Out of our work together on that script a friendship was born that lasted until his death. For thirteen years, during my comings and goings, the house on Tower Road (in which he lived with his wife Sarah, a beautiful, indestructable Jewish madonna, and their three children, Don, Frank and a little blonde angel named Johanna) became for me what the Poors' house had been on the South Mountain Road. Throughout those years he was, variously, my collaborator, my father, my wayward son, my counsellor and a source of inexhaustible stimulation, exasperation and pleasure.

Throughout the fall and winter of 1939 Herman Mankiewicz had lain flat on his back in a cast with a triple fracture of his left leg. (His account of the accident was more than an hour long and was another surrealist movie in itself.) In that recumbent position we had worked without enthusiasm on a couple of radio shows that Orson had thrown his way. But now, as I sat by his bedside and listened while, between grunts, feverish stirrings and panic calls for Sarah, he outlined his notion for a film, I suddenly had the feeling that we might quite possibly have found what Orson was looking for.

It was something Mank had been thinking about for years: the idea of telling a man's private life (preferably one that suggested a recognizable American figure) immediately following his death, through the intimate and sometimes incompatible testimony of those who had known him at different times and in different circumstances.

In one of its earlier versions, the subject of this prismatic revelation had been a celebrated criminal like John Dillinger, whose personality and motivations were to be discovered, successively, through the eyes of his doting mother, the brother who hated him, a member of his gang, his childhood sweetheart, the FBI man who trailed him and the woman who had lived with him for the last month of his life before turning him in for the reward. Then one day an infinitely better idea had come to him. Total disagreement persists as to where the Hearst idea originated. The fact is that, as a former newspaperman and an avid reader of contemporary history, Mank had long been fascinated by the American phenomenon of William Randolph Hearst. Unlike his friends of the Left, to whom Hearst was not the archenemy, fascist isolationist and labor baiter, Mankiewicz remembered the years when Hearst had been regarded as the working man's friend and a political progressive. He had observed him later as a member of the film colony—grandiose, aging and vulnerable in the immensity of his reconstructed palace at San Simeon. By applying his "prism" notion to a figure of such complexity and stature and adding to it the charisma inherent in the public and private personality of Orson Welles, the possibility of a rich and unusual movie became apparent.

After Mank and I had talked for several hours and Sarah had sent our dinner up to his room, I phoned Orson from his bedside and told him I was ready to try. He arrived with a magnum of champagne and we talked on until Sarah threw us out. The next day—no longer as its president but as a writer—I signed a contract with Mercury Productions. At Mank's insistence and remembering how badly I myself had worked with Orson peering over my shoulder, it was stated in the agreement that we would do our work without interference and beyond his reach. Welles would be shown what there was of the script after six weeks and the rest of it, if he decided he wanted to continue, after we were finished. It was felt by everyone, especially Sarah, that our only hope of getting such a difficult script done in such a limited time was to move Mankiewicz out of his natural habitat—away form distractions and temptations. The retreat chosen for us was a guest ranch in the mesa country near Victorville at the top of the Cajon Pass.

Two days later, we set out for the San Bernardino Mountains in a small caravan that consisted of a studio limousine containing Mankiewicz, prone and protesting in the back seat, with a trained nurse and two pairs of crutches in the front, and a convertible driven by myself, containing a secretary, a typewriter and three cases of stationery and research material. The next day we went to work.

Our life at the Campbell Ranch was austere but comfortable; the food monotonous but adequate; the climate temperate, dry and perfect for work, with no distractions for a hundred miles around. Since we were there between seasons we had the place almost to ourselves during the week; weekends were crowded and there were musicales, symposia and folk dancing at night, from which we were excused on account of Mank's leg. He and I shared a bungalow with two bedrooms and a living room which we used as a study. His nurse was a long-suffering German body whom Mankiewicz summoned at all hours of the day and night for unnecessary services. The secretary, discovered and briefed by Sarah, was a patient, efficient, nice-looking English girl. No pair of Internal Revenue agents could have been more diligent in their daily inspection of Mank's room for intoxicants. This precaution proved unnecessary. With no family to make him feel guilty, no employer to hate and no one to compete with except an incomprehensible, cultivated, half-gentile hybrid with a British accent, the mental and emotional energy which had been squandered for years in self-generated conflicts and neurotic disorders was now concentrated on the single task of creating our script. After so many fallow years his fertility was amazing.

We started with the image of a man—a giant, a tycoon, a glamor figure, a controller of public opinion, a legend in his own lifetime—who had entered the world with all possible advantages, exploited them to the full, yet failed to achieve most of what he really wanted from life—including love. As we talked we asked each other how this man had got to be the way he was, made the choices he did. In the process we discovered what persons were associated with him; we learned what brought them together and what he did with them and to them over the years. In deciding who was qualified, personally and historically, to tell his story and reflect his image, in selecting the "prisms" which would most clearly reveal the parts from which we must finally create a whole, we found the dramatic structure of the film gradually asserting itself.

By trial and error we reduced the number of principal witnesses to five—each with different attitudes and subjective versions of the events of this man's extraordinary life: the lawyer-guardian, who had observed him with exasperated and impotent disapproval in childhood, at the height of his fortunes and in his final, predictable collapse; his manager, who followed him with slavish and admiring devotion from the beginning of his career through his greatest triumphs and down again; the friend who understood him better than anyone else and who, for that reason, finally split with him; his mistress, whom he came closest to loving and who, through no fault of her own, helped to destroy him; the servant, who saw only the ruin and the folly and the lonely end.

In the brouhaha that preceded and followed the first Hollywood showings of *Citizen Kane*, amid the accusations and denials, the massive pressures and the truculent refutations, the whole question of Kane's identification with Hearst became confused. The truth is simple: for the basic concept of Charles Foster Kane and for the main lines and significant events of his public life, Mankiewicz used as his model the figure of William Randolph Hearst. To this were added incidents and details invented or derived from other sources.

With the single exception of Susan Alexander whose situation, though not her personality, clearly resembled that of Marion Davies, our "witnesses" had no individual equivalents in the life of William Randolph Hearst. Bernstein was the prototype of the shrewd, unquestioningly loyal business manager. Jed Leland, Kane's best friend, was superficially modelled after Ashton Stevens, the drama dritic, a long-time friend of Hearst, and, incidentally, of Orson's father. Thatcher, the guardian-lawyer-banker, was a wholly fictitious personage, to whom Mank added overtones of J.P. Morgan, including a recent newsreel in which the haughty financier had been subjected, during a congressional investigation, to the humiliation of being photographed with a midget on his knee. This seemingly irrelevant clip was typical of the use Mank made throughout the script of historical material—real, reconstructed and imagined. From this constant cross-fertilization between myth, fact and fiction the film acquired much of its vitality and dimension.

Throughout our work on the screenplay of what later came to be called *Citizen Kane*, we had one special advantage: we were not working in a vacuum, developing a script for some absent producer; we were—and we never for one instant forgot it—creating a vehicle suited to the personality and creative energy of a man who, at twenty-four, was himself only slightly less fabulous than the mythical hero he would be portraying. And the deeper we penetrated beyond the public events into the heart of Charles Foster Kane, the closer we seemed to come to the identity of Orson Welles.

Orson was aware of this. Far from resisting the resemblance, he pushed it even further when he came to shoot the film. Kane's fury was of a special and recognizable kind. The wanton, wordless, destructive rage which Kane wreaks upon the inanimate objects in his wife's room when he realizes that she had left him was taken directly from our scene in the upper room at Chasen's. During its filming, Orson reproduced with frightening fidelity the physical gestures and the blind agony of rage with which he had hurled those flaming sternos against the wall. The cuts he received on his hands on both occasions were, I was told, almost identical.

Our days and nights on the Campbell Ranch followed a reassuring routine. Mankiewicz wrote and read half the night and slept in the morning. I got up early, went riding for an hour—my first contact with a horse since the Estancia Santa Maria. After that, while I waited for him to come to life, I would edit the pages Mank had dictated the night before, which the secretary had typed at dawn. At 9:30 Mank received his breakfast in bed. An hour later, having made an enormous production of shaving, washing and dressing himself on one leg, he was ready for work. This consisted of going over yesterday's material, arguing over changes and seeing how the new scenes fitted into the structure of the whole and affected the scenes to come.

The wranglers' daughters who served us our meals were frightened by our shouting, but we enjoyed our collaboration. Once Mank had come to trust me, my editing, for all our disagreements, gave him more creative freedom than his own neurotic self-censorship. We argued without competitiveness or embarrassment till the middle of the afternoon. At that time Mank, who suffered great pain from the knitting bones in his leg, would retire for his siesta while the secretary and I went over her notes. At six Mankiewicz rose ready and eager for the great adventure of the day, when I would drive him and his crutches to a railroad bar known as the Green Spot, where we slowly drank one Scotch apiece and watched the locals playing the pinball machines and dancing to the Western music of a jukebox. Once a week we visited the only movie, then returned to the Green Spot for dinner. Other evenings we worked until around ten, when I became sleepy from the mountain air. From my bed, through the closed door, I could hear Mank's voice as he continued his dictation, interrupted by games of cribbage which he had taught our devoted secretary.

We were not entirely incommunicado. Sarah drove up every other week to satisfy herself that all was well and seemed astounded to discover that it was. Orson telephoned at odd hours to inquire after our progress. On the appointed day, at the end of six weeks, he arrived in a limousine driven by Alfalfa, read a hundred pages of script, listened to our outline of the rest, dined with us at the Green Spot, thanked us and returned to Los Angeles. The next day he informed the Studio that he would start shooting early in July on a film which, at the time, was still entitled *American*.

The script grew harder to write as it went along. The richer and the more varied the sum of the testimonies became, the harder it got to keep them in manageable order. After each testimony it became necessary to go back into the script and make changes to conform to the new and sometimes seemingly contradictory events and situations that had just been revealed. Since our witnesses frequently appeared in scenes that took place before their own testimony began and stayed in the action long after their own story had ended, these multiple adjustments became increasingly complicated as the script developed.

Finally, after ten weeks, we were done. *Rosebud* had been reduced to ashes in the incinerator at Xanadu. The script was more than four hundred pages long—overrich, repetitious, loaded with irrelevant, fascinating detail and private jokes. We spent two more weeks going through it with machetes—hacking away, trimming, simplifying, clarifying its main dramatic line and yelling at each other all the time. Above all, we worked on the connective tissue, substituting sharp cinematic cuts and visual transitions for what, in the first version, had too often been leisurely verbal and literary expositions. And, for the twentieth time, I reorganized the March of Time, which had become my special domain, to conform to what now appeared to be significant facts in the life of Charles Foster Kane.

Our peace was disturbed, during the last fortnight, by the news that was coming in night and day over the radio. The "phony war" was over: Hitler's invasion of Belgium and France had begun. Mank could not bear to be away from the half-dozen newspapers he was in the habit of reading each day. We extended our working hours. Then, one evening, from the Green Spot, I called the Studio and ordered the limousine for the next day. Mank's leg was almost healed, but he clung to his invalid's privileges. He lay alone, groaning, in the rear seat of the limousine, and I followed in the convertible as we made the reverse journey through the Cajon Pass, down the steep curves of the San Bernardino Mountains, between the vineyards and orange groves of Azusa, through the slums of Los Angeles to the RKO Studio in Hollywood, where, before returning Mankiewicz to his home, we solemnly presented Orson with a screenplay whose blue title page read:

AMERICAN
by
Herman Mankiewicz

That night, in the lobby of the Chateau Marmont, I listened incredulously to the crackling, fading short-wave broadcast of the capitulation speech by the King of the Belgians.

In the days that followed there were moments when I regretted my decision to return to New York. The whole mood of the Mercury unit was suddenly changed: Orson was working, once again, with a concentrated, single-minded intensity that I had not seen since the first year of the Mercury. He took me to his art director's room, its walls covered with hundreds of production sketches, some by Welles himself, in which all our notions of the past three months had begun to find form and substance. He introduced me to Gregg Toland, one of the industry's top cameramen, who had come to him and offered to work on his film. They were making tests that day and the next for the part of Susan Alexander. Having no one in the Mercury company who could play it and determined to use no familiar faces, Orson was working with two contract girls from the Studio. One was Lucille Ball, the other a reddish blonde named Winter, who later resumed her real name of Dorothy Comingore.

I stayed on for three days breathing the dizzying air of an excitement of which I no longer felt myself a part. On the fourth day I asked for a studio car to drive me to the station. I spent my first night and day on the eastbound Santa Fe Superchief rereading a novel to which Mank and I had decided to try and obtain the dramatic rights—Richard Wright's *Native Son*.

Mankiewicz stayed on at RKO throughout the making of *Citizen Kane*, as it came to be called, torn between his enthusiasm over the way Welles was shooting it and his indignation (which grew as he realized what a great picture it was going to be) at Orson's tacit, at first, and then quite open assumption of writing credit on the film. It was a brawl I had seen coming and of which I was determined to have no part.

Citizen Kane is Welles's film. The dramatic genius that animates it and the creative personality with which it is imbued are wholly and undeniably Orson's—just as, in another medium, *The War of the Worlds* owed its final impact to his miraculous touch. But he did not write either of them.

Long before "auteurism" became part of the critical film jargon, it had been generally accepted that a script (no matter how complete, detailed or brilliant) is only the first stage in the creative process of film making. In *Kane*, Welles's direction of his own and the other actors' performances, his pacing, his strong, personal visual concept (including his brilliant use of Toland's deep-focus photography), his audacious cutting and, above all, the theatrical vitality with which he filled every frame of the film—all these add up to make it one of the world's recognized masterpieces. But it could not have been made without Mankiewicz's screenplay.

It is no denigration of Welles's talent to observe that, throughout his career, he has functioned most effectively and created most freely when he was supported by a strong text. Mankiewicz supplied him with such a structure.

Since no one has ever disputed Welles's cinematic authorship of *Citizen Kane* and since its success and fame, like that of *The War of the Worlds*, was overwhelmingly his, how does one explain the furious malignance with which he has attempted to deny both Koch and Mankiewicz the writing credits to which they were entitled? It as always difficult to fathom an ego like Orson's, to understand the alchemy through which any project in which he was even remotely involved became automatically and wholly his own. For this reason he was genuinely surprised and disturbed when, in place of gratitude, his collaborators expressed an unreasonable desire for personal credit. When, like Koch or Mankiewicz (both of whom profited greatly from their collaboration with Welles), they persisted in their demands, he regarded their attitude as disloyal and treacherous.

Writing was a particularly sensitive region of Orson's ego. It was a form of creativity in which he had never excelled but in which he refused to concede defeat. His ability to push a dramatic situation far beyond its normal level of tension made him a great director but an inferior dramatist. His story sense was erratic and disorganized; whenever he strayed outside the solid structure of someone else's work, he ended in formless confusion. This was something his ego would not acknowledge. It was also something which, for more mundane reasons, he could not afford to admit. *"Written, produced, directed and performed by Orson Welles"* was the wording of his contracts with the mass media: it justified the amount of money and the degree of artistic freedom which he was able to demand and obtain from his employers. For anyone else to receive credit—particularly a writing credit—on one of his productions not only diminished him personally but threatened the entire fiction of his superhuman capacity. After the notoriety he had achieved with *The War of the Worlds*, how could he let it be known that a $60-a-week scribbler had, in fact, been responsible for the script? Following a year of false starts, how could he acknowledge that his first film was based on the work of a well-known Hollywood hack?

It was during my last three days in California that I made my final contribution to *Citizen Kane*. Bernard Herrmann had arrived from New York to work on the score, including the opera in which Susan Kane makes her ill-fated debut in the opera house her husband has built for her. Benny had decided not to use a scene from a standard opera but to create one of his own. He decided it should be a French opera and asked me to write him a text. Remembering my father's bathroom recitations, I hurriedly assembled a potpourri from Racine's *Athalie* with some added lines from *Phèdre*. It did not make much sense; as sung by an unknown soprano, lip-sync'd by Dorothy Comingore, it was barely intelligible; but, around it, Orson built one of the great visual sequences of his film. I was not present when he shot it, for by that time I was back in New York and finished for good with Charles Foster Kane though not, quite yet, with Orson Welles.

* * *

For a living I had signed a contract for the fall to be one of two writers on the Helen Hayes weekly dramatic radio show. Free of money worries, I was now able to return to the theater and, more specifically, to Richard Wright's *Native Son*, which had become a national best seller and to which I was eager to obtain the producing rights.

Having learned that Wright was in Mexico, I asked a visiting friend to call upon him and stake my claim. She found him beside a pool in Cuernavaca and learned that arrangements had already been made for Paul Green to dramatize the work. I was disappointed, but it was a reasonable choice: Green was the first white playwright to write sympathetically of Negro life in the South. However, I had my own personal doubts as to Green's suitability for this particular task: *Native Son* was a violent, revolutionary work that did not accord with Green's perceptive and sensitive but essentially Southern, rural attitude towards the race problem in America. However, it was done and the next best thing was to try and secure the producing rights. With my record in the Negro theater this was not difficult, and in July, I was informed that Wright was returning from Mexico and would go directly to North Carolina to work with Green on the play script.

I was there when Wright arrived—a surprisingly mild-mannered, round-faced, brown-skinned young man with beautiful eyes. It was only later, when I came to know him better, that I began to sense the deep, almost morbid violence that lay skin-deep below that gentle surface. At that first meeting I was surprised—not altogether agreeably—by the blandness with which he recounted the shameful story of his return to his native land. At Brownsville, at the border, a Texan customs inspector had pawed through his baggage, suspiciously examined and criticized his manuscripts and books ("Where's your Bible, boy?") and demanded to know where he got the money for travel and clothes. On the train that carried him across the South he had, of course, been denied access to the dining car and the black waiter carrying his meal to the Jim Crow chair car was stopped as he passed through the train and forbidden to serve a nigger on dining-car china with white men's linen and silver.

I spent a day with him and Green, listening to Paul's ideas for the play. I watched Dick Wright for his reactions: I saw nothing. But my own apprehension rose sharply. Paul Green was a man who sincerely believed himself free of racial prejudice. His action in inviting Wright to live in his home during their collaboration was an act of some courage—even in an academic community like Chapel Hill, North Carolina. Throughout his stay, according to Dick, he could not have been more courteous, thoughtful and hospitable in his treatment of his black guest. But, having granted him social equality, he stopped there. From the first hour of their "discussions" it became clear that he was incapable or unwilling to extend this equality into the professional or creative fields. Whether from his exalted position as veteran playwright and Pulitzer Prize-winner or from some innate sense of intellectual and moral superiority (aggravated by Wright's Communist connections), Paul Green's attitude in the collaboration was, first and last, insensitive, condescending and intransigent. The basic and radical premise of Wright's novel—that only through an act of violence could a Negro like Bigger Thomas break through the massive and highly organized repressive structure by which he was surrounded ("The most I could say of Bigger was that he felt the *need* for a whole life and *acted* out that need; that was all")—was something that Green refused to accept, morally or artistically. Resenting what he called Dick's existentialism, he attempted, till the day of the play's opening, to evade and dilute the dramatic conclusion with which Wright had consciously and deliberately ended a book in which he wanted his readers to face the horrible truth "without the consolation of tears."

When I left them to their uneasy collaboration, Green estimated it would take him less than two months for a first draft. Until then there was nothing I could do but tamp down my apprehensions and start making arrangements for an early production, so as to profit from *Native Son's* continued presence on the best-seller lists. I called Mankiewicz to tell him of my progress, listened to his ambivalent ravings about "Monstro" (his latest name for Welles) whom he alternately described as (1) a genius shooting one of the greatest films ever made and (2) a scoundrel and a thief who was now claiming sole credit for the writing of *Citizen Kane.*

Five or six weeks later I got a call from Richard Wright in North Carolina saying that Green's first draft had gone to the typist and that he would be returning to New York. I asked him to wait till I had a chance to read it, but he said there was nothing more he could do. He sounded so discouraged that I told him I'd be down the next day and drive him back. Knowing my mother's passion for motoring, I invited her to drive with me through country she had never seen. The next day I met with Wright and Green, who seemed satisfied with his work. Richard said nothing but on the way up I sensed enough to ask him with some impatience why, if he was so disturbed, he had not spoken up and given me a chance to provoke a confrontation. Wright, who had quit the Party but remained a disciplined Marxist, replied that under no circumstances would he risk a public disagreement with a man like Paul Green. There were too many people on both sides anxious to enjoy a racial dogfight between a best-selling black author and a white Southern writer of progressive reputation—an avowed friend of the Negro people.

Some days later a "first rough working draft" arrived. Structurally it stayed fairly close to the book, which Wright had consciously written in dramatic scene form. ("I wanted the reader to feel that Bigger's story was happening *now* like a play upon a stage or a movie on a screen.") But the "editorial changes"—the additions and modifications—exasperated me. More serious in my opinion was the changed moral attitude that pervaded the script, leading inevitably to a total betrayal of Wright's intention in the closing scene. This was the scene of which Wright had written:

At last I found how to end the book; I ended it just as I had begun it, showing Bigger living dangerously, taking his life in his hands, accepting what life had made of him. The lawyer, Max, was placed in Bigger's cell at the end to register the moral—or what I felt was the moral—horror of Negro life in the United States.

This final facing of the terrible truth of his life was distorted, in Green's version, by giving Bigger "lyric" delusions in which he saw himself as "a black God, single and alone."

I urged Wright to repudiate what I considered a deliberate betrayal of his work. I told him I had no intention of producing the play in its present form. Dick continued to be distressed but repeated that he preferred not to see it produced than to risk a public disagreement with Paul Green. There was nothing more I could do. My option ran for three and a half months longer. I put the script in a drawer, swallowed my disappointment and turned back to my radio work, including a version of *The Trojan Women* that I developed with Virgil Thomson.

* * *

One morning around Thanksgiving I awoke in my raised, red-velvet bed and raged at the thought that I owned one of the hottest theatrical properties in the world and was prevented from doing anything with it by a peculiar combination of Southern moral prejudice and black, Marxist scruples. I called up Dick Wright and asked him to come over to Ninth Street for lunch. I told him I had re-examined the book and Green's dramatization of it: the revised version was structurally sound; wherever it followed the novel it was usable; where it deviated, as in the absurd final scene, it was reparable by returning to his own original text. Dick asked if we would let Green know what we were doing. I said no. The restoration would be done entirely on my authority as producer and I would assume full responsibility for it.

Almost every morning for three weeks, he came over from Brooklyn Heights (where he lived in the basement apartment of a house that was also inhabited by Oliver Smith, Paul Bowles and Wystan Auden) and we would work our way through the scenes, transfusing the blood of the novel back into the body of the play. We had a good time and when we were done I had the script retyped and took it with me to California, where I was flown at the invitation of David Selznick, who was looking for an associate producer to help to run his studio while he rested after his triumphs with *Gone with the Wind* and *Rebecca*. I listened to him talk for four hours, then drove to RKO, where Orson ran the work print of *Citizen Kane* for me. That night, in my first spasm of enthusiasm, I did what I had vowed I would never do again. I gave Orson the new script of *Native Son* and asked him if he would like to direct it as a Mercury production.

He called me in New York two days later and said yes, very much, as soon as he had seen *Citizen Kane* through its releasing pains— probably in mid-February. My feelings were mixed by this time. I had set my heart on directing this one myself. But I was anxious to end my theatrical association with Welles on a note of triumph and I felt that Orson's direction of *Native Son* would be more dynamic than mine. I gave Wright the news and he was delighted. So was Paul Green.

My relations with Orson during the production were different from what they had been during our partnership. Not being so close made it easier for us to work together. He and Jean Rosenthal (who was beginning to achieve fame on the outside) worked out a production scheme in which, behind a vast, permanent, brick-painted portal, ten wagons of various sizes moved past and around each other with never more than a few inches to spare. It took thirty-five stagehands to move them but they worked without a hitch. And, for once, we had no money problems. Since *Kane*, Hollywood was suddenly full of operators eager for a piece of the action—Orson's action. Two of them, in the hope of becoming his partners in future film ventures, put up the money for *Native Son* to the tune of $55,000.

Assembling the cast was a pleasure: it was made up of Mercury regulars (returned from California) and former members of the WPA Negro unit, including Canada Lee who had played Banquo for us in *Macbeth* and whom the role of Bigger was about to make a Broadway star.

For our script we used the text Wright and I had worked on. The few changes we made in rehearsal were all returns to the book. Dick came regularly and seemed to enjoy himself. Then one day I got word that Paul Green would be in New York for the final run-throughs. He appeared in the theater one evening, sat in silence and left without a word after the last scene. The next morning, the day of our first preview, we held a meeting: Green, Wright, his agent, Welles and myself. Green insisted that we reinstate his version—particularly the final scene. I told him it was much too late for that and, besides, we had no intention of being parties to the distortion of a work we admired. Richard sat silent beside his agent, who now informed us that Green's version (credited to Paul Green and Richard Wright) was already in his publisher's hands. I suggested he get it back and change it to conform to the acting version. Green was furious. When Orson began to howl at him, he got up and left and we never saw him again. After our successful opening I called his publisher and pointed out the absurdity of the situation. But it was too late and as long as it remained in print, *Harper's* continued to circulate a version of the play that was radically different from what had been performed on stage.

At the final preview of *Native Son* two sets of pickets suddenly appeared on 44th Street. One, from the conservative Urban League, was protesting the squalor of the book and the bad light in which it put the Negro people. The other represented a small, purist faction of the intellectual Communist Party, which could not forgive Richard Wright for having defied Party orders and refused to rewrite certain sections of his book at their behest. They left after an hour and did not reappear on opening night, which took place on March 24 as a Mercury production presented by Orson Welles and John Houseman.

Native Son was a hit and played for fifteen weeks to predominantly white audiences: it was an expensive show to run and with the coming of the hot weather our Hollywood backers decided to close it. It reopened the following fall in a more economical version, directed by Jack Berry, that was seen in New York and Eastern cities for the better part of a year. In certain places such as Chicago and St. Louis where tensions ran high, it played under police protection in an atmosphere that was close to that of a race riot.

* * *

David O. Selznick, when I went to work for him in the spring of 1941, was at the peak of his success. He had produced *Gone with the Wind*, the most costly and the most profitable film made up to that time, and followed it up with *Rebecca*, Alfred Hitchcock's first American picture—also a winner. He was a dynamic, flamboyant, spoiled, utterly egotistical man. Compared with Orson he was semieducated and uninspired but he had an infallible, instinctive sense of the motion-picture business with its strange blend of blatant romanticism and commercial preoccupation. By inheritance and marriage he was an organic part of the Hollywood establishment. His father was a notorious early freebooter. His brother Myron was the first of the great manipulating talent agents. David himself, through his dynastic marriage to the handsome and brilliant Irene Mayer, had acquired the head of MGM as a father-in-law and future business associate. For all his arrogance and exasperating self-indulgence, he was a man of intelligence and considerable charm—a typical Hollywood combination of oafishness and sophistication. We remained friends long after I stopped working for him—on a superficial, male, competitive basis that usually consisted, when we met, of comparing our weight and the beauty and talent of our respective mistresses. (He once tried to bet me $1000 that, within a year, "his" would be making

$50,000 more per picture than "mine.")

I was under the impression that what Selznick needed, while he rested on his laurels and watched the money roll in, was someone to keep his studio active and to produce pictures in his place with his producing organization. I could not have been more mistaken. David O. Selznick had not the slightest intention of letting anyone make pictures in his studio except himself.

My first assignment for Selznick was to work on Charlotte Brontë's *Jane Eyre*. As usual, David was in a hurry; he had sent Robert Stevenson—an English writer-director whom he had under contract—to New York to work on it with me. Soon after the opening of *Native Son*, we flew back to the Coast together and five weeks after that, with Stevenson doing most of the work, we finished it and presented it to our leader, only to discover that he had not the slightest intention of producing it. Instead he began offering it around, together with the services of Joan Fontaine and Robert Stevenson, at a price so fabulous that it was not until the war-boom a year later that he was able to sell it to Twentieth Century Fox. (It was made in my absence with Joan Fontaine as the nubile Jane, Orson Welles as Mr. Rochester and a troupe of moppets that included Margaret O'Brien and Elizabeth Taylor.)

My second assignment was to work with Alfred Hitchcock. It was no secret that all had not been roses between him and David during the making of *Rebecca* to which Hitch had attempted to apply the very personal creative methods that had made him world-famous. These methods were profoundly repulsive to David O. Selznick, who belonged to the school of the well-made, producer-controlled, strictly-adhere-to-shooting script. As a result I was instructed to use my British background to establish good personal relations with Hitch and to cajole and encourage him into conceiving and preparing an "original" screenplay for his second American film.

In the course of this delicate mission I developed a relationship with Hitch and Alma, his wife, that lasted through the years I lived in California and beyond. I had heard of him as a fat man given to scabrous jokes—a gourmet and an ostentatious connoisseur of fine wines. What I was unprepared for was a man of exaggeratedly delicate sensibilities, marked by a harsh Catholic education and the scars from a social system against which he was in perpetual revolt and which had left him suspicious and vulnerable, alternately docile and defiant. He was an entertaining and knowledgeable companion: books and paintings, dogs, houses and politics all occupied a place in his life. But his passion was for his work, which he approached with an intelligence and an almost scientific clarity to which I was unaccustomed in the theater.

Rebecca had been a distasteful experience for him. Anxious to get started on a new and more individual film, he came up with a notion for a picaresque spy story—a U.S. version of *The Thirty-nine Steps*—with a transcontinental chase that moved from coast to coast and ended inside the hand of the Statue of Liberty. He called it *The Saboteur* and we outlined it to Selznick, who thought it was terrible but gave us the go-ahead—the quicker the better.

Working with Hitch really meant listening to him talk—anecdotes, situation, characters, revelations and reversals, which he would think up at night and try out on us during the day and of which the surviving elements were finally strung together into some sort of story in accordance with carefully calculated and elaborately plotted rhythms. His listeners on this project were Joan Harrison (an able, well-tailored English blonde who had been his assistant in London), Peter Viertel (an apprentice writer in Selznick's stable whose first novel had just been published), occasionally Alma Hitchcock (who had been one of the highest-paid continuity writers in English silent pictures) and myself.

My own enjoyment of the work was diminished by the knowledge that I would have nothing to do with its production, since David had every intention of selling it outright, together with Hitchcock's services as a director, to the highest bidder. (Hitchcock's resentment of what he regarded as exploitation became so deep that it finally affected the quality of the picture. *The Saboteur* was sold to an independent producer who paid so much for the property that he was forced to economize on the making of the film. It was less conscientiously produced than any of the other Hitchcock pictures, but David made a net profit of over $100,000 on the transaction.)

My next activity for Selznick was something I was delighted to do. Ingrid Bergman was between pictures and someone (perhaps herself) suggested that she was a natural for the name part in Eugene O'Neill's *Anna Christie*. I came up with the idea that we do it in Santa Barbara, 100 miles up the coast, where there was an excellent theater and a civilized audience. Within twenty-four hours David had inflated this into a gala summer theater season which he asked me to direct and for which I was rewarded the vice-presidency of David O. Selznick Productions.

Ingrid was a joy to work with. She was eager, passionate, well-prepared and she gave me everything I asked for except the feeling that Anna was corrupted and doomed. (One had the conviction that beneath her period skirt her underclothes were starched, clean and sweet-smelling.) It was a success, with a full Hollywood, Selznick-promoted opening, and we moved it to San Francisco, where we played for another two weeks before Ingrid had to return to Culver City to begin *Dr. Jekyll and Mr. Hyde* with Spencer Tracy.

The night of our San Francisco opening I was taken to Izzy Gomez's bar (supposedly the scene of *The Time of Your Life*), where I encountered William Saroyan surrounded by characters from his works. I asked him if he had a new play we could do in Santa Barbara. He said he had a piece called *Hello Out There!* which he'd finish by the end of the week and send to me. He did and we went into rehearsal with it two weeks later. The boy was played by a young man who later became Harry Morgan of *M*A*S*H* and the girl by a completely unknown young actress whose name Selznick had just changed from Phyllis Walker to Jennifer Jones.

In October familiar faces appeared on the RKO Pathé lot where Orson Welles was beginning to shoot *The Magnificent Ambersons*. We had done it on the Mercury radio show: Booth Tarkington had been a close friend of Orson's father and the Midwestern scene at the turn of the century was very close to his heart. I watched him shoot part of the opening sequence—the long approach through the industrial streets to the family mansion, the slow move up the grand staircase into the glittering ballroom of the Amberson home. In its rough cut, before it was edited to meet the requirements of a normal-length feature picture, it was one of the most extraordinary film sequences I have ever seen.

It may have been Orson's presence on the lot, sharply reminding me of the creative excitement in which I no longer had a part, that finally stirred me to revolt against the well-paid, tranquil, irrelevant life I was leading as vice-president of David O. Selznick Productions. But the discontent had been there for months, running deep under the frustrations of my career; and it had to do, in part, with the state of the world.

Throughout my years with the Federal Theater and during the rise and fall of the Mercury, I had been accustomed to relate my theatrical activity to the historical movements of the time. On WPA this participation had been direct and inescapable. On the Negro theater and later on Project #891 we were reminded daily, by friends and enemies alike, that our work was an essential part of the social and political life of our day. Some of this sense of involvement was carried over into the Mercury, where it directly affected our choice of subjects and our methods of operation.

Now all this had changed. The violent confusions of the Nazi-Soviet Pact leading to the invasion of Poland, the stress of the "phony war" followed by the fall of France and the threatened invasion of Britain—each had its cumulative, traumatic effect and created tensions to which no creative response was possible and to which my theatrical activities could no longer be related. For a time I had been diverted by the constant, furious pressures of the Mercury operation and the personal crises of my deteriorating relations with Orson Welles. When these finally ceased, I found myself suddenly alone and vulnerable.

My outward circumstances had changed—mostly for the better. I was making more money than I ever made in my life and I had acquired a certain reputation in show business. But, under the surface, there was the old frightening sense of isolation, of being hopelessly adrift while I waited (with not the faintest idea of when or from where it was coming) for some great new wind to arise and fill my drooping sails.

Late in November I received a call from my friend Pare Lorentz. He had just arrived to make a movie for RKO, where George Schaeffer, his courage restored by the artistic success of *Citizen Kane*, had decided to try his luck with another maverick film maker. As a result Pare was hard at work on his most ambitious project—a dramatic documentary about the condition of the R.S. industrial worker with special emphasis on the economic and emotional effects of the production line. He called it alternately *Ecce Homo* and *Name, Age and Occupation*, and he had already shot several tens of thousands of feet of industrial footage in Detroit.

I was fond of Pare, impressed by his films and, even more, by his passionate and comprehensive historical sense about the United States of America. He asked me to help with the script and casting of his new project and I leaped at the chance. I pointed out to Selznick that he would be saving several thousand dollars by loaning me out during the idle holiday season. He agreed and I went to work with Pare the next day. It was not the great wind I was waiting for but I had the sense, once again, of participating in the realities of the world.

Our collaboration was less successful than mine with Mankiewicz; Pare's feeling for his material was entirely subjective and personal and he was having difficulty reconciling his documentary approach to the requirements of this, his first full-length dramatic film. We were making slow progress when Pare decided that the moment had come for a trip to New York to discover some of those unknown faces he was determined to use in his picture. We flew east together and interviewed scores of males between the ages of twenty-five and thirty-five. We chose two of them and RKO put them under contract. (Neither of them appeared in Pare's film, which was never made. They both went off to war: one was killed at Iwo Jima; the other, Robert Ryan, returned home and became a star.) In Chicago, during the usual long wait between the trains, we stopped off at the Blackstone Hotel; in the lobby Pare encountered Senator William Benton, who assured us over drinks that we did not understand the real feelings of the country: the Middle West was solidly isolationist; Charles Lindbergh was a popular hero; Roosevelt would never get us into war, no matter how hard he tried. We left him to catch our train, talked and fell asleep. The next day, around noon, speeding through western Kansas, we heard the news of Pearl Harbor over the radio in the club car and stayed there for the rest of the day and night drinking and listening to the news with mixed feelings of exhilaration and terror.

Crossing the desert we heard the President's declaration of war and in California, when we arrived, there was much talk of a Japanese invasion and of enemy submarines off the coast. The next night some of Hollywood's more pugnacious and athletic performers relieved their tensions by putting on their riding boots, going down to Chinatown and beating up a number of Orientals.

A week later I was flying east again on a government priority, in response to a telegram I had received from Washington from Robert Sherwood. (I was familiar with his plays; I had met him socially and professionally over the years and I knew he was close to the White House and had drafted several of the President's most important recent speeches.) He received me in a bare, makeshift office in the old state department building, then led me down the hall to meet a tough, white-haired charmer named William ("Wild Bill") Donovan, a hero of World War I and one of the country's most successful lawyers, whom the President had recently named Coordinator of Information. They surprised me by asking how soon I could come east and go to work organizing what was to be known as the Voice of America. I told them I needed a few days to wind up my affairs in California and took the night plane back to Los Angeles.

It was a tedious flight with a number of stops but it gave me time to consider the exciting new turn in my life which I apparently owed to my mother's fanatical faith in the value of foreign tongues. (There were dozens of men with experience in big-time radio but few, if any, with an intimate knowledge of languages—French, German, and Spanish and a smattering of Italian—that would be most generally used in our wartime foreign broadcasts.) It also gave me time to consider a troubling personal problem that had taken on a sudden urgency—my own uncertain attitude towards the war in which I was suddenly being called to play an important part.

For the past two years my reactions had been not unlike those of a sports enthusiast who, from the depths of his armchair, follows the fortunes of the team with which he has sentimentally identified himself. There was no doubt as to where my sympathies lay: the fall of France had shaken me—particularly the Occupation of Paris, which had been my mother's home for so long and where I had spent many of the happiest times of my childhood. Later, I had anxiously followed the Battle of Britain; many of those being bombed and threatened with invasion were people to whom I was still bound with ties of adolescent memory. Yet never, for one single moment, had I found myself transforming these nostalgic emotions into that sense of personal loyalty and obligation that I might have been expected to feel for a country in which I had lived for so many years and to which I had so desperately yearned to belong.

I could excuse this lack of involvement by telling myself that when I crossed the Atlantic at the age of twenty-two to take up my new life in America I had severed my ties with a society that, I reminded myself, had never fully accepted me. This rationalization worked—up to a point. Though I could not altogether suppress a vague sense of betrayal and guilt, I managed to live with it without serious inconvenience. Now, as America was suddenly and dramatically drawn into the war, I became aware that I was once again being put to the test.

For most of the people around me the shock of Pearl Harbor had been followed by a sense of relief that the long suspense or our uneasy neutrality had come to an end. The Left, enervated by the uncertainties and shifting political lines of the past three years; the impatient Anglophiles; the Jews, eager to avenge the horrors of Nazi persecution; even the America-Firsters and the chronic Roosevelt-haters—they were all united now in a sudden surge of patriotic fervor that I alone seemed unable or unwilling to share.

This alienation was not new but its persistence now struck me as disagreeable and dangerous. I could argue that I should not be expected to feel any strong patriotic emotion for a country of which I was not even a citizen. Yet I had long recognized the United States as my home, where I had been offered surprising opportunities of which I had taken substantial advantage.

I knew I was not incapable of devotion and loyalty. I had proved it with my commitment to the New Deal's WPA Theater in its most difficult times. But those were special circumstances—a combination of love, ambition and a new-found sense of social responsibility fused by the magic of the theater into an irresistible cause. It was quite another thing to extend these emotions to the more general and conventional concept of patriotism.

Perhaps I had changed countries too often. By the time I was twenty-one I had held three nationalities: Rumanian by birth, French by inheritance, English by upbringing and naturalization. I had lived in the United States for the past seventeen years—seven of them illegally, in constant fear of deportation. That situation had finally been corrected: I had re-entered the country in 1936 as a legitimate immigrant and applied for citizenship which, after six years, had not yet come through. But now, with the outbreak of war, things had become complicated again. Having been born in Rumania, I was formally classified as an Enemy Alien!

I did not mention this to Sherwood or Donovan in Washington nor did I draw attention to it in the official forms I filled out at their behest. If I had any private doubts as to my suitability as Head of the Overseas Radio Programming Bureau of the Foreign Information Service of the United States, I kept them to myself as I hurriedly wound up my life in Los Angeles—informing David O. Selznick that he was losing his vice-president to the war, giving up my small house in Laurel Canyon, saying goodbye to friends and generally preparing myself for the job ahead.

Back in New York, where I received my formal Civil Service appointment in the name of Jacques Haussmann, no one, least of all myself, seemed to question the propriety of placing the Voice of America under the direction of an enemy alien who, as such, was expressly forbidden by the U.S. Department of Justice to go near a short-wave radio set. My dilemma soon disappeared: within a few days I had become totally absorbed in the kind of frenzied and all-consuming activity that has never failed to solve my most complicated and disturbing personal problems.

XI
The Voice of America
1942-43

Long after it had become evident that the United States would soon be at war, no official information or propaganda service existed. International propaganda, to the American mind, was something tyrants and fascists resorted to: it was an activity democracies preferred to avoid.

By 1941 this attitude was changing. In that year two new U.S. government agencies were set up:

1) The COI (Coordinator of Information) under Colonel William Donovan, created with "authority to collect and analyze material dealing with national security and to carry out any supplementary activities requested by the President";

2) The FIS (Foreign Information Service), created by Robert Sherwood as an organization devoted to the collection and dissemination of U.S. information overseas.

This assignment of overlapping functions was typical of Roosevelt's method of government. To Donovan and Sherwood, aside from their personal, temperamental disagreements, "psychological warfare" meant two entirely different things. The former saw it as a military weapon with emphasis on covert, underground operations; he was not averse to "lies and deception" and other dirty tricks where they were required for strategic purposes. The latter sincerely believed that "all U.S. information to the world should be considered as though it were a continuous speech by the President."

In January, 1942, the U.S. possessed thirteen dubious short-wave transmitters—against Germany's sixty-eight and Japan's forty-six. These scant facilties were owned and operated by private companies broadcasting a few hours a day with limited staffs. The U.S. Government had no control over what they were broadcasting and no way of ensuring that overseas listeners received a concerted view of American opinion. Soon after Pearl Harbor the President moved to correct this; all existent short-wave transmitters were leased, acquired or commandeered till, by the summer of 1942, there was not one single private American short-wave transmitter broadcasting overseas. (The last holdout, in Scituate, Massachusetts, was taken over, finally, by a detachment of Marines at pistol point.)

Even more controversial than the new agencies' dealings with the private stations were their relations with established government organizations. From the start, the State Department was distrustful of activities which contrasted with its own slow, tradition-bound procedures. "Donovan is a thorn in the side," one official complained and a War Department official described the COI as "a fly-by-night civilian outfit headed by a wild man who's trying to horn in on the war."

Sherwood, with his lower profile and more cultivated manner, was less subject to attack. With access to the White House and the ear of Harry Hopkins, he moved forward with the development of the Foreign Information Service and early in 1942 he was ready to launch his country's psychological warfare activities.

I was back in New York early in January, three weeks after Pearl Harbor, and spent two days moving back into my apartment on Ninth Street with its tall french windows, pale yellow walls, white moldings and raised, red-velvet bed. On the third day I reported to the office of the Foreign Information Service at 270 Madison Avenue.

The man who came out to greet me that first morning and who introduced himself as Joseph Barnes wore unpressed gray flannel slacks and a dark blue blazer with tarnished brass buttons. He seemed to be about my age, with light brown hair and a pale, rather worn face; my first impression was one of subtle intelligence and perfect manners overlaying a core of unmistakable toughness. Later, as I got to know him better, I discovered other laminations of sincerity and guile, rashness and calculation. Knowing little of the newspaper world, I was unaware of Joe's brilliant career as a foreign correspondent. Educated at Harvard, the London School of Economics and the Institute of Slavonic Languages, he went into banking as a young man but left it for journalism, in which he soon made his mark. He was correspondent for the *New York Herald Tribune* in Moscow from 1937 to 1939, then in Berlin for some months before he was called back to become Foreign News Editor. Early in the summer of 1941 he was granted leave by the *Tribune* to join Sherwood in setting up the U.S. Foreign Information Service where he soon became Sherwood's deputy and chief of the New York office.

He led me on a tour of the half-finished premises and introduced me to some of the people with whom I would be working. Some were old friends; among them, in a dark corner next to the men's room, bent myopically over a yellow legal-sized pad, I found my former roommate and co-author, Lewis Galantière, who had left the Federal Reserve Bank to join Sherwood as an expert on French affairs. Also present was Alice Thomas, a wonderful black woman who had been my secretary on the Negro Theater Project.

Others whom I met for the first time that morning were Ed Barrett, formerly of *Newsweek* and now head of our News and Features Department; a young German theater director from Munich named Werner Michel who became my production assistant; Edd Johnson, head of Control Desk—a brilliant journalist with an untidy personal life who became my closest collaborator in the months to come.

Sherwood was away the day I reported. So it was Barnes and Johnson, over lunch at a bar around the corner, who described the work I was expected to do. This was nothing less than to create what would be known as the Voice of America.

Everyone, including our British Allies, was eager for us to begin transmitting our own overseas broadcasts—particularly those addressed to the people of enemy and occupied countries. My first urgent assignment, therefore, was to design, organize, test and produce a daily show in German that would reflect the spirit of America at war and that could then be used as a model for programs in other languages. I asked how soon I was expected to go on the air. "Tomorrow," said Johnson, and ordered us each another brandy. When we got back to the office we found that James Warburg was back from Washington. As head of our Planning Board and an expert on Germany, he would be exerting a decisive influence on the tone and content of our German broadcasts. He was a fluent, attractive man in his early forties, heir to the great international banking house of that name. I found him charming, intelligent, opinionated, somewhat spoiled by habits of power and intolerant of authority and opposition.

It took me two and a half weeks to create a satisfactory German show. I worked around the clock, for I had everything to learn. I spent hours each day in the Monitoring Room, under Edd Johnson's guidance, breaking the law by listening to British and enemy short-wave broadcasts and to what our own transmitters were sending out. And I learned the routines of the New Department, where the day's mass of news was received over the wires of the various news services, selected, rewritten, edited and then sent out through Control to the Language Desks, where it was translated, edited and adapted for its relevance and suitability to the target area for which it was intended.

I spent many hours with our advisers and experts trying to determine just what the tone and content of our first German broadcast should be. Sherwood held to his conviction that "truth coming from America with unmistakable sincerity is by far our most effective form of propaganda." Barnes, more realistically, believed that "we must tell a true story to every area, but to each one we must tell the true story that will best serve our interests."

In reality we had little choice. The news that the Voice of America carried to the world in the first half of 1942 was almost all bad. As Japanese victories and invasions followed one another with sickening regularity and the Nazi armies moved ever deeper into Russia and the Near East, we would have to report these reverses without weaseling. Only thus could we establish a reputation for honesty. Meantime all we could do was radiate self-confidence and faith in our own unlimited technical and human resources—the world's greatest industrial democracy girding itself for a righteous war which, in the end, it had no doubt of winning.

Next came the problems of form and style. We needed to create shows that would sound straightforward, truthful and clear (bearing in mind that many of our audience might be listening at the risk of their lives) but that would also have the freshness and energy associated with the United States of America.

My first decision was to get away from the single-voice news style of the private stations and BBC. The Voice of America would, in our broadcasts, be represented by several voices of different quality and pitch carefully orchestrated to achieve a maximum of variety and energy. And I hoped (though this could never be proved) that with these multiple voices we might penetrate enemy interference more effectively than with the constant tone of a single speaker.

In our dry runs I tried to distribute the varied tonalities of our speakers in a way that related dramatically to the nature of the news. For a week we made test records based on the news of the day, then played them back for Sherwood, Warburg and Barnes and an invited audience. Finally, on February 11, 1942, we were ready to go. The Voice of America in German went out live on all the short-wave frequencies we possessed—and the next day the British Ministry of Information rebroadcast it on several of their medium-wave stations from an acetate recording flown to London by bomber.

(That first broadcast had military news from Russia, the destruction by fire in New York Harbor of the great French liner *Normandie*, the landing of the first U.S. Marines in New Zealand, bad news from Bataan and Singapore and reports of rapidly increasing American war production including planes, tanks, parachutes and landing craft "for the U.S. offensives in 1943.")

The show was considered a success. The State Department was silent, but the White House congratulated us. So did the British by transatlantic phone. Later their underground monitoring stations in neutral and enemy territories reported that the Nazis had done their heaviest jamming of the war ('with whistles, bells, warbling, music and noises which sound like a cross between a tank factory and a rifle range') to prevent this first Voice of America from being heard.

Our German broadcast was followed within a week by three similar shows: in French, Italian and English. Broadcast over our short-wave transmitters and repeated several times a day with such changes as the news demanded, they became the spine of our operation. And, each day, one show in German, one in French and one in English were telephoned over the transatlantic cable to London, where they were rebroadcast over British medium-wave radio. Each of them had the same four-voice format, with slight modifications in tone and text to meet the needs of each particular target. And in each we repeated our promises to produce 50,000 planes and 40,000 tanks before the end of the year.

Between sunspots, magnetic disturbances, storms and enemy jamming, we were haunted, during those first months of the war, by the constant fear that the Voice of America—no matter how carefully we prepared and transmitted it—would not be heard by those for whom it was intended. Before long our monitors reported that the Vichy government was taking cognizance of our broadcasts by publicly rebuking "those in France who have swallowed the false drugs poured out by London and New York." Further evidence that we were getting through was to be found in the Swiss newspapers, which now began to list the times of American short-wave broadcasts in French, German and Italian and to carry advertisements for short-wave radio sets capable of receiving them. Finally, during the summer of 1942, a letter arrived by a circuitous route from Cannes:

You in America cannot imagine how even a few minutes of news from America, heard by a Frenchman, is spread around. An hour after it is heard hundreds, then thousands know the truth.

It was good to know that not all our words were being lost in the atmosphere.

* * *

My friend Virgil Thomson maintains that I derive sexual excitement from overwork. If that is true, then my time with the Voice of America represents one of the most satisfying affairs of my life; it also explains the state of perpetual exhilaration in which I lived during my eighteen months with the Overseas Branch.

I had little or no personal life. On my return to New York I had tried to resume some of my associations but these had revolved mostly around the Federal and Mercury theaters, and what remained of that world had been blown apart by the outbreak of war. There remained a few durable relationships: Jean Rosenthal, who had just opened her own production office on Broadway; Iris Barry, riding high with her Film Department at the Museum of Modern Art; Virgil Thomson, installed at the Chelsea Hotel in the first flush of his fame as music critic for the *Herald Tribune*. But my emotional life that winter and spring was centered on the corner of Madison Avenue and 40th Street.

Psychological warfare could not furnish me with the theater's climaxes or consummations; there was no applause for the Voice of America, no curtain calls or morning-after reviews, no lines at the box office. But the excitement was the same and there was the added, heady sense of direct participation in the history of the world at one of its most dramatic and significant moments.

For me, this was a new world. The journalists, male and female, with whom I was working in the New York office of the FIS formed a different society from any I had known or worked with before. Hastily recruited from all over the country, they were a brilliant, fluid group—one which, to my surprise, I found myself admitted almost immediately on terms of equality. Our relationship, after the first inevitable probings, soon became one of close, creative, intimate collaboration.

Because of the time differences in various parts of the world our working hours were abnormally long. Living for twelve to sixteen hours a day in this feverish atmosphere, immersed in a constant flood of remote and violent news, it became difficult to separate our own concerns and emotions from the historic events in which we found ourselves involved. No matter how late it was or how exhausted we were, we chose to stay together, reluctant to exchange the excitement of our cosmic activity for the cold, dull solitude of our personal lives.

Since we were never free of our work our midnight meetings in neighboring bars took on something of the character of a club or secret society, held together by a common fatigue and the possession of

enough restricted information and inside knowledge to make us wary
of admitting outsiders to our company. This gave our gatherings a
locker-room atmosphere where the day's news and our handling of it
were reviewed objectively like the incidents of a hard-fought sporting
contest—Sherwood vs Goebbels—in which we were all directly and
personally involved.

From these sessions, particularly from Johnson and Barnes, I
learned a lot about the drinking habits of newspapermen. I discovered
that their alcoholism was not a vice or a weakness but a vocational
necessity. There were sensitive areas of the news and significant
political situations that could not be approached in a formal
atmosphere of reserved sobriety; under the releasing influence of
alcohol they could be discussed frankly and openly and clarified by
knowledgeable, civilized men without indiscretion or treason.

Among our regular drinking companions was our leader, Bob
Sherwood. Slow of speech, sentimental, humorous and wholly
determined, he was a very tall, thin man of strong passions and
unswerving loyalties. His shortcomings as an administrator were notorious. He was known to be "slow, unpunctual and moody" as well as
"pugnaciously individualistic and uncompromising, with no
experience of office routine and no gift for the delegation of authority."
There were stories, many of them true, of his indifference to security, of
top-secret directives sent to the cleaners in the pockets of suits he had
worn to his meetings with the Chiefs of Staff. Yet it was Sherwood,
individually and through the personalities of the men he chose to serve
under him, who gave the Foreign Information Service the humane and
civilized quality that distinguished so much of its work during those
first months of the war. It was Sherwood, for all his absences and va-
guenesses, who determined the goals of our operation: it was his
influence that caused a historian to write of the Overseas Branch that "it
seemed to be thinking in terms of a people's war, a gallant crusade
against the forces of reaction that could make the world a better place to
live in."

Early in June, after months of infighting, the long-awaited
"reorganization" was announced. It separated Donovan's "covert
operations" (which became the OSS and later the CIA) from Overseas
Information and Propaganda. This left Sherwood free to move ahead
with his plans for psychological warfare.

No comprehensive history of the Overseas Branch has yet appeared
and it is unlikely that one will be written. But a complete roster of its
employees during the first years of World War II would reveal a
collection of native and foreign luminaries—journalists, authors, poets,

designers, publishers, executives, actors, musicians, economists, philosophers, educators and financiers—of such celebrity in their past and future careers that it is almost impossible to believe that they were all assembled under one roof.

By the end ot 1942 there were close to 3000 persons working in our New York Office, engaged in activities that included publications, posters and a film department under two well-known Hollywood figures—Robert Riskin and Philip Dunne. But our main instrument of propaganda remained The Voice of America which, by this time, was broadcasting close to a thousand shows a day in twenty-two languages including Swahili. These were prepared, under the supervision of the News and Control Desks, by our so-called Language Sections, whose personnel (75 percent alien) formed the population of the Tower of Babel over which I presided for eighteen months with great energy and erratic effectiveness.

Working with them gave me an astonishing insight into the diversity of ethnic prejudices and passions retained and intensified in exile by intelligent and cultivated men and women. Why did the occupants of the Serbian and Croatian desks hate each other so bitterly while supposedly fighting together against a common enemy? (Their disputes could be heard from one end of the building to the other and seriously disturbed the work of the neutral Swedes and Portuguese who were their neighbors.) Why was there such a subtle but deep division between our German and Austrian exiles? Why were the Poles, after centuries of partition and suffering, riddled with anti-Semitism and obsessed by mad dreams of a "Greater Poland"? Why, finally, did I face a mutiny in the sophisticated Italian section over a speech by Vice-President Wallace in which he promised every living man, woman and child in the Free World a quart of milk a day? Did I know that milk was poison and if we broadcast such nonsense every full-blooded Latin male would "puke and turn off his radio"?

It has never ceased to surprise me that no major breach of security was ever discovered among our heterogeneous personnel. God knows there were plenty of people who would have been delighted to find and expose it—among them the Roosevelt-haters in Congress and the disgruntled exiles who felt they should have a greater say in the broadcasts beamed at their own countries.

I doubt if our clean bill of health was in any way attributable to the vigilance of the Civil Service whose employees we were. Its security checks were carried out by a large corps of investigators, most of them trained by management during the labor unrest of the thirties. Almost without exception they seemed more interested in our social views and our moral turpitude than in any possibility of collaboration with the enemy against whom we were fighting a desperate war. It was they who invented and frequently used in their reports the term "premature antifascist." And in their manual for investigators they included the warning that "an earmark of an American Communist today is an advanced degree of patriotism. This makes it difficult to distinguish friend from foe."

The North African landings which took place on the night of November 7, 1942, marked the beginning of a drastic and irreversible change in the function and status of the Overseas Branch. In our first excitement over a successful operation in which we had played a remote but appreciable part we chose to ignore the inevitable confrontation that would soon erupt between our own independent propaganda and that of the Armed Forces facing military and political necessities in the territories they were preparing to liberate. On that first thrilling night we could foresee neither the changes it would bring about in our own organization nor the personal consequences it would have for so many of us—including myself.

On the night of the landings the French section of the Voice of America, led by that great journalist Pierre Lazareff, had outdone itself and we had received congratulations form both the Pentagon and the White House. But, in the weeks that followed, this harmony ended. Shocked and disillusioned by the political compromises being made in North Africa by the State Department and the Armed Forces, Sherwood's idealists did not hesitate to express their dissenting views. This infuriated both the State Department and the military; indeed, General Eisenhower was heard to complain that the Voice of America was doing more harm to the Expeditionary than to enemy morale. This did not prevent him, some weeks later, as our military advances continued, from inviting the help of the Voice of America in launching a major propaganda assault on the Axis. For this purpose, it was reported in the press, "Robert Sherwood, Director of Overseas Operations, will leave soon for London en route to North Africa to assist in shaping radio programs to be aimed at the soft underbelly of Nazi-occupied Europe."

At a meeting held shortly before his departure Sherwood informed me that I was to accompany him to London, then to North Africa, where I was to start setting up a new subsidiary Voice of America program, following the general pattern of our New York operation. My assignment had been cleared with the White House and, to facilitate my dealings with the military, I was to be accredited with the rank of colonel. I should be prepared to leave as soon as I received my passport.

My first reaction was one of satisfaction and pride at having been chosen for such a mission, heightened by a faint, not unpleasant twinge of fear at the thought of finding myself in what was still a combat area. My second was the sobering realization that I was an "enemy alien" who had not held a valid passport for nine years. I discussed this over drinks with Joe Barnes; I explained that my final U.S. citizenship was applied for and overdue. Joe said not to worry: the naturalization process could be accelerated by a little pressure in the right places. I had a second session with Sherwood before he left for London at which we decided that I should go directly to North Africa. He thought I might have to stay there for several months.

My naturalization was soon taken care of. I filled out the required forms, enclosed my draft card and within a few days received a summons to take my oath of allegiance as United States citizen.

And so, on the morning of March 1, 1943, I stood nervously outside the red-brick armory on Columbus Avenue that was occupied by the U.S. Immigration Service. Remembering that moment, I am once again amazed at the violence with which emotional patterns repeat and reassert themselves with no reasonable relation to the circumstances involved. Waiting on that gray late-winter morning, at the age of forty-one, for my final interrogation, I suffered exactly the same feeling of helpless panic as I had felt at the age of twelve, during the First World War, when I had to register as an alien with the Bristol police, or when I had sat for hours in the outer office of the French consulate at Southampton waiting for the precious visa that would carry me home to my mother and my beloved Paris holidays. After twenty-eight years, the threat of official rejection had set off an identical pattern of fear.

The interrogation was perfunctory; my swearing in by the judge, in company with some thirty or forty other grateful new citizens, was conducted with dispatch. And, as I took on the fourth nationality of my life, I formally assumed the name of John Houseman, which I had been using professionally for a dozen years. By 2 p.m. I was back and a photostat of my naturalization certificate was clipped onto my passport application and sent by special pouch to the State Department in Washington.

Sherwood sent a cable from London asking for the date of my arrival. A seat was reserved for me in one of the Army bombers that were carrying VIPs across the Atlantic. And I set about making preparations for my departure. I walked across town in my lunch hour to Brooks Brothers' emporium on Madison Avenue and (overcoming my thirty-year allergy to military garb) proudly ordered the costume in which I would be playing the part of a U.S. Infantry colonel. The military tailors were overwhelmed with orders, and it was six days before the stuff was delivered to my apartment on Ninth Street, where I tried it on in the presence of my mother, on whom it made a profound impression.

The Overseas Branch had set up its own indoctrination center where I now spent three feckless days learning about disguises and simple methods of murder while I waited for my passport to arrive. It was now mid-March; Sherwood had arrived in North Africa and our transportation department had twice changed my bomber date. Barnes called our Washington office which, in turn, called the Passport Division. No answer. Another inquiry at the State Department. Then, one morning, unofficial word came that my application had been refused. No reason was given.

To explain this refusal various theories were put forward: one was that Mrs. Shipley, head of the Passport Division, being herself of Polish origin, was taking revenge for the injuries supposedly inflicted on the Polish government-in-exile by the Voice of America. Then, from some mysterious quarter, came the information that I had apparently been confused with Hans Haussmann—a notorious radical, formerly head of the Communist Party in Switzerland.

After this had been straightened out and my passport denied once again, Sherwood, back from North Africa, sent for me and asked me bluntly if there was anything in my life that justified such a refusal. I reminded him of my years of illegal residence and of my vulnerable position as director of the WPA's controversial Federal Theater. Neither of these seemed sufficient grounds. He then asked me if I had any objection to having my case reviewed by Army Intelligence. I said I would welcome it.

So one day in early April I found myself riding the Congressional Limited to Washington. At the Pentagon I waited for more than an hour in the outer office of General Strong, head of G-2 (Army Intelligence). The General was courteous and pleasant, though it was evident that he was irritated at being called on to arbitrate between two departments of the government. He asked me some questions, referring occasionally to my FBI and Civil Service files, which lay open in front of him. He made it clear that he disapproved of a sensitive wartime position being filled by a man who, until two weeks ago, had been an enemy alien, but added that there was no evidence in my record of disloyalty or subversion and that he would so report to Mr. Sherwood.

I returned to New York that evening to await the result of my interview. Within a few days it became evident that there would be none.

Sherwood was a stubborn man. As a last resort he turned to Harry Hopkins and asked him to apply White House pressure on the grounds that my presence as an international broadcasting expert was urgently needed in an important theater of war. Once again I was turned down—this time by Undersecretary of State Adolf Berle himself.

It was clear by this time that my interdiction was not a personal one but part of the continuing departmental struggle between the State Department and the Voice of America, where my duties, that spring, included supervising our international coverage of the summit meeting being held in Casablanca between Churchill and Roosevelt. From midnight to 10 a.m. on the first day of the conference we made the announcement 548 times—136 in English, 78 in German, 129 in French, 70 in Italian, not to mention Greek, Persian, Turkish, Bulgarian, Finnish and other languages.

One Sunday morning I decided not to go to work; I sat instead in my raised red-velvet bed and wrote two letters in longhand. One was to my agents in California informing them of my imminent return and instructing them so to inform the Paramount Studios where a contract as film producer was awaiting me. The other was a personal letter to Joe Barnes, my immediate superior, informing him of my resignation. Before delivering it I spent a long alcoholic evening with him during which I attempted to purge myself of some of the guilt I felt at walking off the job in the middle of a war. Joe made no effort to dissuade me. It was his considered opinion that our honeymoon with the Voice of America was over and that the Overseas Branch, from now on, would be operating mostly as an adjunct of the Armed Forces rather than as an ideological outpost of progressive American thinking.

I left soon after the Allied Sicilian landings but my connection with the Overseas Branch was not quite ended. I had been in California for three months when I produced a propaganda film that I felt could be better made in a Hollywood studio than in the political atmosphere of New York or Washington. Part fiction, part documentary and part animation, it was intended to clarify the American system of government and to describe our process of national elections in terms that were clear enough to be translated and shown all over the world. It was written by two top Hollywood writers, Philip Dunne and Howard Koch, animated by John Hubley and furnished with a fine score by Virgil Thomson. *Tuesday in November* was completed, translated into twenty-two languages and shown all over the world except in the United States of America.

Meantime, the destruction of the Overseas Branch occurred pretty much as Joe Barnes had predicted. More and more of its best men and women were assigned overseas where they now took their orders from the commanders in the field rather than from the New York office, which was more than ever under continuous and violent attack in

Congress and in the press. Sherwood's obduracy and his continuing influence in the White House delayed the final collapse by a few months. In fact, I was more than halfway through my first feature film for Paramount Pictures when I read in the *Los Angeles Times* one morning that there had been an "upheaval" in the New York office of the Overseas Branch and that resignations had been "requested and received from Joseph Barnes, Deputy Director of Atlantic Operations, James Warburg, Deputy Director in Charge of Psychological Warfare and Edd Johnson, Head of the Overseas Editorial Board." My name, if I had still been around, would quite certainly have been on that list.

XII
The Blue Dahlia
1945

I have lived in Southern California on and off for more than forty years. I have owned houses there, made friends, had love affairs, married, raised children and enjoyed some professional successes. But this still does not protect me from the wave of sickening anxiety that sweeps over me each time I face the sprawling, hideous approaches to the City of Angels. There is something in that air, that hazy, sun-drenched, polluted, subtropical, earthquake-threatened atmosphere that fills me with loathing and gloom. I become used to it after a while; I even get to like it—especially the beach on which I lived for so long. But that first devastating impression persists.

It has its roots, I believe, in the sad, humiliating months I spent in Hollywood as the bankrupt, unemployed husband of an insecure movie star, and then again, eight years later, in the soul-destroying months I spent there as Orson Welles's castrated, ineffectual partner. Both were bad times in which I found myself living on the fringes of wealth and fame, close enough to breathe that exciting air but with little hope of achieving either of them for myself.

My return to Hollywood in the late summer of 1943 was one of the worst. I arrived by car in the company of my friend Virgil Thomson after a twelve-day voyage—with time out for wartime tires and gasoline. The further west we drove, the more we became aware of the steady stream of slow, mile-long, heavy-laden trains, all headed for the Coast with arms and supplies for the war in the Pacific—the tanks and guns and planes I had been promising the world in twenty-seven languages.

We crossed the desert at dawn and arrived in Los Angeles in mid-morning. It took me twenty-four hours (by which time Virgil had gone north to visit Darius Milhaud in San Francisco) to summon up the courage to inform my agents that I had arrived. The next morning I was driven in a black limousine to the Paramount Studio to meet my new master, Buddy DeSylva. He was a tough little infighter born in the orange groves of Azusa. Starting as a ukulele player and prolific songwriter he had gone on to become a successful producer of Broadway musicals and, later, of films. Shortly before the outbreak of war, he had become head of production at Paramount, where he had ridden the wave of the wartime movie boom with a succession of popular pictures. At the I time arrived, his stock was high.

Paramount was a loosely structured, lively, improvisational studio specializing in comedies and musicals and turning out more than forty films a year. Its principal moneymakers were Bob Hope and Bing Crosby; other stars included Betty Hutton, Bill Holden, Paulette Goddard, Dorothy Lamour, Ray Milland and Ginger Rogers. Its producers, directors and writers were a mixed lot: the elegant Arthur Hornblow; Paul Jones, a pear-shaped specialist in comedies such as the Bob Hope pictures; Mark Sandrick, maker of early Astaire and recent Bing Crosby musicals; the celebrated team of Charles Brackett and Billy Wilder; Preston Sturges, then at the height of his meteoric career. Above them all, seldom seen but ever present, was the declining but still Olympian figure of Cecil B. De Mille, after whom the main gate of the studio had been named.

These talents were controlled and maneuvered by Buddy DeSylva, who, as long as he turned out his quota of lucrative pictures, suffered little interference from the New York office or from the titular head of the studio, Y. Frank Freeman, an ignorant and bigoted banker from Atlanta, Georgia (whose main preoccupation seemed to be to make sure that no "niggra"—male or female—ever came into contact, on the screen, with a member of the Master Race).

This was the world for which I had left the Voice of America and which I now entered with all the apprehensions of a new boy on thefirst day of school. My agents had done their best to establish my status through the location of my office—a paneled suite on the ground floor of the Tudor-timbered Administration Building only a few doors down the hall from DeSylva and next door to the head of the Story Department—William Dozier. It was very different from the exposed glass cage I had occupied with the Overseas Branch: it had a heavy carpet, a massive upholstered sofa, a private toilet and a good view of the stars' bungalows and of the dog run in which Y. Frank Freeman exercised his prize boxers.

At our first meeting DeSylva asked me if I had any projects of my own. I replied truthfully that I did not and realized in that instant how ill-prepared I was, emotionally and professionally, for the job on which I was about to embark. As I prepared to make the drastic transition from the realities of contemporary history to the world of make-believe in which movies were created, the chameleon in me was once again preparing to change his color. But it was not at all clear along what lines my new identity should be developed. At forty-one I still had no positive conviction about who I was or what I wanted to do.

My agent had urged me not to be too adventurous with my first projects. I was ready to follow his advice. Deep in debt after eighteen months of government service, haunted by doubts about my own creative capacity (unlike Orson, who never for one instant doubted that his first film would be a masterpiece), I was more concerned with holding a job and establishing myself as part of the system than with satisfying any strong artistic urge of my own. It was a regrettable state of mind in which to be setting out on my career as a motion-picture producer and the results were predictably mediocre.

Since many of the next twenty years of my life were to be spent producing films, it seems desirable to describe briefly what was meant by the term "producer" in Hollywood at the time. His functions varied—depending on the structure of the studio at which he worked. He might do no more than follow the orders of his studio head or he might be the major creative factor in the films that bore his name—selecting the material, developing it with a writer of his choice, engaging the director and cast, supervising its filming and having the final say in the editing, scoring and, even, merchandising of his finished picture.

I fulfilled only a few of those functions during my early days at Paramount, where my first film was a mild horror tale based on an English novel that was already owned by the Studio and shot by a director also supplied by the Studio—an uninspired English hack with whom I found it impossible to communicate on any level. *The Unseen*, of which the *New York Times* wrote that it was "as tenebrous a tale as has come along in some time," did quite well at the box office.

(The truth is that all films were doing well. Through 1944 the film industry was still riding the crest of the war boom. With transport drastically limited by gas rationing, there seemed to be no way to spend money except at the movies. With money pouring into the box office and jobs for everyone who was not in uniform, those were boom days for the film companies and their employees. What is more—absorbed in the fictitious excitements of filmmaking, they sincerely believed that they were contributing to the war effort.)

My second film was based on a moderate best seller by the name of *Miss Susie Slagle's*—a sentimental novel about the famed Johns Hopkins medical school, as seen through the eyes of a houseful of medical students. This time I chose my own director—a young man named Jack Berry who had been one of the mutinous mob in *Julius Caesar* and our stage manager and assistant director on *Native Son*. Both he and my scriptwriter ended up a few years later on the blacklist but the film we made together was conventional in the extreme. It was described in the press as "leisurely entertainment with a great deal of authenticity" and a "cheerful, nostalgic picture of fabricated life." Its main virtue was that it brought Lillian Gish back to the screen after an absence of many years. However, it disappointed the Studio, which had hoped for an American *Mrs. Chips*.

Halfway through my film, DeSylva had a heart attack—a serious one, for he never returned to the studio, leaving me to the tender mercies of Y. Frank Freeman who, from the day of my arrival (and particularly after the production of my government documentary), regarded me as a dangerous radical. Sensing that my days were numbered, I was in the process of negotiating a contract with William Dozier (who had moved to the RKO Studio next door as head of production) when I embarked on my third and last film at Paramount—*The Blue Dahlia*.

Raymond Chandler was fifty-six when we met. By then most of his books had been written—some of them twice: first, long ago, for a pittance from the pulps—*Argosy* and *Black Mask*; then again after he had combined and expanded them ('cannibalized' as he called it) for publication as hardbacks and, later, as best-selling paperbacks. His creative days were almost over, but his success was just beginning: royalties were pouring in now, followed by movie sales. For the first time in many years, Chandler and his wife were able to enjoy such modest Southern Californian comforts as they desired.

Ray had appeared at Paramount a few weeks before I did: he had come to work with Billy Wilder on dialogue and to supply the Los Angeles atmosphere for *Double Indemnity*. It was during that time that our friendship was formed, based on the astonishing premise that he and I alone, of all those currently employed at Paramount Studio, were British public-school men—and, consequently, gentlemen.

I never got to know much about Chandler's life. There was a story around the studio that he had earned his living for a time stringing tennis rackets; there was also a rumor that he had, for some years, been an alcoholic. This was easy to believe, for the first impression Ray gave was one of extreme frailty; it was not until later that you discovered the peculiar strength that lay behind his ashy, burnt-out look and his querulous hypochondria.

He was too inhibited to be cheerful, too emotional to be witty. And the English public-school system had left its sexually devastating mark upon him. The presence of young women—secretaries and extras around the lot—disturbed and excited him. His voice was normally muted; it was in a husky whisper that he uttered those prurient juvenile obscenities at which he would have been the first to take offense if they had been spoken by others. After he left the Studio, we continued to meet occasionally and one Sunday he and his wife Cissie drove me up the coast in the huge, gray-green vintage Packard convertible of which he was justly proud.

(In Hollywood, where the selection of wives was frequently confused with the casting of motion pictures, Cissie was something of a phenomenon. Ray's life had been hard; he looked at least ten years older than his age. His wife looked twenty years older than he did and dressed thirty years younger. Later, after her death—"not by inches but by half-inches"—Ray wrote to me of their "thirty years, ten months and four days of as happy a marriage as any man could expect.")

It was late in 1944 when the management of the Paramount Studio came to the horrifying realization that Alan Ladd—the Studio's top star and the highest-rated male performer in the U.S.—would soon be entering the Army, leaving behind him not one foot of unreleased film. At our next producers' meeting, between the dire threats and fulsome flattery with which the Front Office was wont to entertain us, Y. Frank Freeman let it be know that anyone who came up with an Alan Ladd vehicle ready to go into production within a month would earn the eternal gratitude of the company's management and shareholders. That same day, at one of our weekly luncheons, Ray complained to me of being stuck on a book he was writing and muttered that he was seriously thinking of turning it into a screenplay for sale to the movies. After lunch, we went to his house—a small, Spanish-style stucco bungalow, where Cissie was lying in a cloud of pink tarlatan, with a broken leg—and I read the first 120 typed pages of his book. Forty-eight hours later Paramount had bought *The Blue Dahlia* for a substantial sum and Ray Chandler was at work on the screenplay, of which he dictated the first half—about 45 minutes of film—in under three weeks, at the rate of four or five pages a day. This was no miracle; the situations and the dialogue were already written and carried directly into the screenplay. After the first sixty pages had been mimeographed, a shooting date was set—three weeks away. Everyone was astounded and overjoyed and my stock was high.

Our director was one of the old maestros of Hollywood—George

Marshall, who had been in movies since their earliest days, first as an actor, then as a director. His most famous picture was *Destry Rides Again*, which, according to him, he had practically created on the set. It took a lot of earnest talk from me (although, since I was still a beginner, he didn't pay much attention) to convince George Marshall that *The Blue Dahlia* was one script that he was not expected to rewrite or improvise on the set.

Casting proved no serious problem. The leading part, as written by Chandler for Alan Ladd, was perfectly suited to the special qualities of that surprising star (who had played a part, so small that I barely remembered it, in *Citizen Kane*) and who had remained virtually unknown until the lucky day on which he was cast in *This Gun for Hire*, where he played a professional killer with a poignant and desolating ferocity that made him unique among male heroes of his day.

As a star, Ladd had some say in the choice of his cast. Since he himself was extremely short, he had only one standard by which he judged his fellow players: their height. Veronica Lake was the perfect size for him, but we had trouble over the part of his dissolute wife, who is murdered halfway through the film and in which I had already cast my beautiful dark-haired friend Doris Dowling. Since she was a full half-foot taller than Ladd, he made a determined attempt to get rid of her; we placated him in their scenes together by keeping her sitting or lying down.

Shooting went well from the start. By the end of our first week we were a day and a half ahead of schedule. It was not until the middle of our fourth week that the script girl called my attention to the fact that the camera was slowly but surely gaining on the script. We had shot 62 pages in four weeks; Chandler, during that time, had turned in only 22—with another 30 to go.

Ray's problem with the script (as with the book) was a simple one: he had no ending and no idea who had committed the crime. I was not worried. Ray had written such stories for years, and I was quite confident that sooner or later (probably later, since he seemed to enjoy the suspense) he would wind up the proceedings with an "artistic" revelation (it was his word) and a caustic last line. But as the days went by and the camera went on chewing its way through the script and still no ending arrived, signs of tension began to appear. At one point we held a story conference to review our various suspects. It was during this meeting, early one afternoon, that a man came running down the studio street, stopping at the various windows to shout to the people inside. When he reached us, he shoved his head in and told us that Franklin D. Roosevelt was dead.

We sat stunned for a while. Then we said all the obvious things:

how ill he had looked in the photographs from Yalta; how reckless it had been of him to take that long motor-ride in the pouring rain through the New York streets; how he had looked and sounded on that morning of his first inauguration almost exactly twelve years ago—all the things that everyone all over the country was saying in that moment. Finally we fell silent and sat there gloomily for a while. Then, gradually, we drifted back to our story conference; half an hour later, we were deep in the intricacies of *The Blue Dahlia*, looking for the least likely suspect and trying to decide on whom it would be most satisfying to pin the murder.

Two days later I was sitting in my office when my secretary hurried in to say that Mr. Chandler was outside and was asking to see me. I was not used to this formality, and there was something strange about the way she said it. When Ray came in, he was deadly pale and his hands were trembling. She made him a cup of coffee and, piece by piece, I heard his story. Late the night before, Ray's agent had called him to say the Front Office would like to see him, privately, at 9:30 the next morning. Ray had spent a sleepless night; he was a timorous man, and his agitation was increased by the admonition that he should, under no circumstances, mention the appointment to anyone.

When he appeared in the paneled executive office with its English hunting prints and cream wall-to-wall carpet, Ray was told that the future of Paramount would be seriously imperiled if the balance of *The Blue Dahlia* script was not delivered on time. If it *were*, a bonus of $5000 would be paid on delivery of the final pages.

By never letting Ray share my apprehensions, I had convinced him of my confidence in his ability to finish the script on time. This sense of security was now hopelessly shattered. He had been insulted. To be offered an additional sum of money for the completion of an assignment which he had every intention of fulfilling was by Ray's standards a degradation and a dishonor. Furthermore, he felt that I—as his friend and producer—was being betrayed. That is why he had come straight to me in a state of nervous despair; he assured me that his creative mechanism had been wrecked and that he had no choice but to withdraw from a project to which he had nothing more to contribute.

After he had left, I tried to evaluate our situation. The latest word from the sound stage was that we would complete page 93 before night. That left us with 28 pages of unshot script—less than five days' work. And in ten days' time Alan Ladd would vanish irrevocably into the U.S. Army.

That afternoon I received from the sound stage what, in the circumstances, seemed like good news. During a scene of mayhem, one of our heavies had let a massive oak tabletop fall upon and break another heavy's toe. But when I reached the set, George Marshall told me not to worry; he had found a way for the injured heavy to play the scene from the floor. He also asked where the rest of the pages were.

The next morning, true to the promise he had made me, Chandler reappeared in my office, looking even grimmer than the day before. He said that after a sleepless and tormented night he had come to the unalterable conclusion that he was incapable of finishing *The Blue Dahlia* on time—or ever. This declaration was followed by a silence of several minutes during which we gazed at each other, more in sorrow than in anger. Then, having finished his coffee and carefully put down his cup on the floor, Ray spoke again, softly and seriously. After some prefatory remarks about the esteem and affection in which he held me, he made the following astonishing proposal: I was no doubt aware (or had heard it rumored) that he had for some years been a serious drinker. By an intense effort of will he had overcome his addiction. This abstinence, he explained, had been all the more difficult to sustain because alcohol gave him an energy and a self-assurance as a writer that he could achieve in no other way. This brought us to the crux of the matter; having repeated that he was unable to continue working on *The Blue Dahlia* sober, Ray assured me of his complete confidence in his ability to finish it—*drunk*.

He did not minimize the hazards: he pointed out that his plan, if adopted, would call for deep faith on my part and supreme courage on his, since he would be in effect completing the script at the risk of his life. It wasn't the drinking that was dangerous, he explained, since he had a doctor who gave him such massive injections of glucose that he could last for weeks with no solid food at all. It was the sobering-up that was parlous, the terrible strain of his return to normal living. This is why Cissie had so bitterly opposed his proposed scheme, till Ray had finally convinced her that honor came before safety.

My first reaction was one of pure panic. Such is my own insecurity that contact with a human brain which is even slightly out of control frightens, repels and finally enrages me. On that ground alone I was horrified by Ray's proposal. I also knew that if I was mad enough to take this risk, it would have to be entirely my own responsibility and without the Studio's knowledge. At this point Ray produced a sheet of yellow foolscap paper and presented me with the list of his basic requirements:

A   Two Cadillac limousines, to stand day and night outside the house with drivers available for:

1. Fetching the doctor (Ray's or Cissie's or both).

2. Taking script pages to and from the studio.

3. Driving the maid to market.

4. Contingencies and emergencies.

B Six secretaries—in three relays of two—to be in constant attendance and readiness, available at all times for dictation, typing and other possible emergencies.

C A direct line open at all times to my office by day and the studio switchboard at night.

I asked for an hour to think it over. With great courtesy and understanding, Ray agreed. For half an hour I walked the studio streets. I visited the set, where the director informed me that he'd be out of script by evening of the following day. Then I went back to my office, where Ray was sitting, reading *Variety*. With all the public-school fervor and esprit de corps I could dredge up from the memory of my ten years at Clifton, I accepted his proposal and shook his hand.

Ray now became extremely cheerful. It was almost noon, and he suggested, as proof of my faith in him, that we drive to the most expensive restaurant in Los Angeles and tie one on together. We left the studio and drove to Perino's, where I watched him down three double martinis before eating a large and carefully selected lunch, followed by three double stingers. We then drove back to his house, where the two Cadillacs were already in position and the first relay of secretaries at their posts.

Early next morning the limousines were still there, shining in the sun. The drivers had been changed; so had the secretaries. Ray lay, passed out, on the sofa of his living room. On the table beside him was a tall, half-filled highball glass of bourbon; beside it were five typed pages of script, neatly corrected—Ray's work of the night. In the back seat of the black limousine that rushed me back to the studio, I learned that our murderer was none other than the house detective. The pages I was carrying back to the studio contained his confession and death scene.

I was on the sound stage when a boy on a bicycle arrived with the pages, still damp from the mimeograph machines. George Marshall read them and found them acceptable. I think he had looked forward to saving the day by improvising the last days' work on the set and that he was a little hurt that we preferred the work of a man in an advanced stage of alcoholism to his own. But he behaved admirably. So did everyone else. The film was finished with four days to spare, Alan Ladd went off to the army, Paramount made a lot of money and I had my first big success as a filmmaker.

During those last days of work, Chandler did not draw one sober breath, nor did one speck of solid food pass his lips. He was polite and cheerful when I appeared, and his doctor came twice a day to give him intravenous injections. The rest of the time, except when he was asleep, with his black cat in his arms, Ray was never without a glass in his hand. He did not drink much. Having reached the euphoria he needed, he continued to consume just enough bourbon to maintain himself in that condition. Between eight and ten every evening, he sat in Cissie's room and they listened together to the Southern California Gas Company's program of classical music on the radio. The rest of the time was spent in a light sleep, from which he woke in full possession of his faculties to pick up exactly where he had stopped with whichever of the rotating secretaries happened to be with him. He continued until he felt himself growing drowsy again, then dropped back comfortably into sleep while the girl went into the next room, typed the pages and left them on the table beside him to be reread and corrected when he woke up. As his last line of dialogue in the film, Ray had written in pencil? "Did somebody say something about a drink of bourbon?"

Ray had not exaggerated when he said that he was risking his life for *The Blue Dahlia*. His starvation seriously weakened him, and it took him a fortnight to recover, during which his doctor came twice a day to administer mysterious, reviving shots that cost him a lot more than the "bonus" he received. During his convalescence he lay neatly dressed in fresh pajamas under a silk robe; when I came to see him he would extend a white and trembling hand and receive my expressions of gratitude with the modest smile of a gravely wounded hero who has shown courage far beyond the call of duty.

XIII
Three Interludes and Two Musicals
1944-46

With *The Blue Dahlia* I completed the first phase of my Hollywood film-making. I had been back in California for more than two years and I was beginning to master the business of making movies. My self-assurance had almost climbed back to the level it had reached on the Voice of America, with this difference—that because of my lack of emotional involvement with the films I was making, my work absorbed only part of my energy. The libido that was left over was diverted into three quite different and separate activities.

1. Social Life

The War had brought more people to California than it had taken away and I found myself with more friends and more varied acquaintances in Hollywood and Beverly Hills than I had in New York. The Mankiewiczes were still in their house on Tower Road; Herman was working for Twentieth Century Fox, more aggressive than ever in the expression of his informed but outrageous opinions on world affairs. Geraldine Fitzgerald, with her Irish husband and her son, an infant Gargantua, were living in a haunted home rented from Boris Karloff; Olivia de Havilland had a house off Coldwater Canyon where we spent many pleasant evenings interrupted occasionally by the sudden, unannounced appearances of her demon-lover John Huston. Several of the Mercury actors imported for *Citizen Kane* had stayed on and prospered—particularly Joseph Cotten, who was now a full-fledged film star and who, with his wife, gave musical evenings and elegant weekend tennis lunches. Alfred Hitchcock (still grousing about his master, David O. Selznick) presided nightly, with his wife Alma, over small dinners with superlative wines.

Hitch never formed part of the accredited British colony, of which the social center was Ronald Colman's huge, timbered mansion off Benedict Canyon. Colman was a charming, shrewd, rather stiff man who had recently, to everyone's surprise and delight, married the English actress Benita Hume, who, by a curious coincidence, had been the child bride, many years ago, of my foster brother Eric Siepmann. It was through her that I came to be invited to the Great House where, on Saturday nights, often in black tie, one was likely to sit down at the long, gleaming table with such fellow guests as Mary Pickford, Gloria Swanson, Norma Shearer, Arthur Rubinstein, the Mendels, the Huxleys, Richard Barthelmess, Charles and Pat Boyer, Adolphe Menjou, the Goldwyns, the latest English girl-stars sent over to earn dollars and, occasionally, Oscar Levant.

Other, more unbuttoned evenings were spent in the Valley with Howard Koch who, following *The War of the Worlds*, had become a successful film writer; with the Dowling sisters (Connie was under contract to Goldwyn, Doris to Paramount); with Val Lewton, my former colleague at Selznick's, who had become a successful producer of low-budget horror films; finally, with Sam Spiegel (who, at the time, still went by the name of S.P. Eagle).

He had appeared in California some years earlier, penniless and a fugitive from the police of several countries, and had managed to promote and produce one quite successful film. He had become something of a local legend, and his rented Beverly Hills home was frequented by some of the liveliest and most civilized persons in town.

You came by invitation or were brought and, if Sam approved of you, you kept coming back. The atmosphere was that of a private club, relaxed and sophisticated. Nothing much happened; people (mostly writers and directors, with or without their ladies) dropped in after dinner for a drink and stayed for hours, playing backgammon or gin rummy (at which Sam was a wizard) or simply talking. Among the habitués were Billy Wilder, Luwig Bemelmans, John Huston, Willy Wyler, Geraldine Fitzgerald, Olivia de Havilland, Tim Durant, Otto Preminger and others. It was a unique and agreeable institution—the closest Hollywood came to having a professional if not a literary salon.

Finally, there was Salka Viertel's house in Santa Monica, where the town's most eminent émigrés continued to congregate and where you might find yourself sharing brilliant conversation or a sachertorte with Brecht, Feuchtwanger, Reinhardt, Kortner, Thomas or Heinrich Mann among the literati and theater people; Toch, Korngold, Eissler, Schoenberg and Steuermann among the musicians.

2. Politics

It came as a distinct surprise, some years later, to discover that the vaguely patriotic duties I had once performed as a member of the Hollywood Writers' Mobilization were considered "political." It was even more of a shock to discover that the Mobilization, of which I was vice-chairman for two years, was high on the Attorney General's list of subversive organizations.

The Mobilization had been created early in the war by the Screen Writers' Guild to act as a channel between writers, studios and government agencies—a clearing house for a variety of wartime services that included the drafting of speeches for stars fo deliver at bond rallies, blood banks and Red Cross drives together with theatrical material (jokes and comedy routines) to be used for troop entertainment and overseas broadcasts.

My own first assignment, for which I was recruited soon after my arrival from New York by a curly-headed assistant story editor at Paramount, was a hundred-word exhortation to be uttered at a bond rally by Ginger Rogers. I soon found myself involved in other activities of the Mobilization and was invited (because of my experience of propaganda) to attend meetings where future projects were discussed and assigned.

Since it offered one of the few available opportunities for articulate civilians to participate in the war effort, the Hollywood Writers' Mobilization had developed over the years into an extensive organization that went far beyond its original, limited "service" functions. One of its early achievements was its sponsorship of a National Writers' Congress on the campus of the University of California in Los Angeles. At its opening session, which was attended by leading figures in the film industry, telegrams of good will and congratulation were read from the President and Vice President of the United States. (A few years later some of its distinguished participants would have been pleased to have their presence at the Congress forgotten and their utterances expunged from the 663-page transcript of the proceedings in which their anti-Fascist eloquence, laced with expressions of gratitude and praise for our gallant Russian allies, made embarrassing reading in the first chill of the Cold War.)

I do recall that towards the end of the war, especially after D-Day, the functions and attitudes of the Mobilization began to change. Our wartime activities continued as long as they were required but, as victory approached, we began to concern ourselves increasingly with the future of the country and of the world as it would be shaped by the coming peace. The focus of our concern began to shift.

A letter, sent out by the National Independent Citizens' Committee in March 1945 and endorsed by the Mobilization, invited artists and professionals to:

join in meeting the greatest challenge ever presented to the people of this country...We are faced with the enormous task of securing the peace and a democratic America...Your support is the measure of your strength and effectiveness in shaping our postwar world.

The Mobilization felt morally obliged to participate in meeting this challenge, which had taken on added urgency with the dropping of the atom bomb. Our activities during 1945-46 included two radio series to be know as "Free World Theater" and "Reunion USA." We held conferences with Army psychologists to consider the problems facing the returning GI; we organized a series of lectures and seminars on Thought Control; we helped to sponsor a brilliant animation by John Hubley on *The Brotherhood of Man*. We also contemplated a second Writers' Conference "to consider development of communications agencies in all freedom-loving nations and to consider realistically the possibilities of using the resources of screen, press and radio in a way that will make them more effective instruments in the service of world unity and welfare."

Inevitably such projects had social and political implications; yet they did not represent any organized or consistent political action. The Writers' Mobilization was a loose, voluntary association. Except for its annually elected officers, it was a casual collection of members, drawn for the most part from the ranks of liberal writers and artists of the Left and center. Almost all were New Deal Democrats of one shade or another; many were veterans of the bitter professional conflicts that had raged in Hollywood in the thirties before the Screenwriters' Guild was reluctantly recognized by the film industry. This in itself made them suspect to the Studios and odious to such patriotic organiztions as the Motion Picture Alliance for the Preservation of American Ideals.

When the House Un-American Activities Committee sent its first emissaries to Hollywood to investigate the industry in the spring of 1947, the Mobilization was among the organizations cited for radicalism. Of its first three chairmen two were among those subpoenaed as "unfriendly" witnesses. A number of its members were blacklisted; a few went to jail.

Some of my friends were surprised and shocked to find themselves in such radical company. I was not. Coping with the Party, personally and collectively, had become a habit in my life—in the backroom sessions over the staffing of the Negro Unit of the WPA Federal Theater; in my association with Marc Blitzstein on *The Cradle Will Rock*; in my negotiations over the political heresies of *Danton's Death*; in my collaboration with Dick Wright on *Native Son*; finally, in my dealings with members of the native and foreign news desks at the Voice of America.

As a participant in the councils of the Mobilization, I was well aware of the Communist influences among us. Some of our most active and zealous workers were probably Party members and I knew that in the course of our activities there were undoubtedly times when we were coinciding with, if not following, the Party line, which, once again, advocated a united front. I never at any time felt manipulated or duped. We may have been do-gooders and busybodies, ingenuous and self-righteous. But we were never in any sense subversive. At our most radical we represented a progressive and altruistic element of the Establishment. Looking back, it strikes me that our thinking, socially and artistically, was consistently mild and conventional.

(One of our typical creations was the *Hollywood Quarterly*, which we launched in 1945 in association with the University of California. The nature of this collaboration is reflected in the make-up of its first advisory board: four from the university—including one historian, one social psychologist, the head of the University Press and Kenneth MacGowan (friend and producer of Eugene O'Neill and now Dean of Theater Arts at UCLA). Representing the Mobilization were three well-known film writers—Dudley Nichols, Howard Koch and John Howard Lawson—and one producer—myself.

The *Quarterly* was later denounced as a Communist organ. A glance at its contents during its brief life will show the absurdity of the charge. There was never any doubt in my mind that Lawson, as an active member of the Party's cultural apparatus, welcomed the creation of such a publication with its opportunities for cultural influence; he may even have hoped to see it repeat, in films, the important function played by *New Theater* in New York in the thirties. In fact, our editorial make-up made any such radical developments impossible: the *Hollywood Quarterly* remained an earnest, rather dull magazine—part professional, part academic and sociological. It created no major stir and exerted not the slightest influence on the filmmaking of its time.)

For my own part, I found my work with the Mobilization a source of considerable personal satisfaction; it gave me a sense of belonging that I did not have at the studio and a feeling of collective effort and accomplishment such as I had not enjoyed since the WPA and the Voice of America.

3. Sex

My third activity was not controversial: I loved a movie star. In my exhilaration over my conquest I treated my friend, Mina Curtiss, to some transcontinental erotica:

In the theater an actress brings to her lovemaking some of the warmth and energy or anger and sadness that she has carried over, physically and emotionally, from her performance. She comes to bed charged with some residue of the excitement she has generated in her exchange with her fellow actors and her living audience.

Not so the movie star. At a certain level of stardom she is transformed into a Goddess—with a Divinity's capacity to be in a thousand places at once. Modern technology has made physically real what countless generations of men have dreamed of in myths and fairy tales. At the same moment as I am making love to her in my own private and personal way on a large bed in a dark room in Beverly Hills she is appearing, in one or other of her various incarnations, to millions of others, for each of whom she is a legitimate object of artfully stimulated lust. Those with whom I am sharing her are enjoying aspects of her that I, with my limited sense, cannot hope to perceive. Peering up at her through the awesome twilight of darkened movie houses all over the world, they are seeing her, magnified and illuminated in a dazzling vision that reveals every pore of her skin and every tremor of her muscles; her eyes are great globes of translucent jelly; her mouth (which I know as well as my own) has become a tumescent red cavern and her breasts (which are white and tender and flecked with gold) have been built up into twin mounds—each six feet wide at its base—of suggestively draped and illuminated flesh.

Joan Fontaine has graciously testified that she found me a satisfying lover. I take this opportunity to return the compliment. She was an enchanting mistress—childish, sweet-smelling, elegant, calculating, sophisticated, lecherous, innocent and faithless. I believe she found in my company a temporary refuge from the hard-faced producers who made passes at her and from the handsome British actor whom she had recently divorced. She also saw in her affair with me a sure way to exasperate her sister, Olivia de Havilland.

Ours was what was known in Hollywood in those days as a "romance"—which meant that we slept together three or four nights a week, got invited to parties together, went away together for weekends and sometimes talked about getting married without really meaning it. Our "romance," which lasted a little more than a year, was followed closely in the local and national press. I was never quite sure how much of this information was revealed by the lady herself in carefully timed, alternating bulletins that she issued by phone and in person to Hedda and Louella as part of a highly organized game in which paid publicity, personal vanity and studio politics all played their part and in which "romantic" revelations were regularly traded for professional breaks in the syndicated columns of the day.

I professed to resent it, but it gave our relationship a pressurized excitement that was not altogether disagreeable and probably held us together rather longer than we might otherwise have remained. I have always found wealth and celebrity an infallible aphrodisiac: to be known from coast to coast as the lover of one of the brightest young stars in the Hollywood firmament gave me a satisfaction and a self-confidence for which I was sincerely grateful.

* * *

Having signed my new contract with RKO Pictures for one film a year for three years, I returned to New York in the spring of 1946 in what was planned as some sort of a premature honeymoon. The next day I drove up the Hudson to the small house in New City that had been my refuge for so many years. After my long residence in California, I found the Eastern spring overwhelming in its fierce beauty: within a week of my return I had persuaded Bessie Poor to sell me 10 acres of the mountain land she owned on the South Mountain Road. It was a condition of the sale that her husband, Henry Varnum Poor, design and build me a house there.

Joan and I spent several days following Henry up the mountain, through the dense, second-growth woods, trying to decide on a suitable site for what we had begun, without much conviction, to call "our" home. The hills were covered with poison ivy, and every evening when we got home in the failing light, Henry made us undress and wash all over with yellow soap. We found the perfect place finally—a flat ledge of rock facing almost due south—and Henry set about designing a house with a bedroom that would catch the morning light, a living room that would be illuminated at noon and a kitchen from which one could watch the sunset.

Two weeks after our arrival, Miss Fontaine, following a lot of long-distance telephoning, suddenly announced that she was returning to the Coast. Her departure left me with an aching emptiness that was presently filled by the excitement of a new and unexpected theatrical adventure.

Arnold Weissberger (who had been my lawyer since the days of the Mercury) took me over one afternoon to visit Michael Meyerberg, an eccentric, cadaverous real-estate operator with a passion for the theater and a flair for quality that had led him to give *The Skin of Our Teeth* and, later, *Waiting for Godot* their American premieres. He was now preparing an ambitious production with Mary Martin, based on the Chinese classic *Pi-Pa-Ki*, to be known as *Lute Song*. I spent several hours with him and the next day with Miss Martin and her husband—manager, during which I sensed that the show's most persistent and vexing problem would be the effective blending of a Broadway musical with a Chinese dramatic classic.

Evidently I passed muster, for the rest of my summer was divided between going over Henry Poor's first designs for my house and absorbing Meyerberg's innumerable ideas for the production of *Lute Song*. For his scenery and costumes he had engaged the greatest of all American designers, Robert Edmund Jones—one of whose last and most beautiful shows this became. Some casting had been done. For his music and lyrics he had turned to Raymond Scott, a specialist in instrumental and electronic arrangements, and a young lyricist named Hennigan who had never had a show on Broadway. To appear opposite Miss Martin, Meyerberg had discovered a balding, dynamic, strangely beautiful young man of Russian-Chinese origin whom he had discovered in a White Russian nightclub somewhere, crooning gypsy laments to the accompaniment of a guitar. (I remembered him vaguely as one of our French announcers on the Voice of America.) Neither Mary nor Scott were enthusiastic about Yul Brynner's voice, which was untrained and had a wavering pitch. But he satisfied all the other requirements: a sexy, exotic leading man with interesting speech and a vaguely Oriental look. For the hero's aging parents we chose Mildred Dunnock (it was the first of our many plays together) and Augustin Duncan—Isadora's brother who had not allowed total blindness in middle age to interfere with his acting career. At Mary Martin's suggestion, to play one of the princess's flower maidens, we engaged an attractive but awkward virgin by the name of Nancy Davis (better known later as Nancy Reagan).

Rehearsals began in October. With the help of Nick Ray (who had worked with me on the Voice of America and on *Tuesday in November* and whom I now summoned from California to assist me) I tried to conceal the abject terror that gripped me on that first morning as I tried to suppress the awful fear that my ineptitude would soon become apparent to everyone and that I would be exposed and disgraced at any moment. I had prepared my first day's work with great care and for forty-eight hours I managed to maintain a false air of self-confidence. Then, halfway through the third day, I suddenly realized that everything was going quite well and that the worst was over. On the ninth day we had a run-through of the first act. It meant a lot to me that Robert Edmund Jones was pleased. So was Miss Martin, while Meyerberg informed everyone that he had discovered a new Max Reinhardt.

I had one final problem. The play, in its classic Chinese form, had a beautifully civilized conclusion. The hero, in the final scene, finds himself torn between his deep love for his devoted country wife whom he believed to be dead and has finally found again, and his feelings for the princess (his second wife) who has lovingly elevated him to his exalted rank at the imperial court. His dilemma is solved by the princess, who decides that, since they both love him and need him, he shall, by special imperial decree, remain married to them both—bound by vows of love to the first and by bonds of interest to the second. Mary and her husband decided that sharing a man was unworthy of a star of Mary's magnitude. They harassed Meyerberg into presenting a version in which the princess, amid general rejoicing, generously returns the hero to his village sweetheart. I protested, gave in and never ceased to regret it.

Lute Song opened in New York on the night of February 2, 1946, at the Plymouth Theater (where I discovered that Mary Martin was occupying the dressing room in which I had met and wooed Zita Johann eighteen years earlier during the run of *Machinal*). Reviews were good, though our Chinese transplant was too esoteric to please everyone. The dean of American critics, George Jean Nathan, wrote of "an excitingly beautiful evening in the theater"; others described it as "one of the most exquisite and exciting things ever seen upon a stage" and "having virtually everything within the resources of the modern stage—save vulgarity."

It ran in New York for five months before moving to Chicago where it played thirteen weeks and closed to a net loss of over $250,000 of Michael Meyerberg's own money.

* * *

A few days after the opening of *Lute Song* I started driving back to Los Angeles in the company of two close friends and collaborators—Herman Mankiewicz and Nick Ray. Both were dedicated to their own self-destruction, but their timing was different. Herman was forty-nine; his health was impaired and his wild, reckless days were behind him. It was seven years since we had worked on *Citizen Kane* and he had six years more to live; they were years in which, behind his truculent front, he was worrying about survival and about his health and about the condition in which he would be leaving his family. With *Kane* he had made his statement as a writer and, from now on, he was resigned to making his living as a well-paid studio hack.

Nick Ray, at thirty-five, had worked with me in theater and radio. Our collaboration in film was about to begin. He was a stimulating and sometimes disturbing companion; garrulous and inarticulate, ingenuous and pretentious, his mind was filled with original ideas which he found difficult to formulate or express. Alcohol reduced him to rambling unintelligibility; his speech, which was slow and convoluted at best, became unbearably turgid after more than one drink. Yet, confronted with a theatrical situation or a problem of dramatic or musical expression he was amazingly quick, lucid and intuitive with a sureness of touch, a sensitivity to human values and an infallible taste that I have seldom seen equalled.

From his year's apprenticeship as a scholarship student with Frank Lloyd Wright, Nick had acquired a perfectionism and a sense of commitment to his work which were rare in the theater and even more rare in the film business. But in his personal life he was the victim of irresistible impulses that left his career and his personal relationships in ruins and finally destroyed him. He was a handsome, complicated man whose sentimentality and apparent softness covered deep layers of resilience and strength. Reared in Wisconsin in a household dominated by women, he was a potential homosexual with a deep, passionate and constant need for female love in his life. This made him attractive to women, for whom the chance to save him from his own self-destructive habits proved an irresistible attraction of which Nick took full advantage and for which he rarely forgave them. He left a trail of damaged lives behind him—not as a seducer, but as a husband, lover and father.

Once again we crossed the desert at night and arrived in Los Angeles on a gray February morning. Mank had invited me to stay with him in Tower Road while I looked for a place to live; the next day I drove down to the studio, where I made an astonishing discovery.

My "romance" with Joan Fontaine had not survived our six months' separation. I had not expected it to. We had written occasionally and spoken on the phone with diminishing frequency and growing embarrassment. If I had not been too busy to follow Hollywood gossip I would have been less startled to learn that my successor in Miss Fontaine's favors was none other than my old friend and new executive producer, William Dozier, in whom she had apparently found a more forceful and reassuring mate—for she presently married him.

RKO, of which Bill Dozier had recently become head of production, was a maverick studio with no consistent record of achievement and no discernible policy—artistic or economic. This instability had permitted the production of a number of notable films over the years, including the early Hepburns, *King Kong*, the first Astaire musicals, *Citizen Kane* and, more recently, Val Lewton's small masterpieces of terror from *The Cat-People* to *The Isle of the Dead*.

I spent my first two months reading material and resisting most of Dozier's suggestions for films. Then, from among the piles of galleys, synopses and typescripts with which I was deluged, I came across a short novel—*Thieves Like Us*—by an unknown writer about which I decided, before I was halfway through it, that this was my next film. It was a blend of chase and love story—the brief idyll of two lonely, emotionally stunted young people set in a world in which hunger, fear, treachery and violence were essential components.

I gave it to Nick to read and he liked it as much as I did. Dozier was less enthusiastic but agreed to buy it for me. He suggested several highly paid Hollywood writers for the screenplay. I told him I'd rather work on it quietly with Nick Ray.

I had rented a house high in the Hollywood Hills whose previous tenant was Peter Lorre. It had an amazing view of the city and a small guest house at the end of the garden. Here Nick was installed and started work on a treatment of *Thieves Like Us* that formed the basis of the film we made the following year. While I spent the day at the studio reading the scripts that Dozier kept sending me, Nick was up on the hill working like a man possessed. In the evening and early morning we'd go over what he'd done during the day. And we worked weekends. For by now I was convinced that we were onto something I had been waiting and hoping for ever since my arrival in Hollywood—a film I really loved.

We were making slow but satisfying progress when I learned one morning (from the trades) that RKO had been sold and Bill Dozier liquidated. As usual in show business, all projects initiated by the previous management were automatically canceled or shelved. I managed to keep Nick on the payroll for a few weeks; we finished the treatment, had it mimeographed—all 124 pages of it—and stole a dozen copies for future use.

The change of management did not affect my own contract, which had two and a half years to run. But, if I was not going to make a film, I preferred to wait for the next phase of my contract back in New York. This allowed me to consider an intriguing offer I had received the previous winter from a former fellow worker on Harlem's WPA Negro Theater. Perry Watkins (the only black set-designer working in the New York theater) had come to me during *Lute Song* with a project, still in the dream stage, involving Duke Ellington and John Latouche. Their idea was to update Gay's *Beggar's Opera*, to move its milieu from London's eighteenth-century underworld to the contemporary jungle of our own big cities. (The Brecht-Weill *Threepenny Opera* was still virtually unknown since its failure on Broadway in the midthirties.) It was an attractive idea—all the more since this promised to be a wholly integrated production, beginning with the authors and producers and going right on down through the cast and chorus. I never got to read the script or to hear more than a couple of numbers from the score. But I did talk with Ellington, one of the world's great spellbinders, and with Latouche, whom I had known since the deep Depression days when Virgil Thomson had harbored him in our apartment. (Since then he had achieved success with *Cabin in the Sky* and the nationally admired *Ballad for Americans*.)

All through the spring and summer of 1946, Perry Watkins would call long distance every few weeks to report that all was going well—"full steam ahead" was his phrase; money was pouring in and Latouche and Ellington were "cooking with gas." Still no script arrived. After the collapse of our film plans Nick and I made another of our high-pressure drives to New York to appraise the situation.

The day after we arrived, I drove over the George Washington Bridge to New City to take a look at the House on the Hill that Henry Poor was building for me. It was midafternoon, and the hills above the South Mountain Road were bright with leaves—the lush, heavy green of Hudson Valley summer. I couldn't see my house from below, but a road of sorts had been torn out of the side of the hill, with a huge, curved retaining wall of native stone to keep it from sliding into the ravine. The leaves were still dripping form a summer storm as I came up around the last steep curve with my tires skidding in the wet gravel. And suddenly there it was—rising like a ruined castle out of the rock and the scarred earth, its great fieldstone walls pierced with black, gaping windows that stared out over the trees and the valley below. It was Sunday and there was no one at work; there was no roof yet or doors or window frames; tree stumps and builders' equipment were scattered around under the gray stormclouds; it all had a grim, abandoned look and my first emotion on seeing my dream house was not the excitement and pleasure I had expected but a sudden, overwhelming desire to see it sink and vanish forever into the earth.

Until this instant it had been a remote and vaguely imagined thing, born of a sentimental fantasy and nurtured by what was left each month of my Hollywood earnings. Now, in one awful moment, the conceit had become a reality. Wandering for the first time through the chill half-light of these enormous bare rooms with their tall windows and massive fireplaces, the astonishing, cantilevered concrete staircase, the three-foot-thick stone walls and the gigantic overhead beams, I could see none of its wonders—only the monstrous trap in which I had allowed myself to get caught. Half-finished and empty, it filled me with foreboding and gloom—a terrifying symbol of the perpetual, insoluble conflict between my growing need to belong somewhere and my old, deadly, fear of engagement.

I had told no one of my coming. In my present mood I preferred to be alone. I stayed up on that hill alone for three hours. The storm had long since blown away and the late afternoon sun was flooding the house—just as Henry Poor had planned that it should. By the time I got back to New York my terror had begun to ebb. But it would be more than a year before I was ready to accept the idea that this fantastic castle was really mine.

The following day Nick and I met the producers of *Beggar's Holiday* and were made aware of several things—none of them good. Latouche was not only lazy but he was drinking and he had been working on several other projects during the summer. He had written a number of lyrics but only the roughest draft of our first act and almost nothing of the second. Ellington, teeming with tunes and mood pieces, still had not faced the necessity of composing a musical score. Added to these unpleasant discoveries were others of which I soon became aware: our producers were not only inexperienced and inefficient—they were desperately short of money. Finally, owing to the Duke's enormous list of future commitments, we had no leeway at all but must start rehearsals within four weeks or not at all.

Nick and I weighed the situation with all its attractions and dangers. We had little to lose and the temptation was great. Our coitus interruptus with our film had left us edgy and impatient. We decided to go ahead.

We spent our days planning the production, our nights in a desolate, freezing penthouse on the roof of the Chelsea Hotel, slaving away at the script, trying to give it some shape and motion. A week before rehearsal we had the semblance of a first act: it remained fairly close to Gay's original text, ending with MacHeath's betrayal by Jenny Diver. The second act was chaotic and remained so during rehearsals and throughout our New Haven, Boston and New York engagements.

Our integrated show gave us opportunities for adventurous and exhilarating casting. MacHeath was played by Alfred Drake (whose operatic baritone and lively stage presence had helped to establish the success of *Oklahoma!* and *Kismet*); the Lockits were black; the Peachums were white, with Zero Mostel in his first stage role as the outrageous Mr. Peachum. The pimps and whores were mixed black and white with Avon Long as Filch and Libby Holman as a sultry, overripe Jenny Diver. The dancers, whom we selected with Valerie Bettis, our choreographer, were gorgeous to look at and moved like panthers. The settings, originally attempted by Perry Watkins, were soon, at my insistence, turned over to Oliver Smith, who, in less than a week, delivered designs of such imaginative beauty that he repeated most of them years later (fire escapes and all) in *West Side Story*. Costumes were created by a wild male *modiste* with gold-lacquered hair. They were extravagant and scandalous and exactly right.

Rehearsals began deceptively well. The quality of Ellington's music and the energy of our mixed cast almost made us forget the inadequacies of our book and the absence of a structured score. When we needed additional music, Ellington's celebrated arranger, Billy Strayhorn (know as "Sweet Pea"), would run up to the Duke's apartment and fish out of a drawer, crammed with unperformed music, whatever tune seemed to fit the scene. Some were wonderful and, with Latouche's lyrics, remained for years in the repertory of Lena Horne and other well-known singers. But this did not make up for the absence of a score and a book.

By the middle of the second week we found ourselves mired in our nonexistent second act, and our producer's checks had begun to bounce. Costume and scene shops were threatening to suspend fittings and building for lack of funds when a new angel was unearthed in the person of a small, ill-favored, timid alcoholic who, in a series of desperate scenes of blackmail and tears, was separated over the next few weeks from a substantial part of his inherited wealth. Unfortunately, the money never seemed to arrive in time to re-establish our credit or to assure the smooth progress of the production.

The nightmare continued—growing darker and more frightening from day to day. By now I was so busy dealing with crises that I had little time for the show. New Haven, that familiar testing ground for unready and faltering productions, saw us arrive on a Monday and rehearse for two days on a bare stage because the scenic studio where our show was being built refused to load out the scenery until it was paid for. We were due to open on Thursday night under our new name of *Twilight Alley*. On Tuesday afternoon our alcoholic angel was cozened out of an additional $50,000; early Wednesday morning the scenery was unloaded and erected in a continuous thirty-hour crew call on golden hours. At midnight we began a technical rehearsal that lasted till after dawn. The next day, at noon, eight hours before opening, we began our first and only dress rehearsal, which we were unable to complete.

Even in a town that was used to impromptu openings, ours was unusually calamitous. The last twenty minutes of the show—MacHeath's death dream in the electric chair followed by his reprieve and his reunion with his many wives—were virtually improvised by Drake and the cast before an audience that included the usual number of vulturous ill-wishers from New York.

In the frenetic atmosphere that prevailed, it was never entirely clear to me whether I resigned from *Beggar's Holiday* or was fired. I do remember that on the morning following our new Haven opening I informed the producers that I was leaving the show. They made no attempt to dissuade me and I later discovered that they had already hired the great George Abbott to try to salvage the project.

It didn't help. *Beggar's Holiday* limped into New York and closed after a few weeks. What should have been a triumphal theatrical novelty had been ruined by inadequate preparation and inept production. I have always felt that much of the responsibility for the disaster was mine—for agreeing to go into rehearsal with a show that was nowhere near ready.

Soon after that, while I was nursing my wounds, I received a phone call form Herman Mankiewicz in California informing me that Dore Schary had just been named head of production for RKO. I had never worked with him, but I knew him as an educated, intelligent, progressive filmmaker. I told my agents that I was ready to resume my RKO contract and asked them to notify Schary to that effect. He sent word within a few days that I could start any time I wished. I called to thank him and to ask him, please, to read the treatment of *Thieves Like Us* as soon as possible. A week later I was back in Los Angeles.

XIV
Thieves Like Us
1945-47

1937 had been a miraculous year. 1947 was another. In nine months I produced two films and presented five West Coast theatrical premières—not to mention the opening of a new playhouse, the creation of a gallery of modern art, the formation of the Hollywood Film Society and the publication of the *Hollywood Quarterly*. Most of these activities took place simultaneously—sometimes parallel, sometimes overlapping—and they were all, as usual, unpremeditated and unexpected.

It started with *Thieves Like Us*. By the time Nick Ray and I got back to California, Dore Schary, our new executive producer, had read our treatment and liked it. After five months of torpor following Dozier's departure, the studio was in need of product and Schary was eager to go into production as soon as possible. Our first step was to turn Nick's 124-page treatment into a screenplay. It was, in fact, half screenplay already, with the action, the characters and much of the dialogue of the film we eventually made. What we needed now was a writer of sufficient skill and experience to turn out a script that would be budgeted and shot within the limitations of a medium-priced picture. He must also have the sensitivity and modesty to recognize and respect the quality we had found in the book and that Nick had developed in his treatment.

Nick was eager to write the screenplay himself but I had other plans for him. And I had the writer I needed. Charles Schnee was a friend from New York, a one-time contributor to the Mercury Theater whose recent work on Howard Hawks's *Red River* made him an accredited film writer. He liked *Thieves Like Us* and agreed to work on it. He was a fast writer and within six weeks, working closely with Nick and myself, he had completed a screenplay that was approved by Schary and the production department. One element was still missing—the director.

Several well-known names were suggested. But, this time, I was determined to have my own way and my own director. For the first time since I had begun to make pictures I felt myself wholly committed to a film and that commitment included Nick Ray. I had a problem selling him to the Studio: his aesthetic and moral ruminations made him suspect to the tough, pragmatic men in the production department. Schary was sympathetic, but he had natural reservations about entrusting a feature film to a novice whose only experience was the three months he had spent as Kazan's assistant on *A Tree Grows in Brooklyn*. To solve the argument, I persuaded Schary to let Ray direct our casting tests. They were beautiful and, within a week, Nicholas Ray was formally installed as director of *Thieves Like Us* with a starting date that was less than two months away.

At the Voice of America and during the making of *Tuesday in November*, *Lute Song* and *Beggar's Holiday*, my cooperation with Nick had been a close and affectionate one. This continued throughout the preparation of our film. Then, with the first day's shooting of *Thieves Like Us*, I realized that our association had undergone a subtle but drastic change. Our affection continued throughout its making and for another thirty years. But, suddenly, there was a new balance. Until then, though I had complete faith in his taste and talent and frequently accepted his judgments, Nick had functioned as my assistant. Overnight this was changed. From the first instant of shooting, Nick Ray emerged as an autonomous creator with a style and work patterns that were entirely and fiercely his own. As with Orson in our early days together, it now became my function to maintain a climate within which he could work freely and creatively, without interference from anyone—including myself.

Our first day's shooting was traumatic. We had agreed to make *Thieves Like Us* as much in sequence as possible. Our first shot was an open field in which four escaping convicts and the terrified farmer they have taken hostage are racing in his battered open Model A towards the highway and freedom. Nick wanted to shoot the scene from above, and since no camera crane was high enough or capable of traveling at high speed over rough corn stubble, he decided it must be shot from a helicopter.

Whirlybirds had been used for combat filming during the war and for high, panoramic shots of landscapes and cities but never, to my knowledge, the way Ray was planning to use this one—as an infinite, swiftly moving boom. Ours was not a "big" picture and the production department predictably opposed the idea on the grounds that it involved serious risks. Aside from the possibility of mechanical failure, there were factors of wind, light and human error. Nick was adamant: he insisted it was an essential shot—a unique way to establish the mood and movement of the film in its opening moments. I agreed to let him try.

The next morning we stood in a bare field northeast of Los Angeles, waiting for the mist to clear. A little after nine the pilot announced he was ready to take off. Nick went up in the cameraman's place. For more than an hour our battered Model A bounced over the corn stubble while the whirlybird clattered overhead. Once it almost hit a sandbank with its tailpiece. Finally, with the fourth run, the shape of the shot became clear, and Nick got out and let the operator climb back. The helicopter took off, rose and hovered noisily 100 feet above us as the Model A started off again across the field with its four sweating and desperate occupants. As it approached, the helicopter slowly descended to meet it, drawing closer and closer till they were only a few feet apart. For a few seconds, as they traveled along together, the camera held the car in close focus—close enough to catch the wind in the men's hair and the wild look in their eyes. Then slowly the car started to pull away. The camera was above them now, shooting on the men's backs except when they glanced back to see if they were being followed, moving along slightly above and behind them as they bumped across the stubble towards the highway. When they reached it, the helicopter rose and hovered and the Model A passed under it, becoming smaller and smaller as it raced away along the highway to safety.

The first take was a dud. Over the walkie-talkie the pilot announced he was coming down and, as soon as he'd landed, everyone came running and gathered for a conference clear of the slowly revolving blades. The operator said he needed more time to change his focus as the car passed beneath him. The car went back to its starting mark as the helicopter blades began to turn. This time, as it rose, it barely avoided a scrub oak. It was a few minutes before noon and it was getting hot. Once again the helicopter hovered noisily overhead. The assistant gave the cue and the Model A bounced past us, gathering speed as the camera came down to meet it. This time it worked. The operator reported a perfect take all the way. For protection Nick made two more—neither as good as the first—then broke for lunch.

By now Nick was drunk with power. The whirlybird was ours for the day and, before nightfall, he had shot fifteen more set-ups including one very dramatic shot of a roadside poster, starting with a huge, garish close-up of a girl advertising a local motel, then pulling back to reveal a small human figure crouched at its base, waiting for night to fall.

We returned to the studio exhausted and triumphant, but it was not until the next day at noon when the "dailies" were rushed over from the lab that we were able to see what had been accomplished. If we had got nothing else, that first sensational shot alone justified Nick's use of the helicopter to reveal our three principal characters in violent action and to give that feeling of desperate, dusty flight that was to become the continuing style of the picture. And because of the way it was shot from above, it had a curiously detached, almost godlike point of view that could have been achieved in no other way.

Nick maintained his tempo and, after a few days, even the production department came around. He was working with actors now—mostly with the Boy and the Girl. And as we started to cut and assemble our first few days' footage we became aware of a very special quality not only in our actors' performances but also of the physical and emotional background against which their scenes were played. Most of *Thieves Like Us* was shot on our own backlot or on locations that were within easy reach of the studio. And here Nick's personal experience of hard times in the Southwest, combined with his visual sense, enabled him, with very limited means, to recreate the emotional reality of that world of shabby small towns, abandoned farms and squalid cabins and tourist camps in which the action of our film was taking place. This sense of emotional reality also pervaded the sound track that Nick put together with loving care during and after shooting—the characteristic, commonplace, personal and mechanical sounds of American life, blended with a musical score that forms an integral part of the film. Some of it was authentic source material from radios and jukeboxes—pop tunes of the period mixed up with songs by Nick's friend Woody Guthrie, which were then orchestrated into running themes by Leigh Harline.

Shooting was finished—a day under schedule, and we were editing *Thieves Like Us* when I began to make daily trips over the Cahuenga Pass to the old Universal Studios in the Valley to work on an altogether different project.

The Doziers had re-entered my life. They had set up a producing company of their own of which Dozier was the executive producer and Joan the star. It was an attractive if slightly incestuous set-up and, for their first independent production, they had chosen Stefan Zweig's *Letter from an Unknown Woman*, for which I shared their enthusiasm as a vehicle for Joan. I told them I'd be delighted to produce it for them. To write the screenplay we agreed on Howard Koch. He in turn suggested a European émigré, Max Ophüls, as the right director for the picture. To convince us he showed us a film Ophüls had made before the war, based on Schnitzler's *Liebelei*. It was of the same period and milieu as Zweig's novella. We saw it, liked it, invited Ophüls to join us and, almost before I knew it, I was deep in the preparation of a second film.

Bill, as usual, was in a hurry; Joan had a starting date for film at another studio and we were still working on the screenplay when we went into production. Koch and I were old collaborators and I got on well with Max Ophüls after I overcame his European conviction, aggravated by bad Hollywood experiences, that the producer and the director of a film were natural and irreconcilable enemies.

Letter from an Unknown Woman is bittersweet Viennese. It is the confession of a woman who has been in love for most of her life with a man to whom she has meant so little that—though they have been intimate, in different ways, at three different times of their lives—he does not even remember her. The first two thirds of our story were altogether romantic. They were a joy to work on. Joan Fontaine had proved in *Rebecca*, *Suspicion* and *Jane Eyre* that she was an expert at portraying the emotions of an adolescent girl in thrall to an older man. She had no difficulty at all in playing the teenage Lisa, crouched in the dark stairwell, listening to her idol playing Chopin upstairs in his room. And she was charming and moving as the passionate young Viennese girl giving herself without regret in a romantic ecstasy to the man she has worshipped for most of her life.

The third and last episode presented more serious hazards of writing and acting. The frame of Zweig's novella is a letter written by Lisa as she is dying; it is not a reproach but a profession of gratitude to the man who, without being aware of it, has given her all the love she has ever known. It is a literary device that was valid in print but seemed less convincing when it was transferred to the more specific realism of film. And Joan, with her poignant immaturity, ran into problems of credibility when she was called upon to play a European *femme du monde* in her thirties.

Koch was a sincere writer with a good sense of structure. Vienna was not his territory, but he had Max by his side to guide him and to devise some of the script's most imaginative moments. This was an atmosphere that Ophüls knew intimately and dearly loved: he used it in *Leibelei* and would use it again, years later, in *La Ronde*. All through production he was tireless and insatiable, to the point of exasperation, in his insistence upon authentic atmospheric detail. Above all I remember the touching, entirely original scene of Lisa's seduction in the mock-up compartment of a European railroad carriage with the painted Alpine scenery moving by outside on a slowly rolling canvas cyclorama propelled by a little man furiously pedaling a stationary bicycle.

Yet, as the film moved into its final stages, I detected a disturbing tone of discouragement and diminishing energy. Some of this had to do with Joan's performance; some was inherent in the form of Zweig's novella, to which Koch had scrupulously—perhaps too scrupulously—adhered. Some of it stemmed from Ophüls's own mercurial temperament.

One night, during the last week of shooting, I got a call from him long after midnight. He begged me to drive out and meet him as soon as possible at an all-night joint in the Valley next to the studio. When I got there I found him plunged in a raging gloom. We sat for two hours over drinks and coffee, then walked around the back lot, where the dawn was coming up over our Viennese amusement park. Max informed me that he had spent the previous evening running the rough cut of our film and it was his somber conclusion that our ending was downbeat, maudlin and wholly lacking in dramatic conviction. He blamed Zwieg, Koch, Miss Fontaine and, most particularly, himself for our failure. Once in a while he wept, blew his nose and went on talking. There was truth in what he said, all the more since the censors in the Breen Office had taken much of the emotional shock out of Lisa's last moments with her lover. But at five in the morning, I found his attitude defeatist, self-indulgent and dangerous. I pointed out that it was too late in the day for him to be making these discoveries; that it was impossible, at this stage of the film, to reshape the ending without losing the essential quality of Zweig's story. I assured him that the film was beautiful; I did all I could to send him back onto the set in a less calamitous frame of mind. Three hours later I watched him riding a boom with his usual enthusiasm and that night he called to tell me that our rushes were wonderful.

In the fall of 1947 my future in the film business looked bright. I seemed to have not one winner, but two. While we were preparing and shooting *Letter to an Unknown Woman*, I had continued to work with Nick on the final editing and scoring of *Thieves Like Us*. In September we had two good previews, then cut the negative and began showing it to critics of the trades and magazines under the new title of *Your Red Wagon* (the title of a blues number in the film). Our first reviews were wonderful; Iris Barry gave us a special running at the Museum of Modern Art in New York and word began to get around that we had one of the sleepers of the year.

Then, overnight, disaster struck. Our film was scheduled to be released during the winter of 1947-48. But, before that, the trades carried the dark news one morning that RKO had been acquired by Howard Hughes. His first act was to get rid of Dore Schary and to reverse all arrangements made by the previous management. These included the release of our film, which moldered in a vault for two years before it was finally released under the title *They Live by Night*.

The magazines would not review it a second time or reprint their earlier notices. The daily press treated it as what it had become—a B-picture on the second half of a double bill.

This sabotage of my favorite picture left me with *Letter from an Unknown Woman* as my last hope of establishing my reputation as a serious filmmaker. The Doziers seemed happy; our San Francisco preview had gone well and I was beginning to get congratulatory letters from people whose opinions I valued—such as Preston Sturges and Joseph Losey.

My euphoria was short-lived. In the latter part of April *Letter from an Unknown Woman* was given a hurried national release. The Cold War had started and the general mood was violently anti-romantic. With few exceptions, our reviews were terrible, e.g., the *New York Times:*

Let your imagination picture a beautiful, sad-eyed Joan Fontaine standing outside in a snowstorm, her nose pressed against a window pane, yearning with lonely ardor toward the warmth of a never-to-be romance, and you'll have a fair-sized notion of the nature and atmosphere of *Letter from an Unknown Woman.*

It took several years of European success to restore *Letter* to its honored place in the canon of Max Ophüls' film work. In its day, it was an unmitigated disaster—critically and commercially—and a devastating defeat for us all.

XV
Galileo Galilei
1947

I was well served that year by my compulsive habit of always doing several things at once and by my incurable insistence on jumping out of one medium into another. Throughout 1947, my anxiety over the fate of my two films was diluted by my equally intense concern over the success of the theater season in which I had suddenly got myself involved.

That spring my friend Norman Lloyd had called me in great excitement to report the existence of a beautiful, new, small theater about to be completed on the edge of Beverly Hills. It could be rented for very little; there might even be financing from certain unmentionable sources. I was not interested. I was trying to get two films off the ground and I had a large, unfinished house to pay for in the East. Besides, it had never occurred to me to get involved in theater outside New York.

I was surprised, therefore, some weeks later to find myself signing a year's lease for the Coronet Theater on La Cienega Boulevard and even more surprised to have become president of Pelican Productions and of the Hollywood Film Society. Looking back I can find no reasonable explanation for my involvement in such a reckless undertaking which had all the usual characteristics of a Houseman enterprise—grandiose conception, little preparation and no money.

There was a theatrical slump all over the country but nowhere was this collapse more complete than in Los Angeles, where most of the area's vast new population was unaware that theater existed. Even the educated and the well-to-do had lost the habit of local theater-going. To see a play they flew to New York or London.

When Norman Lloyd and I took possession of our new building, we were agreeably surprised. We had a conventional theater with close to 300 seats, adequate wing space, a spacious foyer and patio and an insulated professional projection booth. For the next eight months this formed the apex of a triangle of which the other two points were the RKO Studio in Hollywood and the Universal Studio in the Valley. Driving between them at high speed and in a state of perpetual excitement I made the circuit twice and often three times a day.

The birth of Pelican Productions had caught us unawares. Overnight we found ourselves in possession of a theater with nothing to put in it, no organization to operate it and no predictable audience with which to fill it. My first move, as usual, was to make a flamboyant announcement of our plans which, in addition to theatrical production, included music, a picture gallery and the Hollywood Film Society.

The latter was an improvisation to which I had, until that moment, given little thought. Finding ourselves in possession of a projection booth and having watched Iris Barry's operation at the Museum of Modern Art, it suddenly occurred to me that such an institution would thrive in a town where a large percentage of the world's films were made. Without bothering to find out if such a need really existed or if anyone was willing to support it, I acquired two of the best and most modern projection machines available and mailed out an elegant three-color brochure announcing several series of films—drama, documentary and experimental—to be shown daily in our theater between the hours of 4 and 7 p.m. In the same mailing, patrons also received the announcement of an exhibition of theatrical paintings and drawings to be held in the foyer of our theater featuring works by Bérard, Tchelitchev, Dali, Chagall, Berman and a number of young local artists. Most of the pictures were loans from local collections including Igor Stravinsky's. (Among my most vivid memories of that summer is that of the world's leading composer balanced dangerously on a tall ladder hammering nails into the walls of our foyer.)

These were the trimmings. Our first and most urgent obligation as impresarios was to find an opening Pelican production that would justify our highfalutin claim that we were about to restore Theater to Southern California. We found it in Bertolt Brecht's *Galileo Galilei* in a translation by Charles Laughton, in which he himself had agreed to appear.

I had met Brecht in the midthirties during the Theater Union's production of Gorki's *Mother*. Joseph Losey had brought us together: he thought Brecht's *Round Heads and Square Heads* might be suitable for production by the WPA Negro Theater of which I was the director. I remember little of that meeting beyond my first superficial impression of an unshaven man, dressed in drab European workmen's clothes with a thin cigar in his mouth. I had heard accounts of his violent and abusive behavior during rehearsals of *Mother*. No such scenes occurred in the weeks that Brecht worked for the Voice of America in the winter of 1942-43 broadcasting a program of his own songs and poems. Since then I had met him personally at Salka Viertel's émigré salon in Santa Monica, where I was startled by the intransigence of his views. "Folk art is a lot of *shit*" he would shout in German and then very forcibly and convincingly expatiate without interruption for the next forty minutes.

Charles Laughton and his wife Elsa Lanchester were old friends but it was Norman Lloyd who, through his friendship with Hanns Eisler (Brecht's musical collaborator after his break with Kurt Weill), brough *Galileo* to my attention and arranged for a reading of the play one evening at the Laughton's home in Pacific Palisades.

From Laughton's first public reading it was evident that this was a noble and important work and that it would be an honor—as well as good business and a thrilling theatrical experience—to present it in its world première. Charles was a fussy negotiator but, by mid-May, a contract had been signed between Brecht, Laughton and ourselves: joint producers would be Pelican Productions and T. Edward Hambleton—a young New York producer with money and a friend of the Laughtons.

At the last moment, we had second thoughts about *Galileo* as our opener. My producer's instinct told me that it was wrong and unfair to open such a great and controversial play on an untried stage under an unknown management and that it would be wiser to present it as our second production. This made the choice of our first play even more urgent than ever.

That problem was solved by the appearance one day in our theater of Carol Stone and her husband with the rights to a West Coast production of *The Skin of Our Teeth*. I had seen Kazan's production in New York; ours (with Keenan Wynn and Jane Wyatt as the Antrobuses, Carol Stone as Sabina and Blanche Yurka as the fortune-teller) was lighter and, in my opinion, rather clearer and more human. For our première we indulged in a little circus showmanship: to add color to our Atlantic City boardwalk scenes, I had made an arrangement with a local school band which played poorly but enthusiastically—not only on stage but also in the patio before performance and during intermissions. Clad in scarlet uniforms, they contributed to the festive tone of our opening which took place on June 10, 1947, before an audience that, according to Hedda Hopper, included Judy Garland, Olivia de Havilland, the Van Johnsons, Angela Lansbury, Charles and Pat Boyer, Gene Kelly and Ed Wynn.

Our reviews were enthusiastic—WILDER PLAY STIRRING—
PELICAN SETS NEW STANDARD—and our success with the public was
such that, following our four-week run, we moved to another theater
where, according to *Variety*:

PELICAN SKIN'S HWD CLICK BRINGS INDEF RUN

We were now ready to present *Galileo*. Brecht's play, which dramatizes
the inevitable conflict between the revolutionary thinker and the
Establishment (in this instance the Church of Rome) had been written
in Denmark in 1938, during Brecht's years of exile and wandering "in
those dark months when many people felt fascism's advance to be
irresistible and the final collapse of Western civilization to have
arrived."

It was Brecht's habit constantly to revise and rewrite his plays. In
Galileo the main changes were made years later in the United States in
response to "a world event of inescapable significance"—the
construction and use of the atom bomb.

Overnight the biography of the founder of the new system of physics read
differently. The informal effect of the great bomb placed the conflict between
Galileo and the authorities of his day in a new and sharper light...Galileo's
crime (his abjuration) can be regarded as the "original sin" of modern natural
sciences.

Credit for direction of our production went to Joseph Losey but the
vital decisions, before and during productions, were all Brecht's. His
preliminary notes form an eloquent summary of his theatrical
convictions:

1. The decorations should not be of a kind to suggest to the spectators that they
are in a medieval Italian room or in the Vatican. The audience should always
remain conscious of being in a theater.

2. The background should show more than the scene directly surrounding
Galileo; in an imaginative and artistically pleasing way it should show the
play's historical setting.

3. Furniture and props should be realistic and above all of social and historical
interest. Costumes must be individualized and show signs of having been
worn. Social differences must be underlined since an audience finds it difficult
to distinguish these in historical fashions.

4. The characters' groupings must have the quality of historical paintings (not
as an aesthetic attraction). The director can help to achieve this by inventing
historical titles for the various episodes.

5. The action must be presented calmly and with a wide sweep. Frequent
changes of position and irrelevant movements should be avoided. The director
must not for a moment forget that many of the actions and speeches are hard
to understand and that it is therefore necessary to express the underlying idea

of an episode by positioning. The audience must be assured that when someone walks or gets up or makes a gesture it has a meaning and deserves attention.

6. In casting the ecclesiastical dignitaries realism is of more than usual importance. No caricature of the church is intended...In this play the church mainly represents authority; as types its dignitaries should resemble our present-day bankers and senators.

7. The actor's portrayal of Galileo should not aim at rousing the audience to sympathy or empathy; they should rather be encouraged to adopt a deliberate attitude of wonder and criticism.

8. The more profoundly the historical seriousness of a production is established, the more scope can be given to humor. The more sweeping the all-over plan, the more intimately individual scenes can be played.

For an account of Laughton's performance as Galileo, I refer the reader to Brecht's own memoir in which he describes with affectionate admiration the "pains of a great artist who is willing to take on the preparation and rehearsing of a role." Published years later in Berlin, it is in sharp contrast with much of what I remember of Brecht's attitude during production. In his determination to achieve the precise style and interpretation he wanted, he was harsh, intolerant and often brutal and abusive. The words *"Scheiss"* and "shit" were the most frequent in the vocabulary with which he voiced his artistic opinions. That he was nearly always right did not diminish the pain and resentment he spread around him during those long, intense weeks of rehearsal.

Besides Laughton himself, there was one element of the production over which there was never any argument and one man whose judgment Brecht never questioned. That was Hanns Eisler—compatriot and fellow Marxist. His *Galileo* music was scored for harpsichord and small orchestra plus some a cappella choral interludes sung by a three-boy choir that introduced each scene of the play. It was a pastiche of sixteenth-century Italian music with a modernity that made it brilliantly and theatrically alive. And it earned Eisler a tribute of unqualified praise from Igor Stravinsky, who came several times to hear it.

In fact, Brecht's violence seldom reached Laughton, who had problems of his own, aggravated by the almost hysterical nervousness that came over him as the night approached on which he was to make his first stage appearance in fifteen years. Inside this complicated, timid, arrogant man a vast panic was building up that became increasingly painful to watch as the days went by. He did not crack; his self-discipline was remarkable. During the last part of July we had a heat wave which stacks of ice, piled up in front of two large electric fans on either side of the stage, were unable to attenuate. Yet, during the long ordeal of costume fittings and technical rehearsals made hideous by Brecht's screeched obscenities, Laughton remained remarkably courteous and calm.

His nervousness took another form—that of a profound and frightening neurotic inertia. The company of *Galileo* was a large one—more than fifty in all, including singers, dancers and costumed musicians—and our dressing rooms were woefully insufficient for them. During rehearsals and for the duration of the run, we rented, for Charles's use, a medium-sized trailer, which stood in our back alley next to the stage door. Here, as opening night drew near, he began to do an inordinate amount of sleeping: not catnaps but deep, heavy slumber into which he would sink at strange and unexpected moments—in the midst of making up, while going over lines and sometimes even between scenes—and from which it became increasingly difficult for our stage managers to rouse him for his next appearance. Brecht had written prophetically (as far back as 1941):

Galileo should not be idealized as a star-gazer, a pallid, intellectual idealist...My Galileo is a powerful physicist with a belly on him, a face like Socrates, a vociferous full-blooded man with a sense of humor, earthy, a great talker. Favorite attitude—stomach thrust forward, both hands on the buttocks, head back, using a meaty hand to gesticulate with; comfortable trousers for working in.

Laughton carried the image one step further. In his nervousness he was inclnced to emphasize the grossness of the man. At our first preview he spent what seemed like several minutes of the opening scene with his hands in his pockets scratching his scrotum and buttocks. On the following night it was discovered just before curtain-time that his trouser pockets had been sewn up. We never found out who did it: the prime suspect was Heli Weigel, Brecht's devoted wife (later the star and director of the Berliner Ensemble), who was helping out in our wardrobe department at the time.

The première of *Galileo* took place on July 30, 1947, by which time every seat had been sold for the entire four-week run. On opening night the world press was represented and among the Hollywood celebrities whose presence was noted in local columns were Charles Chaplin, Charles Boyer, John Garfield and Ingrid Berman, together with countless European émigrés with nostalgic memories of former Brechtian triumphs in Berlin in the twenties and early thirties. Reactions were mixed: the local left-wing intelligentsia predictably found Brecht's dialectic less positive than they had expected. The rest of the audience, unprepared for epic theater, seemed perplexed by its form and content and became rather bored with the piece as the evening wore on.

The next day's reviews reflected this ambivalence: it was referred to as "an arresting footlight event," "a rich new experience" and "erudite but dubious drama." A wholly negative opinion came from a devout Catholic on Hearst's *Los Angeles Examiner*, who condemned the play as "a harangue—and a fussy, juvenile harangue at that."

Galileo gave the Pelican its place in theatrical history but it did nothing to solve our problems. We turned people away every night but our production costs had been enormous. We had hoped to extend our run but Laughton found the part so exhausting that he was unable to go on beyond the four weeks on which we had originally agreed. Once again, we had to find something in a hurry with which to follow our successful double-header. Of the suggestions with which we were flooded, the most sensible seemed Jean-Paul Sartre's *No Exit*. I had seen it in New York the previous winter, directed by John Huston, and it had the virtue, after our first two huge productions, of having one set and three characters. It was followed by *Dark of the Moon*—a curious blend of musical comedy, folk drama, ballet and evangelistic fervor, in total contrast to the European intellectualism of Sartre and Brecht. Its main problem, with its large cast of actors, dancers and musicians (incuding a remarkable young singer with his five-string banjo, named Pete Seeger), was its cost. Like *Galileo* it could never hope to recoup its production cost and, with our 265 seats, we could not even cover our weekly expenses. We did sell-out business, yet each week saw us deeper in the red. We ran for a month and turned away hundreds; then, since no commercial backer could be found to buy us out and move us to another theater or city, we closed to a massive loss of around $30,000.

In addition to our theatrical difficulties there was now the problem of the Hollywood Film Society. Conceived and organized on an impulse, with no prior appraisal of its potential audience, it had cost a lot to set up (our projection equipment alone cost close to $20,000) and it was expensive to run. The first public and press reaction had been encouraging; our opening series were well attended by film lovers, students and a number of distinguished writers, filmmakers and actors. Then, after a few weeks, as our novelty began to wear off, the beaches, the holidays, the social life of Beverly Hills and the falling political barometer each took their toll. Audiences dwindled. By mid-August our average attendance had dipped from several hundred to a few dozen. We began by reducing our showings. Then we eliminated our "experimental" series. Finally, early in October, quietly and without a whimper, we folded, and our precious projection machines lay cold and silent under their hoods.

Pelican Productions was a more painful and complicated matter. For several months we had dominated serious theatrical production in Southern California. Our reputation was excellent and our attendance was consistently high. The idea of ceasing production at the peak of our success was unthinkable. Yet the facts must be faced. What had been a vague uneasiness in August was rapidly turning into a sense of disaster from which there seemed to be no escape but to close the theater as quickly as possible. It was an experience with which I was not unfamiliar. I had lived through the liquidation of the Oceanic Grain Corporation; I had watched the Mercury go from triumph to dissolution in a few months. All these ventures had this in common: their collapse was due to overexpansion and to the absence of sufficient backing to cushion the hazards of a notoriously perilous business.

The decline and fall of Pelican Productions was not solely economic. In July we were the newest and hottest thing in town: by October (with no appreciable loss of quality) we had become just another struggling playhouse in a city that was not interested in theater. It is clear, looking back, that besides my own improvidence and the notorious fecklessness of the Hollywood public, there was another, more significant explanation for our defeat. 1947 was the year in which the Cold War became part of America's foreign policy; it also marked the formal opening of the witch-hunting season in American show business.

Through the previous winter and spring there had been rumors that the House Un-American Activities Committee was about to turn its attention to Hollywood and the film business. Representatives arrived in town as early as May, interviewing what came to be known as "friendly witnesses," building up a case against the "Communists and fellow travellers" who were thought to have infiltrated the industry and injected their subversive propaganda into the nation's motion-picture product. Some of the "friendly" witnesses were executives of major film companies who welcomed this chance to eliminate the activists who had given them trouble during contract negotiations; in some instances the denunciations were made by envious competitors; others were acts of vengeance. (Still others had more grotesque backgrounds—as in the case of my friend Howard Koch. Late in 1942, as one of the Studio's most successful screenwriters, he had been sent for by the Warner Brothers, his employers, and invited to work on the script of a book by Ambassador Joseph Davies—*Mission to Moscow*—which they had recently acquired. Weary from years of uninterrupted work and eager to take a sabbatical, Koch reluctantly declined. The Warners—Harry and Jack—summoned him again some days later and begged and bullied him into taking the job. They repeated that he was uniquely qualified to undertake a patriotic assignment about our courageous allies, which they assured him was particularly dear to the heart of the President of the United States. Five

years later these same brothers were denouncing Koch as a notorious
Red, citing his writing of *Mission to Moscow* as concrete proof of his
Communist sympathies.)

By mid-summer of 1947 it was generally known that a number of
"witnesses," accusers and accused, would be summoned to
Washington to testify before the Committee. From that moment the
whole town was concerned more with political and professional
maneuvers than with entertainment. With Brecht and Sartre the Pelican
had undoubtedly identified itself with the Left; but the truth is that no
vital theater could have prospered in the atmosphere of suspicion,
anger and fear which prevailed in Hollywood during the months that
followed.

Dark of the Moon had just opened when HUAC issued its first
subpoenas. Brecht was among the nineteen "unfriendly" witnesses
who flew to Washington, most of them with the avowed intention of
defying the Committee. (So much has been printed about those
hearings that it will not be repeated here.) It was still running when
they came back—minus Brecht, who left the country the morning after
his hearing. Their return was marked by a big Sunday rally at Sinclair
Stadium, which was normally used for auto races and other sporting
events. The purpose of the meeting was to hear a first-hand account of
what had taken place in Washington, to arouse public opinion and to
plan strategy for the future. I have always disliked such gatherings, but
these men were my friends and I was outraged by the treatment they
had received. (Every one of them was known to me personally: some,
like Koch and Scott, had been my collaborators in the theater, radio or
films; others were fellow guild members and a number of them had
been closely associated with me on the Hollywood Writers'
Mobilization.) The only way in which my situation differed from that
of the men whose mug shots were appearing on the front pages of the
nation's newspapers lay in the investigators' knowledge that most of
them were holding or had at one time held cards in the American
Communist Party. On this technicality I was, for the present, immune
from official interrogation. And this left me in a curiously ambivalent
state of mind. Once again my chameleon's habits and my instinctive
avoidance of social commitment had saved me from the unpleasant
consequences of my own rash behavior. On the other hand, in my first
spasm of agitation and indignation, I felt a certain regret and even a
trace of embarrassment at being left out of a prosecution in which so
many of my close friends and associates were involved.

Later, as I got used to the situation, I made the necessary self-
protective adjustments. But I was confused and troubled as I made my
way early that Sunday afternoon, into the stadium where a few hun-

dred stalwarts of the Left sat scattered around the stands. Since this had been announced as a benefit for a defense fund, I bought the highest-priced ticket available—a box seat directly in front of the improvised platform on which the Eighteen were due to appear. The box was empty; so were the ones on either side of me as I sat down with what was left of my Sunday paper. I was too restless to read and I watched people passing below on their way to their seats. I knew some of them and we exchanged greetings. I think we were all curious to see who would show up that afternoon.

Twenty minutes later the meeting still hadn't begun and there was no sign of the Eighteen. But the press was there in force, reporters and photographers gathered in the center of the field around the empty platform. While they waited they moved around snapping pictures of familiar figures in the stands, shooting some of the same faces they were accustomed to catch at Ciro's and Grauman's Chinese and other Hollywood events. This time I knew that some of the pictures they snapped would find their way into the FBI files or into those of the official and private antisubversive organizations that were proliferating.

A few minutes before three there was some kind of agitation around the entrance to the stadium, which suggested that the Eighteen were about to make their entrance. The crowd was growing and the tension had begun to build. At that instant I became aware of a couple moving into the box next to mine. When I turned I saw that it was Hanns Eisler and his wife.

We had become acquainted during *Galileo* in one of those ephemeral theatrical relationships that seldom outlast the final curtain. He was a charming, humorous, erudite, highly intelligent man with whom I had found it possible to discuss our artistic problems when neither Brecht nor Laughton was accessible. I had not seen him since then, but I had read a lot about him. For, in the two months following *Galileo*, Hanns Eisler had achieved a sudden and unwelcome notoriety. He had, in fact, become the first public victim of the Hollywood Blacklist.

During its preliminary investigation the Committee had turned up an eager "friendly" witness in the person of Ruth Fisher, a former Communist who marked her repentance by revealing that Hanns's eldest brother, Gerhardt Eisler, had long been a leading functionary in the international Communist apparatus. Headlines in the Los Angeles press exposed the horrendous fact that Hanns Eisler, a notorious Communist alien, was currently employed to compose the score for a major Hollywood film. He was fired that same day and a clamor arose to have him deported immediately.

Part of the community rallied to his support; a number of famous figures, including Thomas Mann, Albert Einstein and Charles Chaplin, spoke out on his behalf and Clifford Odets gave him and his wife sanctuary for a while. During the HUAC hearings in Washington his name had come up repeatedly. (The Chairman of the Committee asked Dore Schary whether, "assuming that Hanns Eisler is a great artist; assuming also that he is a Communist, would you rehire him?" To which Schary replied, "I would not hesitate to rehire him if it were not proved that he was a foreign agent." In subsequent testimony he recanted and declared that, if all the Committee's counsel said about Eisler were true, he would not rehire him.)

We exchanged greetings as the Eislers entered their box. As they sat down, less than six feet away, I saw the photographers move in and start taking pictures of this, the most notorious Red in Southern California. At that moment something happened that has puzzled me for almost half a century. Heroism is not my style; physically and socially I have always regarded myself as a rather craven character. But now, sitting in my box, staring at my unread newspaper, I became aware of a mysterious urge. Suddenly it had become necessary for me to get up, cross the narrow aisle that separated me from the Eislers in their box, sit down beside them and talk with them.

Normally, shyness would have kept me from such a move: we were not close friends; I had not seen them for weeks; I had nothing special to say to either of them. (I also felt certain that Eisler himself, as a pragmatic Marxist, would have been the first to disapprove of such a gratuitous, sentimental and pointless gesture.) But I seemed to have no choice. By a process of levitation over which I exercised no conscious control I felt my backside leaving the hard wooden seat on which I was sitting and my legs carrying me, in an action of which I was only vaguely aware, across the aisle towards the neighboring box. I entered it so quickly and unexpectedly that it took Eisler, who was talking with his wife, trying to ignore the photographers, a moment to acknowledge my presence. He rose, smiling; we shook hands formally in that European manner. Without being invited I found myself sitting down between them.

I cannot, for the life of me, recall one word of the small talk we made through the clicking of cameras and the popping of flashbulbs. I do remember that as I sat there, my guts frozen with fear, I was visualizing the front page of the next morning's *Los Angeles Times* with a picture of Eisler and myself over a caption that would quite certainly spell the end of my Hollywood career.

I don't know how long my performance lasted. It couldn't have been more than a few minutes, but it seemed an eternity. The same force that had carried me helplessly into the Eisler's box now held me nailed to my seat, concerned lest my visit seem perfunctory or my departure precipitate. Finally, it was not my own volition that moved me but a sudden stir in the crowd as the Eighteen, at long last, entered the stadium and moved towards their platform. Like filings to a magnet, the photographers were suddenly drawn away towards the center of the field, where someone was making crackling testing noises over the PA system. This seemed the proper time for me to leave.

I rose, excused myself, shook hands once again, turned and moved back across the aisle to my own empty box just in time to hear the first speaker clear his throat. For the rest of the afternoon, through those long, emotional proceedings, I was filled with the intense exhilaration that, I imagine, normally follows the commission of a heroic act.

As it turned out, it was not so heroic after all. To the best of my knowledge, no photograph of Eisler and myself ever appeared in print, nor was my presence at that meeting included in the long list of subversive acts with which I was later charged. One of the photographers, a friend, sent me a print of a picture he took that afternoon: it shows me listening, with a rather wooden expression, to a short, balding, smiling man of bourgeois appearance.

It was in this atmosphere of confusion and rising anxiety that we rehearsed and opened the Pelican's final show—the first professional North American performance of Lorca's *House of Bernarda Alba*. It never quite worked. The possessive, bigoted, protective energy of Lorca's matriarch was beyond our leading lady's range. And the young women, the best we could find among the dozens of girls who were awaiting stardom in Hollywood, remained frustrated, discontented American ingénues rather than the half-crazed, sex-starved, fanatical females of Lorca's creation. With one exception. The hunchbacked Martirio was played by Ona Munson, who had been a famous beauty and a notorious *"grande amoureuse"* best remembered for her flashing Belle Watling, Rhett Butler's mistress, in *Gone with the Wind*. She gave a deeply moving performance—one of her last.

Our reviews were mixed, and our business reflected the audiences' lack of empathy with the play. For the first time since we opened, our theater was only half filled. And this, our first taste of failure, came at a time when our economic woes were reaching their terminal stage. I stuck it out for a few days; then suddenly, in the middle of the run of *Bernarda Alba*, after a particularly depressing night, I could stand it no longer. I called Norman Lloyd and told him I was leaving for New York. Feeling as I imagine Napoleon must have felt as he drove out of Moscow, leaving his broken army to perish in the Russian snows, I left Los Angeles on the morning plane and stayed away for more than a year.

XVI
The Countess and the King
1948-50

To escape the gloom into which my recent reverses had plunged me I retreated once again to New City. Only, this time, it was not in the dark, familiar womb of the small house on the South Mountain Road that I sought refuge but in my own huge empty House on the Hill.

It was far from finished. Lack of money had interrupted the work—especially the landscaping. Because of the steepness of the hill on which the house was set, huge retaining walls had been built and tons of soil brought by truck up the precipitous mountain road, leaving a number of half-finished terraces around the house like the ruins of medieval battlements. The house itself was quite bare: my only furniture during those first weeks was a mattress on the floor of the great white master bedroom and a table and two chairs beside the corner fireplace in the kitchen. This made me even more aware of the miracle of the Eastern spring that presently exploded around me: first, the forsythia, of which two great golden bushes flared overnight outside my living room windows; followed by innumerable dogwoods that brightened the hillside with their dazzling whiteness; finally the peonies, of which dozens had been transplanted from their old beds in the valley and which were exploding around me in large, feathery white and mauve blooms. But most of all, it was the greenness that amazed and excited me—the infinite variations of bushes and grasses and trees, ranging all the way from black to pale yellow, that suddenly surrounded me and threatened to pour, in an overwhelming flood, through the huge, naked windows of my empty house.

Amid so much color and energy my general gloom dissolved and disappeared. This left me free to face the very real and immediate problems that had collected around my personal and professional life. Regarding the former, I had little to celebrate: the frenzy of the past year had eroded most of my personal relationships: the only love affair in which I had been seriously engaged had foundered on my refusal to accept any kind of emotional commitment. And I took a dim view of my professional situation:

What do I do next? The ruins of my career stretch out all around me—before and behind—a grim landscape of unfinished, unrealized, unrelated structures and abandoned, overgrown trails leading nowhere...Will I ever find a way to discipline and control my disorganized and seemingly unlimited energy?

On a more prosaic level I had more than the usual grounds for anxiety. For the first time in some years I was entirely without an income: the film money that had been flowing in a steady, golden stream was cut off and would not resume for some months. My debts seemed enormous; there was money owed for work on the house which Henry Poor could ill afford to advance, but far more urgent and serious were the still unknown debts incurred by Pelican Productions during the eight months of its brilliant but stormy existence. (This included money owed the U.S. Government for admission taxes and Social Security payments that we had purloined week after week to take care of current expenses. I was informed that this constituted a felony.) In the nick of time my agents, reluctant to see a client go to jail, managed to extract a substantial advance from RKO on my next year's film contract. Most of it was used to pacify the Internal Revenue Service, but there was enough left to tide me over for a few months.

Alone in my empty castle, as spring turned into summer, I enjoyed a serenity such as I had not known for years. It centered on the house. The terror and momentary loathing I had felt when I first saw it, half finished, the year before, were now reversed. What I had then regarded as a major folly, an object of anxiety and defeat, was turning into a symbol of my ability, finally, to create something solid and lasting in my life. I had never before owned a home—far less created one. Much remained to be done, inside and out. Visitors from New York were warned that they would be put to work if they ventured up the hill: there were rocks to be moved, beds to be dug, gravel to be spread and brick paths to be laid. With surprising skill and determination, I spent several days high up on a borrowed 30-foot ladder daubing the outer walls of the house with a whitewash solution of lime, sand, Portland cement and water.

I still had my apartment on Ninth Street into which my mother had moved during the war and where she still occupied the back room overlooking the garden. Here I continued to spend one or two nights a week. To make the journey and to negotiate the still-dangerous mountain road, which, after each heavy rain, turned into a quagmire of loose, rutted gravel, I acquired for $270 an ancient Army surplus command car. It was a monstrous vehicle—a dung-colored 1942 Dodge left over from the war with four-wheel drive and iron fenders as thick as the hull of a battleship. It was hell to drive, but it suited me perfectly, and I used it to transport everything from sand, bricks and flagstones to the furniture I was gradually moving from Ninth Street to the House on the Hill.

There were other interruptions of my bucolic life. I was summoned to Washington to appear as a character witness for one of the Hollywood Ten who was about to go to jail for contempt of the Un-American Activities Committee. In fact, I was not called and returned rather sheepishly to New York that same night. But, in the confused hours I had spent in the corridors outside the courtroom with the accused and their witnesses, I realized how far we had traveled and how much our world had blown apart since the Committee's investigators had first come to Los Angeles barely twelve months before.

A few solid friendships survived. Nick Ray continued to call and report on his career as a director, which was off to a good start. Norman Lloyd wrote and called regularly. So did Herman Mankiewicz:

Nothing new: all here are bristling at each other. I miss you, for in the midst of this desert of chicanery, corruption and deceit you remain that lonely oasis—a scholar and a gentleman!

Letters came from the Dowling sisters in Italy with news of their turbulent, unpredictable lives. Alex Knox and Doris Nolan announced their marriage, and there was regular word from Howard Koch and occasionally from Hitchcock. But my most persistent correspondent that spring and summer was Max Ophüls:

John, why are you so self-doubting and depressed? Goethe says: *"Mut verloren—alles verloren. Dan wäre es besser nich geboren."* "Mut" is courage and by "Alles" he means talent. Wake up from your unproductive sleep! Come here! Do something! Let's make a picture together!

Later he wrote that he was leaving for Europe:

where many projects await me. In all my projects I would like to include you. In short, I miss you.   Max

The truth is that I had, for the present, quite lost my "Mut" for films. I was pointed in other directions, including an occasional foray into the uncertain but rapidly growing field of television and the production of several radio shows, in French, for the Voice of America.

More important was the fact that I was beginning to write again.

During dinner one night I had told the story of the Mercury's notorious "Men from Mars" broadcast. Michael Bessie, who was a fellow guest and worked for *Harper's*, suggested that I write it as a piece for the magazine. All through that summer—partly in New City and partly on Ninth Street—slowly, with infinite misery and pain and pleasure, I worked on it. It took me close to three months to finish it and when my fifth and final version was finally typed, I delivered it to *Harper's*, where it appeared in the September issue—the first of five articles I wrote for them during the next four years.

It was my first piece of writing since Desmond MacCarthy had lost the manuscript of my book in Bloomsbury twenty-six years before. But it as not until later that the full irony of this new development in my life became apparent—the realization that without plan or premeditation I was finally, in middle age, achieving my dream of being a writer, which I had vainly cherished for so many years as a young man.

I had just begun to savor my success when I received a second and even more surprising offer. Joe Barnes had been my chief and my very close friend at the Voice of America. From there he had returned to the *Herald Tribune* as foreign editor, then left again in the summer of 1948 to become editor and associate publisher of his own newspaper, the *New York Star*, where he was making a valiant but almost certainly hopeless attempt to start a new liberal daily in New York's shrinking newspaper field. That it was probably foredoomed did not in any way diminish the excitement and pride with which I received Joe's offer to write a weekly column devoted to subjects of my own choosing but all related, in one form or another, to the performing arts and to recent social and economic developments in theater, films, radio and television. It was Joe's idea to call the column "Show Business."

The *Harper's* article and the publication of my first *Star* column (for which I received $50) came in such rapid succession that I had little time to rejoice or worry over my new assignment. Even before the first piece was in print I was at work on the second. Because of my inexperience, those 1000-word articles took up an inordinate amount of time. Tuesday and Wednesday I thought up ideas, did research, made notes. Thursday I started to write and continued in steady agony through the weekend. On Monday morning I typed the final version, took the subway to the *Star* office downtown and delivered my material to my editor—a pleasant, scholarly, meticulous man named Leon Edel (who later achieved fame as the biographer of Henry James).

I wrote sixteen columns for the *Star*, of which Virgil Thomson said that they were written for "people who were intelligent but not informed." I don't know how they rated as journalism or whether they could have existed in a less eccentric atmosphere than that of the ephemeral *New York Star*. But, for me, they were of lasting value—not to mention the elation I felt at finding myself quoted, within one week, in various contexts, by three such disparate publications as *Variety*, the *New Yorker* and the *Saturday Review*.

Howard Teichmann had worked for the Mercury during the harrowing weeks of *Danton's Death* and, after that, as my assistant on the Mercury of the Air and the Helen Hayes Show. Since then he had become a successful radio writer and producer. It was in that double capacity that he now put together a "package" known as *Theater USA*—a thirty-minute variety radio show to be broadcast nationally on prime time and possessing two unusual features: it was produced under the auspices of that prestigious institution, ANTA (the American National Theater and Academy) and it was commercially sponsored by the United States Army and Air Force.

Partly out of friendship and partly because he needed a respectable theatrical name on the show, Teichmann invited me to direct it. Considering how I'd felt, all my life, about the military establishment, the incongruity of my position on what was, in fact, a recruiting show did not escape me. But I needed the job and it promised to be an easy and agreeable assignment.

Our first broadcast, "lovingly performed and respectfully presented by the people of the American Theater to the people of the U.S.A," featured Mary Martin, Tallulah Bankhead, the great comic Willy Howard, Benny Goodman and Alfred Drake. We got good reviews and good ratings: the advertising agency was delighted; so, apparently, were the Army and the Air Force (though they never told us what effect, if any, we were having on recruitment). Our second and third shows were equally successful and I was settling down to a pleasant, lucrative winter when a series of front-page articles began to appear in the Scripps-Howard press exposing the infiltration of American show business by Reds. Among the names listed I discovered my own—together with editorial indignation at the presence on a U.S. recruiting program of such a notorious fellow traveler as myself.

This was my first personal experience of the witch-hunts. For a day or two after the appearance of the first article, there was stunned silence. Then all hell broke loose. First the network and then the advertising agency, on behalf of its clients—the U.S. Army and Air Force—demanded my instant resignation from the show. I refused. At the same time I was loath to embarrass ANTA or my friend Teichmann, who had got me the job. An ingenious solution was found.

ANTA's main claim to fame in recent years had been the production of an enormous, brilliant annual benefit known as the *Anta Album*, featuring innumerable theatrical stars in highlights from their most memorable successes. In response to popular demand an even more elaborate show was being planned for the spring of 1949. It was now suggested to me (in one of those shady arrangements that were not unusual during the plague years) that if I agreed to leave *Theater USA* peacefully I would be invited to produce the upcoming *Anta Album*. Two days later I received the offer and accepted it. It bothered me to discover that I was now irrevocably marked for the Blacklist. On the other hand I was delighted at the prospect of working with such an aggregation of theatrical stars. With the exception of *Lute Song* I had not had much success within the Broadway establishment; now suddenly I was the producer of the New York theater's most glamorous entertainment of the year.

The *Anta Album* was performed on the night of March 7, 1949. By a miracle of efficiency and luck and by asking the audience to limit its ovations to the ends of numbers, we managed to bring down the curtain on the final musical number—"This Was a Real Nice Clambake," with the assembled choruses of four Broadway musicals, *High Button Shoes, Along Fifth Avenue, Love Life* and *Carousel* —only a few minutes after midnight.

The next day's reviews were enthusiastic:

BIG NIGHT AT THE ZIEGFELD

Not in all my long show-going days has the American theater displayed its old sweet self to livelier advantage than last night. It made me an enraptured member of an enraptured congregation.

Among my guests at the Ziegfeld Theater that night was a young woman by the name of Joan Courtney, Comtesse de Foucauld. Born in London during a Zeppelin raid, she had a Spanish-Russian mother and a Scottish-Irish father from Omaha, Nebraska, who, shortly before the birth of his second daughter, abandoned his family and his job as editor of the Paris *New York Herald* to introduce the anthroposophical doctrines of Rudolph Steiner to the United States of America.

Raised in France, educated by Jesuits, tall and strikingly attractive, Joan had supported her mother and sister from the age of seventeen by modeling for two of the great Parisian fashion houses—Patou and Revillon. During the war, sh0w had gone back to work while her husband was serving in the Tank Corps with the Free French. This had kept her in Paris throughout the Occupation, consorting with the surrealists, among whom she performed the normal, dangerous tasks of Resistance. She appeared in New York in the late forties (carrying, as her sole possessions, an etching by Picasso and a small terra cotta Lipschitz "Harlequin") and found work as a genteel, cultivated, underpaid helper at the Museum of Modern Art. Here she came to the attention of Philip Johnson, who saw her an adornment to his architect's office and a private secretary of distinction. Vainly she pleaded ignorance of shorthand, typing and English spelling. He would not listen. Within a month she was out of a job and ended, in desperation, selling handbags for I. Miller on Fifth Avenue.

I first heard of her from Virgil Thomson's friend Sherry Mangan (poet, printer, journalist and dedicated Trotskyite) who had known her in Paris when he was special correspondent for *Time-Life* after the war. Every time I was him that winter he insisted he had the ideal wife for me. When he finally brought the Countess to Ninth Street one night after the ballet she fell asleep almost immediately on my sofa and snored softly for more than an hour while Sherry and I discussed European anti-Semitism in the Middle Ages. When she awoke, in time to be driven home to the cold-water flat she shared with a friend on the edge of the Bowery, I invited her to lunch with me at Voisin's the next day.

In her tailored gray suit and immaculate suede gloves she made me think of Henrietta Bingham, whom she in no way resembled. (Besides the beauty and the elegance there was the same curiously seductive confusion of laughter and melancholy, inertia and liveliness.) Later that week I took her downtown to a hootenanny organized by my friends Will Geer and Peter Seeger at Webster Hall. She seemed quite at home in that gamey atmosphere of rhapsodic protest.

After that we saw each other almost every day. We spoke mostly French together and we became lovers soon after the opening of the *Album*. (In thirty-seven years our relationship has not greatly changed. We have had eighteen homes, two sons and ten dogs; we have lived together in various worlds to which neither of us belonged; we have shared success and despair, cheerful penury and extravagance without security; we have known resentment and boredom and tenderness, the erosion of physical passion and deepening affection and trust. Over the years we have understood and comforted each other and we have continued to speak to each other in unpredictable patterns of mixed French and English.)

With the coming of spring the Countess began to visit New City and the House on the Hill—first for weekends and then as a resident. The absence of comfort did not trouble her; in those huge, empty rooms

with their bare white walls and their great windows overlooking the
flowering hillside, she seemed to find temporary refuge from the Furies
that had pursued her across the ocean. And during her stay she
revealed an unexpected expertise in a craft that she had certainly not
learned in the Parisian salons of Patou or Revillon Frères. Below and
around my house in New City were huge circular retaining walls of
fieldstone into which had been poured hundreds of tons of fill and
topsoil hauled up from the valley below. They formed vast naked
terraces waiting to be covered with flagstones or brick. Joan took these
over as a personal assignment. Within a few weeks of her arrival paths
and terraces appeared as though by magic—conceived and executed
with imagination and skill. She who had sometimes seemed low in
energy and vague of purpose was now up at dawn each day, in an old
torn sweater with a blue stocking cap on her head, moving piles of sand
and pink Haverstraw brick, which she miraculously converted, in the
course of the day, into original and complex floor designs.

My own efforts were directed to the coarser and heavier work of
laying stone. But here too she was invaluable. Our climactic
achievement was the laying of a vast terrace stretching across the entire
front of the house—an epic undertaking that involved numerous
voyages to a stone quarry in New Jersey, where the groaning
command car was loaded with giant slabs of prodigious weight which
were then hauled across the state line and up the hill, unloaded, laid
out and fitted together, like fragments of a gigantic jigsaw puzzle, till
they formed a smooth gray surface, more than 1000 feet square. It was
during this titanic labor, executed over two agonizing weekends—with
our hands torn and blackened and slippery from the damp earth and
the mosquitoes and shad-flies swarming in dark, buzzing clouds
around our sweating faces—that our relationship was tested and
tempered. It was night when we were finally done, and we washed
and went down to the Elms in New City and had two bottles of
champagne and roast beef.

Not all of my energies, that spring and summer, were devoted to
landscaping and love. On Easter Sunday I found myself directing a
national broadcast edited by Archibald MacLeish from the Gospels and
supported by Bach Passion Music performed on open trumpets. For
three months I taught a theater course at Barnard College: I spent time
with Al Capp discussing a musical version of his *Li'l Abner* comic strip
and I toyed briefly with the new medium of television. None was
particularly satisfying and by the end of summer I was ready to return
to the only lucrative occupation available to me.

My relations with RKO were not the best. As my starting date

approached I began to receive scripts—one more repulsive than the
other, but, by August, it had become clear that the sooner I got back to
my $2000 a week the better. All the more since I had had a call from
Nick Ray, who was halfway through his picture with Humphrey
Bogart and who had just read an English novel—*Mad with Much
Heart*—that he was eager for me to produce as a film.

My last two weeks in the East were spent in New City revising a
long piece I had written for *Harper's* on the economics of the Broadway
commercial theater. With the check they sent me and the plane fare I
received from RKO I made a down payment on a small green
Studebaker convertible in which I invited the Countess to accompany
me across the continent. She thought it over for two days, then
accepted on condition that, before leaving, she receive a plane ticket
from Los Angeles to New York. (She still had her return ticket from
New York to Paris.)

We set out at dawn one summer morning: it was my twelfth
crossing of the continent and the first of nine that Joan and I made
together over the years. We took the middle route through Chicago,
Kansas and Colorado. I have always been excited by the unfolding
wonder of this amazing, enormous country: it was doubly moving to
see it now through Joan's eyes, which grew ever wider as we moved
westward into the mythical regions that she knew from films or from
the pages (so beloved by the French) of James Fenimore Cooper. The
sight of her first Indian (*"Mon Dieu! Un peau-rouge!"*) made a deep
impression on her. So did our own nerve-wracking ordeal in the
mountains of Colorado.

We had driven through Denver and around noon, at a roadside
restaurant where we ate mountain trout, we saw signs relating to the
historic mining town of Central City, which I felt Joan should visit. We
had missed the turn-off, which was now some 15 miles behind us on
the highway. But there was the old coach road—unpaved, without
guard rails—that was open in summer and was very beautiful, we
were told. There were restless clouds in the sky but no immediate
threat of rain. And it *was* very beautiful.

We were less than halfway up the mountain when a summer storm
struck without warning. There was no place to turn back or stop.
Within minutes the coach road had turned into a river of quaking mud,
the color and consistency of porridge, through which we churned our
slow, slippery way upward with the rain blurring the windshield and
prodigious thunder crashing around us. The Countess was cool. There
was a bottle of cognac in the glove compartment. She handed it to me
on an average of once a minute. I drank without taking my eyes off the
road and it helped to blunt the terror of that ghastly ascent. Now and

then a car under partial control would come slithering down the mountain, forcing us against the rock wall on one side or towards the soft outer edge where you could no longer tell where the porridge ended and the sheer drop into the valley began.

We had lost all sense of distance and time: our only measure was the brandy bottle, which became empty just as the rain suddenly stopped and we came up over the top of the pass. The sun was shining again and the mud was stiffening on our fenders as we drove into Central City.

Viewed as a test of our relationship it was a brilliant success. We stayed in New Mexico two days longer than we had planned and ran out of money. (It was before the days of credit cards.) We entered the desert at five in the morning with a full tank of gas and 27 cents in my pocket. I had made a collect call to Nick Ray and $50 was waiting for us at Western Union in Victorville, which allowed us to have breakfast. We reached Los Angeles at noon and moved, with my usual feeling of nausea, into a bungalow beside the swimming pool in the Garden of Allah, next door to where Zita and I had spent several miserable weeks.

RKO, under Howard Hughes's management, was very different from the relaxed place I had known on my previous visits. Hughes himself was never seen but his influence was pervasive and sinister and I found the atmosphere of the studio disagreeable and unproductive. When I arrived, there was a memo on my desk about Nick's novel.

This is an unpleasant but powerful story. It is likely to emerge as an "art" production which may receive critical acclaim but no sizeable box-office returns. *NO* for RKO.

This was discouraging but not surprising. The truth was that I, myself, did not entirely share Nick's enthusiasm for the book. I saw what drew him to it but not how he proposed to turn it into a movie. Since he was off on location, I did not have much opportunity to find out but, on an offhand chance, responding to a letter he had written me, I sent it to Ray Chandler. Within a week I had my reply:

Dear John,

Thanks for sending me *Mad with Heart*. I don't feel enthusiastic about it from my possibly warped point of view. It has no humor at all which makes it tough for me. The cop is a ridiculous character. Who sent him into the hills? The blind girl is obviously an idiot. And there's hardly a line of dialogue which would not be pure slop on the screen.

I had also sent it to my friend Robert Ryan, who had become a star with *Crossfire* and who was anxious to work with Ray and me. Using Nick's and Ryan's names and that of Ida Lupino who was willing to play the woman, I struck a deal with the Studio. I could go ahead with our picture if I also agreed to produce a piece of garbage that Mr. Hughes wanted made.

Al Bezzerides was put to work on the script. He was a powerfully built Armenian from Fresno, a friend of Saroyan, who had written two good, tough California novels. He and Nick seemed to understand each other, though I was never quite sure how closely they agreed on the nature of the film we were making. Both combined an elaborate sensitivity with a strong macho streak that sent them out, night after night, in Los Angeles Police Department squad cars, to study the psychopathy of violence.

The film was shot partly on the RKO lot and partly in deep snow in the mountains of Colorado. I was with them for a short time, then returned to Los Angeles to attend to my other chores at the Studio.

Of all the forms of boredom and exasperation I have encountered in a varied career none is more corrosive and deadly than working on a film project that offers neither stimulation nor hope. Such was the one I had undertaken to produce for Mr. Hughes as the price for Nick's picture and on which I labored with revulsion and loathing for the first six months of 1950.

One effect of this professional frustration was to increase the importance of my personal life and to enhance the value of my relationship with Joan. Sarah Mankiewicz had found a house for us not far from her own off Benedict Canyon. It was small and pleasant with a raccoon in its garden. (Not knowing how to drive a car, Joan felt isolated at first until we found a sturdy Model A Ford for $125, which she soon learned to control and in which she triumphantly acquired her driver's license.) For my own part, since my first troubled marriage twenty years earlier, I had not lived regularly with anyone nor faced the problems of uninterrupted cohabitation. I found them engrossing and agreeable on the whole. We lived modestly, since most of my salary was still being snatched at the source to satisfy the Internal Revenue Service and the rest of my dozen creditors. We saw mostly friends from my previous California sojourns—many of them employed in the movie industry. For Joan and her Parisian surrealist companions the dream world of Hollywood films had held a hypnotic fascination but my prosaic colleagues who practiced filmmaking as a profession and a way of life were beyond her comprehension. They were unlike any writers, artists or craftsmen she had known and she found their obsessive preoccupation with the making and merchandising of film bewildering and, finally, exasperating. Her first and closest friend in California was an Englishwoman, the second wife of my old schoolmate Alan Napier, who had settled in Los Angeles, where he made a good living playing elderly British gentlemen. It was in their cabin on Big Bear Mountain, with snow on the ground under a brilliant blue sky, that we spent Christmas—and our honeymoon.

We were wed in Yuma, according to Arizona's instant marriage laws. We had driven from California through the desert and across the state line. In a hotel lobby we encountered a pimp who, for $10, offered to guide us through the nuptial routine. He led us to the Gretna Green Chapel—"The Mecca of Romance"—presided over by a squalid couple that closely resembled the crooked marrying-judge and his wife in *They Live by Night*. At the start of the ceremony the lights dimmed and a record player began to play "Silent Night"; this "crossfaded" into the "Wedding March" while the words, "Kiss your wife," were uttered. We were back in the San Bernardino Mountains before dark.

During our visit to Yuma, we were both aware that we were being united in a ceremony that, besides being unspeakably sordid, was also almost certainly invalid. Joan's husband, the Count, was very much alive and living in Rio de Janeiro. Before she left Europe, vague indecisive steps had been taken towards civil divorce; these could not be completed in Brazil, a Catholic country. Two years later, after our first son was born and we seemed to be finding contentment together, we got married again, this time in Las Vegas, following Joan's six-week residence there. On our return to Los Angeles we acquired two dachshunds and moved into a house on the beach—the first of twelve homes we occupied over the years in the Malibu Colony.

There were some fine moments in Nick's film, now known as *On Dangerous Ground*. Bernard Herrmann composed for us what he later claimed to be his best movie score; but it never quite came together and I found myself in reluctant agreement with the critic of the *New York Times* who described it as "an attempt to get something more than sheer melodrama onto the screen—something pictorially reflective of the emotional confusion of a man," but who felt that "for all Nicholas Ray's sincere and shrewd direction and the striking outdoor photography, it fails to traverse its chosen ground."

Meantime, as my second, detested film ground to its sordid conclusion, it had become clear that my days were numbered at a Studio in which I had no desire to remain. For some months I had been secretely negotiating with Dore Schary, now head of production at Metro-Goldwyn-Mayer. In September, I received a formal offer of a five-year senior producer's contract at the Industry's most prestigious Studio. I accepted and celebrated: it meant the end of my financial troubles and a chance, finally, to produce the kind of picture I now felt myself capable of making.

There was one fly in the ointment. My term at MGM was not due to begin until March—more than four months away. At first I was unhappy about this: I saw myself falling into financial and creative doldrums from which it would take months to extricate myself. Then, overnight, what had seemed like a liability turned into a stroke of luck. I received an invitation to direct *King Lear* on Broadway—and I was free to accept it!

* * *

This offer meant far more to me than just another theatrical assignment (though that, too, would have been welcome after three fallow years). It was my first chance to work on a classical play since my ten years' separation from Orson Welles. As usual, it came out of the blue. I had come to know Louis Calhern when he had acted as master of ceremonies for my *Anta Album* in New York. In California we saw each other occasionally at parties. He called me one night and asked me to come to his house the next afternoon for a drink. There, over a glass of ginger ale, he told me that two young New York producers were suggesting that he play *King Lear* on Broadway. If he did it would I be interested in directing it and was I available? I said yes. On my way home I stopped at a bookshop in Westwood and bought the Variorum, the Granville Barker preface and several editions of a play I had not read in years. As a result, I was able to make some sense when I met Robert Joseph, my producer, the following weekend. He was a curly-headed, overweight young man (the son of the Comptroller of the City of New York) of unusual intelligence and enthusiasm and I followed him to New York, where we spent several days with his partner, Alexander Cohen, discussing the production and holding auditions. This was followed by daily long-distance calls and a huge correspondence while I wound up my affairs at RKO. In mid-October Joan and I drove east and moved back into the House on the Hill, from which I commuted daily to the office on 42nd Street where casting and contract negotiations were being conducted in a flurry of emotion. This confusion continued through the first week of rehearsals. On the second day we changed Cordelias; on the fifth we switched Fools. After that we settled down and, almost before we knew it, we were into run-throughs and facing the horrors of technical rehearsals and the enervating anxieties that form an inevitable part of the "neurotic ordeal" of a Broadway opening.

Our producers were generous. At an added cost of $10,000, they allowed us three dress rehearsals and six previews, which, considering the complexities of the production, went surprisingly well. At our fourth performance Calhern got a standing ovation, and this allowed me to step back and take a dispassionate view of what I had accomplished in those frantic five weeks. With the successful interweaving of the main theme and the subplots, we seemed to have realized something of the symphonic sweep of Shakespeare's tragedy. Calhern himself was better than I had dared to hope; his voice lacked the resonance and the rhythm required to meet the demands of that prodigious Elizabethan verse; but what he lacked in verbal eloquence he made up for with his physical presence and theatrical authority. He was at his best in his moments of action; weakest in his lyrical and philosophical passages. But, overall, his King was a noble, tragic, moving figure and he succeeded in communicating directly with his audience in terms with which they could empathize.

So, irrevocably, we moved towards our opening night. Under the Broadway system there is no second chance: the fate of the production—honorable run or shameful closing—depends entirely on the opening night's reception and on the reactions of a handful of dubiously qualified journalists to that single performance. This knowledge had its unnerving effect on our company, each of whom had knowingly risked a winter's living on the slender chance of the commercial success of one of the world's most notoriously difficult plays. Free enterprise is no respecter of classics. For the satisfaction of sharing in what they hoped would be a memorable theatrical experience, they had engaged themselves, individually and collectively, in what they knew to be a desperate venture—with the odds overwhelmingly against them.

We opened on Christmas night with a good but nervous performance. I went backstage, thanked the cast, looked for Joan but could not find her and disappeared. There was a party for the company, for whom opening night was a consummation and a release. But not for me. I wanted to be alone with my anxiety, waiting for those fateful notices—of which the first would be out in two hours.

I don't remember where I walked that night, only that there had been some rain in the afternoon and that the streets were shiny and slick. By midnight I had walked several miles in circles and suddenly became aware that I was back in the theater district and that my feet had carried me onto what had been, for more than a dozen years, forbidden ground.

The Mercury Theater had stood on the south side of 41st Street, between Sixth Avenue and Broadway. Where it had been, there was now a parking lot from which the rubble had not been entirely cleared. A few abandoned cars glowed dully, still wet with rain, beside a sign that read:

PARK $1

And suddenly the thought struck me that on this same spot, during the winter of 1937-38, it had been possible, for that same sum of money (if you didn't mind sitting high up in the balcony), to buy two seats for the Mercury Theater's first successful repertory season.

The lot on which our theater had stood seemed surprisingly small—so narrow that it was hard to believe that on this irregular strip of asphalt, that now gaped like a missing tooth between the surrounding tall buildings, had stood a shabby, once elegant little theater which, for a few months, had housed Broadway's hottest ticket, the Mercury's *Julius Caesar*. Where the pavement now ended, our bright Mercury electric sign had twinkled over the green and gold doorway that led to the cramped box office and the small gray-blue lobby with the crystal chandelier that was never paid for. Beyond that, where the asphalt of the parking lot now began, had been the orchestra floor. As I stood there, looking up into the rain-soaked sky, the whole ghostly structure seemed for a moment to rebuild itself around me. Under my feet I could feel the lumpy, threadbare carpeting into which the iron frames of our shabby red plush seats had been so insecurely fastened. Behind me rose the stained marble steps leading up to the mezzanine and, beyond that, to my desolate, second-balcony office. Before me was the dark, gaping void of our curtainless stage, crisscrossed with the ever changing miracle of Jean Rosenthal's innumerable light-beams. And below (filled now with the rubble from the battered building) was the rat-infested region in which stood the ailing, rusty boiler that died on us an average of once a week and the toilets that Orson had ordered locked during the Forum scene lest their flushing ruin his silences. Here, in our ill-lit, airless basement under the stage, our extras had crouched and huddled in darkness and sung "La Carmagnole" in *Danton's Death;* here Geraldine Fitzgerald (in this, her first, frightened stage appearance) and Orson (with pounds of putty and a long white beard) had played their strange wooing scene in *Heartbreak House;* here Welles, in his black pinstripe Brutus suit, had been found one night, out cold, after falling headlong down one of his own traps…

I don't know how long I stood there, dreaming. Suddenly I realized that it must be close to one o'clock. I hurried across Broadway to Seventh Avenue and 43rd Street where the *New York Times* had its printing plant and where, on the ground floor, press agents and producers were wont to hover on opening night, waiting for a spy in the basement to slip them an advance word of the Brooks Atkinson review. Sometimes the best they could get was a garbled version of his opening sentence. On this particular night that was sufficient:

Not in our time has *King Lear* had so worthy a hearing in New York...

Without waiting for the rest I went on to the company party. (When I got there I found that my wife had only just arrived. There had been snow in New City, but she had climbed into the command car in evening dress, started down the hill, skidded, lost control and hit a tree halfway down. Barefoot, she had slithered down the icy mountain, hitchhiked to New City, had a shot of brandy at the Elms, caught a late bus and made it, with blood and mud on her dress, to our celebration.)

One by one the notices were brought in and read out loud—most of them amid cheers:

"A magnificent cast in a fine production"..."Forceful, vivid drama...Acting of virtuoso brilliance, carefully planned and rich in detail"..."The finest production in memory"..."An altogether splendid revival of this formidable work."

These favorable reviews of New York's first professional *Lear* in thirty years did not impress Broadway's theatergoers. We played to good houses throughout the holidays; then, during the usual January slump, business fell off. Following the grim Broadway tradition that a show is either a hit or a flop, our management panicked and allowed another show to be booked into our theater for early February. As soon as our closing was announced business bounced back, and for the last three weeks of its run *King Lear* sold out. At its four final performances police were summoned to 41st Street to control the crowd that was besieging the theater for standing room. The usual desperate but futile last-minute attempts were made to extend the run, but by then it was too late.

I was not there for the last night. In mid-January, we closed up the house in New City and set out once more for California with our two dachshunds in the rear seat.

Virgil Thomson.

Joseph Barnes.

Doris Dowling and Howard da Silva in *The Blue Dahlia*.

Raymond Chandler.

Lute Song—Mary Martin and Yul Brynner. J. H., director. (New York, 1947)

Judy Holliday.

Beggar's Holiday—Duke Ellington with Billy ('Sweet Pea') Strayhorn. (1946)

Alfred Drake as MacHeath and Zero Mostel as Peachum.

Oliver Smith's set. [*Beggar's Holiday*]

Nicholas Ray and J. H. at work
on *They Live by Night* (*Thieves
Like Us*).

Pelican Productions. Opening
night of *Galileo*, July, 1947.

The Skin of Our Teeth—with
Hurd Hatfield, Keenan Wynn,
Carol Stone, Jane Wyatt and
Blanche Yurka.

Joan Courtney Houseman.

Pelican Productions. *The House of Bernarda Alba* with Ona Munson as Martirio.

Bertolt Brecht and Charles Laughton.

The honeymoon car, MG-TD.

The House on the Hill, 1956,
inside and out.

May Haussmann with J.H. at
Malibu.

Jasper and Caroline I.

The living room and the
kitchen.

Joan and Michael.

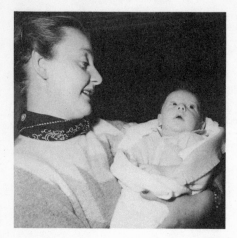

Michael entertains the New York City Ballet on the beach in Malibu.

Family portrait.

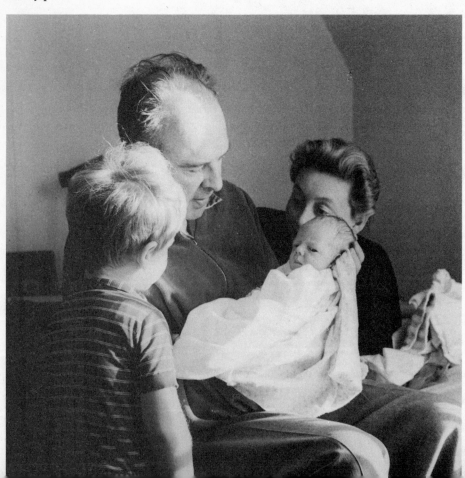

J.H. and Michael.

Sebastian at two and a half.

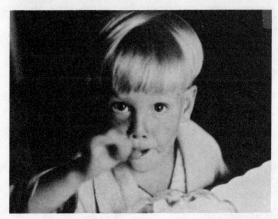

Lunch in Santa Monica: Joan, John, Liliane Montevecchi and Madame Courtney on a visit.

The Fool and Lear (Norman
Lloyd and Louis Calhern).
(National Theatre in New
York, 1950)

J.H. and Dore Schary with a
Scandinavian award.

Keenan Wynn in the scene of
his final binge, *Holiday for
Sinners.* (1951)

Julius Caesar—The first reading.

Conference on the set of *The Bad and the Beautiful*—Lana Turner, J.H., Kirk Douglas and director Vincente Minnelli.

Joan Fontaine in *Letter from an Unknown Woman*. (1947)

Julius Caesar—The making of a scene. '…imperious Caesar, dead, and turn'd to sawdust.'

Julius Caesar—Gielgud and Mason. 'Let not our looks put on our purposes.' (1953)

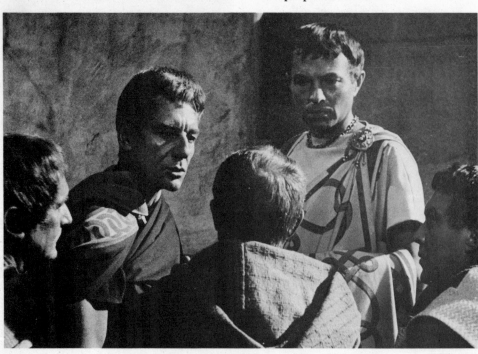

'My heart is in the coffin...there with Caesar,' Marlon Brando tells Roman street crowds, speaking at the funeral scene in MGM's *Julius Caesar*.

Julius Caesar—the making of a scene. Brando with director Joseph Mankiewicz refining a moment.

Coriolanus—Will Geer, not in costume.

Anthony Quinn and Kirk
Douglas with Vincente
Minnelli as referee, *Lust for Life*.

Lust for Life—The cutting of the
ear.

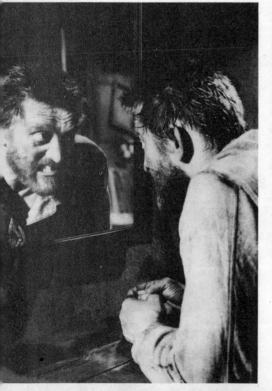

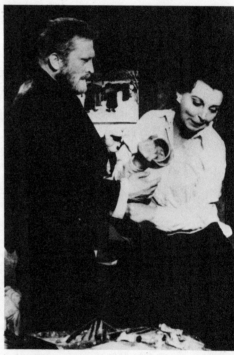

Lust for Life—J.H., producer.
Kirk Douglas and Pamela
Brown as Cristine. (1955)

XVII
The Bad and the Beautiful
1951

Metro-Goldwyn-Mayer was neither the oldest nor the largest nor the most fertile of American motion-picture companies but in 1951 it was still considered the dean of the industry, and its headquarters in Culver City—the home of the Roaring Lion—was generally regarded as the Versailles of Hollywood film studios. Its heart was the Thalberg Building, a four-story, gray-white edifice of no architectural distinction whatever: its grandeur was somewhat diminished by the presence, on its southeast corner, of a funeral parlor whose owners continued to ply their grim, essential function in seeming indifference to the glamor that swirled around them.

I entered the studio on the morning of March 1, 1951, flanked by a pair of well-dressed agents who led me through the executive parking lot, up the wide terraced steps between the sleeping lions, past the reception desk and through the carefully guarded doors—a newly accredited member of Hollywood's élite, an MGM senior producer, responsible only to the head of production, Dore Schary.

His recent appointment marked the latest turn in a long struggle for power between Hollywood and New York, the picture makers and the financiers, and now, more specifically, between Louis B. Mayer, longtime head of production at MGM, and Nicholas Schenck, president of the parent company—Loew's Incorporated.

At Schenck's insistence that a younger man be found to revitalize the Studio, Mayer, increasingly involved in politics and racehorses, had chosen Schary to be his junior associate. In the increasingly frequent disagreements that arose between them over the selection and treatment of film material at MGM, it soon became evident that the full force of Schenck's support was being thrown to Schary.

I was never involved in this conflict. On entering the studio I was formally presented to Mr. Mayer, whom I already knew through his daughter Irene. I was still in the early stages of preparing my first film when he left the studio in a rage: "Nick and Dore want the studio...Well, they can have it and choke on it!" His henchmen remained, ostensibly cooperating with the new management. Like civil servants after a change of government, they continued to exert administrative and executive authority over the Studio and I regarded them from the start as my enemies.

Dore Schary and I were never very close personally and we did not always speak the same language. But we liked and trusted one another. (I shared his enthusiasm for Roosevelt and the New Deal, but not for the New York Yankees.) I think he admired and envied my theatrical achievement; on the other hand he was slightly embarrassed by my continued connections with the left-wing writers, his former associates, who had never forgiven him for his reluctant acceptance and subsequent defense of the Industry's formal pledge not to employ anyone known to have been a member of the Communist Party. As a former newspaperman involved in local and national politics and as a potent member of the Democratic Party, he had a surer sense of what was newsworthy than I did and I benefited from his advice in my selection of film subjects. He was more sentimental than I and there was a vaguely evangelical tone to this thinking which I found unacceptable but he never tried to force a project upon me; for my part, I never pressed him to let me make a film of which I felt he disapproved. I was one of the first of the new producers he had recruited to replace Mayer's Old Guard at Culver City and this gave us a joint interest in my success as a producer for MGM.

Following my first formal interview with Schary and my introduction to the other inmates of the "third floor," I was conducted to my office on the floor below—a sumptuous corner suite with a secretary's outer office, a huge main room complete with paneling, bookshelves, a leather sofa, easy chairs, a thick golden carpet, two huge windows and a desk the size of a Cadillac. After that came a bathroom, and beyond that another chamber, small but luxurious, with a mirror, two Louis XVI chairs and a couch, ostensibly for the producer to rest on after his Herculean labors, though a private exit into a rear passage suggested that it had other, more intimate uses.

MGM—in spite of its recent tremors—was a huge, secure, smoothly functioning mechanism geared to the production and merchandising of high-priced motion pictures. With its superb production plant, its unique stable of stars and its incomparable sales and publicity department, MGM expected nothing less than major films from its producers.

My contract allowed me several months in which to find a suitable subject for my first picture; this gave me time to explore the institution of which I was now a part. My investigations took me all over the huge lot: onto the sound stages which, when I first saw them, seemed vaster and grander than any I had seen before; to the costume and prop shops, where garments and objects of all sorts had been accumulating for more than thirty years—everything from Roman armor, period umbrellas, French furniture and Russian icons to Victorian pisspots— all displayed not in pairs or dozens but in sets of hundreds. And I spent days driving around that amazing back lot—the cottages (including Camille's), the water tanks, battlements and palaces; French, English and Asiatic villages; New York, New England and New Orleans streets; sailing ships and decks of liners; churches, casinos and dozens of staircases leading nowhere.

My frequent companion on these excursions was a tall, slim, attractive, intelligent, socially secure but professionally diffident young man whom Schary, in a nepotistic gesture, had assigned to me as my assistant. His name was Arthur Loew, Jr., and he was a scion of two of the great pioneer families that had created the film industry—the Zukors and the Loews. In his company I overcame much of my "new boy's" apprehension; at noon, in the studio commissary, his luncheon companions ranged from old professionals who had known him from childhood to a group of golden lads and lasses—young actors, dancers and musicians among whom I remember Gene Kelly, Pier Angeli, Leslie Caron, André Previn, Stanley Donen and his companion at the time—a breathtakingly beautiful, dark-haired girl with exquisite coloring and violet eyes by the name of Elizabeth Taylor.

My first few weeks at MGM flowed by pleasantly enough. Joan was pregnant and we were happy in our rented house at the beach in which—until I got going on my first film—I was able to spend more than my usual amount of time. Nick Ray and Gloria Grahame, recently married, moved into a house next to ours; visitors from the East came and stayed with us, including Virgil Thomson, after whom we named our third dachshund.

In the midst of this agreeable hiatus before I began my first film, something happened that might have put a sudden end to my new Hollywood career—but didn't. When Senator Joseph McCarthy was holding his hearings on Communist infiltration of government he devoted some of his time to the Voice of America. One of his chosen victims was my friend and former colleague, Fernand Auberjonois, head of the French Desk, against whom he presented an absurd list of charges—among them that he had consistently "neutralized" the news to France (whatever that meant) and that on some of his cultural broadcasts he had employed, as producer and master of ceremonies, "John Houseman, a notorious Red and Communist sympathizer."

Through a curious piece of luck, Auberjonois' interrogation, which had been reported in full in an early edition of the *New York Times*, was replaced in later editions by the far juicier testimony of the Voice of America's religious editor. No report of the Auberjonois interrogation ever reached the West Coast and there was no mention of it in any of the subsequent "Red" files that the American Legion assembled against me the following year.

My five years in Culver City yielded a crop of nine films produced and eleven in preparation. Of the lot, there are four that I remember with satisfaction.

The Bad and the Beautiful, which I chose as my first "big" picture for MGM, started as a short story. I had found it in a pile of submissions and rejected it because it was about a Broadway producer on the pattern of Jed Harris and I was tired of theatrical stories with protagonists patterned on Jed Harris. I changed my mind after it occurred to me that the time was ripe for a realistic film about Hollywood. (*A Star Is Born*, which I greatly admired, had been made fifteen years before, in 1936, when Hollywood was a very different town.) I asked Schary if he was prepared to make a controversial film about Hollywood that would involve vaguely recognizable figures in the industry. He said he was. I told him I would like to engage Charles Schnee, who had worked so well with me before, to work on the script. He approved that too.

Schnee read the material and became excited at the idea of making a Hollywood film *à clef*. We accepted the original premise (a simpler version of Mank's "prism" structure) of a producer-director of genius whose behavior is recalled by four professional and personal intimates each of whom has benefited by his talent and each of whom has, at one time or another, been exploited, betrayed or injured by him. Unmistakable elements of David O. Selznick's personality are to be found in our hero-villain Jonathan Shields—his ambition and egomania; his talent for discovering, developing and discarding stars; his rather loose amorousness combined with a blend of sentimentality and ruthlessness; his total absorption in film that led him to commit acts of callousness and personal treachery; finally, the circumstances of his decline and fall.

The lost girl who becomes a film star took some time to assume her final shape; her neurotic devotion to the memory of her world-famous father suggests the Barrymores but she became a composite of other ladies, including fragments of Gardner and Fontaine—not to mention

Lana Turner herself. But these resemblances (which were further emphasized while shooting the picture) should not obscure the fact that Schnee, in a remarkably short time, created a rich, well-constructed, entirely original screenplay.

Within an hour of receiving Schnee's script from the mimeographing department I called Vincente Minnelli, whose work I admired and who (following *An American in Paris*) was the Studio's white-haired boy. I invited him to lunch at Romanoff's. Over coffee I handed him the script and the next morning he called and said he was anxious to direct it.

So now, overnight, I had my "package"—a hot script and a big-name director; I never for a moment doubted that we would have all the stars we wanted. Word had got around and the attitude of the men on the third floor had changed: Mannix smiled at me through the mist of the executives' steam bath and Thau was anxious to discuss casting. We went through the roster of MGM stars. Barry Sullivan was perfect for the director, Walter Pidgeon for the loyal, long-lived studio manager. But there was no one at MGM capable of playing Jonathan Shields. Robert Taylor was suggested, but he was wrong; so was the aging Gable. Besides, I had already secretly invited Kirk Douglas to play the part. There was some hassling over price, but this was before the day of astronomical figures and a reasonable sum was soon agreed on. For the girl, Minnelli, Schnee and I all wanted Lana Turner and we got her without difficulty. Also Gloria Grahame.

I have never produced a film on which there were fewer problems. Partly this had to do with the heady atmosphere of success that surrounded us from the first day of shooting; it also related to the fun we were all having with so much inside material. It was Minnelli who thought of reproducing scenes from that silent MGM classic—*Anna Karenina*; we indulged in a good-natured caricature of Alfred Hitchcock; a well-known German actor was cast to suggest Fritz Lang at his most Teutonic and formidable; finally, we all pitched in with ideas to make Shields's first horror film, *The Son of the Cat People*—reminiscent of Val Lewton's shoestring methods at RKO.

I had limited experience working with superstars. Some of ours were reputed to be "difficult," including Lana Turner, but she gave us no trouble at all. In the personal dealings I had with her I found her pleasant, childlike and obstinate in her insecurity; desirable but not beautiful. What fascinated me about her was her behavior *off* the set—star conduct that was reminiscent of the Great Days. In addition to her own private bungalow, she had a special portable dressing room—an apartment on wheels that was hauled by tractor from stage to stage and surrounded by a fence that formed about half an acre of private territory from which unauthorized persons were barred. This corral was inhabited by a troupe of hangers-on—make-up girls, hairdressers, secretaries and servitors of various sorts including a team whose sole function it was to keep the record-player playing loudly at all times. I had been warned that Miss Turner was inclined to extend her lunch break and hold up the day's work. This only happened a few times. (I had also heard that during those lunches emissaries were sometimes sent out with instructions to bring back some particularly handsome or lusty stagehand on whom the star's eye had fallen during the morning. But I was not a witness to any such excesses.)

Our picture offered an unusually large number of good small parts, admirably played by the character actors who have always been so plentiful in Hollywood. One of them, a New York actor by the name of Ned Glass, was involved in an incident that threatened to mar our production. A favorite episode in the film concerned the absurd horror picture (*The Son of the Cat People*) which Shields makes as his first independent production and in which the menace is furnished by three bit-players dressed in ill-fitting black leotards, with huge cat heads and ratty tails. As a harassed but persistently euphoric member of the wardrobe department, Ned Glass gave us a humorous and touching performance. Minnelli fell in love with the sequence and spent longer on it than he should have. At the end of the second day he still had one final shot left over for the next morning.

When I arrived on the set the assistant director was distraught: Ned Glass had not arrived. A phone call to his home elicited the information that the studio security department had called him the night before and told him he would not be admitted to the studio. Further questioning of our embarrassed casting director revealed that Glass and been hired in error: following his appearance, two years earlier before the House Un-American Activities Committee, he had become ineligible for work in any Hollywood studio. To reshoot his scene would involve two days' work. Minnelli was asked if he could edit the scene to exclude the offender. Absolutely not. I was asked if the entire scene could be eliminated. I said no. The matter was referred to the third floor. Two hours went by. Torn between patriotic fervor and a reluctance to spend $30,000 of the company's money to reshoot the scene, Glass was permitted to re-enter the studio and finish his performance.

The incident made it clear to me that, between patriotism and profit, the latter would usually triumph. It was a lesson I remembered the following year when I had problems of my own.

From the start I had objected to the name that the publicity department had given our picture. I had sulked for a day or two, then gradually I accepted it. Months later I sat with Dore, Kirk, Lana, Gloria,

Schnee and Minnelli in that section of the theater that was reserved for Academy Award nominees, bursting with pride and pleasure as the odious title was called again and again and again. *The Bad and the Beautiful* received seven major nominations:

Best Screenplay

Best Actor

Best Supporting Actress

Best Art Direction

Best Costume Design

Best Set Decoration

Best Cinematography in Black and White

It won five Awards. And, as I watched Charles Schnee (Best Screenplay), Gloria Grahame (Best Supporting Actress) and others who had worked on *The Bad and the Beautiful* go up and collect their Oscars, I was prepared to admit that it wasn't such a bad title after all.

XVIII
Julius Caesar
1952-53

Julius Caesar was my second "big" picture for MGM. Early in 1952 I found myself announcing to the world that I "felt humble but confident as I faced the formidable task of translating Shakespeare's bloody and turbulent melodrama into a medium where both mass emotions and personal conflict can be more closely observed and more fully revealed than through the established forms of theatrical production."

I do not remember if it was I who first suggested Joseph Mankiewicz as the director of *Julius Caesar*. Whoever it was, the idea was a good one. He and I soon discovered that we were in basic agreement on the nature of the play's personal and political conflicts and on the dramatic impact we believed it could have, as a popular film, on contemporary audiences. We each did our cutting and editing of the play. Then we exchanged versions and discussed differences with the understanding that Joe, as director, would be responsible for the final screenplay.

In the meantime, our first priority was casting. And here I found myself emerging as the champion of the American actor. Both Joe and Dore, in their anxiety to make America's first Shakespearean film a worthy one, were inclined to play it safe and rely on established British stars. I argued that in that case the film should be made in Europe by a British company—not by MGM in Culver City. I maintained that we had actors in America who could play Shakespeare no less eloquently and effectively than their British cousins and I insisted that we keep an even balance between actors from both shores of the Atlantic. Our first casting was British: John Gielgud as Cassius—a part he had just played with success at Stratford-on-Avon. To balance that I requested Louis Calhern for Caesar—an aging, tired, nervous dictator rather than a triumphant one. (It was a piece of casting that was not unanimously approved but that I never regretted.) For Brutus, Joe suggested his friend James Mason, who, by now, was generally regarded as a

Hollywood movie actor. He had not appeared on the stage in many years, but his training was classical and he had the right quality for the honest, serious man torn between his republican ideals, his personal feelings for Caesar and his moral reluctance to shed blood. To play the wives we used two resident stars, both under contract to MGM, both English-born but both generally accepted in American roles: Deborah Kerr as the devoted, fanatically loyal Portia, Brutus's wife; Greer Garson as Caesar's neurotic and apprehensive mate, Calpurnia. For the small but important role of Casca, the provocateur, I chose Edmond O'Brien, who had made a successful career for himself playing detectives, newspapermen and crooked lawyers but whose training and early theatrical experience had been entirely classical, including his time with us at the Mercury.

This left one major role to be filled—that of Marc Antony. Mankiewicz was in London conferring with Gielgud: he called to say that he was setting up a film test of Antony for the rising British stage star Paul Scofield. I cabled and asked him to wait a few days. I had just had a mad but brilliant idea: that we consider Marlon Brando for the role. The first general reaction was one of disbelief. Most people remembered Brando as Stanley Kowalski and believed that his slurred, Polish bellowing represented his natural and only speaking voice. I knew better. Marlon refused to make a film test but agreed to record a tape, for which he chose Marc Antony's dramatic entrance into the Senate after the assassination. It was a powerful recording that convinced Joe and myself. But the general skepticism persisted, and I did nothing to allay it. (A canard with wide circulation in Hollywood was that Brando had fooled us all: that he had persuaded Laurence Olivier to make the tape for him and that we had fallen for the substitution.)

Joe had demanded and I had firmly supported him in his request (unheard of in motion pictures) for a three-week rehearsal period—in costume and in our own sets. There was strong resistance from the production and contract departments, but our joint firmness prevailed. This was no ordinary film: we needed time for the leading actors to become word-perfect in their enormous parts, for the technicians to accustom themselves to an unfamiliar cinematic form and, finally, for our company (gathered from so many different places and from such diverse backgrounds) to acquire some sense of the "ensemble" acting that this play so urgently called for.

Rehearsals began in an atmosphere of enthusiasm of which Gielgud, from the first moment, set the tone. Not only was he word-perfect and totally secure in the role of Cassius, but he seemed to inspire everyone in the cast, down to the smallest bit-player, with his own high sense of professional dedication. His perfectionism was apparent not only to his fellow actors but to everyone even remotely connected with the production. Hollywood technicians (a notoriously skeptical and bigoted lot) are men of great technical expertise, capable of recognizing and appreciating such skills in others. Whenever Gielgud was working, our "closed" set was invaded by grips, carpenters, electricians and soundmen who left their own stages and dubbing rooms to come and admire the amazing skill of this English master of the spoken word and to debate how such fluent speech could be transferred to film without loss of quality.

One subject of controversy was whether *Julius Caesar* should be filmed in black and white or in glorious color. The Studio favored color: it might be more expensive but it was guaranteed to yield considerable additional revenue, as it had with *Quo Vadis* and *Ivanhoe*. Mankiewicz and I both firmly resisted: our decision (like Olivier's when he chose to make *Hamlet* in black and white after his great success with *Henry V* in Technicolor) was made on purely dramatic grounds. *Julius Caesar* is a drama of personal and political conflict. It calls for intensity and intimacy rather than spectacle or grandeur. In our eagerness to stress the historical parallel between the political intrigues of the last years of the Roman republic and recent European events, we were drawn irresistibly to the use of black and white. Hitler, Mussolini and Ciano at the Brenner Pass; Stalin and Ribbentrop signing the Pact—we had seen these and other personal meetings that soon turned to violence and death in the press photos and newsreels of the past decade; they were hauntingly similar to the tense confrontations of Shakespeare's conspirators before and after the assassination. For the Forum scenes the parallel was even more obvious: inevitably these would evoke memories of the Führer at Nuremberg and of Mussolini ranting from his high balcony overlooking the wildly cheering crowd that would presently spit on his dead body as it hung by its feet outside a gas station.

We had one further reason for our choice. Our budget was limited—one and a half million against $5 million for *Quo Vadis*, most of whose sets were still standing on the back lot. By shooting in black and white we would be able to use many of its big and expensive Roman structures and still avoid a duplication that would be painfully apparent in color.

For our Roman slums we created our own dark alleys and rickety six-story tenements that were quite contemporary in their squalor. And we followed these same principles in our costumes, which were designed for black and white photography—from the simple woolen textures of our patricians to the street mobs which we wanted to look like the crowds of any large city in any period in a warm climate.

It was on the Forum scenes, finally, that the reputation of Mankiewicz as a director and of Brando as a classical actor would depend. In a film, through close-ups and other cinematic devices, the interaction between the speaker and the mob is more closely observed and becomes a more dramatic factor than it can ever be on stage, where the crowd, no matter how brilliantly it is handled, remains a small, faceless group reacting on cue to a star's bravura performance. On film, Antony remains the ringmaster, but the crowd becomes a more equal partner in their mutually generated emotions. It was Joe's job, as director, to control and orchestrate this interplay of feeling observed from three different but simultaneous points of view—that of the speaker, the mob and the audience. Throughout the action he used two and sometimes as many as five cameras, but the form of the scene—its movement and tempo, its suspense and the effectiveness of its climax—had to be created on the set, at the moment of shooting, with a crowd of Hollywood extras (not known for their imagination or zeal) and an actor of acknowledged talent but total lack of experience in classical theater.

The big surprise was Brando himself. Even those of us who recognized him as one of the most exciting young actors of his time were astonished at the quality of his preparation. He came to me one day to share an amazing discovery he had just made. As a member of the Actors' Studio, he was familiar with the uses of affective emotion and the importance of "subtext"—the need to enrich and strengthen a role through subjective exploration beneath and between the author's lines. Now, suddenly, he had discovered that, with a dramatist of Shakespeare's genius and in a speech as brilliantly and elaborately written as Antony's oration, it was not necessary nor even possible to play *between* the lines. Having, in his own mind, created the character and personality of Antony, he must let Shakespeare's words carry the full flood of his own emotion from the beginning to the end of the scene.

He was helped in this by Mankiewicz's faith and patience. Also by the help he received from John Gielgud, who, throughout rehearsals, showed a generosity that is rare among actors. Partly through his example but also by the direct and practical assistance he gave them, he greatly aided both Brando and Mason (whose classical acting was rusty from years of starring in laconic, realistic roles). With Brando, in particular, he spent hours passing on to him, as one actor to another, the sense of prosody he himself had acquired in the cradle and, out of his own long classical experience, the ability to phrase, clarify and sustain the meaning and the changing rhythm of that long, demanding speech.

Some of this coaching is evident in the finished film. But the real credit goes to Brando himself who, during that long week of shooting—many times each day, in close-up and long shot and even when the cameras were aimed at the crowd and not at him—went through his speech, over and over, without once losing his energy or his concentration. When he faltered or flubbed a line he would stop, apologize, compose himself and start afresh. He never pleaded fatigue or questioned the necessity for so much seemingly repetitious coverage. When the scene came to be edited, his performance benefited from the number and variety of his available "takes." It is no denigration of Marlon's talent to point out that his performance in the film was aided and protected by the careful selection and skillful editing of his best moments. On stage his inexperience would almost certainly have betrayed him: he could not have built, night after night, to such a controlled climax of passion.

Not all the elements of our film were as successful as the Forum scene. Our Battle of Philippi was ridiculous. In our Mercury production Orson had completely eliminated all military activity and no one had missed it. But to do this in a film, in a medium that is loved for its ability to handle violent, large-scale action, seemed a craven evasion. After struggling with the problem for weeks (and having no access to the Yugoslavian extras or the Spanish Army) we ended up with an ambush in the best Western style with Brando perched in Indian fashion, high on a hill, and Brutus and Cassius (like the U.S. Cavalry) coming through the pass, totally unaware of the fate that awaited them. When it was finally edited it wasn't quite as horrible as we had feared but it was nothing to be proud of.

The success of *Julius Caesar* was so resounding—in Sydney, Australia, where it opened; in New York and the rest of the country; in the United Kingdom; and finally all over the world—that, for once, I can resist quoting our reviews. In Culver City the jubilation reached its peak when it was learned that *Caesar's* first national weekend box-office take was 5 percent higher than the corresponding gross of *Quo Vadis* had been. According to *Variety*:

CAESAR BAFFLES SHOWMEN

XIX
Executive Suite and Coriolanus
1953-54

In my late forties and early fifties, during my first three years at MGM, a subtle but significant change was taking place in my life. Until then, throughout my interminable adolescence, my career and my personal problems had been painfully and hopelessly intertwined. My dreams of power and my perpetual insecurity had become so closely involved with the anxieties of my work that it was impossible to separate them. Even my sexual yearnings—the need for conquest and the inevitable dissatisfactions that followed—were indistinguishable from my consuming professional ambitions. Between them, they managed to generate a driving, tormented energy that was confused and frequently self-destructive. Now, finally, these forces seemed to be falling into some kind of order. Partly this was attributable to the new sense of continuity I derived from my growing success in the film business. But, even more, it had to do with my marriage.

I had entered the married state with some doubt; it had been difficult for me to accept the commitment and the responsibilities and restrictions I felt it imposed upon me. Now, gradually, it was becoming apparent that, along with the restraints and dissatisfactions, there were positive virtues in marriage—not least the separation of my personal from my professional life.

For this Joan was responsible. During our first months in Hollywood, she had found it difficult, if not impossible, to comprehend or accept the mysterious business of movie-making to which most of my friends seemed wholly committed. In her Parisian childhood and later, among the surrealists, she had thought of films as a miraculous, dreamlike escape—infantile, absurd and beautiful but in no way related to the realities of life. Thus it was not out of insensitivity but from sheer incomprehension that she was unwilling, or, rather, unable, to share in the emotions of my professional life.

Some men might have resented this indifference, regarded it as disloyalty. Not I. I had watched too many of my colleagues poison the air of their homes and permanently infect their wives, children and even their domestic animals with the fever they carried home nightly from the studio. I got in the habit of dealing with my anxieties by myself. Joan, on her part, was grateful to me for not involving her in the incomprehensible fluctuations of my career. Her contribution to our life together was the creation of a private world to which I returned at the end of each day with a sense of relief and wonder. It made my daily 35-minute drive home along the Coast Highway to Malibu more than a commuter's routine; at the end of it was the promise of that very special atmosphere that my wife, with unusual taste and imagination, succeeded in giving to the various rented homes we inhabited during the first years of our marriage.

On our return to California after *King Lear* we had lived for three months in a small house—a sort of tennis pavilion from which we moved into a second home to which our son, John Michael, was brought at the age of three days in November 1951 in the company of a very competent middle-aged nurse. I was pleased by his arrival and thankful to Joan for creating him, but except for an agreeable awareness of his presence and a general satisfaction at his charm and good looks, he occupied only a small place in my life.

For Joan, on the other hand, his appearance represented a profound transformation—the beginning of a new way of life of which she and her son had suddenly become the center. During the later months of her pregnancy her Spanish-Russian upper-middle-class genes had reasserted themselves. Without losing her easy French charm she, who had been casual and vaguely bohemian in her domestic arrangements, revealed a new firmness and competence in her conduct of our household. She was aided in this by our improved financial condition. The tax-collectors had been appeased: in addition to Michael's nurse, a black "couple" had been added to our establishment. There were other accretions: an English bobtailed sheepdog (acquired because Salka Viertel had seen it languishing in the window of a Santa Monica pet shop), two cats, a tortoise and a pair of expensive cars—a royal blue convertible Mercury for Joan and a gun-metal XK-120 Jaguar for myself. Add to this a steady stream of house guests that began with my mother's visit to her new grandson and included callers from New York, Chicago, Paris and the South Mountain Road.

Just when things seemed to be settling down, a new political threat arose to plague me. The witch-hunts had been going on for close to five years but their main thrust had shifted to the East Coast, from films to radio and television. They had caused me occasional alarm and annoyance such as the Scripps-Howard articles and Senator McCarthy's public reference to me during a congressional hearing but, in Hollywood, the main battle seemed to be over. The Right had triumphed and all that remained was a mopping-up operation in which surviving "Red" stragglers were rounded up and finished off to prevent any possibility of their regrouping in the future. Under the banner of the American Legion and under the direction of a Committee composed of a columnist, an actor and a renegade labor leader, these self-appointed patriots began to harass the major studios with threats of boycott of any films with which former "Red sympathizers" were any way connected.

I was high on the list, with one picture in release and two in preparation. Citing the danger of nationwide picketing by the Legion, the Studio presented me with the long, familiar list of my subversive activities over the years and demanded that I clear myself without delay.

What was handed me was, in fact, a transcript of a four-year-old report from California's Tenney Committee together with extracts of a statement by an even less competent investigator whose main source of information seemed to be old newspaper clippings—most of them from the *Daily Worker*. Some of their findings were correct but irrelevant: they were also surprisingly incomplete in their omission of activities that would have been far more awkward for me to explain. Under pressure from the Studio, I took time off from production to compose a long letter of rebuttal in which I considered each successive item and undertook to refute or explain it. My letter was returned to me as unacceptable since it expressed no acknowledgement of my errors and no contrition over my evil associations. What was wanted of me was a confession and an apology; also an admission that I had been "duped"—none of which I was prepared to give.

When my second letter was returned as unsatisfactory, the Studio became disturbed. Dore Schary (whose own position was none too secure) summoned me and pointed out that something must be done if I hoped to continue producing pictures for MGM. He offered me the services of one of the town's leading lawyers to find a tone and a phraseology that would satisfy the Committee and to which I was willing to sign my name. At a cost that must have run well into five figures, several conferences were held at which every sentence and phrase of my statement was examined and balanced.

My final letter was seven pages long and began with a preamble in which I declared categorically that I was not and never had been a member of the Communist Party. It then considered, one by one, each of the seventeen accusations listed in the reports. These included references to my service with the Federal Theater and the Voice of America; my authorship of the script of *Jane Eyre*; my production of three films for Paramount and a number of Broadway plays that included *Native Son* and *The Cradle Will Rock*. I admitted my modest financial contributions to the Abraham Lincoln Brigade, to Pete Seeger's *People's Songs* and the Yiddish People's Theater. I denied my appearance at a party given for Harry Bridges but admitted my presence at several of Charles Chaplin's; I admitted my connection with the Hollywood Democratic Committee, the Hollywood Independent Citizens' Committee for the Arts and Sciences and the Hollywood Writers' Mobilization—all of which had ended up on the Attorney General's list of subversive organizations. More than two pages of my letter were devoted to my activities with the Mobilization, including my presence on the editorial board of the *Hollywood Quarterly*.

If there were Communist elements in the Mobilization or among the editors and contributors to the *Hollywood Quarterly*, may I repeat that they did not at any time sway or influence my thoughts or actions or writings.

Half a day was spent on the wording of the letter's final paragraph:

I trust the above explains my position with reference to the items listed in these two reports. I repeat that I have not any time supported or approved of the Communist Party. My record of loyal and devoted service to the government and institutions of the United States is long and varied. I am sorry if, at any time, my efforts or my name have been used to help further activities that were in any sense disloyal or subversive. I would do what I could to correct any such unfortunate results.

Sincerely,

John Houseman

In signing it, I made it clear to the Studio and to its lawyer that this marked the final limit of my weaseling. My statement was grudgingly accepted and I was free to proceed with the preparation of my third picture for MGM—*Executive Suite*.

Such was Hollywood's timidity during and after the witch-hunts that a film about Big Business—a struggle for power among corporate executives—was considered an audacious project when I announced it in the winter of 1952-53. *Executive Suite* was a best-selling novel that Dore Schary brought to my attention with the suggestion that the time might be ripe to make such a picture. I agreed, feeling that it was a good follow-up to *The Bad and the Beautiful* and *Julius Caesar*. (It was my third consecutive film to concern itself with the pursuit of power.) During its preparation I acquired a new and valuable associate—a young man in the publicity department who had some producing experience. His name was Jud Kinberg and he worked as my general assistant and associate producer on *Executive Suite*—a position he occupied on a number of my projects during the next seven years.

It was he who found us a writer for the delicate task of turning this long and complicated chronicle of big business into a viable screenplay—a slender, sandy-haired, nervous young man named Ernest Lehman. He had been a Broadway press agent and a supplier of stories, gossip and jokes to Walter Winchell and Milton Berle, from which he had found material for two highly charged novellas about show business. I was impressed by the intensity of his writing, the quality of his dialogue and his technical knowledge of business procedures. I enjoyed working with him—though he now claims that I was difficult at times and swears that I once accused him of approaching a scene "like a man having at the Hope Diamond with a meat-axe!"

Once again I knew exactly whom I wanted as my director and this made it easier for me to reject the impressive names which the Studio tried to thrust upon me. I wanted a young man named Robert Wise whom I had known since his days as a film editor at RKO, where he had worked on *Citizen Kane, The Magnificent Ambersons* and *The Cat People*, and who possessed the essential virtues of coolness, modesty and technical expertise.

No director with a nervous temperament or a visible ego could possibly handle a cast made up of one of the largest collection of stars ever assembled for a dramatic picture—except possibly *Grand Hotel*; only a brilliant film technician could organize, shoot and edit the final twenty minutes of that film where all eight of them sit together in their Gothic boardroom and determine the fate of the company while the camera twists and hovers around them in an endless series of master scenes, two-shots and close-ups.

In two other respects *Executive Suite* was an abnormal picture. We had spent so much on actors' salaries that we had nothing left for production. With Wise's collaboration I decided to shoot the film entirely in existent sets: they looked fine, with a used look that gave them unusual authenticity. We also eliminated all music (even under the opening and closing titles) and I have never doubted that, on this particular occasion, we helped the film with our silence.

Because of the subject matter both *Time* and *Newsweek* gave us their covers. According to *Newsweek*:

Hollywood has finally discovered the U.S. business drama. The businessman's daily problems are part and parcel of the national life, and they often determine the nation's political policies. Oddly, for all of this, the modern businessman's story had never stirred up much interest among American playwrights or scriptwriters...This week Hollywood went a long way toward making amends for this long omission. *Executive Suite* moves with the pace and tension of a fine detective story.

Our success was repeated in Europe and particularly in France, where our film was released under the title of *La Tour des Ambitieux* and was described as having *"grand style."*

* * *

I produced one more picture that year and prepared two others. Between films, I found time to go to New York for six weeks and direct Shakespeare's *Coriolanus* for T. Edward Hambleton and his newly formed Phoenix Theatre. It was exciting to be back in the theater with a play that presented the double challenge of its modern political parallels and of a hero whom even the great Henry Irving had not succeeded in making theatrically acceptable. To play the heroic but ungrateful part I had thought for a moment of Orson Welles (but that was out of the question) and then of Brando (who was otherwise engaged). Then it occurred to me (as a vague notion at first and later with growing enthusiasm) that many of the qualities of this stiff-necked, emotional warrior might be portrayed in an unconventional but convincing manner by my friend Robert Ryan. He was black-Irish, an athlete with a disturbing mixture of anger and tenderness who had reached stardom by playing brutal, neurotic roles that were at complete variance with his true nature. His physical presence was magnificent—six foot four with a heavyweight boxer's body and a head that, with a slightly augmented nose, had all the required look of nobility and dark power. In his "cloak of humility" he would be a magnificent and formidable figure. His voice was pitched rather higher than it should have been in a man of his size, and his speech, though educated, had the ineradicable nasality of his Chicago origin. We both knew the risk he would be taking by appearing before the New York critics in such a famous classic role. He said he was willing to take the chance—if I was.

Volumnia, the part made famous by the great Mrs. Siddons, was played unconventionally but effectively by Mildred Natwick; for the remaining parts, among the best and the most ambitious of New York's younger actors, I found a cast of unusual reality and energy. (It was no surprise to me when several of them, within a few years, moved to the very top of their profession as directors and actors.)

That left two parts that, in my politically oriented version, took

on an unusual importance. In most productions the Tribunes of the
People are treated as troublemakers—inciters and manipulators of an
unthinking, greasy, dangerous mob. I preferred to regard them as
the voice of the people (union leaders or labor MPs), demagogues to
be sure, but also defenders of the common man against the elitist
arrogance of Coriolanus and his friends. This led me naturally, with
Hambleton's complete approval, to cast my Tribunes with actors
who were inclined to hold radical opinions of their own. My first
was John Randolph, a former associate from the Federal Theater,
who was already under a season's contract to the Phoenix. For the
second, the more eloquent of the two, I spent days weighing the
relative merits of two close friends—both of whom had been
destroyed by the witch-hunts and both of whom desperately wanted
the job. Zero Mostel, once a star, had been reduced to earning a
scant living in third-rate nightclubs at cut-rate wages. Will Geer was
an even closer friend who had been with us in *The Cradle Will Rock*:
deprived of his living as a film actor, he had moved back into the
theater where the political climate had kept him unemployed for
almost two years. I finally decided on Geer on grounds of credibility
and greater classical experience and Zero did not speak to me for
several years.

   We opened to reviews that, according to *Variety's* box score of
major critical verdicts, registered "6 approvals and 1 pass." According
to Atkinson of the *Times*, "Unless life starts improving enormously
New York is not likely to see, for many years, a performance of
Coriolanus as good as the one that opened last night at the Phoenix."

   The day after our opening the phone rang. I was in the tub and
Joan called out that it was Dore Schary on the phone from Culver City.
We were all packed and ready to be driven into town to catch the
Twentieth Century Limited back to California. She brought the phone
into the bathroom and I sat in the warm water as I listened to Dore
Schary speaking somewhat sorrowfully:

   "Good morning, John."

   "Good morning, Dore."

   (a pause)

   "Well, John, you've done it again!"

   "What have I done? What is it this time?"

   "You hired Will Geer."

   "Yes, I did."

   (a long pause)

   "Do you know what that means, John?"

   I knew very well what it meant. A call to California from Chicago
and another during a stop in Albuquerque left me in no doubt as to the

reception that awaited me in Culver City. There had been hostile comments in the trades and two violent articles in the witch-hunters' official journal, *Counter-Attack*. The day I got back, flushed with pride over the fresh batch of airmailed reviews I found waiting for me at the studio, I was summoned to the third floor. On my way up I looked in on Schary, who wished me luck and sent me off to fight my own battle upstairs.

All the way across the country I had been evaluating my hand and I had come to the sober conclusion that for once, in the strange game we were all playing, I held the cards. First, I had a distinct feeling that in this, the second half of the first Eisenhower administration, the political climate was changing. McCarthy had passed his peak: very gradually the country was losing its enthusiasm for witch-hunts and "blacklist" was becoming a dirty word. Second, and more important, were the financial considerations. *The Bad and the Beautiful*, with its five Academy Awards, was still running worldwide; so were two other million-dollar films with my name on them as producer. To recall them and take my name off would be costly and legally questionable and would inevitably result in a serious loss of revenue. It was a risk MGM had no intention of taking—no matter how great the pressure.

As I entered the star chamber, even before I could sit down, the assault began. Did I know what I had done? Had I no brains at all? Did I realize that in employing a notorious Communist I had betrayed and embarrassed not only MGM but the entire industry of which I was a member? Where was my loyalty? My patriotism? My sense of obligation? I had been protected once before from the attacks of the Legion; I had been allowed to make whatever films I chose. Was this my gratitude?

I replied as patiently as I could that it was not I who had engaged Mr. Geer. I was the director of *Coriolanus*, not the producer. I had auditioned Mr. Geer and found him well suited to the requirements of the part. It was Mr. Hambleton, the managing director of the Phoenix, who had engaged him. Our reviews had been excellent. And I pointed out, with an innocence that fooled no one, that there was, in fact, no reason why the Phoenix should *not* hire Mr. Geer since *no blacklist existed* in the New York theater.

This was my trump card, and its effect was immediate and devastating. At the mention of that dangerous phrase, Eddie Mannix exhibited all the symptoms of angina pectoris. He called me a son of a bitch and worse and slammed out. Mr. Thau asked me in a venomous whisper if I was suggesting that there was a blacklist in Hollywood. Like Pilate, he would not stay for an answer and I was left alone with Mr. Sydney, the studio manager, who stared glumly through me until I left the room and returned to my office.

This was the year in which my friend Herman Mankiewicz died. He had been failing for some time but persisted in working till within a few weeks of his death. Both he and Sarah became fond of Joan and, in addition to the annual Passover meal we celebrated together, we often dined with them in their house on Tower Road. Herman and I had remained close friends but, between my work at the studio and the growing demands of my household, I saw less of him than I used to. He was sincerely pleased by my success; my encounter with the Legion afforded him particular amusement and furnished him with fresh occasions for withering sarcasm about Hollywood's affluent "radicals." Some months before his death he had sent me his last serious piece of writing: a screenplay based on the life of the notorious evangelist Aimee Semple McPherson. Before I had a chance to discuss it with the Studio as a possible project, Mank himself sabotaged the entire venture by sending a copy of the script to the evangelist's daughter who threatened to sue for libel if it were ever produced.

In his last few days—spent mostly in an oxygen tent—Mank attempted to put his tangled affairs in order. To his eldest son he gave instructions for his funeral: "Put in the paper a notice that says 'No flowers'," he commanded. "Then add, 'In lieu of flowers, contributions may be given to plant trees in the Arab section of Palestine.'" To his brother, Joe, after expressing his final wishes, he announced that he was now ready to meet his maker. Then after a pause, remembering his numerous debts and loans, he added, "Or, in my case, should I say 'co-maker'?"

I was unused to death and could not bear the thought that he was gone. Mank himself, with his Freudian expertise and his penetrating understanding of human behavior, would have had some interesting things to say about my own curious conduct on the day of his funeral. I got hopelessly lost in the streets with which I was perfectly familiar and missed the eulogy delivered by his close friend Nunnally Johnson who perfectly expressed what I felt about him:

I was never with him that I wasn't stimulated. I looked forward to what he had to say—and I carried it home and repeated it for the pleasure of others. I was never with him that I didn't feel in some peculiar way that I had actually benefited—either in my thinking or in my emotions. I have never known the like of his wild wit and imagination—in which there was always a natural wisdom and the kind of blood-curdling perceptiveness that disposed of all nonsense and confusion and laid bare the bones of truth clear for anyone to see.

That was also the year in which Joan and I acquired our first home in California—Salka Viertel's house on Mabery Road in Santa Monica.

By the midfifties the great era of Salka's "salon" was over. So was her privileged position at MGM, where she had been Greta Garbo's accredited companion, writer and adviser. Most of the celebrated émigrés who had used her house as their meeting place during and after the war had returned to Europe. Many of her friends and neighbors (like Donald Ogden Stewart and Ella Winters) had been driven to Europe by the witch-hunts. Now Salka herself was hard up and the house was growing shabby, though its atmosphere and its glamor remained, kept alive by the occasional presence of Greta Garbo with whom Joan and I dined there several times, bemused by the superhuman beauty of that amazing face.

It was a good house in a pleasant street, with large, well-shaped, book-lined rooms, a rose garden and a distant view of the sea. We spent several months making the changes Joan had decided on, with that strangely successful blending of period and "modern" that was her specialty. In designing the nursery, arrangements had been made for a second occupant: Joan was pregnant again and hoping for a daughter. Her gynecologist was a celebrated Beverly Hills doctor who believed in intervention and had fixed on the evening of December 28 as a convenient time for the event. That evening we drove into town, stopped at the Beachcomber, ordered double "zombies" (two apiece), then drove on to the hospital, where Joan disappeared into the delivery room while I sat in the father's room and worked on a screenplay. Around eleven I was admitted to see my second son—Charles Sebastian, and his smiling mother, both of whom were brought back two days later to Mabery Road.

XX
Lust for Life
1955

My commitment at MGM had almost a year or more to run but my agents were already deep in negotiations over a new deal. Early in 1955 they came up with one that surprised everyone including myself. It was a miraculous contract for seven years of which I needed to work only four: the rest of the time was mine—at my choice and at full salary. I was preparing to adjust to this bonanza when two things happened that completely changed my professional and personal life.

The first was a new film that was different from any I had produced before—a project that took me to Europe for the first time in twenty-five years.

Minnelli and I had made two films together and were looking for another. Among the projects we considered was a property the Studio had owned for almost ten years but had never come close to making. *Lust for Life*—Irving Stone's account of the tragic life of the painter Vincent Van Gogh—had been shelved on the grounds that a painter's life was unsuitable material for a motion picture. Now the climate was changing. A recent international Van Gogh exhibition had been attended by hundreds of thousands; reproductions of his "Sunflowers" hung in every students' dormitory in America. More immediately significant was the fact that John Huston's *Moulin Rouge*, a fictionalized life of Toulouse-Lautrec, had recently been a moneymaker.

Still, things might have hung fire indefinitely but for one circumstance: in checking MGM's contract with Irving Stone it was discovered that the rights to his book had been acquired by the Studio for a period of ten years and that those ten years had barely nine more months to run. It was now mid-March and, unless the picture were completed by the end of the year, all rights reverted to the author, who had been approached for an extension, which he had categorically refused. Early in March we got the word that we could go ahead with *Lust for Life* as our next picture on one condition—that principal photography be completed before January 1, 1956.

Kismet, Minnelli's current assignment (from which his producer had no intention of releasing him), would not finish shooting until the second week of July. On the other hand, it was generally agreed that all the exteriors of *Lust for Life* must be filmed in the original European locations—most of them in bright sunshine. This meant that all but the sombre Dutch and Belgian sequences must be shot during Europe's comparatively brief summer; it also meant that we must be in production by late June or early July at the latest.

The script was the least of our problems. We had our scenario in the ineluctable course of Vincent's own race towards madness and death; we had Vincent's own words as they appeared in the hundreds of letters that passed between him and his beloved brother Theo. What we needed was a writer with the skill to select and arrange the words and events of Vincent's life with a sense of structure and poetry. I called Norman Corwin, who had done much of this kind of writing during the great days of radio. He was familiar with the material and, within a few weeks, working twelve hours a day, we were able to present the Studio with a shooting script, a copy of which was immediately forwarded for budgeting and scheduling to our unit-manager in London.

From the start we were spared one problem—the casting of our leading man. The perfect Vincent Van Gogh was available and eager to play the part—Kirk Douglas, who had done so well for us in *The Bad and the Beautiful* and who bore a striking physical resemblance to Van Gogh. His red-blond hair, sharp nose and chin and flashing eyes required no make-up to resemble the doomed painter. Equally available was a Paul Gauguin who was perfect in looks and manner—the Mexican-born actor Anthony Quinn. With these two signed, our main casting problems were over: most of our other parts would be cast in Europe with French or English actors.

Our production would be divided into two parts: first and more difficult was the shooting of our European exteriors in their original locations, followed by the shooting of interiors in our own Culver City studio to match our European locations. Besides these, there would be another kind of filming entirely—the photography and reproduction of the paintings that played such an essential and dramatic part in Van Gogh's life. We sent for John Rewald, of the Museum of Modern Art in New York, for consultation; we questioned international art-dealers, Swiss printers, photographers and museum heads as to the best way to proceed.

One thing they all agreed on: using a movie camera was the worst possible way to photograph paintings, not to mention the fact that most museums and private collectors would not permit their paintings to be subjected to the intense heat generated by motion-picture illumination. After much technical talk a campaign was devised: we would send experts into museums and private collections all over the world, armed with old-fashioned portrait-cameras, with which they would make time-exposures without excessive light: these would then be converted into enlarged transparencies which, in turn, would be backlit and rephotographed by movie cameras with "insert" equipment and special lenses. Except for a tendency to show the colors of the paintings a trifle brighter than they really were, the results were perfect.

It was fortunate for us that Van Gogh was such a prolific artist and that his paintings were so widely scattered in collections all over the world. For, early in our quest, and from Holland in particular, we received a number of evasions and some flat turndowns. Our principal adversary was Van Gogh's nephew, Theo's son, who, personally and through his influence with the Dutch museums, controlled a large number of his uncle's pictures. He had disliked Stone's book and I suspect that he was loath to encourage any project that threatened to reveal the hereditary physical ills that had afflicted the Van Gogh family. His final, formal objection was that paintings were made to be seen and admired on the walls of homes and museums and not to be used as props in a melodrama. (Later, according to John Rewald, he saw the film and was not displeased.)

By mid-June our schedule was laid out. For logistical and meteorological reasons, we would follow Van Gogh's life in reverse—with one major exception. He had spent his childhood in Holland, his young manhood in Belgium, his early days as an artist in Paris, his most creative years in the South of France and his final agony at Auvers-sur-Oise, not far from Paris. For climatic reasons we had to begin with his death.

Vincent died in 1890 at the age of thirty-seven following a self-inflicted gunshot wound incurred at the time he was painting "Wheat Field with Crows," which shows a field of ripe wheat rippling under a stormy sky. Our unit-manager had located what might well have been the very field in which Vincent was painting on that fatal day. We rented the field—for a price that included any damage we might do to the grain in the course of shooting. Before long that accursed field had become the symbol of all our difficulties with the film.

Summer came early to Europe that year. During the last week of June we received word that our wheat field was ripening fast—and Minnelli was not due to finish Kismet till mid-July! On July 3, Joan and I boarded the Scandinavian Air Lines polar flight to Copenhagen and then to London, which I had not seen for more than twenty-five years.

In a suite at the Savoy, overlooking the river, I conferred with members of our crew, met Freddy Young, our cinematographer, and interviewed a number of British actors and actresses whom we hoped to use in the film. I had no time for nostalgia and I made no attempt to see any of the friends of my youth. But one night, in a London restaurant, I encountered a figure out of my more recent past.

The Caprice was a nightspot where actors and audiences met for supper after the theater. Our companions that evening were members of an American theatrical company, headed by Helen Hayes, which was touring Western Europe under the auspices of the U.S. State Department. One of them—Brenda Forbes—reported that Orson had promised to come over after his show—his own version of *Moby Dick* which had just opened successfully in the West End.

Welles and I had not met in years. Now that we were both in Europe, I knew that I would run into him sooner or later. Whatever pleasure I might have taken in introducing Joan to London's nightlife withered in the agitation with which I now awaited the appearance of my onetime friend and partner.

By 12:30 most of the others had gone off to bed. I was tired, and I had a hard day ahead of me, but an overwhelming compulsion kept me glued to my chair, making small talk with my wife while I waited for this meeting that I so feared and desired. Around 1 a.m. a faint but insistent *blip* on my private radar warned me that the Wonder Boy was approaching. With that same sense of levitation that I had experienced in Sinclair Stadium I found myself rising from my seat. Propelled by a potent blend of nostalgia, curiosity and terror, I began to move towards the doorway in which I never for an instant doubted that Orson was about to appear.

He did. He came suddenly into view—a huge figure in a dark suit, emerging from a small crowd of familiars and waiters. As I continued to move towards him I had not the faintest idea of what would happen. Either he would hurl himself upon me with a roar of rage, swinging and flailing as he so often had during our five years' partnership. Or he would fling his giant arms around me in a choking, passionate embrace. Either way, it would be dangerous and dramatic.

Under my feet I felt the softness of the carpet change to the smooth hardness of the dance floor across which I continued to advance. Then came the moment when I knew that Orson had become aware of me. With no change of expression on that big, round face, he separated himself from his party and started in my direction, so that we were now moving slowly and silently towards each other across the deserted floor like a pair of classic Western gunfighters approaching each other for the final shoot-out. I could feel the muscles of my arms tensing—ready to fly up to parry the haymaker that would be aimed at my head or to return the bear hug in which I would be enveloped.

We were less than three feet apart when the silence was shattered by a bellow of "Jacko!" and patrons of the Caprice were treated to the surprising spectacle of two very large men, locked in a frantic, clumsy embrace, whirling slowly, like a giant top, around the dance floor. Finally we stopped and moved to Welles's table, where champagne was served. Then for an hour we were deep in the past—at the Lafayette in Harlem, the Maxine Elliott, the moldering Mercury and the smooth, acoustical walls of CBS Studio One—repeating the epic, familiar, ever moving stories of triumphs and disasters, terrible fights and absurd reconciliations, all laced with gargantuan laughter and a feeling of indescribable bliss. (In the pain of our breakup I had forgotten how inexpressibly seductive and endearing Orson could be when he tried.)

It was then that I made my first mistake. I mentioned that I had a hard day ahead of me and I made a move to leave, ignoring what I should have remembered from similar situations in the past—that Orson detested departures and leave-takings that were not initiated by himself. I assured him that we would be seeing each other again, since I was eager to see his *Moby Dick*, of which I had heard and read such good things.

Next, out of carelessness or perversity, I did a really idiotic thing: I told him I was not sure which night I would be coming to his theater. I explained that I had only three days left in England and that I was waiting to hear from Stratford, where Laurence Olivier was playing *Macbeth*, to which it was virtually impossible to buy a ticket.

I could have bitten off my tongue even as I said it. It was too late. The glasses on the table leaped and crashed as a huge fist slammed onto the table. Orson was on his feet. His eyes were glazed and his face had the sweaty gray-whiteness of his great furies. Underlining each word as though addressing a child or a halfwit, *"It is no more difficult to get seats for* Macbeth *than it is for* Moby Dick!" he said. Then, before I could dispute his palpably false statement, his voice rose to a shout that reached to every corner of the Caprice: "For twenty years, you son of a bitch, you've been trying to humiliate and destroy me! You've never stopped, have you? And you're still at it!"

Early in our association I had learned that it was futile to try to stem such rages. I took my wife's arm and started my exit, making our way, with all the dignity I could muster, between the tables and the startled stares of the few remaining customers while, behind us, I could hear Orson bellowing (much as he had at Chasen's more than fourteen years before) that I'd better not stick my filthy nose into his theater; if I did he'd come down off the stage and personally throw me out!

I never got to see Olivier's *Macbeth*. But I did see Welles' *Moby Dick* the next night and I loved it. It had all the excitement and magic that were Orson's special theatrical virtues. He did not throw me out, but he and I did not speak to each other again for close to twenty years.

Two days later our relentless unit-manager carried me off to Paris, where personnel and equipment for our expedition were being assembled. Our main concern at that moment was still that accursed wheat field where the grain was ripe and ready for harvest. The farmer was threatening to cut it any day now. If he did—there went the climactic scene of our film! There was only one solution: to buy his entire crop and hope that God would spare the wheat until Minnelli arrived. (*Kismet* was moving slowly to its conclusion: it was three days behind schedule.)

There was also the question of the *crows*. A striking feature of Van Gogh's last painting is a flight of crows rising from the windswept wheat field. For centuries French farmers have waged a relentless war against crows, which they accuse of devouring their crops: this meant that we might be unable to find enough crows locally to fill our scene. At my command, word went out all over France that the Americans were in the market for crows, at five francs a crow—said crows to be delivered alive at Auvers-sur-Oise on or before July 20. By the middle of the month they had begun to arrive, in crates, sacks and baskets, and we had to put on a special crew of keepers to keep them alive.

I spent ten days in Paris waiting for Minnelli to arrive and conferring with our French production staff—a competent and charming group. Jud Kinberg arrived, accompanied by our "art expert"—a Post-Impressionist specialist recommended by John Rewald. I immediately put him to work to paint us a credible, unfinished copy of Van Gogh's wheat field of exactly the right size and state of completion, at which Kirk Douglas could daub away while fighting off a flock of exasperated crows.

Finally, in the last week of July, Minnelli arrived, exhausted, harassed and vile-tempered. He flew in on a Saturday, and we were scheduled to start shooting the wheat field on Monday morning. He asked to see the unfinished "Wheat Field." It was a disaster. Our "expert" was a scholar but no painter. We called Beverly Hills and got the name of a young French artist—Claude Garrache, a good painter in his own right and an expert faker. A squad of assistants were sent out to find him and bring him to our hotel, together with six canvases of the right size. He arrived at two in the morning and labored all that day and far into the night. Monday at dawn we set out for

Auvers-sur-Oise with two acceptable, unfinished copies of "Wheat Field with Crows" in the prop truck. By noon we were in the field, and Kirk, in a faded blue shirt and battered straw hat, was fighting off a flock of crows whose legs were secured with fine piano wire so that they could be yanked back and forth for another and yet another attempt to get that difficult and all-important shot.

By dusk we had the scene shot from all its various angles, and that night the negative was flown to America for developing. Two days later, when word came that all was well, the farmer moved in and harvested what was left of his overripe grain. (That left us with several dozen ailing and exhausted crows on our hands. Our natural instinct was to release them; the neighboring farmers and the local police threatened us with arrest and enormous fines if all surviving specimens were not immediately destroyed or shipped out of the region. The next day no crows were visible and I preferred not to know what happened to them.)

We spent a week in Auvers. It was a charming village, rich in flowers and Impressionist history. Pissarro had lived and painted there; so had Docteur Gachet, who had befriended Vincent in his last days. We filmed several scenes in the Doctor's garden—including one mentioned by Vincent in a letter to Theo a few days before his death. After work, Joan and I would go and dine at one of the small restaurants along the river banks.

All too soon, our idyllic days were over and our great caravan started out on its long trek along the highways of France, Belgium and Holland. It numbered between twenty and thirty vehicles—two generators, a camera boom, three trucks filled with camera equipment and electronics of various sorts, dressing rooms, portable toilets, make-up and hairdressing supplies, props and several vans crammed with costumes, old clothes and ragged, local garments of the period.

Our first southern location was Arles, where we had constructed our own "Yellow House" on the site of the original, which had been destroyed by the British when they bombed the bridges across the Rhône. With that exception, most of the scenes and places Van Gogh had painted and described still existed or were easy to reconstruct: the flower market, the Public Garden, the streets and squares, the Hospice—hardly changed in sixty years—the surrounding countryside with its fields and orchards and even one or two of the original small wooden drawbridges.

Occasionally Minnelli would become so entranced by something he saw during the day that Jud and I would sit up all night writing a new scene that could be shot in this new location. When these were viewed in Culver City they invariably evoked cables of protest—either from Norman Corwin, who accused us of mutilating his script, or from the production department, which resented every additional hour we spent on location.

Our next move in Provence was to the village of Les Baux, some 30 kilometers away. It lies at the foot of a towering cliff on which sits the haunted, historic, abandoned town of the same name. At its base was a luxury hotel, where we stayed for almost a month and which the company used as its base of operations for the rest of the filming in Provence.

Under a burning sun that beat down on us mercilessly day after day (as it had on Van Gogh), we shot the dried stubble fields cut up by irrigation ditches, the orchards that were no longer in bloom and the small villages that had not changed appreciably since Vincent painted them. But most of our time was spent in and around the asylum in which Vincent had been confined in semiliberty for so many months. It was abandoned now, but its solid stone walls and corridors were still there; so were the rows of cells with their small windows overlooking the garden; the public rooms described in letters to Theo; the olive groves and the dark, flaming cypresses Vincent had painted against a bright sky full of whirling stars.

All things considered, and notwithstanding the screams of anguish that emanated daily from Culver City, our work was going surprisingly well. As the weeks went by Minnelli's panic subsided—so did his irritability. He was not accustomed to the physical hardships and limitations of a remote location and he had never before gone into production with so little preparation. Yet, in spite of the hard time he gave us I never for a moment doubted that he was the right man for the job. His visual sense (he had started his career as an artist) proved invaluable in the delicate task of reconciling the scenes and backgrounds of the film with the surface and spirit of the paintings. He was aided in this by the creative collaboration he received from our strange mixed Anglo-French crew. He drove them half mad with his exacting and often unreasonable demands; but the film—when the developed prints came to us from Provence to Paris to Houston to Los Angeles and finally back to Provence, where we ran them at midnight in a local movie house in Avignon—had a richness and a brilliance that fully justified the toil and anguish we suffered in shooting it.

For my own part, in spite of all our difficulties, I was finding our European voyage exhilarating—especially our time in the South. Though French was our habitual language at home, Joan and I had never been in France together before and neither of us knew Provence. On Sundays when I was not writing or preparing for the coming week's shooting we drove to Nîmes, to the Camargue and to the amazing dead city of Aigues Mortes, which St. Louis had used as his port of embarkation for the first Crusade more than seven centuries ago.

Early in September, Joan returned to Paris to be with her mother, and the company started on its voyage north, headed for Holland and Belgium. There were more than thirty-three vehicles in our caravan by now; I looked down on them from the plane that was flying me to Amsterdam—a motorized army crawling like a long, dark caterpillar across the French countryside.

No two landscapes could have been more different than the burnt yellow plains of Provence and the lush, green, low-lying meadows of the Netherlands. Neunen, the village in which Van Gogh's father had had his modest church and where we were able to stage family scenes in the original parish house, was less than 50 kilometers from Amsterdam. This was the home of the Potato Eaters whose huge, coarse peasant features were identical with those of their grandparents, whom Van Gogh had drawn and painted in their dark, smoke-filled huts. In Amsterdam, we were able to shoot in the former home of Vincent's wealthy uncle which contrasted with scenes of Vincent's squalid life with Cristine, the whore who became his common-law wife and by whom he had a child. She was played with wonderful harsh pathos by the great English actress Pamela Brown. I can still see her—her hair falling about her pale face under a gray shawl as she moved along the narrow streets that run beside the canal in what is still the red-light district of Amsterdam, with the plain, quiet-looking girls sitting in the lighted windows doing their knitting or needlework while they wait for a customer.

From Amsterdam our caravan moved southeast into Belgium, into the gloomy depths of the coal-mining region known as the Borinage. It remains unspeakably grim—an area of poverty, unemployment and fear where conditions had not materially improved since Van Gogh worked there as an ineffectual preacher and made his first, dark, clumsy pictures before his health collapsed and he had to go home.

Finally, we were done! I spent a few days in Paris, closing our caravan and saying goodbye to our European crew. Then we were off to California to shoot what remained of the picture. We were accompanied across the Atlantic by our French faker-painter and by certain British members of our cast, including Pamela Brown and James Donald, who was playing Vincent's brother, Theo.

Our work in the studio, though it included many of our biggest dramatic scenes, was less exciting than the locations, where we had the constantly thrilling sense of feeling the same burning sun, treading the same dry earth and reacting to the same violent colors that had helped to drive Vincent into madness three quarters of a century earlier. Still, the work went well—particularly Van Gogh's scenes with Gauguin and Cristine, which were among the critical moments of the film.

On our return to Europe we had been able to examine and appraise what had been accomplished by our special-effects departments in their treatment of the paintings that we had assembled from all over the world. Their work was magnificent and so thorough and abundant that we finally used fewer than half the paintings they had so painstakingly reproduced.

We had been living so long with the film that we had done most of our editing as we went along. Less than a month after we finished shooting, it was ready to be viewed—without music and with a number of special effects still missing. Even so, it was an impressive running. In March a successful sneak preview was held in Santa Barbara; except for a few cuts and visual changes in the ending there was little more to be done.

Lust for Life opened five months later, preceded by a disgraceful advertising campaign. Once again the sales department had distorted and demeaned the product and attempted to make it a "popular" attraction with lurid pictures of a maniacal artist in the act of raping a nude model. Our première was held at the Plaza Theater as a benefit for the Metropolitan Museum of Art; it was attended by the heads of every museum and art gallery in New York City and elsewhere. Many of them had allowed us to photograph their paintings; now they were nervous over their own connection with a project that had been so crudely advertised. By the end of the evening apprehension had turned to enthusiasm: our reception in the art world and the press was one of unqualified approval. In Europe, particularly, it was the subject of general astonishment (as it had been with *Julius Caesar*) that Americans could produce so artistic and sensitive a picture. From the Academy we received one award and four nominations and our financial results around the world were equally satisfying. From Europe *Variety* reported that "local box-office ranks *Lust* as another *Mogambo*."

* * *

A year earlier all this would have filled me with delight. Now I hardly cared, for before our first preview I had instructed my agents to inform MGM that I was taking a year off—as provided for in my new contract.

The news was received with stupefaction by my employers,

outrage by my agents and incredulity by most of my friends. But those who knew me better merely noted that I had done it again. Once more I was upsetting the apple cart, screwing up my career, throwing away my hard-earned success and disrupting the smooth, upward course of my life. The years I had just spent in Culver City represented the longest and most productive employment I had ever known. My position at MGM was wholly enviable; there were few men in the industry who would not gladly have changed places with me. On a personal level, I had everything to content me—a good marriage, a beautiful home, a well-run household and a new financial security that exceeded my wildest dreams. Out of sheer perversity, animated by my old spirit of self-destruction and a neurotic yearning for change, I was giving all this up—exchanging it for a new and hazardous endeavor in which the odds were overwhelmingly against me.

In fact, there was rather more to it than that. For more than a year now I had been growing restless: my sexual and cultural moonlighting and my restless assumption of film projects that I had no real desire to complete were all symptoms of a growing tedium that the agitations of *Lust for Life* had only momentarily assuaged.

I was not being altogether capricious. By now, at the age of fifty-three, I was beginning to know myself and to understand the complicated engine that drove me. I knew that uncertainty and fear were essential elements of my own creative drive and that once they were removed I was easy prey to boredom and my own dangerous kind of corruption.

Finally, on a more realistic and pragmatic level, there was the feeling, awakened by the sensitive antennae that I had developed during so many years of alienation and fear—that all was not well in Culver City; that Schary's situation was not as secure as it had been; that with any weakening of his authority my own position at the Studio was directly threatened. I was also aware that, for the past five years, I had enjoyed miraculous luck; I had a nagging premonition that those halcyon days were coming to an end.

For all these reasons Lincoln Kirstein (though he did not know it) had chosen a good moment to rouse me from a deep sleep and to ask me bluntly, on the phone from New York, in the middle of the night, whether I would be interested in becoming artistic director of the American Shakespeare Festival Theater for the coming year.

I cannot recall my sleepy answer but it must have been sufficiently positive for him to go ahead with his lunatic scheme. Two days later Joseph Verner Reed, whom I knew as a millionaire patron of the arts, had arrived in Los Angeles. We had lunch together and met again for several hours the following morning. He outlined the situation in

Stratford and the nature of my function as Artistic Director of the American Shakespeare Festival Theater. I made it clear, on my part, that my authority must be absolute and unquestionable, in the choice of plays and in the selection of actors, designers, composers and artistic staff. I also inquired about the financial status of the Festival: Joe Reed assured me that he, personally, was underwriting the coming season. All in all, I made a great show of toughness but my mind was already made up to accept their offer.

We had a lovely family Christmas—our last in Santa Monica. (At the top of our tree was a golden angel of Swedish origin; it had belonged to Greta Garbo, who had left it in our attic together with a packet of unopened international fan mail.) Then Joan and I flew to New York and moved back within a few days into the House on the Hill in New City. Two days after that our two boys, with their Scotch nurse and three dogs, arrived by train in a blizzard. Snow, which they had never seen, excited them wildly: for my own part, I found it strangely moving to see my wife and sons occupying this house which I had started to build ten years before either of the boys had been thought of.

XXI
Festival: King John and Measure
for Measure
1956

The three ruling members of the American Shakespeare Festival's executive committee were Lawrence Langner, Lincoln Kirstein and Joseph Verner Reed. They were the ones with whom I had my official dealings and each of them had to be treated in a separate and different way.

That I had long disliked and mistrusted Lawrence Langner and felt suspicious and ill at ease in his presence (I'm sure the feeling was mutual) does not alter the historic fact that he was a man of great energy and skill who, between World War I and his death in 1962, played a highly constructive part in the development of serious theater in America. A Welsh Jew by birth and a patent lawyer by profession, he was one of the group that had founded the Washington Square Players (later the Theater Guild)—the most progressive and durable producing organization in the history of the American theater.

Like Ulysses, Langner was a man of many devices and the idea of an American Shakespeare Festival was entirely his. He had spent years of effort and much of his own money creating it amidst general indifference in the hope that "many thousands of Americans who can't afford a trip to England will be able to witness the finest Shakespeare productions during the summer vacation period."

By 1951, as a result of his incessant activity, money in substantial amounts had been raised from major foundations and a bill had been passed by the Connecticut state legislature establishing the American Shakespeare Festival and Academy as a non-profit educational corporation in that state. Four years later the theater had been constructed and opened—amid speeches and congratulatory telegrams from President Eisenhower and Winston Churchill who hailed this newest of the Shakespeare festivals as "completing the three sides of the triangle" with the Stratfords in Warwickshire and in Ontario, Canada. Organized and staged with insufficient thought and preparation, the Festival's first season had been a failure. Its productions of *Julius Caesar* and *The Tempest* had been received with disappointment verging on hostility.

I had known, when I accepted the job, that my relations with Langner would be awkward. My absolute authority over an organization that he considered his own had been wrung from him by his own associates, who considered him mainly responsible for the confusions of the previous summer. I knew that Langner himself never really accepted the new arrangement and I had the constant uncomfortable feeling that he was sitting back, waiting for me to break my neck.

Joseph Reed was generous, insecure, modest, conventional, eccentric, unreliable, entirely selfish and deeply dedicated—a tall, slender, elegant gentleman with a prominent nose and a passion for petit-point tapestry, of which he usually carried a frame to rehearsals and conferences together with a huge basket of fresh fruit from his farm in Greenwich. His personal income (derived from inherited holdings in copper mines) was reported to be in the neighborhood of $1 million a year—of which an appreciable amount went into the haphazard backing of artistic ventures. He had a passion for the Bard and once wrote to me that "there's not a night that passes that I don't awaken at some time around four o'clock to wrestle with Shakespeare."

Emotionally, he was divided: one side of him seemed to enjoy trouble and turmoil; the other yearned for harmony and success. He was sensitive and callous, with the combined diffidence and presumption of the very rich. Though his attitude towards me was consistently cordial and friendly, I felt that he never ceased to regard me as a slightly dangerous and alien figure to whom he was never quite sure he should entrust his beloved Shakespeare.

My relations with Lincoln Kirstein were of another order altogether. They went back more than a quarter of a century to the year in which I first arrived from Europe. I first met him as a teenager at his sister Mina's house at a time when he was still at Harvard, where he founded and edited the brilliant literary and artistic quarterly, *Hound and Horn*. I had read his poetry and his first moving, troubled novel and, over the years, I had followed and admired the tenacity and courage with which he and Balanchine pursued and finally achieved their dream of creating a great American ballet school and company. We had never worked together but I was consistently impressed by his erudition and fertile intelligence. I was also aware that Lincoln's enthusiasms and artistic opinions were subjective, arbitrary and unreliable. Within the span of an hour he would express two directly conflicting views—each with equal conviction and vehemence—depending on changes in the emotional situation in which he found himself.

Throughout our association I tried to profit from the quality of his taste and from his vast fund of ideas without being swayed by the violence of his opinions, which were often in opposition to my own. For a while he accepted these denials with good grace and without apparent resentment. He did not, until much later, use his support of me as leverage with which to try and impose his will upon me.

During my first few months with the Festival my work was done in New York. I continued to live with my family in New City, driving in and out across the George Washington Bridge every day in the blue second-hand jeep I had acquired soon after my return. The boys (aged two and five) got over their amazement at the sight of snow and ice and happily accepted the House on the Hill as yet another of the constantly changing homes in which their brief lives had been spent. John Michael attended the Rudolph Steiner Day School in Spring Valley while Sebastian crawled around the terrace whose bricks his mother and I had laid seven years earlier. The only unhappy one was Joan, who hated the Eastern cold and grieved for her house in Santa Monica. She did her best to adapt to our new life but received scant comfort from me—obsessed as I was with the immediate challenge of the Festival.

Our New York office that spring was a bare suite with a borrowed desk and a single telephone, where, in the company of a small, red-haired, very efficient secretary left over from the previous year, I settled down to the task of planning a program for an organization that was badly shaken by the failure of its first season and unsure of its own future direction. For my own part, I was swinging, almost hourly, between my familiar poles of exhilaration and terror.

Except for my brief foray with *Coriolanus* at the Phoenix in 1953, I had been absent from New York theater for close to six years. Thus I found myself, from the moment of my arrival, looking around for help of all sorts in a field—classical repertory—that had lain virtually fallow in the American theater for many years. On the technical side I had the support of my beloved Jean Rosenthal. In the fifteen years since we had worked together she was little changed: the cherubic child's head, framed with dark curly hair; the snub nose, the smiling lips; the strange body, perfectly formed from the waist up and almost dwarflike below. But professionally she had come a long way. She had designed the lighting for numerous Broadway shows and for such institutions as the New York City Opera and Light Opera companies. But her most consistent and important functions had been those of technical director and lighting designer for Martha Graham and for the New York City Ballet Company. It was Kirstein who had brought her into the Stratford Festival; with her at my side, there were no physical or technical difficulties I did not feel confident of overcoming.

On a chill, rainy New England afternoon, I made my first voyage to Stratford with Lincoln Kirstein and Jean Rosenthal to look over the Festival Theater. I found it surprisingly handsome, with a stage-house that rose tall and clear above the surrounding fields, blending into the New England countryside. The interior was less satisfying. The more I looked the more concerned I became. On my way back to New York I made it clear to Lincoln that certain changes must be made—particularly in the relation of stage and auditorium.

In the meantime it was becoming urgently necessary for me to announce my choice of plays and actors. From the start, as soon as I stopped dreaming and got down to the practical problems of the summer season, one thing had become clear: following the disappointments of the first year it would be difficult, if not impossible, to lure any established stars onto our Connecticut stage. For that reason it would be folly to attempt any of the Bard's major works—each of which carries its accumulated burden of expectations and comparisons. With *Coriolanus*, I had discovered the excitement of introducing audiences to a little-known Shakespeare drama. This confirmed me in my conviction that my only hope for this hazardous second season lay in the bold, imaginative production of unfamiliar, contrasting plays, performed by a vital company of young, comparatively unknown actors. I delayed my announcement as long as possible while I devoured every obscure work in the canon—works I had never seen or had read so long ago that I had entirely forgotten them.

The day came when I could delay no longer. I had to reveal my program—first to the trustees and then, in a public announcement, to the press. The two plays I selected had only one thing in common: their complete unfamiliarity to the audience and to all but a handful of critics. Of all Shakespeare's works I doubt if any two are more unlike in theme, in tone, in period, in acting requirements and production styles than *King John* and *Measure for Measure*—to which I added, for later in the season, *The Taming of the Shrew*.

This choice of plays, though it shocked some of our trustees, provoked the public reaction I had hoped for: surprise, skepticism and a grudging admiration for our daring. Two weeks later I announced the names of the acting company. We could boast of no single major star, but my list included many of the best young and middle-aged actors in the American theater. (At the last moment Morris Carnovsky was added to our cast; he was a former companion from the Group Theatre, whose vast theatrical experience had not yet included the playing of Shakespeare. He offered me his services on condition that he play only small parts for the first season while he faced the new acting problems involved in the speaking of Elizabethan verse.)

The following Sunday found me riding my favorite hobbyhorse onto the front page of the drama section of the *New York Times.*

For many years American acting was an honorable branch of the British theatrical tradition. Then, with the rise of native American drama, there gradually developed an unfortunate and ever-widening chasm between the classic and realistic schools of performance in this country. In the past two generations most of our best young actors have been concerned with the inner mechanics of expressing emotions—the much discussed "method" and its derivatives. Of late, however, there has been a growing preoccupation with a more styled and eloquent theater, a rising impatience with the limitations of the naturalistic stage and a general desire for a freer, more fluid and more lyric communication between stage and auditorium, between the dramatic creation and its audience.

Having made this sanguine announcement, I faced the problem of the effective production of the plays I had chosen. The three works selected had the widest possible range: the crude, savage historical conflicts of *King John*; the sophisticated, equivocal morality of *Measure for Measure*; the simple, lusty, mountebank mood of *Shrew*. For the presentation of three so widely different plays in repertory, a new, more flexible stage must be devised within the existing structure of the Festival Theater—one on which it was hoped "to combine the blunt immediacy of the Elizabethan platform stage with the visual variety that lies within the depths of a dramatically lighted proscenium arch."

In pursuing this ambitious objective I found myself depending increasingly on the aid and advice of a young man whom I had chosen as my Associate Artistic Director. Jack Landau was from the Middle West; he had lived in England for a time—first as a student, then as a junior staff member of the Old Vic Theatre School under George Devine and Michel Saint-Denis. He had also served as observer-assistant to Peter Brook at Stratford-upon-Avon. On his return to New York he had directed successful off-Broadway productions of *The Clandestine Marriage* and *The White Devil*. I interviewed him, among many others, and found him unusually intelligent and knowledgeable. At the same time I was vaguely repelled by his somber and unappetizing appearance. He was squat, dark, sallow, with dark hair and the molelike look that very thick lenses give their wearers.

When I began to audition actors for the company he proved invaluable. I noticed that many of the young actors whom I favored had worked with him and admired him and I found him the only person, besides Kirstein and Rosenthal, with whom I could frankly and seriously analyze and discuss the season's artistic and practical problems.

The main responsibility for designing our physical productions fell upon a discovery of Lincoln Kirstein's—a slender, elegant young man with the resonant Armenian name of Rouben Ter-Arutunian. He was born in Russia and reared in Germany; with his shaven head and the dark, liquid eyes of a doe, he resembled a figure in Persian miniature. After weeks at his drawing board—with Jean Rosenthal hovering at his side to check the technical and economic feasibility of his designs—he came up with a model that was startling in its simplicity and beauty and formed the basis of what came to be known as the "Festival Stage."

It was a "floating" architectural unit supported on thin, set-back, almost invisible legs, through which he had solved the double problem of closing in the vast stage and losing the hard frame of the existent proscenium arch. It was one of my requirements for our new stage that it should have the functional qualities of an Elizabethan theater, with its great variety of playing areas and its multiplicity of exits and entrances. On Rouben's new Festival Stage there were *eighteen* of them, including six entrances from the sides, four upstage and the rest served by steps set at various angles together with ramps, counter ramps and strategically located "traps."

The problem of "masking" such a large open area was a serious one. Rouben solved it by hanging walls of thin wooden strips, in double layers, all around the stage in a solid-seeming surface. These were made up of strips of crating, painted various shades of silvery brown, all equally spaced one inch apart and rigged, like a Venetian blind, in such a way that each could move separately and independently up and down to form an infinite variety and combination of shapes that suggested gates, doors, windows, colonnades, tunnels, chambers and passageways.

Most of the ideas for the new stage were developed on Rouben's drawing board, but many of them underwent growth and change as the result of experiments and observations on the stage itself. In fact, some of our problems were not finally solved until we were able to see our actors on the stage during the final week of rehearsal.

Actors' Equity had allowed us six weeks for the rehearsal of our first two plays. Just before we began I went through my usual panic, aggravated by the general sense of anxiety that pervaded the Festival organization. As a result, I found myself turning more and more to Jack Landau for support and counsel. Having less to lose, he seemed less appalled than I was by the perils of the program we were undertaking.

King John was the longer, heavier, and more complicated of our two productions; I began rehearsals with that—with Jack Landau as co-director—and followed it after a few days with *Measure for Measure* which I had intended to direct by myself. But it soon became apparent that these two productions were indivisible. Since rehearsals inevitably overlapped, with many of the company playing important parts in both plays, continuous close cooperation between their directors was essential. In time this became functional and automatic, but during those first weeks it called for exceptional tact and understanding between two men (one half the age of the other) who barely knew each other and had not worked together before. In our dealings with our actors it was essential that we give an impression of complete unity of concept and interpretation. Above all, there must be no suggestion of rivalry.

Rouben's new stage was built in New York and moved to Stratford in sections. Now it had to be installed and lit. This was Jean Rosenthal's domain and here our long, affectionate association proved of immeasurable value. That summer—as at all other times that I worked with her—she showed amazing skill in coordinating the various conflicting elements of production; in spite of her feminine handicap and her diminutive size, she maintained amicable but firm authority over our stagehands—a tough crew most of whom had been imposed on us by the New Haven and local Bridgeport unions.

In the third week of June the entire company of two dozen actors, twenty student apprentices and fourteen technicians, stage managers, wardrobe women and hangers-on moved up to Connecticut. For our children and dogs this was yet another inexplicable change of residence. For Joan, it was one more bewildering episode in a life that was only slightly less confused than my own. Her reaction to New England was conditioned at first by the perpetual chill of a belated spring and by the realization that once again she would be living with a man who was under such stress that, most of the time, he was less than half present and whose emotional crises and releases had almost no relation to her or to the children.

The truth is that during those final weeks of rehearsal, the pressure with which I was living had become almost unbearable. What I was facing was not the normal risk of theatrical success or failure; it was the entire future of an enterprise in which I had become deeply involved and on which I had placed professional and emotional bets that were far beyond my means.

Rouben Ter-Arutunian, besides designing the new Festival Stage and the scenery for our first two productions, was also responsible for our costumes. To convey the archaic, historical tone of the play, it had been agreed that the actors in *King John* should have an oversized, "epic" appearance. Rouben fulfilled the assignment and went beyond it. The costumes he designed, particularly those for the military figures, were not only "epic"; they were gigantic.

For economic and theatrical reasons we had decided against real chain mail. In its place our warriors were encased in padded, oversized suits of armor made up of brightly painted plaques of wood, plastic and synthetic rubber. These were handsome to look at but so bulky that when the actors inside them attempted to move they suggested the inflated figure of the Michelin Man. Besides, they became so costly that they were issued only to kings, nobles and military leaders. For the rest, Rouben raided half the Army and Navy surplus stores in New York and came out with a collection of pea jackets, padded vests, life jackets and rubber rafts which, when cut up and sewn back together into medieval uniforms, delighted him with their formidable mass.

All martial figures were supposed to wear tall leather hip boots. Since these too were far beyond our resources, only the élite received them. The lower ranks were supplied with huge gray-green rubber waders (acquired in stores specializing in fishing equipment) which rose all the way to the crotch and which proved almost impossible to work in on account of their volume and weight but even more because of the fiendish heat generated in their airless depths when the stage lights hit them.

On the day of our dress parade the temperature at Stratford was close to 90 degrees at noon and had gone down only slightly by midafternoon when the company arrived at the theater and began putting on its costumes. From where I sat in the house I became aware of some grumbling rising from the dressing rooms below, which increased as the frailer members of the cast struggled to drag themselves and their boots up the steep steps that led to the stage.

Instead of the usual dress parade, I had decided, for lack of time, on a "run-through" in costume. Early in the first act an apprentice, a stripling in his teens, suddenly collapsed. With all that rubberized material on him he made a strange soft slurping thud as he fell. Peter Zeisler, our production stage manager, appeared from backstage with an assistant and dragged him off while the run-through continued. Rouben was seated beside me taking costume notes; I gave him a questioning look, to which he responded with a shrug. The gravity of our situation was not yet apparent.

Halfway through rehearsal, with the embattled forces of France and England confronting each other while Jean Rosenthal checked and adjusted her light cues, that ghastly slurping thud was heard again and then repeated with increasing frequency as, one after another, singly and in pairs, the warriors of both armies began to collapse. After the seventh had gone down I glanced at Rouben. While he muttered "Amateurs" and "Sabotage," another keeled over and then another and another. Before long there were twelve dehydrated bodies (five nobles and seven soldiers) lying on our new shining platform—some out cold, others still conscious and writhing as they struggled to tear off their boots and jackets.

I called off rehearsal and gave the actors a two-hour dinner break. When they returned from their long dinner they found that their boots and jackets had been punched, pierced, gouged and lacerated to permit the passage of air and the removal of several hundred pounds of cotton padding. During the next few days many additional rents and punctures appeared—most of them made by the actors themselves. By the time we opened, our soldiers had a ragged, thoroughly "medieval" and "epic" appearance and the fainting rate was down to one or two a week.

Except for the costumes, Rouben's scenic conception for *King John* proved handsome and functional. To the accompaniment of Virgil Thomson's somber military fanfares, the tall wooden walls rose and fell in constantly changing shapes and openings that formed a dark, impressive background for the groupings of our actors and permitted the action to move, without delays of laborious scene shifts, through the play's grim world of castles, walled town, camps, battlefields, sea costs and dungeons to its tragic climax in the orchard where the wretched King lies dying in agony to the muffled booming of an abbey bell.

Finally and painfully, we came to our opening night. Following the example set by Stratford, Ontario, it had become the accepted habit of festivals to open the season's first two shows "back to back" on successive nights. The New York and Boston critics (unwilling to make the journey twice) arrived in the afternoon and were dined and wined before attending the first play. They wrote their reviews on the premises, phoned them in in time for the final edition and then went to bed and rested until the following evening, when they covered the second show before departing. This was rough on the company and the crew and often resulted in productions being reviewed before they had a chance to shake down. But it did substantially improve the odds of our getting quotable reviews from a first-string critic at the start of the season.

I had always known (and it had become daily more evident) that

King John's chances of receiving general approval were slim indeed. I figured that to follow this crude and savage historical tragedy with a sophisticated comedy like *Measure for Measure* would form a valuable contrast and would offer convincing proof of the range and versatility of our new Festival Company. Now this elaborate and risky strategy was about to be put to the test.

Among the mixed reactions to *King John* one drama critic had commented that "the Stratford authorities are beginning to find the nucleus of a young, vigorous, well-spoken company," but added, "the salvo that will announce the contemporary American theater's coming of age in its long bout with Shakespeare has yet to be fired."

So now our survival hung precariously on the fate of *Measure for Measure,* which the crew had set up during the night and which was about to open in a few hours. It was a frail vessel into which to pour so much hope.

During our final pre-opening period Jeannie and I had fallen back into the patterns of those earlier times with the Mercury when we were spending days and nights together in our darkened theater, slowly and painfully making our way through scene after scene, discussing effects, setting focuses and organizing transitions for the next run-through. Around six in the morning, with sunlight pouring in through the skylights in the stage-house, we would finally quit, go to our separate houses, sleep an hour or two, eat breakfast and be back in the theater in time for technical rehearsal at ten. These hours of shared exhaustion and exhilaration created an intimacy between us that was far closer than if we had spent the night making love.

June 27 was such a time. Most of the night had been spent changing sets and setting lights: at 10 a.m. a technical rehearsal was scheduled; a preview with an invited audience at 1:30; a formal opening at 7:30.

Though the crew was dead on its feet, the changeover and the morning's technical rehearsal had gone smoothly. Seated next to Jean Rosenthal in the auditorium as she called and checked her light cues, I found myself marvelling at the changes our stage had undergone since the night before. For *King John,* our hanging "slats" had been used as vast, dark surfaces—the somber walls of fortresses and dungeons and the stormy backgrounds of battles and midnight slayings. The same slats—with the addition of a great chandelier, crimson draperies, garish lighted windows, prison bars and the shadows of trees—were now illuminated to suggest the ducal palace, streets, a brothel, a jail and public gardens. Our props included chains and manacles, festoons of flags for the finale, a leather hatbox capable of holding a severed head, two pedigreed wolfhounds and a headsman's block.

Our actors had been called for noon. As they straggled into the basement they were tense and gloomy from reading their *King John* reviews which had reached Stratford during the morning. While they were getting into their costumes (lighter and more colorful than those of the previous night) the crew returned from lunch and Jeannie had them check a few final focuses. The 32-foot ladder was dragged up onto the stage and set up on the slanting surface of Rouben's platform. When it was steadied, Joe Patterson, our head electrician (who had been with us at the Mercury nineteen years before), clambered up it; with his legs wrapped tightly around its swaying upper extension, he reached out perilously for the instruments hanging high up inside the proscenium and adjusted them to Rosenthal's specifications. When he was done there were still a few minutes left before we let the audience into the house—just enough time to slip a crimson velvet sheath over the bare wires that held up the main chandelier in the ducal palace.

While "half hour" was being called over the intercom, an electrician, a burly middle-aged local grip, started up the ladder; halfway he turned and the red sheath was handed up to him. Drawing it up behind him, he climbed on up to the top and reached out to slip it over the bare, hanging wires. He couldn't quite reach it. He shifted his weight, reached far out, slipped and lost his balance. We saw it happen; he hung in the air for a moment while the sheath, like a long, writhing, crimson snake, fell out of his hand to the floor. A fraction of a second later his body followed it down. It took him a long time to fall those 32 feet and he landed on his buttocks and the small of his back with a grunt and a dull, hollow sound.

There, for two or three seconds, he lay quite still. Then the men who had been holding the ladder ran forward to where he lay. He stirred. He wasn't dead. Spread-eagled on the floor on his back he looked older and heavier than he had in the air. As someone ran to telephone for an ambulance he moved slightly—first an arm, then one leg—till Joe Patterson ordered him to stay still. Down in the basement, over the intercom, the actors had heard the sound of the fall and the sudden silence that followed. Some of them came up, half dressed, and now they stared in shock at the body.

As I stood there, beside Joe and Rosenthal, looking down at the dark, motionless form and hoping desperately that he was not seriously hurt, my thoughts were less for the injured man than for myself and the Festival. With that hollow thud, my last hope had been shattered. Tired and enervated as they were, the crew would not go back to work—certainly not until a report had been received from the hospital. And by that time it would be too late and the preview would have to be canceled. Without it, the evening's opening would be a shambles.

I could cancel that too, invoking the accident as an excuse. In that case the first-string critics would go home (there was no hope of holding them for a third night) and their judgment of our season would be based entirely on their dubious appraisal of *King John*. In that case the Festival was down the drain.

All this had taken half a minute or less. And then suddenly, as I watched in amazement, Joe Patterson got up from beside the still-motionless body, gave Jean Rosenthal a quick, knowing look, walked briskly over to the foot of the ladder, where the red velvet sheath lay coiled on the floor. He picked it up and started to climb. The men, grouped around their injured comrade, looked up, hesitated, then moved forward to the base of the ladder and held it firm. High above them, with his legs wrapped tightly around the top rung while he strained to slide the long sheath over the wires, Patterson continued to issue orders for the coming run-through. Again the men hesitated, then moved at his bidding. By the time he was down and the ladder was dragged off the stage, the paralysis was over and morale had been restored.

Jean was still checking cues when the house was finally opened and actors began to take their positions backstage. The preview had been delayed a few minutes while the paramedics carried the man to the waiting ambulance. It was evident by then that his injuries were not grievous. (He was back at work within a week.)

Measure for Measure opened with a fanfare of hunting horns as a small procession of pink-coated retainers appeared at the head of the stairs, carrying the departing Duke's belongings to the carriages waiting below and leading two magnificent wolfhounds tugging at the leash. As the Duke (in an Inverness cape) and Escalus (in a stovepipe hat) followed them onstage, they got weak applause from the small audience.

That afternoon's run-through was tense, slow and labored—a perfect preparation for whirling action of that evening's opening performance. It was as though all the frustrations of *King John* and all the adrenalin accumulated during the near-tragedy of the afternoon had been suddenly released into a show that went far beyond anything that had been seen in rehearsal. It was the first time the play had been seen by a real audience, and their delighted reaction made it clear that we had found the right formula for this equivocal play. There was enthusiastic applause, but that did not prevent the critics, scuttling silently up the aisle, from looking blank and mysterious as they followed our press agent towards the building where they would be writing their reviews.

At the opening-night party which was given in the lobby of the theater (under the eye of Van Soest's celebrated portrait of the Bard that had been presented to the Festival by Lincoln Kirstein) spirits were high. Everyone was exhausted and so eager to relax after the exhilaration of the recent performance that the dubious reviews of *King John* were forgotten.

Then, just after midnight, when the gaiety was at its height, the second dramatic event of the day occurred. When our press agent arrived at the party (after taking care of the critics, helping them to make their telephone connections and escorting them to their cars) he reported that Brooks Atkinson (who wrote his reviews in longhand) had been the last to leave and had apologized for taking so long. After he had finally driven off, Ben had gone back into the house to lock up. On an impulse he had glanced into the wastebasket beneath the desk where Atkinson had been writing. In it he had found a small, dark, crumpled ball of carbon paper which he now handed to me.

I snatched it and ran with it to my office, followed by Landau and a secretary hastily plucked from the party. By holding the creased carbon up against the light, we were just able to make out what, it now appeared, was the first page of Atkinson's all-important handwritten review for the *New York Times*.

It took some time to decipher and for the secretary to type. When it was done I rushed out, broke up the party and read it out loud:

A LOVELY, ROLLICKING FARCE AT STRATFORD

To play *Measure for Measure* in modern dress as the American Shakespeare Festival did last evening is to accomplish two things that are not in the rule book. A complicated harum-scarum plot becomes simple and clear. An acrid comedy becomes amiable and pleasant. Add something else to these attractive dividends: the company plays *Measure for Measure* with elegance, humor and harmony. Shakespeare's bitterest comedy has never seemed so delightful and the acting on the Stratford stage has never seemed so accomplished. I urge you—

There the page ended, but it was enough. The cheering and the huzzahs went on and on. Though there was a matinée of *Measure* the next afternoon, no one went to bed before dawn, waiting for the phone calls to come through from New York with the rest of the reviews. Almost all were good; some were raves—including the rest of Brooks Atkinson's in the *Times*, in which he described *Measure for Measure* as "a particularly winning piece of theater—lightly devised, ingeniously staged, played lightly. It deserves a hundred and one performances in this inviting theater on the Housatonic River."

On the night of June 27, 1956, the tide turned for the American Shakespeare Festival Theater at Stratford, Connecticut. Attendance remained spotty over the Fourth of July, then built gradually through July and August, when *The Taming of the Shrew* was added to the repertory and the number of performances of *King John* was reduced. By the end of August, standing room only was habitual on weekends.

Our third show, *The Taming of the Shrew*, had been selected as a concession to conventional programming. When I first announced it I was not at all sure it would ever reach the stage. But after the success of *Measure* and with the steady growth of our audiences, its production became a necessity—one that caught me unprepared. Neither Landau nor I was eager to direct it; we were both exhausted and felt that to make *Shrew* viable, a fresh, entirely new energy was needed. This was supplied by my friend Norman Lloyd, who had played the fool for me in *Lear* years ago and who had just scored brilliantly for us as Lucio in *Measure*. He had worked with our actors before and his early vaudeville background made him the perfect director to galvanize that old piece into new, comic theatrical life.

He did a wonderfully theatrical job. The *New York Times* was enchanted by the "inspired madness" of the production and declared, "It would have surprised no one if Harpo Marx had suddenly been lowered from the ceiling on a rope."

With full houses and no more productions to worry about, life was becoming leisurely and agreeable on the banks of the Housatonic. It had been a good season: the weather was beautiful, morale was high, and I was becoming visible, occasionally, to my wife and children.

Around the middle of August I talked with the executive committee about the Festival situation and about my own plans. I made it clear that my own Hollywood commitment was irrevocable and I gave them my views on the future of the Festival and repeated these in letter to the Board.

After all the work and hopes we've put into this venture, is it to be no more than a summer theater? Is that really all you want? Or does the Festival Company offer the basis for the foundation of a permanent American Acting Company? Aren't you interested in that?

Then, just before Labor Day, with the Festival in its final week, I read in the *New York Times* one morning that there had been a blowup at the MGM Studio and that Dore Schary was out as head of production. I called my agents, who confirmed the news.

So now (as so often in my life) everything was suddenly and totally changed. With Schary gone, I would be the lame-duck survivor of a discredited regime, at the mercy of whatever new executive was brought in to run the studio. I remembered my bad times at RKO and shuddered and took another look at my future. If I went back to California I would be, at best, repeating something I had already achieved. To stay in the East and to create the first American classical repertory company seemed in every way a more exciting prospect. The enormous drop in income which it entailed played almost no part in my thinking: my behavior about money has always been entirely irrational.

I called Lincoln Kirstein and informed him confidentially of the situation. There was the expected resistance from Langner and it was not until after the trees in New City had begun to change their color that I was able to inform my poor wife that she would be spending the next few years on the Eastern seaboard. Lawyers were summoned and an agreement was drawn up in which I was named Artistic Director of the Festival (with Jack Landau as my associate) for the next three years, with the same authority as I had demanded and obtained during my first year. Throughout these negotiations I used my film contract as leverage. Now, on October 16, a telegram was sent to my agents in California to negotiate a settlement with MGM "on the best possible terms."

By now I was in a hurry to abrogate my film contract—not only because of Stratford but for another reason altogether.

XXII
Festival: Othello, The Merchant
and Much Ado
1957

Early in October Louis Cowan asked me to lunch with him in the Oak Room of the Plaza Hotel in New York. He and I had worked together on the Voice of America, where he was our contact with the Pentagon on the shows we were broadcasting to our armed forces all over the world. We had remained friends ever since.

In private life, before the war, Cowan had been a public relations expert specializing in religious groups; he had gone on to become a successful producer of radio programs, including *The Quiz Kids* which he created and owned and which he later transferred to television together with a number of other nationally rated quiz shows. As a result, he had recently been offered and accepted the presidency of CBS Television, to whose vast profits his programs had substantially contributed.

Like many of his kind Cowan combined a sincere yearning for "better things" with a shrewd, irresistible appetite for money and I listened with wandering attention while he outlined his plans for the network. He seemed particularly excited over a new show—*The Seven Lively Arts*—that was to be broadcast on Sunday afternoons. With dessert he came to the point: since I was known to be "ass-deep in culture" (sic), I might be the very man the network was looking for to develop and produce this prestigious project.

I rose to the bait and within a few days I had met with Hubbell Robinson, head of production for CBS, and with "the chairman," William Paley himself, with whom I had not communicated since the "Men from Mars." Three weeks later, on the same day that I signed my contract with the American Shakespeare Festival Theater, I signed a two-year contract (for more money than I had ever earned before) to produce *The Seven Lively Arts* for CBS Television.

No one questioned the propriety of my conducting the Festival season and the *Seven Lively Arts* series at the same time and I was careful not to raise the point with either organization. As a result, beginning in mid-November, I began to divide my days between the preparation of my next Stratford season and the long-range task of creating an organization capable of conceiving, organizing and broadcasting twenty-six original hour-long television shows.

The more I looked into it, the more evident it became that *The Seven Lively Arts* was a project about which everyone was enthusiastic but no one had any clear or definite ideas—beyond the feeling that it must be original, entertaining, instructive, prestigious and, of course, popular. With so much lead time (it was not due to go on the air until November 1957) my initial approach to its problems was leisurely and discursive. Dozens of ideas and projects were discussed, considered, developed or rejected: they comprised "live" drama, film documentary, animation, music, dance—or all of them combined. To develop a series of shows out of such infinite possibilities three teams were chosen for their diverse talents and for their experience in various forms of television. It became their collective assignment to convert these sundry notions into viable television programs.

The first of these units was under Robert Herridge—a young TV writer and director, with the head of a gladiator and a rising reputation for serious "live" television drama. To balance him (on Ed Murrow's recommendation) I engaged "Shad" Northshield, a man dedicated to the creative recording of documentary material, whom I named head of our film unit. Finally, from California, I summoned Jud Kinberg (who had been my associate producer on eight films at MGM) and invited him to join my own production unit on *The Seven Lively Arts.*

Having set up the beginnings of an organization capable of producing the most hazardous and highly publicized series of the 1957-58 television season, I continued to devote the greater part of my time that winter and spring to the preparation of my Stratford program.

Our first season had been successful without the presence of major stars. Now, with our artistic credit somewhat restored, Langner had made approaches behind my back to a number of stars of whom a few had expressed interest but made no commitment. I was not surprised or disappointed; I continued to believe that our most important task was the development of a company of our own and that we must eventually create our own stars through the performances they gave on our stage. On the other hand, as a Shakespeare festival, we could no longer avoid presenting at least one of the major tragedies each season. How to cast it? We had no outstanding Hamlet in the company. No

Macbeth. No Lear. We did have an Othello.

A young black actor named Earle Hyman had played Othello off-Broadway with considerable success. Now, some years later, it seemed good repertory policy to let him play it again on a bigger stage, with a stronger company and a larger audience. Also, as it happened, I had an excellent Iago.

Alfred Drake was an actor with whom I had worked before and in whom I had great faith. Knowing how eager he was to get out of musical theater into classical acting, for which he was thoroughly trained, I asked him if he would like to play Iago; he said yes and inquired what his other part would be. While I was preparing to answer him, something happened that caused our whole summer's repertory to fall suddenly into place.

Lawrence Langner was a man of great tenacity. He had never accepted Kate Hepburn's refusal of his invitation to appear in Stratford that summer. Early in March, when he called her for the umpteenth time, she told him she might, after all, be able to join us. Her first suggestion, as a part for herself, was Portia in *The Merchant of Venice*, in which she had appeared with the Old Vic Company on a recent Australian tour.

Following the horrors of the Holocaust, *The Merchant* had been rigidly excluded from the American theater as offensively anti-Semitic. During the previous season, however, we had placed a questionnaire in our program listing eight of Shakespeare's plays and asking the audiences to number them in the order of their preference. To our intense surprise the choice,well ahead of *Hamlet* and *Midsummer Night's Dream*—had been *The Merchant of Venice*. This enabled us to accede to Miss Hepburn's request; it also allowed us to offer a great role to a member of our own company. If there was one actor in America physically and mentally capable of playing Shylock as an understandable and tragic rather than a hateful or grotesque figure, it was Morris Carnovsky, who had served his classical apprenticeship with us the previous season.

One further decision remained to be made. Both Kate and Alfred had made it a condition of their coming to Stratford that they each appear in *two* plays. Since we now had in our company a lively Beatrice and an eloquent Benedick, it did not take long to decide what our third production would be.

So, finally, we proudly announced our repertory for the American Shakespeare Festival's 1957 season: *Othello, The Merchant of Venice,* and *Much Ado about Nothing*. And we were able, in our brochures and advertisements, to blazon the names of our two bright stars, Hepburn and Drake.

The results—in press coverage and advance sales—were immediately perceptible. But the problem of absorbing two such luminaries into the company was a serious and delicate one—particularly in the case of Miss Hepburn, who was an international star and who was known to be willful, opinionated and domineering and to have Lawrence Langner under her thumb. Following our first interview with her in her small house in Turtle Bay, Jack Landau and I spent hours in earnest consultation as to how to deal with this magnetic personality without endangering the morale of our young company. We decided that I would start the season with *Othello* while Landau took on *The Merchant*—with me standing by and ready to throw my weight around in case of emergency.

By and large this strategy worked, though it did not take into account Kate's overwhelming charm and the fact that, within two days of the start of rehearsal, not only Landau but everyone else had fallen deeply and irresistibly under her spell. Kate, on her part, soon came to appreciate the quality of the company. When the star problem did come up, it occurred not with Kate but over *Othello*.

When he played Othello off-Broadway, Earle Hyman had been surrounded by actors whom he dominated. With Drake he found himself confronted by an Iago who had the weight and presence of an established star in addition to a superb baritone voice—more trained and powerful than Earle's. If there is one quality that is essential for an effective performance of *Othello*, it is the ability to dominate the stage at all times. Hyman did not have it. I had hoped he would achieve it through the intensity of his passion but, for all his fine figure and the striking costumes Ter-Arutunian had designed for him, it was Iago to whom you gave your attention when they were on stage together. As a director I did what I could to redress the balance. I should have done more. I knew Hyman was going through hell and I was torn between pity and exasperation that made it difficult for me to help him. As we approached our opening night his mental distress was transformed into physical failure: his voice began to go. The local doctor diagnosed laryngitis, for which he attempted to give local relief. At our final preview our Othello was virtually inaudible and I sat up half the night with Landau and our press agent going over possible alternatives, including postponement, all of which were disastrous.

Early on the next morning one of our stage managers drove Hyman to New York to visit the country's leading throat specialist, who, as expected, forbade him to open his mouth for a week. Under protest, he gave him emergency treatment, and that evening we opened with an Othello who was muted but audible through the first half of the play.

Our reviews were about as expected. The *New York Times* wrote of a "fine but lopsided presentation in which Iago is so splendidly acted that our sympathy is with him rather than with the Othello," whose performance he described as "more like a chronicle in small beer than a bath in steepdown gulfs of liquid fire." Once the trauma of the opening had worn off, Hyman's voice and courage slowly returned. Later reviewers compared his Othello favorably with that of Paul Robeson; but the harm was done.

Miss Hepburn arrived the day after the opening of *Othello* and immediately went into rehearsal. Working on *Merchant* while playing *Othello* eight times a week did not leave members of the company much leisure, but they seemed to find time for swimming, sunbathing, shopping, lovemaking and some social intercourse, most of which took place late at night after the show in the back room of the town's single, depressing bar known as Ryan's. If the tone of the summer was generally more relaxed and playful than that of the previous year, this was due mainly to the influence of Miss Hepburn, whose presence in our midst was pervasive, inescapable and very welcome.

As an inducement to come to Stratford, Langner had offered her a number of historic houses. She chose instead a red, broken-down fisherman's shack built over the Housatonic River which, at that point, swollen by the tides, runs wide and strong into Long Island Sound. She moved into these cramped quarters while her ever present companion and secretary occupied a room with a local family across the road. According to a local reporter:

She sleeps in a screened-in porch where, early in the morning, she hears the birds call from a marsh across the river and, underneath her, the water laps gently at the pilings. The other day she spied a white heron. She has a red outboard motorboat. Recently, when the wind-gauge was registering seventy miles an hour in gusts, she was in her boat getting drenched by the water and reveling in it.

In her contacts with the company Kate was friendly but wholly professional. She had her favorites, but her favors were bestowed, generally, only on those whose work or character she respected. She admired audacity and strength in others; any show of weakness or fear or undue complication brought out the worst in her. She was opinionated and bossy and, in her determination to have her way, she used charm and the weight of her prestige in equal proportions. Landau was putty in her strong, slender hands.

But where Kate's influence was really decisive was in the matter of company morale which needed bolstering after the early dubious reaction to *Othello*. Here she proved an unqualified asset. The conscientiousness of her professional behavior, the fact that, from the first day of rehearsal, she was line-perfect, the first to arrive and the last to leave, a model of dedicated and concentrated energy—all this had a salutary effect on members of the company, who (though some of them may have questioned her presence in the beginning) now derived comforting reassurance from their association throughout the summer with a major star to whom they knew they owed the exhilaration of the full and enthusiastic houses to which they found themselves playing.

Rehearsals for *Merchant* went smoothly, with Landau fighting a rearguard action to retain some of his own ideas. What might have been a problem was avoided by the circumstance that, except for their final confrontation in court, Portia and Shylock never appear on stage together. This meant that Jack could rehearse Kate and Carnovsky separately in their own styles and with their own very different approaches to the play. Kate's manners were perfect and she never, directly or through Landau, attempted to influence or even to comment on a conception of Shylock that differed radically from the baroque manner in which Robert Helpmann had played the part on their recent, joint tour of Australia. When Portia and the Jew finally did meet in the Doge's court, her very personal and surprisingly subdued rendering of the famous "Mercy" speech (of which one critic wrote that "she so breaks it up that she seems literally to have forgotten her lines") could not fail to affect and condition Shylock's behavior in his climactic scene.

The Merchant of Venice opened on July 10 to phenomenal business and mixed reviews. But there was one subject on which there was unanimous agreement: Carnovsky's Shylock. The *New York Times* reported, "He has delivered to us a performance that is a beautiful counterpoint of comedy, romance, melodrama and pathos." Henry Hewes described it as "the best major performance in the three-year history of the Festival." John Gassner affirmed, "If ever there was a better Shylock than Carnovsky's in the entire stage history of *The Merchant of Venice*, it is not apparent to me from my personal experience or my reading."

Kate took her mixed notices in stride (she was quite accustomed to them). So did the trustees of the Festival, who found in the lines at our box office and the enthusiasm of our audiences more than sufficient compensation for a few critical reservations.

It was Kate's idea, I believe, to move *Much Ado about Nothing* from fifteenth-century Italy to nineteenth-century Texas. It worked wonderfully well. The great house with its flocks of armed and unarmed servants; the comic-opera plots and forays; the morality surrounding the courtship of the ingénue and the exaggerated sense of family honor; finally, the translation of Dogberry from rural constable to Texas sheriff; these all made perfect sense on the banks of the Rio Grande. Kate and the ladies of the house looked ravishing in their mantillas and, in their tight embroidered pants and jackets, our men looked like a troupe of sexy bullfighters, choreographed to their best advantage by George Balanchine in the masked, ballroom scene.

For the first time in a year Jack Landau and I were once again co-directing. Our relations, after two years of working together, had become somewhat like those of a pilot with his co-pilot. The final decisions were mine but, for functional collaboration in running every aspect of the Festival, I counted on him continually and without reservation.

The next problem we found ourselves facing was one created by the presence on our stage of two very different stars. Kate's self-confidence was the result of years of stardom in the theater and in motion pictures. Drake's position in the theater had been achieved as the star of such enormously successful musicals as *Oklahoma!*, *Kiss Me Kate* and *Kismet*. As a proud and ardent Italian baritone, it had been his habit, whenever possible, to extend his romantic stage association with his current leading lady into real life. I am sure that he cherished no serious hope of adding Miss Hepburn to his conquests but he did, I suspect, entertain visions of a gallant, glamorous stage relationship with his fellow star.

Kate's idea of fun was altogether different. She loved a fight, a contest of wills in which her regard for her antagonist varied in direct proportion to the energy with which he returned her assaults. With her Benedick, she may have felt that such backstage sparring would add spice and vitality to their onstage courtship. When Drake stubbornly refused her challenge, she pressed her mocking provocations, hoping to sting him into some kind of suitable masculine retort. Alfred refused to play her game and made it clear that he found her behavior unfeminine and unprofessional.

These one-sided skirmishes extended into rehearsal. In their scenes together Drake was a polished, witty, somewhat conventional and slightly pompous wooer; Kate countered with readings that were so outrageous and bits of mischief so brash and unexpected that they threw him off balance—as she intended them to. And she laughed at him in front of the company.

The day came when he could stand it no longer. When I went backstage after one particularly lively rehearsal, I found Kate, whose dressing room I visited first, weary but exhilarated, like an athlete after a stiff contest in which she felt herself the winner. When I went to Alfred's room he handed me his resignation. I reminded him that he had a contract; he declared that he refused to work with that bitch.

That storm blew over and Kate tempered her aggressions. But she and Alfred never entirely forgave each other. Onstage they finally became an accomplished, humorous and attractive couple, but they never quite formed the glamorous team they might have been.

XXIII
Seven Lively Arts
1957-58

Since the Festival company had been playing, for its last seven weeks, to total capacity, our Stratford season was extended for one week beyond our announced closing day of September 7. By then, I was back in New York struggling with the prodigious task of readying *The Seven Lively Arts* for the air.

My three teams had done their work over the spring and summer: we had five shows approved and ready. But my personal efforts in the weeks that followed were concentrated on the preparation of what was to be our first, all-important broadcast. It was called "The Changing Ways of Love" and it was the network's idea of a blockbuster which I had accepted with some reservation. It was an ambitious venture: it was also a risky one with which to start a series that was already suspect and controversial and still lacked a commercial sponsor.

The idea was to investigate and illustrate the changing sexual, social and sentimental behavior of American men and women over the past thirty years, as revealed and exploited through popular examples of theater, film, music, drama, radio and, finally, television.

Using the overwhelming mass of research that Kinberg and his staff had accumulated over the summer, "The Changing Ways of Love" was divided into three parts:

1/ The Jazz Age of the Booming Twenties;
2/ The Years of the Great Depression;
3/ World War II and its Aftermath.

Each of the sections would have its own narrator whose reports would be introduced and coordinated by our own master of ceremonies, who would thus assume a position of great importance and would help to set the tone and character of the entire show. To discover a suitable MC for this and subsequent programs occupied much of our time and thought, as we sought to find a figure who would give an impression of authority, erudition and charm.

Finally he was found. 1957 was the year in which the quiz shows reached the peak of their popularity. The most successful of these pseudointellectual contests was *Twenty-One*, from which a young scholar named Charles Van Doren had recently emerged to win the hearts of the entire nation. He had everything in his favor—youth, looks, distinction and brains: he was even sexy in a scholarly way. By midsummer (after two epic struggles in which he defeated a sophisticated jockey and a well-informed but unlikeable professor) his winnings exceeded $100,000 and he had made the cover of *Time*.

At that point the network decided that Charles Van Doren would indeed make the perfect master of ceremonies for *The Seven Lively Arts* and contracts were being drawn up when, suddenly, the sky darkened. An insidious rumor began to circulate of skulduggery on the quiz shows; it was suggested and then confirmed that certain candidates had been given advance notice of subjects and questions. At the first suggestion that young Mr. Van Doren's encyclopedic knowledge might not be entirely his own, the world turned against him; national enthusiasm changed to fury, admiration to contempt. He was hauled before a grand jury, exposed and stripped of his ill-gotten gains, including his contract with CBS on which the ink was not yet dry.

We had little time left in which to find a substitute. Clifton Fadiman, of the *New Yorker*, who had once been a leading candidate, was no longer available, and things were beginning to look grim when the heads of the network had a second inspiration—John Crosby. Such was their excitement at discovering that he was available that he was engaged before I had a chance to meet him.

There is no equivalent today of John Crosby. He belongs to the Golden Age of Television: as critic and columnist for the *Herald Tribune* syndicate, he had, within a few years, established a unique national reputation for literate, independent and fearless reviewing that made him the darling of the middle-brows and the terror of networks and advertisers. His highly publicized and ethically dubious appointment as master of ceremonies for *The Seven Lively Arts* received a predictably mixed reception in the press and in the trades but generated a lot of publicity as we met to discuss the nature of his functions on the show.

He was to act as general consultant on the series (most of which was already prepared and written); he was to create and edit his own material and he was to speak it on the air. It was in this final capacity that he came to play a tragic part in the future of the series.

John Crosby's charisma was essentially literary. In person he was mild-mannered and myopic. And, though this was by no means abnormal or shameful, I felt that thick glasses would not add to his popular image as our jaunty MC. I suggested that he visit an oculist and get a prescription for the new contact lenses that had recently come into general use. He agreed and the most expensive optician in the city was put to work on two pairs of contact lenses with the assurance that they would be available long before the start of rehearsals.

With that detail satisfactorily disposed of I was able to turn my attention to other more urgent matters of production. By mid-October we were able to announce the line-up of our first three broadcasts and the elements of our opening show seemed to be falling into place.

"The Changing Ways of Love" was an elaborate contraption—half film and half "live"—complete with animations, dancing girls, dramatic sketches and social commentary. At our first reading Crosby appeared without his glasses (a distinct improvement in his public persona) and though he complained mildly about his new lenses they enabled him to read without difficulty. During the next few days, as we ran through the show, he seemed to be at ease and to have no problem following his cue cards.

On Saturday, November 2, halfway through our final on-camera rehearsal and twenty-four hours before air time, Crosby asked to speak with me in private and informed me that his lenses were driving him mad—to the point where he had decided to appear without them. I said if that's how he felt, he should go back to wearing his glasses. He said he wasn't going to do that either. He assured me that he had a prodigious memory and was entirely confident of his ability to MC the show without either glasses or lenses. I objected but he was adamant.

The atmosphere in the studio was tense that Sunday but not more so than at most premières of a major TV show. I was tired and nervous; Kinberg, as usual, was wallowing in anxiety and despair. Yet, our dress rehearsal at noon had gone surprisingly well for such an elaborate show. Crosby was a bit stiff, but he sounded intelligent and sincere and he seemed quite capable of deciphering and/or memorizing his cue cards. At 3:55 p.m., we retired into the control room and sat staring at the studio's electric clock as its second hand moved towards air time. We had piles of telegrams of good wishes from both coasts.

A few seconds after four we went on the air. We opened with a carefully selected gallery of the love goddesses of the twenties—Swanson, Pickford, Naldi, Bow, the Talmadge sisters, Harlow, Garbo and the rest. "This is the face of love," Crosby declared as the montage ended and he himself made his first appearance in a close shot that filled the screen. He informed the nation that his name was John Crosby and that this was the opening program in a new series called *The Seven Lively Arts*. He explained that our first show was about Love:

Because love is not only an art in itself but is the constant theme that runs through all the other arts. Love, theoretically, is eternal. Its objectives and techniques shouldn't change much whether you are in a penthouse or a haystack. They shouldn't, but they have. How? Let's go back to the twenties and find out. For this leg in the journey we have with us—

The world never found out what we had. For, at that moment, Crosby's voice stopped in midsentence and a look of abject panic came over his face. For a second or two we waited, confident that he would recover himself and go on. Instead, the face on the monitor froze; the mouth went slack, then hung open like that of a dead man. The only thing that remained alive in his sweating face were the eyes, desperately attempting to focus on the boob card that the assistant was waving in front of him. Then, as he gave up, the eyes, too, glazed into a rigid stare of utter despair.

In the control room we sat helpless and numb with horror. No one moved. Even our technical director's hands seemed frozen to the controls. (The next day, running the kinescope of the show, we clocked the time during which millions of Americans stared at the silent death mask of John Crosby. It added up to eighteen and a half seconds. It seemed like six months. And it made TV history.) Finally, like members of Sleeping Beauty's court, we returned to life. Orders flashed over the intercom. Our dancing girls, warming up in a neighboring studio, were herded onto the set and into the "Black Bottom." Sid Perelman, the narrator-historian of our first act, pacing nervously backstage behind a flat, was grabbed and hustled before a camera which caught him in a state of bewildered alarm as Crosby's voice, partially restored, reading from a cue card that the assistant was holding directly under his nose, introduced him as "S.J. Perelman, the celebrated humorist, Academy Award winner for the screenplay of *Around the World in Eighty Days* and himself a survivor of the reckless twenties." Whereupon Perelman, his glasses flashing and his voice supercharged with forced gaiety, heroically launched his jocular commentary into a void of bewilderment and despair.

Slowly the blood began to flow back into our bodies. We were still alive, but we were ruined and we knew it. Such an occurrence on major network television was unprecedented and unforgivable. After such a disgrace there was only one way to go—to disappear and never come back! But, for the moment, we had no choice; we had to go on with the show and it was agony. As face after glamorous face appeared on the monitor, they all seemed to be smiling at our humiliation. The frantic dances of the twenties were dances of death; Rudy Vallee, whose voice Perelman introduced as "the velvety, nasal woodnotes of our first radio troubador," was crooning our funeral dirge. It was not until we were deep into the erotic melancholy of Scott Fitzgerald's "Winter Dreams" that the show finally moved back into focus.

"It was a wonderful world while it lasted," observed Perelman as the lovers went off into the dark to the strains of a Cole Porter melody and the sudden sharp clicking of the ticker tape announced to the world that the great Crash of 1929 was upon us—and that the first act of "The Changing Ways of Love" was finally and mercifully over!

During the station break I ran down into the studio to restore morale and to check on Crosby's condition. He seemed to have recovered some of his composure—or maybe he was still in shock. He looked pale but determined as he prepared for the second act—the Years of the Great Depression—of which he was himself the narrator and which contained, among other things, a scene from Clifford Odets's *Awake and Sing*. Our third act, whose presiding deities were Hayworth, Grable, Lamour, Sinatra and Presley, dealt with the sexual revolution brought about by World War II and was efficiently narrated by that relentless investigator, Mike Wallace.

Our reviews were about as expected.

ROMANCE AT RANDOM

A CONFUSED, INERT PICTURE OF LOVE

Reported the *New York Times*, while *Variety* pronounced it "a lively if not entirely inspired hour."

Predictably, the critics' principal victim was John Crosby, whose colleagues from coast to coast made no attempt to conceal their delight over his discomfiture. They found in his "cathode baptism" comforting evidence that "critics can be human" and "should be read and not seen." They reported gleefully that "he was better at roasting than hosting" and "tense as a terrified titmouse." Others were even more personal: "Crosby grunted as if in constant pain and close-ups did him few favors for they presented his face with a seemingly endless mouth which, when speaking, seemed to be pulled apart vertically by unseen strings."

*

One of the blessings of television is that it leaves you no time to brood over your failures. Within hours we were in rehearsal with our second show—"The World of Nick Adams." This was a loose assembly of five early stories by Ernest Hemingway, produced by Robert Herridge and directed "live" with simplicity and feeling by Robert Mulligan. (On neither this nor the next show did Crosby have much to say on camera.) Our third, produced by Shad Northshield, investigated the behavior of "those men and women, black and white, who dedicate their fanatical energy to bringing people to God." It started with film footage from the Deep South, where, in a broken-down barn, a black preacher, Cat-Iron Carradino, whipped his ragged congregation into a rising fever of frenzied devotion. This was followed by scenes of immersion, some "healing" rituals and brief visits to Billy Sunday and Aimee Semple McPherson. The last third of the broadcast was devoted to that most successful of all modern evangelists, Billy Graham. According to *Time*:

After scoring last week with "The World of Nick Adams," *The Seven Lively Arts* established itself as one of the season's brightest new corners with "The Revivalists."

But, in the harsh world of national network television, a series is judged by the success of its première. Since ours was generally considered a disaster, we found ourselves more than once, in the months to come, replaced by football games and other, more popular network events. And around CBS and the industry in general I felt myself treated with nervous commiseration as the leprous creator of the season's biggest turkey.

We continued to turn out shows, including a "filmed essay" by E.B. White and two programs produced in collaboration with the choreographers George Balanchine and Agnes De Mille. Then, before the end of the year, we delivered a blockbuster:

The Seven Lively Arts came into its own yesterday with a brilliant and exciting program on Jazz. The spontaneity and artistry of modern music were presented with more authenticity, understanding and appreciation than television has ever managed before.

Historically the show was notable for being one of the last public appearances of the great Billie Holiday before her final eclipse and death. Among other jazz giants scattered around the sound stage were Count Basie, Lionel Hampton, Teddy Wilson, Thelonious Monk, PeeWee Russell, Coleman Hawkins, Jimmy Giuffre and Roy Eldridge.

*

The Seven Lively Arts left the air prematurely but with honor. For our final broadcast we presented what I still believe to be one of the most moving dramatic broadcasts I have ever been associated with. "The Blast in Centralia Number Five" was the true story, reported in *Harper's* magazine by John Bartlow Martin, of an Illinois mine disaster that cost 120 lives. It was a tragedy that everyone knew was coming and that no one, neither management nor the union nor the U.S. Bureau of Mines, made one single move to prevent.

Its dramatization, which combined documentary realism with personal tragedy, was directed by George Roy Hill and performed by Maureen Stapleton and Jason Robards; it evoked tributes that were emotional and nationwide: "A truly great example of television at its finest.' 'A tragic, memorable documentary." "A searing indictment of government red tape, of big business, of union inertia and of a politically appointed bureaucracy."

It was ironic that these tributes were also our obituaries. This, our final show, was broadcast on the afternoon of Sunday, February 16, 1958, after eleven shows instead of the originally scheduled twenty-six. We had been off the air for some months when we received the National Academy of Television Arts and Sciences' Award for the best new program of the 1957-58 season. *Time,* looking back on the season in television, described us as "the season's liveliest artistic success and costliest financial flop."

* * *

In March, soon after the demise of the television show, Joan and I took our first vacation in years—from work and the household. We flew to Veradero Beach, a modest resort outside Havana, Cuba, remote from the big hotels, that had been discovered by friends. This was the last year of the Batista regime and military police in white helmets rode American jeeps through the streets. We drank rum at night and lay in the hot sand by day looking out to where a huge manta ray was clearly visible in the bright blue water a hundred feet offshore. Gradually some of the past year's tension began to slide away. Then the phone began to ring and within ten days I was back in New York facing the problems of the new Stratford season.

Within a few days of my return I received an invitation from Louis Cowan to lunch once again at the Plaza with him and Hubbell Robinson. I went reluctantly, anticipating an embarrassing explanation of why CBS would not be picking up my option. Instead, over our second martini, I was informed that I had been selected as one of three producers of *Playhouse 90* for the coming season. I accepted, provided it did not interfere with my direction of the Festival, which remained my prime artistic obligation. This presented no problem: the eight TV shows assigned to me were scheduled to be broadcast from California during the fall and early winter and would in no way conflict with my Festival activities in the East.

That spring, as though I were not busy enough already, I took on one additional assignment. This followed an urgent call from Nate Kroll (musician and minor impresario) who begged me, as a long-time friend of Martha Graham, to look at a film he was producing with her and her company. Photographed in black and white by a young cameraman named Peter Glushanek, it was as beautiful a piece of dance film as I had ever seen, with a physical and spiritual energy that I had seldom seen caught in a motion picture. Filmed in leotards in a low-ceilinged dance studio, it showed the Graham company at work, illustrating some of Martha's basic concepts of dance through fragments from some of her most celebrated works. In its carefully rehearsed simplicity, it had extraordinary beauty and strength.

Having lured me with the quality of his film, Kroll explained that he was in terrible trouble, from which apparently only I could save him. As originally conceived, *The Dancer's World* was to alternate the dance segments I had seen (with voice-over commentary by Graham) with three short, intimate scenes in which Martha herself would appear in her dressing room, discussing her ideas and her feelings about her work. It was when the time came to shoot these personal scenes that the trouble arose. Martha, in her perfectionism and her immeasurable vanity and pride, was terrified at the prospect of intimate contact with an instrument (the movie camera) with which she was unfamiliar and over which she felt she had no control. She admired Glushanek's work with the women in the company but, when it came to her own close-ups, she refused to let him photograph or direct her. Finally, after two days of silence, she told Jean Rosenthal that she could think of one person she'd be willing to work with.

Martha Graham and I had been friends for more than twenty years—ever since the distant days of *Valley Forge* and *Panic*. We had remained in remote but constant touch—mostly through Jeannie, who was very close to us both. I had observed Martha's rising fame; she, on her part, had followed my erratic career—first in the theater and later in films. What now brought us together was a purely technical consideration on her part. Throughout her aesthetic and spiritual flights Martha never lost her strong, practical sense of showmanship. What she needed for her first personal appearance on film was not artistic advice but supervision by a professional who had produced Hollywood films for such accredited sex figures as Lana Turner and

Joan Fontaine—not to mention such mature ladies as Greer Garson and Barbara Stanwyck.

I ran Glushanek's film with her and told her in all honesty how much I admired it and how important I felt it was for her to complete it. Then we sat down in her apartment and went over the three short scenes in which she insisted on appearing in full make-up and costume of her most celebrated roles. I reminded her that I was not a film director but that I would be standing behind the camera and that she would, in fact, be talking not to the camera but to me. If she or I felt anything was wrong, we'd stop and shoot it over—as often as she wanted. Concerning her lighting, Jean Rosenthal would work with Glushanek and she would look on film just as she did on stage. With all these pledges, she agreed to perform her scenes.

Except for my reassuring presence and the few suggestions I made concerning continuity, I contributed little to this remarkable film, on which I am proud but slightly embarrassed to find my name listed as co-director. Later, Martha's talks about the dance and about her work became an integral element of her triumphal appearances throughout the world. But there is something intense and personal, if a trifle stiff, about that first, frightened appearance on film that has a particularly poignant quality. And it cemented a relationship that has survived for another twenty-five years and enabled us both, later, to come through a serious professional crisis.

XXIV
Festival: The Dream, Hamlet and All's Well
1958-59

My third Festival summer is one I remember with satisfaction and pride. Not only was our season varied and popular (including the addition of our first successful School Season) but we seemed to be moving, slowly but surely, towards the creation of a permanent classical repertory company. We had no single stars in the cast that year but, of the thirty-two actors who assembled for rehearsals in late April, less than one third were new to the company and most had worked together before.

There were some changes in our organization. Virgil Thomson was in Europe; to take his place I invited my old associate Marc Blitzstein to compose music for the *Dream* and *Winter's Tale*. A more serious absence was that of Joseph Verner Reed. His large, regular contributions to the Republican Party had been rewarded by his appointment as cultural attaché to the U.S. Embassy in Paris. His going was a grievous loss. Not only was he our main financial supporter but he was my only real and reliable contact with the board of trustees; for all his vacillations and quirks, he had been a constant, sympathetic and constructive ally whose going had the most serious consequences for the Festival and for myself.

To fill the vacuum of his absence, an attempt was made by Langner to induce Eugene Black, head of the International Bank and a Shakespeare enthusiast, to assume a more active part in the organization. Among the forms this took was his offer of a young man from his own staff to be our general manager. I would have preferred someone with more theatrical experience, but Langner insisted that we accept Black's offer—all the more since Mr. Black was prepared to pay his full salary. Tom Noone, a personable, energetic, handsome young man in his midthirties and three-piece suits, moved from Washington to assume his new functions. He was eager and efficient and might have become a good general manager if he hadn't stepped on a land mine soon after his arrival.

By 1958 the worst of the Eastern witch-hunting was over. McCarthy was gone and people were slowly drifting back into the jobs from which they had been blacklisted during the previous decade. But the House Un-American Activities Committee, though generally discredited, refused to die and announced a new set of hearings, this time in New York City. By now there were few "Reds" left to expose, but a handful were found who had been overlooked in earlier sessions. Needless to say, they included a number of my friends—among them Joseph Papp, head of the Public Theater, and, closer to home, Marc Blitzstein, the Festival's chosen composer, and Bernard Gersten, our production stage manager.

Most of those interrogated followed the normal practice of "taking the Fifth," and after a few days the committee returned to Washington, leaving little wreckage behind them. Blitzstein had already delivered his score for *Dream* and we were using it in rehearsal: he was well into *Winter's Tale*, which he was completing in Stratford—some of it on the piano in our house. As for Gersten, he clearly fell under a recent ruling by Actors' Equity which stated categorically that no Equity member could be dismissed from his job for political reasons. As a result I was able to ignore the investigation and to proceed with our preparations for the summer.

We opened the School Season with *A Midsummer Night's Dream* and the Festival Season with *Hamlet*. Once again we discovered that, under Festival conditions, Shakespeare's comedies are easier to pull off than his tragedies. Fritz Weaver's angular, intellectual, neurotic personality was perfect for the Prince's early tormented scenes of feigned madness but limited him later when, as a man, he must finally face the reality of his destiny. His Hamlet was received with mild favor: the *Dream* was a smash hit. Our fairies were glamorous, our lovers athletic and handsome, and, in Richard Easton, we had an energetic, endearing Puck. But it was in the performances of the "rude mechanicals" that the production was outstanding: only in repertory could a group of such actors be assembled to play such parts and only in a permanent company could a quality of ensemble playing be achieved that caused Brooks Atkinson, critic of the *New York Times*, to wonder "if, in the entire history of the play, there has ever been a better team of comics to play these roles."

With our double bill of *Hamlet* and *Midsummer Night's Dream* the Festival was enjoying its best season yet. We had begun with a substantial advance, all the more satisfying since it was achieved in the absence of stars. Attendance was continuing to build as we went into rehearsal with our third production—*The Winter's Tale*. Then, one Saturday afternoon shortly before our matinée of the *Dream*, three young men appeared on the lawn in the front of the theater—carrying crude, hand-lettered signs protesting the presence of a *Red* stage manager in the Festival company.

I was shocked but not altogether surprised. Stratford was a suburb of Bridgeport, and Bridgeport was a notoriously reactionary town which had always regarded the Festival with suspicion. Still, I was not too disturbed. I felt sure that these pickets were temporary, that they would not affect attendance and that they would disappear after a few days. I was right about that, but I was wrong in my estimate of the harm their appearance would finally do to the Festival.

When the pickets first appeared, Tom Noone, our new manager, was having lunch. When he returned he ran smack into them as he drove up to the theater. He was appalled and came storming into my office. I told him to relax. I understood his agitation but there was nothing we could do about it except hope the louts with the signs would soon go away.

"Shouldn't we negotiate with them?" Noone asked.

I told him that was the last thing we should do. Whoever had sent them would demand Gersten's dismissal, and when we refused we'd be in worse shape than before.

"In that case, why don't we pay Gersten off and get rid of him?"

I found it necessary to remind him of the Equity ruling that none of its members could be dismissed on political grounds.

Noone was on his way to call his master in Washington when he ran into Lincoln Kirstein, who was in one of his dark moods. Lincoln told him not to be a horse's ass, to mind his own fucking business, and to keep his goddamned mouth shut. Didn't he know that half of our company were Communists and that if we fired Gersten all the others would quit? And we'd have no season? Is that what he wanted? Noone stared at him openmouthed, and Lincoln, having achieved his dramatic effect, climbed into his car and drove off for the weekend. Noone took one last, nervous look at the pickets, got into his car and drove straight to La Guardia Airport and from there to Washington to carry his alarming news to the head of the International Bank.

Lincoln had, as usual, exaggerated. But, as usual, there was truth in what he said. We had in the company, to my personal knowledge, no fewer than *five*, besides Gersten, who had taken the Fifth

Amendment—not to mention half a dozen "fellow travelers," of whom I was, myself, the most notorious. Gersten's firing would in fact have blown the whole Festival apart.

Eugene Black's reaction was predictable. He requested an emergency meeting of the board, which took place a few days later in a room at Yale University, of which he was a trustee. Black (who was there with his fellow banker, George Woods) explained his position. He loved Shakespeare and appreciated what had been achieved by the Festival. But, as a public figure holding a key position with the United States government, he could not remain associated with an organization that was being publicly accused of harboring subversives.

Langner, torn between his long-standing liberalism and his eagerness to keep our two bankers on the board, stayed on the fence. He raised the question: if Gersten were paid his full salary for the rest of the season and let go, would that violate Equity's interdiction against political dismissals? I replied that I would not even consider such an action and we were deadlocked once again. The meeting ended in disarray. And the next day, though the pickets had disappeared, Black and Woods resigned, thus depriving the American Shakespeare Festival of its last remaining money-raising trustees.

The effects of their departure were not immediately evident. The festival appeared to be flourishing and *Winter's Tale* was a joy to rehearse. The company was exhausted but tuned to a fine sensibility. Our two Nancies (Wickwire and Marchand as the Queen and Paulina) gave great emotional power to the melodrama of the Queen's trial and to the corny but always moving final scene in which the Queen's statue comes to life. A newcomer, Inga Swenson, was a fresh, delicious Perdita and the production was enhanced by the notion (originally Kirstein's, brilliantly executed by Dorothy Jeakins) of locating the entire action in the world of Mediterranean tarot cards.

When the season came to an end after Labor Day, I had every reason to be satisfied. Our press had been good, our audiences large and enthusiastic and the company's morale had never been higher. This did not blind me to the growing divisions that were becoming apparent in the internal affairs of the Festival. Our financial base had always been precarious: with the departure of the munificent Joseph Reed and our bankers' resignations it suddenly crumbled. Throughout the latter part of the season Langner missed no opportunity of reminding me that, though he admired my integrity, I had almost certainly wrecked the Festival with my intransigence. This view was generally reflected in the attitude of our trustees at whose board meetings our summer's successes were submerged in the deepening gloom of our deteriorating financial condition.

Such was the prevalent mood when I flew to California in September to produce my six television shows for *Playhouse 90*, leaving Jack Landau to hold the fort and deal with our worsening situation. For the first time in two years no winter activity had been planned for the Festival Company; the 1959 summer season remained uncertain, dependent upon delayed financial decisions by the trustees. I hated to leave things in such a mess but I was delighted to get away.

* * *

I arrived in Los Angeles in time to take part in what turned out to be the last season of "live" TV drama. The previous year a way had been found to coordinate videotape and sound; by the following year it had become possible (though still time-consuming) to edit tape in much the same way as film. After that it was just a matter of time before "live" television drama declined and finally withered away.

In its day and at its best, "live" television drama was a highly creative dramatic form, practiced mostly by quite young men, many of whom later became great figures in the film world. Working alongside them was a group of writers (some of them from radio) who were finding in TV drama creative opportunities that were denied them in the shrinking commercial theater and in the highly structured film industry. Among them, week after week, they produced a large number of dramatic shows, not all of which were distinguished but which, in the aggregate, displayed a remarkable range of energy and courage—in their choice of subjects and in the dramatic and technical skill that went into their creation.

As flagship of the leading network and the only dramatic show running longer than 60 minutes on the air, *Playhouse 90* enjoyed special privileges as regards budget and rehearsal time. Our normal production schedule was sixteen days. Of those, eleven or twelve were taken up with readings, corrections of the script and "blocking" in rehearsal rooms large enough for sets to be marked out on the floor with multicolored tape. These rehearsals were attended by a scene designer and a technical director to make sure that nothing was rehearsed that could not be executed when the show moved into a major studio. This move took place during the weekend preceding our Thursday broadcast; by that time our sets were already standing in various stages of completion and actors were at work in them, watched by lighting and camera crews. On Wednesdays, like a dark swarm of mechanical monsters trailing hundreds of feet of black cable behind them, the electronic cameras and their crews moved onto the floor while the director retired into the control room, in which, surrounded by banks of flickering consoles and monitors, he and his technical director would start shaping and editing the show.

Thursday was a day of madness—a tense and hair-raising experience—with actors grouped in the center of the studio as four moving cameras, on their various mountings (including one on a tall crane), waltzed in silence around them in moves every one of which was watched and regulated by the director and his technical aides from the control room above. As each scene ended, hell broke loose; there was a sudden rush of actors from one set to another, followed by the four cameras and their troops of handlers—ready to take up their new positions and to begin a scene that within a few seconds would be going out over the air to millions of viewers. For one trained in the leisurely tempo of filmmaking, the speed and skill with which these improvisations were carried out was a constant source of amazement. Once in a while disaster struck; an actor would miss an entrance or forget his lines or, in a frenzy, enter through the wrong door; on almost every show a hovering stagehand, a mike boom or a camera would appear unexpectedly on the electronic screen. Such accidents were instantly and calmly corrected.

Stupefied by terror, I remember almost nothing of my first two shows—except that they were broadcast without major incident or disgrace. With my third, "Seven Against the Wall," I found my stride and began to enjoy myself. This was a thoroughly immoral show, the script of which I had bought from a former FBI agent: a detailed and accurate treatment of the St. Valentine's Day Massacre in which Capone and his boys knocked off seven of Bugs Moran's henchmen in a Chicago garage. Meticulously researched and brilliantly executed, it was a perfect example of what later came to be known as "docudrama." It was directed by that great craftsman, Frank Schaffner, with so many sets that we had to use *two* vast connecting stages to hold them all. Except for a gang execution in a phone booth (which, on account of the danger from flying glass, was shot ahead of time, on film) it was a "live" show, in which Capone, in his bloodthirsty agitation, twice used a four-letter word on the air (that was instantly "blipped" out by the ever vigilant censor).

To divert possible unfavorable public reaction I engaged that paragon of journalistic probity, Eric Sevareid, to narrate it and to express "our concern with social and economic phenomena and with the dangers of underworld power in the structure of our national life." Our press was excellent: "This was big television...a gripping, unsentimental and marvelously thorough recapitulation." And it brought me the dubious honor of having started the renaissance of gangster shows, which continued to thrive through the midsixties.

The other broadcast I recall with satisfaction was a version of Henry James's *The Wings of the Dove*. There was a general conviction that James and his works were unsuited to the mass media. I tried to disprove this with a script by Meade Roberts, ravishing period costumes by Dorothy Jeakins and a distinguished international cast. It proved viable TV drama and provoked one particularly gratifying response—from James Thurber who, in the *New Yorker*, described it as:

closer to the James tone and closer to perfection of total production than any other dramatization I have seen. Miss Swenson must have been recruited by James himself from among the angels.

The day after "Wings of the Dove" went on the air I was back in New York to supervise my Christmas Day broadcast of *The Nutcracker*. And with that my year's participation in *Playhouse 90* came to an end. At year's end we once again received an Academy Award as the best dramatic series of the year and I was re-engaged as one of its producers for the following season. In the meantime I was free to devote myself to renewing my acquaintance with my family and to facing the growing problems of the American Shakespeare Festival, whose budget for the 1959 season, when it was finally approved by its nervous trustees, represented a substantial reduction in the funds available for production.

This was not allowed to interfere with the ambitious plans Landau and I had cooked up for our 1959 season. Our belated circulars announced a three-week school season and a program of four productions instead of the usual three. They were *Romeo and Juliet*, *The Merry Wives of Windsor*, *All's Well that Ends Well* and *A Midsummer Night's Dream* (repeated by popular demand).

With a few gains and few losses, we had assembled the same company as the previous year. But, from the first day of rehearsal, I sensed a change. There was the same general feeling of professional dedication but some of the buoyancy and fervor of the previous year seemed to be missing. This may have been due to the unusually long hiatus between productions; it may also have been a reflection of my own dissatisfaction; finally, it may have been aggravated by an event that could not help having a serious effect on our operation.

I have mentioned Jean Rosenthal's position with Lincoln Kirstein and his ballet company, whose lighting designer and technical director she had been for more than ten years. That winter, without explanation or warning, she and her staff were replaced by a young man who had been at Stratford for two years, first as an apprentice and then as one of our assistant stage managers.

This came as a stunning blow to Jeannie who, for all her growing fame, still regarded the New York City Ballet Company as her home and permanent base. Yet, strangely enough (not so strangely if you considered his complex and mysterious personality), it was not on Jeannie but on Lincoln that the break had its most immediate traumatic effect. It was consistent with his intensely emotional nature that the grief and guilt he felt over the abrupt dismissal of someone to whom he had been so close for so long should be followed by feelings of embarrassment that were soon transformed into revulsion and hatred. Jean continued to work with us at the Festival, but her name was no longer mentioned between Lincoln and myself and it finally got so that he could no longer bear the sight of her; if he entered the theater and became aware of her sitting in the darkened house or even heard her voice over the intercom, he would turn and leave and not come back rather than face the possibility of encountering her. All this occurred at a time when the storm clouds were gathering about my head and I desperately needed him as an ally and confidant in the crisis that was developing.

There is nothing better than overwork for actors' morale. With *Merry Wives* the company seemed to recapture some of its *joie de vivre*. But it was not until the last show of the season, when everyone was exhausted, that we fully recovered our stride. *All's Well that Ends Well*, though it went into rehearsal in an atmosphere of rising apprehension and ill feeling between the trustees and myself, seemed to draw its members together and gave our work a quality of intimacy and harmony that was reflected in our production.

Nancy Wickwire had simplicity, clarity, beauty and a sense of passionate independence that made her Helena, instead of a lovesick ninny, a "new woman" determined to get her man, almost in the Shavian manner. Her scenes with her elders—the Countess of Rousillon, the ailing King of France and the wise, courtly Lafeu—were played with a combination of respect and self-confidence that was in direct contrast to her humble but relentless pursuit of her reluctant lover.

With the launching of *All's Well* late in July our summer's repertory was complete. Now a visitor to Stratford could spend a long weekend on the banks of the Housatonic and see four of Shakespeare's plays. Each evening (except Monday) and twice on matinée days, the wide green lawns that ran down to the river were crowded with couples and families: our warning bell sent hundreds of picnickers scurrying to dispose of the remains of their alfresco meals (from foie gras to hot dogs and from Coke to Dom Pérignon) before they streamed into the air-conditioned darkness of the Festival Theater.

Publicly things had never looked better; we played to full houses and our press—except for *Romeo*—had been consistently good. But, behind the scenes—in New York, in Westport and in Stratford—sides were forming for the inevitable confrontation between the Executive Committee and the Artistic Director. With the start of rehearsals a kind of armed truce had been declared; the summer's receipts and advance sales had eased our cash-flow crisis, but, beneath the surface, personal animosities and suspicions continued to ferment and sour. What brought them to a head was the growing awareness that my contract as artistic director was drawing to a close. Relations had been so strained and communication so desultory over the past nine months that the matter had never been openly or formally discussed. However, I had made it quite clear to everyone that I had no intention of continuing as director unless I received credible assurances that my demands for the future of the Festival would be met. Having worked for four years to raise the Festival to its present honorable estate, I had no intention of presiding over its retreat and ultimate dissolution.

The annual trustees' meeting was scheduled for mid-August, and, as that date approached, the true nature of the conflict became more apparent. On Langner's side were a number of trustees, mostly from the professional theater, who liked to be consulted on matters of policy and programming, and who had long resented what they considered my arbitrary decisions and overbearing behavior. Others were divided. Whenever they visited Stratford they were generous with their praise of our productions and voluble in their appreciation of what had been accomplished. But that did not mean that they were prepared, as trustees, to support demands which, in the Festival's present financial condition, they felt to be unrealistic.

Supporting me were most of the working elements of the Festival, together with the press, which I had so assiduously cultivated over the past four years. I was heartened by their support, yet I knew that neither would be of much help to me in the struggle ahead. In spite of the Festival's continued success, I was well aware that my position was weaker, in some ways, than it had been during our first two years, when Lincoln Kirstein, Joseph Reed and I had formed a solid and effective triumvirate. Now Reed was gone and Kirstein, once my staunchest supporter, had become an uncertain ally.

I wrote a personal letter to each member of the company—actors, staff and crew—inviting them to my house for "a chance to talk to all of you personally and to tell you how things stand at this time." They all came one night after the show, and I read a statement, prepared by Landau and myself, summarizing the Festival's growth over the past four years and outlining my bright hopes for the company's future. I pointed out that these were conditional upon certain assurances of support by the trustees: extended employment for the acting company; expansion of the repertory; the opportunity to perform in places other than Stratford, including a regular classical season in New York City.

My statement was received with enthusiasm by members of the company. And it formed the basis of the memorandum I presented in person to the trustees the following Sunday, together with a list of my current grievances and of the ways in which I felt the Festival was being "betrayed" by what I considered the board's inadequate and unimaginative methods of fund-raising.

I read my statement and made my exit, leaving behind me a disturbed, angry and puzzled board. My tone was aggressive and must have come as a disagreeable shock—especially to those casual trustees who knew only the pleasant things they had read in the papers. Even my friends must have wondered what I hoped to accomplish by forcing the issue as I did. Either I was pulling a dangerous bluff or I must be too drunk with power to realize that I was jeopardizing my own future and that of an institution I had worked so hard and so successfully to create and develop.

After a quarter of a century it has become possible to view my behavior in a somewhat different perspective and to face the fact that it may not have been quite as impulsive or altruistic as it seemed. My wife, who has long been a passive but perceptive observer of my personal and professional manipulations, maintains that whenever she sees me growing righteously indignant she knows that I am up to something devious and that my expressions of outrage are often nothing but a mask for my own feelings of self-reproach. According to this interpretation, my indignation rises in direct proportion to my sense of guilt.

With this, I step into an emotional hornets' nest: for all my enthusiasm for the Festival, my very real love of the company, my intense pride in our achievement and my deep dedication to the creation of a national classical repertory company, was I, in fact, looking for a way out? After the first exhilaration of victory against seemingly overwhelming odds was I once again becoming bored? Had the crises of the past year—Jeannie's trouble with Lincoln, the Gersten affair and our deteriorating financial situation—merely triggered my chronic desire for change? Was I blowing up my differences with Langner and the trustees into a self-righteous excuse for abandoning a project that I was, in fact, beginning to find stale and unprofitable? Finally, was the exaggerated hostility I expressed towards the trustees for denying my demands a reflection of my own guilt over my imminent betrayal of a cause to which I had so publicly committed myself?

For four days following the board meeting I remained sulking in my tent, waiting for reactions that did not come. Then, before attending my next meeting with the Executive Committee, I dictated the final version of a release I had prepared and gave it to our press agent to mimeograph and hold until I gave him word to distribute it. If it came to a break (and now I felt sure it would) I wanted my resignation reported to the press in *my* way—and *first*.

After four years as Artistic Director of the American Shakespeare Festival Theater, John Houseman today announced his resignation. He attributed his departure from Stratford to divergences with the Festival's Executive Committee over the basic policies governing the management of the Festival.

The points of disagreement include the continued failure of the Board of Trustees to provide the necessary working funds to extend the activities of the Festival on a year-round basis with national scope.

I concluded with an expression of "regret and deep gratitude to all working members of the Festival who have so devotedly collaborated with me over the years."

At 5:30 p.m., as I left the Executive meeting, I had my statement released by telegram so that the New York papers carried it the next morning together with local reactions: "Shocked by Resignation," "Stratford Cast Takes Director's Side," "Festival Backs Houseman." It provoked a bitter letter from Langner complaining of my premature and unilateral announcement to the press, followed by a formal letter of separation.

It was several days before either of them reached me in my House on the Hill in New City to which I had retreated after leaving Stratford in a howling thunderstorm during a matinée of *All's Well*. There I fell into a deep inertia not unlike what I had felt on other similar occasions: the bankruptcy of the Oceanic; the end of my first marriage; my departure from the Federal Theater; the break-up of my partnership with Orson Welles; my decision to desert the Voice of America and, after five successful years, to abandon MGM. Following a period of intense and consuming effort, I was left each time in a state of emotional exhaustion in which sadness, anger, exhilaration and a deep sense of relief were all equally present.

The network was pressing me to fly out to California for preparation and casting of my next *Playhouse 90* season. Before leaving, Joan and I gave a farewell party in the House on the Hill. It was a highly emotional occasion, complete with speeches, tears, embraces, excoriations, dancing and a lot to drink. One car (an old white Porsche) was wrecked between Stratford and New City with no serious injuries, and Morris Carnovsky, on behalf of the company, formally presented to me a set of Shakespeare's complete works in the Nonesuch edition. At some time in the evening Nancy Wickwire, wandering into the night to cool off between dances, plunged 30 feet over the edge of our ravine, landed against a rock, got up and returned, muddy, bleeding a little but smiling, to dance some more.

Two days later the family's westward migration got under way. The boys left by plane with the larger of our two poodles. I drove out in my aging Chrysler 300 weighed down with books, household effects, my 79-year-old mother and Virgil, the black dachshund. We made it in three and a half days, and my mother could not remember ever having had a better time. Joan, my secretary, and two more dogs followed in a second-hand blue Mercedes.

By the end of September we were all settled in a large, ramshackle house on the beach. Joan was glad to be back in Malibu but indignant at having to live in a rented house instead of her own beautiful and comfortable home in Santa Monica, which I had sold without consulting her the year before.

Soon after I reported to the CBS Center, I became aware once again I was working for an organization that was past its peak of success. *Playhouse 90* was no longer the network's flagship but a leaky vessel that we were trying to keep afloat. It was having trouble competing for viewers with the new prime-time favorites, of which the most sensationally successful was *The Beverly Hillbillies*. The era of TV "ratings" had begun.

My own first show was a melodramatic but well written "original" about a fictional revolution in a Latin American country ruled over by a dictator played by George C. Scott. My third was a version of G.B. Shaw's *Misalliance*. Produced, against the network's strong opposition, it was carried by the extraordinary cast we were able to assemble. With Claire Bloom as the ingénue, Isobel Elsom as her mother, Robert Morley as the father, Kenneth Haigh as the burglar and Siobhan McKenna as the Polish acrobat-aviatrix, it was all more like a West End stage performance than a TV show. They all behaved in the great tradition of British actors: they quarrelled, they gossiped, they back-bit and bitched incessantly but performed brilliantly in a broadcast that provoked a lot of talk and received a mixed reception from our diminishing audience.

Meantime, in my need for a regular, six-figure income, I had allowed my agent to engage in negotiations with the new management of MGM. With mixed feelings I signed a contract for two pictures a year for three years. Then, just after we had moved into our new house and a few days before I was due to go to work, the Screen Writers' Guild called a major strike against the studios for residual rights. The companies invoked the *force majeure* clause that allowed them to suspend all existing contractual commitments for the duration of the strike.

I spent close to three months waiting for the Studio to reopen. My first reaction was one of alarm. Later I became aware that during this involuntary calm a watershed had formed that conditioned my attitudes for the rest of my life.

XXV
Watershed
1960

With our return to the beach, some of the clouds that had hung low over our lives during the past two years seemed to lift. My own loathing of Southern California gradually dissolved in the subtropical sunshine. The boys too seemed to recover a sense of freedom and physical well-being which (except for John Michael's enchanted sojourn in a summer camp named Blueberry Cove in Maine) they had not generally enjoyed in the East.

We celebrated Christmas and New Year's with Joan's customary Russian rituals. After that, we began to receive visitors. Our new home had a guest house which my mother, who was approaching eighty, occupied for several months. It had a large, sunny bedroom overlooking the ocean from which she seldom stirred before midafternoon but where she presided, amid clouds of cigarette smoke, over a court of children and dogs whom she seduced with tidbits of various kinds. In March she returned to her beloved Paris, where she was to spend the next thirteen years of her life.

The first consequence of my enforced leisure was a gradual renewal of my acquaintance with my wife and family and, through them, with the person I myself had become during a decade in which I had been so wholly and perpetually absorbed in crises that I had little time or energy for anything else.

I spent those months of unemployment making conscientious attempts to establish social and cultural contacts with my sons. With their merciless children's observation they recognized these tardy approaches for what they were: my evening readings were only moderately appreciated—partly due to the difficulty of finding suitable common material for auditors of such different ages. The concerts I organized and played on the family record-player were listened to with polite but wandering attention. Family walks on the beach (in the company of two poodles, a basset hound, two dachshunds and a nervous cat) were more popular. On the rare forays on which Joan joined us, she used the occasion to introduce the boys to the salty delights of the *fruits de mer* in which the beach abounded—mussels, clams, winkles and prickly sea urchins—which Sebastian was always the first to sight and dig up but which Joan and John Michael were the only ones to relish.

As I began to make their acquaintance, I was surprised to discover how very different these two small persons had become during the brief span of their lives. Both were healthy and charming without apparent ill effects from their incredibly diverse genes—Spanish and Finnish-Russian combined with Nebraska Scotch-Irish on Joan's side, Alsatian-French-Jewish crossed with Welsh-Irish on mine. Both were tall, handsome and fair, though Sebastian's platinum was finally darkening, and they seemed passionately devoted to each other.

John Michael, the elder, was not unlike what I might have been at his age, only more secure and gregarious, with a wholly egotistical interest in people that rarely outlasted their physical presence, and an aptitude for mathematical and abstract conjecture in which I had been totally deficient.

Sebastian, almost from birth, revealed astonishingly keen sensory perceptions combined with a prodigious obstinacy that kept him from conforming to normal disciplines or to any sustained effort required of him. His attendance at Malibu's Catholic school was punctuated by fearful scenes with the French-Canadian nuns including dunce caps, handslapping with rulers and standings-in-the-corner, all of which he suffered in defiant silence. This same defiance persisted during his grilling by the local police when he and a friend (known as "Kevin-the-Bad" to distinguish him from another local boy known as "Kevin-the-Good") were caught breaking into an occupied beach house where they performed mysterious rites at dead of night: the burned-out stubs of several dozen candles were found, set in an uneven circle, on the wooden floor of the highly flammable gazebo.

If the boys squabbled more loudly and frequently with their mother than they did with me, it was because they were more closely and uninhibitedly involved with her. With Sebastian, in particular, Joan had similarities of temperament that led to frequent conflict based on an intuitive sense of each other's motivations. Yet her deeper maternal feelings were for John Michael, her first-born, who could reduce her to sudden tenderness, anxiety or suffering without the slightest awareness of what he was doing.

Overall, I failed to qualify, then or at any other time, as a concerned, effective or authoritative father. Looking back, I realize that almost every decision affecting our children's health, education and welfare (including, at Joan's insistence, their belated baptism) was made and executed by their mother. I am also aware that, over the years, I achieved a far closer empathy with associates and played a more effective parental role with some of my actors and students than I ever succeeded in doing with my sons. However, during those three months of idleness, I did make some progress and managed to establish a remote, perplexed but mildly affectionate relationship with both of them that has persisted, without much change, to this day.

Between Joan and me it was less a matter of discovery than of recognition. After twelve years of living together we held few surprises for each other but, during my long periods of physical and emotional absence, I was inclined to forget or overlook certain basic facts about my wife that never failed to startle me when, in our periods of resumed intimacy, I once again became aware of them and realized how they underlay and conditioned our close and lasting relationship.

First of all was the realization, which never failed to astound me, that, as a Jesuit-educated, though lapsed, Catholic, my wife believed in the Resurrection of the Body (*le corps glorieux*) and remained secretly and painfully convinced that by marrying me while her first husband (the Count, now a resident of Brazil) was still alive she had, in the eyes of the Church, committed a deadly sin.

Another thing I was inclined to forget was Joan's unshakable conviction, in which her mother had indoctrinated her, that all men were, by nature, irretrievably sinful and dangerous. While this did not immediately affect our relationship, it no doubt colored our life together and probably helped her to put up with some of my egomaniacal behavior more philosophically than she might otherwise have done.

But, finally, the main impact of this hiatus was on myself. I found it strange and disturbing, after so many years of furious energy, to wake up in the morning and reflect that I had no bus or subway to catch, no office or theater or studio to drive to or immediate crisis to face, and that my principal activity during the day would be a long walk along the sand and my only worry the possibility that I might come home with oil sludge on the soles of my feet.

It was not unlike the shock one experiences at the end of a long flight or after hours of cross-country driving, when the motor is turned off and all motion suddenly ceases. What I felt in the unfamiliar stillness was neither relief nor peace but a sense of emptiness, bordering on panic. It was a lost, lonely feeling that I could share with no one—least of all with Joan, who had been the principal sufferer from the succession of frenzies that had consumed me over the past twelve years and who was greatly relieved by my temporary inactivity.

In my solitary walks, as I slowly unwound and caught my breath after the frantic exertions of the past decade, I found myself looking back and trying, if not to understand all that had happened to me during those busy years, then at least to achieve some awareness of the forces that had driven me to such unrelenting, egotistical activity—forces I knew to be rooted in old subconscious anxieties: the primal terror of cold and hunger aggravated by my mother's recurrent economic panics over my father's reckless speculations and my own long-standing fears of rejection, failure and, finally, annihilation.

This had taken the form, early in life, of a deep, nervous inertia that had been condemned by teachers and employers alike, under the general heading of laziness. Later this had been transformed, through ambition and terror, into the compulsive energy that had served me so well in my long battle for personal and professional survival. By my midfifties I had achieved some of the success I longed for and made my breakthrough into the big time of show business. My personal and professional reputation seemed reasonably assured and the lengthening column of my credits was finally eliminating the fear of oblivion against which my life, until now, had been an unceasing struggle.

But it was a hollow victory. Far from assuaging my fever, success seemed to aggravate it: each successive achievement was followed by a compulsive need for new risks and for ever more difficult and dangerous undertakings. My perverse insistence (almost unique among theater workers of my generation) on jumping around between the various media was such a reaction, though, in fact, it had begun as a form of professional self-protection. In my deep insecurity and fear of failure, I figured that if and when I failed in one venture I should have a fall-back prepared in another. With the years, this had become a regular working pattern in my life. I had come to believe that I was likely to achieve my best results through the intensified effort of working on two or more projects at one time. This need to divide my energy was not a professional eccentricity but followed an emotional pattern that had been set in my childhood, as I tried to adjust to the conflicting demands of the two worlds which I inhabited on either side of the Channel.

In show business this had taken on a form that my associates, my agent, my lawyer and my bank manager found particularly foolish and dangerous. This was my habit of oscillating between work that I did for professional and financial gain and work that involved me in some form of public service. In vain I tried to explain the difference in the degree and quality of gratification I derived from these two different kinds of activity. In my work for the U.S. government (with the Federal Theater and the Voice of America) I had the exhilarating and almost mystical feeling that I was participating in some sort of historical event and contributing, alien though I was, to a significant and valuable national cause. At Stratford, my sense of accomplishment had been of a similar kind. During the four years I worked there, for all my frustrations and disappointments, I enjoyed a godlike sense of having created order out of chaos and of having succeeded, against overwhelming odds, in building an organization equal to those of other countries in the presentation of the world's greatest playwright.

Yet the true explanation of my behavior, as I came to understand it during those weeks of self-examination, was rooted, once again, in my childhood. At Clifton, where I had spent more than ten of my first twenty years, generations of boys (the dumb no less than the bright) had been brought up with a strong sense of public service. The great majority of them went into His Majesty's Navy or Army or Civil Service, at home or abroad. The rest were expected to become teachers, clergymen or professionals of various sorts. With this tradition of public service went a deep prejudice among boys and teachers alike against what was still referred to as "trade," and few went into commerce or industry.

Not being British, I found much of this patriotic instruction irrelevant. Besides, by the time I was ready to leave Clifton, the dissolution of the British Empire was well under way and it had become apparent that most of those "services" for which we were being trained were no longer required. This did not change the nature or the tone of our education; for years after I left school, I carried the burden of a deep and obscure sense of guilt over the obligations I had failed to fulfill. Much later, when I chose to go to work for minimal salaries, first for the Works Progess Administration, then for the Office of War Information, it is possible that I felt I was belatedly and subconsciously atoning for the betrayals of my youth.

My activities, during those months, were not limited to parental solicitude or self-examinations. While I waited to resume my career in films, I found myself once again, and quite unexpectedly, becoming involved in the theater.

I had been visited in Stratford the previous summer by the head of the rapidly expanding Adult Education "Extension" of the University of California. To his numerous programs he had recently added "Living Theatre." Remembering my exciting though difficult days with Pelican Productions in the midforties, I had agreed to become an absentee member of his advisory board. During the summer, this newly formed organization (known as the Professional Theater Group of the UCLA Extension) had presented a brief but distinguished season of play readings on the UCLA campus. Encouraged by the response they received and anxious to progess to fully mounted performances, they had invited me (once it became known that I was again a resident of California) to become the Group's artistic director. Still smarting from my Stratford experience I said yes, with no clear notion of what was expected of me, and started to lay the ground for my sixth theater company in twenty-five years.

I wasted no time. By February I had selected the play I would open with and its cast. Robert Ryan (who had played Coriolanus for me in New York six years before) had been one of the original proponents of the Theater Group, and it seemed appropriate that he should appear in our first production, for which I had chosen T.S. Eliot's *Murder in the Cathedral*. He was not the ideal Archbishop. He had done some work on his voice, which remained flat and unresonant but, as in *Coriolanus*, his vocal weakness was offset by his physical presence, his intelligence and his understanding of this profoundly Catholic play. His clerical supporters, his tempters and his murderers, as well as the women of Canterbury, were played by actors many of whom I had worked with before. By arrangement with the UCLA Music Department we had the use of Shoenberg Hall, a 500-seat auditorium intended for chamber music but ideally suited to theatrical production. The acoustics were excellent, the stage adequate in size and depth, with a hydraulic elevator that gave us opportunities to create levels, steps and a variety of exits and entrances.

Murder in the Cathedral was a deliberately simple production intended to clarify Eliot's thought and to emphasize the theatrical and literary quality of his text. It played ten performances to good houses. In contrast to my artistically distinguished but financially disastrous Pelican season of 1947, the Theater Group, with its university backing and its vast Extension audience, seemed ready to launch an economically viable as well as an artistically exciting program of theater in Southern California.

XXVI
All Fall Down and King Lear
1961-63

The Writers' Strike was settled by the end of March but, since it took the industry some weeks to resume normal operations, it was mid-April before I formally re-entered the MGM lot in Culver City. Within an hour of driving through the main gate, I became aware of the difference between this and the institution I had left five years before. My friend Dore Schary was gone; so was the sinister triumvirate that had ruled the third floor. But there were other, more basic differences, of which the most obvious was the fact that television companies, with their small casts and skimpy sets, were occupying many of the sound stages that had once been devoted to the grandeurs of *Ben Hur*, Esther Williams and *Singin' in the Rain*.

Some of the surface luxury remained: I was installed in a suite that was even more sumptuous than the one I had occupied during my previous residence. But the sense of confident supremacy that had once permeated the studio was absent. And in my own situation something was changed. Though I began to function, from the day of my arrival, in the same lavish and energetic way as before (acquiring three expensive properties within a month of my arrival) there was a difference in my attitude towards filmmaking that partly explains the failure of my second sojourn in Culver City.

When I first went to work for MGM in 1951, I had the feeling that this was my last chance: I must make successful films now or go under. I had succeeded and confirmed my victory by walking away at the height of my success. Now, five years later, I was returning to the scene of my triumphs in a very different state of mind, preparing to repeat something I had done before and hoping to recapture the excitement and the success of that earlier time. I never did. From the start there was something wrong with the mix—perhaps the absence of terror. During the two and a half years of my second tenure, I prepared six pictures for MGM and produced three of which only one—the first—

gave me the slightest satisfaction or pride.

All Fall Down was an intriguing, sensitive novel that had been received with critical approval and moderate sales. It was suggested to me by William Inge whom I had known during the years of his Broadway fame. As his star dimmed and he became subject to discouragement amounting to melancholia, he became eager to move to California to work in films and seemed particularly well suited to deal with this story of a neurotic Midwestern American family.

Not everyone shared my enthusiasm for *All Fall Down*. It was offbeat, it had a dubious hero, a flawed heroine, an unsympathetic mother, censorship problems and a tragic ending. But, in the absence of formal objections, I moved ahead with its preparation. Inge, as a playwright, was accustomed to working fast. In less than four months he had finished and revised the screenplay, which I gave to John Frankenheimer (one of my former directors of *Playhouse 90*) who was acquiring a name in films and who eagerly accepted the assignment. And, almost before I knew it, I had acquired a young leading man for the ambivalent role of our charming but worthless hero.

Inge had suggested him and Warren Beatty himself had done the rest. In an astonishing campaign of self-promotion, this young man, whose only previous film appearance had been in Elia Kazan's *Splendor in the Grass* and whose only other claim to fame was his fraternity to Shirley MacLaine, had managed to get pictures of himself, together with articles, into every major magazine in the counrty. Using charm, sex and unmitigated gall, he kept the nation's female columnists in a tizzy. Before we had shot a single frame of film, he had turned a tall, nice-looking but rather awkward and completely unknown young man into one of the hottest names in the business—completely eclipsing such well-established fellow players as Eva Marie Saint, Karl Malden, Angela Lansbury and the former child star, Brandon de Wilde.

Throughout the shooting our most serious problem remained young Mr. Beatty. With his angelic arrogance, his determination to emulate Marlon Brando and Jimmy Dean and his half-baked notions of "Method" acting, he succeeded in perplexing and antagonizing not only his fellow actors but our entire crew. While the company was on location in Key West, our veteran cameraman, Curly Lindon, became so exasperated with him that he flew a camera-bearing helicopter within a few inches of his head. And on the last day of shooting, in a secret agreement with the local police, Warren Beatty was left to languish in a bare cell of the Key West jail while the company flew back to California.

All Fall Down's advance reception in the "trades" and magazines was encouraging. *Newsweek* assigned it "a place of its own among eccentric American family stories—between *You Can't Take It with You* and *Long Day's Journey into Night.."Show* hailed it as "one of the best domestic movies in a decade." It was chosen by the American Motion Picture Producers' Association and by the Festival's own selection committee as the U.S. entry at the Cannes Film Festival. Then, as with *They Live by Night*, disaster struck. In direct violation of its promise to open the film in small or medium-sized theaters, the MGM sales department, responding to unpredictable market pressures, suddenly switched its entire campaign. With no time for publicity or preparation, our sophisticated little film was thrown into dozens of oversized movie palaces that habitually house major spectacles and musicals in color. Inevitably it withered and died. Most local critics were influenced by the cavernous gloom of the empty theaters in which they viewed it.

Their principal victim was Warren Beatty. The *New York Times* described him as a "disgusting young man who is virtually a cretin" and "a noxious young brute who provokes a reasonable spectator to give up in disgust."

This was my earliest intimation that my second sojourn in Culver City might not be repeating the triumphs of the first. Show business has its own mysterious rhythms of success and failure, its seemingly irresistible upward and downward curves. Looking back on the history of the Mercury Theater I had observed that, whereas in our first season we could do no wrong, in our second, no matter how hard we tried, we could get nothing right. The same seemed to be true of my second term with MGM.

My next project was based on a novel the Studio had acquired at enormous cost: Irwin Shaw's *Two Weeks in Another Town*. It is not one of Shaw's best books and there was front-office interference in its casting and final editing.

But the basic mistake was mine in thinking I could duplicate the success of *The Bad and the Beautiful* by mechanically assembling the same creative elements. In the years that had passed we had all undergone drastic personal and professional changes. I was no longer the frightened, desperately eager and indefatigable producer I had been in 1951; Charles Schnee, beset by poor health and marital troubles, was not the flexible, imaginative writer he had been nine years before; Minnelli (with whom this was my fourth picture) was worn out from grinding out one film after another for MGM; finally Kirk Douglas was no longer at that stage in his career where his furious drive for fame and recognition coincided with the roles he was playing.

Two Weeks in Another Town gave me a luxurious month in Rome and almost nothing else. This was even truer of my next venture, which I have consistently refused to include in any list of my productions. It was a depressing love story which I had undertaken for two reasons—both bad. The first was to assuage my agents who, in order to assure the extension of my lucrative contract with MGM, were constantly nagging me to produce more pictures. The second was personal and reflected a growing restlessness. My Roman voyage, for all its problems, had stirred up my long-repressed yearning for travel. Much of the action of *The Cool of the Day* was laid in Greece; its production would involve an extended voyage for Joan and myself to such places as Athens, Delphi, the Gulf of Corinth, the Greek islands and the Peloponnesus at the best time of the year.

It is almost impossible, once you get started, not to become infected with the excitement of a major film. In the weeks that preceded our departure for Europe all kinds of decisions had to be made. Among them was the problem of creating a new personality for Jane Fonda, who had scored a personal success as a teenage hoyden in *Walk on the Wild Side*. Our efforts to transform her were not wholly successful. Someone devised a hairdo for her that bore a close and unfortunate resemblance to Elizabeth Taylor's Cleopatra. Several such dark, helmet-like wigs were made at enormous expense, and no matter how much we fiddled with them later they completely destroyed the mobility and fascination of that expressive face. For her clothes she chose a fashionable designer whose elaborate creations turned out to be curiously unattractive and unconvincing. Finally, Jane insisted on wearing high spike heels throughout the film—even on the rocky slopes of the Parthenon.

Jane Fonda, whom I hold to be one of the outstanding women of our time, has always shown a wonderfully feminine capacity for taking on the color, the attitudes, the opinions and even the personalities of her men. During the first days of shooting I discovered that she was currently playing Trilby to the Svengali of a young Greek comrade from the Actors' Studio, who accompanied her on the set and remained there throughout rehearsal and filming. Under his tutelage, before each take of an emotional scene Jane emitted a chilling and ear-splitting primal scream. After each take her first look was to him for approval over the heads of her director and of a perplexed Peter Finch, with whom she was playing most of her scenes.

(Years later my wife spoke of our Greek voyage with nostalgia though, at the time, it was my impression that it disturbed and frightened her. Partly this had to do with the devastating heat; partly, it was her strong emotional reaction to the immense power of those battered but still furiously living stones. At Delphi, in the shrine in which she asked to be left alone for an hour, this backsliding French Catholic claimed, in all seriousness, to have had a personal interview with the oracle. Addressing her in French, a woman's voice had told her that she would never find peace (*tranquillité*) until she got rid of the anger (*rancoeur*) in her heart. We drank champagne to the sybil that night in a modern hotel whose windows looked down over the endless olive groves that run sheer down to the valley and out to the sea. To this day my wife is convinced that on that sunny afternoon she recaptured some of the peace she had lost during the troubled years of the German occupation.)

The concluding scenes of the picture were to be shot in England. While we were in Greece the physical excitement of our locations had kept us together. Now suddenly the whole thing fell apart. For more than twenty years, ever since my first tentative producer's steps into *The Unseen*, I had, for better or for worse, managed to maintain control over the style and tone of my productions. Now, in the hostile atmosphere of the MGM Studio at Borehamwood, I felt utterly helpless and impotent as I watched *The Cool of the Day* drift towards its hopeless and shameful close.

Two days before the picture ended I received a call from Washington inviting me to represent the U.S. on the jury of the Venice Film Festival. I packed my evening clothes, abandoned my battered film, flew to Paris, where I picked up Joan, and flew on to Milan and from there to Venice. We arrived before dawn and were taken across the lagoon to the Lido by speedboat as the sun rose.

My wife spent her days cruising between the Lido, Harry's bar, the Biennale and the churches. My own duties with the Festival kept me so busy that I didn't get to see much of anything. We were expected to view between three and five films a day and we attended nocturnal functions to the point of exhaustion. I soon found that my interest focused less on the films we were being shown than on the machinations of which the Festival was the center. I had been warned that there was an unholy alliance between the Russians, the Italians and some of the French to tip the scales against Hollywood and in favor of the socialist countries. I soon discovered that the pressures on the jury from both sides were constant and unrelenting and that most of our awards that year were negotiated—the result of deals and compromises arrived at between the two sides of this artistic cold war.

I did not stay for the formal presentation of the awards but flew directly to California. The day after I arrived I sat in a projection room in Culver City and was able to see for myself that my film was every bit as dreary as I feared. I have noticed that neither Jane Fonda nor I ever list it among the films we have made.

My contract with MGM still had a little over a year to run but, before leaving London, I had instructed my agent to terminate it on the best possible terms. Back in California, my melancholy lifted and my battered self-confidence returned. This process was speeded by an unexpected offer I received from the Dallas Opera Company to direct Verdi's *Otello*. (Among its attractions was the knowledge that I would be working once again with two favorite members of my Stratford team—Jean Rosenthal as lighting designer and Gordon Davidson as stage manager.) I do not read music: so, for three weeks, I listened daily to records of the opera and followed them as best I could in the score, so that when I arrived in Dallas in mid-October I was sufficiently familiar with the work to collaborate effectively with the conductor and my two celebrated stars in the persons of Mario del Monaco (the most illustrious Otello of the decade) and, in the role of Iago, Ramon Vinay (who, before his voice deepened, had been Toscanini's favorite Otello).

I left immediately after our opening and reached Los Angeles in time to approve a settlement of my MGM contract (my remaining nine months' salary, to be paid over the next two years) and to sign a deal with CBS Television to produce a historical series the following year. This allowed me to concentrate for the next few months on what had, in fact, been my main preoccupation during the past year—the artistic direction of UCLA's Professional Theater Group.

My successive film failures would have had a far more lasting and demoralizing effect had it not been for the satisfaction I continued to derive from the theatrical activities of the Group, which was not only thriving locally but had already achieved a unique position among American regional theaters as the only professional company performing regularly within a major university structure.

There were two main factors to explain our success. Increasingly, with the supremacy of television, Los Angeles had become the main gathering place and residence of many of the country's best actors—not only of stars but of a wide range of performers of all ages. Many of them had started in the theatre and yearned for a chance to refresh and recharge themselves through work on the stage and contact with living audiences. The Theater Group offered the advantages of a brief, local engagement and of a chance to appear in good parts before an audience, part academic, part professional, that was sophisticated and starved for serious theater. It was of great help to me in my early programing to be able to present plays that would have bene considered standard fare in some communities but which, after years of theatrical drought, we could offer as genuine "West Coast Premieres." (These included, during our first two seasons, *Murder in the Cathedral*, *Three Sisters*, *Six*

Characters in Search of an Author and *The Iceman Cometh*.)

To these we added novelties such as Three Plays of the Absurd, Dos Passos' *U.S.A.*, Paul Shyre's dramatizations of O'Casey's *I Knock at the Door* and *Pictures in the Hallway*, Frisch's *The Chinese Wall*, a revival of Odets's *Rocket to the Moon* and the world première of John Hersey's *The Child Buyer*.

For two years our attendance was consistent—limited only by the size of the house and our occupancy of the theater, which was ours for only half of each year. This created the need for a permanent theater of our own and, soon after the opening of *The Child Buyer* (for which we received national reviews), we received a miraculous communication from the Ford Foundation informing us that we were receiving a grant of $500,000 "to be used toward the construction and operation of a theater on the University of California at Los Angeles campus." According to the formal citation:

The Theater Group has established a new pattern for a professional theater company. Through its activities over its first three years, professional theater has been added to the community resources traditionally provided by universities.

With that our fondest hopes seemed to be realized. We had a company and an audience. Now we were acquiring a home. No one seriously doubted our ability to raise the rest of the money required to erect a suitable playhouse on the fine plot of land that had been allocated to us by the university. In an interview with the *Los Angeles Times* I confidently predicted that the new theater would be ready for operation during the 1964-65 season: "With a house that will seat around 1000 and by presenting up to ten plays a year the Theater Group hopes to establish a regular audience of around 40,000 who will be looking forward to a stimulating evening in the theater ten times a year. Can anyone ask for more?"

This had been the state of our affairs when I departed for Europe, leaving the Group in the joint but divided charge of Abbott Kaplan, head of the UCLA Extension, Lamont Johnson, our associate director, and Ethel Winant (formerly of *Playhouse 90* and now my associate producer at MGM). On my return I was met by two pieces of bad news: the first that, in his enthusiasm, Lamont Johnson had mounted an ambitious summer season of classics (Lope de Vega's *Peribanez* and John Ford's *'Tis Pity She's a Whore*) which were difficult to produce and beyond our audience's comprehension. As a result they had lost most of the $45,000 we had so painfully accumulated over the past two years.

The second was far worse. At a board meeting held shortly after my return I was informed that the project of a playhouse on campus, though formally approved by the chancellor, required the official sanction of the university's regents of whom the most powerful, by far, was Dorothy (Buffy) Chandler, owner by marriage of the *Los Angeles Times* and a figure of enormous power in Southern California who was herself engaged in raising huge sums for the creation of the Los Angeles Music Center. When she heard of the Group's intention, she categorically forbade any further theatrical fund-raising until her own drive was completed. Since her word was law (all the more since the chancellor was, in fact, about to leave the university for a position in the Chandler organization) all plans for the Group's theater were being called off, and the land allocated to our building was being reassigned to more urgent uses.

The board was disappointed but unwilling to raise an academic storm. I had no such scruples. With my usual tact, I accused them of selling out to Mrs. Chandler and added that if the best we could hope for was to continue to function indefinitely as guests of the university, dependent for acting space on the whims of the Music and Humanities Departments, I, for one, was no longer interested.

The blow was a particularly painful one, coming so soon after my debacle at MGM and after what I still considered my betrayal by the American Shakespeare Festival. Once again, after a brilliant start, I had been defeated in my attempt to create a lasting theater organization.

My gloom was brief. Once again I was saved from demoralization by my ability to leap from one project to another and from one medium to another. *The Great Adventure* was announced to the world as a new, hour-long, weekly television series "based on American history and designed to furnish family viewing that is both exciting and entertaining."

In the spring of 1963, accompanied by Ethel Winant, I moved back to the CBS Television Center and into the same office I had occupied during *Playhouse 90*. And, while researchers on both coasts were digging up material and sifting through the mass of suggestions that had begun to come in, I was able to pay some attention to my personal life, which was not without problems.

Joan had had an operation that gave us momentary concern; Michael was off in Europe in a school near Paris and she missed him. Sebastian, aged eight, was in his usual disciplinary difficulties and came close to losing an eye when a neighbor's child shot at him point-blank with an air gun loaded with gravel. But my most immediate crisis was material. With the purchase of a big new house in Malibu, I suddenly found myself in such financial difficulties that my mail was once again filled with exasperated letters from my bank manager and my lawyer warning me of tragic consequences if I did not mend my ways. Glumly I accepted the first reasonable offer I received for the House on the Hill in New City. Joan had never been happy there and its sale eased my immediate financial problems; the loss of the first and only home I had ever built for myself roused deep secret feelings of guilt and remorse which presently dissolved in the pleasure we had both begun to take in our beautiful new home on the beach.

Joan had furnished it with her usual skill—mostly with things from New City and from our New York apartment (including hundreds of books making their third transcontinental crossing). One of her local purchases was a huge California farm table which, surrounded by the tall, straw-seated, rustic chairs I had bought in Rome, allowed us to increase our Sunday lunch parties to twelve and even sixteen. We had our "regulars," but we tried, through constant infusions of Eastern visitors and people not engaged in show business, to keep our parties from becoming routine Hollywood gatherings. Shop talk was inevitable, but too much of it was discouraged, and, over the years, a number of artistic and theatrical associations were formed there; a "monster" film was shot there one weekend by Andy Warhol; several love affairs started there—also two international marriages and a number of interesting "happenings" of which Anais Nin was often the organizer and star.

During our preparation for *The Great Adventure*, Ethel Winant and I were frequently reminded that the series was expected to be commercially as well as critically successful. By midsummer we had collected a dozen stories, half of them already in script form. Increasingly, as we approached production, we were subject to pressures from the network to make the series more "popular" and "patriotic"—with more shootings, more violence and, if possible, more sex.

Our first five shows were varied and exciting. (They dealt successively with the building and operation of the first small, man-driven submarine, an Indian massacre, Harriet Tubman and the "underground railroad," and the California farmers' war against the Southern Pacific.) But the pressures continued and I knew that more "popular" scripts were being prepared behind our backs. On July 27, more than two months before the first of our shows was due to go on the air, a columnist was writing in the *Los Angeles Times*:

There are indications that John Houseman's troubles with *The Great Adventure* spring from his going too "long hair"—in other words, taking too much time and spending too much money for a quality which the network bosses felt might not be appreciated by an early evening audience of kids (7:30 in the East, 6:30 in the Midwest).

All five of our shows were filmed and broadcast. They received uniformly favorable reviews and fair ratings. But, by then, I was no longer around.

This time, at Ethel Winant's insistence, I kept my mouth shut and refrained from my usual gesture of resignation. As a result, CBS Television had to pay me over $100,000 for the unexpired term of my contract. As for *The Great Adventure*, it stayed on the air for a few weeks after the last of my shows, then vanished without a trace.

* * *

Here I sit on my secluded, well-guarded beach, complete with wife and children and animals, waiting for lightning to strike. I have no immediate financial concerns and no projects or ambitions that go further than tomorrow morning. The more I try to peer into my future, the more murky it seems—shrouded in mists of fatigue and boredom—made denser by a new, sobering sense of the irrestistible approach of old age!

Writing to my friend, John Bartlow Martin, in Santo Domingo, where he was U.S. Ambassador, I was exaggerating, as usual. But this letter, written in the fall of 1963, accurately describes my state of mind at the time. After the adrenalin of my successive crises had drained off, I was left with the sobering realization that the two major show-business organizations (MGM and CBS) on which I had depended for more than a decade for lucrative employment were both closed to me for years to come. Following the settlement of my two contracts, I feared I might be acquiring the reputation of being, at best, a troublemaker and, at worst, a loser.

The knowledge that I was better situated financially than I had ever been helped me to face this new crisis without undue panic. But the new and chilling element that now appeared for the first time in my thinking was reflected in the final sentence of my note to John Martin.

At sixty-one I could say in all honesty that a sense of age had never played the slightest part in my planning. I had been a late starter—in my choice of work, in my emotional development and in my assumption of personal and professional responsibility. Having started late, I had so far to go and I was in such a frantic hurry to get there that I had remained quite unaware of the passage of years.

In fact, I might have continued to ignore my age entirely had it not been for my recent defeats. These forced me to face certain disturbing questions about my future. Was my recent succession of disappointments attributable to the normal odds of an uncertain and speculative business? ("You can't win them all!") Or was it due to my own gradual deterioration—a reduction of energy that was normal in a man of my age? In taming my ego and shedding the worst of my fears had I also lost some of my will to win?

These questions came up as I found myself considering some of the alternatives I was facing. Retirement was out of the question. Show business remained my chosen field in which my ever growing list of credits was such that I had little of my old terror of unemployment. What had begun to worry me was my own attitude towards my work. Previously, when I made my frequent, sometimes inane leaps from one activity to another, I made them thoughtlessly, with the tailwinds of fear and ambition blowing so strongly that it was all I could do to hold on. Now things were different. My spasms of despair and terror were less frequent and intense than before—but so were my libido and my blind drive to succeed. The tides that had raged around me for thirty years had swept me to a considerable height; but they had not prepared me for thoughts of declining productivity nor for the acceptance of such limited objectives as could be expected by a man who was entering the last quarter of his life.

It was during these months of uncertainty that I made my first undirected attempts to work on the account of my life in the theater that my friend Joe Barnes kept urging me to write. The little I achieved was not satisfactory, either as personal therapy or as contemporary history. The best I was able to squeeze out of my personal probe of the past was a series of disconnected notes and reminiscences. They afforded me some nostalgic satisfaction, but they proved quite worthless when I finally came to face the real problem of turning them into a book.

Once again I was distracted from my self-examinations by the offers of work that came my way. One came to me through the famous architect and designer, Charles Eames, who called me one day to ask if I would be interested in taking over a film he had agreed to make for New York's 1964 World's Fair but which he now found himself too busy to undertake. It was to be a fifteen-minute film dealing with the history of immigration in the United States over the past two hundred years. I said yes and flew once again to New York where I was informed that the film was being made at the express request of President Kennedy to help create a favorable climate for the new immigration laws he was about to submit to Congress. Otherwise I was free to choose my own form and content.

Given the brevity of the film, the immensity of the subject and the short time at my disposal, it soon became evident that *Voyage to America* (as it came to be called) could best be told through a dramatic and imaginative use of existing graphic material (photographs, drawings, cartoons and engravings of the period) of which there was an extraordinary wealth. Since Nick Ray was off in Europe, I found three local associates: Richard McCann, film critic and West Coast correspondent for the *Christian Science Monitor*, Ben Jackson, a young filmmaker just out of UCLA; Dorothy Jeakins, on whom I counted for the research and selection of material.

By early November we had assembled the draft of a script and some choice graphic material that I took east with me to submit to the White House for approval. I was lunching in the Oak Room of the Plaza Hotel, discussing the script with one of Kennedy's bright young men, when the news came—in whispered disbelief at first, then confirmed on radio and ticker tape and spreading like wildfire—that the President had been wounded and, a moment later, that he was dead. I remember drifting, aimless and incredulous, from table to table and then out onto Fifth Avenue, where drivers sat frozen behind the wheels of their cars and pedestrians stared at one another or talked in bewildered whispers.

In January I sent a first rough print of the film to Virgil Thomson with a request for another of his great American fugues—such as he had composed for *The River, Louisiana Story* and *Tuesday in November*. Within a month it had been recorded by Eugene Ormandy and the Philadelphia Orchestra. Projected on the back wall of the vast entrance hall through which the crowds streamed into the U.S. Federal Pavilion, *Journey to America* achieved a record of sorts by being shown more than fifty times a day (five times an hour for ten hours a day) over a period of several months. According to one patriotic reviewer, "it should be shown every twelve minutes around the world."

I enjoyed making it, yet I never quite got over the feeling that it would have been a more original and striking film if Charles Eames had been able to execute it.

My decision to live in Europe came as a surprise to everyone, including myself. I consulted no one and gave little thought to the consequences such a violent change would have on my own life and on the lives of my wife and children. (When I broached the subject to Joan, I discovered that she was, as usual, far ahead of me and had faced and accepted the prospect of total upheaval some time before.)

I was well aware of the recklessness of my move and of the great risk I was taking in throwing away my professional safety nets and giving up a security it had taken me more than half my life to achieve. But, like most of my crucial decisions (such as lingering in Argentina instead of going to Cambridge; sailing suddenly to America at twenty-three, leaving my English life behind me without thought or regret; walking penniless into the theater at the age of thirty-one without experience or prospects of any sort), this one was made suddenly and arbitrarily in response to some deep, subconscious, irreversible urge that was quite impervious to sense or reason. Once I had made it, I never had one single moment of hesitation or misgiving, even though it was not entirely clear to me or anyone else exactly what this mad excursion was expected to accomplish.

On the negative side, there was the growing mood of vague discontent into which I had been drifting over the past few years, together with the lack of commitment without which I was finding much of my work stale and unprofitable. This restlessness extended to my personal relationships. There was nothing wrong with my marriage or my family or the large circle of my friends. In that respect my situation compared favorably with that of most of my peers. But it lacked motion: it was predictable and monotonous. In that sense this voyage was an escape—a flight from what I felt to be the diminishing returns of my life.

Another, more positive motive for this self-imposed exile was the hope that I might finally be able to write that book I was always talking about. Progress so far had been ridiculously slow: Joe Barnes' attempt to encourage me by giving me a publisher's contract and a modest advance had not helped. Perhaps in Europe, free of the distractions and inhibitions with which I went to such pains to surround myself at home, I might finally feel free to write the story I was so eager to tell.

By late spring, my bridges had been burned: my decision to move to Paris was final, and the machinery for the liquidation of our lives in Malibu had been set in motion. This involved renting the house, getting the boys out of school, disposing of animals and automobiles, and dealing with the logistical problems involved in such a major migration. As usual, the bulk of this tedious and painful labor fell on Joan who executed it with her usual reluctant efficiency. Only, once in a while, I would catch her looking wistfully around the rooms of our house, her eyes misting at the thought of once again leaving one of her beautiful homes in which she was convinced she would never live again. As usual, she was right.

Before leaving for Europe there was one final duty I had to perform. I wanted my association with the Theater Group, on which I had lavished so much love and energy, to end with a bang, not a whimper.

I called Kaplan and told him that, before leaving, I wanted to direct *King Lear* for the Theater Group, first at UCLA and then in an outdoor amphitheater in Hollywood Hills, known as the Pilgrimage Theater, which had a good stage, remarkable acoustics and an intimacy that was rare in outdoor theaters.

To do *Lear* you must have a King and, by good fortune, I had one. I had seen Carnovsky's *Lear* at Stratford the previous summer and admired it (though, with a normal director's ego, I had found things I would have done differently). I had run into him at a party and asked him if he had any desire to do Lear again. Morris replied that he did. Now I called and repeated my question. He said he was available and intrested and we fixed a date for rehearsal.

This West Coast *Lear* bore little physical resemblance to what I had done in New York fourteen years before. In place of my raked platform, I ordered six massive towers of abstract form which, set in a rough semicircle at the rear of the stage, could be turned and moved to form walls, gates, battlements, a jousting ring and, simply, the ominous background for a storm or battle. They were designed and hand-painted by a young sculptor in the UCLA Art Department named Oliver Andrews.

I had known, from the beginning, that I would never entirely recapture the exhilaration and terror through which I had lived during the production of my first *Lear*. And I had faced the fact that Calhern and Carnovsky would be very different Lears. Neither was a master of theatrical verse but each, in his own way, had the stage presence and vocal power that are essential for the part. Morris lacked the personal beauty and the decaying elegance that made Calhern's King such a moving and tragic figure. But he had a massive nobility of his own and he made effective use of the patriarchal tradition that has distinguished so many of the great Lears in the Jewish theater.

We opened successfully in Schoenberg Hall on June 8, though there were moments when I feared that the walls of that small auditorium would explode with the violence of that superhuman tragedy. Once again the Theater Group was hailed as having "reached the summit of its existence."

Two days later we began rehearsal on the outdoor stage of the Pilgrimage Theater. To take advantage of this new location, I made drastic changes, particularly in entrances and exits and in the physical scope and projection of the production. And I invited Gordon Davidson, who had been my stage manager in Stratford, to fly out and join me as assistant director. Another welcome reunion was with Jean Rosenthal, who happened to be in California as consultant for the new theaters being built in the Music Center, and who contributed new miracles of light to our outdoor production.

Carnovsky's finest performances were given in the Pilgrimage Theater, and in my own memory it was this outdoor production that justified the huge effort of restaging *King Lear*. It gave the play a stature that could never be achieved indoors: the storm scenes, in particular, were the best I have ever seen—the small, tattered band of the King and his followers coming down the steep, wooded hill, their clothes flapping and their torches blowing in the wind, is a sight I shall never forget.

The *New York Times* sent its first-string critic to the West Coast:

In a year of many Lears the finest is being performed by Morris Carnovsky in a dramatic outdoor theater carved out of the side of a Hollywood hill. With the rocks towering darkly in the background, it takes on the terror of a primeval force and the pity of the inescapably tragic human condition. Supported by a cast of high caliber, the curve of his performance is now irreproachably sustained. It moves like pitiless fate from stubborn wrongheadedness through intemperate wrath to disbelief, madness, humility and tenderness to a final redemptive strength.

Now I had only a short time left to savor my success and to wind up my affairs in California. To the Theater Group my parting gift was the suggestion that Gordon Davidson be invited to succeed me as artistic director. My advice was taken and greatly affected the future of theater in Los Angeles.

For my own part, even if I had wanted to change my mind at the last moment, it was too late. The liquidation of my life in Malibu had gone too far. Our house was easy to rent; a wealthy tenant had been found, and this monthly income, added to the severance payments from MGM and CBS, assured us of a comfortable life in Europe for two or three years.

Our numerous animals happily found new homes—all except Joan's diminutive Yorkshire terrier, Mousy-Cat, who would, of course, accompany his mistress to Paris. Our fleet of cars, four in all, was easily parted with, except for a vintage Thunderbird to which Joan was particularly attached and which we decided to take to Europe with us. Finally, there was the dispersal and disposal of personal and household possessions.

As soon as I began to look into the question of how to move two grown-ups, two boys, a vast amount of baggage, one car, a mass of household equipment and a very small dog from Southern California to France without spending half our year's income on travel, it became evident that it must be by ship. (We were in no great hurry; a leisurely decompression from one world to the other was actually desirable.) Investigation revealed that a French line had a fleet of freighters, running a regular schedule through the Panama Canal between the Pacific Coast and Le Havre.

I booked passage on the motorship *Maryland*, due to sail during the first week of August. By the time *King Lear* opened we had said goodbye to our animals, buyers had taken possession of our automobiles, and our liquor (except for a few vintage wines that were put into storage) was being drunk up in a long series of farewell parties.

Our sailing turned into something of a happening. Getting our goods and chattels to the dock was a massive undertaking: two hired trucks and a procession of cars including the departing Thunderbird carried some forty or fifty persons down the coast from Malibu to Long Beach, where the *Maryland* lay at her berth. Like pirates boarding a prize, we swarmed aboard, took possession of our cabins (one for Joan and me, one for the boys), then invaded the upper deck and opened the champagne. From there, as the afternoon wore on, we leaned over the railing and watched our possessions, including the Thunderbird, being lowered into the darkness of the ship's gaping hold. At dusk the ship's bell was rung and the last of our well-wishers was ordered ashore. We watched their unsteady descent and continued waving to them on the dock as the *Maryland* moved slowly out to sea. Soon after that, the oil wells on Signal Hill faded in the smog. But it was not until the last low hills of the Southern California coast had sunk into the sea that the full enormity of what I was doing was finally borne in on me.

XXVII
Paris
1964-65

In this flawed world there may not be such a thing as a perfect month, but our three and a half weeks' voyage aboard the *Maryland* brought us closer to it than we had thought possible.

For twenty-four days the sun shone and the sea was smooth as glass. The gentle motion of the ship became part of our lives; it rocked us to sleep at night and gave a pleasant, tidelike motion to the sea water in the canvas swimming pool the crew had rigged on deck and in which John Michael and Sebastian spent several hours of each day—spidery pink figures against the pale blue of the ocean.

We discovered, after our well-wishers had left the ship, that there were only nine passengers aboard, including the four of us. (Three got off at Aruba, leaving only two others.)We also discovered that the ship's food was delicious (French *cuisine bourgeoise* washed down with two wines at every meal) and that our crew, mostly Bretons, was made up of agreeable, intelligent men. They invited the boys into the wheelhouse for an hour every morning to steer the ship and joined us in ruthless games of shuffleboard in the late afternoon. In the evening John Michael and the captain played backgammon.

Our cabins were comfortable if not spacious and I soon transformed the ship's saloon into a private study where I sat every morning, looking out of the window as I forced myself back in time and struggled to find a form for the book to which this voyage had irrevocably committed me. It was a curious feeling to be delving into the remote depths of my European childhood while staring out at the sunlit tropical Pacific Ocean. But around that small desk in the corner of that paneled room I did manage, for hours at a time, to create a vacuum which allowed me to float free of the present and to drift back into those remote regions where my life had been formed. After three weeks I had less than a dozen pages to show for my six to eight hours of concentrated daily work. But, finally, a start had been made.

The weather held as we crossed the Atlantic and it was not until our twenty-fifth day, as we approached the coast of France, that we became aware of an extreme barometric change. The first officer warned us that we were heading into foul weather. As we entered the Bay of Biscay our radio picked up reports of ships in distress, and once, off to starboard, faintly through a curtain of rain and spray, I caught sight of a small ship wallowing in that awful steel-colored flood. Late the next afternoon, in a sudden, unnatural calm, we docked at Le Havre. By eleven the next morning we were through customs and in possession of the Thunderbird in which the four of us (five, including Mousy-Cat), together with a mass of hand luggage, were squeezed into a car built for two. In our excitement at being together on French soil we ignored our discomfort as we drove south towards Paris, where we arrived just in time for the magnificent fireworks display with which General de Gaulle chose to celebrated the anniversary of the liberation of Paris.

The next day we moved, bag and baggage (including the thirteen trunks and packing cases that arrived by road from Le Havre), into an apartment we had rented by long distance near the Parc Monceau. It was a typically over-decorated upper-middle-class Parisian flat—pretentious and expensive and not entirely suited to our needs, with its elaborate green Directoire salon, its formal dining room and elegant master bedroom.

Here we spent our first five months in a city which for each of us represented something entirely different. For Joan it meant a return, after sixteen years, to the place in which she had spent the first thirty years of her life, including the bad years of the Occupation. It was a return she had dreaded but to which she adjusted far more more readily than she expected. Within a few weeks she had renewed her close relations with her mother and re-established a number of friendships in what was left of her Paris world of the thirties and forties.

For John Michael and Sebastian, Paris represented yet another change of surroundings. Armed with what French John Michael had acquired during his year in France and with what they had both absorbed by osmosis from Joan and me at home and, more recently, from the crew of the *Maryland*, they were soon familiar with the Parisian transportation system and roamed the city at will in total disregard of the cultural itineraries laid out for them by their two grandmothers. They found the open spaces around the Palais de Chaillot particularly suited to skate-boarding, and their photographs appeared one morning in the *Paris Herald Tribune* as pioneers in this, the latest American sport to cross the Atlantic.

Mousy-Cat, on his part, took to Paris like a duck to water. The sidewalks offered smells that were more heady and varied than those of the Malibu beaches, and the lush green lawns of the Parc Monceau seemed particularly seductive. Not even the stiff brooms with which he was threatened by certain ill-tempered concierges of the neighborhood could dampen his spirits.

My own reactions were more complicated. During our filming of *Lust for Life* I had been overwhelmed by the city's incredible beauty. This time I was no longer a visitor, living it up in the cosmopolitan luxury of the Hotel Georges V. I was here now as a resident with the calculated and dangerous purpose of recapturing the most impressionable years of my life.

Within a few days of our arrival I resumed the work schedule I had set up on the *Maryland*. I started at eight each morning adn went on until I could work no longer. Then, to clear my head after hours of painful and seemingly useless effort, I would wander, without aim or direction, through the concentric, tree-lined avenues that had been laid out in the previous century by my namesake, the Baron Haussmann. Often, as I walked, I had the feeling that I had been there before; the buildings and shops and trees that lined those wide, well-tended streets had the vague familiarity of a landscape in a recurrent dream. Even the street sounds, far from seeming strange, confirmed this sense of recognition.

One afternoon, quite by chance, in one of those short, steep streets that link the Avenue Friedland to the Champs-Elysées, I suddenly came upon the small residential hotel in which my father and mother had lived for so many years. And, instantly, I understood that within this modest building lay the heart of the mystery I had come here to unravel. It was here, in my parents' bedroom, that my tonsils were bloodily removed; here, while munching croissants dipped in *café au lait* in my parents' warm bed, that I had listened in wonder to my father reciting Corneille, Racine and Victor Hugo over his washbasin. It was to this place that my father had come home in great agitation one evening in August 1914 to announce that France was at war with Germany. And it was here, above all, that I had created that secret universe of fantasies and desires in which my mother was queen and I was her only beloved son—that private Garden of Eden for which I had yearned so desperately throughout the desolating loneliness of my English schooldays and for so many years after that.

This discovery released such a flood of nostalgia that, for some weeks, I found myself living on two quite separate and often conflicting levels: that of our well-organized family life at 99 Rue de Prony and that other, more exciting world I entered the moment I was alone and shared with no one: a world of sights and sounds and intimate memories that had lain buried for more than half a century. Gradually my world of ghosts became more vivid and satisfying than the realities of the present. Then, as the first thrill of rediscovery wore off, it became evident that these journeys into the past were becoming an end in themselves and that they had gone far beyond the needs of the book of which they were supposed to furnish the emotional base.

After several sterile weeks I decided to take advantage of an offer Virgil Thomson had made me. He owned a small apartment on the Quai Voltaire in a building in which Ingres had once painted. For close to two months this became my daytime refuge and hiding place, the laboratory in which I struggled to make the agonizing conjunction between the past and the present, between my childhood memories and the personal and professional events of my adult life.

Among the baggage that had emerged from the hold of the *Maryland* was a massive but delicate German tape recorder through which I now made daily explorations of the various layers of my past. They followed no chronological order. Each day I would choose one or more specific memories with which to begin and from which I wandered freely as one recollection evoked another. Sometimes I talked, without stopping, for the two hours that a tape lasted. Sometimes I fell asleep in the middle of a sentence and went on when I awoke. At other times I would fly off in an entirely different direction, following some bright splinter of memory that had surfaced during my sleep. It was a painful but enormously exciting and satisfying process that left me drained and dizzy.

Within a few weeks several dozen reels had accumulated in a corner of Virgil's room. They contained miles of tape on which an intimate but disorganized and fragmentary account of the first two dozen years of my life had been recorded in several hundred thousand words. They might have remained in that form for ever but for a fortunate accident. My former MGM secretary, Marian Fenn, had accompanied her current husband to England, where the Living Theater was opening its first major European tour. I got an urgent call one night from London, where the première had been such a disaster that the company was temporarily disbanding. Did I have a job for her? I urged her to come over immediately and found a room for her in a horrid little hotel not far from the Quai Voltaire. She was a lightning typist and, since she was being paid by the page, she sat there, day after day, before a rented American typewriter, transcribing those miles of often obscure and occasionally embarrassing tapes, stopping only when her sight failed or when her fingers froze on the keys. When the last tape was transcribed she took her money and flew back to

California, leaving me 680 triple-spaced pages to struggle with. Much of it was repetitious, self-pitying and useless. But when *Run-Through* was finally written several years later, the first part of it was, in fact, a corrected, reorganized and drastically edited version of that outpouring.

The completion of these tapes coincided with a sudden change in our lives. We had rented our apartment for one year but, after five months, Joan persuaded the owner to release us and moved us all to an entirely different part of town, much closer to her own former haunts. It was a smaller, cheaper, less elegant but more likeable apartment in the heart of Montparnasse, only a few blocks from those favorite establishments of the intelligentsia, the Dôme, the Rotonde and the Coupole. A few hundred yards away, on the other side, was the Montparnasse cemetery, in whose Jewish section my father lay buried and, a few blocks beyond that, the little house which had been Joan's mother's home for so many years and where Joan herself had grown up. Here we lived among local shops, cafés, seedy nightclubs (including one notorious Lesbian establishment) and run-down hotels to which the cheerful, hard-working ladies who plied their trade on every corner were in the habit of conducting their customers.

The move had a stimulating effect on us all. John Michael and Sebastian had recently celebrated their respective birthdays (thirteen and ten), and they too welcomed this new environment, in which they lived a freer and more colorful life than in the middle-class respectability of the Rue de Prony, where no flame-swallowers, escape artists or other mountebanks had ever appeared after dark as they did almost every evening in the Boulevard Edgar Quinet. A bus from the American School came for them every morning and the boys seemed to board it less reluctantly than before. (It was not until months later that we discovered that, as they sat each morning outside the corner bistro waiting for their bus to arrive, they were both fortifying themselves, like the French workmen around them, with a brimming glass of Calvados.)

For my part, with my 680 pages of confession safely stowed in a suitcase under my bed, I was finally getting around to dealing with the current problems of life with Joan in Paris. Among the contacts I established were several with former members of the French section of the Voice of America, including the red-haired peanut-faced Lazareff himself. Since their return to France, in the midforties, Pierre and his wife, Hélène, had become dominant figures in French journalism, publishing, film and television. It amused Pierre to introduce me to his partners over lunch at the Berkley as *"mon boss américain,"* and on Sunday Joan and I drove out in the Thunderbird to one of the famous lunches that he and Hélène gave in their country house near Versailles, where, in the course of a few hours, we seemed to meet every French figure of prominence from Coco Chanel to the Pompidous.

I had arrived in Europe with an assignment from a New York theatrical magazine, *Show*, to write a series of articles about the French and, later, the Italian and German theaters. I had ignored it during my months of self-exploration, but I returned to it now with renewed energy. Finding myself back in the theater, even as a spectator viewing plays in another language, broke down some of the isolation in which I had been living for the past seven months.

The truth is that by the spring of 1965 I had begun to enjoy my life in Paris. At the same time I was starting to worry, once again, about money. The gloomy communications I received from my lawyer in New York indicated that our expenses abroad were running far higher than expected. The three years of travel I had promised myself were reduced to two—one of which was more than half spent. These financial concerns may have been the spur I needed. I went to Brentano's on the rue de Rivoli, bought *Roget's Thesaurus* in its latest edition and began writing. Within a week of finishing my first theater article and sending it off to New York, I was deep into an entirely unpremeditated piece for *Harper's* magazine which described the strange manner in which Raymond Chandler and I had completed the screenplay of *The Blue Dahlia*. *Harper's* accepted it and it appeared (with some cuts and dramatic subheadings of which I disapproved) in the July issue.

Soon after I had sent off the *Harper's* piece I received two transatlantic phone calls within a few days of each other. The first was from Ray Stark, whom I had known for years as one of Hollywood's sharpest and most ambitious agents, and more recently as a successful Broadway and film producer. His latest project, a starring vehicle for Natalie Wood and Robert Redford, was a film based on Tennessee Williams's *This Property Is Condemned*. Ray offered me $50,000 plus living expenses if I would come to Los Angeles and produce it for him: the whole thing would take up no more than three or four months of my time.

I had never before taken over a film prepared by someone else, for which a script had alredy been written and the leading actors selected. However, it was the first big-time offer I had received in fifteen months and, as I pointed out to Joan, it would buy us another year abroad.

I don't know how much I was swayed in my decision by another transatlantic call I received a few days later. This was from New York, from the head of the Juilliard Music School. It was entirely unexpected

and opened up such astonishing vistas that all I could say to him was
that I would soon be in America and would prefer to discuss the
proposal in person. I told Joan of the call but not of its implications.
And that night I called Ray Stark in California and accepted his offer.
As usual, he was in a tearing hurry and he urged me to fly to California
within a week.

Ray Stark's Seven Arts Company occupied an entire floor in a new
bank building in Beverly Hills. Here he operated in an atmosphere of
feverish activity and here, on the morning of my arrival, I encountered
a dark, bearded, intense young man who was introduced to me as
Francis Ford Coppola. He was a recent graduate of UCLA's film
department whom Ray kept locked in a small cell, turning out
first-draft screenplays at the rate of around one a month for a
minimum wage. The script of *This Property Is Condemned* was mostly
his.

To direct his film Ray had wooed John Huston and failed. In his
place he now sought my approval for a newcomer by the name of
Sydney Pollack, whom I knew from television and as an observer who
had sat in on my rehearsals at UCLA. He was a dark, neurotic young
man of considerable talent and furious ambition. No sooner had he
signed his contract than he set about compulsively trying to undermine
my position and to form an alliance with Natalie to gain control of the
film. This maneuver was facilitated by the fact that we were shooting a
weak screenplay, publicly repudiated by Tennessee. In the weeks
before and during shooting, as many as five writers were assigned to
the script, each working to please a different person and each trying to
strengthen the film's contrived and dubious love story. While this
troupe of writers was slaving away I took a long weekend and flew to
New York for my meeting with Peter Mennin at Juilliard. He was a
composer of repute as well as a calculating executive who had become
convinced, after much consultation, that I was the man best qualified to
set up and head Juilliard's new Drama Division. Our first meeting was
tense but positive. I came away with a number of questions still
unanswered, but, with two months still to go on the film, I had plenty
of time to consider my decision. It was agreed that we would meet
again when I returned to New York and that I would give him my final
answer at that time.

Our first location for *This Property Is Condemned* was a modest
resort town on Mississippi's Gulf Coast, not far from the Louisiana
state line. It had a one-track railroad station and a spur of track along
which we could work undisturbed except for the passage of two
freights a day. From there we moved to New Orleans, which I found
sadly changed from the romantic city in which I had dwelled briefly in

the fall of 1927 (supervising the loading of wheat shipments to Europe). We shot for two weeks in the French Quarter, then flew back to California for another month of studio work on the Paramount lot. By now I was so discouraged and irritated that even Pollack's continued manipulations failed to disturb me. Some of our footage, particularly the scenes between Natalie and Kate Reid, had real dramatic quality, and Charles Bronson lent his own special kind of energy to the scenes at the water hole. But our love scenes (the combined product of five well-paid Hollywood writers) made no sense at all.

The film had been rough-cut as we went along. I left the final editing to Pollack and Stark and, within a few days of the end of shooting, I was on my way back to New York for my decisive meeting with Peter Mennin.

It was not until I was halfway across the Atlantic that I began to rehearse what I would say to Joan about what had just been decided. We had spoken on the phone; she knew of the Juilliard offer and, though I had given her few details, she could not fail to be aware of its consequences. Knowing me as she did after fifteen years of living together, she must also have known that I would accept it. When I informed her on the night of my arrival, over a welcoming glass of champagne, that we would soon be returning to America and that our home, for the next few years, would be Manhattan and not Malibu, she had already made her adjustment to the situation. What I did not dare to tell her until later was that before leaving New York, in my exhilaration over my new life, I had spent most of the money I had just made on Stark's film buying an apartment on Gramercy Park.

XXVIII
Juilliard
1966-68

The Juilliard School was half a century old and was generally regarded as one of the world's leading musical conservatories. When the Rockefellers, early in the fifties, decided to created a vast new midtown art center that would include the Metropolitan Opera, the New York State Theater, a repertory theater and a branch of the New York Public Library, they decided that they also needed an educational arm. Juilliard Music School was invited to Lincoln Center, to occupy what was to become, architecturally, the most distinguished building in the new complex. It was agreed that if Juilliard was to be a true conservatory of the performing arts, it must add theater to its curriculum.

Since the Juilliard building was the last to go up, Peter Mennin, when he assumed the presidency of the Music School in 1962, had several years in which to make his decisions about his new Drama Division and its personnel. A preliminary study had been made some years earlier by an outstanding figure in the field, the Anglo-French director and educator Michel Saint-Denis. (Starting as an actor under his celebrated uncle, Jacques Copeau, he had formed the Compagnie de Quinze before moving to England and organizing the London Theater Studio where he had been an inspiration to Gielgud, Olivier, Redgrave and many others. After the war—in association with George Devine, Glen Byam Shaw and Tyrone Guthrie—he had set up the celebrated Old Vic School.)

Saint-Denis had spent eighteen months in the United States, observing the theatrical scene from coast to coast and making suggestions for a training program to meet the current needs and conditions of the American theater. When he returned to Europe, the opening of the School was still several years away: he left his findings at Juilliard where they became known as "the Saint-Denis bible."

Meantime, the Lincoln Center for the Performing Arts had slowly risen out of the ground. Last of its structures to open was the Beaumont Theater where the repertory company was having its own problems of artistic management. It had been assumed that the repertory company and Juilliard's Drama Division would be closely allied: it now became evident that the school must be set up independently with a strong director and a firm theatrical viewpoint of its own.

I have never known how many candidates were considered for the position, nor how my name finally rose to the top of the pile. I have always believed that one of the prime movers in my appointment was the unpredictable Lincoln Kirstein. We had had our artistic and emotional differences, but we shared a sense of continuity and a firm belief in the classics as a basis of training. I do know that my candidacy was supported by McNeill Lowrie of the Ford Foundation who qualified his approval, I learned later, with the warning that I was a prickly and opinionated character who would not be easy to deal with.

On my part, unlike many of my crucial decisions, this one was not lightly or hurriedly made. Whatever I decided now, at sixty-four, seemed to constitute a final commitment, one that would directly and permanently affect what was left of my life. Juilliard represented a position of prestige and security. At the same time it meant my acceptance of the fact that my best days in show business were over and a final surrender of the illusion, so dear to every man and woman in show business, that the Big Break is just around the corner. Also, it meant a drastic drop in income at a time when our boys were about to enter the expensive part of their education. It also meant living once again in New York and I knew that this would create a serious problem for Joan.

My decision to accept Mennin's offer had been motivated, finally, by none of these things. It was made in response to the challenge offered by this unexpected opportunity to attempt something new and entirely different. Offered the opportunity to create and direct the country's most advanced and effective theater conservatory, it became absolutely necessary for me to prove that it was something I was capable of doing.

With my usual mixture of modesty and arrogance, I made a conscientious appraisal of my capacity to organize such an institution. As an educator my experience was limited; but conducting a conservatory, like running a theater, called for a delicate balance of creative and executive authority and energy, and these I felt I possessed to an unusual degree. I had organized no fewer than seven theater companies; I had produced and/or directed a great variety of professional classical productions in New York and elsewhere. And I had been involved, in one way or another, with most of the significant American theater movements of the past thirty years.

Timing too played its part. I felt that this was a particularly propitious moment for the creation of such a school. Following the recent renaissance of regional theater in America, there were, by now, several dozen active, viable, effective theaters in operation throughout the country—with more on the way. These new companies made entirely different demands on their artists than either Broadway or the mass media. They called for an ability on the part of their actors to work in a wide range of periods and styles. In consequence, one of the most important and vital functions to be fulfilled in today's American theater was the creation of a carefully planned and developed actor-training program suited to meet these new professional needs. To create the model for such a program appealed strongly to the combination of personal ambition and the urge for public service that had played such a persistent part in my professional life.

I was back in Paris in time for the family Christmas rituals and for the sixteenth anniversary of a marriage which, all passion spent and in spite of certain areas of chronic misunderstanding, had come to represent, for Joan and myself, the only real and durable relationship in our lives.

I had been away for close to five months—our longest separation yet—but on the Boulevard Edgar Quinet little seemed to have changed in my absence. The same ladies of easy virtue stood on the same corners; the market booths were still set up before dawn every Tuesday and Friday; the fire-eaters and escape-artists still performed during the weekend.

Soon after the turn of the year I went traveling again. My first and most distant voyage was made at the invitation of my old, dear friend Rosamond Gilder. A theater conference was being held in New Delhi under the auspices of UNESCO and the International Theater Institute and she urged me to accompany her. As future head of America's leading theatrical conservatory, it behooved me to attend such a function; I met her in Paris and went on with her from there, with a stop in Beirut.

On the night of our arrival in Delhi, after an exhausting flight, we were driven to a ceremony held on a vast plain outside the city, of which the traditional climax was the setting alight of brightly colored 50-foot-high wicker effigies by flaming arrows, while hundreds of thousands cheered as they collapsed and were devoured by flames. The next night there was an exhibition of Kali dancers—bright, oversized and masked, in their slow, interminable, gyrating ritual combats ending with the fall and death of the villain from whose gaping mouth long reels of scarlet tape unwound and covered the stage with paper blood. My strongest impression, finally, was not of the Taj Mahal, to which we were duly conducted, but of the neighboring red marble palace at Fatehpur Sikri, which, in the splendor and extravagance of its formal planning, made me think of the structure erected by the Sun King at Versailles a century later.

The theater conference itself, the first of many I attended in my new academic role, was of limited interest. The fashion that year was antiliterary—to decry the written text in favor of improvisation and spontaneous creation by actors and director. There were long speeches on the subject, including mine, in opposition, and I was introduced to Madame Gandhi.

A shorter but more productive voyage was one I made the following month to Stratford-upon-Avon to visit Michel Saint-Denis. I had not seen him in seven years (since he had lectured for us at Stratford) and I found him older and frailer but still full of energy and ideas. I spent two days with him and his handsome Russian wife, Suria, in their house near the theater (where I saw *The Tempest* and *Cymbeline* with Vanessa Redgrave as Imogen) and discovered that the chances of obtaining the Saint-Denis' collaboration in the organization of Juilliard's Drama Division were not as remote as I had feared. I found Michel receptive to my proposal that he and Suria join me as consultant directors of the Drama Division. With his consent I sent a cable to Peter Mennin informing him of the Saint-Denis' availability. Michel and Suria would be going to France in a few weeks; at that time we would meet again in Paris, put our agreement into final form and discuss the structure of the new school.

The time was approaching when I must return to America—on Juilliard business and because it was time to enroll our son Michael in an American school. Joan decided to stay on with Sebastian till the end of the school year, then to join me in California where I had promised her we would spend the summer. I left with regret, for suddenly, as I was leaving, I had fallen in love with Paris. The spring had been miraculous: there was lilac blooming in Joan's mother's garden and along the walls of the Montparnasse cemetery, into which I wandered with Michael one afternoon to take a last look at his grandfather's grave.

While I was busy packing and preparing for departure, the Saint-Denis arrived from London. We held a series of conferences in which we laid down as much as we could o the Drama Division's curriculum. I was impressed by Michel's vast experience and by the energy and clarity of his ideas and I felt we accomplished a lot. We worked hard—seven or eight hours a day: I noticed that by midafternoon Saint-Denis would grow tired and vague and, except for an occasional sharp, emphatic interjection, leave most of the talking to

Suria. We made a date to meet again in New York during the summer but, on the night following our last meeting, while my son and I were in midair over the Atlantic, Michel Saint-Denis suffered the first of a series of strokes that diminished and, within a few years, completely destroyed him.

We had a good summer in California in a modest but agreeable house on a hilltop with a spectacular view of the ocean. Our own house in the Malibu Colony had been rented and then sold at twice what we had paid for it, but this failed to console Joan for its loss. She spent much of her time dismantling the home she hated to leave and shipping things to a city that she had always feared and detested and in which she seemed condemned to spend the next ten years of her life.

Joan's distress was aggravated by the visit we finally paid to the New York apartment I had acquired to impulsively the previous spring. What I had described as a glamorous duplex in one of New York's most desirable locations turned out to be considerably less than that. In the state in which it had been left by its former occupant (an extremely old, bedridden lady who had lived there for half a century) it looked drab, musty, cheerless and ridiculously cramped for a family of four. Joan grieved for a while, then set about converting it, at considerable cost, into one of the most attractive small dwellings in New York City. But there was nothing she could do about its size and we remained crowded and constricted throughout the three years we inhabited it.

My contract with the School called for my full employment by the winter of 1966. Since our new quarters would not be ready for a year or more, I was given an office on the ground floor of the old building on Claremont Avenue. It was a large, dark, gloomy space (formerly used as a faculty room) into which I moved with Marian Fenn, who had re-entered my employ with the new title of administrative assistant. Our equipment consisted of two ancient desks and one filing cabinet, two telephones, busts of Beethoven and Brahms and a huge, exploded sofa. Here I spent eighteen months laying the foundation of the Drama Division. This involved much reading, innumerable interviews and endless correspondence and phone calls to schools, universities and theatrical institutions all over the country, informing them of our existence and asking them for suggestions and recommendations. It meant humble visits to major foundations and consultations with the Department of Education in Albany; also visits to regional theaters, universities and even high schools that had acquired a reputation for theatrical training. I also spent many hours with the controller going over budgets and with the dean checking the academic requirements that would give the new Drama Division an accredited university standing.

My longest voyage (undertaken once again in the company of Rosamond Gilder) was to Sweden, to attend one of a series of international theater conferences at which members of theater schools and conservatories discussed the problems of actor training. This one took place in Stockholm and had as its subject *"le baggage culturel de l'acteur"* (cultural equipment for the actor). Though, in my shyness and ignorance, I kept my mouth shut during the four days of the conference, I found it absorbing, not so much for the pedagogic information I collected as for the glimpses it gave me into the personalities and activities of my future colleagues on both sides of the Iron Curtain. And I took advantage of the Saint-Denis' presence to continue working with him and Suria on the development of our plans for the School.

Though my attention was focused on Juilliard that year, I found myself, following my incurable habit, scattering my energies in various other directions. One was an entertainment I devised for the opening of the new auditorium at the California Institute of Technology in Pasadena; it was a potpourri of dramatic material, all realating to marriage, that included Strindberg, Ibsen, Samuel Butler, Shaw, and Beckett's *Happy Days*. Another was my growing involvement in the artistic affairs of what had become one of the most lively theatrical organizations in the country. Known as the APA-Phoenix, it was a partnership of Ellis Rabb's Association of Performing Artists and T. Edward Hambleton's Phoenix Theater, with both of which I had been vaguely associated since their formation. Their recent union resulted in three successful seasons of New York repertory—the first in a small theater uptown, the second and third on Broadway in the famous Lyceum Theater.

During the off season the APA-Phoenix was in the habit of presenting its repertory (which, that year, included *The Wild Duck, War and Peace*, Ionesco's *Exit the King* and George Kelly's *The Show-Off*) in Ann Arbor, Michigan, Toronto and Los Angeles where, in the summer of 1967, we opened the new production with which I was most directly concerned—*Pantagleize* by the great Belgian playwright de Ghelderode, which Ellis Rabb and I had adapted together and which we were now co-directing. Throughout its initial rehearsals in New York, Joan had been our production assistant. Now we all met again in Southern California for final rehearsals.

Pantagleize is described by its author as "a farce to make you sad." Its main character is an innocent, Chaplinesque Everyman whose casual remark, on awakening, that "it's a lovely day" triggers a revolution and projects him into a fantastic and finally tragic destiny. The production was a demanding one, requiring imagination and skill, most of which was provided by Rabb, as director and star. Once again, as with Welles years before, I was surprised (given my own competitive nature) by my ungrudging willingness to subordinate my ego to an associate whom (in this instance at least) I considered my superior in creative ability.

Pantagleize had a good engagement in Los Angeles and improved as it moved east where it was variously described following its Toronto and New York openings as "an intellectual charade," "a major work of twentieth-century drama," and "a tale told by an idiot signifying everything." According to the *New York Times*, "the whole thing is funny, thoughtful, stimulating and entertaining." For my own part I found it enormously rewarding and I enjoyed working with Rabb.

My final activity of the year came as a surprise and was literally thrust upon me. For its major production of the year Juilliard's Opera Theater was preparing a new opera, *The Mines of Sulphur*, by the English composer Richard Rodney Bennett. Its director had fallen ill with what was presently diagnosed as terminal cancer. Reluctant, at this stage, to seek an outside director, Mennin invited me to stage and produce it. Anxious to establish relations with the other divisions of Juilliard, I accepted and took over rehearsals.

We opened to reviews that had reservations about the music but none about the production. "Quite the best Juilliard has presented in a long time...This is the modern style of American operatic acting at its best." It was good for my morale and helped to consolidate my unusual position at Juilliard. And it set a precedent: over the next eight years I came to direct most of the new works performed by the Opera Theater. These included such varied items as Honegger's *Antigone*, Ernst Block's American première of *Macbeth*, Virgil Thomson's *Lord Byron* and a percussive opera about Hell's Angels for which the program credits included thanks to "Ghost Motorcycle and Harley-Davidson Company of Manhattan" and "the Humble Oil Refining Company for the loan of their fuel-pumps."

My time, that year and the next (aside from work on my book), was spent in a continued investigation of the current state of actor training in the United States. I audited classes in New England, New York and California; I observed theater games in Chicago; I appeared at various universities and made speeches before such bodies as the National Theater Conference and the National Educational Theater Association.

Everywhere I encountered curiosity and excitement about the new school for which I spent several months preparing a comprehensive brochure describing those elements of our training that would distinguish us from other schools in the country. By November I had completed such a document, in consultation with the Saint-Denis in London and based largely on the Saint-Denis "bible." Prominently displayed were the questions: "What kinds of theater artists do we hope to train at Juilliard? And what sort of theater are we training them for?" And the answer:

We are trying to form an actor equipped wth all possible means of dramatic production, capable of meeting the demands of today's and tomorrow's ever-changing theater—an actor who is capable of participating in those changes and who is, himself, inventive enough to contribute to them. For in the final analysis, whatever experiments may be attempted through fresh forms of writing, on new stages, using the latest technical devices, everything ultimately depends on the human being—the actor.

The rest of the brochure, aside from housekeeping details, was an outline of how we proposed to train such actors.

Early in 1968 Peter Mennin and I had one of our doom-laden lunches. Did I really feel, he asked, that we should launch the Drama Division in the fall? Would it not be wiser to postpone our opening until after our move to Lincoln Center? He listened to my indignant reaction and to my proffered resignation if such a postponement occurred.

This was our last hesitation. Early that spring I set about making arrangements for our first students' auditions, knowing that on the quality of the human material we discovered and on the choices we made in selecting our first year's students depended not only the fate of the school but, I sincerely believed, the future of actor training in the United States. It was a responsibility I was unwilling and unable to face alone. Saint-Denis, who should have shared it, was off in London and too frail for the rigors of such a voyage. Jack Landau, on whom I had counted to take his place, could not accompany me for an even more valid and tragic reason.

In the years since our collaboration in Stratford, Landau and I had kept in touch and discussed numerous projects, none of which were consummated. When I accepted the Juilliard assignment he was one of the first to whom I turned for advice. To avoid premature speculation and to give Saint-Denis the courtesy of participating in our final decisions, no contracts had been signed and no announcements made concerning the new Drama Division's faculty. But, for months, there had been an understanding between Landau, Michel and myself that Landau would be my second-in-command and (since he himself had been part of the Old Vic School) a valuable intermediary between the

Saint-Denis and myself. One evening I asked him to come over and discuss some question of organization; he was currently working on a documentary series for a TV station in Boston but he said he'd come by for a drink on his way to the airport. Joan asked him to stay for dinner; he said he had a breakfast meeting in Boston and must catch the 9:00 p.m. plane from La Guardia.

I was at the school next morning watching a rehearsal when someone came down the aisle and said there was a call for me. It was from Landau's agent and close friend who asked if I'd heard from him: he had not shown up for his early appointment in Boston and when they called his apartment the phone seemed to be disconnected. Forty minutes later she called again. A man from the TV station had gone to the apartment, found the door unlocked and Jack's body on the floor—dead from seven stab wounds and three neckties knotted in a garrotte around his throat.

By mid-February the Drama Division had received more than 600 written applications from students all over the country. Since I was determined to make this a national rather than an Eastern school, I decided to hold our first round of auditions in seven major American cities, each the center of a regional area. Later we would hold auditions on the East Coast.

I left New York on the evening of March 10, 1968, carrying a horribly heavy box that contained additional applications and several thousand appraisal forms on which to record our impressions of candidates. My companion was a tall, dark, handsome, nervous young man named Michael Kahn, who had flown very little and who spent most of his time in the air in alternating states of ecstasy and panic. I had selected him finally to fill the place left vacant by Landau's death. It says something about my own taste in collaborators that they were both young, intelligent, mercurial, Jewish and basically unstable. Kahn had a more attractive and dynamic personality but lacked Landau's cultural experience and stubborn organizing ability. This tour was a test of his competence and of our compatibility.

Auditioning candidates for an actor-training program is a delicate and tricky process. Faced with the challenge of assembling a brilliant first class for a school which was still in formation, I had decided, in making our choices, that we would set a higher value on originality and temperament than on the more conventional standards of looks and competence. Our auditioning procedure was simple. We gave candidates fifteen minutes each, during which we would meet and talk with them and they would perform two short pieces—one classical (preferably in verse) and one realistic and contemporary. If this was not sufficient to tell us what we needed to know about them, Kahn would put them through a number of simple exercises which would give us further insight into their personality and imagination.

Our first stop was Kansas City. Our applicants were a mediocre lot but we gave qualifying marks to one ingénue and to one plump boy with a fine voice (a bookie's son who had been recommended to me by his English teacher at the University of Kentucky at Bowling Green).

The next day we were in Little Rock, Arkansas, where a performing-arts center had been in existence for two years but was now being dissolved. Its director hoped that some of his students might qualify for Juilliard. We rated four of them acceptable, plus a local boy of sixteen, a high-school football hero, and moved on to Chicago. Of the twenty-three applicants who showed up, five qualified and two were outstanding: a strange, wild girl from a convent school in Minneapolis and a nervous, bow-legged black youth, Steve Henderson, who made an enormous impression on us both. In Dallas we had slim pickings and moved on to Southern California where we found seven "possibles," of whom we qualified five, including a very tall, talented blonde who told us she was a white witch and who later left us to marry a warlock.

Our New York auditions, which were open to students from all over the country, extended over a full week during which the record shows that we auditioned thirty-two on one day and forty-three on another. In May we held a last-chance audition and when it was all over we found ourselves with close to fifty young people who, in our opinion, qualified for admission. Since we had decided that the number of admissions must never exceed thirty-five, the next painful step was to eliminate a dozen or more of those who had initially qualified. After much argument and shuffling around (that included inevitable considerations of financial need and scholarship requirement) we finally selected twenty-two males and twelve females to form what turned out to be the most variegated, successful and troublesome class that ever attended the Drama Division of the Juilliard School.

Michel and Suria Saint-Denis were due to arrive from Europe in late August. I asked them to come two weeks earlier and I persuaded the Rockefeller Foundation to give me a special grant of $10,000 with which I set about organizing a two-week "retreat" in Washington, Connecticut, in the spacious premises of a famous young ladies' establishment known as Wykeham Rise. Here, while the girls were away on their vacation, I proposed to assemble all those whom I was seriously considering for teaching positions at Juilliard. Here they would meet the Saint-Denis and each other; be confronted with the teaching methods we intended to employ; discuss and demonstrate their own theory and practice of actor training; finally they would test their personal and pedagogical compatibility with the other elements of the new school. To aid us in this task I had made an arrangement with Canada's National Theatre School in Montreal to lend us four of their second-year students (two male, two female) to be used as "guinea pigs" for demonstrations of the various disciplines.

As the date approached and as I grew increasingly nervous at the prospect of starting an entirely new career at the age of sixty-six, I found myself, for the first time in my life, resorting to a journal in which I proposed to record the birth and growth of the School.

12 August. The Saint-Denis arrived this afternoon from London. I watched from the observation platform as Michel came limping painfully down the steps. Suria tried to help him but he knocked her hand away. He seemed exhausted and bewildered as we drove across the Triborough Bridge and into Connecticut.

14 August. Washington, Conn. Worked all morning on a schedule for the Retreat. My present intention is to let Saint-Denis start us off with a brief, general introduction—then devote the first two days to Speech and Movement. This will give the Saint-Denis time to meet the faculty and to prepare Michel's major statements.

15 August. Today Michel seemed quite lucid and lively, but the prospect of working with him in this condition is alarming, especially since Suria has built a protective screen around him of mingled helplessness and intransigence that is hard to deal with.

16 August. First general meeting at noon. Bad beginning. Introduced Saint-Denis, who, very rattled, made a disastrous start, referring to notes he couldn't follow and was unable to recall the simplest dates and facts. To make matters worse, his hearing aid was bust. Serious alarm and concern—especially among those who are meeting him for the first time. Then, slowly, with Suria at this side, he recovered himself. Flashes of his old authority and charm returned. Between them, they outlined the various "disciplines," using such phrases as "the discovery phase," "improvisation," "nondramatic reading," "speech delivery," etc., which meant little to most of us. A few questions. ("When do we *teach* acting?" Kahn wants to know and gets an answer that doesn't satisfy him.)

17 August. Today, amid protests and nerves, the faculty "demonstrations" began with "Speech" and "Voice" as taught by Edith Skinner and Elizabeth Smith. Everyone is nervous, feeling that they are being tested, which indeed they are! They are being observed and appraised by the Saint-Denis, by their future peers on the faculty and by me—for quality and adaptability to our program.

19 August. Thunderstorm in the night and awoke to the news of the Russian invasion of Czechoslovakia. With the Democratic national convention going on in Chicago—with its riots, tear gas, clubbing and general violence—our delegates to the Retreat have plenty to watch on television in the evening.

We found some new transistors yesterday at the village drugstore for Michel's hearing aid which is now working so effectively that he's able to follow everything that is said in demonstrations and in personal conversation.

In the morning Michael Kahn gave a lively demonstration of "theater games." I'm not sure how much the Saint-Denis got out of it, particularly in view of Suria's instinctive resistance to anything that is not already part of the Saint-Denis system.

The rest of the day spent on body training with Anna Sokolow doing a 90-minute class with the "guinea pigs" that left them panting and groaning and everyone exhausted—just from watching—and the Saint-Denis worried about "tension."

They feel that Anna's work is altogether too violent and energetic and directly opposed to the "relaxation" which they consider so essential during the first year. Anna, on her part, insists she is not afraid of tension and believes in the building of strength and muscle to enable performers to deal with whatever is required of them on stage. Later in the day we discussed "nondramatic texts" but the demonstration was poorly organized and the Saint-Denis will have to be much more specific about the true function of this discipline.

25 August. Spent the night in New York then back early to Connecticut for the Big Day of the Retreat. By noon today we had twenty-six people assembled at Wykeham Rise; gradually the Retreat is assuming the scope and vitality it lacked during our first week. This afternoon we got around to the subject of "improvisation." To avoid a repetition of last Sunday's disaster I read from Saint-Denis's paper for the Bucharest Conference, pausing now and then for comments by Michel and Suria. This was followed by Suria's not so lucid description of the more elaborate exercises such as "transformations," "dreams" and, finally, "group improvisation, and use of masks with special emphasis on the relationship between the mask and the individual and their absorption into each other."

By way of demonstration, Saint-Denis himself donned one of the character masks, with sensational effect. The character he created before our eyes—half-comic, half-tragic—was essentially the one of which he described the creation half a century ago while working with Copeau. As we watched we forgot the physical frailty and the failing brain, entirely captivated and convinced by the imaginative energy of the spirit inside that papier-mâché shell! With professional questions from Kahn, Bedford, Yakim and Auberjonois, the two hours were full of electricity.

Afterwards drinks and dinner of roast beef and baked Alaska. General and private talks in which Michel played an active and creative part. Before long half of us were juggling and tumbling while others were having mask confrontations with themselves in the mirror. Others dancing. I watched this with proprietary satisfaction and began to feel some sort of a collective, creative identity emerging.

26 August. In the cold light of this morning's dawn I couldn't help feeling that last night's minor debauch was a highly creative occasion. Unfortunately Michel, exhausted by his activities of the past forty-eight hours, had retired to bed, watched over by Suria. Without them nothing can be done.

27 August. Final day of the Retreat. We have done all we can. Saint-Denis's failure to reappear and his consequent inability to explain and illustrate the progression from "improvisation" to "interpretation" makes it pointless to hold any more general sessions at this time. Discouraging but not serious.

So the first hurdle had been cleared. The Retreat was not as successful as I had hoped, but it was not as discouraging as I feared it might be. For my own part, it left me more conscious than ever of my deficiencies but less disturbed by them.

A later entry in the journal reports "a big lunch at Gramercy Park to celebrate my sixty-sixth birthday. Delicious food, good talk (mostly in French) and early to bed to face the terrifying fact that *my School opens tomorrow*, God help me!"

* * *

Years later, after the School had achieved success and I had become a film and then a television star, I used to think of my first years at Juilliard as a time of comparative calm and of the school as an academic refuge from the pressures and anxieties of show business. Nothing could be further from the truth. Personally and professionally it was a time of insecurity and constant overwork unrelieved by the cathartic climaxes and consummations of the entertainment business.

Immediately following the Retreat, contracts had been signed with members of the faculty. I had made it clear to Peter Mennin that I was engaging the entire teaching staff from the beginning even though they would have only thirty-four students to teach. In their off hours they were expected to attend each other's classes and to become familiar with each other's instruction. This resulted, later, in a fully informed and integrated teaching staff.

We still lacked a home but the Rockefellers gave us the daytime use of an entire floor, including a ballroom, at International House across the street from the Music School and this was more than sufficient for our temporary needs.

Within a few weeks we could begin to assess the quality of our faculty and of our student selections. There were the usual surprises, good and bad, but overall we seemed to have collected the sort of variegated and malleable human material we had dreamed of assembling for our first year. Many of our students' problems in the beginning (especially those from the South and Middle West) stemmed from the fact that they came from medium and small towns and had trouble getting accustomed to life in New York City. This maladjustment took various forms—from acute homesickness and culture shock to exposure to the big-city drug scene which, for many of them, came as a complete and destructive surprise.

Today one of the boys from Little Rock, the handsome, sensitive one, fell apart, started crashing stores along upper Broadway, harassing shoppers and finally removing his clothes...Friends and Marian Fenn are sitting up with him all night to prevent him from jumping out the window of his room.

He was finally taken to St. Luke's Hospital but his collapse had a disruptive effect on the school and confirmed the complaints of those who felt we were pushing our students too hard.

A later entry describes how "another of the boys from Arkansas went berserk this afternoon in the middle of Edith Skinner's speech class and started to smash up the furniture." Yet another reports "Woudjie Dwyer ran out of class this morning, scribbled a note resigning from the school and was later found by the police, standing in the middle of Riverside Drive trying to get hit by a car."

Soon after Christmas we began the "dramatic readings" prescribed in the Saint-Denis curriculum. When we got to the Greeks—*Trojan Women* and *Oedipus*—I took a chance and invited Saint-Denis to join us. I felt he might benefit from revisiting one of the scenes of his own former theatrical triumphs. Suria agreed and our invitation seemed to revive and inspire him. For five days he functioned effectively and brilliantly and his presence was an inspiration for the students. Then, as he became emotionally involved, he began to fall apart—to fuss and repeat himself. Two days before the final reading he suffered a minor stroke during the lunch break and had to be taken home in an ambulance. This marked the end of his active work with the school.

From then on his appearances among us were infrequent and this had its inevitable reaction on Suria, who even when she was with us was, in reality, only half present, worrying all the time about Michel, alone in his hotel room. Her concern grew with the months as the doctors began to talk of irreversible brain damage following the last two strokes and to question the wisdom of keeping Michel in America. (All I could do was to reassure her that, no matter what happened, their financial arrangements with the school would remain unchanged, including the royalties they would both receive as consultants for years to come.) When, at the doctors' insistence, the Saînt-Denis left for London just before the end of our first school year, we knew we were seeing Michel for the last time. Throughout his long final illness, Suria managed to fly to America twice a year; after his death she continued to spend several months a year with us as Michel's surrogate and the school's conscience.

The last weeks of our third term were filled with tensions: tests, reviews, confrontations and incessant faculty meetings in which we made appraisals of the year's work and final decisions on what were euphemistically called "separations." This was a form of pruning, favored in the best theater schools, from which, it was generally believed, that the survivors emerged stronger and better. (It is certainly true that in acting classes where the work is largely collective and involves intimate collaboration and mutual dependence, a weakness in one or more students may prove seriously injurious to the progress of the entire group. It is equally true that the ever present threat of dismissal creates a state of apprehension which, while challenging and stimulating to some, can have a harmful effect on the insecure or the oversensitive.)

Our "separations" fell into three categories. The first, largest and easiest to determine affected those first-year students of whom it was generally felt that they should never have been accepted in the first place—young men and women with physical or psychological defects which, in the faculty's opinion, rendered them unfit for a productive career in theater. Over the years the purges on these grounds averaged as high as one third of each freshman class.

The second, later and more controversial separations included those of students who had qualified physically and emotionally during their first year but about whom it was felt, after a second year of instruction, that their capacity and temperament would prevent them from ever rising above a mediocre level of theatrical achievement. These were the most painful of our executions—a delicate area in which the faculty's unanimous and objective judgments were difficult to obtain.

The third and final category of "separations" included some of our most creative and original students of whom we never doubted that they would have a brilliant future but about whom we felt, for one reason or another, that there was little more we could teach them and that, for all their evident talent, they were not suitable material for the acting ensemble which we regarded as the major and final objective of our training.

Whatever their merits, those annual "separations" tended to bring out not only our students' but also our faculty's most contentious and neurotic behavior. Edgy and tired from eight months of intense commitment to a group of young people with whom they had developed strong professional and personal ties but on whose individual merits they often held widely divergent views, teachers fell to arguing and intriguing among themselves—particularly on this critical subject of purges. My ruling that the verdict must be unanimous added to the intensity of the faculty discussions; that the final act of execution had to be carried out personally by me added to my own profound distaste for those final days of the school year.

XXIX
Juilliard
1969-72

My first awareness of death had come to me at the age of seven in Lucerne, Switzerland, induced by the paintings in the overhead panels of the ancient, covered wooden bridge I had to cross twice a day on the way to and from the hotel where my mother and I were spending the summer. It was a traditional, medieval Dance of Death, depicting several dozen scenes of public and private life, in each of which there appeared a cloaked and grinning skeleton with a scythe preparing to carry off some unsuspecting citizen to the boneyard. With the coming of night the recollection of these scenes, mingled with the misery I felt at being abandoned in my hotel room by my beautiful mother, had set up a pattern of terror and sadness that was as strong and deep as anything I can remember feeling before or since.

It was not fear of dying that distressed me. At the age of seven my own death seemed quite remote and, with my loose, cosmopolitan upbringing, I was not burdened with religious fears of purgatory or hellfire. What I remember feeling was an overwhelming sense of loneliness and despair at the idea of annihilation; of utter desolation at the thought that all living things, including my mother and myself, were inexorably doomed to extinction and must disappear utterly and for all eternity into a black void of nothingness.

Those vague childhood terrors lasted for no more than a few weeks and never returned in their full force. My father's death, when I was fifteen, filled me with sadness but no sense of awe: I had passed through two wars virtually untouched by personal loss; my own later brushes with sudden death (one on U.S. 5 between New Haven and Hartford when I fell asleep at the wheel one winter evening on the way to deliver a lecture and, again, six months later, in my own bed at Gramercy Park of virulent septicemia) had not revived my child's dread of mortality.

But now, gradually, as I approached my seventieth year, the Man with the Scythe was moving back into my life—no longer a fanciful figure in a remote costume drama, but an immediate and insistent threat from which there was no escape. He was present in the crowd at the public deaths of that decade—at both Kennedy assassinations, at Kent State, in Vietnam and at the shooting of Martin Luther King. And, all the time, he was coming closer, moving in among my friends and associates, picking them off one by one with a regularity that gave me an uneasy feeling of being, if not responsible, then, in some way, related and involved in their deaths.

The list kept growing. It had begun soon after my departure from Stratford with the sudden death of Lawrence Langner while, several thousand miles away, Edd Johnson, my close associate at the Voice of America, had perished in a Mexican plane crash as he was taking his dog to the vet at Cuernavaca. Joseph Verner Reed had died soon after; so had Judy Holliday and Edna Giessen, my agent, who was found dead at her desk one morning with one of my lecture contracts in front of her. James Warbug was gone; so was Hallie Flanagan—my dynamic and fearless chief at the Federal Theater of the WPA, and beautiful Constance Dowling, found dead in her Bel-Air bedroom; Marc Blitzstein murdered on a Caribbean island, Jack Landau stabbed and garrotted in a rented room in Boston; finally, my dear friend, Henry Varnum Poor, who had built my House on the Hill and whose great heart had finally given out peacefully one night in his own stone house on the South Mountain Road. Still Death kept coming nearer and moving among my closest and dearest friends.

Joe Barnes was more than a friend. He was one of the very few men I have known with whom I had worked closely and intimately without a trace of that competitive rage that has darkened and distorted so many of the male relationships in my life. As my immediate superior at the Voice of America I had found him a generous and loyal colleague. Later, as editor and co-publisher of the short-lived *New York Star*, he had given me my first writing assignment. Finally, he had risked his status as senior editor of Simon & Schuster by giving me a contract and an advance on a book I might never finish and in which no one but he had the slightest faith. These were the professional debts I owed him. Beyond that, there was the intense stimulation and the active pleasure I derived from his company and the strange sense of wisdom and inherent goodness I never failed to feel in his presence.

At some time during the previous year I had heard of a recurrence of his cancer: I had spent one weekend with him during the summer in Connecticut and I had lunched with him at the Century late in the fall to talk about the book and been saddened by his appearance. Soon after that I heard from his wife that there had been another operation; that his case was hopeless and that he had asked to die at home. I left a rehearsal of *The Caucasian Chalk Circle* I was directing at Juilliard and walked down to the Barnes's apartment in Chelsea. Joe was lying on a day bed in the living room in the fetal position; his voice was little more than a croak and he gave out a sense of endless unbearable pain. Worst of all was the look of abject resignation I saw in his eyes.

It was our pretense that I had come to report on the progress of the book we both knew he would never see. With his customary courtesy, in what amounted to an apology for dying, he thanked me for coming "on such a feckless mission." Presently our talk drifted to our days at the Overseas Branch and from that to the beavers we had watched together in Joe's stream in Connecticut the previous summer. He asked about the school and I started to tell him. Then, sensing his exhaustion, I got up to leave. As she was seeing me to the door, his wife told me what I already knew—that he had only a few days to live.

My next loss was that of Jean Rosenthal.

Throughout the winter I had regularly visited Lincoln Center to watch the progress of our new building and, in particular, of the workshop-theater that Michel Saint-Denis had helped to design for us and on which Jeannie was our consultant.

I had not seen much of her recently. Our activities had taken us in different directions: we had not worked together since *King Lear* but I had followed her progress and I had heard of the surgery she had undergone the previous year. Now, seeing her at work, clambering all over that steep concrete shell, full of imaginative and ingenious theatrical suggestions, I became directly aware, for the first time, of how sick she really was.

After one of these work sessions I went back with her to her apartment for drinks and supper which she apologized for having in bed. She was exhausted and frighteningly pale but she talked eagerly of the future and particularly of a project on which she was working with Martha Graham and in which she wanted me to take part. She reminded me of the last time we had worked with Martha and I promised to get in touch with her and see if I could help. Then we went on to talk of other things—mostly of the mad things we had done together in the theater and of things we might do together in the future. Soon after, when she was back in the hospital for transfusions, she sent word that she'd see me when she got home and not to try to visit her. On the opening night of the *Antigone* I was directing at Juilliard and on which Jeannie was to have helped with the lighting, a telegram was delivered:

ALL MY LOVE HOPE I CAN BE
THERE TO SEE IT. LOVE JEAN

A week after that, numb with despair and the awful knowledge that
something irreplaceable had been torn out of my life, I spoke at the
service that was held in Jean's memory around the corner from the
unfinished Juilliard building at the Ethical Culture School she had
attended as a child.

Martha was at the service and I spoke to her briefly. Later in the
week I went to see her. We spoke about Jeannie and how desperately
we would both miss her. I mentioned my talk with her and asked
Martha what I could do to help with her coming project.

I had not been alone with her for years and I found her at
seventy-five as extraordinary as ever—beautiful, inspiring, feminine,
willful, appealing and full of wiles. She told me that the Ford
Foundation had just given her a grant of $250,000 to record a number
of her works on film—"for posterity." Instead, Martha had persuaded
the Foundation to let her spend the money on a 90-minute television
show—made up of three works from her current repertory: "Cortège of
Eagles," "Seraphic Dialogue" and "Acrobats of God."

What she and Jeannie (as her technical director) had been looking
for was someone with professional authority and experience of
television production who would also have sufficient understanding of
Martha's work to help her to translate it, without loss of identity, into
the medium of television. Remembering our happy experience with *The
Dancer's World*, I offered to work with her and almost immediately
regretted it.

What I had failed to appreciate in that first interview with Martha
was how much things had changed for her and what a difficult time
she was having. For close to fifty years—much of the time entirely
by herself—she had fought and struggled to create, with her brain
and her muscle, a body of highly personal and dangerously original
work. During that time she had assembled a company of high
quality and held it together under terrible conditions of deprivation
and public indifference. Finally, in her sixties, worldwide recognition
had come to her as a choreographer and performer of her own
works.

Now, in her midseventies, her strength was finally beginning to
wane. During her current New York season, she had received some
dubious personal reviews and diminishing public response. As a
result, she found herself torn between fear that she could no longer do
justice to her own works and a furious reluctance to surrender them to
anyone else.

Though she never spoke of it, I think she may have regarded the coming television show as a possible solution to this grim dilemma: she may have hoped that in the controlled technical perfection of big-time television lay her chance to continue presenting her creations beyond their normal theatrical span. This, combined with her inevitable panic at the prospect of working in an unknown medium, made our production of *Three by Martha Graham* something of a nightmare.

As the time for production approached, Martha's panic grew and, with it, the feeling that I was no longer a friend and an ally but a possible enemy. In one single afternoon I received three conflicting messages from her, the last of which stated, "Miss Graham finally and categorically refuses to appear in the film."

I called her back and, for close to an hour, she covered the full dramatic range—from rage and despair to remorse, love and hope. She ended with a vow to "go to the country for a week and get in shape." Two hours later, when I got back to New City, there was another call: within twenty minutes of the end of her conversation with me, she had summoned her manager, screamed at him that "Houseman is forcing me! You're all forcing me!" and forbidden him ever to mention the film again.

The next afternoon, while performing at the City Center, she had received a standing ovation, after which, between matinée and evening, she signed her contract with the Public Broadcasting System for her television show. This did not prevent her from occasionally announcing, during rehearsals, that the film was going to be a disaster and that she had every intention of making it one!

From the moment we got before the cameras everything changed. The energy and the perfectionism returned; the challenge of the new medium seemed to revive her spirits and give her her fresh life. We shot for four days, ten hours a day. By midafternoon she and her dancers were drained and pale with exhaustion but such was her discipline and theirs that no trace of fatigue ever showed on the screen.

We finished only a little behind schedule amid expressions of gratitude and embraces. The show, broadcast months later, was generally admired. But the suffering had been such that Martha herself never fully enjoyed its success. And it did not help to resolve the agonizing problem of her continued appearance in her own works.

Following the broadcast, her harassed and bewildered entourage approached me in desperation and begged me, if only temporarily, to take on the presidency of the Martha Graham Dance Center. I hesitated and then, in what I now regard as an outrageous piece of meddling, I offered, in view of our old friendship, to have a meeting with Martha in which I would try to obtain a clearer view of her present feelings about her future and that of the company.

I went to see her one afternoon in her apartment and once again I had the feeling, as I always did when I was alone with her, of being in the presence of greatness—a greatness frayed, at this moment, by age and despair. She knew why I was there and she must have hated the sight of me. Yet, for our first hour together, she was her usual seductive, manipulative, female self. There were occasional interruptions, brief visits to a side room from which she returned each time with brighter eyes and heightened energy. She offered me a sea shell that she declared "perfectly combines art and homemaking"; she presented me with a striking photograph of herself in "Acrobats of God." Each of these gifts called for a trip to the side room and her speech had begun to blur a little when she finally got around to talking about herself.

"I'm a proud, vain, spoiled woman, John, and have been for forty years...My analyst tells me I'll realize one day that I'm not a goddess."

These were among the words I remember as, gradually, layer by layer, the full depth of her distress was revealed—hurt and anger she felt at the realization that there was a general sense among audiences and among her own people that her performances were becoming a liabilty to herself and to her company and that it was her artistic obligation to let younger women replace her in the great roles she had created for herself over the years but which it was still impossible for her accept as being danced by anyone else.

"There is no reality in this piece except the inner reality of feeling eternal in all of us." So she had written in her published notebooks about one of her works. And this is what she felt now. I believe she was convinced that without her presence these intensely personal creations of hers would cease to exist or, rather, that they would lose their "reality" if they were separated from her own physical and spiritual identity.

When I spoke to her of the repertory and of the irreparable loss it would be to the world if it were not kept alive, I had the impression that, in her present mood, she would just as soon pull the temple down about her head and perish in the rubble!

I would hesitate to record this whole painful episode were it not that the story has a triumphal ending. On the night of June 20, 1975, some five years after our broadcast and two years after her own close brush with death, Martha Graham presented her revived dance company on Broadway in "one of the year's great galas of Show Business." It was the first of the annual Graham apotheoses that have followed each other with dazzling regularity ever since. The *New York Times,* in reporting the celebration of the company's *fiftieth* anniversary, described the historic curtain call "with Dame Margot Fonteyn and Rudolph Nureyev, the living embodiment of classic ballet flanking the divine Martha, the incorruptible and true spirit of modern dance."

Another critic, describing her triumph, perceived a note of sadness in the 82-year-old dance pioneer's quoted statement: "I'd rather be dancing than choreographing...I'll always miss it."

* * *

Our move to the new Juilliard building in Lincoln Center took place gradually over the summer of 1969. As we took possession of our offices, classrooms, studios and theater, it became apparent that we had been presented with one of the most spacious and best conceived theater-training plants in the world. It had far more space than we would be requiring that year or the next but, with the eventual addition of two more classes over the next two years, our enrollment would rise to well over one hundred, working on four separate schedules and requiring every inch of our new space.

Meantime, it was all we could do to adjust to our new home and to become accustomed to our new grandeur. There had been one major administrative change during the summer. A few days before the end of our first year, Marian Fenn had suddenly announced that she intended to start a new life in the West with one of of the male Canadian "guinea pigs" we had used during the Retreat. I missed her sharpness, her skepticism and her devotion. But the young woman with whom I replaced her had qualities of her own that prevented me from ever regretting the change. She was the product of a progressive American university and a well-known British drama school, a former dancer with administrative experience and unlimited energy. Her name was Margot Harley and, during the next eighteen years, she was to play a dominant part in our affairs—first in the conduct of the school and then in the creation and operation of the Acting Company that grew out if it. Among Margot's first duties as administrator of the Drama Division was the assimilation of the twenty-two survivors of Group I with the thirty-three freshmen whom Michael Kahn and I had selected during our second national auditions and who now became known as Group II.

Our first impressions of our second-year choices were favorable. Its members seemed calmer than their predecessors and less likely to give us trouble—individually or collectively. They seemed to adjust more easily to the perils of the big city and to submit more readily to the rules and disciplines that Group I (having no precedents to guide them) had consistently questioned and resisted. As a result, our own attitude towards Group II was more relaxed, more like that of parents towards a second, seemingly well-adapted child. The surprises came later. Meantime, Group I remained the main object of our preoccupation and affection. They were our first-born; we felt that we had created the school together and that our future was closely interwoven with theirs.

Generally our curriculum continued to develop along the lines laid down with the Saint-Denis in Paris and at Wykeham Rise. Michael Kahn, despite his emotional caprices and occasional absences, remained our most creative teacher of acting and our faculty's most enlightened and far-sighted educator. Steven Aaron, Gene Lesser and Marian Seldes, together with the recently added Boris Tumarin, formed our acting and directing faculty; William Woodman (who had been one of my stage managers at Stratford) played a valuable double part as director and and executive assistant in charge of the enormous and complicated labor of scheduling.

Our regular disciplines followed predictable lines under their respective head. Voice and Speech—both were under the strained joint leadership of Edith Skinner (with her authority and wealth of experience) and Liz Smith (with her dedication and overwhelming energy)—was probably our most consistent and effective department. Movement fluctuated with its changing and mercurial teachers: Anna Sokolow remained a storm center and a catalyst; Yakim (an Israeli dancer) was energetic but erratic; Liz Keen was a welcome addition but inclined to impinge on emotional areas that our teachers of acting regarded as theirs. Judith Leibowitz, on her part, maintained a steady level of constructive and valuable work with her first- and second-year classes in Alexander Technique, a mind-body exercise in general use in theatrical circles.

Secondary but fascinating activities such as judo, folk dancing, circus acrobatics and choral singing were conducted by part-time teachers; there were also classes in art appreciation, theater history, costume, make-up and style, to which must be added a number of reluctantly attended academic courses required for the BFA degree. All this led to constant complaints (supported by certain members of the faculty but consistently ignored by me) that our schedule was overcrowded and exhausting and did not give our students time to "think."

That year, besides that problems of adjusting to the new building, an unexpected element was added to our teaching problems. For many months student unrest had been growing throughout the country, with tempers rising and protests becoming more audible against the war in Vietnam and against academic structure in general. Juilliard, as a professional conservatory, was never in the vanguard of student activism but, by midwinter, the gathering storm could no longer be ignored, even in a privileged stronghold of culture such as Lincoln Center. There was one demonstration in which members of our school marched across town to the United Nations building where they performed an improvised Dance of Death, dressed in black with dead-white faces to the accompaniment of the slow movement from Beethoven's *Eroica* performed by Juilliard's music students, to protest the casualties in Vietnam. And there was another day in which several hundred of us—students and faculty alike—lay as dead for an hour and covered the entire pavement of Lincoln Plaza with our bodies in silent protest against the bombing of Cambodia.

But our real problems arose with the "student strikes" being organized with varying degrees of effectiveness of the country's leading campuses. Juilliard was among the last to be affected but, midway through our third term, a number of hirsute young men and intense girls in battle dress appeared among us, evading the security guards and mingling with the students to explain and promote "strike action." They and little effect at first. Of our musicians, dancers and actors the majority were apolitical and obsessively concerned with their own artistic and professional futures. But as weeks went by and the strike date approached, the gap began to widen between pro-and anti-strike elements in the Drama Division. The latter—mostly female—maintained that they were studying to be actors and that such external disturbances represented an unwelcome threat to their training. Those who favored the strike did so almost entirely for histrionic reasons. Knowing nothing and caring little about the national and academic issues involved, a number of our students got themselves elected, through their energy and dramatic sense, to key positions on the various committees and delegations which began to conduct negotiations with a bewildered and outraged administration. Using the actors' disciplines ("improvisations," "adjustments" and "choices") we had taught them so assiduously over the past months, they suddenly revealed vivid and colorful personalities, some of which had remained unsuspected till now. One girl, for instance, was changed overnight from a tense, stiff, inhibited California beauty into a flushed, wild-eyed, utterly infuriating verson of La Pasionaria—an academic firebrand urging her laggard associates to acts of reckless audacity. Schramm, the talented but indolent Kentucky bookmaker's son, did some hurried reading of *Ten Days That Shook the World* and emerged in a black jacket, a new-grown Trotsky-style goatee and a bright-red scarf knotted about his arm, to lead the people's armies against the forces of reaction.

Peter Mennin, supported by his board and a generally conservative faculty, took a firm stand and announced that if Juilliard were closed by a strike, it might never reopen. Nobody believed that, but things went so far that one final, critical meeting was called in the main Juilliard Theater, in which the strike issue was actually put to a student vote. Some of our drama students were among the most eloquent advocates of a strike, which was blocked at the last moment through the efficient, hard-nosed parliamentary maneuvering of an associate dean.

A week later everyone was back at work. But I have always believed that this brief, superficial exposure to political passion played a vital and highly valuable part in Group I's theatrical development. No matter which side they were on, the crisis furnished them with an emotional experience of which the more complacent classes that succeeded them never had the benefit.

The unrest that accompanied the last years of the war in Vietnam had other strange and baleful side effects on the school. I have spoken of Group II's reasonable behavior and easy adjustment. Before the end of the school year, these turned out to be altogether fallacious. Group I, on the whole, had been dominated by males: in Group II the talents that gave the group its identity and its quality were predominantly feminine.

Sherry Rivers was a small, quiet blonde from a conventional background whose temperament revealed itself only in her work. Kayla Spillson was a rangy, handsome girl whose father owned a hotel in the Middle West; she had a warm, open personality and unusual authority as a performer. Both were model students; yet it was at their hands that I received the two most shattering blows dealt me during my tenure at Juilliard. Both, on the same morning, announced their intention to leave the School. In Sherry's case this represented an escape through religion from the violence and horror of the contemporary world. She had found a young man who shared her views; they were getting married and would live a simple, dedicated life in a minibus with a canoe on its roof. Kayla's case was simpler and more urgent. She had been living for some time with a young man who, as a conscientious objector, was being forced to seek refuge, like so many others, in Canada. She had decided to follow him and was leaving to join him in a few days.

Their desertion completely disrupted Group II which, we now

discovered, had been held together and animated by the creative energy
of those two young women. With their going Group II disintegrated; by
the end of the year it had shrunk to half its original number.

My own political problems that year were evenly divided between
school and home. My son Michael, having graduated with honors from
his Dominican school in New Hampshire, in a sudden awareness of his
Jewish heritage, had chosen Brandeis over Harvard as his university.
He had also discovered sex and decided to spend part of his vacation
hitchhiking with a young woman through the Middle West. Shortly
before departing, he received a communication from his draft board to
which he replied with a long, somewhat self-righteous letter in which
he explained that, on religious and moral grounds, he found it
impossible to accept their invitation to register for the draft or to
participate in the war in Vietnam.

This letter, which he read to us with considerable pride, became
the subject of heated family discussions. Joan, whose mother had been
a "revolutionary" in her Russian girlhood and who had herself, during
the German occupation, been actively involved in the French
Resistance, was divided between her satisfaction over her son's
nonconformist spirit and her maternal horror at imagining him in
prison. For my part, in view of my own long subversive record, I was
not shocked by his activism but, since admission to Brandeis
automatically assured him of a military deferment, I regarded his
action as a gratuitous bid for martyrdom.

Months later he was served with a subpoena summoning him to
appear as a witness before a grand jury in New York City on a charge
of "conspiracy," which puzzled and disturbed the Civil Liberties
Union's lawyer who was handling his case. Michael himself was
divided, by this time, between apprehension and anticipation; between
fear of arrest and a vision of himself delivering a historic antiwar
oration before an admiring judge and jury. Recalling my own
experiences at the time of the Un-American Acitivities Committee, I
assured him that that was not the way things worked: his attempts at
reason or eloquence would be ruthlessly and legally suppressed. His
lawyer told him the same thing.

He was kept waiting in court for a day and a half before being
called to the stand. After he had taken the oath and answered a few
general questions, the prosecutor (for a reason no one ever understood)
thrust a sheet of paper at him and (over the legal objections of his
lawyer) told him to sign his name *ten* times. He was on the sixth
signature when an attendant burst into the courtroom with the news
that there was a bomb in the basement. The case was recessed, then

postponed, and, finally, dismissed and Michael returned to Boston richer by $117—representing his travel expenses and the per diem allowance he had incurred as a witness. The mystery of his "conspiracy" was never solved and, later, when he faced a routine hearing for draft evasion he received a suspended sentence of one year, which was expunged two years later, by which time his political and religious ardor had subsided and had been replaced by a mounting concern with comparative religions, including the Hebraic studies in which Brandeis was particularly distinguished. Those led indirectly to anthropology, which he eventually made his life's work.

Otherwise, Joan and I spent a pleasantly peaceful summer together—a summer made notable by our return to the House on the Hill. (I had heard a rumor that spring that it might be for sale. It was, and I bought it back for only a little more than I had sold it for three years earlier.) Back on the South Mountain Road, for the first time since leaving Paris I was able to follow a regular routine on my book. It was painful and difficult work that left me emotionally drained; but, by the time I had to stop and start preparing myself for the new school year, I was over the worst and halfway through the account of my association with Orson Welles.

XXX
The Acting Company
1972

The third year of the Drama Division was marked by a number of changes. Our enrollment was now close to a hundred, including Group III and a few so-called "advanced students" whom we had auditioned and chosen with great care the previous spring from among a select group of college graduates and young actors. Their presence made a new set of demands on our faculty who were now faced with the problem of absorbing young professionals who were at a different (though not necessarily higher) level than our own third-year students.

This assimilation was aided by the public performances we began to give that year in the New York public schools. Performing Molière's *Scapin* (sometimes under a hail of broken paperclips) was a young company that had among its performers such future stars as Kevin Kline, Patti LuPone, Ben Hendrickson, David Schramm, Mary Lou Rosato and David Ogden Stiers.

At the same time and with the same cast we were preparing two major productions for the final demonstrations of the year: Middleton's Jacobean tragedy *Women Beware Women* and *The School for Scandal*. Before embarking on Sheridan's comedy of manners, Group I had worked all winter with Pierre Lefevre on advanced improvisation and "character" masks; they had also done considerable work on seventeenth- and eighteenth-century style followed by a full month of master classes in the more elaborate aspects of high comedy. As a result, our production reached a new level of performance and production.

As the Drama Division entered its fourth year, I continued to waver between worry and pride; between alternating moods when I doubted if results justified our enormous efforts and moments of triumph when, for a few days, it seemed as though all our doubts and anxieties were over for ever.

The autumn of 1971 was such a time. The school was running at full strength, with four groups in operation. Group I had shown remarkable quality in its third-year performances and I had made the decision, during the summer, that the time had come for the Drama Division to throw off its wrappings and reveal itself to the world. The most effective—as well as the most dangerous—way to do this was to present Group I in a full-scale New York repertory season open to the public and the press.

Part of our repertory for such a season already existed. *The School for Scandal* and *Women Beware Women* had been shown and admired as student productions in the spring. After they returned from their long summer vacation, members of Group I resumed daily classes in Voice, Movement and other disciplines but the main emphasis from now on was on performance and on preparation for the fateful repertory season on which I had decided to risk our reputation as America's leading theatrical conservatory. By late November our repertory of four plays was ready: *The School for Scandal, Women Beware Women, The Hostage* and Gorki's *Lower Depths*.

Early in the fall we had sent out several thousand mailings in the red-black-and-white format we had established for our brochures, announcing our repertory and dedicating the season to the memory of our beloved co-director, Michel Saint-Denis. We had apparently underestimated the general curiosity about our work for, by mid-Novermber, we had sold two thirds of our tickets for a season that was still several weeks away. Later I wrote personal notes to the New York drama critics explaining that we did not expect them to review us but that we would be happy if they would visit us during our season and appraise the work we had been doing at the school over the past three and a half years.

We opened with *School for Scandal* on December 7 and closed with *The Hostage* on the night of December 16. The following Sunday we read the first and possibly the most important notice we ever received. It occupied four full columns in the *New York Times*:

Anyone worried about the future of the American theater should have seen the new Juilliard Acting Company in action, presenting a season of true repertory and doing it splendidly...This is a repertory that would challenge any company and it does, but each reveals, in performance, a first-rate ensemble of actors. Why can't we keep them here intact as a permanently expanding company, performing great plays in repertory?

This and the rest of our New York reviews set off an immediate and insistent demand for our repertory in a number of Eastern and Midwestern universities. To satisfy these unexpected requests we hurriedly set up booking services for which we were totally unprepared: between January and the end of April we successfully presented our program at Harvard; at Princeton; at Urbana, Illinois; at Toledo, Ohio; at Ann Arbor, Michigan; and at the University of Indiana in Bloomington.

Their success and the many inquiries we were receiving about engagements for the following season added to the difficulty and urgency of a decision that had to be made immediately—and by me alone.

I had two alternatives. My first and easier choice was to let Group I graduate and accept individual theatrical employment which, in view of their proven quality, they would have little difficulty in finding. In this way we would have fulfilled our function as a conservatory. But this meant the dissolution of something we had spent four years creating with love, sweat and tears—a skilled and cohesive acting ensemble. Did we have the right to do that? Having created such a precious theatrical instrument, could we now abandon it?

The answer to that question raised an acute personal problem. Over the years I had been involved in the birth of no fewer than seven theatrical organizations. I was proud of my connection with each one of them, but now, at the age of seventy, I needed an eighth (with its inevitable anxieties, personal crises and financial and artistic hazards) like a hole in the head. I was torn between love of my students and strong reluctance to get involved once again in the hazards of an art-theater operation, until something happened that resolved my dilemma.

For years now I had regarded the School as my major concern and my final achievement in the theater. There was a part of me, however, that had never totally accepted this resignation and had never ceased to yearn for the agitations—the sudden triumphs and disasters, defeats and victories of show business. So it came as a welcome surprise one morning when I received a call from an agent of my acquaintance who asked me if I knew Clifford Odets's *Country Girl* and did I like it? When I asked him to explain, he told me that his client Jason Robards was about to play it in Washington, D.C., as the first production to be presented at the Kennedy Center in its newly opened Eisenhower Theater. Would I be interested in directing it? Jason had suggested my name and I had been approved by the other two actors already engaged—Maureen Stapleton and George Grizzard.

It is a commonplace that everyone in the theater is convinced, between engagements, that he or she will never work again. In my case the feeling was confirmed by the bitter realization that in more than four years I had not had one single serious offer to direct and had given up all hope of ever receiving one. Now, suddenly, I found myself asked to work with three of the most highly regarded actors in America.

The Country Girl is not difficult to stage: I had seen it in the theater with Uta Hagen and on the screen with Grace Kelly. But, with Maureen Stapleton in the role of Georgie, it presented a somewhat different challenge. There was little I could do to add to Robards's very personal and credible performance of the alcoholic actor; but the relationship between his wife and his director needed to be adjusted to the personalities of the actors who were playing the parts. I succeeded, according to audience and critics—first in Washington where "one relishes watching three actors with roles of equal balance reacting to each other's nerve-ends," and, later, in New York, where Clive Barnes in the *Times* described it as a "most delicate production in which Maureen Stapleton, despite remarkable acting opposition, is totally, indelibly memorable."

The success of *Country Girl* may, in fact, have given me courage to make up my mind about the Acting Company. But, looking back, I can see that the issue was never really in doubt. My final decision was precipitated by a proposal we received that spring from Saratoga, offering the Company a four-week repertory season as part of an arts festival that included, among its performers, the Philadelphia Orchestra under Eugene Ormandy and George Balanchine's New York City Ballet. How could we refuse to appear in such company?

Our Saratoga season opened in mid-July and repeated our New York repertory. For the Company it was a wonderful combination of work and holiday. Four major productions performed seven times a week (plus one children's matinée of *Scapin*) kept them fully occupied but did not prevent them from attending occasional ballet and concert performances or from sunning themselves daily around the vast swimming pool that was situated a few hundred yards from the theater.

Attendance was fair at first in a community that had known no theater for several years. It grew from week to week till it reached an average of 60 percent of capacity on week nights and full houses on Fridays and Saturdays. But the true value of our Saratoga summer lay in the opportunity it gave our young actors to settle down, find their professional identity and prepare themselves for their transition from a brilliant graduating student class to a permanent professional company.

It was typical of my paternalistic attitude that I had never really consulted members of Group I on the subject of the Acting Company and that they, on their part, were prepared to follow me unquestioningly into the treacherous, uncharted waters of professional theater. This blind faith was touching but it aggravated the responsibilities to which, in our first flush of success, I had as usual failed to give realistic consideration.

Our Saratoga season was due to end in mid-August, at which time the company would receive its final check from the Arts Center and all formal connection with Juilliard would cease. As the weeks went by I began to have serious doubts about our prospects of survival, together with a rising fear that, in my enthusiasm, I might have led my students into a dead end.

My wife, quite rightly, saw in my creation of another theater company nothing but a new source of anxiety and overwork. Margot Harley was the only person with whom I could honestly discuss the Company's future. Together we came to the grim conclusion that we had less than a month in which to determine the fate of what we had come to think of as the Acting Company. If we were not in active production by Labor Day we must face the shameful necessity of calling off all plans and letting the Group scatter.

As I hustled around New York that summer, desperately seeking a doorstep on which to deposit this, my latest infant, I could not help recalling my attempts to launch the Mercury Theater thirty-five years earlier. For all their differences of time and circumstance, the two projects were strangely similar: both were improvised and utterly reckless; both were finally pulled off through ingenuity, luck and a little larceny. And both were finally made possible by an unexpected windfall. In the case of the Acting Company this took the form of a grant from the Rockefeller Foundation of $25,000 towards the organization of a New York repertory season. Most of that was spent converting our actors from a student group to a professional company by having them all join Actors' Equity at a gross cost of close to $10,000. But, at least, it set the ball rolling.

My next approach was to Richard Clurman, an executive of Time-Life and the new president of the New York City Center, with the suggestion that he adopt the Acting Company as the Center's dramatic arm. He was startled but receptive and our agreement was signed within a week and announced forty-eight hours before the time Margot and I had set as our final deadline.

The next step was to find a suitable place in which to present our first New York season. I had refused to occupy the huge City Center theater on 55th Street: I felt the Acting Company should make its first professional appearance in a place that was modest in size and tone; yet it must be well located and possess a stage capable of holding all four of our productions. By a minor miracle, the perfect place was available. That it happened to be located within 100 yards of the Juilliard School was pure luck.

The Good Shepherd-Faith church was a survival from the days when the West Sixties formed part of a slum known as Hell's Kitchen. With the construction of Lincoln Center the church had lost most of its congregation but it continued to function under its progessive pastor as a social center rather than a place of worship. For two years I had passed it every morning on my way to work without ever suspecting its theatrical possibilities. Besides being reasonable to rent and perfectly located, the Good Shepherd-Faith church had exactly the right tone of calculated modesty and eccentric distinction which I was trying to create for our young company.

Since the church was literally penniless, negotiations with its pastor were brief and pleasant. The next morning the New York papers, under the headline 6 SHOWS IN 4 WEEKS, carried the announcement and complete schedule of the Acting Company's first New York repertory season.

In preparing our budget, we had estimated our probable attendance at 65 percent of our 230 seat house and that's just about what we got. But we greatly underestimated what it cost to present repertory in New York City. Douglas Schmidt, our designer, and Joe Pacitti, our technical director, had done a brilliant job of adjusting our massive scenery to the rudimentary conditions of the Good Shepherd church. By raising and extending the platform on which the altar once stood, they created a stage that was smaller but not unlike that of the Juilliard Drama Theater and gave audiences (seated in stiff, narrow and quite uncomfortable pews) perfect sight lines and tolerable acoustics. Our main problem was that the church was on the mezzanine and that every prop and every piece of scenery had to be dragged by hand up and down a cramped and twisting stairway. The same was true of our switchboards and lighting equipment, which had to be affixed to the walls and ceiling of a building that was about to collapse from age and neglect.

I hoped that by playing in such an unconventional location we would provoke talk—and we did. We also created a few special problems of which the most serious became evident only two days before we opened. Our theater had two toilets, both located in the area assigned to the actors as dressing rooms. What of our audience during the long stretches and intermissions of our classical repertory? We considered routing them to Juilliard but felt that Dr. Mennin might not appreciate such a use of his conservatory's facilities. Nor were the delegates of the Chinese People's Republic, whose legation was across the street, likely to welcome our theatergoers into their well-guarded building. Finally someone suggested renting four portable toilets from the construction company that was building a school next door. A deal was made and one of the curiosities of our first repertory season was a row of four maroon portable chemical outhouses lined up in the parking lot behind the church.

Our advance sale was helped by an eight-column photograph of the Company in its *School for Scandal* costumes that appeared on the front page of the *New York Times*'s entertainment section the Sunday before we opened. Three nights later, on September 17, 1972, after two previews, the Acting Company launched its first professional New York repertory season.

What I hoped for from New York critics and audiences was praise for our opening show and general appreciation of the company. We got both.

The School for Scandal is the wittiest show in town. Be good to yourself and rush to buy tickets...The birth of a repertory company is headline news and the birth of such a fine one deserves page-one play.

So wrote Clive Barnes in the *New York Times*. In fact he found our *School for Scandal*

in many respects a better performance than that being currently given by Britain's National Theatre...I enjoyed myself and what is more I enjoyed the prospect of a new repertory company that New York can grow up with. Welcome!

We never equalled the overnight, smash-hit "hottest-ticket-in-town" status of the Mercury's *Julius Caesar*. But our audiences were steady and our press consistently favorable. *Scandal* was followed by *The Hostage* and this, in turn, by *Women Beware Women* and *The Lower Depths*. To these we added two performances each of Dos Passos's *U.S.A.* and James Saunders's *Next Time I'll Sing to You*, which was described in the *Times* as "one of the most fully realized and entertaining works in the repertory and a personal triumph for Patti LuPone."

Two days after the close of our New York season the company set out on the first leg of a national tour that has continued without interruption and without loss of energy or quality for more than fourteen years.

Norman Lloyd and J.H. during rehearsals of *Taming of the Shrew*.

J.H., Kate Hepburn, Jack Landau and Lawrence Langner. (1957)

Hepburn and Alfred Drake in *Much Ado* on the Rio Grande.

Joan and J. H. at an opening-night party.

Robert Ryan in *Murder in the Cathedral*. (UCLA)

'Madame Spivy' as Madame Pace in *Six Characters in Search of an Author*. (UCLA, 1960)

John Crosby, *The Seven Lively Arts*.

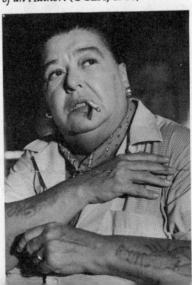

J.H. and William Inge at MGM during work on the script of *All Fall Down.*

J.H. backstage with Bernard Bersten and William Woodman. (*The Winter's Tale,* 1958)

The Theatre Group rehearsing *Antigone* with John Kerr, Joanna Barnes and Mariette Hartley as Antigone.

J.H. with Gordon Davidson
during *Lear*.

Jane Fonda and Peter Finch in
The Cool of the Day.

Morris Carnovsky making up
for the opening scene of *King
Lear*. (UCLA)

Sebastian and Michael at the
beach. (1964)

Joan and Mousy-Cat return to
the U.S.A. (1965)

Michel and Suria Saint-Denis.

J.H. and Elizabeth Smith at the 'Retreat.'

Ellis Rabb and J.H. during APA-Phoenix.

Patrick Hines and Christopher Walken in *The Chronicles of Hell.*

The 'Retreat' at Wykeham Rise—Michel Saint-Denis explaining 'Mask Improvisation.'

The last and most dramatic of
our mass protests against the
Vietnam War.

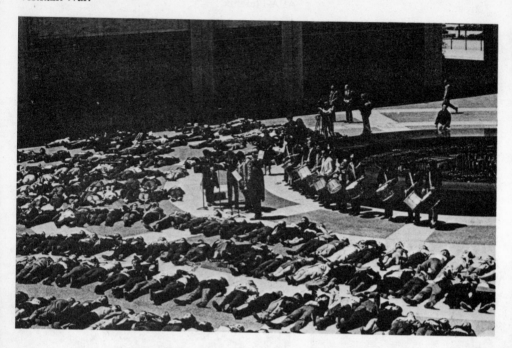

J.H. directing. (UCLA)

Martha Graham making up as
Clytemnestra.

Kevin Kline and Patti LuPone
in *The Beggar's Opera.*

Reading our first great review
in *The New York Times.*

Lord Byron at Juilliard. Left to right, Jack Larson, Virgil Thomson, J.H., Peter Mennin and Gerhard Samuels.

Jason Robards, J.H., George Grizzard and Maureen Stapleton in the first reading of *The Country Girl.*

J. H. as Professor Kingsfield in
The Paper Chase.

James Bridges and J.H. during
filming of *The Paper Chase* in
Toronto.

J.H. contemplating his own
mask at Juilliard.

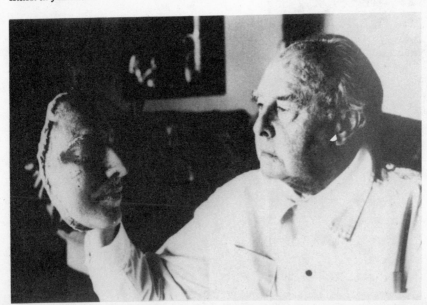

Douglas Fairbanks, Jr., Fred
Astaire, J. H.,Melvyn Douglas.
(*Ghost Story*, 1980)

John Gielgud and J. H. in *Marco
Polo*. (1984)

"For heaven's sake. It's John Houseman."

Joan says farewell to Malibu.
(1964)

May Haussmann lunching at
New City at the age of 96.

J.H. during the filming of *Ghost
Story*. (Winter, 1980)

Berry's World   By Jim Berry

'Do you realize that, lately, you have been
on TV almost as much as John Houseman?'

J.H. accepting Academy
Award from Ernest Borgnine
and Cybill Shepherd. (April,
1974)

XXXI
Paper Chase and Run-Through
1972-73

In the middle of the Acting Company's New York repertory season something happened which, at first, seemed just another diversion but which was eventually to change the course of what was left of my life.

The agent of this transformation was a young man from Paris, Arkansas, whose first play had been performed in a small theater in Los Angeles in the early sixties. His name was James Bridges and he had come to work for our UCLA Professional Theater Group as a stage manager until I recommended him as a writer on the Hitchcock suspense series. There he wrote eighteen scripts before moving into motion pictures, where he soon established himself as that rare and valuable commodity—a writer-director. At the time of *The Paper Chase*, Bridges was a young-looking man of thirty-five, boyish and balding, full of charm and affection but very shrewd and tough and determined underneath.

(One of the most endearing things about him was his combination of sophistication and naïveté. He once told me that at the age of twelve he had run home from school—a distance of several miles—during his lunch hour, to get a glimpse of his elder sister's boyfriend who, it was rumored, was a *Jew*. He had never seen one and was determined not to miss the chance.)

Bridges and I had stayed in touch over the years and he regularly kept me informed of his personal and professional progress. Then, in the spring of 1972, he called one day in great agitation to tell me that he had just signed a contract to write the script and direct a film about Harvard Law School. He had already engaged Timothy Bottoms (the star of *The Last Picture Show*) for the leading part of a freshman law student and was hoping to get James Mason to appear opposite him as a formidable dean of the Harvard Law School. He sent me the script, which I liked, and we dined together when he came to New York to audition young actors for the roles of law students. Then he told me that Mason had failed him and, as the weeks went by, I detected a growing anxiety over his inability to cast the essential role of Professor Kingsfield. Having tried and failed to get Melvyn Douglas, Edward G. Robinson, John Gielgud and Paul Scofield, among others, Bridges observed, not altogether in jest, that I might end up having to play the part.

During the last week of September Bridges and his crew were moving into Toronto where *The Paper Chase* was to be shot. He had his cameraman (Gordon Willis) and his heroine (Lindsay Wagner) but he still lacked a Kingsfield and again suggested that I play it. I replied that since he now had his crew, I was prepared to fly up to Canada for a day and quietly make a test. If it stank we'd burn it.

I flew to Toronto carrying two suits, a selection of bow ties and some Xeroxed pages of the professor's most eloquent scenes. When I got there him said he also wanted to shoot Kingsfield's opening address to his class. I sat up half the night with a bottle of brandy memorizing my speeches which I delivered the next morning to a class consisting of the camera crew and a second assistant director. Both my scenes were shot by midafternoon and I flew back to New York the same evening.

Two days later Jim called in great agitation. He had just seen the test and it was "fabulous."

I had been in and around show business for forty years and the idea of becoming an actor had never, for one single moment, entered my head. For that reason and because it had all happened so quickly, I went to work on *The Paper Chase* without a trace of the anxiety which normally accompanied the start of a new venture. I had some secret misgivings about my ability (in my seventy-first year and without previous experience) to memorize the long speeches that were to be uttered by the professor. But, once I realized that these presented no serious difficulty, I found playing the scholarly curmudgeon an agreeable and easy task—all the more since Bridges and I had known each other for years in a relationship that was not altogether unlike that which existed in the film between Kingsfield and Hart.

It felt strange, after so many years of producing and directing, to find myself suddenly on the other side of the camera. But I soon got used to the idea and, throughout the shooting of the film, I found my experience as a director and producer of constant help in my performance. Thus I was able to take full advantage of the strategy through which Jim and Gordon Willis, his cameraman, planned to heighten the impact of the formidable professor's outrageous behavior. Throughout my early classroom scenes I was to be consistently photographed in close-up and at angles that gave me weight and stature, in contrast to the long shots and diminishing lenses through which young Hart and my other helpless victims were photographed. I'm not sure how much my playing of those scenes was affected by this knowledge, but I'm sure that it added authority and color to my performance.

Owing to the lateness of my engagement I had done little preparation and almost no research into the legal aspects of my role. I talked to a number of lawyers about the relations between law professors and their students and I did what reading I could about "Bull" Warren, the Harvard professor who was the principal model for Kingsfield. Also, through long talks with John Osborn, the author of the novel on which the film was based, I learned not only the details of the Law School routines and the workings of the so-called Socratic Method but also some of the philosophy that lay behind the dry legal facts and the tyrannical classroom behavior.

Looking back, I am astonished to find how little time I actually spent in Toronto. My contract called for me to start shooting in November, for four weeks. I arrived, shot for ten days, then flew back to spend two days at Juilliard and the weekend with Joan in New City. I was back in Toronto on the 19th and worked through the 25th, when I flew to Philadelphia to do advance publicity for the Acting Company's Christmas engagement. The next day I was back in Toronto shooting my final scenes, including the night work in Kingsfield's home, climaxed by my inopportune return to find Hart in bed with my daughter.

On the last day of the month I attended the Drama Division's term-end "exercises" and, for the last time, conducted the personal interviews and year-end dismissals I always found so distressing. Beginning that year I decided that—since the faculty made the decisions—it was only fair that they should also assume the unpleasant task of executing them. Looking back, I realize that this was only one example of a tendency that was becoming increasingly apparent in my conduct of the school. By handing over to the faculty many of the decisions and duties for which I had insisted on assuming sole responsibility during our early years, was I being a wise and thoughtful administrator or was I, in fact and perhaps unconsciously, once again preparing for my exit?

* * *

1937 had been a year crammed with surprises and miracles. 1947 was another. So was 1972.

In this breathless account of my activities during that eventful year

I have almost forgotten the most startling event of them all—the publication of my book, *Run-Through*. The previous spring, four years after Joseph Barnes's death, I had finally delivered my manuscript to Michael Korda, who had succeeded Barnes as my editor. Throughout the summer I had spent hours at Simon & Schuster selecting photographs and going over my script with the copy editor, the art director and the legal department. My galley proofs had been my Christmas present from Korda and I had received them with strangely mixed feelings.

It was exciting and satisfying, after so many years of frustration and false starts, momentary exhilaration and utter despair, to see those hundreds of thousands of words reduced to a few hundred pages of print. At the same time it represented a finality that I found frightening. This thing with my name on it that was about to be issued to the world—was it a book or an ego trip? Was it something people would read with interest and sympathy? Or would it be exposed as a huge chunk of self-serving nostalgia, a futile attempt to convince the world and, particularly, myself that my life had not been entirely wasted?

Reassurances that I had done something more than rid myself of a heavy load of self-doubt came first from Virgil Thomson and then in a brief note from Christopher Isherwood, to whom, on an impulse, I had sent my page proofs with an apology and a request, if he felt like it, to give me his sincere opinion of the book. He was an old acquaintance but not a close friend and I had chosen him as a kind of literary litmus paper. His favorable response was a certificate of quality that was of infinite comfort to me in those anxious weeks before publication.

Early in February 1972 I was summoned to meet the head of promotion for Simon & Schuster, who led me into an office where, piled like Ali Baba's treasure, I beheld several hundred copies of my book awaiting my signature.

It was a moment of unqualified bliss. For half a century I had yearned to be a writer. I had come close to it at twenty-one, only to have a dream snatched away and buried under years of business and travel. Following my bankruptcy at the age of twenty-eight, I had been horrified to discover that I had absolutely nothing to write about. Now, forty years later, by a long and complicated route, my dream had come true. Here I was, in a small, cluttered office high up in Rockefeller Center, surrounded by copies of a thick, shiny books that bore my name and my picture in profile on the back cover together with complimentary comments by Christopher Isherwood, Russell Lynes, Brooks Atkinson and Virgil Thomson!

In the last week of February I was sent out by my publisher on the usual author's tour of major cities—Boston, Washington, Chicago, Minneapolis, San Francisco and, finally, Los Angeles, where a huge and splendid party was given for me; it was distinguished by one of the rare social appearances of Alfred Hitchcock and by being the very last occasion on which Oscar Levant played the piano in public.

Back in New York, a week later, overwhelmed and exhausted, I attended a party in Virgil Thomson's apartment at the Chelsea Hotel. It was similar, I imagine, to dozens of literary parties given by publishers to launch their authors' books but, for me, it was a unique and historic occasion. When it was over and the glasses and canapés had been cleared away and I had thanked Virgil for the loan of his apartment and the two efficient and decorative young women from Juilliard for pushing the drinks, Joan and I took a cab uptown and stopped at the newsstand on Times Square to pick up the early edition of the *New York Times* on the off chance that it might contain a review of my book. It did—and it was good.

The following Sunday, to my amazement, the entire front page of the *New York Times Book Review* was occupied by Walter Kerr's review of *Run-Through*.

'Memoir' is too slight a word for this substantial, satisfyingly detailed, gracefully written account of an exciting period of American theater.

The *New York Post* reviewer described it as "one of the most brilliant volumes of theatrical reminiscence I've ever read," and Robert Kirsch in the *Los Angeles Times* found it "so good on so many counts that by the time one has finished reading it, that overused and exploited adjective 'great' does not seem an exaggeration." It was difficult to believe, but there was a similar tone to the dozens of clippings that began to pour in from San Diego, Oklahoma City, New England, Seattle, Minneapolis, Miami, etc. The weeklies followed suit. *Life* called it "a true chronicle of the American theater...the best show in town."

One critic concluded his perceptive review of *Run-Through* with the regret that—

for all its theatrical sugar and spice, what remains most curious is its portrait of a man who remains the collaborator, the behind-the-scenes organizer, the vital supernumerary. It's all great fun, to be sure, but also sad and unresolved—a run-through without the excitement of a finished performance or the applause of the final curtain.

I would have liked to explain that a "run-through," in theatrical parlance, takes place *during the rehearsal period* and does not admit of a final or "finished performance." My memoir was written in mid-career;

it dealt with events, the most recent of which had taken place more than thirty years earlier. It covered a period of my life when, for all my frenzied activity and the steady growth of my ego, I remained totally insecure and continued to take refuge in an attitude of anonymity that was deliberate and self-protective. What I did not know and therefore could not tell the reviewer was that the "final curtain" whose absence he regretted was still more than half a century in the future.

The Acting Company's second season was due to begin in July. This gave us barely two months in which to give our exhausted actors a rest, to rehearse our new program for the coming season and to deal with the first serious financial crisis in our brief history.

Until now, all our shows had originated as student productions: the sets and costumes had been paid for by Juilliard and most of our rehearsals conducted on Juilliard time. Now, though our relations with the School remained cordial, we faced the grim necessity of paying for our own productions and rehearsing them at full Equity salaries. That sent our budget soaring and made the mangement of the Company a source of continuing and agonizing financial anxiety which I anticipated but from which I would often have given the world to free myself.

To help us deal with our latest financial crisis we appealed to our various sponsors and benefactors and our two major contributing foundations; also to the New York State Council on the Arts and the National Endowment for the Arts, all of whom were generous in their understanding of our problem. By anticipating the date of their grants they made it possible for us to make the necessary commitments for our new season, in which we were further aided by advances from the Saratoga Arts Center.

Since we could afford only two new productions, we decided to repeat *The Hostage* and to throw in, as an additional attraction, Ann Jellicoe's *The Knack*, a four-character play in which Kevin Kline made his first major breakthrough as a comedian. Other productions included Chekhov's *Three Sisters*, for which our company was particularly well suited. Our sisters were Mary Lou Rosato, Mary Joan Negro and Patti LuPone and it remained in our repertory longer than any of our productions. Since it seemed desirable finally to include a Shakespearean play in our program, I decided to repeat my "Viennese" production of *Measure for Measure* that had worked so well at Stratford and in California.

This second summer season was generally considered equal or superior to the first. As a result, we were invited to remain for three additional weeks during August, during which we produced Gay's

Beggar's Opera, featuring Patti LuPone as Lucy Lockit and Kevin Kline as MacHeath.

Before the start of the Saratoga season the Housemans had enjoyed another brief summer reunion in the House on the Hill. Michael's final year at Brandeis had been a good one: he ended up on the dean's list for academic achievement. In his final semester he had taken a graduate course in anthropology which had so excited him that he had enrolled in a field trip organized for the summer in the mountains of Haute Savoie, in eastern France. Sebastian had scraped through the Storm King School and graduated. Having decided, with my consent, not to apply for college, he was getting ready to see the world in the form of a visit to a lady of his acquaintance, a nightclub stripper in Miami, Florida—where he spent the next few months incommunicado except for the occasional arrival in the mail of surprisingly detailed and beautiful drawings in the style of Gustave Doré.

Halfway through the summer an event occurred that, for a few days, interrupted all other activities. Passing through New City one morning, I found a letter in our mailbox in my mother's unmistakable, bold and still firm handwriting (except that now the end of each line sagged slightly) in which she informed me that she had finally resigned herself to leaving her beloved Paris. Coming to America seemed the sensible thing to do—all the more since it would bring her closer to me. But she was worried about the trip. I spoke to her on the phone and told her that I'd come over (before she changed her mind) and that we'd made the flight back together.

For more than sixty years, with few interruptions (World War II and her sister's long, final illness) my mother had lived in Paris. Her apartment had been taken from her during the war and she had moved to a small hotel on the rue de Rivoli where she continued to live alone past the age of ninety. In her eighties she had been hit by a Paris taxicab and spent some weeks in the hospital. This left her with a stiff back that make it difficult for her to move around but did not otherwise interfere with her life. At ninety she was still beautiful, vain and opinionated. It was her custom to spend the early part of the day in bed smoking, reading books, the French newspapers and the *Herald Tribune*. At 1 p.m. she had a light lunch in bed. At three she arose and began to make up. Around five she was ready and walked down the street to Rumpelmeyer's where she met friends and had tea and several cigarettes, followed by the first Scotch-and-soda of the day before moving on, in company, to a well-chosen dinner in one of the better restaurants of the neighborhood. Every Sunday afternoon, for fifteen years, she had taken a taxi across town and had tea with Joan's mother in Montparnasse.

After ninety she tired more easily and one night she fell and lay for nine hours on the floor of her room where she was found half-conscious in the morning by the maid who was bringing her breakfast. I flew over and urged her to move to America: she insisted on remaining in Paris in a very expensive and somewhat sinister nursing home where she was well cared for but increasingly incapacitated, bored and restless. Now, two years later, she had finally changed her mind.

I spent three days in Paris, mostly with my son, Michael, whose stay in Haute Savoie had been a great experience for him—so much so that he had decided to remain in France and study anthropology at the University of Nanterre. He had no language problem and had already found a part-time job in the Paris branch of the Organization for Economic Cooperation and Development (where he started off as an office boy and presently became a junior statistician). He was at the airport to see us off.

With my habitual insecurity, I had dreaded the embarrassments of a transatlantic flight with my 93-year-old mother in her frail condition. Contrary to all expectations the flight was a delight. She had always been an enthusiastic traveler and the excitement of a long journey after the months spent in the boring seclusion of a French nursing home helped to bring about a startling transformation in her condition. It as a long and beautiful summer's day; everyone was sympathetic and kind; Air France's food was excellent, champagne flowed and, in the eight hours it took to cover the distance from Orly to New York, my mother and I found ourselves closer than we had been in years.

At the airport an ambulance was waiting to take us along the familiar Hudson River route into Rockland County and by late afternoon, with the sun still shining, May was installed in her room at the nursing home in which she contined to live for the remaining six years of her life. Two days later she was having lunch with Virgil Thomson and Bessie Poor in our House on the Hill and following her habitual regimen of two Scotch-and-sodas and half a pack of cigarettes before and during lunch.

A few days after that I drove into Manhattan one evening for the first "sneak" preview of *The Paper Chase*. Word seemed to have got around and I saw a number of acquaintances in the theater. As a spectator, I enjoyed the film and felt that, except for the end, which I found soft and unclear, Jim Bridges had done a good job of filmmaking. But Professor Kingsfield really disturbed me.

I had been puzzled and slightly contemptuous when Joan Fontaine told me, years before, that she threw up every time she had to look at herself on the screen. Now I understood. I sat there, staring up at the giant image of myself engaged in actions with which I was familiar (since I remembered playing them) but that had no relation whatever to the *me* that sat frozen in my seat in the darkness below. One hour and forty minutes of being whipsawed between these two versions of myself left me limp and exhausted and quite incapable of exercising any kind of objective judgment about my performance. When the picture was over and the light had come back, I sat there for a while, drained and incredulous.

I forget who first uttered the words "Academy Award" but I remember that several ladies, including Irene Selznick and Cicely Tyson, hugged me on the sidewalk. By the time I'd made the long trip back to Saratoga I was over my excitement and immersed once more in the affairs of the Acting Company. Then, within a few weeks, *The Paper Chase* began to take over my life. Early in September, escorted by a platoon of publicists, male and female, Bridges, Bottoms, Wagner and I descended on Atlanta, Georgia, where a film festival was in progress. In their desperate anxiety to secure the world premiere of a major Hollywood film, its promoters had made a not-so-secret deal with Twentieth Century Fox by which they guaranteed that *Paper Chase* would be awarded the Golden Phoenix and seven other prestigious awards, which we accepted with the appropriate gratitude in the presence of the governor of the state, Jimmy Carter. Soon after that the reviews began to appear. They were generally favorable. But there was one aspect of the film on which there seemed to be no disagreement whatever and that was the character, personality and potency of Professor Kingsfield.

Dazed and incredulous, I read in *Time* magazine of "a forbidding, superb performance catching not only the coldness of such a man but the patrician crustiness that conceals deep and raging contempt"; in the *New York Times* of "one of those uproarious, all-stops-out, fiendishly expert, domineering and exhilarating performaces which come along once in a blue moon of movies."

A more sober attitude prevailed among my own students in the Drama Division. Some days before the film's release I invited the entire student body to a private running of the film. Their behavior was exemplary; they arrived on time, laughed in the right places, applauded politely when it was over, thanked me and left in silence. The next morning at school I waited for their reactions. I had been giving severe critiques of their performances for years and I felt it only fair that they have a chance to do the same for mine. Nothing happened. Not a word. On the second day I waited for the lunch break, when they would be gathered in their dressing rooms and passages, and appeared among them. Still nothing. Finally I could stand it no longer and confronted them. They said they had enjoyed the film and that they felt Bridges had done a nice job of direction.

"How about the performances?" I inquired.

They played it cool. They said they had liked Timothy Bottoms, Lindsay Wagner and some of the others.

"What about *me*?" I insisted. "What did you think of *my* performance?"

"That was no performance," they said. "That's exactly the way you behave around here."

(My mother, who had been taken to see *The Paper Chase* at the local movie house, categorically refused to recognize or acknowledge me, declaring that the dreadful old man on the screen was an impostor and bore absolutely no relation to her beloved son—whom she still thought of as being in his middle thirties.)

During the winter of 1973, for all my rising excitement over *The Paper Chase*, my main concern continued to be for the School and for the Acting Company, whose second national tour had taken us, during the fall, through Texas, Colorado, Louisiana, Missouri and New Jersey. During the Christmas holidays, we were planning to give our second New York City repertory season—this time in a regular Broadway theater.

This was an engagement to which I had been opposed at first—partly because of its excessive cost and partly because I feared the fickleness of New York audiences and press and the heavy odds against rekindling the enthusiasm we had aroused with our first maverick appearance. My mind was changed by the Billy Rose Foundation, which contributed generously to our season besides giving us free use of the Broadway theater it owned.

Our reception was friendly but, as I feared, it lacked the excitement of our first adventurous engagement. With attendance at around 60 percent of capacity (including student and cut-rate tickets) our houses looked good but our net loss for the season exceeded $100,000 that we could ill afford.

I myself missed the last few days of our season when I flew to California in response to an urgent call I received late one night from two men, neither of whom I had ever met. One was Mike Merrick, Harry Belafonte's manager; the other was a writer for television by the name of David Rintels. They had been in rehearsal for ten days with a one-man show about the famed trial lawyer Clarence Darrow, starring Henry Fonda. Now suddenly Fonda seemed to have lost faith in their director and in the script and was talking of quitting. Would I fly out, diagnose the trouble and, if I thought it was curable, take over the show?

Attracted by the possibility of working with Fonda, I agreed to fly out and watch a run-through before making my decision. I was aware of Fonda's reputation as a perfectionist and of his habit of becoming depressed and discouraged halfway through rehearsals when things were not measuring up to his expectations. Sitting for two and a half hours in a shabby little Hollywood theater, I found *Darrow* an absorbing and dramatic show. With some trims, a few structural transpositions and, above all, a change in climate, it stood a good chance of becoming one of the outstanding performances of Fonda's long and distinguished career.

That evening, in Fonda's house high in the Bel-Air hills, I told them, as honestly as I could, how I felt about the show. The idea of replacing another director (who, I felt, was getting a raw deal) was repulsive to me. But, if their minds were made up, I was willing to take over the show. That night I took the "red-eye" flight back to New York. Three days later, having handed the last week of the Acting Company's season over to Margot Harley, I returned to California.

We had less than three weeks before our out-of-town opening, but that was enough. The script which Rintels had put together from Irving Stone's biography—augmented by additions from Darrow's own writings and from court records of the time—was filled with eloquent, colorful and sometimes humorous material. We did some editing, changed our act ending and worked on the scenes of Darrow's first marriage with which Fonda was not satisfied. I believe I gave Hank confidence and I was of some value in bringing variety and movement to his two-hour soliloquy. But such was his intelligence, his sensitivity and his own flawless taste that my main use to him as a director, during our final rehearsals, lay simply in my being out front and supplying him with a living mirror in which to check the truth of his performance.

For me, it was a revelation and gave me the sense, once again, of being in the presence of theatrical genius. His was the kind of acting of which I had little personal experience and which I had been inclined to lump in the limiting category of "naturalism." As such, it was quite different from what we were teaching at Juilliard. Yet, to my surprise, I found that, when practiced by an actor of Fonda's stature, it conformed in every respect to those standards of "reality" and "style" which were the final goal of our instruction.

Darrow opened in New York in the last week of March. We had a brief, terrifying flare of trouble with the sound system on opening night but Hank's triumph was complete and unqualified. The overwhelming reviews he received echoed the feelings of admiration and affection I had come to feel for this reticent and dedicated man.

* * *

There had been times, during my first years at Juilliard, when I felt that in accepting my appointment as head of the Drama Division, I had settled for a future of limited opportunity and slow, professional decline. Now, seven years later, I could look back with stupefaction on a series of unpredictable achievements which, besides a successful graduation, included two Broadway hits, the publication of a book and a starring role in a Hollywood film—not to mention the creation and administration of the country's most advanced theater school and the formation of a young acting company that stood alone in the contemporary American theater.

All this should finally have satisfied me and allowed me, in my midseventies, to rest on my laurels and enjoy the fruits of so many years of unrelenting toil. Instead, I was about to be subjected, without warning, to the most violent and unexpected shock of them all.

I am well aware that luck has played an overwhelming part in my affairs. I am also aware of the furious effort and incessant manipulation to which I have habitually resorted over the years to take advantage of these repeated accidents of fortune. What was different and curious about this latest tremor was the apparent calm with which I received it.

Early in 1974, just about the time the Acting Company had concluded its second New York repertory season and Henry Fonda was making his move with *Darrow* from Chicago to Washington, the names of those nominated for the 1973 awards of the Academy of Motion Picture Arts and Sciences were made public. Mine was among them but my first real recognition of what was happening to me came during a long-distance call I received one evening from my friend Norman Lloyd in Los Angeles. He reported that Nick the Greek in Las Vegas had just lowered the betting odds against my winning the award from 5-1 to 3-2!

My first reaction was one of incredulity and vague pleasure, followed by a sense of embarrassment at the realization that for most actors of my age an Academy Award or even a nomination comes as the hard-earned culmination of a long and dedicated career: mine was the reward for ten agreeable days spent with a friend in Toronto!

In the weeks that followed there was a steady increase in the number of interviews and TV appearances set up by the Studio to publicize *The Paper Chase*—to all of which I submitted, reluctantly at first and then with rising competitive excitement. The image of myself as the "septuagenarian novice" was one that was giving interviewers something to work on. Having, until then, carefully avoided all thought and mention of age, I was beginning to enjoy this new situation that had suddenly opened up a whole fresh area in which to exercise my ego.

The one person who might have kept me sober during those fevered weeks was not around. Joan's persistent refusal to become emotionally concerned with the competitive aspects of show business would have been invaluable during those final, lunatic days of elaborately and deliberately contrived suspense. Unfortunately she had taken advantage of my departure for California to pay an overdue visit to her family and friends in Europe.

I did my best to keep myself occupied—with the School, with the Acting Company and with the New York opening of *Darrow*. Then, one morning, my peace was shattered by a call I received from the president of the Hollywood Foreign Press Association inviting me with suspicious urgency to fly to California the following night to attend the annual Golden Globes ceremony, which was generally regarded as the prelude to the Academy Awards. I called Jim Bridges in California and asked him to take my place. He called back the next morning and said he had my Golden Globe on his desk and what the hell should he do with it? The next day in Vegas my odds went to even money.

On April 1, I made an embarrassing appearance with two of my rivals on one of the early-morning shows, where, with hypocritical smiles, the three of us wished each other success. The next morning I left for Los Angeles.

In Beverly Hills' three major caravanserais, madness reigned. Arriving nominees and celebrated presenters were installed in suites and were set upon by packs of ferocious reporters who kept asking the same ridiculous questions. When I could stand it no longer I called down, pleaded fatigue and canceled all further interviews. Then I went quickly through my growing pile of telegrams and messages and made some telephone calls to friends and to my escort for the evening. (I had given much thought to whom I should invite to share this dramatic moment. Finally I had the brilliant notion of inviting an old, dear friend, Sarah, the widow of my beloved collaborator Herman Mankiewicz, for whom I hoped the occasion would revive happy memories of the night her husband had been honored for his screenplay of *Citizen Kane*.)

Because of the time difference with the East Coast, we had been instructed to be in our seats by 6:30. This gave me two and a half hours. I undressed, slept for ninety minutes and was awakened by a call from the lobby from someone whom I had not seen or thought of in a long time—a lovely lady whom I had desired for years but with whom it had never seemed possible or appropriate to consummate my lust. We opened one of the bottles of champagne with which the suite was cluttered and talked until it was time for me to get ready for the ceremony. We said goodbye and I retired to shave and bathe. When I came back, the lady was lying in my bed smiling—with a glass of champagne in her hand. "For luck!" she said, and we spent the next twenty minutes, without sentiment or pretense, engaged in the eager, impersonal pleasure of making love.

There were several dozen limousines waiting below. One of them drove me to Brentwood to pick up Sarah Mankiewicz and on down to the Chandler Pavilion, where we arrived in broad daylight and made our way into the theater past screeching bleachers and minefields of cameras and microphones. I was seated next to Bridges and in the same section as Paul Newman and George Roy Hill (nominated for *The Sting*). I was completely numb by this time and only dimly aware of what was going on as presenters, award-winners and musical numbers followed each other relentlessly on that huge, overlit stage and Burt Reynolds, who had been pressed into service as MC at the last moment, fumbled his uncertain way through the evening. As in a nightmare, I kept repeating in my head fragments of the various acceptance speeches I had been composing for days—alternately praying for an Oscar and dreading the moment when I might have to go up there and receive it.

There was a brief, welcome interlude when that year's inevitable "streaker" made his bid for fame—a pitiful, pale, knock-kneed nude who ran across the stage but was soon intercepted and dragged away. After that I lapsed back into my torpor until, feeling Sarah tugging at my sleeve, I became aware of a dark, squat man and a ravishing blonde beauty in a low-cut dress approaching the stage-left podium, and I realized with horror that the moment had come and that these were the presenters of the award for the best performance by a male actor in a supporting role. I could see their lips moving as they listed the names of the nominees and heard their voices coming from what seemed to be an entirely different place. Finally the girl in the low-cut dress held up the envelope and unsealed it. Her mouth opened. "The winner is John Houseman," she said.

I rose to my feet and made my way, in what felt like very slow motion, past Jim Bridges, Paul Newman, Joanne Woodward and a number of young women with escorts I didn't know, down the aisle and in the direction of the stage. As I started up the steps I heard a sound behind me that remains my most vivid memory of that night.

All through the evening, each successive winner had been greeted by a salvo of applause that varied in volume and quality with the nature of the award and the popularity of the victor. The announcement of my name had started the kind of reaction that could be expected to greet the announcement of the first of the evening's major awards. But then, as I completed my climb up the shallow carpeted steps, turned and started on my long, flat-footed, self-conscious walk across the stage, the sound of applause, instead of dying down, seemed to rise and spread. What had begun as an automatic reaction to the surprise victory of a septuagenarian dark horse was turning into a minor ovation—a spontaneous expression of personal recognition and affection.

There were 3300 people in the Chandler Pavilion that night—most of them professionals, of whom at least one quarter were men and women with whom, at one time or another, directly or indirectly, in one way or another, in theater, radio, films or television, I had collaborated over the past forty years. What I believe they were applauding at that moment, over and above my fluky victory, was their own sentimental memory of work we had done together.

The next thing I knew I was being handed a gleaming brass figure, which I found larger and heavier than I expected. Then, as the applause died away, I found myself standing all alone, staring out over that sea of faces with not one word left in my head of all those sincere and elegant phrases I had been preparing for days. I opened my mouth and, according to the official record, this is what came out:

For the first time in a long and tumultuous life I find myself almost incapable of speech. I cannot begin to describe to you the emotions with which I receive this great honor at your hands. I do, however, have a few personal gratitudes I need to express: first, to all those who worked with me on *The Paper Chase*, for the great kindness and generosity with which they accepted the presence of a mysterious and inexperienced intruder in their midst; second, to Gordon Willis, whose extraordinarily dramatic camerawork did so much to help me create the character of Dr. Kingsfield; thirdly, fourthly and fifthly, to my dear friend Jim Bridges, as the writer, the director and as the extraordinarily reckless young man who had the unspeakable gall to select an aging and obscure schoolmaster to play this perfectly glorious part in his picture.

As I started offstage, escorted by my keepers and still clutching my Oscar, I remember wondering if Orson Welles was watching the show.

XXXII
Unfinished Business
1974-88

Preoccupation with time has not been one of my problems. I have friends, male and female, for whom reaching the age of thirty has been a disturbing experience; others have attained the age of forty with a chilling sense of having lived more than half of their lives; a fiftieth birthday is a favorite occasion for neurotic behavior while, at sixty, the threats of impotence and enforced retirement present rich opportunities for apprehension and gloom.

Not for me. Throughout my life I have been too busy fighting my ill-organized battle against oblivion to worry about such mundane considerations as the passage of years. In three-quarters of a century my life has undergone innumerable transformations, each of which has demanded its own drastic adjustments—changes of activity and identity in which age has played only an incidental part.

Memoirs are normally undertaken in the latter part of a life when most of the returns are in and the final result (what we have come to call the "bottom line") can be appraised with some degree of assurance. Mine have met no such requirements. They were written over a period of more than thirty years of incessant flux during which the relation of the past to the present was continually and violently shifting. Most of the events of my life have been recorded between twenty and thirty years after they occurred. My recollections of them have inevitably been colored by the changing circumstances of the present in which I wrote them.

When I began work on *Run-Through* I intended it not as an autobiography or a confession, but as a factual narrative describing certain incidents that occurred in my 30s and 40s, of which I had been a witness and in some of which my friends and I had played an active part. As I moved into middle age and found that more and more of my associates were disappearing, I became increasingly disturbed at the thought that many of the exciting and significant theatrical and social events in which we had taken part were likely to remain unrecorded and, finally, unremembered. Hence these memoirs, which begin in Bucharest, Rumania, in September, 1902, and end on the stage of Hollywood's Pantages Theatre in the spring of 1974.

The first volume—*Run-Through*—which ends a few days after Pearl Harbor, was begun in Paris in the fall of 1964 and completed in New York during the summer of 1971. The second—*Front and Center*—came out seven years later and covers events that took place between 1942 and 1958. The third—*Final Dress*—published in 1983, ends with the surprise of my Academy Award nine years earlier. The fourth has not been written.

In the Brothers Grimm's familiar fairy tale of the Frog Prince, the transformation that followed the kiss of the King's Daughter was total and instantaneous. Mine was more gradual; it took Professor Kingsfield and myself more than five years to reach the peak of our celebrity. Yet, in their final effect, there is little difference between the frog's miraculous transit from the pond to the palace and my own metamorphosis from an aging, semi-retired veteran of the theater to one of the most highly publicized and familiar figures in American Show Business.

For some years after the release of *The Paper Chase* I remained with the Juilliard School where, following my usual pattern, I had begun to transfer my enthusiasm from the Drama Division, which I had successfully directed for seven years, to the newer and more exciting operation of the Acting Company, which I had recently created. I resigned from Juilliard in the summer of 1976 to appease the anxieties of its president and trustees, who had begun to fret about my advanced age. This left me free to devote my energy and affection to the Acting Company which, of the eight theatrical organizations I have formed in my lifetime, has been the longest-lived and the most effectual. All the others, including the brilliant Mercury Theatre (which actually lasted for less than two years), had been mavericks recklessly created outside the theatrical mainstream of their day. The formation of the Acting Company coincided with the birth of institutional theater and with a general acceptance of the value of actor-training and ensemble playing in the American theater. I have remained its director for 17 years.

Following my Oscar I began to receive occasional offers to appear in films. The first and most interesting were *Three Days of the Condor*, a spy story shot in New York and Washington, and *Rollerball*, a futurist film shot in Munich in the stadium built by Hitler for his 1938 Olympic Games. In one I played the head of the C.I.A.; in the other I was

president of one of three ruthless international consortiums that
controlled the world.

Others followed. There is a limit to the number of parts available to
an actor in his late seventies but, over the past decade, I have played
Winston Churchill in his decline, several grandfathers, a senile parish
priest, the Patriarch of Venice and the governor of Hong Kong. I have
appeared as an art-historian with a close resemblance to Bernard
Berenson, the Chief Justice of the U.S. Supreme Court, the conductor of
a symphony orchestra, General Winfield Scott, a first-century rabbi and
a mad scientist bent on the destruction of the human race in general
and of the Bionic Woman in particular.

These performances were evenly divided between film and
television. Some were satisfying; others were shameful. I enjoyed them
as novelties but never entirely accepted them as a serious part of my
life.

It took *The Paper Chase* six years to move from film to television. It
was not even considered for TV until the fall of 1977 when it was
produced by CBS as one of the three hundred trial "pilots" spawned
annually by the networks. Written once again by James Bridges, it was
rated one of the best pilots of the season but too "high-brow" for
commercial television.

The following spring CBS surprised us all by including *The Paper
Chase* in its prime-time evening TV schedule for the coming season.
Our enthusiasm was tempered by our discovery that the air-time
assigned to us was Tuesday evening at 8 p.m. (a slot know as "The
Graveyard" or "Murderer's Row") where our show would be
broadcast in direct competition with the nation's two most popular
sit-coms—*Happy Days* and *LaVerne and Shirley.*

Our reviews were good; our "ratings" abysmal. According to the
Nielsen Company's calculations, we were being watched in the fall of
1978 in 8.5 million homes by 19% of the nation's viewing public. In
other words, we had an audience of around 15 million against our
rivals' 35 to 40 million. Normally this would have spelled instant
cancellation but, once again, to everyone's surprise, CBS, for reasons of
its own, renewed us on a week-to-week basis and kept us on the air for
the rest of the season.

"PAPER CHASE STAYS," reported *Variety*, and we became famous
for some weeks as "the show Nielsen couldn't kill."

Predictably we were not included in the CBS prime-time lineup for
the following season. In reply to complaints by critics who had
admired the show and to the several hundred thousand letters of
protest received by the network from outraged viewers, CBS explained
that, much to their sorrow, *The Paper Chase* "had not generated enough

public support to make it a viable program."

But, by now, it no longer mattered. In his twenty-one appearances on prime-time television, Professor Kingsfield had been accepted as one of the mythical figures of American television. Through a strange combination of circumstances, what had begun as a realistic characterization of a great teacher of contract law had been transferred through the mysterious alchemy of the Mass Media into that rare and precious commodity known as "credibility." A national survey conducted by one of the country's leading advertising agencies in the summer of 1978 revealed the surprising information that, next to Walter Cronkite, the highest "credibility" enjoyed by any male television performer in the United States was that of Professor Kingsfield, a.k.a. John Houseman.

This credibility was soon put to work promoting the sale of such diverse products as automobiles (foreign and domestic), the oil of sunflower seeds (guaranteed free of cholesterol), a leading fast-food franchise and the services of a well-known financial institution whose frequently repeated assurance that "they make money the old-fashioned way—*they earn it*" became something of a national slogan and vastly increased their profits during the boom years of the stock market. (A national cartoon that appeared that same year showed a Presidential aide comforting his troubled master with the reassurance that "lately you've been seen on TV almost as much as John Houseman!")

With such exposure of its leading character *The Paper Chase* was soon resurrected. Our CBS shows were revived on Public Television and, soon after that, Showtime, the second largest of the country's new cable networks, desperately looking for a dramatic series that would give it an assured audience and a reputation for quality, decided that *The Paper Chase* satisfied both requirements.

Between 1982 and 1985, in addition to my commercials, we created thirty-seven new episodes in which the Professor began to show signs of age while his students moved from first and second year to the final stages of their legal education. That made *The Paper Chase* the only television show on record to be broadcast three times in prime-time—first on a major network, then on Public and finally on Cable Television. By then it had also been shown in England (on the BBC) and in fifty-one other countries, including Ireland, Germany and most of Europe; also in South and Central America, Israel, Australia, Malaysia, India, Singapore, and Zimbabwe.

It has been a source of wonder and occasional bitterness to reflect that in my half-century of dedicated service to the American theater I received only a fraction of the recognition I achieved in my mid-seventies through this one performance of a supporting role in a moderately successful film. What has made the situation particularly ironic is my awareness that my sudden celebrity and the extravagant rewards I have been receiving for more than a decade are in fact only remotely related to my own performance as an actor.

The whole thing becomes even more fantastic with the realization that this "credibility" which has been put to such various uses is, in reality, not mine at all, but belongs to a fictional character for whom I have supplied the voice, the physical features and certain individual characteristics. Professor Kingsfield is, in fact, the joint creation of a budding novelist, a great cinematographer and an ambitious and talented young writer-director making his first major film. From the legendary personality of a former professor of Harvard Law School (with all his intransigence, his passion for the law, his savage humor and his obstinate integrity) there emerged a public figure with whom I have become so solidly identified that it has become impossible for me to separate his personality from my own.

Throughout our long association, I have always regarded Professor Kingsfield as a senior partner: I am well aware that the strangers who approach me on the street, in planes, hotel lobbies and university campuses are under the impression that they are addressing the formidable professor and that the audiences which regularly fill the halls, theaters and gymnasia in which I lecture have not come to hear John Houseman's views on the Performing Arts but to take a closer look at a figure with which they have become familiar on their television screens. I have often wondered how many of the multicolored academic hoods that hang in the closets of my home as visible symbols of the thirteen honorary degrees I have received over the years are truly mine and how many were intended for the Professor.

This confusion extends to other aspects of my life. I cannot, for example, fill out a questionnaire (for a credit card, health insurance or a passport application) without experiencing a twinge of doubt and embarrassment as to what I should give as my occupation. For more than a dozen years acting, in one form or another, has been my main source of income and reputation, yet I remain reluctant and somewhat embarrassed at the idea of describing myself as an actor.

It always surprises me to discover how little effect our prosperity has had upon Joan's and my personal way of life. In fact, our new opulence has given us a sense of security which has eliminated the need for some of the symbols of conspicuous wealth that my wife and I once found it necessary to display: Dom Perignon has been replaced for Sunday morning consumption by Spanish champagne; Porsche and Jaguar have been supplanted in our garage by Honda and VW Rabbit; our animal population has shrunk from six to one.

The same is true of our dwellings. Throughout the thirty-nine years of our marriage the houses we occupied have played a significant, emotional part in our lives. The House on the Hill in New City and the Big House in the Malibu Colony were both impressive evidences of success. Both have been sold. For the past dozen years, commuting between California and New York and, occasionally, Europe (where Joan has a small house in East Sussex), we have lived in a succession of medium-sized dwellings, each of which Joan has filled with her own special atmosphere. The first, acquired in haste when we moved to Los Angeles for *The Paper Chase*, was a perilous, ship-like structure perched on tall wooden stilts on the most exposed corner of the Colony's beach, directly in the path of every drifting log and piece of floating wreckage that made its way down the coast during the atrocious California winter of 1978-79. The house quivered and shook incessantly but it survived and doubled in value during the two years we lived in it.

With the proceeds we sought safety high on a bluff known as Big Rock, where we had a 300-degree view of the Pacific Ocean. We lived there for two years but when we returned from Tunisia (where I had been playing the part of the Rabbi Gamaliel) I was shown a cleft—forty feet long, one foot wide and quite deep—running from one end of our house to the other. It was caused, I was told, by a mudslide that was endangering the entire mountain. A few days later our house was condemned as unfit for human habitation. We moved back down to the beach, two doors from the Big House we gave up in 1964 to go and live in Paris, and only a few houses up the beach from the bungalow we occupied when we were first married forty years ago.

In the pursuit of my career I have flown hundreds of thousands of miles but, until recently, Joan and I never found it possible to travel together for our pleasure. A month's motor trip through Spain with our two sons and a magical Aegean cruise followed by a voyage up the Nile and a visit to Tahiti on the way back from Australia whetted our appetites for more. We still commute between California and New York and we fly to Europe at least once a year. But, between us, our health has forced us to reduce the range of our future voyages.

Professionally, between 1980 and 1985, besides playing in thirty-seven episodes of *The Paper Chase*, nine *Silver Spoons* and a number of commercials, I appeared in three TV "miniseries"—shot in

Florence, Yugoslavia and North Africa. Two more of my books have been published—one here and one in England—and I have produced two films, both for television. One was about the Supreme Court's famous "Gideon" decision affirming the individual's rights to a lawyer in a criminal trial; the other concerned the Maryknoll nuns who were murdered by government soldiers in El Salvador. Surprisingly, for films on such such contentious subjects, they were both seen by audiences of twenty million or more. Meantime, I continue to play small parts (known in the trade as "vignettes") in films of various kinds and I still deliver lectures—mostly variations of previous ones—in locations that range from Oregon to Mississippi and Florida.

My obstinate refusal to acknowledge the passage of time was finally shaken a few years ago when a television writer in search of an original situation for *The Paper Chase* created an episode in which Kingsfield's worshipful students risked the Professor's ire by presenting him with a huge cake, obscenely loaded with candles, on the occasion of his—and my—eightieth birthday. My ceremonious extinction of those four-score lights was more than a test of lung-power; it made an effective scene on television and created a sudden awareness of age from which I have never entirely recovered.

Over the years I have had two narrow escapes from death. Neither time did I feel much sense of fear. The same is true of the pulmonary embolism that hit me a year ago. The sudden blackout that landed me with my face on the floor under my wife's Louis XIII oak table; the prompt appearance of two paramedics escorted by member of the New York City police force; the six hours spent in the emergency room, followed by five days of intensive care—all these disturbed me not because of any physical suffering I underwent but because of the solicitude of the doctors and nurses who cared for me with a zeal that suggested that my case was a serious one. In my eighty-sixth year I began to think about death.

Having ceased to regard death as a threat, I now accept it as the last of the many surprises of which my life is the sum. My awareness that I have only a short time to live has conditioned my attitude toward the years I have left. The calamities with which mankind is constantly threatened (the "big" earthquake, if you happen to live in California; nuclear Armageddon no matter where you may be) hold few terrors for me, secure in the knowledge that I shall not be around to see them.

Physically, I face the normal problems of my age: diminishing strength and miscellaneous aches and pains that come and go without warning or explanation, accompanied by a vague sense of never feeling quite as well as I once did. Familiar obstacles such as stairs, whose ubiquitous presence I once took for granted, have forced me into a new reliance upon railings and banisters for which I feel the same resentment as I have long felt toward eyeglasses, hearing aids and other mechanical devices upon which I have become increasingly dependent. I continue to drive my car, to walk on the beach (preferably after a high tide when the sand is smooth and firm) and, when I am at home, to spend between four and six hours a day at my desk. I still have a prodigious memory for incidents and people but a difficulty in recalling names that has become a serious social embarrassment.

Sleeping or waking, much of my life, these days, seems to be spent in the past, and this conditions my attitude toward the present. I, who once had such exasperating energy, find myself, certain mornings, resisting the need to get up—not out of illness or idleness or because the weather is uninviting or because I have personal or professional problems I prefer not to face—but out of sheer boredom at the prospect of going through the familiar routine of washing, shaving, dressing, brushing my teeth and hair and renewing contact with the world. I have come to understand the truth of Francis Bacon's observation that "a man would die, though he be neither violent nor miserable, only upon a weariness to do something so oft, over and over." In my increasing leisure I read more than I have for years—biography and history mostly, together with some of the great works I first read years ago in French and English. These second readings give me the double satisfaction of memory and discovery.

I remain an avid newspaper reader. During my early years of loneliness and frustration, it was my habit, after I had read the news in the morning paper, to turn to the social columns—to the space devoted to local engagements and weddings. From my contemplation of so many dozens of nubile young women all trying to look their best as they stared into the camera, I found relief from my isolation and a partial satisfaction of my libido.

Today, half a century later, it is no longer to the social columns that I turn but to the obituaries—with special attention to those of persons who have exceeded their span of three score years and ten and have approached or gone beyond my own age. Where the demise recorded is that of a former associate, it takes on an added interest and a twinge of personal loss. But the principal comfort I derive from these announcements is a sense of relief—a feeling that there, but for the grace of God, go I! In addition, I enjoy a sense of sympathy and comradeship with those who, like myself, have weathered the terrors and crises of their long time on earth and managed, for so many years, to hold off annihilation.

* * *

Some months ago I received a phone call from a lady who said she worked for the *New York Times*. Since one does not refuse a summons from that greatest of American newspapers, we met the next day at a neighboring restaurant. While I drank my sherry, she explained that it was her function to update and check facts on those persons about whom the *Times* expected to publish obituaries in the foreseeable future.

My first reaction was one of revulsion such as I might have felt on discovering that I was lunching with an eager mortician or an enterprising burial-plot salesman. However, the lady was attractive, lively and knowledgeable; for added reassurance, she referred me to a list of aging friends and colleagues whom she had recently interviewed. Halfway through lunch I found myself reminding her of certain facts in my life that she seemed to have overlooked and giving her additional suggestions for my obituary.

We parted amicably and, in the months that followed, I have come to the conclusion that (unlike the Skeleton with the Scythe on the Swiss bridge whom, as a child, I had seen hustling his victims to the boneyard) the *Times'* Angel of Death is benign and patient. Of the half dozen persons she listed as subjects of her necrological investigations, all six (including one who recently celebrated his hundredth birthday) are, as I write, alive and well.

THE END

Index